ROUTLEDGE LIBRARY EDITIONS: LITERARY THEORY

Volume 24

GENETIC CODES OF CULTURE?

GENETIC CODES OF CULTURE?
The Deconstruction of Tradition by Kuhn, Bloom, and Derrida

WILLIAM R. SCHULTZ

Routledge
Taylor & Francis Group

LONDON AND NEW YORK

First published in 1994 by Garland Publishing, Inc.

This edition first published in 2017
by Routledge
2 Park Square, Milton Park, Abingdon, Oxon OX14 4RN

and by Routledge
711 Third Avenue, New York, NY 10017

Routledge is an imprint of the Taylor & Francis Group, an informa business

© 1994 William R. Schultz

All rights reserved. No part of this book may be reprinted or reproduced or utilised in any form or by any electronic, mechanical, or other means, now known or hereafter invented, including photocopying and recording, or in any information storage or retrieval system, without permission in writing from the publishers.

Trademark notice: Product or corporate names may be trademarks or registered trademarks, and are used only for identification and explanation without intent to infringe.

British Library Cataloguing in Publication Data
A catalogue record for this book is available from the British Library

ISBN: 978-1-138-69377-7 (Set)
ISBN: 978-1-315-52921-9 (Set) (ebk)
ISBN: 978-1-138-68976-3 (Volume 24) (hbk)
ISBN: 978-1-138-68977-0 (Volume 24) (pbk)
ISBN: 978-1-315-53742-9 (Volume 24) (ebk)

Publisher's Note
The publisher has gone to great lengths to ensure the quality of this reprint but points out that some imperfections in the original copies may be apparent.

Disclaimer
The publisher has made every effort to trace copyright holders and would welcome correspondence from those they have been unable to trace.

GENETIC CODES OF CULTURE?

The Deconstruction of Tradition by Kuhn, Bloom, and Derrida

William R. Schultz

GARLAND PUBLISHING, INC.
New York & London / 1994

Copyright © 1994 William R. Schultz
All rights reserved

Library of Congress Cataloging-in-Publication Data

Schultz, William R., 1953–
   Genetic codes of culture? : the deconstruction of tradition by Kuhn, Bloom, and Derrida / by William R. Schultz.
      p.   cm. — (Garland reference library of the humanities ; vol. 1701. Wellesley studies in critical theory, literary history, and culture ; vol. 6)
   Includes bibliographical references and index.
   ISBN 0-8153-1299-7 (alk. paper)
   1. Literature—History and criticism—Theory, etc. 2. Kuhn, Thomas S. 3. Bloom, Harold. 4. Derrida, Jacques. I. Title. II. Series: Garland reference library of the humanities ; vol. 1701. III. Series: Garland reference library of the humanities. Wellesley studies in critical theory, literary history, and culture ; vol. 6.
PN441.S35   1994
801'.95—dc20   94-6495
                                                                      CIP

Printed on acid-free, 250-year-life paper
Manufactured in the United States of America

To Liana,

a Source of Both Culture and Life

Contents

List of Illustrations..ix
Preface: The Rhetorical Situation..xi
Acknowledgments..xiii
List of Abbreviations.. xv

Prologue: Are There Genetic Codes of Science, Poetry, and Philosophy?... 3

Part I: Overview of the Three Careers and Theories

1. Overview of the Three Careers 43
2. Overview of the Three Theories.. 69

Part II: The Three Theories of Tradition

Section A: The Start of a Tradition Form
3. The Start of a Scientific Theory 117
4. The Start of a Poetry 137
5. The Start of Derrida's Philosophy 163

Section B: The Middle Stages of a Tradition Form
6. The Middle Stage of a Scientific
   Theory... 231
7. The Middle Stage of a Poetry.. 237
8. The Middle Stage of Derrida's
   Philosophy 247

Section C: The End of a Tradition Form
9. The End of a Scientific Theory 259
10. The End of a Poetry 281
11. The End of Derrida's Philosophy 305

Part III: Conclusion: Judging the Three Theories by Comparison and by Reference to the Standard of a Cultural Genetic Code

12. Judging Kuhn's Theory 361
13. Judging Bloom's Theory 401
14. Judging Derrida's Theory 435

Epilogue: Proposal for a Transductive Method 453

List of Secondary Works Cited 487
Bibliography 497
Index 603

Illustrations

Painting: "A Golden Thread" 165
Figure 5-1: The Three Fates, Who Define the Cycle and the Fate of an Individual Human's Life 167
Figure 5-2: Bricolage Is Like a Change from One Perspective Drawing to Another 172
Figure 5-3: The Ouroboros or The Serpent of Time Represents the Cyclical, Circular, and Finite Nature of Cultural Works 191
Figure 5-4: Sartre's Dualistic View of Human Progress 195
Figure 5-5: Creation as a Circumscribing Knowledge: the Total Former Thought Processes Become Represented as a New Object of Knowledge 199
Figure 5-6: The Idea of Difference Is Related to Sartre's Closing Concept by Derrida's Ideas of Trace and Erasure 205
Figure 5-7: Tradition Takes One Step Forward by Isonomizing the One before It, Or by Finding a New Universal Principle of Ordering Tradition 210
Figure 5-8: Not Only Does Each New Whole Step in Tradition Redefine the Totality of What Went before, But Also Each Major Stage in a Cultural Work Is a New Stance toward the Past ... 211

Figure 11-1: A Cultural Work Has a Perspectival Meaning by Redefining a New Position in Tradition at Each New Main Stage 333
Figure 11-2: Each New Cycle of Philosophy and Poetry Has within It a Triadic Genetic Code 347

Figure 13-1: Bloom's Insufficiently Cyclical Definition of a Poetry 428

Figure 14-1: Derrida's Philosophy Belongs in the Canon; This Means It Is One Step Forward in Tradition, Like Many Previous Such Steps 437
Figure 14-2: One Horn of the Dilemma of the Supplement and a Suggested Alternative.. 444
Figure 14-3: A Second Horn of the Dilemma of the Supplement . 445

Figure Epi-1: A New Genetic Code Is Generated in the Change of Disciplinary Matrices 460

Preface: The Rhetorical Situation

In a preface it seems fitting to speak about the rhetorical situation of the work that follows. How does the work relate the author and readers?

Genetic Codes of Culture? The Deconstruction of Tradition by Kuhn, Bloom, and Derrida has been designed for different audiences: for students just starting their university careers in science, poetry, or philosophy; for advanced students; for very knowledgeable people in one field who often are not so expert in a second or third field; and for people in fields other than science, poetry, and philosophy who can apply some ideas suggested by the author to their own fields. In this way, the book attempts to be both introductory and advanced, interdisciplinary and specialized.

The organization of the book has been based on some principles of technical writing to allow various audiences to benefit to the degree and in the way that they can. This is especially necessary because of the interdisciplinary nature of the book. The book is divided according to the start, middle, and end of a science, poetry, or philosophy. Further divisions within chapters allow for selective reading--the concentration on some topics more than others. Experts may choose to read only those passages dealing with a topic relating to their research. Short introductory and summary passages before the main discussions help readers who may not have an advanced background but who may be able to follow some if they are guided by those non-technical passages.

This work has various related purposes. No discussion of the idea of tradition in deconstruction has yet been attempted on such a scale, and this idea is crucial for the contemporary intellectual scene in many fields, as each one is tending to regard its activity more on the model of a genetic code or on what I will call a "tradition form": the idea that any new science, poetry, or philosophy--or any field--

changes tradition has come into the center of new ideas pregnant with the future, especially in the work of Jacques Derrida. More specifically, the purposes are to isolate and present the ideas of Kuhn, Bloom, and Derrida on tradition in the respective fields; to compare the theories; to criticize them; to redefine the boundary between criticism and creation; and to propose a new direction for critics and scholars. The author believes the proposal is significant for any field of culture, for any human formative activity making a tradition.

The method of this work is unique; although other works are also comparative, this one on tradition gains power by assuming a fundamental cooperation of human activities in the building of civilization. Strategies of one author can be applied to another if science, poetry, and philosophy each make a tradition in their own ways. That any cultural field essentially makes a form of tradition has great value for future scholarship.

The exposition and criticism of the majority of the book lead to a more creative proposal about the practice of critical scholarship; if a model of a genetic code is followed, criticism can come closer to the sources of creation than it has thus far.

Finally, of least concern to most readers but nonetheless an essential component of the rhetorical situation, the author uses this work to make one step closer to writing original philosophy or to developing a new theory of literary criticism. Through the five years of this project the author's idea of how creation takes place has changed. From criticism to creation there is a threshold most very knowledgeable scholars cannot pass through. The author feels more prepared to face this mystery and hopes the readers will, too.

William R. Schultz
English Department
University of Athens
Greece

Acknowledgments

I would like to thank the many fine scholars whose works have influenced me, especially Geoff Bennington, Joseph Campbell, David Fite, Rodolphe Gasché, Frederick T. Griffiths, Irene Harvey, James Jakób Liszka, Jean-François Lyotard and Stanley J. Rabinowitz, not to mention Kuhn, Bloom, and Derrida.

The many librarians at The University of California at Berkeley deserve much thanks for helping me to locate a large number of sources which contributed to the following project.

Conversations with Professor Donald Philip Verene (The Department of Philosophy, Emory University, Atlanta, Georgia) helped me to frame some of the fundamental ideas.

Lewis Fried, co-compiler of *Jacques Derrida: An Annotated Primary and Secondary Bibliography*, has helped me tremendously-- locating articles, books, and bibliographic references, a process quite difficult if attempted only from Greece.

Professor Spyros Iliopoulos has helped me during our cooperation on literary articles when ideas of this book were discussed.

Dimitris Armaos provided very expert, valuable assistance in the use of drawings and figures.

In more ways than I can mention, my wife Liana, scholar and poet, has helped me explore the limits of criticism and creation.

List of Abbreviations

KUHN'S WORKS

CR	*The Copernican Revolution*
CG	*Criticism and the Growth of Knowledge* (Containing "Response to Critics" and "Logic of Discovery or Psychology of Research")
ET	*The Essential Tension* (Containing "Comment on the Relations of Science and Art"; "Second Thoughts on Paradigms"; "The Essential Tension")
SSR	*The Structure of Scientific Revolutions* (Containing "Postscript--1969")

BLOOM'S WORKS

Agon	*Agon: Towards a Theory of Revisionism*
AI	*The Anxiety of Influence*
BA	*Blake's Apocalypse*
BV	*The Breaking of the Vessels*
FC	*Figures of Capable Imagination*
KC	*Kabbalah and Criticism*
MM	*A Map of Misreading*
PI	*Poetics of Influence: New and Selected Criticism*
PR	*Poetry and Repression*
RT	*The Ringers in the Tower*
SM	*Shelley's Mythmaking*
VC	*The Visionary Company*
WS	*Wallace Stevens: The Poems of Our Climate*
Yeats	*Yeats*
DC	*Deconstruction and Criticism*

DERRIDA'S WORKS

AF	*The Archaeology of the Frivolous*
DS	*Dissemination*
Ear	*The Ear of the Other*
OR	*Edmund Husserl's `Origin of Geometry': An Introduction*
MP	*Margins of Philosophy*
OG	*Of Grammatology*
OS	*Of Spirit*
LIM	*Limited Inc...*
POS	*Positions*
PC	*The Post Card*
SP	*Speech and Phenomena*
TP	*The Truth in Painting*
WD	*Writing and Difference*

OTHER WORKS

BN	*Being and Nothingness* (Sartre)
EM	*An Essay on Man* (Cassirer)
ETR	*Einstein's Theory of Relativity Considered from the Epistemological Standpoint* (Cassirer)
LR	*The Lyotard Reader* (Edited by Andrew Benjamin)
SF	*Substance and Function* (Cassirer)

Genetic Codes of Culture?

Prologue:

Are There Genetic Codes Of Science, Poetry, and Philosophy?

Of all the biological kingdom, only we humans have evolved the possibility of being the cause of our own development. While animals remained in the jungles, humans created their own artificial environment of houses, buildings, cities, nations; they changed the way the whole planet looks.

The difference seems to be the power of making traditions, for it is through the continuity of learning, through the accumulation of knowledge, and through the transmission of it that the human race has changed itself so much. Even though chimpanzees can be taught to use various signs--a kind of "language ability"--they do not teach their young these signs, and the young do not transmit the knowledge while increasing it through the generations. Similarly, human children have been lost, abandoned in wild areas, raised by wolves, and then found by society. Typically, they can hardly be taught language and the benefit of thousands of years of human civilization cannot simply be invented by the lone individual. But by a miracle making us human, the child in society can eventually come to receive the accumulated knowledge of civilization in some specific fields and even extend this knowledge. It is as if all the individuals in history can come to act as one mind, one ever-growing human being.

In this process there must be a determining factor, there must be some way to tell how to advance the knowledge accumulated thus far. The following book contributes to the understanding of how this human miracle can occur.

Does Cultural Inheritance Resemble Biological Inheritance?

Nobel Prize winner George Beadle raises a question omnipresent in discussions of our time:

> We have learned to write down messages that are equivalent to DNA. We have developed through speech and writing very effective methods of communication. These methods of communication and the ability to reason, to store information in our nervous systems, to take it out, to rearrange it, and to communicate it, make possible the evolution of a cultural inheritance, which we alone among all creatures on earth possess. This inheritance includes language, religion, music, literature, art, technology, and science. No other organism has added...cultural inheritance to its biological inheritance. We accumulate our cultural inheritance individually; we transmit it to our fellow man, and we transmit it to the next generation in a cumulative fashion. Our educational institutions are engaged in the process of systematically transmitting such information to the next generation and in adding to it in a cumulative way from one generation to the next. This is in addition to and separate from our biological inheritance in its manner of accumulation, storage and transmission. ...The two types of inheritance [biological and cultural] are complementary. (*The Norton Reader: An Anthology of Expository Prose*, Ed. Arthur M. Eastman. W.W. Norton & Company, N.Y., 1969, 1294-95).

Beadle goes so far as to derive cultural inheritance in a direct, continuous line from biological inheritance:

> The assumed evolutionary sequence from hydrogen to man has proceeded through a fantastic number of steps, each almost imperceptibly small. Each

> represents a chemical change such as the fusion of hydrogen to form helium or the modification of a DNA "letter" by a simple chemical reaction. Through science, which is a part of our cultural inheritance, we have identified many of these evolutionary steps. The humanities, too, are a part of our cultural inheritance. In this sense, the two areas are closely related. If we are to understand and appreciate our total cultural inheritance, as we believe liberally educated men and women should, we cannot reasonably disregard any of its major components (1295).

Increasingly, thinkers of our time have been defining "evolutionary steps" in the arts, humanities, social sciences, and all fields formerly not thought to be evolutionary. Such discussion places all fields on a par as modes of developing our common heritage of culture.

To discuss the analogy of cultural inheritance to the biological, it is best to remember main traits of the latter. Francis Crick, winner of the Nobel Prize for Physiology of Medicine in 1962, has written explanations of the genetic code for a general educated audience, and these supply an accurate basis for our discussion. What strikes him as "the absolutely central requirement" of a genetic code is "for some rather precise method of replication" (63 *LI*). This requirement is a good definition of what is meant by the term `genetic code'. The organic molecules making up the genetic code replicate the giant chains of DNA and RNA such that they have "a regular, repeating structure" (46). DNA and RNA do "very little except replicate and code for proteins," making them into genetic material. "Fit mainly for reproduction," DNA and RNA are called "self-replicating systems," for they produce a copy which can itself be copied (72, 175). Such a basis for the continuity of individual living things is necessary for them to be capable of evolution. Life itself--the title of Crick's general book--being such a highly organized state of matter could not have arisen except by a very long series of small steps. And after life had leaped ahead of dead matter, culture could ahead of mere biological life.

"What is not quite so apparent," Crick writes, "is the marvelous capacity of such a system [the genetic code] to improve itself. ...The first thing to grasp is the continuing nature of the process. To achieve anything striking, the system must effectively go on forever" (56). Might this description not apply to cultural inheritance? Haven't the various traditions of the sciences, arts, humanities, and social sciences been continuous? Haven't they improved themselves and us? Don't many traditions seem to have gone on forever, beginning in prehistory? In them, too, it is worthwhile to consider if there might not be recurring structures uniting the generations.

Researchers in other fields besides science have found the link of cultural inheritance to the biological to be of paramount importance. Even more than Beadle, Thomas Sebeok, renowned semioticist--a researcher of signs and meaning, considers the idea of a genetic code to be crucial to his field and even to all others, the arts, humanities, and social sciences included. Taking Beadle's suggestion further, Sebeok writes,

> Numerous observations confirm the hypothesis that the internal organic world descend in a straight line from the primordial forms of life. The most remarkable fact is the omnipresence of the DNA molecule. The genetic material of all organisms known on earth is in great measure made up of the nucleonic acids DNA and RNA that contain in their information structure, transmitted by reproduction from one generation to another and furthermore gifted with the capacity of self-reproduction and imitation. Briefly, the genetic code is universal, or almost. ...It is obvious that the genetic code must be considered the most fundamental of all the semiotic networks [systems of signs], and therefore a prototype of all the other systems of signaling that animals use, man included. From this point of view, molecules which are systems of quanta and behave like stable vehicles of physical information, systems of animal semiotics and cultural systems, including language, constitute a continuous chain of stages, with always more complex energy levels, in the framework of a universal unique evolution. It is therefore possible to describe either language or living systems from a unified cybernetic point-of-view. For the present, this is only a useful

analogy or a prediction. A reciprocal rapprochement between animal communication and linguistics can lead to a complete knowledge of the dynamics of semiotics, and such a knowledge can be revealed, in the last analysis, to be nothing less than the very definition of life" (Quoted from 106-07 Baudrillard).

For Sebeok, the genetic code is "the most fundamental of all the semiotic networks, and therefore a prototype of all the other systems"--the arts, sciences, humanities, and social sciences. Sebeok's idea would permit the extension of operations of the genetic code to cultural forms. The idea of a "unified cybernetic point-of-view" makes all the fields of culture share common functions, makes them more comparable than many scholars have thought. A common prejudice after Darwin has been that science is evolutionary, whereas art and other fields are not. It is time to rethink the unity of human traditions.

The perspective of Sebeok, as well as other semioticists, has its historical precedent in the writings of Charles Sanders Peirce, self-proclaimed founder of semiotics. From Peirce's "procreation" model of the production of signs Sebeok argues for a "fundamental identity of the processes of biological reproduction and semiosis."[1] Even if no identity exists, cultural evolution may be like the biological.

The founder of semiology wrote about the new science as dynamic, biological: "a science that studies the life of signs...is conceivable; ...I shall call it `semiology'. ...Linguistics is only a part of the general science of semiology; the laws discovered by semiology will be applicable to linguistics" (825 Tedlock; elisions by Tedlock). Particularly important are the words "the life of signs" for a discussion of cultural and biological inheritance. In his theory of `interpretants' Peirce expressed much the same idea in non-biological terms; the meaning of a symbol is its translation into other symbols; the meaning of a sign can be explained by another sign; the meaning is in some sense another sign.[2] In Peirce's words, "A sign is anything which determines something else (its interpretant) to refer to an object to which itself refers (its object) in the same way, the interpretant becoming in turn a sign, and so on ad infinitum."[3] This "unlimited semiosis" can begin the explanation of the unlimited possibility for the accumulation of knowledge as civilization develops. About such progress, Walter Lowe wrote of a "life-story of three dialectical moments, which is remarkably consistent from the one thinker to the other," serving as an "undergirding framework." Triple repetitions are common cultural patterns, as when Boris Eichenbaum, Russian Formalist literary critic writes of "the triple repetition common in tales" (116 Lemon and Reis). Other examples are the Hegelian dialectic; Newton's three laws; Freud's id, ego, and superego; great paintings such as Christian tryptichs showing three parts of a story or Salvador Dali's "Metamorphosis of Narcissus"; and the Holy Trinity. Not just random patterns, the triple pattern is at work in the internal replication of DNA and seems to be essential for explaining unlimited semiosis or never-ending tradition (See Crick's Appendix to *LI*).

Semioticists by no means agree on the degree to which cultural inheritance can be identified with biological. Umberto Eco expresses reservations about G. Prodi's claims of bio-logic being the "materialistic foundation of the `cultural' logic" (184 *Semiotics*).[4] More significant is Eco's observation that the interpretation of one sign by a next one is the basis for growth in the process of interpretation.

Extending these ideas into social theory, Jean Baudrillard uses the idea of DNA to explain all meaning in contemporary society: "The process of signification is, at bottom, nothing but a gigantic *simulation model of meaning*" (160-161 *For a Critique...*). And concerning DNA as a model of social meaning, Baudrillard writes, "It is in effect in the genetic code that the `genesis of simulacra' today finds its most accomplished form".[5]

From these thinkers representing various cultural fields it is clear that the genetic code may be useful in interpreting the evolution of human traditions.

Myth Is Related to the Genetic Code

If an essential trait of the genetic code for cultural fields is that it is `self-improving', then myths might also be used in their explanation, since they are at bottom traditional tales accumulating the knowledge of the past.

Just as Beadle and others linked cultural inheritance to its biological origin, many scholars have traced the roots of various disciplines to mythic origins. One of the most famous mythologists, Joseph Campbell, speaks about the common origin in unusual terms:

> It would not be too much to say that myth is the secret opening through which the inexhaustible energies of the cosmos pour into human cultural manifestation. Religions, philosophies, arts, the social forms of primitive and historic man, prime discoveries in science and technology, the very dreams that blister, boil up from the basic, magic ring of myth (3 *Hero*).

Quite glowing, the description is unusual because he speaks of myth as being a formative power in contemporary culture. True, he believes, as many do, that fields historically *arose* from myth; but for an explanation of how contemporary fields resemble myth we shall have to look at other writers.

One way in which the power of myth may still be a creative force in contemporary non-mythical products has been expressed by the respected mythologists, Mr. and Mrs. H.A. Frankfort: mythical imagery "represents the form in which the experience has become conscious."[6] The structure of myths may lead their creators to new and higher values, and this structure, albeit transformed, may be simulated in modern disciplines.

Concentrating on the process of myth and describing it as a code, Baudrillard writes, "But myths are not comprised of content. They are a process of exchange and circulation of a code whose *form* is determinant" (159 *For a Critique...*). Here in the process of myth the creators are very much aware of the form the myth is taking; this form may lead us to the determining factor in human self-improvement, the source of our freedom, our distinctive nature.

And in *Simulations* he relates myth to DNA by their operation: "It remains to be seen if this operationality [of capital as an "interminable machine" or "social genetic code"] is not itself a myth, if DNA is not also a *myth*. Once and for all there is posed, in effect, the problem of science as discourse" (112-113). Why would the problem of science as discourse be a problem of the operation of myth or DNA? Baudrillard does not give a direct answer, for he has other goals, concerning social theory. Surely for this French thinker the answer lies partly in the awareness of the total form being represented in its formation, and partly in the self-perpetuation of DNA and RNA, "interminable machines."

For myth and DNA to be self-perpetuating they must operate by forming cycles. Jean-François Lyotard has written much about the operation of tradition through "narrative cycles." The mode of linking the cycles and the mode of linking within the cycles are crucial for the success of the continuity of myth and DNA. Within the cycle of the formation of new DNA there is an internal process of self-replication of its parts until the whole previous structure is reproduced. Such cycles of self-replication characterize myths. Lyotard explains these cycles by concentrating on their transmission as the most important factor:

> I, an Aryan, tell you, an Aryan, the narrative of our Aryan ancestors' acts. The single name *Aryan* occupies the three instances in the universes of the narrative phrase. ...The closed narrative cell operates prescriptively. ...If you hear, tell or do. If you tell, hear or do. If you do, tell or hear. The implications are reicprocal. You don't therefore enter into the narrative cycle, you are always already there, or you are never there. Such is the genre of mythic narrative. It is not cyclical in theme, but in its (if you will, pragmatic) transmission. That is why tradition obeys a ritual protocol: I, an Aryan, tell you this story that an Aryan told me, so tell it, carry it out, Aryans" (105 *Differend*).

Important for the issue of cultural inheritance, this passage describes how narratives can form similar cycles and be self-perpetuating--interminable machines of unlimited semiosis. To do that narratives must contain within themselves a reference to the narrative that went before ("the narrative of our Aryan ancestors' acts")--and notice that the past is spoken of as accumulated, and a reference to the narrative that will follow ("tell you, an Aryan" who must in turn tell the tale but in his/her new way). Such necessary connections between generations resemble the human life cycles from parent to child, to child of the child, and so on. Here Lyotard is writing about myths; how can the same principle of cyclical transmission apply to science, which isn't a story? Using different vocabulary more appropriate for science, this discourse could still be explained to be self-perpetuating if it contained a reference to the previous theory and some reference to what a subsequent theory would need to do. Such references could be integral to the structure of the science. These suggestions will be elaborated in the course of what follows.

A problem--only partially surmountable--of relating myth and DNA is the difference in the language styles scholars in the two areas have. Philosophers of science typically would reject any suggestion that scientific discourse as a tradition resembles myth, a common synonym for mistaken anthropomorphic beliefs and superstitions, just as scholars of myth tend to avoid assigning truth or false values to myths, preferring instead an explanation based on final causes. Thomas S. Kuhn, historian-philosopher of science, is somewhat unorthodox when he admits that science today is in a very important way not more scientific than that of centuries ago, which was intermixed with myth (2 *SSR*). He writes,

> ...historians confront growing difficulties in distinguishing the "scientific" component of past observation and belief from what their predecessors had readily labeled "error" and "superstition." The more carefully they study, say, Aristotelian dynamics, phlogistic chemistry, or caloric thermodynamics, the more certain they feel that those once current views of nature were, as a whole, neither less scientific nor more the product of human idiosyncracy than those current today. If these out-of-date beliefs are to be called myths, then myths can be produced by the same sorts of methods and held for the same sorts of reasons that now lead to scientific knowledge. If, on the other hand, they are to be called science, the science has included bodies of belief quite incompatible with the ones we hold today. Given these alternatives, the historian must choose the latter. Out-of-date theories are not in principle unscientific because they have been discarded. That choice, however, makes it difficult to see scientific development as a process of accretion (2-3 *SSR*).

When Kuhn claims that science of the past is not less scientific, he does not therefore claim that science has not improved; rather, he points out a continuity of the operation, the processes, the requirements of scientific discourse. Comparing scientific discourse to the operation of DNA it should be noted that biologists have determined the remarkable consistency of structure throughout thousands of years, and they measure the rate of change through time (such research was carried out at The University of California at Berkely and the California Polytechnic State University by removing DNA from ancient bees enclosed in amber). As a second main point in the passage, the acceptance of a *continuing* essential bond of science to myth seems to cast into doubt the progress of science by accretion. Perhaps science does not simply add some new ideas to some old ideas without changing them. Radical change in scientific meaning further casts into doubt the assumption that the purpose of science is to produce true or false statements about the environment.

Such an assumption is hard to apply to myth, for it seems to our common sense to lack a concern for truths about nature. Wild stories about dragons and demons; angels and underworlds; speaking rocks; ancestral parrots,--the often anthropomorphic fantasy has no one-to-one connection with the physical environment. In contrast to science, myths seem to express human powers and activities.

Myth does, nevertheless, develop according to some sense of truth values or at least increasing knowledge. The succession of myths in human history has been developmental, as it served to lead up to the traditional cultural discourses of today. Lévi-Strauss, structural anthropologist of the first rank, echoes Kuhn's idea of a structural identity of science through time when he writes about the continuity of myths. "Every myth is a mediation," he writes, "between a binary opposition." [7] This binary opposition comes from a previous myth so that myths are essentially traditional; their purpose is to take a step in tradition, not explain the external world. "The purpose of myth is to provide a logical model capable of overcoming a contradiction" (229 *Structural Anthropology*). Myths relate to the ones before and after such that three generations are needed to see the full cycle, this triadic context mirrored as a feedback mechanism within the myth itself. [I have researched for a few years the succession of ancient myths from the Babylonian Creation Myth through Homer, through Hesiod, through Pherecydes of Syros, and then through the tradition of Greek philosophy; and I might suggest that the myths move toward more integrated systems of ideas in a developmental process, thus accumulating the knowledge from the past and increasing the power of mind.] To speak of myth in terms of a logical model is quite foreign to the expectations of many philosophers of science who would reserve truth value for discursive "scientific" modes of thinking. Here we can find a bridge, albeit still small, between the tradition-making activities of myth and science. In Peirce's language, in some respects midway between the logicism of philosophers of science and the teleologism of mythologists, a scientific theory interprets a previous one and is in turn re-interpreted by a subsequent. If such a process in general did not occur, how could the continuity and development of science be explained? Musn't theories interlock like chains and build on the past like ascending steps? By mediating oppositions of previous myths and in their turn having oppositions that they produced mediated by subsequent myths, myths not only transmit their code of formation but essentially improve upon one another as the process is one of interpretation (involving comprehension), of totalizing the past in principle and improving it. The form of past myths explicitly enters new ones as factors of creation; such a cycle comprehending previous cycles would be "a determining factor within the phenomenon of development," which the Viennese art historian Alois Riegl deemed necessary and actually present (9). This knowledge of how to create may make cultural genetic codes, if there are any, of a higher more developed order than biological codes improving only as a result of chance, not self-determination. To be human is to be free, and to be free is to choose, thought Sartre.

"It has always been the prime function of mythology and rite," writes Joseph Campbell, "to supply the symbols that carry the human spirit forward... " (11 *Hero*). Might not such a building of tradition be the prime function of science? Certainly, if this is correct, other purposes might still be achieved through science, such as the control of the environment, the making of technological devices, products, lifestyles.

Scholars in the twentieth century have begun to regard myth not as a mistaken product of superstition and ignorance but as a mode of traditon-making. Geoffrey Kirk places myth in the more general category of traditional tale, as does Walter Burkert (1 Burkert):

> ...myth is a traditional tale with secondary, partial reference to something of collective importance. Myth is traditional tale applied; and its relevance and seriousness stem largely from this application. The reference is secondary, as the meaning of the tale is not to be derived from it...; and it is partial, since tale and reality will never be quite isomorphic in these applications" (23 Burkert).

Lyotard also writes about myth as "traditional narrative," a process in which "a ritual fixes the extension of myths and their recurrence" (152 *Differend*). Myths are designed to be recurring steps in tradition by which the individual enhances the entire human tradition. According to Campbell,

> The standard path of the mythological adventure of the hero is a magnification of the formula represented in the rites of passage: *separation--initiation--return*: which might be named the nuclear unit of the monomyth. *A hero ventures forth from the world of common day into a region of supernatural wonder: fabulous forces are there encountered and a decisive victory is won: the hero comes back from this mysterious adventure with the power to bestow boons on his fellow man*" (30 *Hero*).

Northrop Frye "identified the central myth of literature, in its narrative aspect, with the quest-myth" (25). J. Hillis Miller, renowned literary critic, describes a life quest of the individual, who must first assimilate tradition and then, to be an individual, must repeat traditional knowledge but in a new way, providing a benefit to the entire human community" (109-110 *The Form of...*). (The life quest resembles the stages in psychological development from the id to the ego to the superego.)

Not only do myths *perform* the process of an individual extending tradition but they also *discuss* this problem as their subject. A good example is the bright crimson and yellow mythical bird, the phoenix as the Greeks began to call it, whose original Egyptian name was `Ennu'. It visited Egypt after the death of its father and buried its parent in the shrine particularly dedicated to it at Heliopolis, divine city of the sun, a symbol of recurrence and regeneration and the source of life. When near death, the phoenix made a nest for itself from which arose a new phoenix. As with most myths there are variations through time; the most popular version is that only one such bird existed at any one time, which would burn itself from whose ashes a new young phoenix arose. The bird used in literature symbolizes the soul, its immortality, its capacity for rebirth. Can we add "tradition"?

To close this section on myth as a possible starting point, along with DNA, for the explanation of some link between cultural and biological genetic codes, the idea of the phoenix has been suggested to be a model. Any specific tradition form--be it a scientific theory, a style of painting by one painter, Beethoven's music, a sociology, a form of the novel--any must have a life-cycle like the phoenix. The individual and his/her cultural products are limited, but in that limitation there is the power to be an individual as handed down by the community; no one could start without any knowledge of the past and develop a more advanced science, as shown by the examples of "wolf children" who did not on their own invent language. Using an idea like the phoenix to explain the humanities are the words of Georg Simmel, quoted by Ernst Cassirer in *The Logic of the Humanities*:

> For we define a tragic fate--in contradistinction to one which is pitiable or comes as destruction from external causes--as one in which the destroying forces are not only directed against a being but originate in the deepest recesses of this very being; it is a fate in which a destiny is completed in a self-destruction which is latent and, so to speak, the logical development of the very structure by means of which that being has attained its positive existence.[8]

All living things die but their kind can continue beyond them. Musn't specific scientific theories, myths, literary works, and other tradition-making fields form life-cycles? Musn't they be able to continue their kind beyond themselves? Musn't there be some cultural genetic codes?

Both Myth and the Genetic Code Describe Features of Human Traditions

For a time in the physics of the early part of the twentieth century there was a problem of characterizing some phenomena as waves or alternatively as particles yet not at the same time. Eventually, a higher more integral notion lay behind the separate concepts. Such a situation applies to a possible relation between myth and the genetic code. How do they operate in similar ways? What is a more fundamental category than either for the description of evolutionary processes in human civilization? The answer, begun in this following section and further developed in this book, is a "tradition form."

A "tradition form" is an actual cultural life-cycle; for example, Eliot's poetry, all Einstein's theories, Freud's entire psychology. It is the size of a life, for it represents the structure of all the work by one individual. It repeats the pattern of the field and provides the structure from which a successor will develop a similar pattern. It always means a life's work in one specialty; for example, in science, it is better than "scientific theory," because different parts of his total work are often given the name of a theory separately--the Theory of Special Relativity, the Theory of General Relativity. Similarly, it could be a poetry as opposed to a poem, literature providing the distinction missing in science between the whole body of work and one part in it. "Tradition form" emphasizes that to be a cultural form is to be a unit in tradition.

The question, "What is a unit of tradition in science, poetry, or philosophy?" is identical to the question, "What is a science, a poetry, a philosophy?" At any level throughout history, any science contains the latest understanding of the idea of science--in modern terms science contains meta-science. Specific scientific theories evolve the idea of what science does for the human race.

How can cultural fields be limited to specific steps in tradition? In the words of Baudrillard, the unity of a science is nothing but "the coherence of a certain *discourse*, and all scientific movement is nothing but the space of this discourse, never revealing itself as such..." (113 *Simulations*). The form of a science is its "coherence," the uniting of one concept to another within a relatively closed body of concepts, here called a "space"--a term used by others such as

Gaston Bachelard and Jacques Derrida. There is a "scheme of scientific discourse" known to itself. If there weren't criteria of scientificity accessible to scientists, how could they ever know an improvement has been made? Worse yet, how could there ever be any improvement?

A coherence, a space, a scheme of scientific discourse must represent itself as part of the process. With this need in mind Northrop Frye offered valuable suggestions about defining literature systematically, which is only possible if literature itself has a systematic character (20). By no means is the idea that literature makes systematic products widespread outside of literary criticism. Frye finds a possible systematic quality in literature's representation to itself of its total process: "An archetype [of literature] should be not only a unifying category of criticism, but itself a part of a total form, and it leads us at once to the question of what sort of total form criticism can see in literature" (20). "Total form" indicates a unity of literature akin to the coherence, the space, the scheme spoken of by Baudrillard. Within it creators of literature can make archetypes again, which means that they are realizing how the total form is made--its tradition form. And besides the systematic character of literature, it must have an orienting effect, much as a map can only function if we imagine our present location in the grid of relations; literature, too, contains within itself directions as to how to ascend the stair steps of the evolution it effects in our total being.

The unit of a science or any field is that unit which can reproduce itself, to use biological language, or that unit which can become understood and improved upon by a succeeding similar unit, perhaps typically in a threefold movement. "Our example," writes Lyotard, "clearly illustrates that a narrative tradition is also the tradition of the criteria defining a threefold competance--`know-how', `knowing how to speak', and `knowing how to hear'--through which the community's relationship to itself and its environment is played out. What is transmitted through these narratives is the set of pragmatic rules that constitutes the social bond" (21 *Postmodern*). The three generations here correspond to the three phases of myth outlined by Joseph Campbell: separation--initiation--return, forming a rite of passage, a process of maturation or coming into being. For cultural fields to be traditional, there must be knowledge of the past, new knowledge, and knowledge of how to discover in what has been learned how to learn more. (Cultural forms regularly close themselves with the knowledge of the new creative process just traversed, as will be discussed at length.)

As Derrida writes, "The quality and fecundity of a discourse are perhaps measured by the critical rigor with which this relation to the history of metaphysics and to inherited concepts is thought. Here it is a question of a critical relation to the language of the social sciences and a critical responsibility of the discourse itself" (282 *WD*). As a tradition form, any cultural work criticizes the work before it and, since its quality depends on the rigor of the criticism, a form must come into being for the sake of remaking its tradition.

In art history Heinrich Wölfflin interprets the primary function of painting, sculpture, and architecture not to be an imitation of nature, as science is most often thought to be its explanation, but rather to be a new step in tradition, a new cycle in the total history of art. Using almost biological terminology that is quite foreign to most descriptions of science, he writes,

> The history of forms never stands still. There are times of accelerated impulse and times of slow imaginative activity, but even then an ornament continually repeated will gradually alter its physiognomy. Nothing retains its effect. What seems living to-day is not quite living to-morrow. This process is not only to be explained negatively by the theory of the palling of interest and a consequent necessity of a stimulation of interest, but positively also by the fact that every form lives on, begetting, and every style calls to a new one. We see that clearly in the history of decoration and architecture. But even in the history of representative art, the effect of picture on picture as a factor in style is much more important than what comes directly from the imitation of nature. Pictorial imitation developed from decoration--the design as representation once arose from the ornament--and the after-effects of this relation have affected the whole of art history (230).

Here "the effect of picture on picture as a factor in style" suggests that creation occurs as a reaction to tradition, that what is made is a new form of tradition, that a similar kind of step is taken forward. Literary works, too, remain within the tradition by repeating a pattern and nevertheless extend it as well.[9] In this way, and not as accretion of permanent facts, is there accumulation of knowledge: not mere addition but cultural evolution.

It is the nature, essence, definition of a cultural work to develop as a reaction to a work before it. The creation and validity of a discourse are determined by its own principles. The ideas of science or the images of poetry "cannot be defined by relation to a substance which is alien to them. As Tynyanov observes, `The function of each work is in its correlation with others...It is a differential sign'" (252 *Poetics of Prose*).

It is harder to admit that science is not fundamentally an explanation of nature than that art is not fundamentally an imitation of nature. But underlying them both is a determining factor made known through the traditionalizing process. Lévi-Strauss sees myth as akin to science when he writes about the operation of myth: "Myths...were simply making a general application of the processes according to which thought finds itself to be operating, these processes being the same in both areas, since thought, and the world which encompasses it, are two correlative manifestations of the same reality."[10] If this is true of science, then scientists by making science would become more aware of the science-making process, of a power of their own minds, and never could they compare their concepts to a world unformed by previous science or perception unafffected by science. If science is a continuous *progressive* tradition, musn't previous science-making processes become known to new scientists? If so, science--the greatest examples of it--would reflect the operation of the mind and be for us primarily a way to develop ourselves in the course of civilization, notwithstanding secondary technological benefits undreamed of by the greatest scientists. The great epistemologist of science, Ernst Cassirer, bases his view of science not on correspondence with nature but on the continuity of a type of discourse through generations when he writes, "But above all it is the general form of natural law which we have to recognize as the real invariant and thus as the real logical framework of nature in general"; the *form* of natural law is the invariant, the coherence of scientific discourse, the space, the scheme, the tradition form (374 *ETR*). The individual culture-maker brings about the perpetuation of the field's code, or way of doing things, almost as if in repayment for having been given the power of self-fulfillment by past codes. The individual and the human community are so closely cooperative that a kind of symbiosis occurs; each lives through the other.

Though not many people would be at first willing to agree that science is more a mode of individual and species development than explanation, there are additional truths in support of this view. Consider the function of science to make civilization continuous. Beginning before 1000 B.C. the sciences of mathematics and astronomy have endured through the millennia, or perhaps it is the human kind that have endured because of it. Science and other cultural fields are the means by which we have a common identity; without the past on which to build no one in any society would have had the level of thought and life that they had; they would be reduced to "wolf children." So there is a growing sense of the human community. The continuity for science so often defended by philosophers of science should be applied to literature and the arts as well. In the words of Curtius, "The literary tradition is the medium by which the European mind preserves its identity through the millenniums. Memory (Mnemosyne), according to the Greek myth, is the Mother of the Muses" (395). The human capacity of cultural memory may be unlimited, for at each new step in a tradition the whole past was comprehended and added to. Or, rather than being a matter of quantity, it is better, more intelligible to think of it as a performing of mind's own nature--as the distinctive function of human mind to operate as a tradition-making process. Then there need not be an explanation for the seemingly unlimited power of remembering the ever-increasing quantity of knowledge, feeling, perception in any one specialty.

More precisely than before, I can describe the unit of tradition as the step by which an individual can receive the whole of the accumulated knowledge in a specialty and then can make a definite contribution to the whole accumulated knowledge of human history. In *The Hero with a Thousand Faces*, this title suggesting the common identity of human beings, Campbell describes the interplay of individual and community contributions:

> The tribal ceremonies of birth, initiation, marriage, burial, installation, and so forth, serve to translate the individual's life-crises and life-deeds into classic, impersonal forms. They disclose him to himself, not as this personality or that, but as the warrior, the bride, the widow, the priest, the chieftain; at the same time rehearsing for the rest of the community the old lesson of the archetypal stages. All participate in the ceremonial according to rank and function. The whole society becomes visible to itself as an imperishable living unit. Generations of individuals pass, like anonymous cells from a living body; but the sustaining, timeless form remains. By an enlargement of vision to embrace this super-individual, each discovers himself enhanced, enriched, supported, and magnified. His role, however unimpressive, is seen to be intrinsic to the beautiful festival-image of man-- the image, potential yet necessarily inhibited, within himself" (383).

In the manner of Campbell, we "all participate in" science "according to rank and function," meaning that science is a value for the whole community but not the same value for each member; some--most-- cannot understand the greatest science as the creators or successors could, and so the meaning of the activity must vary within the community. And also in the manner of Campbell, we can say that the "whole" of science "becomes visible to itself as an imperishable living unit." More specifically, in order to remember the entire cultural past in a specialty it must be comprehended in an abbreviated form or in principle, that is, by a new figure of science. The relation of Einstein to previous physics warrants such a suggestion, as we shall see later.

If both myth and the genetic code suggest features of the more integral idea `tradition form', and properties of myth apply to science, then science may be revealing of myth, humanities, the arts, and social sciences. "...The sciences provide a particularly promising area," concurs Kuhn, "in which to explore the role of forces current in the larger society in shaping the evolution of a discipline which is simultaneously controlled by its own internal demands. That study, if successful, could provide models for a variety of fields besides the sciences" (160 *ET*). Conversely, Kuhn described his originality as having applied methods or assumptions about art or philosophy when discussing the history of science (348 *CR*). Placing science and art within some common category, he writes, "That science and art are both products of human behavior is a truism, but not therefore inconsequential" (351 *ET*). On the contrary, that they both are products of human behavior, which is traditional, suggests that the study of one can enrich the study of the other. Kuhn's statement that the gains of scholarship on science could be applied to other fields highly valorizes the evolutionary quality and could suggest that those fields manifest this quality in a lower degree, making them less evolutionary or less `scientific', systematic.

The idea of interdisciplinarity, which became prominent in the structuralist movement, especially through a chief promoter of it--Jean Piaget, raises questions concerning the influence one field has on another. Can principles be translated from one discipline into another? Can there be some cross-fertilization? Does a change in one field necessitate, cause, or influence a change in another field? Are changes in one field parallel to those of another because of a common spirit of the age? Does Jung's idea of synchronicity--that two events may have the same meaning and occur at the same time but not be causally related--apply to interdisciplinarity? If all cutural fields have implicit links affecting their development, then do they form a complex of cooperating activities as the senses silently agree with one another to form a unified world?

In this book dealing with science, poetry, and philosophy no claim is made that a change in one field *brings about* a change in another, nor that there is an identity of meaning among various cultural activities. There can be relevance and value of one field for another without the assumption of identity of meaning or production in another one. Rather, the study of each field enriches the others due to their common status as modes of forming tradition, of changing the level of human existence. Being phenomena of tradition they may be discussed as sharing some functions and qualities. Though their agreement may be silent, cultural fields may nonetheless tell us how they effect a level change, each in its own way, thus contributing to the common purpose of civilization.

Another great obstacle to studies of more than one discipline has been the dispute over the use of teleological explanation. Typically, science is not characterized by final causes, nor does it use them; art, in contrast, uses them but is not evolutionary in the same definite sense of accumulating knowledge, getting better. By limiting this dispute to the issue of creation in science versus art, we can see an underlying prejudice, present in the best of minds. The great philosopher Immanuel Kant wrote, "Thus we can readily learn all that *Newton* has set forth in his immortal work on the Principles of Natural Philsophy, however great a head was required to discover it; but we cannot learn to write spirited poetry, however express may be the precepts of the art and however excellent its models."[11] Here is a prejudice for science and against art in the form of a false analogy: the understanding of science is compared to the creation of art. But shouldn't the *creation* of science be compared with the *creation* of art? Or shouldn't the understanding of science be compared with the understanding of some poems? There are two questionable assumptions behind this common faulty view both, it seems to me, placing art on a lower level of human achievement. First of all, Kant's statement assumes that many people *fully* know Newton's principles, yet isn't there a limit to their knowledge preventing them from being creators? The understanding of science may mean that `scientists' can solve motion problems using Newtonian formulas. But using formulas is a much easier mental feat than creating a system of formulas describing the entire physical universe. Understanding science in this sense is a lower level of scientific knowledge than creation is. Secondly, Kant confidently asserts without discussion, "we cannot learn to write spirited poetry, however express may be the precepts of the art and however excellent its models." A questionable assumption, art is deficient with respect to science because it lacks the means by which to determine its direction; art is less objective, less epistemic, more subjective, more mysterious; it hardly has a tradition. Some better alternative lies buried in the words of Kant when he mentions the excellent models art may have to base itself on. In their use the opposition of evolution (the prerogative of science) may be reconciled with teleology (the prerogative of art and the humanities) by a deeper unity of the relation of work to work, model to model. If the evolution of science is construed as limited to individual steps without the assumption of the same final cause guiding the entire history, then it may use final causes to show itself its own form during the creation process: science must become aware of its own causes. Only by representing its processes to itself could science change them and accumulate them; psychologists say that a child's memory begins to form a personal history only when a self concept can be formed. The awareness of science's own processes, however, can only be limited to science at a specific level of development. In this way science is actually less explicit than it was thought to be, and the greater divergences in successive art forms can be explained not by the failure of art to have a single goal guiding the entire history but by a step--a definite step--being made beyond the previous artistic level. Whether in science or in art, each renews itself by modeling on past forms, all of which success is limited to the specific conception of science or art at that level, this conception acting as a final (but limited) cause. These important ideas shall be discussed further and in different ways.

Literature Improves Itself through Narratives (as Do Myths and the Genetic code)

Since the change in the arts seemed more irregular than that in science, and since science seemed to be more continuous as it produced more and more useful technology, the arts and humanities have often been thought not to be evolutionary. After all, most people can more readily see the change in everyday objects than in the spirit of a culture.

It is commonly thought that all cultural fields evolved from myth; this does not mean, however, that myths are precultural, that they are mistakes before culture begins seriously, nor that they lack forces in them leading beyond themselves. They must themselves have been evolutionary, or how else could they have led up to more advanced cultural fields? Furthermore, not all cultural works of ancient Greece and before can be grouped indifferently as myths, for scrutiny reveals definite lines of transmission through different kinds of mythical works. Kuhn quite astutely remarks that some scientific traditions can be traced to prehistory, such as astronomy and mathematics. It is more accurate to speak of mythical astronomy or mathematics than to speak of all myths as isomorphic.

Concerning literature the evolution from myth is clearer, more acceptable, whereas such a link in discussions of science usually result in the denial of myth, the denial of it having any scientific, evolutionary qualities. Literature improves itself through narratives, and it can do so because its specific bodies of work act like myths and the genetic code; they are tradition forms: forms in which tradition moves itself forward.

Harold Bloom, very celebrated American literary critic, based his first book on the mythical qualities of Shelley's poetry: *Shelley's Mythmaking*. In it he agrees with scholars who trace the origin of literature to a transformation of myth: "myth became a certain kind, and tradition, of poetry" (4 *SM*). The common term between myth and poetry here is tradition. If this is the main function making these types of discourse relatively continuous, an analysis of the tradition-making would illuminate the nature of literature.

The continuity of the literary tradition can be explained by its transmission from one generation to the next. Like the phoenix, each great body of literary work, each great poetry, each great group of novels and of plays, has a cycle of development. What makes the cycle possible is that parts of the process refer to the whole of literature undergoing the labor of revision. This holomorphism of literary figures, their having some of the structure of the whole, is a difficult but salient point for understanding the `immortality' of literature in human civilization. More simply, literature has as its subject the whole of literature, which is in process; truths about social reality or psychology are secondary at best. As only preliminary evidence, with more to follow later, consider the description of this creative feedback mechanism in the words of Lyotard, philosopher, especially of art:

> If the dream can be described as a game, it is not simply because it has `an effect upon the world', but rather, because it is articulated as a struggle, as a conflict whose resolution can only be provisory and partial. And this resolution always implies a narrative. That is why the `pragmatics' of the dream is reminiscent of that of the `narration of popular tale' as analyzed in *Just Gaming* (and also in *The Postmodern Condition*). According to this analysis, the privileged term in these tales is the narrated, not as a content,

> but as an interminable and indeterminable `relaying'. For every effort to determine it becomes itself a variation and continuation of the story. Thus it can be said that `we are always immanent to stories in the making, even when we are the ones telling the story to the other' (110 *Just Gaming*).

This passage describes a struggle to resolve a conflict; the resolution must be performed by a narrative, a literary process. Earlier in this Prologue the trait of myth to mediate binary oppositions of previous myths was mentioned. Evolving out of myth, literature retained the struggle over a conflict; all plot has some struggle, some suspense for the reader, some dynamism of development. The conflict seems to concern people or events, whereas Lyotard is saying that the conflict is about the whole of the literary proces: "the privileged term in these tales is the narrated [the whole of the literary process currently underway], not as a content, but as an interminable and indeterminable `relaying'." Secondly, Lyotard claims that every effort to determine the whole process moves the process on to new events. A literary representation of the whole process moves the narrative or is the dynamism of creation. So, thirdly, each point at which a narrative attempts to represent the whole process can have only partial success or resolution of the struggle to do so--until a total form of a poetry, novel, or drama is achieved. The partial success even at the most mature phase of a body of literature is necessary to explain why the work, likened to a myth, produces some binary opposition, some conflict of aesthetic representation of the whole of literature to make a subsequent literary work necessary. The feedback mechanism in literature by which it knows how to create depends upon the representation of the whole idea of a literature in strategic points in a work. While more determinate than commonly thought, the process is nonetheless limited insofar as all writers know the whole of literature only as the specific form they give to it; there is no single idea which all writers use identically as a model. The process can be truly evolutionary only if literary history is not predetermined by a final cause that cannot change.

Literary works model themselves on previous ones, as Gregory Ulmer writes, "Literary or plastic texts...are not analyzed but are adopted as models or tutors to be imitated, as generative forms for the production of another text" (x-xi *Applied Grammatology*, Baltimore: Johns Hopkins University Press, 1985). Frye discusses the modeling of literary works on the larger whole of literature, and then a poetry, for example, is a model of literature at a certain level. According to this view, it is understandable that each work would represent the whole of literature as it is being revised. Works would also model themselves on previous ones, essentially the last great one, representing the whole of literature and handing it down in its individual form. For literature to be understood as any science would, claims Frye, there must be "a co-ordinating principle, a central hypothesis which, like the theory of evolution in biology, will see the phenomena it deals with as parts of a whole" (18). [Even stronger theorists of literature as evolutionary are the French scholar Ferdinand Brunetière, the Russian Formalists Alexander Veselovsky, Yury Tynyanov, and Viktor Shklovsky.] To know how to advance itself, literature must constantly remind itself of the current idea of the whole of literature; it must give itself a mirror.

In the modeling of novels on previous novels, poetries on previous ones, and so on, there is conflict, struggle, and development of a new ideal of literature. The behavior of literary works toward one another, initial parodying leading to extension of the art and culminating in a literary dead end awaiting a revival, is mirrored within the works. "Shakespeare's plays," writes Howard Nemerov, himself a poet laureate of America, "are always about the transfer of power from one generation to the next, and the struggle for power among the young siblings--they may be brothers, or friends, or cousins, but it's always happening. And that, of course, gives the drama an immense power, because we'd like also to have them brought down to our level--at least in the respect that they have the same family troubles we have" (52). Such conflict of generations is represented within literature as its subject matter and also describes the process of the work in relation to its predecessor; this mirroring is a determining factor in the accumulation of knowledge, in the revision and extension of literary form. How universal this conflict is! Think only of ancient Greek myths and tragedy, with its most famous son Oedipus, who provided different models throughout history--even to the non-literary field of psychology, Freud's `Oedipus and electra complexes' in particular.

From these preliminary ideas about the improvement of literature, we can conclude that the transformation of myth into literature helps to show the latter's continuity and self-determination. The transformation is an evolution, not a case of interdisciplinarity. The discussion ended in reference to the value of Sophocles' *Oedipus* for Freud. Does this influence show one discipline can produce new ideas in another? I think such a conclusion is too hasty. Instead, it seems that both activities, drama and psychology, are tradition-making activites, and that Sophocles' representation of this process of drama within his works helped Freud to realize he needed an analogous powerful representation--a representation of the tradition-making activity of psychology within his psychology, a representation of tradition within his tradition form. On this suggestion, the id, ego, and superego are directly concerned with various human beings' individual psychology, but more importantly the conflict in them may have represented to Freud the developmental criteria of psychology as a science. This view does not mean that psychology can directly use drama as a creative force; it does mean that drama and psychology both make traditions.

The traditon-making is re-encoded in each new body of literary work. The work has as its purpose this new encoding. So the conflict of works, their differences, are essential to the process. In the words of Eco in "A Logic of Culture," "...a text (for instance a literary work) does not perform a `code-abiding' operation, but a `code-making' one: this involves a type of discourse which `announces' a possible code, which `produces' a new articulation of the culture (as Julia Kristeva shows)" (16). The announcing of a possible code acts as the operation of final causes; literature represents to itself a new model or ideal as a constitutive factor in the creation process.

Kuhn, Bloom, and Derrida All Describe Tradition Like a Genetic Code.

Thomas S. Kuhn, historian/philosopher of science; Harold Bloom, literary critic; and Jacques Derrida, philosopher, all describe tradition like a genetic code.

Kuhn is interested in the evolution of science, in "the processes by which scientific concepts evolve and replace their predecessors" (4 *CR*). The evolution from what he calls "the two-sphere universe" is compared with giving birth:

> The Copernican universe is itself the product of a series of investigations that the two-sphere universe made possible: the conception of a planetary earth is the most forceful illustration of the effective guidance given to science by the incompatible conception of a unique central earth. That is why a discussion of the Copernican Revolution must begin with a study of the two-sphere cosmology which Copernicanism ultimately made obsolete. The two-sphere universe is the parent of the Copernican; no conceptual scheme is born from nothing (41 *CR*).

Even though he describes the relation of one life-work of science with another as a birth, as an evolution on its smallest scale, he predominantly understands the relation as a "revolution"; his main work is *The Structure of Scientific Revolutions*, not `The Structure of Scientific Evolution'. "Revolution" suggests a more complete change than the less violent "evolution."

For Harold Bloom, too, there is a difference between generations revealing an evolution, and this change is often referred to with words suggesting it to be a process of bearing children. But in poetry, Bloom claims, the struggle between generations is stronger, more central to its purpose. Furthermore, the biological functioning of his field is much more emphasized. Tradition, as critics have pointed out, is very central to Bloom's whole concern.[12] He writes about "the tradition pattern" in romanticism (223 *PR*) and of "paradigms"--a word Kuhn's theory of science made commonplace.

This pattern is "a triad" and "a life-cycle"--in general like biological inheritance: "Poems stay alive when they engender live poems, even through resistance, resentment, misinterpretation; and poems become immortal when their descendants in turn engender vital poems" (99 *PR*; 7 *AI*; 200 *MM*). Bloom's generations of great poetries sound much like the relations of DNA to its offspring. Not only does a triad characterize the structure of a poem, or of a poetry, but a triplicity of generations characterizes the life-cycle of a poetry. Thus, in order to define it clearly, determinately, completely there must be a situating of the poetry among the generations immediately before and after. Since "the poems themselves are acts of reading," the process of creating poetry is self-critical (26 *PR*). There is a feedback mechanism or mirroring in poetic creation to act as a determining factor.

The triadic pattern Bloom found confirmed in a medieval Jewish doctrine of creation, "Kabbalah," meaning tradition, and he believes this doctrine is an analogue to Derrida's work (44 *MM*). There are other approving remarks about the work (1 *PR*).

Derrida, like Kuhn and Bloom, is most concerned with tradition and, more like Bloom than Kuhn, he writes about cultural creation on the model of a genetic decoding and encoding: `Hence, let me beg leave to repeat it, there is a necessity of making a new combination of ideas, beginning with the most simple ideas transmitted by the senses, and framing them into complex notions, which combined in their turn, will be productive of others, and so on" (62 *AI*). Speaking of evolutionary processes of the mind, Derrida claims one of his key concepts can "transgress nature and yet remain within it" (187 *OG*). Such terms make clear that the essential purpose of a cultural work is improvement. In his philosophy this transgression and repetition describes the relation of generations.

Like Bloom, Derrida understands the idea of tradition through three generations of successive works:

> Under these conditions, Condillac's relation to Locke will be analogous to Locke's relation to his predecessors. The science of human understanding, as properly inaugurated by Locke, is repeated, corrected, and completed by Condillac--particularly concerning the decisive question of language (43 *AF*).

Again, tradition is modeled on a genetic code, on an almost biological relation of three generations--on a network of environing relations, which define the code and which were set up by it. And, the relations between generations resemble the relations between myths insofar as Derrida claims one generation "corrects" the previous one and, as has been mentioned, myths resolve oppositions affecting previous myths.

In the case of myth, however, as opposed to the analogy of the genetic code, there is a clearer sense of final causes, of an idea of the process represented in it, of a determining factor in creation capable of explaining the non-arbitrary direction in progress and thus raising cultural inheritance above the automatism of mere biological reproduction.

The evolution of one generation to the next--notice that one usually speaks of evolution on a very large scale of time and change--is based on analogy. One body of scientific work, say Einstein's, is developed by analogy from a physics preceding it. Philosophers of science would criticize the idea of analogy as being inexact, for all analogies break down. Yet, Derrida does not agree that *his* understanding of the relation of generations is inexact; in fact, it is exact and so can be extended from science to other fields to explain evolution from one work to the next:

> So let us see how analogy makes us speak in this science, and we will know how it ought to make us speak in the others. That is what I propose. Thus mathematics, which I will treat, is in this work an object subordinated to a much greater object. The question is showing how this exactitude can be given to all the sciences, an exactitude believed to be the exclusive lot of mathematics.[13]

Combined with the previous passage from Derrida on "repeating, correcting, and completing" the preceding work, this one means to assert an exactitude for the analogy by which one work creates itself from another.

Do All Three Belong to the Intellectual Movement called "Deconstruction"?

Kuhn, Bloom, and Derrida are all very concerned with tradition; however, whether they all belong to the same intellectual movement is a controversial issue, worth introducing now, only to be answered fully after much detailed discussion.

Are they all "deconstructionists" *because* of their concern for tradition? This term, coined by Derrida, in preliminary terms means a reaction of one philosophy to a preceding one--revising, extending, and completing what the earlier couldn't. Does the same process of forming a new step in tradition characterize science and, if it does, does Kuhn think so? Does the same process apply to poetry in Bloom's theory?

It is less clear that Kuhn is a deconstructionist than it is for Bloom. Kuhn's most famous work was written in 1962--five years before Derrida published his main deconstruction: *Of Grammatology*. Apart from this temporal difference, Kuhn's work manifests other differences, to be discussed in detail. More striking at first are some strong similarites. Regarded by many scholars to be controversial when published such as "incommensurability," "crisis," "conversion," and "paradigm," these key ideas on revolutions have reverberations in the work of Bloom and Derrida. What is more, Kuhn has an idea of the "reconstruction" of previous science that positions his work closer to deconstruction than to other views by philosophers of science.

There are many reasons to place Bloom in the movement called deconstruction. The most prevalent reason has been the publication of *Deconstruction and Criticism*, containing an essay by Bloom, one by Derrida, and others now commonly identified as proponents of deconstruction. Here is Art Berman's view:

> Deconstruction in America has come to be defined through the work of four critics, J. Hillis Miller, Paul de Man, Geoffrey Hartman, and Harold Bloom... . The attempt to integrate Derridean analysis, especially its ramifications for selfhood, is compromised in their writings (5-6).

Berman explains how each of the mentioned authors attempts to integrate Derrida's philosophical developments, his deconstruction. When Berman discusses Bloom, he claims there is only one respect in which that critic can be called a deconstructionist: "only in his use of the idea of indeterminacy does he resemble the deconstructionsts" (6). Derrida is similarly charged with indeterminate views; deconstruction, however, is a very determinate intellectual operation of one text in relation to its precursor, as Derrida claims in several publications.

At any rate, the issue of who is a deconstructionist should be separated from the issue of the determinacy of interpretation. Moreover, when discussing indeterminacy everyone must ask for whom are the views indeterminate and in what ways?

Perhaps *seemingly* idiosyncratic or unintelligible ideas of Bloom (and Derrida) give Berman and others such an impression; consider the following: "the heart of Shelley's central myth" is "the defeat of, the unmaking of myth" (111 *SM*). Such ideas sound like deconstruction, indeed express a function of it--the change or `undoing' of tradition, yet they are not indeterminate, being elaborated in more than fifteen books through a complex analysis of poetic relationships. Deconstruction is not synonymous with the view that interpretation is indeterminate. Derrida does limit the degree in which any text can be known, especially by its creator, but a limitation of determinacy is not its complete denial. All in all, this question, requiring a knowledge of the whole philosophy or theory of poetry, is too complex to be solved in a Prologue.

The best way to determine whether Kuhn and Bloom do perform deconstruction is to determine first what Derrida meant; doing so will lead to determining the relative merits of their views, which outweighs tagging them with this or that group membership.

The Three Authors Are Contemporaries with Much Popularity and Influence.

The three authors to be discussed in the following book are all celebrated but controversial sons of their time, each publishing his main work within approximately ten years of the others (Kuhn 1962, Derrida 1967, Bloom 1973). Not only do their writings have in common the interest in tradition but they also have the advantage of being unusually famous and so belong in the same category of very influential thinkers of their time

Kuhn mentioned his fame in the following way: "Part of the reason for its success [*The Structure of Scientific Revolutions*] is, I regretfully conclude, that it can be too nearly all things to all people" (293 *SSR*).

The "highly influential" work of Kuhn has been praised by I. Bernard Cohen, himself a theorist of scientific revolution, :

> In 1962, Thomas S. Kuhn's *Structure of Scientific Revolutions* radically altered our thinking about scientific change. Few books in the history of science have stimulated so much interest and so continuing a dialogue. Even those who do not follow Kuhn's analysis in all detail have been provoked to consider that the advance of science is not necessarily a cumulative process, that there are successions of great revolutions and intermediate ones, and that a revolutionary process is part of the regular pattern in the increase of scientific knowledge (22-23).

And further on, Cohen writes of "the dramatic influence Kuhn has had on the spread of the use of the concept of revolution."

Of all books in the history or philosophy of science in Kuhn's time, his was the "most widely read" according to T. Kisiel (89): "*The Structure of Scientific Revolutions* thus became the most widely read and translated book in the shift in perspective which has led to the `displacement' (*Aufhebung* [Hegelian term for the cancellation and raising of a concept to a higher level of meaning]) of the older logical approaches by more historical approaches to science" (87).

Kuhn's influence extended to fields other than science. Crediting Kuhn in a statement of purpose, Remi Clignet was inspired to write *The Structure of Artistic Revolutions* which, however, was not inspired enough to be widely read as its model was. Another extension to art by Suzi Gablik (*Progress in Art*) discusses Kuhn's views at length in a wider, more determined intellectual context of the time than in Clignet's book. Perhaps it was Kuhn's own limited extensions of his views to art that particularly engendered studies in that area so seemingly removed from science. Studies inspired by Kuhn in other fields can be found among the 1,700 listings of works on or by Kuhn in the University of California at Berkeley library, as of autumn 1992. So influential has Kuhn been that ironically or even somewhat humorously advocates of his work have refused to accept the disclaimer late in his career of the term `paradigm', preferring the earlier, more pure usage (578 Cohen).

While the fame of Kuhn is not often matched by scholars, Bloom has enjoyed it at least equally. There are several indications of the fame. In *The Dictionary of Literary Biography* series Helen Elam describes it well:

> In 1973 a small book was published under the title, *The Anxiety of Influence.* It was to mark Harold Bloom's dramatic entrance into literary theory and was to mark as well the theoretical discourse of our century. Since the publication of this book, it has been impossible to discuss theories of influence and tradition without reference to Bloom. ...This criticism transformed the conventional landscape of literary history into a battleground..." (33).

Clearly, Bloom stands in the forefront of his profession. The fellow deconstructionist Paul de Man also described Bloom at the forefront: "It will probably turn out that, in his understanding of the patterns of mis-reading, as in his understanding of Romanticism, Harold Bloom has been ahead of everybody else all along" (276 *Blindness*...).

A strong supporter and original poet, John Hollander argues Bloom's "revisionary ratios" go far beyond Frye's archetypes (xxi).

> In *The Anxiety of Influence*, Bloom sought to reinterpret the idea of poetic tradition as it has been most widely received. Going beyond Northrop Frye's introduction to the notion that the formation of literary canons is as much part of the *res* of literature as the composing of texts, Bloom believed tradition to be internalized in the psyche of each major (or, as he calls it, `strong') poet. Instead of a mere conscious acknowledgment of great formal or thematic predecessors, a profound and pervasive deliberateness, operating at many levels of consciousness and avowal, commits the poet to a total stance or attitude toward his precursors (xx).

Hollander's general idea of Bloom's theory corroborates previous initial claims in this Prologue; for example, (1) Bloom "sought to reinterpret the idea of poetic tradition"; (2) literature, on Bloom's view, struggles to reform its own canon, that is, to preserve the continuity of it by reformulating a new ideal, represented in the works; (3) the creative process occurs through a greater "deliberateness" than has been typically defined.

David Fite, who wrote a full-length study on Bloom's theory, expresses its fame while providing an overview:

> The critical project of Harold Bloom, taken as a whole, has many merits that even his detractors would not deny. Bloom's fourteen major volumes feature countless seminal readings of important Romantic and modern poetic texts, all the readings invested with a passionate erudition entirely appropriate to an exegete of the grand Romantic tradition, none of them completely compromised by our disagreement with the hubristic designs of the map for misreading. Bloom has introduced an unarguably sophisticated mode of psychopoetics and psychohistory into the generally moribund realm of the traditional scholarly study of literary influence, thereby compelling a trenchant reexamination of those *idées reçues* concerning influence, self, and the role of psychobiography which for so many years have stultified critics interested in the dynamics of literary tradition. Yet to suggest that Bloom's enterprise is most notable for his accomplishments in the mode of `practical criticism' (*AI*, 13) that he has always claimed to value is to ignore the larger significance of his work. Perhaps above all, what Bloom has given us, with his self-styled critical prophecy for a belated age, is an *idea of criticism* whose deliberate extremes and contrived rhetoric of crisis do not so much address as *reflect* the very real crisis in vision troubling not only the profession of literary criticism but also the entire tradition of humanistic culture in the last half of the twentieth century (188).

Although not all of these conclusions can be accepted, this passage does give a sense that Bloom has had influence. A recent computer search of writings by Bloom yielded more than 1,500 entries, mainly because he edited some very large series of criticisms of the entire history of literature, and the search yielded a large number of secondary works, though the number is not accurate owing to the fact that Bloom is mentioned in many more writings that do not discuss his views at length.

Another measure of fame, the compiling of citations, was carried out by John W. Kronik in his 1990 "Editor's column" for the *PMLA*, a publication produced by the largest, most recognized association of language and literature. The numbers indicate the citations by authors in *PMLA*. Kronik referred to the earlier counting of citations by Joel Conarroe in 1980, in which both Bloom and Derrida rated very high. Ten years later Kronik's larger sampling of 235 *PMLA* articles from 1981 to 1990 yielded these results: "Top billing on my accreditation list goes to the same French thinkers who dominated Joel Conarroe's count ten years ago: Roland Barthes and Jacques Derrida, tied at 58 entries each. ...The favored Derrida text is, not surprisingly, *Of Grammatology*" (202). In this sampling Harold Bloom had 20 citations (out of 235 articles)--a high figure relative to others, though it gives little indication of the frequency of citations in other publications besides *PMLA*.

Another, perhaps better way to gauge Derrida's fame is to refer to *Jacques Derrida: An Annotated Primary and Secondary Bibliography* by the present author and Lewis Fried. In 886 pages there are more than 3,500 items as of 1991, and these are from many disciplines and in many languages.

Yet another way is to read the unique, fine article by Sociologist Michèle Lamont, "How to Become a Dominant French Philosopher." The rise to fame is analysed and explained. A surprising conclusion, Derrida seemed to be more famous among American literary critics than among philosophers, whether in America or in France.

Purpose of This Book

The following book attempts to answer the question, `Whose theory of tradition is the best--Kuhn's, Bloom's, or Derrida's?' The validity of such a comparison cannot fairly be rejected before the evidence is given. In asking this question, and in comparing three very related writers still extremely influential in our common intellectual climate, a second more general question arises, `Are there genetic codes of science, poetry, and philosophy?' If there are, there probably are for other cultural fields as well. This latter question is being asked incompletely, inarticulately, inexplicitly in so great a number of intellectual discussions that it appears as the most widespread common problem of all cultural fields. For with a thorough knowledge of this issue may come the awareness of the determining factors by which the sum of human knowledge in specific fields may be extended--all for the greater dignity and power of our human spirit.

NOTES

1. Quoted from 829 Tedlock; the original is on 181 of Sebeok's *Perfusion of Signs*, Ed. Sebeok, Bloomington, Indiana University Press, 1977.

2. Quoted from 261 *Poetics of Prose*; Todorov elaborates the idea as operating on different levels of human meaning, from less to more general.

3. Quoted from page 12 of Eco's "A Logic of Culture" in *The Tell-Tale Sign*.

4. See Prodi, G. *Le basi materiali della significazione*, Milan: Bompiani, 1977; *La Storia Naturale della Logica*, Milan: Bompiani, 1982; and Sebeok, Thomas A., "Semiotica e Zoosemiotica," *Versus* Vol. 15, 1-3(1971), p.7.

5. Quoted from 79 Kellner; see Baudrillard's *Simulations*, 103.

6. Frankfort, Henri; Mrs. H.A. Frankfort, John A. Wilson, Thorkild Jacobs. *Before Philosophy*. London: Penguin, 1949, 22. Also quoted in 3 *SM* by Bloom.

7. For this idea see 149 Burkert; also see 229 of Lévi-Strauss' *Structural Anthropology*. N.Y. 1963; Burkert adds evidence that myths mediate oppositions of previous myths by referring to A.G. Dundes and G.S. Kirk, 44 and 48 of *Myth: Its Meaning and Function in Ancient and Other Cultures*. Berkeley. 1970.

8. Page 187 in *The Logic of the Humanities*; 251 in Simmel's *Philosophische Kultur*. Leipzig: A. Kröner, 1911.

9. For this idea concerning fiction, see 121 *Novel Epics*: "To investigate how *The Brothers Karamazov* presents itself within the monumental tradition and as an extension of Gogol's epic vision... ."

10. Quoted from 161 Nancy; the original is on page 678 of Lévi-Strauss' *Naked Man*.

11. Quoted from 228 *An Essay on Man*, by Cassirer; for the original see Kant, *Critique of Judgment*, secs. 46, 47. English trans. by J.H. Bernard (London, Macmillan, 1892), pp. 188-190.

12. See Bové 1980, p. 19; and Brooke-Rose, p. 33.

13. Quoted from 83 *AI*; Derrida is agreeing with Condillac: *La Langue des calculs*, in *Oeuvres Philosophiques de Condillac*, Ed. Georges Le Roy. II, Corpus Général des Philosophes Français. Paris: Presses Universitaires de France, 1947-51 for 3 vols. pp. 419-20.

Part I:

Overview of the Three Careers and Theories

Chapter 1:
Overview of the Three Careers

KUHN'S IMPRESSIVE CAREER

Introduction

The purpose of this section is to present a very general orientation for those readers unfamiliar with Kuhn's theory; the two following sections, on Bloom and Derrida, have a similar purpose. Probably in most cases readers who are quite knowledgeable about the topics will be thoroughly acquainted with only one of the three figures, as they do belong to separate specialities. In any case a general orientation makes subsequent detailed and advanced discussions more intelligible.

Originality of Kuhn's Theory

Kuhn's theory is original, even bold, for applying principles of artistic and philosophical development to science.
In contrast to other theorists Kuhn felt his originality consisted in the idea of a paradigm as an exemplar, an actual problem solution serving as a model ("Postscript"). "With respect to gross developmental pattern," writes Kuhn, "my originality, if any, was only the insistence that what has long been recognized about the development, of say, the arts or philosophy applies to science as well....one must

also be prepared to discover a number of revealing differences in developmental fine structure" (348 *CR*).

Concerning the originality of his *Copernican Revolution*, Kuhn wrote, "Creative interdisciplinarity ties like these play many and varied roles in the Copernican Revolution. Specialized accounts are inhibited both by aim and method from examining the nature of these ties and their effects upon the growth of human knowledge. This account of the Copernican Revolution therefore aims to display the significance of the Revolution's plurality, and that object is probably the book's most important novelty" (viii *CR*). By "interdisciplinarity" Kuhn means his general, wide-ranging style of speaking about changes in science, which necessarily extend beyond the specialty originating the change.

More specifically, his most original ideas--at the same time his most controversial--are "paradigm," (which is the most disputed), "conversion," "crisis," "disciplinary matrix," "normal science," "extraordinary science," and the gestalt switch of "revolutions." Kuhn felt "the paradigm as shared example" was the most novel, least understood idea of his theory (187 *SSR*); this usage contrasts with paradigm as disciplinary matrix--this difference is discussed below in **"Changes in Theory."**

Influences on Kuhn

Some main influences on Kuhn were Ludwig Fleck, Sir Karl Popper, Alexander Koyré, Herbert Butterfield and R.K. Merton, Frank Barron, F. Reif, E.A. Nida, Dudley Shapere, Stephen Toulmin, Clifford Truesdell, among others, including gestalt psychology.

There are many distinguished names in the philosophy of science whom Kuhn cites as influences: in the 1930s, Ludwig Fleck (wrote on `thought collectives' in science which foreshadowed Kuhn's gestalt approach to revolutions); 1935, Sir Karl Popper, the thinker most often contrasted with Kuhn (*Logic of Scientific Discovery*, original in German); 1939, Alexander Koyré (*Etudes galiléennes*); 1949, Herbert Butterfield (*Origins of Modern Science*); 1957, R.K. Merton ("Priorities in Scientific Discovery"); 1958, Frank Barron ("The Psychology of Imagination"); 1961, F. Reif ("The Competitive World of the Pure Scientist"); 1964, E.A. Nida ("Linguistics and Ethnology in Translation Problems"); 1964, Dudley Shapere ("The Structure of Scientific Revolutions,"); 1963, Stephen Toulmin (*Foresight and Understanding* and in 1968, "Conceptual Revolutions in Science,"); N.R. Hanson (*Patterns of Discovery*); 1967, Clifford Truesdell ("Reactions of Late Baroque Mechanics to Success, Conjecture, Error, and Failure in Newton's *Principia*"); and many others.

Kuhn describes the background of his main work, *The Structure of Scientific Revolutions* 1962, in the Preface. He felt the project was conceived in principle 15 years before publication. During this period the early essays "deal with the integral part played by one or another metaphysic in creative scientific research. Others examine the way in which the experimental bases of a new theory are accumulated and assimilated by men committed to an incompatible older theory. In the process they describe the type of development that I have below called the `emergence' of a new theory or discovery" (vii). In 1958-59 Kuhn had the chance to spend time working with behavioural scientists and he became very interested in their disagreements about fundamentals in their fields. The answers of researchers in the natural sciences didn't seem more permanent or certain, yet there did seem to be fewer or less severe controversies about fundamentals.

> "Attempting to discover the source of that difference led me to recognize the role in scientific research of what I have since called `paradigms'(vii). These I take to be universally recognized scientific achievements that for a time provide model problems and solutions to a community of practitioners. Once that piece of my puzzle fell into place, a draft of this essay emerged rapidly" (viii).

Kuhn's chief notion is undoubtedly "paradigm."

Purpose

In the most general terms Kuhn's purpose is "to describe or analyze the evolution of a particular scientific tradition" (43 *SSR*).

As an historian, claims Kuhn, he should set himself two tasks: 1. to find out who made a particular discovery or theory and when; 2. to describe the superstition obstructing the advance of science (2 *SSR*). Any reader of Kuhn quickly realizes that he is not concerned with constructing a *genealogy* of scientific discoveries--the names, dates, and relations of specific concepts. The discussion is more wide-ranging, dealing with science in general, as a social force of a time. When speaking of the "Scientific Revolution" (that seemingly greater creativity of science starting in the 1700s), he states the need for a "multidimensional cultural history" (159 *ET*). In addition, technicalities--formulas, special terms, theorems are avoided completely.

Value

Kuhn believes his theory has the value of yielding a new, unique understanding of science, perhaps one from which scientists themselves may benefit (viii *CR*).

Though Kuhn seems to say that scientists could benefit from his historical studies, at first this does not appear to be possible because there are no formulas, special terms, or scientific concepts in their own idiom. Does he mean that scientists would be better able to create after having read his works?

More probably, the new sort of understanding Kuhn offers in his philosophical history helps non-scientists to understand features of science that many professionally trained scientists might not know.

The Structure of Scientific Revolutions was very widely read in many fields because it was written for non-specialists; often it is taught as a text in technical writing classes.

Main Publications

Spanning 1957 to 1977, the period of his main publications defines an entire philosophy of science.

Kuhn published less than Bloom or Derrida. The main works are:

> 1957--*The Copernican Revolution*
> 1962--*The Structure of Scientific Revolutions* and revisions in 1969

1970--Essays in *Criticism and the Growth of Knowledge*
1977--*The Essential Tension: Selected Studies in Scientific Tradition and Change.* (A collection of essays)
1978--*Black-body Theory and the Quantum Discontinuity*

The original concepts do not appear in 1957, and the revisions in the 1969 revised, enlarged edition of *SSR* do not really change his theory much, nor is there much new development of the ideas in *SSR* later.

Chronologically, the trajectory of the career can be divided into four phases: 1. The Formative Phase; 2. The Phase of Main Publications; 3. The Phase of Refinements; 4. The Most Recent Phase: Summary and Review of Stated Views.

1. The Formative Phase

1947

Kuhn "stumbled upon" the idea of scientific revolution. Kuhn describes the need for the project of his main work as about 15 years before 1962 (Preface in *ET*).

1949

Kuhn was influenced by J.S. Bruner and Leo Postman, "On the Perception of Incongruity: A Paradigm," *Journal of Personality* 18(1949), 206-223. There is a psychological resistance to the perception of incongruity, because "paradigm categories" or "conceptual categories prepared by prior experience" "are built into the nature of the perceptual process" (*SSR*, 62-63); thus something learned can become a way of knowing, of gaining knowledge.

2. The Phase of the Publication of the Main Theory

1962

The Structure of Scientific Revolutions. This essentially contains his theory. It is perhaps best to let Kuhn explain what the book accomplishes:
"To the extent that the book portrays scientific

development as a succession of tradition-bound periods punctuated by non-cumulative breaks, its theses are undoubtedly of wide applicability. But they should be, for they are borrowed from other fields. Historians of literature, of music, of the arts, of political development, and of many other human activities have long described their subjects in the same way. Periodization in terms of revolutionary breaks in style, taste, and institutional structure have been among their standard tools. ...Conceivably the notion of a paradigm as a concrete achievement, an exemplar, is a second contribution. I suspect, for example, that some of the notorious difficulties surrounding the notion of style in the arts may vanish if paintings can be seen to be modeled on one another rather than produced in conformity to some abstracted canon of style" (208 *SSR*).

3. The Phase of Refinements
   March 1969
   "Second Thoughts on Paradigms." Prepared for a conference held in March 1969. "Some of the same ground" is "retraced" (Kuhn's words, *ET*, xx) in "Relfections on My Critics" and next in the "Postscript--1969" to the enlarged edition of *SSR*. So "Postscript--1969" is the latest version of his theory.

4. The Most Recent Phase
   1977
   The "Preface" to the collection of essays called *The Essential Tension: Selected Studies in Scientific Tradition and Change* explains the relations of all these collected essays to his main work, whether prior to and leading to the main development in *SSR* or whether a refinement, a change of terms. The title of the book dates back to Kuhn's 1959 paper by the same name.

Changes in Theory

Kuhn made a controversial change in his main idea: "paradigms"; he substituted two terms to replace it: "exemplars" and "disciplinary matrix." Even though the change is controversial, it may not be a radical one.

In 1969 Kuhn changed his most important idea, "paradigms," in response to much criticism, especially Margaret Masterman's and Dudley Shapere's. Masterman found 20 or so meanings of "paradigm" in Kuhn's work. Criticized by other philosophers of science as well, Kuhn decided to choose two meanings for "paradigm," and to disclaim the term for two other ones: "disciplinary matrix" and "exemplars." These *two* terms carry the weight of meaning formerly united in "paradigms." "Exemplars" are actual problem solutions serving as models for much scientific activity and application. "Disciplinary matrix" is more wholistic, referring to the unity of a scientific discourse. The examples, the formulas, the laws are constituents of the matrix but unlike it are not all of a piece (182 *SSR*).

Originally, Kuhn explains, "paradigm" was meant to express a "standard example"--"its central function and use," although most people mistakenly thought it was a "disciplinary matrix." A standard example of problem solving, an exemplar, is easier to discuss than a disciplinary matrix; the example formulas can be isolated, refuted, accepted, applied, compared, taught, altered to solve new puzzles; the disciplinary matrix, however, as the unity of the scientific discourse is difficult for Kuhn or anyone to convince many people about, since it is more abstract than the examples. Yet, it is the matrix or source of the examples, and so a higher knowledge of science is needed to grasp them. Kuhn's disclaiming of "disciplinary matrix" as not his main intention is a way of refusing what is harder to defend oneself for claiming. But, if it is the concept revealing a higher knowledge of science, shouldn't it be discussed, whether controversial or not?

The full discussion of the change would require a definition of many concepts, since the theory is systematic. In these preliminary remarks, however, it can be said that the change may merely be linguistic; he did not deny that previous meanings of paradigm were true; he merely separated the meanings into different terms. His idea of incommensurability between successive generations of science did not change. (See 318-319 of the 1969 edition of *SSR*.)

Main Criticisms

Cohen summarizes the main criticisms well: "...the term `paradigm' was used by Kuhn in a number of different senses (Masterman 1970; Kuhn 1970); another, that all revolutions do not necessarily arise from a crisis; yet another, that the whole scheme seems to work out better for the physical sciences than the biological sciences (Mayr 1976; Greene 1971)" (27).

As other criticisms, ones that Kuhn also responded to, Kuhn is said to be subjective, irrational, illogical; his concepts of conversion and incommensurability between competing paradigms bring out these criticisms the most. Full discussions of these ideas occur later in this book. (See "Reflections on My Critics," in *Criticism and the Growth of Knowledge*.)

Summary

Overviews by Cohen, Kisiel, and Gablik can orient the reader for the more detailed discussions to come.

Cohen provides a general idea of Kuhn's work:

> In his seminal study, Kuhn set forth no ordinary history but rather a social dynamics of scientific change in terms of a sequence of revolutions alternating with what Kuhn calls `normal science'. Kuhn's schema has been applied to such diverse areas as historical-political theory, science and public policy (with respect to the application of biomedical knowledge), and the nature of the modern university, in addition to the history, philosophy, and sociology of science. One major response to Kuhn's bold presentation has been to challenge some features of his analysis, to show that his schema is not universally applicable but limited to certain sciences or to special

periods or selected episodes. Another has been to question the precise meaning (or to explore the ambiguities or multiple meanings) of his technical terms (notably `paradigm'). Doubts have been raised concerning the propriety of using the concept of revolution in relation to scientific change (23).

Kisiel offers a more logical-technical overview:

Kuhn's first use of the term `paradigm' was in a crucial paper presented at a conference on scientific creativity in 1959, reprinted in his selected essays and providing that collection with its overall title. The title of the paper, `The Essential Tension: Tradition and Innovation in Scientific Research', reflects Kuhn's central thesis at its simplest: science in its maturity advances by way of complementary phases of tradition-bound and tradition-shattering activities, the pursuit of normal science on the one hand and the occurrence of scientific revolutions on the other. Normal science is governed and directed by a coherent tradition of accepted scientific achievements which Kuhn calls `paradigms'. Research in normal science is an effort of paradigm-articulation, where the basic aim is to bring about a closer match between the paradigm and the subject matter under investigation. The extraordinary research which culminates in revolution seeks to switch from an extant paradigm which is proving inadequate to emerging problems to a more promising new paradigm. Normal science, as paradigm-articulation, and extraordinary research, as paradigm-switch, are thus both defined in terms of paradigm, `a fundamental unit...of scientific development' (*SSR*, p. 11), which accordingly carries the entire burden of Kuhn's theory of scientific advance (91).

Gablik, while seemingly less technical than Kisiel, offers other salient points about Kuhn's project as a whole:

A paradigm is a unifying ground of presuppositions that influences and makes possible certain ideas and practices, and provides model problems and solutions to the scientific community. (This describes a scientific tradition, but it is also true for stylistic traditions within the artistic community.) But the paradigm is even more, since, according to Kuhn, it is also an organizing principle which can govern perception itself or a new way of seeing. (There is an unconscious element here which resembles Foucault's *episteme*.) In any epoch, man sees the world in terms of a particular paradigm, which serves as an unconscious conceptual framework by which many different facets of the universe can be and are meaningfully related to each other.

Kuhn has defined scientific activity as fundamentally a matter of creating frameworks (paradigms) and of fitting systems together, rather than of simply discovering the `truth' about nature (158).

BLOOM'S BRILLIANT CAREER

Originality

Bloom forms a highly original theory of poetic influence, especially applicable to English romanticism.

Like Kuhn, Bloom develops a few concepts that are so much his own that they at first inspire debates; the debates inspire supporters; and finally when recognized as important ideas they are applied in many ways he might not be able to recognize as his own. To some extent, the ideas have become institutionalized during the course of twenty years of disssemination. Bloom's most original are the "anxiety of influence" (the most general original term), "revisionary ratio" (the most complex but systematic), "misreading," "misprision," "anagogy," and the six "revisionary ratios": "clinamen," "tessera," "kenosis," "daemonization," "askesis", and "apophrades." Though there are actually many more in his "map of misreading," they are less important, less original, and are defined through these--such as "metalepsis," "transumption," "belatedness," "introjection," and "projection." Whereas Kuhn's main idea of "paradigm" occurred in the context of the philosophy of science before Kuhn's main work, Bloom's ideas are a larger departure from the criticism just before him.

An important critic often categorized with Bloom, Paul de Man described the originality in the following way:

> Though Bloom could sound turgid and overemphatic at times, the originality of his reading of English romanticism cannot be sufficiently stressed. He may well have felt that he had to raise his voice to be heard, for in his understanding of the catchall term "imagination" he was philosophically shrewder and, in some respects, better informed than all the other historians and theoreticians of English romanticism, including Frye, Abrams, Wasserman, and others. Ever since his book on Shelley, Bloom has always

> implicitly understood that, all appearances to the contrary, the romantic imagination is *not* to be understood in dialectical interplay with the presumably antithetical category of "nature" (269)

Specifically, this passage is more like praise than a detailed listing of original features; the shrewdness of his idea of the romantic imagination is the main feature.

More details concerning Bloom's originality are offered by Helen Elam:

> Even before the publication of this book, Bloom was a distinguished literary critic. His works on Romanticism had helped bring about a re-evaluation of Romantic poetry and of the critical stances through which Romanticism was being read. His five books published prior to *The Anxiety of Influence* (1959-1971) rejected the modernist and New Critical assumptions which had devalued Romantic poetry. Bloom's re-reading of this tradition, along with Geoffrey's monumental studies of Wordsworth and Paul de Man's significant work on the Romantics, had the effect of reestablishing the fortunes of British Romanticism (33).

Elam claims Bloom developed a new critical approach helping to revive British romanticism.

Bloom believed his originality consisted in criticism becoming closer to the poetic idiom: "...criticism teaches not a language of criticism (a formalist view still held in common by archetypalists, structuralists, and phenomenologists) but a language in which poetry already is written, the language of influence, of the dialectic that governs the relations between poets as poets" (258 *AI*). (A more complete discussion of Bloom's work in relation to that of previous critics can be found in Donald Fite's fine *Rhetoric of Romantic Vision*).

Influences on Bloom

The main influences on Bloom were poets and critics--Meyer Abrams, Walter Jackson Bate, Ernst Robert Curtius, Angus Fletcher (*Allegory*), Northrop Frye, Geoffrey Hartman; psychologists--Freud; philosophers--Nietzsche and Derrida; religious thinkers--medieval Jewish writers on creation and Kabbalah (meaning `tradition' and appearing in Bloom's title *Kabbalah and Criticism*).

The influence of critics on Bloom can be readily seen, even though he does not engage in extended polemics as some critics do. He thought the work by Ernst Robert Curtius on tradition was the best he had ever read. Curtius was interested in the idea of "literary citizens of the first rank" and their membership in the canon; he wanted to choose the greatest, most classical works, and determine the rules of their formation. The process leads to an interest in tradition. One particular idea he had was "belatedness," an idea Bloom develops beyond Curtius' limited usage. From Frye, Bloom gained an interest in myth in poetry, and the systematizing tendencies of Frye are developed further. With regard to the other critics mentioned above, Bloom refers to them in isolated passages usually to develop rather specific points or ideas.

The greater influences are not literary critics. "Nietzsche and Freud," claims Bloom, "are, so far as I can tell, the prime influences upon the theory of influence presented in this book" (8 *AI*). From Nietzsche, he got a sense of the antithetical side of the aesthetic vision, and from Freud he transformed the mechanisms of defence into a more poetic notion of revisionary ratios. Throughout his works, Freud is definitely the stronger influence.

Religious thinkers influenced Bloom very much. At first, in the 1959 *Shelley's Mythmaking*, Jewish ethical writer Martin Buber is a very strong influence; poetic meaning is defined partly in terms of the I-Thou-it concepts from Buber. In later writings, however, these terms are dropped. Without a doubt the stronger influence was that of the medieval Jewish doctrine of "Kabbalah," meaning "tradition." Bloom had already come to his idea of revisionary ratio before he let it be further articulated by Kabbalah. Its threefold movement in creation supports Bloom's whole pattern for the relations of two great poetries. It is clear from the sequence of the main works that Freud was a stronger influence in the initial conception of a revisionary ratio but that Kabbalah helped Bloom to formalize and systematize the ratios.

From philosophy Bloom seems less influenced. There are positive references to Derrida, especially concerning his interpretation and use of Freud's idea of the "Scene of Instruction" (the situation in which creation begins or "a place cleared by the newcomer in himself" [55 *MM*]). The Scene of Instruction defines priority, according to Bloom; "priority" meaning the first step of a poet which is paradoxically before the first step of his/her predecessor. Another favorable reference to Derrida occurs at the start of *Poetry and Repression*, the location and meaning suggesting that Bloom's purpose is parallel to Derrida's. And there are negative references, not so much to Derrida as to deconstructionists; of course, Derrida is the chief one. Speaking quite generally about other critics, Bloom regards them as afflicted with two problems: either they are "over-spiritualized or under" (79 *MM*). The over-spiritualizers are Auerback, Frye, and supporters; the under-spiritualizers are heirs of Nietzsche and the Deconstruction school, including Derrida, de Man, J. Hillis Miller (79 *MM*). Bloom criticizes deconstruction in other ways as well.

Purpose

The purpose of Bloom's theory presented in *The Anxiety of Influence* and subsequent books is to present a theory of poetry, not poetics. The theory offers a "practical criticism": one that can actually be used in the interpretation of individual poems, and Bloom did this in much detail, unlike Kuhn.

By providing a theory of poetry, not a theory of poetics, Bloom means that he does not present a theory about how to *create* poetry; rather he presents a theory of how to *read* poetry to see what it means. The meaning can be found by "charting" "the substitutive interplay of figures and of images..." (87 *MM*). In contrast to Bloom's explicit claims, his theory does more than teach its readers how to read. As John Hollander writes, "It [*The Anxiety of Influence*] provides a myth of poetic creativity at a point close to the sources of self-assertion and questioning" (xvii *PI*). Though Bloom may not *intend* to present a theory of creativity, his theory does provide much insight into the processes.

Questions that Bloom asks are "What is literary tradition? What is a classic? What is a canonical view of tradition?" (31 *MM*) and, even clearer, "What is Shelley doing to tradition here?" (102 *PR*). His theory of poetry is a theory of influence; poetry is not *about* anxiety but *is* an "anxiety" about a poet's relation to the previous poet (94 *AI*). The poetic meaning of "anxiety" must be defined at length using the revisionary ratios. "Anxiety" here means not a feeling so much as the poetic realization of the position a new poet can occupy in relation to the previous great poet; "the poet feels no proper work remains for the poet to perform" (148 *AI*).

Value

Bloom believes his theory has value first of all as practical criticism for interpreting individual poems and whole poetries; secondly, he believes that poets are helped by critics, who can serve as precursors (95 *AI*); thirdly, literary critics can even "perfect and extend the canon" (413 *PI*).

Bloom's theory provides a practical criticism in a very important way. Some theories are so abstract that it is hard for people to use them to interpret individual poems, and the theorists themselves may not interpet many individual poems with the theory. In sharp contrast is Bloom's theory, which includes extensive application of the principles about reading poetry. So university teachers can use the interpretations and students can get help in understanding what poetry does. From the vantage point of decades of thorough reading Bloom can help others come closer to the highest poetic meaning, which he himself may not have if it requires a great poet to see it.

The value of Bloom as a precursor for creative poets is doubtful. It is true his theory could point the way to begin creation but, according to his theory itself, a great poet must develop from a previous one. So, the great poet *must* revise a previous poetry, though he *need not* have read Bloom's theory.

Similarly, the claim that criticism can "perfect and extend the canon" is exaggerated. A great poetry perfects and extends the poetry before it; Bloom's criticism does not relate to a specific great poetry as the successive great poetry does. In my opinion, Bloom makes such claims for criticism because it helps to make his theory self-reflexive, that is, applicable to his criticism. He transfers the ratios *in* his theory to the theory's relation to great poetry. Similarly, he often explains how poetry is about poetry.

Main Publications

Bloom's main publications--and he was prolific--extend from 1959 to 1988 and present in detail a theory of poetry with several complete interpretations of the work of great poets. The following main points are meant merely to give the reader a general idea for the sake of following chapters. A thorough discussion would itself be hundreds of pages--Bloom was very prolific and profound.

The first phase of the main publications begins in 1959 with *Shelley's Mythmaking*. The book differs considerably from *The Anxiety of Influence*, which interprets actual poetry less than it presents a critical model to be accepted. The earlier publication contains some terms and interests not to be found in the later works, such as "anagogy" (preferred over the analogical meaning of a poem), terms from Buber's philosophy, and the preoccupation with myth. Some of the notions, however, such as "anagogy" are bold; perhaps they should have been developed in some way in subsequent works.

The next phase starts in 1973 with *The Anxiety of Influence*: a theoretical book having its own terminology, discussing complex relations, and interpreting individual poems less than the works from 1959 to 1973. This book presents essentially all of his theory of criticism.

In 1975 with *A Map of Misreading*, *Kabbalah and Criticism*, and *Poetry and Repression* the relations discussed previously are defined in a more formal, more articulate, more developed way. Now Bloom has a "map of misreading," which shows more integration of his earlier ideas such that he could network them. The doctrine of `Kabbalah' from medieval Jewish theorists of creation is more important in this period and seems to overshadow the Freudian meaning of the revisionary ratios. These books do represent development.

The next rather theoretical book, *Agon: Towards a Theory of Revisionism*, 1981, does not change the terminology already developed by Bloom.

The next `turn' of his publications is in 1984 when he begins to serve as the editor for the Chelsea House Library of Literary Criticism. In 1985 he also served as the editor for *The Art of the Critic* series, and the *Modern Critical Interpretations* series, both by Chelsea House. Altogether there are several hundred volumes.

The most recent work is *The Book of J*, with David Rosenberg, which does not change, nor extend, the system of criticism published in 1973-75.

Changes in Theory

Bloom's theory, while even more consistent through time than Kuhn's, did change in tone and style, not to mention a few minor changes in ideas.

A striking change in Bloom's career was that from *Shelley's Mythmaking* to *The Anxiety of Influence* 14 years later. Some of the more esoteric concepts and interests are dropped, and the ideas implicit in the earlier work become explicit, more systematic, more technical. The use of Buber's ideas, the principle of anagogy to refer to poetry's ultimate meaning, the discussions of the mythical nature of Shelley's poetry,--all these make the book quite unique in literary criticism; there is a prophetic tone of the divine glow on Bloom's face from a vision. As bad as this may sound to common sensical interpreters of poetry as based on analogy, poetry as a stylized description of ordinary life, something may have been lost in the transition to the 1973 theory. Granted, the theory of influence *is* a very definite development, especially of the revisionary ratios. However, if Bloom had pursued the idea of anagogy more, he might have learned more about poetry by attending less to his own model and more to new great poetry, with a vison of poetic finality, an anagogy. One can realize the truth of this suggestion even more if great poetries change and deepen the poetic ability of the earlier ones.

Also, the idea of misreading changed in a way successors of Bloom's should know. In the 1959 book "misreading" means what it sounds like in ordinary language: a mistaken reading (197, 206,

237). In 1973 and 1975, however, "misreading" is the natural, proper re-envisionment of previous poetry. It is called "mis-" reading because a new great poet interprets the previous poetry in a way not `meant' by that poet: the new poet experiences a change in the perception of the previous poetry, and this change is misreading. The prefix quite subtly could show the succesor's feeling that a different interpretation must be wrong, for the precursor was so great. Nevertheless, all the time it is Bloom who has the right interpretation, standing above any sequence of great poets. He may be standing too far away from necessary poetic decisions. Although this idea merits detailed examination, which it will receive in subsequent chapters, here the suggestion can be made that Bloom is unwilling to say with the newer great poet, `the previous poetry was founded on an inadequate aesthetic and a whole new basis must be found'.

Both Bloom's ideas and Kuhn's become "institutionalized" during the course of their publication history. This change can be likened to that described by Stephen Jay Gould in "A Biological Homage to Mickey Mouse." Mickey had a long successful career as both Kuhn and Bloom have had. Mickey started out as a mischievous or even cruel prankster, mildly hurting animals, acting impolitely, speaking loudly and generally being unpredictable. As his success grew his appearance changed to a more smiling, better looking mouse. In recent years Mickey has become well-mannered, insipid, inoffensive, and his appearance has become more juvenile. Clubs were started for children to groom them in the ways of Mickey. In these ways Mickey became "institutionalized"; he became more acceptable to a larger audience; he became a household word. His audience wanted him to be different, and different he became. Kuhn's career somewhat resembles Mickey's--and I mean no disrespect to the famous contribution (of Kuhn)--because Kuhn disclaimed some of his terms after much criticism. Some of his ideas became weakened; for example, he claims that he did not really mean to claim anything about a "disciplinary matrix" but only "exemplars" (Postscript-- 1969). It is easier to discuss the latter notion; more people can accept it. But there is a great loss in the features of science that are explained. Actually, no harm is done, for Kuhn does not say, `what I said before was wrong'. Instead, he says, `I didn't mean to try to prove that; I only meant to try to prove something easier'. We readers still benefited from the full theory. He also altered his stand on the incommensurability between successive scientific theories; the idea that there could not become full communication between proponents of both theories was weakened to mean there were some language difficulties but no difficulties of scientific understanding. This is weaker because it means there were no real differences of the conception of truth. Kuhn's ideas were guided in a small degree by the institution he addressed. Bloom's work also became less mysterious, less esoteric from *Shelley's Mythmaking* to *The Anxiety of Influence*. Whereas the former has a prophetic tone, the latter has an argumentative. His mid-career works all explain and defend the same theory in numerous books. He has a theory and he has to defend it. Meanwhile, some of the mysteries of the earlier work (for example, I-thou-it, anagogy) fade into the unobjectionable past. The latter work is more formulaic, more prescriptive, and this has its advantages for convincing fellow members of the profession and teaching undergraduate classes. It is not the case that Bloom's ideas became weaker exactly, as Kuhn asserted his terms should become; rather the growth was directed to what could be assimilated more easily, not necessarily what would have led Bloom to a greater knowledge of poetry. Did Bloom discuss many very contemporary poets? Not thoroughly. Did Bloom become a great poet? Why not? Some institutional forces may have brought his work more in line with stylistic restrictions for successful critics. The institution allows people to be successful if they allow it to be. Kuhn's remark that his success stems from it being all things to all people ironically affected him. This principle also applies to Derrida's work who, though less like Mickey, is partly successful because such a great number of people were able to comment, criticize, praise, adapt, and mention the unusual ideas requiring an interpretation. Derrida partly became controversial because controversy is good for allowing people to publish and giving them something to react to. In this way many people have elected Derrida to be their employer. Notwithstanding this limited cynicism *about the reception* of Derrida, Kuhn, and Bloom, their ideas merit a great deal of attention.

Summary

With such a prolific career these ideas about Bloom's career can only be preparatory for the detailed discussions to follow. The several full-length interpretations of great poets and several theoretical books merit detailed discussion and rereading. For the purposes of this book, his main interest is in poetry as a phenomenon of tradition: it gets its meaning as a movement of the poetic tradition.

DERRIDA'S GREAT CAREER

Originality

Unlike Kuhn and Bloom, Derrida is original in a different sense; his theory is not only `about' philosophy, it *is* philosophy, and so he is original in the sense of adding to the tradition he criticizes, being the next step. Kuhn's theory is not itself a science, nor is Bloom's a poetry, even though he may at times blur the distinction between criticism and poetry. (Whether an idea about science can be completely accurate if it is not itself part of the science is a difficult question to be raised later.)

The new philosophy is called "grammatology," a science of writing, worked out fully in *Of Grammatology*. It reacts to the tradition as a whole by rejecting the "transcendental signified" presupposed by all previous philosophy; in these preliminary marks, this word can be defined as the inconsistent assumption of a signifier that cannot in turn act as a signifier; it is "transcendental," or apart from the series of other concepts. The *Tel Quel* intellectual circle of the 1960s, of which Derrida was a chief member, had the common goal of rejecting the transcendental siginified. He finds this fault in Husserl and Saussure most often in his writings, but it is Sartre who assumed the concept in its most classical form.

Another way to describe (not yet prove) Derrida's originality is to say that he repeated the classical coherence, scheme, space, or tradition form of philosophy, inherited from Sartre though ultimately passing through the best philosophers of the entire Western tradition. He has the originality of DNA: he changes the whole of what went before while repeating a pattern or "code" of philosophy, and from his work a new philosophy could arise.

Some concepts that he originated are "deconstruction," "grammatology," "difference," "differance," and "the supplement", among a great number of other coined expressions. The most general term, "deconstruction," has been widely used by thousands of scholars and, not surprisingly, the meaning differs from Derrida's own.

Influence

Derrida was influenced most by Rousseau, Hegel, Husserl, Saussure, Freud, and I would like to claim Sartre.

The influence of Husserl's writings is beyond dispute--in regard to the quantity. Due to Derrida's introduction and translation of Husserl's origin of geometry the French philosopher was invited to the United States to discuss his Husserl interpretation. Saussure, though a linguist, should be referred to along with Husserl because both are mentioned often enough to be recognized as strong influences and both provide clear examples of the transcendental signified.

In *Of Grammatology* Derrida presented a comprehensive deconstruction of Rousseau's thought. He finds the term "supplement" there and adapts it to become a philosophical concept with a classical role.

Derrida wrote essays about Hegel and Freud; there are references to these thinkers in various writings; and Derrida wrote a book half on Hegel, called *Glas*, which is left untranslated in the English version.

While discussing these influences in detail would be very worthwhile, I will provide reasons for deriving Derrida's philosophy more from Sartre's, despite the fact that Sartre is mentioned much less than Husserl or Freud or Saussure.

Purpose

Derrida's purpose is to revise the Western tradition of philosophy as a whole. "The fundamental condition" of his philosophy is "certainly the undoing of logocentrism" (74 *OG*).

In rejecting the "logocentric" philosophies of the entire Western tradition, Derrida is rejecting the idea that knowledge can be based on a pure "presence," a term partially synonymous with "transcendental signified." His aim is to perform a "deconstruction" of Western philosophy. For the preparatory remarks here, this term means a kind of change *and* extension of tradition; a destruction that constructs something new to take its place.

Value

As the value of Derrida's philosophy, he "perfects and extends" the canon, to use Bloom's bold words for critics; in other words, he recreates the pattern of Western philosophies but on a more advanced level than his main predecessor (Sartre).

The highest value achievable by a philosophy is to produce new philosophy of the highest order, of the most classical kind. A classic is the best form achievable. In cycles they appear, like the phoenix, only one at a time; one can be found to be the best--there is a measure. The measure is the total form or tradition form. If a philosophy has the pattern of classical philosophies, gained from a great philosopher, then the highest philosophical value is achieved.

What the philosophical value is for society remains unexplained, however. The question is obliquely addressed by Derrida in his article "Biodegradeables," in which he describes the process of dissemination of ideas throughout a culture as their being biodegraded, reduced to a lower order, broken down. There has been great value for many scholars who wrote about Derrida's work, adapted it, criticized it, praised it, compared it, explained it.

To emphasize, the value of Derrida's philosophy is to have taken the human race's possession of philosophy one more traditional step forward. And he has value as a starting point for a new philosophy.

Main Publications

A tremendously prolific career, Derrida's works extend from 1962 to today, with perhaps the three most central works being published in 1967. I refer the reader to *Jacques Derrida: An Annotated Primary and Secondary Bibliography* for annotations of many other works.

Before these three works, enough to establish a position in the tradition, the main one is the translation and introduction to Husserl's *Origin of Geometry*, 1962. In the period leading up to 1967 he was also writing essays for *Writing and Difference* (1967).

Derrida described his three main works as a related group:

> One can take *Of Grammatology* as a long essay articulated in two parts (whose juncture is not empirical, but theoretical, systematic) *into the middle* of which one could staple *Writing and Difference*. *Grammatology* often calls upon it. In this case the interpretation of Rousseau would also be the twelfth "table" of the collection. Inversely, one could insert *Of Grammatology into the middle* of *Writing and Difference*, since six of the texts in that work preceded--*de facto* and *de jure*--the publication in *Critique* (two years ago) of the articles that announced *Of Grammatology*; the last five texts, beginning with "Freud and the Scene of Writing," are engaged in the grammatlogical opening. But things cannot be reconstituted so easily, as you may well imagine. In any case, that two "volumes" are to be inscribed one *in the middle of* the other is due, you will agree, to a strange geometry, of which these texts are doubtless the contemporaries. ...It [*Speech and Phenomena*] is perhaps the essay which I like most. Doubtless I could have bound it as a long note to one or the other of the other two works. *Of Grammatology* refers to it and economizes its development. But in a classical philosophical architecture, *Speech*... would come first: in it is posed...the question of the privilege of the voice and of phonetic writing in their relationship to the entire history of the West..." (4-5 *Pos*).

This passage declares a very close interconnection between the three works and a departure from the entire tradition of Western philosophy. For the purposes of this book, how such a departure from the entire tradition can occur needs to be explained at length.

Many works follow the 1967 presentation of a whole, complete new philosophy. These works discuss new themes previously not discussed, such as art in *The Truth in Painting*, ideas on creation in *The Archaeology of the Frivolous*, and ideas on Hegel, Genet, Heidegger, Searle, among other topics. This fact of the writings after 1967 would tend to be consistent with Bloom's explanation of the very last phase of poetic form, in which the precursors are rewritten or seen to be derivative of the current creator (apophrades); Picasso "repainted" great paintings of his predecessors during his last phase of painting. Such a trait of the end of a tradition form shows that the creator sees the pattern of his/her field, albeit in a specific limited tradition form of a philosophy or poetry. The best way to categorize the works after 1967, to give a general sense of Derrida's main publications, is to say that they tend to explore the limits of his philosophy as already known in *Of Grammatology*. *His philosophy is structurally complete in that work, but these concepts can be indefinitely refined and applied to new topics as Derrida did. There does occur some genuine extension of knowledge, some further understanding of the concepts of 1967; Derrida tries to understand the limits of his ideas more and more, and this process could go on for the rest of his life, creating what Bloom called a space of the imagination (which is infinite for the individual). Some of the writings lose their clear connection with the tradition, and so they call to mind blinded Oedipus*--a visionary who wanders contemplating the inner vision of the fate he underwent.

Changes in Theory

Unlike Kuhn and Bloom, Derrida does *not* himself change his theory, making it more capable of being received by the profession, though he did quite a lot in practice to inform the academic institutions of his work.

The writings may even become more idiosyncratic or less institutionalizable after 1967, though writing on literary and other topics helped critics to institutionalize his work. The best discussion on this topic is that by Michèle Lamont, "How to Become a Dominant French Philosopher: The Case of Jacques Derrida" (*American Journal of Sociology* 93[1987], 584-622).

Some reasons may be offered as to why there are no changes, no disclaims. One reason might be that Derrida's philosophy is more all of a piece than the theories of Kuhn or Bloom. This comment does not mean that their theories are disunified. On the contrary, it means that Derrida's work constitutes a whole schema of philosophy having a form inherited in general outline from the tradition. Neither Kuhn's nor Bloom's is canonical, is a tradition form, is a member of a series capable of reproducing a classical schema that can itself reproduce something of the same type, and it can reproduce another, and so on--in the manner of a genetic code. Another way to describe the coherence of Derrida's philosophy as greater than those other theories is to use the analogy of a magnet. A magnet has a direction in it, and Derrida's philosophy does, whereas Kuhn's and Bloom's theories don't; they do not take a specific step in the tradition of which they speak, leading to another. Also, the opposite poles of a magnet attract each other; the end of Derrida's philosophy guarantees its start; the end and the start "attract" each other.

Summary

These preparatory remarks point out a difference between the work of Kuhn and Bloom and that of Derrida. From the standpoint of our concern with tradition, Derrida's original ideas relate to the tradition of which he speaks differently from the way either Kuhn's or Bloom's theory does. It is a question of the critique having or not having the form of that of which it criticizes. Kuhn did not effect a specific revolution from a predecessor. His theory of science does not have the form of science, it is not a science, and so one might expect that scientific meaning cannot remain undistorted by ordering principles not totally its own. Similarly for Bloom, his theory is not a specific contest with one poet. Even though the ratios are defined in the same relation as they occur in great poetry, still Bloom's "apophrades" (the self-closing of a poetry), for example, is not a poetic expression but a critical concept. In his case too, it should be questioned whether poetic meaning can remain undistorted outside of its principles of ordering. Instead of "distorted" a better word, following Derrida, might be "biodegraded" into a lower order of meaning.

The following sections will discuss the three authors' ideas of tradition as a whole, in preparation for detailed discussions in the central chapters of this work.

Chapter 2:

Overview of the Three Theories

KUHN'S THEORY OF TRADITION AS A WHOLE

Introduction to "Kuhn's Theory of Tradition as a Whole"

For Kuhn, science can form a whole, continuing tradition because it is a "continuing cyclic process" and its concepts are "repeatedly destroyed and replaced" (264 *CR*). Bold and innovative and controversial, Kuhn shocked many philosophers of science who believed the tradition formed an infinite continuous straight line, each theory adding to the unchanged results of the previous one.

Tradition as a Whole

Kuhn questioned the common sense view of scientific tradition as a line of theories each adding to some past ideas unchanged.

The whole of tradition is an indefinitely extended series of cycles. Some sciences began thousands of years ago and all can be continued indefinitely. By describing a step in tradition as a cycle Kuhn is stating that successive sciences repeat the patterns of previous ones, as a genetic code would reproduce a slight variation of the `same' code.

Regularity is then a characteristic of scientific theories. One would expect them to be regular in structure if the same name is applied. But Kuhn was somewhat bold in defining the regularity of revolutions, which had seemed to be non-regular events. Perhaps Bloom acquired his interest in revolutions out of the feeling that the irregularity of revolutions must be explained, ironically making them regular. In other words, it may have seemed vexing to think of some necessary feature of science as irregular or undeterminable.

Since cycles require some start and end, a primary aim of Kuhn is to emphasize the revolution, being both end of one theory and start of another. "As science progresses," writes Kuhn, "its concepts are repeatedly destroyed and replaced, and today Newtonian concepts are no exception" (265 *CR*).

From Kuhn's actual statements a reader could infer that each new cycle or theory comprehends the entire tradition; this idea, however, is clearer in Bloom's and Derrida's work. According to Kuhn,

> As long as the continuous tradition of Western learning survives, scientists will be able to explain the phenomena first elucidated by Newtonian concepts, just as Newton was able to explain the more restricted list of phenomena previously elucidated by Aristotle and Ptolemy. That is how science advances: each new conceptual scheme embraces the phenomena explained by its predecessors and adds to them (264 *CR*).

A very important consequence, knowledge can grow or increase in power if each new cycle comprehends *all* the past tradition. Of course, this idea does not mean that scientists know every idea of the past; the comprehension of tradition is not a quantitative matter so much as a qualitative change of perspective, a change in fundamental assumptions.

How does science accumulate its knowledge throughout history? The linear cumulative view of scientific progress is the common one for textbooks, which tend to be written in terms of the present level of science ignoring the legitimate claims of past (especially ancient) theories to be equally scientific. Kuhn rejects this view: "From the beginning of the scientific enterprise, a textbook presentation implies, scientists have striven for the particular objectives that are embodied in today's paradigms. One by one, in a process often compared to the addition of bricks to a building, scientists have added another fact, concept, law, or theory to the body of information supplied in the contemporary science text" (140 *SSR*). The cumulative view is wrong, because "the destruction of a paradigm" is required (96 *SSR*); in this respect Kuhn's view resembles Derrida's deconstructive views. Many views of Bloom and Derrida can be found in Kuhn's work if one searches minutely, for often they are less developed.

In theorizing about tradition as a whole Kuhn thinks of it not only as a sequence of scientific theories but also as a way the profession researches: its methods, puzzles, instruments, questions. As a result, sometimes Kuhn speaks of a research tradition as unified by subject matter--by optics, statics, classes of phenomena like heat and electricity (36 *ET*). In contrast, for Bloom, the "subject" of poetry is its own form or process; on such a view there is a greater continuity of forms, because the subjects in Kuhn's view could and do change. They also overlap fields, so that a tradition cannot be defined only by subject matter or else there would be a confusion of fields.

Are the sciences one or many? Is there one tradition of science or several? In contrast to Bloom, who concentrates on one tradition of literature, Kuhn makes claims about science as if one tradition, as if there were no differences between a tradition of physics and that of biology, for example. Kuhn understands science through external factors: "Virtually all the authors now regarded as internalists address themselves to the evolution of a single science or of a closely related set of scientific ideas; the externalists fall almost invariably into the group that has treated the sciences as one..." (31 *ET*). He would not like to be thought of as only an externalist; he wants to balance external and internal approaches (33 *ET*). Nevertheless, his scholarly practice emphasizes the external. He often speaks of tradition as divided into periods of time, rather than as divided into different systems of concepts.

During the course of history the sciences became more separate (60 *ET*). A division in the sciences eventually occurred, and so the number of specialties increased (170 *SSR*). Such a description uses an external approach for the definition of tradition; "external" refers to historical facts, common divisions found in textbooks, changes in subject matter, and so on. The approach avoids the question of analyzing a specific separation or division.

Tradition lies at the heart of Kuhn's definition of science. Without a history before it there can be no science (1 *SSR*). Furthermore, science is that discipline which progresses (161 *SSR*). If it does not progress toward a goal known at the beginnings of science, then he reasons it moves toward "an increasingly detailed and refined understanding of nature" (170 *SSR*). In forming more symbolic generalizations science increases in power and precision (100, 183 *SSR*). Despite rejecting the cumulative view based on a permanent goal, this explanation of progress sounds rather close to the view it criticizes.

To present this view more strongly, this progress depends upon changes like gestalt switches: there is "a global sort of change in the way men viewed nature and applied language to it, one that could not properly be descried as constituted by additions to knowledge or by the mere piecemeal correction of mistakes. That sort of change was to be described by Herbert Butterfield as `putting on a different kind of thinking-cap'..." (xiii *ET*).

A curious view at first, the tradition as a whole took a giant step forward with the Scientific Revolution (1700-), and science created much faster than it had (59 *ET*). "The bulk of scientific knowledge is a product of Europe in the last four centuries. No other place and time has supported the very special communities from which scientific productivity comes" (168 *SSR*). "Through the scientific revolution science won the great new role that it has since played in the development of Western society and Western thought" (2 *CR*). This view may confuse a proliferation of technological applications with increases in the frequency of great scientific ideas. In "an age as dominated by science as our own" many people would agree with Kuhn's historically based conclusion about faster science.

Scope of Revolutions

There are some questions about the size of revolutions and what is included by them. Kuhn offers a variety of answers, making a problem of exact definition for his readers.

Does Kuhn's theory apply to the whole history of science or to just a part? In one passage he claims his theory does not apply to optics before Newton (12 *SSR*). Certainly, Kuhn does not give examples from ancient Greek science. Did it progress by revolutions? All in all, his theory is meant to apply to any science at any point in history.

Some scientific revolutions seem more `revolutionary' or seem larger in scope than others.

Perhaps this emphasis stems from the feeling that some changes in science are so complete, so far reaching as to redefine science and as to require explanation.

Frequently, Kuhn regards some revolutions to be larger than others. At one point he raises one scientific revolution above all others: "No other work known to the history of science has simultaneously permitted so large an increase in both the scope and precision of research" (30 *SSR*). "More clearly than most other episodes in the history of at least the physical sciences [the episodes of Copernicus, Newton, Lavoisier, and Einstein], these display what all scientific revolutions are about" (6 *SSR*). "Most large-scale upheavals in scientific thought produce similar conceptual disparities" (229 *CR*). "Some revolutions are large, like those associated with the names of Copernicus, Newton, or Darwin, but most are much smaller..." (xvii *ET*). There are "large-scale shifts such as the Copernican, Newtonian, chemical, and Einsteinian revolutions" ; and there were "somewhat smaller, because more exclusively professional, changes in paradigm" (66 *SSR*). Some "minor shifts" in paradigms occurred between Aristotle and Galileo (119 *SSR*). More specifically, "...one set of reasons for the transformation of the classical sciences lies within their own previous lines of development. Although historians differ greatly about the weight to be attached to them, few now doubt that some medieval reformulations of ancient doctrine, Islamic or Latin, were of major significance to figures like Copernicus, Galileo, and Kepler" (52 *ET*). This quote introduces an important principle concerning tradition: Kuhn bases development on continuity (lines of development) and implicitly on the regularity of the structures appearing successively along the line. This idea, if developed, would clear up the problems with the scope of revolutions.

Revolutions seem larger than others, because some seem to cause more change in society or other fields. The Copernican Revolution was unusually large because more than most it changed other scientific fields, nonscientific thought, society, and eventually daily life (4 *CR*). The reconciliation of other sciences with Copernican astronomy formed the basis of the Scientific Revolution--that general turn of humanity toward a more rational society with experimental science leading the way. "We shall gradually discover how difficult it is to restrict the scope of an established scientific concept to a single science or even to the sciences as a group" (2 *CR*).

They also seem larger because of the *degree* of change; "radical alterations in man's understanding of nature" occurred (1 *CR*); "an epochal turning point in the intellectual development of Western man" (1 *CR*). As Cohen astutely put it, "In many cases scholars who have used the term `revolution' may have had in mind nothing other than a historical metaphor for a great change, a truly significant invention" (24). The degree of change may be an illusion of hindsight; that is, Plato was not regarded to be such a monumental figure of culture in his own time; the intervening centuries enlarged his reputation because of the number of references to him and the centuries. Consequently, people think he was one of two or three others in 3,000 years with such stature. History must have heros and periods of time for it to do its work.

In fairness to Kuhn, he denies that his concept of revolution is limited to big ones (350 *CR*). The emphasis, nevertheless, occurs so often and in so many ways that the size of revolutions may have been a factor in the choice of the word "revolution," say, as opposed to "evolution."

Kuhn theorizes about the structure of "scientific" revolutions in contrast to the structure of revolutions in physics, astronomy, chemistry, or any specialty.

The generality of the definition indicates that other factors besides changes in concepts determine its meaning. To some extent, a "revolution" is an historical, not a scientific idea. The differences between revolutions are often marked by time periods. Perhaps revolutions did cause changes in time periods, historical eras, though Kuhn's approach seems to be the reverse. He often speaks about revolutions in terms of a few big names separated by centuries: "the ancient astronomical tradition" [extending from Ptolemy to Copernicus] (2 *CR*); "post-paradigm period in the development of thermodynamics" (32 *SSR*). Also, the Copernican Revolution was described as incomplete until completion by Newtonian physics a few centuries later (243 *CR*). This transhistorical scope of a revolution contrasts with Bloom's idea of struggles between poets from one generation to the next. The idea of a `revolution' for Bloom is much more regular than it is for Kuhn, and without large differences of size.

The unclear scope of a revolution produces ambiguous answers about some questions. Maxwell is cited as having had a paradigm that was difficult to get rid of, though Einstein did so (107 *SSR*). Elsewhere Kuhn claims a direct connection between Einstein and Newton: "the transition from Newtonian to Einsteinian mechanics" (102 *SSR*). For an historian there can be links between sciences thousands of years apart, but can there be for science? Was Maxwell's revolution a minor one only for professional circles? Kuhn does not clearly answer the question, "Does it have the same form as Einstein's revolution?"

Start of a Tradition

Many scientific traditions have "always existed" (20 ET), though some come into being when they have built a (regular) history (1 SSR).

Kuhn believes the sciences increased in number, divided, and became more specialized, as was mentioned. The period when thoughtful reflections were *not* science could lead up to it if successive transitions began to occur from one paradigm to another (12 *SSR*). "More and more sciences," he claims, "`crossed the divide' between what the historian might call its prehistory as a science and its history proper" (21 *SSR*). Clearly, science means to make, use, or have a paradigm.

In 1750 *the* tradition of science changes insofar as science takes the supreme cultural role as "historical prime mover" (131 *ET*).

"Prime mover" is a concept from Aristotle's philosophy, meaning "that which moves the whole universe but is itself not moved."

Kuhn does not explain why a new scientific tradition starts but rather that it does as a revolution and to a lesser extent how.

The explanation of the onset of a paradigm from a nonscientific background is vague and unconvincing. Explaining a first paradigm in ancient statics, dynamics, and geometrical optics, Kuhn believes a first paradigm is obtained when facts "speak with sufficient clarity" (16 *SSR*). Furthermore, "When it [the discovery of the Leyden jar] began, there was no single paradigm for electrical research" (61 *SSR*).

Unit of a Tradition

The unit of the tradition of science is a "paradigm." The following remarks present a general orientation for the detailed discussions of succeeding chapters.

Kuhn does not distinguish separate traditions for physics, astronomy, biology, chemistry, and the other specialties. Science is one tradition.

Unlike Bloom who discusses the tradition of only one branch of literature, poetry, Kuhn writes about the single tradition of all science together. The problem is not that a more detailed study of just one field would not yield the same results as those obtained by Kuhn; the problem is that an analysis of a specific tradition in the group of sciences could yield a deeper knowledge, a more detailed knowledge of tradition and of science.

Because all science is treated as one activity, the unit of tradition tends to become a time period, an historical grouping, a designation of fame (88 *SSR*).

The unit of tradition is a "paradigm," a conglomerate notion composed of various meanings: models or "exemplars of past achievements"; "a disciplinary matrix," or a total "framework for the organization of knowledge" (41 CR); a community of researchers with common problems; and to a lesser extent a mode of vision.

From the beginning to the end of his theory, Kuhn argues for a paradigm as "an exemplary past achievement": "One sort of element in that constellation, the concrete puzzle-solutions which, employed as models or examples, can replace explicit rules as a basis for the solution of the remaining puzzles of normal science" (175 *SSR*). Scientists learn their field by modeling problems on previous problems and their solutions. This continuity from one step in tradition to another shows a regular, reoccurring structure like DNA.

Besides being an exemplar, a paradigm is "a disciplinary matrix" or a general conceptual scheme or framework of a scientific theory: "They [paradigms] always cover the entire range of conceivable natural phenomena" (20 *ET*). Similarly, Bloom and Derrida claim their theories apply to the whole of experience; the universal applicability of a cultural form seems to be part of its formal goals.

According to this meaning a paradigm must be whole or not at all, and it is integral to science:

> Once a first paradigm through which to view nature has been found, there is no such thing as research in the absence of any paradigm. To reject one paradigm without simultaneously substituting another is to reject science itself. That act reflects not on the paradigm but on the man. Inevitably he will be seen by his colleagues as `the carpenter who blames his tools' (79 *SSR*).

Here Kuhn speaks as if there could be found an historically first paradigm, but he gives no example of one. Both Bloom and Derrida question a specific origin for the whole series--it would be like the spontaneous generation of a very highly organized life form from a much lower non-organic chemical compound, while they would agree with Kuhn that a cultural form essentially must come from one similar such form before it.

A paradigm shift is a shift from one unit of tradition to another; it is not a shift in isolated facts, formulas, or ideas (125 *SSR*). In this process, the problems and their standards of measurement or truth change (106 *SSR*). There is "a network of new regularities" (125 *SSR*). There is a redefinition of science itself, despite the necessary continuity of a similar--*not identical*--general framework (103 *SSR*).

The idea that a paradigm means some unit beyond a specific scientific field is not clear. For example, electromagnetic theory is said to be "a paradigm for many scientific groups" but "not the same paradigm for them all" (50 *SSR*).

"Paradigm" is a conglomerate notion, for it also refers to the identity of a community of researchers, being a sociological idea. In some passages Kuhn prefers to think of it as a group of researchers, not as an ordering of subject matter.

Some passages about the community of scientists reveal much about Kuhn's idea of science. The group in each specialty may be as few as 100 members worldwide; these are the ones who make and validate the paradigm (178 *SSR*). Also, Kuhn is less interested in proving why one science is better, than he is interested in describing the community change from paradigm to paradigm (153 *SSR*). One consequence is that readers should not look for proof of changes in science, since only general historical descriptions are given.

The unusually strong sense of cooperation and consensus in science may have helped Kuhn to keep the difficult idea of a paradigm always in mind (164 *SSR*).

A final main meaning of "paradigm" (more than twenty meanings were found by Masterman) is a mode of vision. Kuhn describes a "gestalt switch" from paradigm to paradigm, meaning a shift in the entire way of seeing nature.

So famous did Kuhn's idea of paradigm become that it generated a great deal of controversy. To get a sense of the amount of discussion, and its increasing complexity, consider the following passage from Cohen's encyclopedic work on revolutions:

> J.P. Stern wrote about Lichtenbergian paradigms in 1959, three years before the publication of *The Structure of Scientific Revolutions*, and so did not relate

this eighteenth-century idea of paradigm with its twentieth-century successor. But in Stephen Toulmin's *Human Understanding* (1972, 106), Lichtenberg was cited as a predecessor of Kuhn and it was pointed out, furthermore, that in the twentieth century the term `paradigm' had been used before Kuhn by Ludwig Wittgenstein, W.H. Watson, N.R. Hanson, and S. Toulmin. (The general history of `paradigm' in relation to the understanding of science and its growth has been explored by Daniel Goldman Cedarbaum.) A careful analysis of all these usages makes abundantly clear the high degree of originality with which both Lichtenberg and Kuhn used the concept of paradigm in the context of science (519).

Though Cohen's purpose is not an exhaustive list, he does give a sense of the interest in "paradigm." Two writers not mentioned here are J.S. Bruner and Leo Postman, "On the Perception of Incongruity: A Paradigm," 1949.

Method

Calling himself an historian of science, Kuhn defines some revolutions according to periods of time or to communities of researchers, and his method cannot wholeheartedly be called "deconstruction" despite some strong resemblances of major concepts.

Kuhn should be studied along with Bloom and Derrida because like them he is very interested in tradition. In fact, he believes, to study revolutions one must study tradition. The direction of Copernicus' research was often directed by fields outside astronomy (vii *CR*). Unlike them, however, Kuhn often thinks of tradition as an historical construct rather than as a specific form of a specialty defined in its terms. The word "tradition" occurs many times in his writings, often with general rubrics marking off historical periods:

Ptolemaic astronomy, the Copernican world view, the Newtonian tradition, and so on.

The Contents page of *The Copernican Revolution* offers a good example of Kuhn's method. The seven chapters are divided into two main parts: the first being the "scientific part," and the second the "intellectual history"; however, the scientific part constitutes only two chapters out of seven.

Kuhn uses examples in a way neither Bloom nor Derrida tend to. Whereas Bloom offers detailed line-by-line interpretations of individual poems, Kuhn's examples are brief and unanalyzed. Being more illustrative than argumentative, more decorative than decisive, they constitute proof less than examples do in the cases of Bloom and Derrida. Derrida offers extended intensive readings of particular writers *within* his original philosophy; for example, the reading of Rousseau in *Of Grammatology*, the reading of Condillac in *Archaeology of the Frivolous*, and so on.

Kuhn's method differs from Bloom's and Derrida's in another important way. To find what are revolutions, Kuhn the historian looks at non-scientific data such as organizations, dates, journals, and textbook divisions (51 *ET*). "Since a few of my conclusions depend upon the particular list of names selected for study, a few words about the selection procedure seem essential. I have tried to include all the men who were thought by their contemporaries or immediate successors to have reached independently some significant part of energy conservation. To this group I have added Carnot and Hirn, whose work would surely have been so regarded if it had been known..." (69 *ET*). He looks at the literature referred to. Bloom does not depend on the judgments of the community of poets to determine who is a great poet; he explains why a poet is great through the original works themselves as understood by formally defined interpretive concepts he develops. In a way, Kuhn's approach to finding revolutions externally, that is, not through the meaning of scientific concepts directly, assumes the truth of what he is trying to show.

While any limit of the amount of proof does not *disprove* Kuhn's ideas, it may point to a less developed theory of tradition. A defender of Kuhn would likely mention the value of nontechnical examples to reach a general audience and, while being true and praiseworthy, this defence is patronizing of poetry and philosophy, which are then not thought to have to avoid technicality, the prerogative of science.

The tendency to understand science by marking off historical periods has been mentioned. When Kuhn writes about "the Baconian sciences" and "the Baconian movement", he is choosing a point in history by which to relate scientific contributions (49 *ET*). Even clearer, the historian discovers "a penumbral area occupied by achievements whose status is still in doubt, but the core of solved problems and techniques will usually be clear. Despite occasional ambiguities, the paradigms of a mature scientific community can be determined with relative ease" (43 *SSR*). Here Kuhn seems to assume which changes are revolutions, but isn't this what he needs to prove? Bloom has an opposite approach, for he begins with the relations of poetries, explaining them at length, and then infers what can be called historical groups of writers (romanticism). Bloom's formalization of ideas about poetic tradition come after detailed, line-by-line studies of the corpus of some poets.

The periodizing tendencies of Kuhn can be compared with an idea about historical method by Ernst Curtius, much discussed literary scholar. Historical scholarship resembles map making: an aerial photograph can constitute a map, as can a detailed on-the-ground close-up of the same area (ix). These two approaches must both be used, according to Curtius. In contrast Kuhn emphasizes the aerial photograph to the neglect of the detailed on-the-ground map. Had he undertaken some detailed analyses of three successive revolutions perhaps his general principles might have been different. With Bloom's and Derrida's theories, as we shall see, there are more details telling the reader how to get from one point on the map to another, how to get from one poetry or philosophy to another.

The ordering principles of Kuhn's historical approach should be noted. Textbooks, he claims, differ from the original historical texts (4 *ET*). The textbooks order the material and select it by starting with the present and making the science proceed in as straight as line as possible to the present level. The sense that scientists disagreed with others, changing previous science, is completely absent. In the original texts there is a more genuine, more complete sense of what was true then and perhaps not now. Between these paths Kuhn attempts to write "narratives" of the developments to present the changes often hidden in textbooks. This issue of the role of narrative in science and also the issue of narrative in tradition forms will be discussed again.

Kuhn has an "historiographic" approach. He does not want to write only about the permanent contributions of science but also about "the historical integrity of that science in its own time" (3 *SSR*). Brave as he is in circles of philosophers of science, he does not fully allow science to have some kinship with myth:

> If these out-of-date beliefs are to be called myths, then myths can be produced by the same sorts of methods and held for the same sorts of reasons that now lead to scientific knowledge. If, on the other hand, they are to be called science, then science has included bodies of belief quite incompatible with the ones we hold today. Given these alternatives, the historian must choose the latter" (2 *SSR*).

Many philosophers of science would regard previous myths as not an essential part of science or as "pre-scientific." Any error attributed to science would be very limited, according to Kuhn. True enough, there are passages in which he speaks about a change in world view, a total revision of assumptions; all these enthusiastic observations, however, are moderated by the change being a matter of consensus of the community of scientists who are then seen to be in full knowledge and control of the process.

In fact, the method is at bottom "fundamentalist." In religion the term refers to the view that the Bible has just one correct interpretation, often a literal one. Not providing proof in the technical idiom of science, Kuhn regards its truth in this way, suggesting there is no problem of choosing the revolutions, being well-known, and suggesting all scientists know what the true geneaology of science is. If there are revolutions, there are problems in determining who is right and why, not consensus as if by group decision. And if there is a distinction between normal and extraordinary science, then the normal scientists by definition know less about their "disciplinary matrix" than the extraordinary, and the normal would not agree sometimes about the interpretation of revolutions. To attempt to present Kuhn's view strongly, I would say the normal scientists only know less than the extraordinary ones when a new revolution occurs. The question remains, if they had the level of knowledge of an extraordinary scientist, why would they not create a new paradigm?

For Kuhn, there are no problems of interpreting science directly; there are no problems of choosing which changes of concepts are revolutions; the problems involve making an historical narrative of periods. Lyotard has called such projects "grand narratives" or "meta-narratives" of history (*The Postmodern Condition*).

Innovative and insightful, Kuhn's method does resemble the operation of deconstruction in important ways. The idea that a scientific conceptual scheme would have to be destroyed and replaced by one similar in structural features is deconstructive. The idea of incommensurability between proponents of different theories also fits in with deconstruction, for it suggests that there is no meaning outside a theory, a system of differences, and so proponents of different paradigms cannot communicate completely; if they could, it would imply a language above and outside of any two paradigms. Only Kuhn the philosopher of science can rise above the historical series of theories (but perhaps he would say the extraordinary scientist also does this when he changes a paradigm--yet probably he would say, if we draw the implications of his explicit remarks to their limit, this vision does not have the generality of the philosopher of science). Many other features of deconstruction are not known to Kuhn. Bloom is more of a deconstructionist, for he discusses in depth the simultaneous process of destroying the old tradition while constructing a revised version of the same cultural form.

Conclusion about the Unity of the Doctrine

Kuhn's work cannot be split into distinct early or late doctrines. The use of the same name for the 1977 collection and the 1959 paper--"The Essential Tension"-- combined with close reading reveals no major change or shift or revolution in his theory throughout the years of discussion, 1959 to present. His "thinking cap"--as he has said--was the same one; the refinements were clarifications and accommodations to critics, the major one being the rejection of the polysemia of the notion of "paradigm" and the adoption of the term "disciplinary matrix" to cover some uses of the previous term. These uses, he then claimed in response to criticisms, were not his main interest, and he really did not want to develop his theory on them, which disclaimer is a weakening and limitation of his theory, a concession to critics with more common sensical views but a less profound understanding of science, Kuhn's weakening due to his scientific desire to have objective views in agreement with others.

Summary

Kuhn's idea of tradition as a whole is innovative, sometimes bold, and also too general, too descriptive, even questionable. The idea of the tradition as a series of cycles is innovative, bold. Also, the idea of a paradigm--in all its meanings, including the wholistic ones--touches on the most central questions: "What is scientific tradition? What is science?" Nevertheless, there are some questions about the scope of a revolution, the start of a tradition, and the method. All these issues shall be elaborated in very detailed discussions, both of Kuhn's theory and again through Bloom's and Derrida's. This chapter only prepares the reader.

BLOOM'S THEORY OF TRADITION AS A WHOLE

Introduction to "Bloom's Theory of Tradition as a Whole"

Bloom's theory resembles T.S. Eliot's theory of tradition in "Tradition and the Individual Talent" and also basic features of Kuhn's. A striking feature, Bloom emphasizes the one-to-one *struggle* of great poetries in succession, based on the individual efforts of a new great poet; in contrast Kuhn emphasizes *consensus* after a paradigm change, based more on community effort.

Tradition as a Whole

Just as it was for Kuhn, tradition is a continuing series of cycles, yet Bloom defines the changes in the development in much more detail. There is more vocabulary for the process, more in-depth study of figures--notwithstanding Kuhn's study of the Copernican Revolution, which, though extensive as it is, is nevertheless more descriptive than argumentative, more historical than theoretical.

Whereas Kuhn's theory seems to apply to science throughout human history, Bloom explicitly restricts the validity to British romanticism and its descendents, along with an American tradition beginning with Emerson: "I have been tracing the visionary company that inhabits two shadows of influence, the Miltonic tradition that goes from the poets of Sensibility to its culmination in Yeats, and the Emersonian tradition from Whitman to its completion in the last phase of Stevens" (193 *MM*). I think the restriction is an understatement. In other passages Bloom claims his theory concerns the "subject of poetry for the last three centuries" (148 *AI*). In brief references to poets before Spenser--namely, to Dante, Virgil, and Homer--Bloom believes his ratios apply. Moreover, he seems to speak of a plurality of traditions when he places romanticism in the history of other traditions. Above all, because of the nature of the relation between one poet and the next, there is no reason why the series should have an end or clear "first" great poetry. Tradition would not start in 1740 with the romantic movement (36 *MM*). Bloom's theory does allow for its extension to figures before and after the romantic tradition. He declares his intention: to write about *canonical* figures. "Canon" means "standards accepted as axiomatic and universally binding." Instead of a canonical poetry people more often say a great poetry or a classic. "Canon" gives more the sense that rules can be stated to explain why poetries belong in the group of the best ones.

The tradition forms a canon, a growing body of poetries, containing the principle of its self-perpetuation, the primary function of biological genetic codes. Giving a more telling definition of canon, Bloom writes, "a contrapuntal musical compostion is two or more voice parts in which the melody is imitated exactly and completely by the successive voices though not always at the same pitch" 34 *SM*). The "melody" of poetry is "a triple rhythm of contraction, breaking apart, and mending" (39 *Kabbalah* ...). Here is a sense of contrast, as there is between a new poet and the poetic father; repetition, just as a poet repeats the pattern of poetry; and extension, insofar as the new poet alters the previous pattern or code slightly to deepen the poetic principles. In this way the canon according to Bloom has features of the genetic code : "A *strong* reading can be defined as one that itself produces other readings--as Paul de Man says..." (17 *Kabbalah*).

Bloom develops the idea of a single series of great poets in a relation like parent to child, similar to Eliot's idea. Figures he situates in this series are Spenser, Milton, Wordsworth, Shelley, Keats, Tennyson, Browning, Yeats, and later Stevens and Ashberry. From Spenser to Tennyson, Bloom confidently analyzes the relation of poetic father to child through various works. After Tennyson it is uncertain who the unique primary father is. Poems have fathers; "...no poet can write a poem without, in some sense, remembering another poem..." (199 *MM*). New poets who are becoming great "misread" the previous poetic father to extend poetic history by beginning a new poetry.

Notwithstanding several feminine criticisms against the use of "father" and not "mother," Bloom's theory does not depend on this gender difference. He might have said in more gender-neutral, less felicitous terms: one poetry comes from a previous one *like* the origination of one DNA molecule from another.

Poetic tradition, for Bloom, can be defined by reference to only great poets, in contrast to Kuhn's inclusion of the entire profession. The view seems quite elitist but, if the idea of tradition is more articulate, limiting tradition in this way may not be a mistake. Curtius, like Bloom, spoke of "literary citizens of the first class" ("classicus"): the poets who make the classics forming a canon (34 *MM*). Rather than being elitist, this view seems to offer a standard for determining and defining what is the best poetry. Imagine a pyramid. At the point on the top would be great poets, and various levels would be below. Bloom provides a way for defining the poetry on the top. Only the poets on the tops have a vision of the previous poets. "Classic" means "serving as a standard of excellence; traditional, enduring; of the highest rank." By comparison to Kuhn's view of eventual community consensus, Bloom seems to be quite an elitist, or perhaps he defines standards undefined by Kuhn.

Although the series of poetries contains those of the highest rank, each one gets better. Bloom elaborates, "Browning goes on to posit a mighty ladder or authentic poets, in an objective and subjective alternation, who will replace one another almost endlessly in succession, concerning which, `the world dares no longer doubt that its gradations ascend'" (176 *PR*). Kuhn hesitates to speak of the history of science as evolutionary; often avoiding evaluative terms, he resists speaking about scientific theories as changing from inferior to superior, for this progress might suggest the presence of regular error in the unquestionable, the holy process of science. Regrettably, though Bloom is more willing to admit improvement through the history of poetry, not much explanation of the improvement in fact occurs, whereas it does in Derrida's concern with the history of philosophy.

Scope

Bloom believes some great poets surpassed others, and the main tendency is toward reducing the differences in the sizes of poetic contribution among great poets, rather than to describe the greater size of scientific contribution by some great scientists.

In Kuhn's theory there are questions about the relations of paradigms; can they extend for centuries? In general the question is, even though all great theories achieve the best possible at their time, are some better than others? Of great theories, can some be greater than others? Recall the saying (by Huxley or Orwell), everyone is equal but some people are more equal than others. Does a theory's being great mean that, with regard to structure, successive ones are on a par? Eliot preferred to regard poetries as equally poetic, despite the deepening of poetic vision, to some extent as Lévi-Strauss regarded cultures as equally cultural. Kuhn does not raise this question; more of it can be seen in Bloom's work, and more yet in Derrida's. Bloom's term "revisionary ratios," to be discussed at length in subsequent chapters, suggests the question of how to explain the equality of all great poetries *and* the improvement of one on another.

Only on a few occasions does Bloom make comparisons across centuries, a process that may suggest the `greater greatness' or one poetry in relation to another. The much more prevalent process is to compare two poets between whom there was a struggle. Much less ambiguity affects the defining of revolutions in Bloom's theory. However, sometimes he speaks about a "composite precursor" or a "prime precursor" (11 *AI;* 158 *MM*). The idea of multiple precursors runs counter to the idea of poetic form as the result of a one-to-one struggle between generations (through a change of poetic code, a set of specific "revisionary ratios"). As the main doctrine, a poetry has one other poetry as its father [or mother, but Bloom, after Freud, uses "father"].

Several passages declare some great poets to be greater than others, just as Kuhn did, though Bloom emphasizes the regularity of the series of poetries forming tradition. "Of all Milton's poetic descendants,...Wordsworth was the strongest, so strong indeed that we must face a dark truth. Wordsworth's greatest poem, "The Prelude," was finished, in its essentials, a hundred and seventy years ago, and no subsequent poetry written in English can sustain a close comparison with it, no matter what fashionable criticism tries to tell us to the contrary" (60 *PR*). Later in *Poetry and Repression* he claims no one has surpassed Wordsworth (82 *PR*). In one passage Milton is exalted along with Wordsworth above other great poets in the canon: "In our time, the situation becomes more desperate even than it was in the Milton-haunted eighteenth century, or the Wordsworth-haunted nineteenth, and our current and future poets have only the consolation that no certain Titanic figure has risen since Milton and Wordsworth, not even Yeats or Stevens" (32 *AI*). Some great poets are described to be "smaller" than others (11 *AI*). This tendency is more exaggerated in Kuhn's historical work, which defines periods of science.

Sometimes Bloom applies the revisionary ratios and technical terms including "misreading" to non-canonical figures (Blake, whom he denies the status of canonicity with respect to Wordsworth; Emerson) and non-poetic figures (Freud, Nietzsche, 56 *AI*) and to himself (start of *AI*). This application is a mistake, for it shows that Bloom does not believe the genetic line of poets is pure: he does not believe with complete consistency that a poem comes from another poem; rather, it may be mixed with non-poetic influences, one of them being the critic's. The dominant tendency is to regard a poem as directly coming from a previous poem, or a poetry coming from a previous poetry.

In a way clearer than Kuhn's, Bloom understands a great poetry to comprehend the entire tradition before it.

The scope of a poetry is "everything, space and time included," and in this way it resembles the universal scope of the sciences. The scope also includes the whole of the tradition, since poets change poetic history: "...it was Tennyson's transformation of Keats that was the largest single factor in British and American poetry from about 1830 until about 1915" (144-45 *PR*). In *Shelley's Mythmaking* Bloom speaks of the wholistic change by asking what Shelley is doing to tradition. Though Kuhn speaks of changes in world views, and though later theories include the laws of previous ones as limiting cases, the sense that a new theory is meant to accumulate the entire tradition is not strongly expressed. As it seems, Kuhn would like to avoid making previous theories illusory or mistaken if subsequent ones are thought to completely replace them. Kuhn would regard it as an illusion to cast into doubt *all* the results of previous science.

Bloom describes the poet as similarly having illusions about the scope: "to be productive it [a strong reading] must insist upon its own exclusiveness and completeness, and it must deny its partialness and its necessary falsification" (17 *Kabbalah...*). The critic, on

Bloom's view, does not have this illusion about the poet's work; knowing the boundaries, the critic does not allow himself/herself the unlimited scope of the vision felt by the poet. Ironically enough, in so questioning the scope of a poet's claim to the complete poetic vision, Bloom places himself above even the great poets.

Start of Tradition

Poetry originates as a transformation of ancient myths. Bloom's theory applies to a specific tradition beginning with Milton.

For Bloom, the whole tradition of poetry begins as a transformation of myth, and the similarities between the developmental structures of myth and poetry reveal much about the transmission of poetic knowledge. Like many mythologists (e.g. James Jacób Liszka), Campbell has a threefold pattern for the life-cycle of myths:

> [STAGE ONE: SEPARATION FROM THE COMMUNITY]
> The mythological hero, setting forth from his commonday hut or castle, is lured, carried away, or else voluntarily proceeds, to the threshold of adventure. There he encounters a shadow presence that guards the passage. The hero may defeat or conciliate this power and go alive into the kingdom of the dark...or be slain by the opponent and descend in death (dismemberment, crucifixion). Beyond the threshold, then, the hero journeys through a world of unfamiliar yet strangely intimate forces, some of which severely threaten him (tests), some of which give magical aid (helpers).
>
> [STAGE TWO: INITIATION INTO MYSTERIES BY ORDEAL OR BATTLE]
> When he arrives at the nadir of the mythological round, he undergoes a supreme ordeal and gains his

> reward. The triumph may be represented as the hero's sexual union with the goddess-mother of the world (sacred marriage), his recognition by the father-creator (father atonement), his own divinization (apotheosis), or again--if the powers have remained unfriendly to him--his theft of the boon he came to gain (bride-theft, fire-theft); intrinsically it is an expansion of consciousness and therewith of being (illumination, transfiguration, freedom).
>
> [STAGE THREE: THE RETURN TO THE COMMUNITY]
> The final work is that of the return. If the powers have blessed the hero, he now sets forth under their protection (emissary); if not, he flees and is pursued (transformation flight, obstacle flight). At the return threshold the transcendental powers must remain behind; the hero re-emerges from the kingdom of dread (return, resurrection). The boon that he brings restores the world (elixir) (245-46 *Hero...*).

Bloom's model is similarly threefold, three pairs of "ratios," meaning relations of a poet to predecessor.[1]

> Indeed, I propose that the succession and alternation of the three pairs of ratios form the pattern of what has been the central tradition of the greater modern lyric, from its ancestors in Spenser's *Prothalamion* and Milton's *Lycidas* on through its major establishment in the Coleridge-Wordsworthian crisis lyric, with the crucial descendants in the most famous shorter poems of Shelley, Keats, and Stevens down to the best poems being written today. Whatever their formal divisions into stanzas, a remarkable tradition divide argumentatively and imagistically into three parts, very much on the model of the "Intimations Ode." These are: *first*, an initial loss or crisis, centering on a question of renewal or imaginative survival; *second*, a despairing or reductive answer to the

question, in which the mind's power, however great, seems inadequate to overcome the obstacles both of language and of the universe of death, of outer sense; *third*, a more hopeful or at least ongoing answer, however qualified by recognitions of continuing loss" (96 *MM*).

Instead of Cambell's "separation, initiation, return" he usually uses "limitation, substitution, representation" from the medieval Jewish doctrine of Kabbalah. In limitation the new poet limits the validity of the previous poet's aesthetic, making way for a new one. In substitution, the new poet expresses a new and greater difference of his/her new poetic ability in relation to the ability of the predecessor. In representation, the poet permits some association of his aesthetic principles with those of the predecessor provided that they be interpreted to be on a lower poetic level. The "community" is the historical series of great poets, which the new one finally joins. This cyclic process is progressive, for a "higher type" of poetry is achieved. Unfortunately, Bloom does not explain this idea in detail: what constitutes poetic superiority? He does, however, explain in great detail the fact of the change of one great poetry into another, and the fact of some specific change is used to support his theory. He might have used some lines of one poetry to *justify* their superiority to lines in a predecessor's rather than to justify his theory. The concern for the superiority of one poet over another is replaced by the concern for proving Bloom's theory.

In preferance to showing the superiority of one poetry over another Bloom shows the struggle to achieve a similarity of structure, albeit one's own. The cyclic creation of poetry allows it to be immortal: an unlimited tradition making continuous the efforts of poets for thousands of years. The series of reproductive cycles of the human family, in which parents have a child, the child has a child, and the grandchild is also fertile suggests a necessary assumption for the explanation of tradition. Each unit, each poetry, must fit into such a series; each must be like a genetic code. Bloom's theory is closer to such a model than Kuhn's.

The tradition his theory applies to begins after Milton. "He [Milton] surpassed them in greatness, since what he could do for himself was the cause of their becoming unable to do the same for themselves. His achievement became at once their starting point, their inspiration, yet also their goad, their torment" (127 *MM*). In the same passage, though, Bloom cites Milton's belief in Spenser as his "original" (conveyed by Dryden's statement reported from Milton). So, British romanticism begins with Milton but Milton had his beginning in Spenser before him. The revisionary ratios also apply to Spenser. In principle Bloom's theory applies before the romantics. The theory if true must have universal applicability, since tradition is an on-going phenomenon.

Less factual and more explanatory than Kuhn, Bloom is more concerned with the motives for the process of any new contribution to poetic tradition.

Literary tradition begins again with each new poetry. Each beginning fulfills the following conditions: "when a fresh author is simultaneously cognizant not only of his own struggle against the forms and presence of a precursor, but is compelled also to a sense of the Precursor's place in regard to what came before him" (32 *MM*).

The Unit of Tradition

There is some ambiguity concerning whether the unit of tradition is a poem or an entire poetry.

In theory, Bloom understands the unit of tradition to be an entire poetry, rather than an entire work of literature, which might include fiction or drama, in contrast to Kuhn, who thinks the unit of tradition is a scientific theory in general, which indifferently applies to specific sciences. However, in practice, Bloom applies his critical principles to individual poems, which raises the question whether Bloom does not also regard a poem as the unit of tradition.

A poetry has its "life-cycle" (10-11 *AI*) between two poetic dead ends; for Kuhn, science was limited by two revolutions. About creativity and the tradition Borges has said that the artist's "victory, if you like, is that he confronts an intellectual dead end and employs it against itself to accomplish new human work." ² This point is crucial for understanding creation, and it is remarkably similar to Bloom's view. The Russian Formalist literary critic Boris Eichenbaum sees new literary forms implicit in the dead ends: "The creation of new artistic forms is not an act of representation, but of discovery, because these forms are hidden in the forms of preceding periods. Lermontov had to discover the poetic style needed for an escape from the poetic dead end that took shape after the 1820s. This style already existed potentially in some poets of the Pushkin period" (162 *The Formal Method*).

The overcoming of an aesthetic dead end at the end of a poetry resembles a birth. Joseph Cambell explains, "Freud has suggested that all moments of anxiety reproduce the painful feelings of the first separation from the mother--the tightening of the breath, congestion of the blood, etc., of the crisis of birth. Conversely, all moments of separation and new birth produce anxiety."[3] Bloom's idea of the start of any new poetry is a moment of separation and new birth, and this moment causes anxiety.

To say that a poetry has a "life-cycle" is to liken it to the genetic code (10-11 *AI*).

While agreeing with Kuhn that there be a paradigm or total recurring framework for tradition, Bloom goes one step further by defining the internal recurring pattern of the cycles like a genetic code.

Seeing the same constellation of types of images and the same relations between poetries led Bloom to form a theory about the single pattern of "the High Romantic paradigm" (277 *PR*), using language like Kuhn's.

In the life-cycle of the paradigm Bloom distinguishes six "revisionary ratios" (10-11 *AI*). These are poetic expressions equivalent to parallel schemes of rhetorical tropes and psychological defenses. At first Kuhn thought Freud's defenses were the closest analogy to the ratios; then he thought the Kabbalah was; at any rate he came to the notion of ratios before reading about Kabbalah (95 *MM*). The word "ratios" means equal "relations with the predecessor," suggesting that poet and predecessor are equally poets. The word "revisionary" means "a changing stance toward the precursor," suggesting that a subsequent great poet improves on a previous one.

Bloom's key concept of revisionary ratios can be explained in the following preliminary way: they are the six steps of the process of one poet struggling against a previous poet, to come into his own as a great poet. In the structure of poetry, as a change of assumptions is thought by Kuhn to be in the structure of science, all great poets do "not consent to make way for others" (154 *AI*); they foretell the decline of poetry, an artistic dead end. They seem in Bloom's psychological, sometimes personifying terminology to prevent a successor. In terms more comparable to Kuhn's, all great poetries present the poetic equivalent of an unsolvable problem requiring a change in assumptions of the entire world view--there is a poetic paradox.

This proclamation of no more poetry is internalized by a new poet-to-be as an internecine conflict: the sense of poetic belatedness, coming too late, conflicts with the need to create for oneself. This anxiety, this nervous anticipation to create a space of poetry for oneself despite the predecessor, continues until the new creation is complete. A new poetry is a space of imagination renewing the individual's power to accumulate tradition.

The whole-to-whole process (149 *SM*) of development, one poet developing from a specific poetic parent, follows a single, specific line. Remember the following line from Wordsworth: "Another race hath been, and other palms are won" ("Ode: Intimations of Immortality," line 200) as well as this bible verse from 1st Corinthians (9.24): "Know ye not that they which run in a race run all, but one receiveth the prize?" So, to become a great poet, one must enter into a kind of competition with the last great poet. The winner gains the prize for all humanity until a new victor comes.

For Bloom, the anxiety of influence is a poetic, not a psychoanalytic process of six revisionary ratios, six steps toward greatness. The theory very much resembles main ideas of T.S. Eliot's famous "Tradition and the Individual Talent." According to Eliot, a new poet does not become great by "following the ways of the immediate generation before...in a blind or timid adherence to its successes" (2207 *Norton Anthology*). This idea resembles Bloom's that successive generations struggle. Secondly, Eliot believes that a new great poet changes the aesthetic of not only the previous great poet but also simultaneously all preceding great poets. This domino effect is described often by Bloom when he mentions several precursors that have been improved upon by the great poet (11 *PR*). Thirdly, Eliot states that the new great poet measures and is measured by the preceding great poet, reciprocally. Bloom also describes the process as a continuous reference to the precursor, a continuous change, as the name "revisionary ratio" implies. It is partly because of it that the domino effect takes place. The struggle with the predecessor drives the poet all the way to his mature work until the successor has joined the company of great poets, has achieved a structure of similar type.

One poem particularly exemplary of the six revisionary ratios is Shelley's "Ode to the West Wind" (103-106 *PR* and 91 *SM*; and see the *Norton Anthology*, pp. 1819-1820). The poem has three movements, each with a pair of revisionary ratios: 1. clinamen/ tessera; 2. kenosis/ daemonization; and 3. askesis/ apophrades.

In the first movement Shelley breaks away from Wordsworth; in the second he further distances himself from Wordsworth and individuates him as just one powerful predecessor; and in the third movement Shelley shows a greater power than Wordsworth, by doing (or having done) what Wordsworth had denied could be done.

In the title, "West Wind" refers to an unseen presence as a "destroyer and preserver," a deconstructive theme which fits Bloom's idea very well that a poem is about another poem, about the anxiety of influence, about the process of writing poetry, as was Wordsworth's "Intimation's Ode" before it.[4]

Of course, the wind is mentioned by the precursor Wordsworth to signal the coming of inspiration and is important in the first movement of Shelley's poem. In the second movement Shelley further isolates himself from Wordsworth by altering Shelley's own previous assessment of Wordsworth's treatment of nature by poetry.

The third movement resolves the conflict between Shelley and Wordsworth by a prayer. In stanza five Shelley makes clear that he is in effect writing a poetry by measuring it against a previous standard, against Wordsworth's art (the falling leaves), when he writes

Make my thy lyre, even as the forest is:
What if my leaves are falling like its own!
The tumult of thy mighty harmonies

Will take from both a deep, autumnal tone,
Sweet though in sadness. Be thou,/
Spirit fierce,
My spirit! Be thou me, impetuous one!

Drive my dead thoughts over the universe
Like withered leaves to quicken a new birth!
And, by the incantation of this verse,

Scatter, as from an unextinguished hearth
Ashes and sparks, my words among mankind!
Be through my lips to unawakened Earth

The trumpet of a prophecy! O Wind,
If winter comes, can Spring be far behind?

Shelley's act of showing greater poetic power, Bloom believes, can be found when there is a change of images used by Wordsworth: "Where Wordsworth began the third movement of `Intimations' with a sublimating image of `embers', Shelley concludes with `ashes and sparks', his version of `something that doth live' [a poem]. These images especially when located at the end of a poem call to mind the myth of the phoenix, the ancient sunbird, who would die or kill itself and rise from the ashes. The end has the significance that Shelley has raised poetry from Wordsworth's ashes and that Shelley will scatter these live embers among mankind, thus in his turn limiting the fertility or creativity of any would-be successors.

Shelley did to Wordsworth what Wordsworth had done to Milton. Bloom does believe his revisionary ratios form a synchronic pattern for a genetic code of poetry, to use my terms. In the handing down there is a complex opposition; in Bloom's words, "The stronger poet not only performs the dance more skillfully than the weaker poet, but he modifies it as well, and yet it does remain the same dance" (270 *PR*). The precursor is both in Bloom's words the new "poet's muse and enemy" (226 *PR*).

To summarize the threefold movement of ratios between Shelley and Wordsworth, like that between any two great poets, in the first movement Shelley's poetry resembles Wordsworth's but Shelley treats it ironically or parodies it. This stage resembles the Freudian id in child development. In the second movement Shelley gets a stronger sense of a difference. This movement resembles the development of the ego. In the third movement Shelley completes a poetic perspective vis-à-vis Wordsworth's. Emancipation from Wordsworth is finally won as Wordsworth is subordinate in poetic excellence. This movement resembles the Freudian concept of the superego.

Method

Bloom's method warrants the name deconstruction more than Kuhn's does, though Bloom himself criticizes the movement. Applying `deconstructionist' to Bloom is controversial, as many scholars have pointed out.

Before discussing views about the status of Bloom's theory as deconstruction, it is more helpful to quote what might be the most important statement by Bloom on deconstruction. While not helping to classify Bloom, it nevertheless reveals much about his criticism, features that happen to show his kinship with deconstruction. "Deconstructing any discourse by Ralph Waldo Emerson would be a hopeless enterprise, extravagantly demonstrating why Continental modes of interpretation are unlikely to add any lustres to the most American writers. When there are classic canons of construction, protrusions from the text can tempt an unravelling, but in a text like *Nature* (1836) all is protrusion" (105 "Emerson: The American Religion," 1985). What makes this statement so important is that it tells us what can be deconstructed: only a work with a classic canon of construction; only a work with a standard pattern, its genre's genetic code. Many other passages through his writings declare his intention of interpreting only "strong"--that is, great--poets, and passages state that the ratios apply to strong, canonical poets. Elitist as this view may seem, some way to define the best seems necessary in any system of grading anything from worst to best.

Helen Elam does not classify Bloom as a deconstructionist. Here are her reasons:

> His [Bloom's] reaction against deconstruction runs just as deep, but ironically he is sometimes labeled a

> deconstructionist by virtue of his association with the other Yale critics. Bloom's arguments against deconstruction develop over a period of years and through several books. He insists on the priority of psychoanalysis over epistemology, voice over text, a psyche that resists deconstruction's idea of the self as an effect of language. He respects de Man's epistemological analyses (he calls de Man the one critic that "wounds" him), but counters de Man's position with the argument that repression and forgetting offer a clearer account of the intricate relations between one text and another and of the way a text finally reads itself. De Man's *aporia* gives way in Bloom to Nietzsche's will-to-power and to Freud's theories about psychic defense. Poets lie to themselves, and to others, because lying is a poem's defense against time which permits it a kind of triumph over its own belatedness. When Bloom calls for a "diachronic rhetoric" that can take into account the domain of the lie, he is emphasizing the importance of psychic strategies... (35).

In *The Rhetoric of Romantic Vision*, a full-length study of Bloom, Donald Fite has a mixed reaction to classifying Bloom as a deconstructionist:

> While Bloom shares with deconstruction, then, an emphasis on the ineluctable primacy of interpretive activity and, concomitantly, an awareness of the labyrinths of intertextuality that implicate any given utterance, he departs once again from the deconstructionist regimen insofar as he transforms the activities of interpretive textuality into gestures grounded by the dark enduring *logos* of the Romantic will. As such, the mixed poetics and rhetoric of his own work represent an especially extreme instance of the sort of creative criticism that his colleague at Yale, Geoffrey Hartman, has eloquently called for and much more hesitantly embodied (194).

Christopher Norris defines the similarities of Bloom's work to deconstruction a little more definitely and concretely:

> [KINSHIP WITH DECONSTRUCTION]
> Up to a point there is much in common between Bloom's "revisionary ratios" and the practice of deconstruction. Both start out from the idea that literary history, in so far as it exists in any genuine sense, has to deal with texts in their relationships one with another, through a process of perpetual displacement which can only be described in rhetorical terms. Both dismiss the subjectivist illusion of the poet as self-possessed creator of meaning, an individual subject expressing the truths of his own authentic vision. To interpret a text is to seek out the strategies and defensive tropes by which it either confronts or evades the texts that precede it. Bloom is in accord with Derrida when he insists that textual origins are always pushed back beyond recall, in a series of hard-fought rhetorical encounters that make up the line of descent in poetic history.
>
> [DIFFERENCES FROM DECONSTRUCTION]
> Where the difference emerges is in Bloom's countervailing argument that the "strong" poet must always strive to create at least a working-space of presence for his own imagination. In other words, Bloom wants to halt the process of deconstruction at a point where it is still possible to gauge a poet's creative stature in terms of his overriding will to expression. It could hardly be otherwise, given Bloom's intense involvement with Romantic poetry, and his efforts to rescue that tradition from the classicizing canon of Eliot and his followers. It is therefore not surprising that in his recent books Bloom should seem torn between a defence of poetry which holds to the ethos of Romantic individualism, and a deconstructive poetics which tends to dissolve such themes into something approaching an abstract system of tropes

> and relationships. In the last resort, however, Bloom is always willing to invoke the terminology of "voice," "presence" and subjective origin which Derrida so resolutely tracks down to its metaphors (118 *Deconstruction, Theory, and Practice*).

Norris' idea that interpretation deals with the relations between texts points out a major deconstructive feature of Bloom's criticism.

Bloom defines his main difference from deconstruction in the following way:

> As the verbal mechanisms of crisis have come to dominate lyric poetry, in relatively fixed patterns, a striking effect has been that the strongest poets have tended to establish their mastery by the paradox of what I would call *an achieved dearth [lack] of meaning*. Responding to this achieved dearth, many of the strongest critics have tended to manifest *their* skill by attributing the dearth to their own synchronic view of language and so to the vicissitudes of *language itself* in producing meaning. A diachronic phenomenon, dependent upon Miltonic and Wordsworthian poetic *praxis*, is thus assigned to a synchronic cause. Deconstructionist criticism refuses to situate itself in its own historical dilemma, and so by a charming paradox it falls victim to a genealogy to which evidently it must remain blind (12-13 *DC*).

Bloom's charge here that Derrida `refuses to situate himself in the historical dilemma' cannot be refuted in full. Let me say, however, that Derrida's philosophy may turn out in the forthcoming chapters to be much more historically situated and determinate than Bloom's critical model, which seems too synchronic--ironically--contrary to Bloom's statements.

One key feature of deconstruction in Bloom's work is the dialectical revision and extension of tradition. Many remarks by Bloom show his dialectical/ deconstructive approach to tradition; for example, when he claims it is not form itself that gleams in a poem but the breaking apart of form (1 *DC*). Also, "the `Triumph of Life' is a myth-unmaking poem, and is properly Shelley's last work" (220 *SM*). Poets "break and remake the forms again" (253 *PR*). Seemingly echoing Derrida's concept of *bricolage*, involving an intervention and change of meaning in any rigorous reading, Bloom writes, "one must be an inventor to read well" (169 *MM*). Kuhn, in contrast, would prefer to think of his exposition as factual, non-inventive.

Concerning the method of Bloom its fundamentalism should be discussed. He asserts a passage can be paraphrased and a correct paraphrase can be given (250 *SM*). Fundamentalism means the belief in one true interpretation, as a fundamentalist would have a literal interpretation of the Bible. In the following passage notice the belief in a common understanding of critics of the real text (contrary to the charges that Bloom destroys the profession mentioned below). "Knight, even where misleading," writes Bloom, "is valuable as a warning; his work, especially at this point, illustrates the danger of criticism of visionary poetry passing over into independent vision. The motive is altogether generous; the desire is for understanding, but the actuality suddenly becomes the creation of an individual and inferior poetry. Rapt in the consequences of poetry, Knight develops the poem's anagoge for himself. Valuable as this may be (to himself and to others), it ceases to be criticism. ...the ostensible object of criticism has been abandoned" (196 *SM*). The object of criticism is an understanding of the poet's text from that perspective, suggesting that there is one real interpretation and a critic--the profession of critics--can find this meaning.

As an initial critical reflection on this fundamentalism, to be elaborated later, fundamentalism may ignore a level of poetic meaning specific to an actual great poetry. In other words, new great poetries arise, and the new are better, and the new revise the tradition as a whole; then, does it not follow that each new poetry brings a deeper understanding of poetry? Does a model of poetic meaning necessarily common to several poetries, as Bloom's is, catch this progressive meaning?

Bloom makes a provocative remark: criticism "always leaves a remainder" of meaning not yet interpreted; the interpretation of a text can never discuss everything (77 *SM*). This remainder perhaps should show that the purpose of criticism cannot be to find a common single true meaning. Or, perhaps, criticism is forever bound by a fundamentalist chain to the text as authority about poetic meaning. Due to the second-hand character of the knowledge some meaning may be not accessible.

To balance the idea of the remainder, Bloom rightly claims, "...no poetic figure will stand pressing past a certain point" (77 *SM*), meaning that there is a limit of reduction or translation and, I think, that criticism can achieve a relative completion.

Main Criticisms of Bloom's Work

Two common criticisms of Bloom's work were voiced by Elmer Borklund in a large work surveying contemporary criticism. The ratios are "grandly obscure": "...Bloom unwisely affects the prophetic manner himself" (79). Fite at times agrees, claiming Bloom "hurls dark truths into the faithless void like visionary lightning bolts" (194). Secondly, Borklund believes the criticism endangers the profession, because there is "no language of criticism but only of an individual critic" and no method of criticism. "Bloom has returned poetry to history, or at least to an atomized, violent kind of history.

Another criticism centers on the abstract model Bloom gives. Voicing this criticism toward structuralism, Ann Jefferson finds a preoccupation with abstract models rather than individual texts (91, 95). In *The Anxiety of Influence* and *A Map of Misreading* Bloom discusses individual poems less than he had.

Summary

The theory of the anxiety of influence proposes a pattern by which British romanticism--and all canonical poetry, I suggest on behalf of Bloom--can be read. The pattern is composed of six revisionary ratios defining the internal structure of a life-cycle. They define the changing stance of the new creator to the work of the previous great poet. Since the cycles of poetry form a series, Bloom's pattern of influence called the map of misreading (composed of the six ratios) resembles a somewhat synchronic version of a genetic code of poetry.

DERRIDA'S PHILOSOPHY OF TRADITION AS A WHOLE

Introduction to Derrida's Philosophy of Tradition as a Whole

The three theorists of tradition agree that tradition can be accumulated such that one theory can change all that has come before--much in the same way that each person contains some version of the genetic code with its thousands and even millions of years of evolution. And more definitely than Bloom, Derrida believes his theory applies to the whole of the tradition. In fact, he believes he has a critique of the entire history of philosophy and replaces it with a superior philosophy. In general the French philosopher's view of tradition is more normative; he can justify the claims of one step in tradition being better than another. Neither Kuhn's nor Bloom's theory can claim to change their respective fields, thus not extending the tradition to make room for one's own place.

Tradition as a Whole

Derrida gives a specific definition of the entire tradition before him. In the case of Kuhn and Bloom their knowledge of the series is not expressed from the standpoint of any one unit in the series. Neither Kuhn nor Bloom believes his theory includes the entire past of science or poetry.

Since Derrida is not concerned with speaking about tradition but changing it, he does not express the view that tradition is a continuous series of philosophies, similar to Kuhn's and Bloom's recurring cycles; nevertheless, Derrida's stated views allow for that comparison, as the following comments show. Derrida finds a presupposition of the entire Western tradition of philosophy and because this can be done he is able to revise the principle and start again. This claim of his sounds grandiose, but this excess can be tempered with the knowledge that all great philosophers did this, every new generation. The faulty presupposition (the idea of a transcendental signified, to be explained later) ordered the entire tradition toward seeking impossible concepts, which he calls pure presences. All that can be done in the short preliminary space of this chapter is to introduce these terms Derrida uses to revise the entire tradition, as non-technical preparation for complete technical discussions to follow.

The steady progress toward a transcendental signified is "logocentrism." Derrida wants to change the direction of philosophy:

> My justification would be as follows: this and some other indices (in a general way the treatment of the concept of writing) already give us the assured means of broaching the de-construction of the greatest totality--the concept of the epistémè and logocentric metaphysics--within which are produced, without ever posing the radical question of writing, all the Western methods of analysis, explication, reading, or interpretation (46 *OG*).

It is important to notice Derrida's "deconstruction of the greatest totality," --in other words the entire tradition. Kuhn also thought a new paradigm included previous theories--as limiting cases, though he wanted to preserve some of the results of previous science, as if unchanged, not erroneous. Bloom's emphasis is on the comprehension of one poet of the immediate predecessor, but his statements could be extended to claim a poet supercedes all previous poetic vision.

Scope of a Unit of Tradition

The distinction of big and small philosophies is not made, as it was for the other two thinkers. Each new one is "bigger" than past ones in some way.

Derrida does not address this issue directly. Yet, his revising of the tradition and comprehending it shows a belief that a new philosophy is "bigger" (more comprehensive) than a previous one. This improvement is a regular occurrence in the change of great philosophies so that it cannot serve to differentiate them; rather it serves to show how philosophies do the same thing.

Derrida's theory--itself a philosophy--encompasses the entire tradition, unlike the theories of Kuhn and Bloom which are not universal, not comprehensive. Derrida, like Bloom, writes about a specific specialty, not about a group of specialties.

There are many passages in which Derrida declares his philosophy applies to the whole tradition. In *Of Grammatology* he asserts that his philosophy (grammatology) is not one science among many (83 *OG*). It can provide ordering principles for all phenomena in experience, a universal framework. Both Kuhn and Bloom believe the cultural forms they study claim to be able to include everything encounterable in experience, from the standpoint of a distinctive type of cultural activity.

Start of a Tradition

The whole tradition can be traced to mythical prototypes in ancient Greek thought and maybe even before; however, the attempt to give meaning to philosophy by finding a particular origin for it is useless, for all origins are arbitrary. There is no absolute point of departure.

In *Edmund Husserl's `Origin of Geometry': An Introduction* Derrida writes about the origins of that scientific field. Each new geometry must be an origin; he does not look for an historical origin.

For his own philosophy, he claims its point of departure is not absolute; that is, its concepts depend on those he criticizes. The concept of *bricolage* in "Structure, Sign, and Play in the Discourse of the

Human Sciences" indicates the necessity of intervening in the previous philosophy to create a new one. If the tradition of philosophy is like a long staircase, then Derrida could not have gotten to the last step by himself. It is as if he began on the step of his predecessor. The new creator does not have to repeat all the steps of the entire tradition, for the immediate predecessor has brought humanity up to a certain level, the comprehension of which moves one to the next level higher.

Instead of describing indifferently the motives for a new step in tradition, as Bloom did, Derrida gives his own reasons for changing the entire tradition. Examining them can tell us more about the start of a philosophy.

Derrida changed the assumption of the Western tradition because it did not allow the extension of philosophical concepts beyond a certain point. Also, the perspective was not, after all, consistent and unified as Derrida's predecessor had thought. There was a situation of "crisis," the same word used by Kuhn.
The condition of any origin is a "rupture" from the past, from its origin (291 *WD*).

The Unit of Tradition

As it was for Bloom, the unit of tradition is a particular tradition form, namely an entire philosophy, without the ambiguity of deciding whether the unit of tradition is a poem or the entire poetry. Derrida defines the unit more determinately than either Kuhn or Bloom by limiting the meaning to unique cycles. The theory has historical concreteness.

In Derrida's view a unit of tradition must be historically situated to a greater extent than Kuhn or Bloom knew. The concept of *bricolage* in "Structure, Sign, and Play in the Discourse of the Human Sciences" shows the need for a direct, specific link between a new philosophy and an old. The person performing *bricolage*, the *bricoleur*, is different from the "engineer" who creates the entire pattern. The entire pattern of philosophy cannot be "invented" by an individual. In contrast, a new philosopher, or a creator in any field, must create by "borrowing...concepts from the text of a heritage which is more or less coherent or ruined" (285 *WD*). Both Kuhn and Bloom actually try to make the entire pattern, or at least discover it. So both think they have more knowledge than is possible. Whatever sense of the pattern of a field can be known must be known in a particular example of it, itself acquired by "borrowing."

Method

Derrida coined the controversial term "deconstruction." There are three main preliminary points that are important to mention here. First of all, while many scholars claim Derrida's philosophy is merely negative, explicit statements by Derrida contradict this view. Secondly, deconstruction is a dialectical operation. Thirdly, although many scholars from many fields use it as a method, he claims it is not one. This usage requires explanation.

First of all, scholars misinterpret deconstruction when they see it as merely negative, as not bound to the tradition it criticizes. Derrida elaborates this point:

> Within the closure, by an oblique and always perilous movement, constantly risking falling back within what is being deconstructed, it is necessary to surround the critical concepts with a careful and thorough discourse--to mark the conditions, the medium, and the limits of their effectiveness and to designate rigorously their intimate relationship to the machine whose deconstruction they permit; and, in the same process, designate the crevice through which the yet unnameable glimmer beyond the closure can be glimpsed. The concept of the sign is here exemplary. We have just marked its metaphysical appurtenance. ...Treating as suspect, as I just have, the difference between signified and signifier, or the idea of the sign in general, I must state explicitly that it is not a question of doing so in terms of the instance of the present truth, anterior, exterior or superior to the sign, or in terms of the place of the effaced difference. Quite the

> contrary. We are disturbed by that which, in the conception of the sign--which has never existed or functioned outside the history of (the) philosophy (of presence)--remains systematically and genealogically determined by that history. It is there that the concept and above all the work of deconstruction, its "style," remain by nature exposed to misunderstanding and nonrecognition" (14 *OG*).

Many scholars think deconstruction is a kind of scepticism, that it rejects the tradition. Here Derrida asserts the necessary association of his philosophy with the concepts it criticizes.

Other passages also indicate the operation of deconstruction to be based on *bricolage* and thus not to be negative merely. Criticizing the Heideggerian destruction--not deconstruction--of metaphysics, Derrida writes

> But all these destructive discourses are trapped in a kind of circle. This circle is unique. It describes the form of the relation between the history of metaphysics and the concepts of metaphysics in order to shake metaphysics. We have no language--no syntax and no lexicon--which is foreign to this history; we can pronounce not a single destructive proposition which has not already had to slip into the form, the logic, and the implicit postulations of precisely what it seeks to contest (280 *WD*).

Derrida also writes, "The movements of deconstruction do not destroy structures from the outside. They are not possible and effective, nor can they take accurate aim, except by inhabiting those structures" (24 *OG*). By "inhabiting those structures" Derrida means in some other way than confirming the oppositions there; in other words, the oppositions would be revised and used to form new concepts (41 *POS*). Elsewhere, he writes about slowly detaching concepts "from the classical discourse from which I borrow them" (46 *OG*). These ideas call to mind the replication of DNA, in which complementary chains of molecules separate and each part generates its own new complement. Derrida's new concepts must be modeled on previous concepts they nevertheless oppose; only in this way could something be made both the same in type and yet a better version.

Any new philosophy is bound to the one before it. "Logocentrism would thus support the determination of the being of the entity as presence. To the extent that such a logocentrism is not totally absent from Heidegger's thought, perhaps it still holds that thought within the epoch of onto-theology, within the philosophy of presence, within philosophy itself. This would perhaps mean that one does not leave the epoch whose closure one can outline (12-13 *OG*). Derrida's closure of the epoch before him does not mean that he can simply "move on to something else" (14 *OG*).

The second main point about deconstruction, it is dialectical. The "dialectical self-creation of new forms" like that accomplished by Derrida was described by the Russian Formalist literary critic Victor Shklovsky:

> Each new literary school heralds a revolution, something like the appearance of a new class. But, of course, this is only an analogy. The vanquished line is not obliterated, it does not cease to exist. It is only knocked from the crest; it lies dormant and may again arise as a perennial pretender to the throne. Moreover, in reality the matter is complicated by the fact that the new hegemony is usually not a pure revival of previous forms but is made more complex by the presence of features of the younger schools and with features, now secondary, inherited from its predecessors on the throne.[5]

Derrida, too, does not intend to ignore the tradition of philosophy, to discount it entirely. He subordinates it to his new philosophy, which rises to "the crest." Bloom believes there is a period of dual identity when a great poet-to-be must understand but grow beyond the precursor.

The operation of deconstruction is dialectical; it "conserves and annuls." About Lévi-Strauss, Derrida writes, "At once conserving and annuling inherited conceptual oppositions, this thought, like Saussure's, stands on a borderline: sometimes within an uncriticized conceptuality, sometimes putting a strain on the boundaries, and working toward deconstruction" (105 *OG*). "By retracing the true generation of knowledge, by going back to the principles, an actually inaugural practice of analysis can finally dissolve, destroy, decompose the first first philosophy [sic: "first first"]. That means, in the end: replace the first first philosophy while inheriting its name" [thus creating philosophy] (35-36 *AF*). The difficult term "first first philosophy" suggests each philosophy becomes the first in relation to the preceding ones; each establishes new principles of a higher order or level on which the previous ones can be seen to necessarily have depended, unknown to the precursor.

Deconstruction is a struggle of a new philosophy with a former one. This idea of evolution was stated well by Yury Tynyanov:

> When one speaks of "literary tradition" or "succession"...usually one implies a certain kind of direct one uniting the younger and older representatives of a known literary branch. Yet the matter is much more complicated. There is no continuing direct line; there is rather a departure, a pushing away from the known point--a struggle....Any literary succession is first of all a struggle, a destruction of old values and a reconstruction of old elements.[6]

The third main point about deconstruction, Derrida insists it is not a method. It is difficult to speak about deconstruction if not as a method, for the intellectual operation does not occur in ordinary daily behavior. Quite definitely, Derrida denies it is a method. The essential feature of a method is that it can be applied indifferently to many subjects. Derrida denies that his deconstruction does this: "I am not sure [polite denial; he is sure] that deconstruction can function as a literary *method* as such. I am wary of the idea of methods of reading. The laws of reading are determined by the particular text that is being read" (124-125 Kearney, *Dialogues with Contemporary Thinkers*). This view is more complex than Bloom's map of misreading, which does constitute a method, a repeatable procedure for what Bloom calls "practical criticism." From this passage just quoted and others we should conclude that Derrida's deconstruction is a reaction to a particular text: it is a one-time operation. It is Derrida's overcoming of the tradition of philosophy before him; it is Derrida's struggle with a particular philosopher before him. Of course, thousands of applications of deconstruction have been written, but they seem to be "biodegraded" versions; that is to say, the meaning of deconstruction is not completely understood, so a not quite accurate view is used. This process, while couched in pejorative terms, is actually the normal process of the influence of the highest level of cultural knowledge on lower levels. [The idea of the necessary "Biodegradation" of cultural knowledge during its dissemination through society is discussed by Derrida in "Biodegradeables: Seven Diary Fragments," *Critical Inquiry* 15(1989): 812-73.]

Main Criticisms

He explicitly contradicts the frequent charges of scepticism or nihilism or indeterminism in critical knowledge of texts. He is thought by several scholars to deny the determinacy of meaning and thus to impugn scholarship. He is also thought to misapply philosophical principles outside its proper domain, namely, in literary criticism. He is often thought to be an obscurantist--the dark Derrida.

Summary

In some fundamental ways Derrida would agree with Kuhn and Bloom: the series of tradition forms is cyclic; the whole of a tradition can be changed (Kuhn equivocates on this); the change in tradition is a struggle involving a general reorientation of mind. But there are basic, quite definite differences. Derrida's theory is much more detailed than either Kuhn's or Bloom's. The unit of tradition is more historically situated, thus determinate. The movement from one step of tradition to another can be explained by Derrida as a move for the better. Most of all, Derrida's theory differs insofar as it is not merely *about* tradition; it is itself a step forward. The overview in this chapter must mention some technical words to be explained at length later. If all concepts are truly of a piece, then the fullest knowledge of any one is only gained when all the pieces have been considered. Yet, one must begin with some separate pieces to build up the whole network of meaning.

NOTES

1. Wallace Steven's idea of poetry is also threefold. See 188 *MM*.

2. Quoted from Betsy Draine's "Writing, Deconstruction, and Other Unnatural Acts." *Boundary 2* (1981), 425-36.

3. Quoted from 52 *Hero*; for the original see Sigmund Freud, *Introductory Lectures on Psycho-Analysis* (Translated by James Strachey, Standard Edition, XVI; London: The Hogarth Press, 1963, pp. 396-97. (Orig. 1916-17).

4. The same idea that poems are about poems is stated by Byron Raizis in "Yeats's Preoccupation with Spiritualism and His Two Byzantium Poems," page 301: Yeats's Byzantium poems are "visual dramatizations of the `process' of attaining artistic perfection, and of the special `status' (secular and spiritual) of the Poet who has attained excellence." [And previously he quoted Yeats as speaking of Keats in the same way.]

5. Boris Eichenbaum is quoting Shklovsky on 135 of Lemon and Reis, *Russian Formalist Criticism*.

6. Quoted from Boris Eichenbaum in Lemon and Reis, *Russian Formalist Criticism*, 134.

Part II:

The Three Theories of Tradition

Chapter 3:
The Start of a Scientific Theory

Introduction to Kuhn's Definition of the Start

The start of a new scientific theory is a revolution. It occurs because a crisis forced a scientist to develop a new conceptual scheme, a new paradigm, for all the concepts of nature. Whereas Bloom writes in detail about the start of a poetry in relation to the previous one--analyzing the meaning of many lines and comparing the poems--Kuhn does not do something similar for science. The discussions are more general.

Revolution

All scientific theories, that make a complete step forward in tradition, that are "tradition forms," begin as revolutions. At first there are anomalies in the existing theory and then a crisis. A whole new fabric of thought must be created to allow research to continue. The term "revolution" suggests cycles of science.

According to Kuhn, failures to unify phenomena lead scientists to a re-evaluation of tradition. "In these and other ways besides, normal science repeatedly goes astray. And when it does--when, that is, the profession can no longer evade anomalies that subvert the existing tradition of scientific practice--then begin the extraordinary investigations that lead the profession at last to a new set of commitments, a new basis for the practice of science. The extraordinary episodes in which that shift of professional commitments occurs are the ones known in this essay as scientific revolutions. They are the tradition-shattering complements to the tradition-bound activity of normal science" (6 *SSR*).

When the anomalies lead to a self-contradiction, there is a shift to a new paradigm. Kuhn gives the example of Copernicus' famous preface (69 *SSR*). If the contradiction is solved, science can continue to grow once again (169 *SSR*). The contradiction stops research. Rather curiously, Kuhn asserts that the crisis points can be seen prior to the onset of the problems (75 *SSR*). In other words, the crisis points can be seen prior to the crisis, or prior to normal science seeing the problems. Extraordinary science must see these points beforehand if they are seen then. Though Kuhn does not draw conclusions about the significance of this fact, it must mean that crises develop within the natural development of the form; they are not something that could simply disappear from science in some more advanced generation. In this way Kuhn's idea is deconstructive like Bloom's and Derrida's.

Other philosophers of science would support Kuhn's idea that a new science begins to preserve the unity of its tradition which is threatened. Ernst Cassirer argues that Descartes' basic postulate of the unity of science led to the discovery of analytic geometry.[1]

Kuhn defines a revolution as follows:

> ...a displacement of the conceptual network through which scientists view the world. ...For these men [the specialists] the new theory implies a change in the rules governing the prior practice of normal science... That is why a new theory, however special its range of application, is seldom or never just an increment to what is already known. Its assimilation requires the reconstruction of prior theory and the re-evaluation of prior fact, an intrinsically revolutionary process that is seldom completed by a single man and never overnight" (7 *SSR*).

Two key features of a revolution are wholistic change and the presence of controversies: "And each transformed the scientific imagination in ways that we shall ultimately need to describe as a transformation of the world within which scientific work was done. Such changes, together with the controversies that almost always accompany them, are the defining characteristics of scientific revolutions" (6 *SSR*).

Revolutions are surprisingly community-based activities. Kuhn felt a philosopher of science should first understand the community more; if he was to re-write *The Structure of Scientific Revolutions* he would begin with a study of the community.

Also, revolutions include more than one thinker's contribution:

> The construction of Newton's corpuscular world machine completes the conceptual revolution that Copernicus had initiated a century and a half earlier (261 *CR*). ...
>
> The conception of a planetary earth was the first successful break with a constitutive element of the ancient world view. Though intended solely as an astronomical reform, it had destructive consequences which could be resolved only within a new fabric of thought. Copernicus himself did not supply that fabric; his own conception of the universe was closer to Aristotle's than to Newton's. But the new problems and suggestions that derived from his innovation are the most prominent landmarks in the development of the new universe which that innovation had itself called forth. The creation of the need and the aid supplied in its fulfillment are the contributions to history that constitute the Copernican Revolution (265 *CR*).

Kuhn's conception of "world view" might be too literal here; it could be an idea of the vision provided by a specific scientific theory but instead is a vision supplied by several theories. The unity of scientific discourse is endangered. Astronomy is tied to the other sciences and to nonscientific thought as well (264 *CR*).

Does Kuhn have a clear idea of structure? Gablik, much influenced by the structuralist Piaget, sets these standards for a sense of definite structure: "The concept of development, in the sense in which we have been using it here, involves two essential components: the notion of a system which possesses a definite structure, and that of a sequential set of changes within that structure in its mode of operation" (151). Does Kuhn delineate a definite structure between revolutions? Are there characteristic changes as research unfolds. Kuhn's actual discussions are evasive in a crucial way; ostensibly the theory is about revolutions, yet most is written about what happens before and after a revolution, not during.

Gablik has a legitimate question when he writes "The difficulty is, however, that Kuhn never really explains the source of the Gestalt-switch which signals a change of paradigm. He does not really state where paradigms come from nor how they are formed. What determines which body of scientific beliefs is admissable at a certain period? How do scientists make the choice between competing paradigms?" (162)

Kuhn, as was recently mentioned, does say a revolution arises from a contradiction. An isolated statement hardly constitutes a full explanation. Bloom has written much to explain the reasons and process of change. Mainly, it is the idea of revisionary ratios. Gablik notices the lack of something like Bloom's ratios: "What he [Kuhn] fails to consider is the way in which scientific evolution creates successive levels of integration, each characterized by its own laws, or how these levels are coordinated among one another by the continual restructuring of previous acquisitions" (163).

Gablik in his *Progress in Art* defines an idea of "evolution," not "revolution." Being concerned with art, he ironically rejects the language of art historians and prefers the language of the social sciences. In the following quote he does not substantially change the *idea* of the art historians but their *language style*:

> I wish to claim that what Wölfflin could only formulate in crude terms as `the apparatus of apprehension fulfilling itself', and Riegl as `the will-to-form', becomes more explicable once we have taken into account the cognitive determinants of artistic development. There is no need to postulate either a dialectical process impelled by polar oppositions or the unfolding of some Hegelian World Spirit to explain the history of art, once we introduce the idea of a directed evolution which is based on the development of cognitive structures. Such an evolution would then be neither mysterious or supernatural; it is `predetermined' in

> so far as it aims at the realization of certain thought forms in the mind, but it is independent of any final cause or goal. Even if we cannot discover any teleology in the evolution of art, we can nevertheless discern a direction--towards an increase of (internal) means for coordinating knowledge. It should be stated once again, however, that evolution which has a direction from simple to more complex function--that is mediated by more and more complex structures--in no way presupposes a steady improvement in aesthetic quality. I am concerned here not with value judgments but with trying to understand what sorts of factors generate this complexity (150).

The change of language style is significant for any discussion comparing Kuhn to Bloom and Derrida. There would be opposition from Kuhnians if the language did not sound logical, precise, authoritative, nonmysterious. I cannot imagine Kuhn using Bloom's idea of "anagogy." Nonetheless, such an idea--stated obliquely in this passage--would help Kuhn's theory explain more. Gablik believes form is predetermined: the scientist or creator [note the difffference in language] has a sense of the kind of "thought forms in the mind" he wants to create. Just as Gablik denies any teleology in the evolution of art, Kuhn denies a cumulative theory of progress. What Gablik does not notice and what may help to make Kuhn's theory more complete is the operation of a sense of the form of discourse as a final goal directing all the creation. True, there is not one definite goal through all the history of science, past, present, and future. There can, however, be shorter goals, goals not valid beyond a specific scientific theory. The similarity of these goals through history would suggest the discourse has a decoding and encoding function; in some ways it is like DNA, the object of which is to realize something like itself which can in turn reproduce.

Gablik's last remarks here raise some questions. In attempting to eliminate all mystery, does Gablik attempt to master a process he himself cannot do? If so, the evasion would be similar to a Freudian defense reaction. And, when he expresses his interest in "trying to understand what sorts of factors generate" the complexity of a new level of science or art, musn't the new level explain or reveal these principles in ever new ways? If scientific discourse and artistic form are not reflexive in some ways, then how are there standards accessible to the great figures? When Wölfflin describes `the apparatus of apprehension fulfilling itself', this language style can be changed into "the cybernetic status of scientific theory formation" [my words]. Wölfflin was pointing out the necessary self-reflection in all cultural, traditional forms, and the idea is not dissimilar to Gablik's pre-determination as the realization of certain thought forms in the mind. The change in language styles by Gablik may suggest a reaction to the authority of the creator through a defense of the critic's role. For Wölfflin's ideas quoted above attribute the authority of full understanding to the creator, whereas Gablik's near-paraphrase can make the process "explicit," shareable by many people; creators may need critics, Gablik.

Related questions that will be answered in the course of the discussion of Bloom's theory are, Is the form known ahead of time? How can it be known before the science or art is complete?

The discussion of revolution does not end until all of Kuhn's concepts are discussed. A resolution of revolution in science does occur in actual practice when a new way to extend research is shown to be the fittest and to open large new areas (172 *SSR*). This idea should be compared to Bloom's idea of the clearing of an imaginative space, the making of the space of poetry again as one's own, to be discussed.

Paradigm

More important than even `revolution', `paradigm' explains what changes during a revolution and why the change is so complete or radical so as to be called a `revolution'.

"Paradigm" means the framework of particular scientific concepts, the scheme, the space, the conceptual web, the tradition form. The wholistic status should be noticed: "To make the transition to Einstein's universe, the whole conceptual web whose strands are space, time, matter, force, and so on, had to be shifted and laid down again on nature whole. Only men who had together undergone or failed to undergo that transformation would be able to discover precisely what they agreed or disagreed about. Communication across the revolutionary divide is inevitably partial" (149 *SSR*). Not only did the formal laws change with the presuppositions but also the physical referents or structural elements changed (102 *SSR*).

Besides internal crises, external crises and discoveries can lead to paradigm change, though none of these factors by itself must (66, 154 *SSR*).

Theory and fact change together to reformulate tradition: "theories do not evolve piecemeal to fit facts that were there all the time. Rather, they emerge together with the facts they fit from a revolutionary reformulation of the preceding scientific tradition, a tradition within which the knowledge-mediated relationship between the scientist and nature was not quite the same" (141 *SSR*). The boundaries of the chemist's "domain" changes (132 *SSR*). This idea of Kuhn's would suggest that the boundaries are at issue in a revolution and, even more fundamental, form is a setting of these boundaries for discourse. First principles change (163 *PR*).

Paradigms start science again, they form a new start. A new paradigm begins when scientists realize the current ones "no longer define a playable game" (90 *SSR*). This fact points out the cyclic nature of tradition. In paradigm shifts there is "a reconstruction of the field from new fundamentals" (84-85). This statement suggests that science tries to make a form--here called a "field" or domain of discourse. If this idea is carried further than Kuhn did, the relations between one scientific form and the next (say, Maxwell's theory and Einstein's) would be analysed in detail, something Kuhn does not do.

Like the predetermination of form, quantitative laws are often guessed "with the aid of a paradigm years before apparatus could be designed for their experimental determination" (30 *SSR*). In addition, "None of those who questioned the validity of Newton's work did so because of its limited agreement with experiment and observation" (32 *SSR*). This historical fact suggests only the paradigm is needed to make the laws, although Kuhn would like to claim that normal science has a role. Similarly, Kuhn believes detail was seldom required for "extension of existing theory" (43 *ET*). Experiment alone cannot create new theories (136 *ET*).

The priority of a paradigm over individual contents can be seen in another way. On Kuhn's view, physics is right "by comparison with nature..." (27 ET). For the sake of understanding rather than criticizing, a different view would declare physics is right because it fulfills the needs of the form; the pattern is repeated.

The priority of a paradigm can be seen in the way it starts. Its rules "no longer define a playable game" and so another set must be conceived to take their place (90 *SSR*). The paradigm deals with the rules of the game, and so it is more important than specific applications of those rules.

Paradigms are prior, because in any debate the criteria of validity are contained within the choice of paradigm. Proponents of different paradigms cannot fully communicate with others.

Paradigm shifts follow a deconstructive pattern. A paradigm is "declared invalid only if an alternative is ready to take its place" (77 *SSR*). Derrida's deconstruction is not merely destructive; destruction goes hand in hand with construction. "Deconstruction" also means understanding how a previous theory was made and remaking that process.

A question arises concerning this idea of valid criticism and replacement. If "the decision to reject one paradigm, is always simultaneously the decision to accept another (77), this fact might suggest a new paradigm is the proper understanding and criticism of the previous one. So a paradigm isn't fundamentally right because it matches nature--all do to some degree; it is right because it repeats the pattern of the paradigm before it while changing everything at least slightly. Kuhn gives various statements about how much is changed of the predecessor's paradigm. Sometimes he claims all is, sometimes the changes are only partial.

If the primary meaning of a paradigm is not through nature, then through what? Through the previous paradigm, Bloom would say as he did of poetry.

Kuhn opposes the idea of "progressive agreement finding" as the progress of science; rather it is greater power and precision, power meaning a wider range of phenomena is explained (26, 66, 147, *SSR*).

The question whether there are "intrinsic reasons" for paradigm changes shows a big difference between Kuhn and both Bloom and Derrida. Kuhn rejects the idea, claiming that they do not derive from the logical structure of scientific knowledge; the new theory is simply a "higher level" theory uniting many lower theories without substantially changing them (95 *SSR*). This idea does not seem consistent with the idea that paradigms can know the onset of problems before they happen (75 *SSR*). In Kuhn's case I do not think there is a contradiction; instead, the comparison of passages and their contrary implications point to issues not systematically thought out by Kuhn. For both Bloom and Derrida there must be change of the lower theories when united.

Creation

The creation of a new paradigm through revolution occurs thanks to the cooperation of two types of scientist: the normal scientist and the extraordinary scientist (a distinction Kuhn consistently phrases in non-personal terms: normal science and extraordinary science).

Any theory of creation must have an idea of the reinterpretation of a previous theory. For Kuhn, there can be no direct comparison of components of theories with each other (19 *ET*). The change takes place whole-to-whole. Kuhn gives the example of an experiment in which subjects were given lenses to wear that inverted all the images. Then he writes, "Rather than being an interpreter, the scientist who embraces a new paradigm is like the man wearing inverting lenses. Confronting the same constellation of objects as before and knowing that he does so, he nevertheless finds them transformed through and through in many of their details" (122 *SSR*). The recognition of the "same" constellation means "the same but not as I thought of it before" or "the same but now wrong." In the experiment of the inverted lenses, after a while the subjects' eyes and minds correct the position of the images, even with the lenses on. In the case of science, this correction corresponds to the finding of a new paradigm, the restoration of the order that paradigms bring. About the disorientation at the start of creation, Kuhn writes, "Like artists, creative scientists must occasionally be able to live in a world out of joint" (79 *SSR*).

The feeling leading up to creation was described by Einstein: "It was as if the ground had pulled out from under one, with no firm foundation to be seen anywhere, upon which one could have built" (82 *SSR*).

The reinterpretation involves a change of the basic relations of identity and similarity. The change cannot be reduced to laws of transformation because no criteria can be found outside of or above these similarity relations (17 *ET*). For this reason "theory invention" cannot be taught (301 *ET*). Of course, theory invention cannot be reduced to rules which could be transferred *with certainty* to scientists who would then create without fail. The rules after all would change with each new science. On the other hand, if there is no transference of the knowledge of how to do science, then how does a new scientist know his science *is* a science? The rules bound with a particular scientific theory must provide the means for making a repetition of the pattern of scientific discourse, a genetic code of science.

The moment of creation occurs when a new unity is found. Kuhn speaks of it as a "sudden unity" like the finding of a solution to a problem in a flash of insight (72 *ET*). The sudden finding of the new unity shows that the change of interpretation is not part-by-part, not single concept by single concept. The fact that a new unity is found shows that science changes when it revises its sense of its tradition, which forms a unity or continuum. A change in scientific theories is a change in the meaning of science, just as mutations in genes can bring about gradual, cumulative changes in the species of living thing.

The creation also involves "the primitive recognition that the pieces fit to form a familiar, if previously unseen, product" (17 *ET*)-- suggesting the idea of a genetic code, repeated in a different way and known to make the creation continuous with what went before. When a scientist creates, he has a sense of what to expect, a sense of the requirements of scientific form (65 *SSR*). In Bloom's terms science-- that is, any individual science--is canonical; the work of any great scientist must meet certain conditions if it is to belong to the canon. During the formation of new concepts, possible solutions are measured against the previous paradigm. T.S. Eliot wrote in "Tradition and the Individual Talent" about a reciprocal measuring process between a new and old great poetry, during which the rules of the canon can be transferred to mold a new member. Kuhn's idea is less developed than Eliot's, and the discussion of this concept of measuring the new according to the analogy of old requirements of form will be resumed in the corresponding sections on Bloom's and Derrida's theories.

Does the solution to a crisis come from experience, from experiments or observation? Kuhn has a perhaps ambiguous answer: "the two-sphere universe [Ptolemy's scheme] is a product of the human imagination. It is a conceptual scheme, a theory, deriving from observations but simultaneously transcending them" (36 *CR*).

It is important to ask, How conscious is creation? Kuhn does claim "The sources of scientific inspiration are notoriously inscrutable" (95 *ET*). The creation resolving a crisis is "an unstructured event" (122 *SSR*)--which Kuhn nevertheless tries to structure. He even mentions "unconscious creation" in isolated references (86 *SSR*). Still, he does not want to argue that science depends upon "unanalyzable individual intuitions" (191 *SSR*). If no analysis were possible, there could be no room for a theory of scientific revolution. If creation were a completely explicit self-conscious process, creators could reveal their processes without the need for theorists like Kuhn.

The middle ground defining creation is neither induction nor deduction alone (45 *ET*); the answer from Kuhn lies vaguely in these words:

> Sometimes the shape of a paradigm is foreshadowed in the structure that extraordinary research has given to the anomaly. Einstein wrote that before he had any substitute for classical mechanics, he could see the interrelation between the known anomalies... . More often no such structure is consciously seen in advance. Instead, the new paradigm, or a sufficient hint to permit later articulation, emerges all at once... (89 *SSR*).

Next Kuhn denies that the process of invention can be scrutinized. The answer to the question how conscious is creation lies in the words "foreshadowed in the structure" and a sufficient "hint" in advance. Neither exclusively induction nor deduction, creation is some kind of transference from the previous scientific theory, perhaps not unlike the transmission of a code of the species' structure from one living thing to its offspring. At the point of transference, the anomaly or crisis necessitates further integration of the concepts. The integration can be only a specific answer. This idea will be discussed later, especially in the Epilogue, as a transfer of genetic determinants, "transduction" (which is a name also used there for the critical process of discovering the transfers already accomplished by others). The form--

a coded message for its successor to create from--can only be "decoded" in a specific way. Kuhn's theory is a kind of attempt at decoding, explaining science by a non-scientific idiom, but when a creator "decodes" a previous theory, whatever "decoding" or increased understanding of the previous processes takes place can only do so in the form of a new instance of the code.

This understanding of creation *by critics* as a transductive process goes beyond the limits of Kuhn's theory. [In the Epilogue a new term is suggested for the understanding of creation *by creators*.] It seems necessary, however, to provide a middle ground between conscious and unconscious creation, between a source of creation in observation and a source in the mind by itself. Art historian Heinrich Wölfflin asks how creation is determined by the artist:

> Here we encounter the great problem--is the change in the forms of apprehension the result of an inward development, of a development of the apparatus of apprehension fulfilling itself to a certain extent of itself, or is it an impulse from the outside, the other interest, the other attitude to the world, which determines the change?[2]

Gablik criticizes this idea of Wölfflin: Wölfflin is unable to say whether the development is internally or externally determined, whether by mind's inner movement or outer conditions, like what Kuhn calls internal and external factors. Gablik's criticism suffers from the same unproductive assumption as does Kuhn's ambivalent position: the source does not have to be either inner or outer. If the previous theory has within it all necessary ingredients for further creation, as does the genetic code, then this source is neither purely inner or outer. The previous theory is "outer" in the sense that another person invented it; it is ready made and coded in sensible forms. Yet, the theory is also inner, for the development comes from understanding the previous crises enough to be guided by their pointing to a new development.

Kuhn's words embody the germs of this answer: "Produced inadvertently by a game played under one set of rules, their assimilation [fundamental novelties of fact and theory] requires the elaboration of another set" (52 *SSR*). The process of creation here is transgenerational or trans-paradigm. One scientific theory requires a succeeding one. "Inadvertently" shows that the scientists cannot plan ahead of time and know how previous concepts will require succeeding ones. Just as the units of language only have their meaning if specific other units follow them, so too crises have their proper meaning only if they can be followed by concepts with a specific meaning. These conclusions are ones I find undeveloped in Kuhn's words; they are not positions he explicitly argues.

While the process of creation has been described in terms of the product, it can be described in terms of the scientists. Scientists perhaps intentionally attempted to model solutions to problems on previous solutions. Referred to by Kuhn, Clifford Truesdell describes "solution modelling," which asserts the existence of successive similar solutions in post-Newtonian mechanics; unfortunately, the discussion is somewhat general. Scientists have a sense of how scientific discourse develops, but assistance from the previous theory is needed in creation. This process makes creation trans-generational, an idea much more developed by Bloom, and this crucial subject of solution modelling, though treated very briefly, is one of the most profound for the issues of tradition and creation.

Redefinition and "Misunderstanding"

When paradigms change, former ideas become "redefined" by a change in their relations to a new generalization, a new basis of a science (133 *SR*).

New paradigms begin with the vocabulary of the old:

> Since new paradigms are born from old ones, they ordinarily incorporate much of the vocabulary and apparatus, both conceptual and manipulative, that the traditional paradigm had previously employed. Within the new paradigm, old terms, concepts, and experiments fall into new relationships one with the other. The inevitable result is what we must call, though the term is not quite right, a misunderstanding between the two competing schools (149 *SSR*).

The term "misunderstanding" is not developed enough here to be treated as a technical concept, nor a very important part in the theory, not like "crisis" or "incommensurability." Bloom has an idea of "misreading," which he develops much further than Kuhn's "misunderstanding" and which lacks the sociological emphasis. In both authors, though, the terms for redefinition of a predecessor's views have a negative prefix, as if something is wrong in the redefinition. This guaranteeing past theories or poetries their value may be the necessary result of assuming a critical standpoint above any theory or poetry in the series; Derrida does not attach negative value to a subsequent philosophy, and his theory is a *new* member of the series he criticizes.

The idea from this passage that "old terms, concepts, and experiments fall into new relationships" merits further discussion. Kuhn offers an extended example of a scientific revolution:

> For Dalton, any reaction in which the ingredients did not enter in fixed proportion was ipso facto not a purely chemical process. A law that experiment could not have established before Dalton's work, became, once that work was accepted, a constitutive principle that no single set of chemical measurements could have upset. As a result of what is perhaps our fullest example of a scientific revolution, the same chemical manipulations assumed a relationship to chemical generalization very different from the one they had had before (133 *SSR*).

Dalton's law of fixed proportions was not established by experiments. It became a constitutive principle in subsequent research. It changed the relations of the elements of the theory (the chemical manipulations) to the ordering principles (chemical generalization). The example suggests that the elements of a theory get their meaning from the paradigm; the paradigm does not get its meaning from particular observed things.

The shift from one paradigm to another brings about a generalization of the previous laws. In Dalton's case it was clear a new way of practicing research in chemistry had come into being (134 *SSR*). There were new regularities as well.

The improvement of scientific knowledge as generalization is attractive to Kuhn, for he does not have to admit that science could be wrong. He argues for the truth of Newton's theory despite Einstein's: "Subject to this condition [small relative velocities of bodies in comparison to that of light] and a few others, Newtonian theory seems to be derivable from Einsteinian, of which it is therefore a special case" (99 *SSR*). Such assertions by Kuhn do not seem to me to be consistent with other assertions: new paradigms evolve by paradigm "destruction." That the former paradigm had to be destroyed suggests that it was wrong. But, to try to see Kuhn's theory in its most consistent light, he would explain himself in the following way. A former scientific theory can be seen as of a lower type, a lower level of ordering, less general. To make the former theory of a lower type, its anomaly or anomalies are made lawlike (97 *SSR*). A greater more essential order is found.

The generalization requires a reorientation, and the reorientation suggests a change in the interpretation of the former ideas. The reorientation is a reversal, a change in the former views:

> During the transition period there will be a large but never complete overlap between the problems that can be solved by the old paradigm and by the new paradigm. But there will also be a decisive difference in the modes of solution. When the transition is complete, the profession will have changed its view of the field, its methods, and its goals. One perceptive historian, viewing a classic case of a science's reorientation by paradigm change, recently described it as "picking up the other end of the stick," a process that involves "handling the same bundle of data as before, but placing them in a new system of relations with one another by giving them a different framework." Others who have noted this aspect of scientific advance have emphasized its similarity to a change in visual gestalt... (85 *SSR*).

Besides generalization, the changes in the interpretation of former theories consist in changes in the modes of solution to problems, changes in the method for the whole field, changes in the goals of the whole field, changes in the field's structure or framework, and changes like a shift in visual gestalt.

The change in visual gestalt brings along with it a change in perception. Concurring with Herbert Butterfield, Kuhn views the change as `putting on a different kind of thinking cap' (xvii *ET*). This idea calls to mind the idea of the Copernican revolution often used as a metaphor outside science to mean a reflection on one's perspective and a consequent change in all behaviour. The philosopher Immanuel Kant used the term for his own developments based on a process of seeing how his predecessor made his concepts. This is one of the first stages of any deconstruction.

From Resistance to Conversion

Undergoing the difficult process of revolution, of paradigm change, the scientific community experiences resistance from groups within it and conversion of some groups.

Kuhn's most general concern--revolutions--are complementary to normal science (8 *SSR*). A revolution is a radical change for normal science and so it resists.

Normal science is deemed to be "professionalization," causing "an immense restriction of the scientist's vision and to a considerable resistance to paradigm change" (64 *SSR*). A new paradigm creates "an incommensurable world of research," and so normal scientists eventually--after resistance--undergo a gestalt switch, for some as strong as a conversion.

The resistance makes normal science possible; that is, part of the function of normal science is to institutionalize and apply recently created laws of a paradigm (152 *SSR*). So strong is the resistance that new paradigms would hardly arise if they had to be judged only by normal scientists interested in relative problem-solving (157 *SSR*). Some scientists never admit the legitimacy of the new paradigm. Darwin looked to young naturalists to accept his views, and Max Planck believed the old stubborn scientists must die and a new generation arise before the community in general follows the new paradigm (151 *SSR*).

The source of the resistance is the belief that normal science will eventually solve all its problems of application (151 *SSR*). Kuhn does not see the resistance as something that could be avoided; rather, it reveals the nature of scientific revolutions, and for him the belief in the new paradigm seems to be more a matter of allegiance, more a sociological matter than a matter of proof.

I suggest a reason beyond Kuhn's. Normal scientists resist paradigm changes because they do not actually understand the scientific discourse as a paradigm, a whole framework; only the extraordinary scientists do. The resistance is an emblem of lack of understanding. If they did understand the previous paradigm, they would not engage in work that is second best, or that does not help to evolve a new paradigm. Kuhn sees science as a paradigm-seeking activity. If this is true, and if normal scientists could understand the paradigm as a general framework, then why would they not work to become more scientific and evolve a new paradigm? Plato wrote that no one can choose evil; a person aways chooses what is thought to be the better of alternatives. If much of the community never understands science deeply enough to get to the level of a paradigm-maker, then of course they would resist, for they do not understand the kind of proof needed to make a new paradigm. More discussion of this difficult issue at the breaking point of Kuhn's theory will occur later.

But eventually scientists begin to think the alternative paradigm is correct: "Something must make at least a few scientists feel that the new proposal is on the right track, and sometimes it is only personal and inarticulate aesthetic considerations that can do that" (158 *SSR*).

Resistance leads to conversion, and Kuhn is often criticized for this idea, seemingly making him an irrationalist. "Still," Kuhn defends himself, "to say that resistance is inevitable and legitimate, that paradigm change cannot be justified by proof, is not to say that no arguments are relevant..." (152 *SSR*).

"Conversion" is curiously enough a religious and scientific term. Cohen has some valuable remarks on its etymology: "...in classical times `conversio' meant a revolution in the old cyclical sense, and even in religion `conversion' retains some of the ancient sense of spiritual rebirth. But the modern use of this term, especially in science, implies radical change and the acceptance of a wholly different point of view" (472). Kuhn's "conversion" is of a piece with his "revolution" and his discussions of gestalt switches. Cohen points out how striking the number of incidences of conversion are in the history of science (468). It will be important to keep in mind: who undergoes conversion--the creator or his non-creating followers?

SUMMARY

From this discussion of Kuhn's theory about the start of a scientific theory, some conclusions can be drawn. Before a revolution there are crises. While Kuhn wants to assign to normal science a legitimate participative role in creation, it is doubtful whether normal scientists form ideas of crises in the way creators do--if for no other reason than that some revolutions occur before normal science realizes there are serious problems. Some questions arise concerning Kuhn's ideas of creation. Not a matter of consistency so much as a matter of the degree of development of his concepts, Kuhn does not have a clear idea whether creation is determinate or indeterminate, whether it can be caused only by internal factors, or also by external factors. In all fairness to Kuhn, the idea of "paradigm" is more developed. Its sociological senses seem to hinder Kuhn from developing the idea of paradigm change further than he did, both between paradigms and within.

There are three main points of comparison between Kuhn's theory of the start of a scientific theory, a tradition form, and the corresponding phases of Bloom's and Derrida's theories, not yet discussed. First of all, the degree to which the change from one step of tradition to another is explained is decisive for comparisons. Secondly, equally important is the degree to which the unity or requirements of a tradition form--a scientific theory, a poetry, a philosophy--is explained. Thirdly, the ideas of redefinition and understanding should be compared. The change in attitude toward the previous theory shows how much each theorist understands the processes of his field. These comparisons cannot, of course, be made until the other theories have been discussed.

NOTES

1. The idea was taken from p. 94 of *Ernst Cassirer: An Annotated Bibliography*, by Eggers and Mayer, New York: Garland, 1988. The original is "Descartes et l'idée de l'unité de la science." *Revue de Synthèse* 14 (Paris, 1937), 7-28. German trans. in *Descartes: Lehre--Persönlichkeit--Wirkung*.

2. Quoted from 148 Gablik. The quote comes from the close of Wölfflin's *Principles of Art History*.

Chapter 4:
The Start of a Poetry

Introduction to Bloom's Idea of the Start

Bloom defines the start of a poetry in much more detail than Kuhn does for the more general "science." After having studied Bloom's theory, one can look back at Kuhn's to see some salient ideas more developed by Bloom. Instead of "revolution," Bloom has an idea of a struggle between a precursor and his/her successor. To describe this conflict he develops the ideas of "misreading" or "misprision," "clinamen," and "tessera."

Preliminary Idea of the Tradition Form in Bloom's Theory

It has some features of the genetic code. Before DNA becomes complete, it goes through a process of replication. In Bloom's theory some "revisionary ratios" of poetry develop from previous ones having similar structures. The ratios of one poet relate to the poetry of the predecessor. In non-Bloomian terms, one might refer to the revisionary ratios as recurring structural points in the pattern of poetry making it belong to the canon, the tradition.

Bloom has an idea of "a map of misreading," which can be thought of as a genetic code in two main ways. First of all, each poetry has in it a similar pattern or genetic code; namely, the pattern of revisionary ratios. Secondly, before DNA is complete it duplicates portions of its own structure. Poetry does something like this as well, for Bloom's ratios each have a structure generally like that of the one it develops from; all are dialectical.

The map of misreading is different from the genetic code in an important way. Bloom's notion is actually somewhat more synchronic, because the genetic code is seen as changing in each successive manifestation. Bloom does define six ratios in each successive canonical poetry, yet he almost ignores any discussion of the differences in these ratios from one poetry to the next. Each successive manifestation should be a revision of the recurring figure. Had Bloom described these differences, his view would be more diachronic, even more like a genetic code.

A question to keep in mind, Would Bloom's theory of the anxiety of influence be better if it were more like the genetic code? If so, in what ways?

The Initial Relationship between Predecessor and Successor

The predecessor does not make way, but paradoxically no creation is possible if the poetic power and difficulty is avoided (154 *AI*).

Bloom agrees with Derrida on the way any cultural text acquires its meaning. Concerning Derrida's "Freud and the Scene of Writing," Bloom asserts,

> Psychical life thus is no longer to be represented as a transparency of meaning nor as an opacity of force but as an intra-textual difference in the conflict of meanings and the exertion of forces. For Derrida, writing is pathbreaking... Derrida's keenest insight, in my judgment, is that `writing is unthinkable without repression', ...Derrida has made of writing an intra-psychical trope, which is a making that necessarily pleases any reader who himself has made of influence an intra-psychical trope or rather a trope for intra-poetic relationships (48-49 *MM*).

Any text has its meaning through intra-textual differences; these differences begin by differences between texts, author to author.

Bloom's idea that a great poet refuses to make way for a successor requires explanation (154 *AI*). It does not matter if the previous great poet is dead or not, still the poetry has in it as a structural element (part of its end) to speak of poetry as entering a decline or not having any more different rebirths. If one looks in the works of Derrida, one can find the same "resistance to passing," the predecessor's attempt to limit or foretell the limits of future developments (See "Qual quelle," the 1971 essay on Valéry).

The new poet-to-be cannot create great poetry if he/she simply rejects the work of the previous poet, for a new poet to be great must do what the former did, only better. In positive language Bloom does not use, the previous poetry implicity contains or contains in an encoded way the direction that a new one should take. While the precursor cannot see this direction, the successor can by modifying the code of poetry known to the precursor.

The overpowering by the previous poet forces the successor to "misread" the previous one (51 *AI*). This change in interpretation involves making new aesthetic principles changing the sense of the precursor in relation to his/her precursor. This idea of "misreading" or "misprision" will shortly be discussed in its own right.

Initially, as a person moves toward the act of creation, defences begin to operate, forces against change and growth (92 *MM*). In Freud's psychology the change is blocked because it might disturb the ego as a stable psychic component. For a defence to take place, there must be repression--in a poetic sense. In the simplest terms, repression means that the upcoming poet tries to avoid representing the correctness of the previous poet (287 *PR*); there has been a change from complete admiration to reinterpretation.

Instead of being an instinctual drive or desire, repression serves to prevent the representation of the drive or desire in an image (143 *PR*). In other words what the precursor failed to do is not countered with a direct alternative, at least at the start of a poetry. The opposition to the precursor also requires an acceptance, or else the new person could never hope to join the established ranks of great poets. The "double-bind relationship" necessitates a middle path between identity and opposition: the precursor poem is absorbed as impulse, as intuitive sense of the requirements of form, not entirely explicit, but based on a thorough understanding of the making of the previous form (144 *PR*). In this way Bloom's theory follows Freud's of the id, which is the absorption of the comforts of the mother as impulses. Bloom sees repression as a power, not as something bad, to be corrected; the pattern of the predecessor can only be transferred if the newcomer avoids simple identification or rejection. The middle path is a dialectical one of raising the level of the previous activity.

Sometimes admirers of great poetry do not begin to see it in a new way, resulting in the overdetermination of the poetry (71 *AI*). More detail is known about the poetry than is necessary for subsequent creation, and not enough is known about the poetry as a whole in the series of tradition. Creation cannot occur if the interpreter always has a literal interpretation (108 *AI*).

Bloom gives a Freudian definition of tradition: it is "equivalent to repressed material in the mental life of the individual" (109 *AI*). Literally, this means a poet delays the representation of tradition obstructed by the precursor. A great poet coming into being searches for a wholeness lost by the precursor, although this "larger representation" is "kept in abeyance" through to the end of the poetry (109 *MM*). Cultural repression requires some blindness, some lack of explicitness, or else creation cannot occur: "if any poet knows too well what causes his poem, then he cannot write it, or at least will write it badly. He must repress the causes, including the precursor-poems, but such forgetting..." (5 *PR*).

In the preliminary stages of creation there is an internalization of the precursor. The internalization occurs while the upcoming poet believes a new interpretation of the predecessor is the right one and the predecessor is deficient aesthetically. The new interpretation is thought to be "exclusive" and "accurate" (70 *MM*).

Anxiety accompanies the redefinition of the precursor's poetry as deficient. Bloom calls this "the moral problematic of the idea of poetic tradition": how can the predecessor be criticized when he/she is a legitimate great poet standing at the top of accumulated tradition, as if atop a pyramid (141 *MM*)? Could any poetry after this height be the best ever? Could something different be poetry? In general the upcoming poet has "anxiety toward any danger that might `end' him as a poet" (58 *AI*). In the separation from the previous great poet, there is a danger that the new poetry will be too different and thus not belong to the same kind of cultural product; and there is a danger that the new poetry will be too similar, and thus not be original creation. In entirely Freudian terms, Bloom defines the anxiety of influence: "both a kind of separation anxiety and the beginning of a compulsion neurosis, or fear of a death that is a personified superego" (58 *AI*).

The great poet-to-be is set on a quest very much like that spoken of by Campbell (and James Liszka); first separation from the precursor, then initiation into the mysteries of poetic tradition--a rite of passage, and finally the coming into maturity when the new great poet has created a total form that could serve as an alternative to the predecessor's challenge.

In terms almost like Kuhn's, Bloom views the start of a new poetry as questioning the possibility of previous poetry-making (91 *SM*). It was founded on a polarity, a contrast of the product versus the means of its production.

In summary, the upcoming poet experiences much anxiety, much discomfort at not being able to create new great poetry because of the predecessor's perfection. The struggle resembles an Oedipal conflict of generations; killing the father means not wanting to be a mere follower of the poetic father, and marrying the mother means wanting to be one's own source of poetry and of the precursor's poetry. Bloom explicitly rejects the interpretation of his theory as Oedipal because, I believe, he wants to emphasize its poetic meaning. He intends to transplant psychological terms into the context of poetry so that they may be adapted to yield a new critical awareness of poetry.

The Moment of Conception, Creation

Defining the point of change from one poetry to another more than Kuhn did, Bloom sees it as the attempt to rescue or renew poetry. A poem answers a previous poem, and the second is in its turn answered by a future one (1 *PR*).

To create, a poet must form a "Scene of Instruction" (207 *PR*). It is a Freudian term for the conditions in which creation occurs; Bloom translates the psychological idea into poetic terms: "the state of heightened demand that carries a new poet from his origins into his first strong representations" (207).

The riddle of this Primal Scene is a riddle of imaginative priority: how can the successor come to claim he/she forms the riddle? (72 *AI*) "If he [the upcoming poet] is not to be victimized, then the strong poet must 'rescue' the beloved Muse from his precursors" (63 *AI*); this means a new poet offers a changed idea of poetry produced by a new standpoint in tradition.

The moment of creation requires (1) isonomization (equalizing) of one's immediate precursor with the one before, and (2) internalization of the precursor's pattern of poetry. Bloom quotes from J.H. Van den Berg's *Metabletica*: "...the impoverishment of things to a uniform substantiality--and the disposal of everything that is not identical with this substantiality into the `inner self' are both parts of one occurrence" (63 *PR*). That occurrence for Bloom is the moment of creation.

It is an issue of the self-preservation of poetry, for the precursor limited all future poetry and the upcoming poet wants to extend poetry past a limit set by the precursor. The imagination in poetry speaks of itself. Bloom would agree with Victor Shklovsky, who believes "the awareness of form constitutes the subject matter of the novel" (35 Lemon and Reis).

According to Bloom, in the start of a new poetry "the very idea of poetic tradition" is at issue. This idea can be meaningfully elaborated by the following passage from Frederick Griffiths and Stanley Rabinowitz:

> Just as the meaning of a part of the work is not exhausted in itself, but is revealed in its relations with the other parts, a work in its entirety can never be read in a satisfactory and enlightening fashion if we do not put it in relation with other works, previous and contemporary. In a certain sense, all texts can be considered as parts of a single text which has been in the writing since the beginning of time. Without being unaware of the difference between relations established *in presentia* (intratextual relations), and those established *in absentia* (intertextual relations), we must also not underestimate the presence of other texts within the text (244 *Novel Epics*).

Applied to Bloom's ideas, the passage suggests that the reinterpretation of a previous poetry depends upon seeing it in a different relation within the growing tradition. The change of this idea of the previous poetry at the same time places the upcoming poet at the new frontier of poetic tradition.

The passage also contains the idea that a canonical text (the last one in the series of tradition) is like a single text "which has been in the writing since the beginning of time." In the Prologue was mentioned the idea that tradition gives the power to the individual mind to be like the single human being who has been developing throughout all of civilization. This interplay of individual and the whole of humanity resembles the capacity of one DNA molecule to carry the instructions evolved through millions of years while yet having the power to alter them.

In passing comments Bloom suggests how a later poet understands the totality of the precursor, or the precursor's aesthetic in principle. "The new poet `himself' determines the precursor's `particular' law" (42-43 *AI*). The way the precursor created poetry is known to the successor completely. Yeats described the comprehension in the idea of the Condition of Fire: "in that flame he [the poet] views the last of them [the precursor-questers], and unlike them he both sees and knows what he sees" (115 *MM*). The successor understands the precursor in a way the precursor cannot: the cultural processes as a whole can become a new object of knowledge. To be absolutely self-comprehending seems to be a misnomer. One's own perspective can only truly be seen as a whole by another person; this limitation on the individual is a principle of the role of the psychoanalyst, who can see the psyche of a patient more comprehensively than the patient can, and for which reason the analyst-to-be must himself/herself undergo analysis to see any possible interfering factors hidden from self-conscious view--even that of one trained in psychoanalysis. Similarly, Cassirer uses the phrase physics "cannot jump over its own shadow," meaning all individual minds and all their products must be limited according to a source of knowledge (assumptions), which can give way to another (478 *The Philosophy of Symbolic Forms*, III, Trans. Ralph Manheim, Yale University Press, 1957).

A new poetry starts when the previous poetry is seen as having an origin and end different from what the precursor thought. This origin and this end are understood in relation to the new positive sense of poetic origin and poetic end, given by the upcoming poet to himself. In Bloom's words, "a strong poet invents himself" (7 *PR*). Campbell wrote about the dual focus of myth at both its origin and end, and as a result a myth is not wrong solely at its end but at its start as well. This idea does not mean no progress was made; rather, a change in a step of tradition requires modification of the entire world view, no matter how slightly some of the previous ideas in it may be changed in meaning. Certainly, this change is a revolution in Kuhn's sense. However, he always spoke of the beginning of a science as a victory while also arguing for the complete change of a paradigm to bring about a new world view. It is not completely true to speak of the end of a cultural form as faulty while thinking of the beginning as correct. Perhaps even the notion of faulty does not apply to a tradition form and should be replaced by language emphasizing the raising of the level or understanding of the previous processes, which do correctly lay the ground for successors. Bloom resisted any description of the positive role one form had in preparing the way for a successor.

So the question of the end of a poetic form is ultimately bound to the question of its origin. Changing the end of the former poetry is only done properly when a new origin is conceived. From the first moment of creation, there is a sense of a new end of poetic form, a sense of new destination to replace the old "faulty" one. Kuhn's mentioning of solution modelling indicates that the goals of the previous form are not rejected but re-envisoned. Gablik addresses this issue important for Bloom, although not entirely satisfactorily:

> Even though the kind of experimental thinking we find in art is set (like other forms of thinking) to solve problems in a step sequence, it is never satisfied with this; it must continually achieve new openings and new possibilities. A distinction must be made between a development which is fixed in advance by the end state that it must reach--as with Loewy's and Gombrich's model of progress--and a sequence of events that is open-ended to the future because its specific outcome is not foreseen. Cognitive psychologists have stressed the anticipatory nature of cognitive activity and the constant tendency of the mind to go beyond the information given. Microphysicists, for instance, continually seek new modes of conceptual organization from which the finding of new entities will follow (160).

Two types of development are contrasted: "a development which is fixed in advance by the end state that it must reach" and "a sequence of events that is open-ended...because its specific outcome is not seen." Although for Gablik the two types of development are in contrast, for Bloom they are not. Both are true if the final cause of the new poetry is sensed by analogy from the previous poetry, yet not actually explicit until the end of that poetry. During the process the understanding of this final cause or end of form becomes progressively clearer, more complete. Quite astute is Gablik's claim about microphysics continually forming new modes of conceptual organization, from which new entities are found. Similarly, in poetry new aesthetic principles allow the poet to find new images, new feelings, a new sense of what poetry does.

To find a direct relation between a successor and a predecessor, Bloom does not read bibliographies of journal articles and also textbooks as Kuhn does. Bloom finds the words of the successor that are the "antithetical use of the precursor's primal words, that must serve as the basis for an antithetical criticism" (66 *AI*). "Antithetical" criticism means "the juxtaposition of contrasting ideas in balanced or parallel structures, phrases, words" (65 *AI*).

Misprision or Misreading

Kuhn's undeveloped idea of the redefinition of former concepts is for Bloom a more developed doctrine of a transformation in one's total outlook.

Misprision or misreading is not a step before creation: it is creation. The process "clears imaginative space" for the new poet and for poetry (5 *AI*). The previous poetry can no longer be seen as a self-subsistent whole denying real progress after it. In the words of Campbell, "A god [predecessor] outgrown becomes immediately a life-destroying demon. The form [the whole of the poetry] has to be broken and the energies released" (338 *Hero*). Bloom, too, speaks of the "breaking of the vessels," which begins a new poetry (*The Breaking of the Vessels* 1982). The previous poetry is seen as fundamentally disunified, and then relatively unifiable according to a different start of poetry.

Sometimes Bloom uses ideas from Kabbalah to explain the change in interpretation of previous poetry. According to the Kabbalistic notion of Tzim-Tzum, God, who fills the whole universe, was obliged to make room for the creation by contracting himself. If Bloom had placed more emphasis on the developing needs of the unity of poetic tradition, misreading would be less of an individual's personal choice. The negative prefix, to be discussed further later, means not bad reading but intentional alteration of the meaning actually found; a still better approach would make the change in poetries a matter of an increase in value. For now, it seems as if Bloom's critical practice has two faces; on the one hand, "misreading" allows the critic to stand above any poets, who intentionally alter the interpretation of poetry for their ends, and on the other hand, the idea shows a lack of confidence in the comprehending of one poetry--indeed the whole tradition--by a subsequent poetry.

Misreading for Bloom consists of six revisionary ratios, since a poetry *is* a misreading of a previous poetry. [Of course, by poetry I mean great poetry, in the sense of a tradition form.] Their name suggests a revision of previous poetry, and they also revise one's own previous ratios. At six stages in the making of great poetry, the upcoming poet measures himself/herself against the preceding poet, changing the understanding of that former poet while progressively building an alternative sense of the final goal of poetry. The ratios are spoken of in pairs belonging to the same movement. In the first, the two ratios (clinamen and tessera) strive to correct or complete the dead poetry (122 *AI*). In the second (kenosis and daemonization), the pair works to repress the memory of the dead poetry or to further individuate the new poet(122). In the third (askesis and apophrades), the two poets experience the contest proper, the match to the death and the reconciliation with the dead (122). It is a reconciliation with one's poetic father, one in which the father is seen on a lower or earlier level. The new poet finally has cleared an imaginative space in answer to the limitation (and challenge) of the previous poet.

Bloom forms his idea of misreading into a "map" which can be found on page one of *Poetry and Repression* or page 84 of *A Map of Misreading*. The map represents a definite advance in Bloom's understanding of his own concepts, because the map integrates previous ideas and so defines them further. The map has three overall movements, each movement having three phases of the same names as the overall movements. This holomorphism, the part sharing the structure of the whole form, corresponds to the trait of myths to develop in contexts of three generations and to mirror the threefold context within the myth as a three-stage process. The definition of the whole myth through relations among three generations of myths is mirrored within the myth. Bloom's three movements of a poetry were taken from Kabbalah.

The map can be seen as having four lines of development each synonymous with the others: images in the poem, rhetorical tropes, psychic defenses, and revisionary ratios. Bloom finds characteristic types of images defining the developing phases of poems. These images come into being by serving as rhetorical tropes of earlier images; these tropes come from the history of literature and rhetoric. The psychic defences come from Freud's psychoanalysis; their ambivalence makes them good analogies for a dialectical development. The revisionary ratios are the most original of Bloom's ideas.

Clinamen or the Swerve from the Predecessor

Defining the start of a poetry more than Kuhn did for a science, Bloom defines the first step in a new poetry as "clinamen," a swerve from one's predecessor.

The term "clinamen" comes from Lucretius, meaning a swerve of the atom to make change possible in the universe (14 *AI*). To ground a new poetic step in tradition, a successor must swerve from the predecessor, must make change again possible.

"Clinamen" means "swerve"--the new poet swerves from the previous one, meaning the development does not occur without a change of perspective on former poetry.

Clinamen arises as an attempt to rescue the poetic enterprise from the predicament it was left in by the precursor. In de Man's words, "the polar structure" [at the end of poetries] should itself be questioned if there is to be a "reversal of valorization" (269 Review of Bloom).

Clinamen in one stroke revises the entire accumulated poetic tradition of the human race. The revision, however, is not in detail, nor in fact. In other words, Shelley, for example, does not revise every detail of Wordsworth's poetry. Also, Shelley does not in fact revise all previous poets. Since the subject of poetry is its own tradition, the meaning of this whole can be increased in principle, not in quantity. The increase is an increase in poetic power; Bloom infrequently mentions "greater inwardness" to explain improvement. Derrida claimed to change the entire tradition, and certainly he did not revise every detail, not every figure throughout the history of Western philosophy. There is some way that the whole past tradition can achieve a specific representation and thus be revised, worked on as if clay.

In a somewhat uncharacteristic passage Bloom defines the guiding thread of clinamen more in terms of the continuum [of poetry] than in terms of an individual's will to alter it:

> The clinamen or swerve, which is the Urizenic equivalent of the hapless errors of re-creation made by the Platonic demiurge, is necessarily the central working concept of the theory of Poetic Influence, for what divides each poet from his Poetic Father (and so saves, by division) is an instance of creative revisionism. ...the clinamen stems from a `Pataphysical' sense of the arbitrary. The poet so stations his precursor, so swerves his context, that the visionary objects, with their higher intensity, fade into the continuum. The poet has, in regard to the precursor's heterocosm, a shuddering sense of the arbitrary--of the equality, or equal haphazardness, of all objects. This sense is not reductive, for it is the continuum, the stationing context, that is reseen, and shaped into visionary; it is brought up to the intensity of the crucial objects, which then `fade' into it... (42 *AI*).

Here Bloom calls clinamen the central concept in his whole theory; elsewhere he calls another one at the ends of poetries (metalepsis in Askesis) the central concept of interpretation. Anyway, both are crucial--both the start and the end. Here, in more detail than almost all other passages, Bloom states the swerve to be a swerve of the *context* of the predecessor. This move shows a totalizing, unifying, comprehending, accumulating operation. Poetry begins as the gathering of its own tradition, and its form is made by reconceiving the past of poetry and redesigning its future. The subject of poetry is its own continuum, its stationing context. As we shall see, the ends of poetries bring about a completed new continuum, imaginative space, to replace the former one.

While a new great poet is re-making the continuum, the sense of it changes and matures. Clinamen is not a mistake because the continuum at the end of the precursor's poetry was facing an unsolvable crisis. The successor sees the precursor's poetry as *having already wandered* from the continuum; the only way to see the former poetry is from a higher level, for it cannot be unified beyond a certain point if its own perspective is used. The wandering of meaning is a point in the ever-developing continuum seen from a more developed point. Even within a poetry does a poet come to see the wandering of meaning until the structural threefold unity of the poetry is complete. The individual poet cannot stop its development but can earn the right to develop it and be developed by it. To come into existence a new poetry must reconceive its stationing context, thus revising tradition as a whole.

It has been my experience that scholars have a hard time understanding, or more politely agreeing, with Bloom's idea of the wandering of meaning *within* a poetry. Bloom claims:

> The great lesson that Kabbalah can teach contemporary interpretation is that meaning in belated texts is always wandering meaning, even as the belated Jews were a wandering people. Meaning wanders, like human tribulation, or like error, from text to text, and within a text, from figure to figure. What governs this wandering, this errancy, is defense, the beautiful necessity of defense. For not just interpretation is defense, but meaning itself is defense, and so meaning wanders to protect itself (82 *Kabbalah...*).

The idea of a revisionary ratio is that a poet revises the precursor's sense of the continuum as well as his/her own while the new one is being formed. In this constantly changing quest, meaning wanders; the continuum guides the poet, as the thread of Ariadne was a guide for the way out of a labyrinth after having been laid down on the way in; this process is rather deconstructive, for a successor lays down the thread while criticizing the predecessor and can return or form a new poetry by following the steps in reverse, as it were. Bloom speaks of this wandering in terms of clinamen; a poem has "an opening awareness that it [the previous poetry] must be mis-read because its [the previous poem's] signification has wandered already" (71 *MM*). This passage in effect places the blame for the change on the precursor, whereas most passages about misreading seem to treat the act of the successor as negative in some way or at least arbitrary and intentional.

In one passage Bloom claims "the precursor went wrong by `failing to swerve', at just...one angle of vision" (130 *AI*). Here, by implication, the swerve is a positive action by the successor. I do not think this statement, however, is very consistent with others. For, if a poet restations the context of the predecessor, not only the end of the previous poetry undergoes misreading but also its start. Hence, it is not accurate to say a swerve should have occurred at a specific point. A whole new basis of poetry is brought about, not just a partial correction of the last phase of a poetry. Perhaps Bloom wanted to speak of the swerve as a function of the virtually self-changing continuum--as it is manifest in the different orientations of two great poets in succession. Poetry becomes different from itself at points, called tropes by Bloom, not in the manner of logical inconsistency but more in the manner of a metamorphosis.

The dead great poets live in their successors. At the end of a successor's own poetry, (s)he finally gets a sense of the whole process of creating a poetry beyond that of the precursor: "A poet dare not regard himself as being late, yet cannot accept a substitute for the first vision he reflectively judges to have been his precursor's also" (19 *MM*). Any poet is bound to the predecessor; more important, any poet must explain the change in poetic vision; once this is explained fully, there is an answer to the precursor: a new poetry. In these senses the predecessor lives on as a directing force up to the end of the successor's poetry.

The dead poets live in their successors in the following way. A new great poet cannot reject everything of the predecessor but must "compound with" his/her reality to be able to create (38 *MM*). In personal psychology the ambivalence appears as identity and opposition to a parent; in poetry, images, characters, situations, and tone may be repeated from a previous author. The total literary use of these elements, however, differs. The Russian Formalist literary critics studied parody as the form in which stylistic change takes place. The idea of parody comes close in meaning to Bloom's rhetorical trope of irony for the revisionary ratio "clinamen." Parody shows that one poet makes of the previous one an object to develop for one's own new purposes.

An example of parody transferring the holy light of literary life is given by Griffiths and Rabinowitz:

> Dostoevsky, as we know, began his career by "re-reading" seminal works of Gogol, by refashioning Gogol's Akakii Akakievich ("The Overcoat") and Major Kovalev ("The Nose") into the more emotionally complex characters of Makar Devushkin ("Poor Folk") and Yakov Petrovich Golyadkin ("The Double"). Nor are we surprised to find other standard Gogolian techniques throughout all of Dostoevsky's work, especially name symbolism. The very name of Dostoevsky's fictitious town "Skotoprigonevsk" ("Cattle Corral") has an absurdly Gogolian ring to it (165 *Novel Epics*).

Characters are repeated and become "more emotionally complex." Other techniques from the predecessor are used throughout a writer's works. To further associate parody with irony, I should point out that Bloom, Griffiths and Rabinowitz understand irony to be the form of the relation of one author to the previous one as this relation is known to the second succeeding author: "Gogol discusses irony purely as a matter of communication, not introspection. His accounts of his relations with Pushkin and the Russian audience center on questions of irony" (114). Creating poetry has the significance of revising tradition, the canon of poetry. "They [the Russian Formalists] were very adept," writes the historian Victor Ehrlich, "at assessing the role of an author in the literary process, at determining how boldly he moved beyond the canon inherited from his immediate predecessors" (280).

One of the best studies of parody was carried out by Yury Tynyanov who believes parody is "an act of literary `warfare'" showing how one author evolves out of another author.[1] An author is both "a product of, and a challenge to" an immediate predecesor. This idea corresponds very much to Bloom's "clinamen" and in general to "revisionary ratio."

Parody or irony can represent the greater literary consciousness of a successor, which is still nonetheless intermingled with the predecessor's. Tzvetan Todorov describes the increase in literary mind:

> For some time James [Henry] followed in Flaubert's wake; when we mentioned his "exercises" it was to evoke precisely those texts in which he perfects the use of synecdoche (we find such pages to the end of his life.) But in the tales which concern us here, James has gone a step further: he has become conscious of Flaubert's sensationalism (or anti-essentialism), and instead of simply employing it as a means, he has made it the constructive principle of his *oeuvre*. We can see only appearances [when Flaubert's ideas are represented in James' fiction], and their interpretation remains suspect; only the pursuit of the truth can... (151 *Poetics of Prose*).

Irony or parody shows the attainment of an aesthetic vantage point above the predecessor.

Fundamentally, Bloom's criticism concentrates on the conflict of poets, whereas other critics discuss the missing positive side of literary evolution. Bloom discusses admirably how one author seems to hinder any followers, this obstruction being built into the end of poetic form as part of its means of closure (the end will be discussed in detail later). It is a way of projecting a vision of the poetic enterprise into the infinite, ideal future, thus safeguarding the integrity, the universality of the vision provided by the form. Cultural forms do this. Bloom does not discuss, however, how one author *helps* another to become a successor. Even though the predecessor may be dead, his/her poetry has within it what the successor needs. The satire, parody, or irony is not merely negative; it does not merely reject what came before; it continues the previous literary art (4 *Novel Epics*). Any great poetry suggests an aesthetic problem, which is at the same time a challenge and opportunity. Faulty presuppositions or aesthetic dead ends point the way to finding new alternative rejuvenating ones. According to Alois Riegl,

> However, in place of those earlier presuppositions for artistic creation it [late Roman art] has substituted new ones which constitute the basis for the gradual development of the practice of linear perspective in the following periods. In order to avoid an easily engendered misunderstanding, it has to be emphasized most emphatically that beside its negative role of demolition in order to make room for the new, late Roman art always had positive aims, which have to date remained unrecognized, because they appear so different from our accustomed ideas of the aims of modern art which to some degree are the aims of classical and Augustan-Trajanic art (11-12).

Parody and irony mean the demolition that is at the same time a construction and extension of the tradition. The fact that Riegl speaks of "presuppositions" should not be overlooked. They permit Riegl to explain how the end of artistic forms can point the way to a new form without actually providing the new principles, and the idea of presuppositions shows the dependence of thought on something outside itself, just beyond. If artistic and other forms are guided by presuppositions, then a successor can accumulate the previous cultural development by becoming aware of the former presuppositions--no one being aware of his/her own. In a non-quantitative sense the accumulation of an entire tradition can occur, because presuppositions supply the means for a successor to totalize, to comprehend what has been done.

Although Bloom's theory allows for a cyclic sense of poetries, Bloom does not develop this sense strongly enough. If he had, he would have explained how one poet does not merely obstruct the successor who then rejects the former; but the poet has his work continued and even prepares the way for this further development.[2]

Unfortunately, despite all the help Bloom can offer to take his readers closer to the well-springs of poetry, he does not describe the positive improvement in poetic tradition enough. Other critics (Mikhail Bakhtin) do describe progress:

> Every *true* reader of Dostoevsky, who perceives his novels not in the monologic mode and who is capable of rising to Dostoevsky's new authorial position, can sense this peculiar *active broadening* of his consciousness, not solely in the sense of an assimilation of new objects (human types, character, natural and social phenomena), but primarily in the sense of a special dialogic mode of communication with the autonomous consciousness of others, something never before experienced, an active dialogic penetration into the unfinalizable depths of man (68 *Problems of Dostoevsky's Poetics*)

There is an analogy between poets not being able to create and critics not being able to see the positive help a precursor gives a successor. Creation requires less criticism of the precursor than the constant attention to a new whole of poetry, based on analogy with the predecessor:

> ...the continuation of *Dead Souls* [novel by Gogol] required more the talents of a poet than of an artist: "But in general one should focus not on *censuring* others but on *contemplating* one's own self. If the creation of the poet does not contain within it this quality, then it is merely...the fruit of the temporary state of the artist" (163 *Novel Epics*).

Transference of the Pattern from the Precursor

The twofold attitude of the anxiety of influence, acceptance and denial, begins the transfer of the pattern of great poetry--perhaps a genetic code--from precursor to successor.

In "Tradition and the Individual Talent" Eliot notices a process of recognition during the creation of great poetry; the poet knows that the pattern of poetry has been pursued and found again.

The pattern of poetry can be transferred because poetry has for its subject its own tradition. Literary critic Leo Bersani finds a transference of the pattern of fiction by Joyce into works of a superior nature: "The Joycean intertext rescues Western literature from the deconstructive effects of the intertext itself. The parodistic replays of Homer, Shakespeare, and Flaubert--not to speak of all the authors `quoted' in `Oxen of the Sun'--are neither subversive of nor indifferent to the fact of cultural inheritance; rather, Joyce relocates the items of that inheritance with *Ulysses* as both their center and belated origin."[3] Griffiths and Rabinowitz have noticed "an absorption and reconstitution of canon in *Ulysses*" and "the restaging of the tradition" by Dante. They attribute to Bloom the finding of a similar absorption and reconstitution of tradition by Milton: "Milton's inversion of time may derive from the scene in the *Aeneid* (8.626-728) where the baffled Aeneas looks on a divine shield summarizing the history of a Rome that has not yet been founded."[4] The divine shield is an example of the whole of poetic tradition being represented and then capable of being revised through the representation. A creator cannot give a circumscribing representation of his/her own work, for an infinite regress of such circles would be required. Each new successor circumscribes the poetic process of the predecessor and thereby of the whole tradition. "By arranging his precursors in series," explains Bloom, "Milton figuratively reverses his obligation to them..." (138 *MM*); Milton's predecessors are seen as depending on Milton, who has a vantage point. This reversal of perspective on tradition, from seeing oneself as too late to create to seeing oneself as earlier or prior to one's predecessors, is a regular feature of poetry in Bloom's theory.

The pattern cannot be transferred identically, nor can transference be absent if a poet is to become great, to create canonical poetry. Bloom elaborates,

> The compulsion to repeat the precursor's patterns is not a movement beyond the pleasure principle to an inertia of poetic pre-incarnation, to a Blakean Beulah where no dispute can come, but rather is an attempt to recover the prestige of origins, the oral authority of a prior Instruction. Poetic repetition quests, despite itself, for the mediated vision of the fathers, since such mediation holds open the perpetual possibility of one's own sublimity, one's election to the realm of true Instructors (59 *MM*).

In the most simple terms a new poet must do what the previous did, only better. More specifically, Bloom is saying that an upcoming great poet attempts to subordinate the predecessor or to see the former as having a lower level of poetic vision; the lower level is spoken of in temporal terms as being "belated"; the superior position is "early" or "prior," which has both temporal and normative or logical meanings. The "mediated vision of the fathers" means the revised interpretation of the previous poetry--this revision being itself a new poetry. The goal of poetry is to form a revised stance of the predecessor's poetry, so that an upcoming poet constantly compares his/her own poetry to that of the predecessor. Whatever goal the new poet has in mind at any time in the unfolding of the poetry, and this goal is constantly maturing, is known by reference to a whole of poetry lost by the precursor [because (s)he could not allow a successor to remake the entirety of poetry, thus violating what had been done]. In this sense the precursor cannot prescribe what the successor must do. In contrast the precursor's aesthetic acts as if it were part of the poetic id, not a poetic superego. The successor understands the precursor as saying, "Be like me but unlike me" (70 *AI*).

Ironically, in an Oedipal fashion, the resistance to the father brings about a closer association with him. The proper rejection of the previous canonical poet causes that pattern to be reproduced in a new way.[5] Oedipus in the classic play was sent away because of his parents' desire to reverse the decreed fate of the boy's killing his father and marrying his mother. In the end the fate was realized ironically; the boy left his foster home for a new land in order to avoid the decreed fate only to go to the land where his real parents were and to make possible the fulfillment of the prophecy. The irony dramatizes the opposition of the father and son's opposition. With reference to Bloom's ideas, the poet is set on the quest of restoring the lost wholeness of the poetic continuum but is unable to do this until a whole poetry is developed as alternative. The irony is that the opposition cannot stop until the newcomer does what the former did, and Bloom sometimes expresses this, as we shall see, as an acceptance of the precursor but on new aesthetic terms.

Victor Shklovsky wrote about Sterne's "conscious manipulation and violation of traditional plot schemata" (169 *Theory of Prose*). The words "traditional plot schemata" suggest the subject of literature consists in the schemata of its tradition. All canonical poetry is constantly revising the whole tradition.

The transference of the pattern or code of poetry in the indefinitely extending series of human history reoccurs in cycles. The upcoming poet tries to understand the poetic production of the predecessor, and in so doing the poet finds a guiding thread to developing an alternative poetry. This complete poetry will in its turn challenge another upcoming poet to understand its processes of production, and again the attempt leads to the creation of still another poetry.

The Goal Constant Throughout the Transference of the Pattern, Code

The poet who is becoming great strives to stop being influenced and to become an influence by demanding "a mental space," a poetry, of his/her own. Though Bloom states the idea anthropomorphically, it can be seen as a necessary function of a tradition form. At the beginning of one's cultural work one must be influenced by the past, but at the end the work must be able to influence a successor to do the same type of work if the activity is to form an indefinitely extending tradition.

Common sense understands poetry as a pretty, perhaps revealing description of ordinary life, real events; Bloom disagrees (182 *SM*). Poetry attempts to understand the production of previous poetry and to restore its lost vision of the poetic continuum, its forbidding of a new total revision. In less abstract terms, the attempt resembles the attempt all people must face to develop their own personalities from their parents. The very first tendencies at identifying with one's parents do not complete the personality until the child can differentiate, perhaps oppose, the new personality and values to those of his/her parents. So a poet-to-be desires to "come into his/her own" as a poet, these words of Bloom's also being commonly used for the maturing of the personality.

According to Bloom the deepest desire of a poet is to be an influence rather than to be influenced (12 *MM*). Analogous to this desire is the desire of animals--all life forms--to reproduce. A comparison can also be made to the desire of people to have their children live beyond them and in turn reproduce, in order to grant the parents a kind of immortality. However, at the beginning of a poetry, as during the years of growing up, influence has a negative connotation for Bloom. Since the influence from the predecessor seems to stop any real creation by a successor, influence means an end to one's chances of having one's own imaginative space or poetry. In Fletcher's words, the poet demands `a mental space, a referential vacuum, to fill with his own visions' (66 *AI*). Doing what the precursor said could not be done, making the new space, would complete the quest of a poetry.

Thomas Mann has a sense of the goal constant throughout the making of a new canonical literary work[6]:

> ...The bond with the father, the imitation of the father, the game of being the father, and the transference to father-substitute pictures of a higher and more developed type--how these infantile traits work upon the life of the individual to mark and shape it! I use the word `shape', for to me in all seriousness the happiest, most pleasurable element of what we call education (Bildung), the shaping of the human being, is just this powerful influence of admiration and love, this childish identification with a father-image elected out of profound affinity. The artist...can tell us of...a career which after all is often nothing but a reanimation of the hero under very different temporal and personal conditions... .

Bloom feels this passage is concerned with the overcoming of the anxiety of influence discussed by Nietzsche and commented on by Mann. For this book, the passage gives a sense of what is constant throughout a poetry: "the transference to father-substitute pictures of a higher and more developed type." In other words, the poet must do what the precursor did, only better--on a higher poetic level. The dead end of the previous poetry sets the task of restoring the lost whole of poetic vision by making possible a newly defined whole or space. This task eventually requires a complete new vision of a similar type (in the passage, "a reanimation of the hero").

From Clinamen to the Next Ratio, Tessera

The swerving from the predecessor leads to the need to use one's new principle to complete the poetic vision of the world, the needs of poetic form, left in doubt by the predecessor; Bloom calls this "tessera," antithetical completion.

The term "tessera" comes from mosaic making: "the fragment say of a small pot which with the other fragments would re-constitute the vessel" (14 *AI*). The vessel means the poetic continuum, described as being broken when seen by the fresh eyes of a newcomer as it excludes the latter. The vessel is the poetic perspective. The repaired pot resembles the new poet's first stage in the recreation of the continuum: "the later poet provides what his imagination tells him would complete the otherwise `truncated' precursor poem and poet, a `completion' that is as much misprision as a revisionary swerve is" (66 *AI*). The first step of a poetry reconceives the sense of the tradition to make room for the newcomer, but this solution turns out to be incomplete, as we shall see.

Summary

The start of a poetry can be defined to be a movement of clinamen and tessera, two revisionary ratios. A reinterpretation of the precursor must take place, called "misreading" or "misprision." This act differs from the more partial reinterpretation in daily life, because the new poet revises the entire previous tradition by changing the principles on which the aesthetic was produced. Clinamen uses irony and parody to show its change of style. During this first movement away from the precursor, the upcoming poet realizes he/she must develop a whole vision from the new poetic building block discovered through clinamen. The result is a universalization of clinamen into tessera; at this point in poems the previous types of images are extended to all of nature or life. "Tessera" means the attempt to make an antithetical completion of the precursor. While it does do this, this move is insufficient to gain what the predecessor had lost, as explained by the next pair of revisionary ratios, and so the poet must develop the sense of poetry further.

NOTES

1. From 258 Erlich. The passage should be helpful for anyone wishing to understand the evolution or the genealogy of fiction: "The Formalist observations on the role of parody cast an interesting light on the mechanics of literary change. In his masterful study, *Dostoevskij and Gogol, Tynyanov* demonstrated that the relationship between these two writers was a much more complex phenomenon than was generally understood. Dostoevskij's indebtedness to Gogol', he observed, is undeniable, attested as it is by a wealth of Gogolian echoes in Dostoevskij's early novels, e.g. *Poor Folk, The Double, Netochka Nezvanova*. But, according to Tynanov, there is also another aspect, unnoticed by most literary historians: in his novel *The Friend of the Family* (Selo Stepancikovo) Dostoevskij was parodying the ponderous rhetoric of Gogol's *Correspondence with Friends*. Now parody, continued Tynyanov, is a sign of emancipation, indeed an act of literary `warfare'. If *Poor Folk* and *The Double* are a proof that Dostoevskij evolved out of Gogol', *The Friend of the Family* clearly indicates that its author was moving beyond Gogol'. Dostoevskij's literary art, concluded Tynyanov, was both a product of, and a challenge to, Gogol's `romantic naturalism'."

2. Griffiths and Rabinowitz explain how Dostoevsky extends Gogol's vision: "In presenting epic more as cycle than as genre, as a mode of other genres rather than a form unto itself, we propose a new meaning to the familiar designation of an "epic tradition" in the Russian novel. For it is not just scale and calling that define the category but the quality of memory that attaches the novels to the prophets of other nations--Homer, Virgil, Dante--and novelist to novelist, as in Dostoevsky's implicit sense that he is not just replicating or rivaling Gogol's vision but materially continuing his project, as we shall see" (39 *Novel Epics*).

3. Quoted from 155 *Novel Epics*. The original passage occurs in Leo Bersani's "Against *Ulysses*," *Raritan* 8, no. 2(Fall 1988): 21.

4. The idea of Griffiths and Rabinowitz is on 155 of *Novel Epics* Bloom's ideas can be found in *MM*, 138.

5. Bloom's idea is contained in the following passage: "But what is the Primal Scene [discovery of the project of a new poetry], for a poet as poet? It is his Poetic Father's coitus with the Muse. There he was begotten? No--there they failed to beget himself--he

must wait for his Son, who will define him even as he has defined his own Poetic Father" (36 *AI*).

6. Quoted from 52 *AI*. The original passage can be found in Mann's *Freud and the Future*. Bloom unfortunately gives no page number nor other publishing information.

Chapter 5:
The Start of Derrida's Philosophy

Introduction to Derrida's Definition of the Start

The corner stone for the new edifice of philosophy is the concept of difference--his definition of the start. This concept is gained by rejecting a negative (false and implicit) presupposition of Sartre, much like the point outside a perspective drawing. Derrida can change the entire tradition by changing its latest presupposition. "Difference" and "the chain of differences" resemble Bloom's clinamen and tessera very much--in so far as these figures function to change the precursor's thought and develop tradition.

Preliminary Idea of Derrida's Philosophy as Tradition Form

Derrida's philosophy as a tradition form resembles the genetic code more than Bloom's theory does. The philosophy is a cycle like that defined by the three fates (or moerae, parcae). Derrida's whole philosophy places a greater emphasis on the object of knowledge being traditional, and this is why he is concerned with writing: "The Possibility of Writing will assure the absolute traditionalization of the object, its absolute ideal objectivity" (87 *OR*). Derrida's philosophy is about tradition and it performs a new step in the Western tradition.

"I [Derrida] will be permitted to recall, here [Note 24, 102 *Pos*], that the first text I published concerned particularly the problem of writing as the condition of scientificity." Derrida emphasizes writing because it is a sensible representation that has helped traditions to be built up. Of all human artifacts writing seems more malleable to reinterpretation through the centuries while it also serves to unite the people of those eras. Writing is a kind of metaphor for tradition. The interest in it arises through the specific criticism of the transcendental signified.

Bloom's theory is somewhat more synchronic than a genetic code, even though to a large extent the map of misreading functions like the code. Since the map does not change with each change of a poetry, it is less diachronic than the genetic code (no two people can have exactly the same set of genes, and now DNA tests are used to identify criminals in trials merely by bits of skin or hair or bodily fluid). From the start of Derrida's philosophy it is clear that the idea of tradition is more like a genetic code, more diachronic, for Derrida's founding idea is bound to ideas of the immediate predecessor, due to the concept of *bricolage* (from "Structure, Sign, and Play in the Discourse of the Human Sciences"). His idea of tradition is historically determinate. Also, Derrida's philosophy is more like a genetic code because it repeats the pattern of the philosophy before it, whereas neither Kuhn's nor Bloom's theory is canonical. Derrida's philosophy is fertile like the genetic code; Bloom's theory cannot `reproduce itself'. This same conclusion applies to Kuhn's theory even more; it is not itself canonical, though it explains the canon of science.

Besides the genetic code, Derrida's philosophy can be likened to the cycle of life defined by the three fates from ancient Greek thought. The three fates appear in various philosophical and literary works and also artworks through the centuries after Homer. Both Homer and Hesiod mention the fates, and Plato does at the end of the *Republic*. Often pictured with the fates are the goddess of birth, Ilithyia, and the goddess determining death, the Keres. The cycle of life is bounded, just as the meaning of any cultural form is.

To illustrate the cyclical nature of cultural forms and in particular of Derrida's philosophy, I would like to refer to John Mehuish Strudwick's painting "A Golden Thread" (1885) as shown on page 165. The painting pictures the three fates, always represented as women, determining the "portion" or the "lot" of one's life. I don't think this is only a quantitative "portion," because they determine a person's destiny. Together they perform different functions on two threads defining the continuity of life, one gray and the other golden and universal (like life and death principles). The first

"A Golden Thread"

fate is Clotho, the Spinner, who is pictured spinning the thread of life; that is, making the thread from loose fibers or flax. This represents the start of Derrida's philosophy and also the start of a poetry, clinamen, according to Bloom. A new constituting element is found to generate a vision of human experience, but no specific word in Kuhn's theory articulates this first building block.

The second in temporal succession is Lachesis, the Disposer of Lots, who measures off the thread of life, its length. In other artworks Lachesis is pictured with a scroll or globe and does not only measure but weaves the thread into a fabric. Lachesis calls to mind Derrida's "differance" and "infinite differance," and Bloom's ratios of kenosis and daemonization. Differance, to be discussed in detail, serves to further distinguish Derrida's own concepts from those of his predecessor, Sartre; Bloom describes those ratios as similarly providing an individuating function of successor from precursor. The measurement of the thread by Lachesis symbolizes this further distancing.

In Strudwick's picture Atropos (the Inflexible or the Inevitable) is ready to cut the thread of life that is being spun and measured--actually the two threads, gray and golden. In other artworks Atropos has shears, a pair of scales, or else is drawing a lot as in Figure 5-1 on page 167. In Derrida's philosophy the concept of the supplement (and its advanced version, the festival) corresponds to this function of limiting the thread of thought. In Bloom's theory the two ratios askesis and apophrades limit the precursor, the creator and any successors so that the creator is assured of a *humanly* infinite or indefinite imaginative space of poetry within limits no other individual with the same immediate predecessor could pass.

The successor of a poetry or philosophy or a scientific theory must find these two threads in the precursor's thought. The gray thread represents the negative presupposition that the successor will reject. The golden thread represents the new founding principle that the creator can use to begin restoring a new imaginative space for humanity--whether in poetry, philosophy, or science. Deconstruction finds the threads. It sets a new boundary on the life cycle of the precursor's work. It rejects the gray thread and continues the golden, metaphorically speaking.

In "A Golden Thread" Strudwick splits the painting horizontally, putting the three fates on the bottom, as if a picture in a picture. On

Figure 5-1: The Three Fates, Who Define the Cycle and the Fate of an Individual Human's Life

From *Harper's Dictionary of Classical Literature and Antiquities.* Edited by Harry Thurston Peck. New York: Cooper Square Publishers, (n.d.), p. 1051.

In the figure above showing the three fates, although Atropos does her work the last, she is pictured here in the middle, as in Strudwick's painting "A Golden Thread." I suggest this position indicates a finalizing, mediating function in relation to the actions of the previous two fates. This suggestion is consistent with Bloom's idea of Apophrades and Derrida's idea of the supplement (the advanced form called the festival). A correlation in the history of philosophy is the role of Kant's third critique in relation to the preceding two critiques.

the top in a separate part are pictured an angel and a person whose destiny is being determined. So too might the workings of philosophy be determinative of a person's life without being on the same plane of meaning.

It would make much sense if the life cycles of culture evolved from biological life cycles and still followed some features of the earlier, lower type of organization, while remaining associated with it. Biological limits cannot be surpassed; people die. Yet they can be indefinitely extended through the traditional or cultural activities making all humans into one being growing through the millennia. We still read the ancients, and so they have in a sense outlived their biological lives; however, new thinkers surpassed them, and so even cultural life cycles have their limits, though in relation to the biological they seem to be capable of indefinite extension through time and culture. The limit of a cultural form to a cycle is necessary for a new individual to be able to understand it as a whole, thus accumulating all previous knowledge into a new form of the same.

The caption under the painting reads:

> Right true it is that these
> And all things else that under Heaven dwell
> Are changed of Time.

The limited life cycle defined by the three fates seems to apply to cultural life cycles in science, poetry, philosophy. The picture of the three fates also shows the inner transformation of the human being defining its distinctive life process in the animal kingdom, and this presentation and performing of a transformation of being are represented in all great paintings; consider Salvador Dali's "Metamorphosis of Narcissus" (1937) in which Narcissus at three stages of his life is shown. In the first he is seen in the background as he originally was; in the second he is kneeling at a pool where he falls in love with his image; in the third he is seen holding an egg and a flower, the Narcissus, which the gods had transformed him into because of his sin of self-love. The egg shows the fertitlity of the completed threefold transformation--like a genetic code. Throughout the history of painting one can see parts of a masterpiece related to each other to present and perform a transformation; the Christian Tryptichs, which tell stories in three parts, are clear examples.

More attention should be given to the idea just mentioned that Atropos resembles Bloom's askesis and apophrades in limiting the precursor, creator, and any successor while in so doing giving to the creator his/her unique imaginative space, a new unit in tradition. This distribution of functions, this establishment of a hierarchy as it will be called later, resembles the function of Freud's superego. The psychoanalyst tries to stabilize the boundaries of the id-ego-superego, neither giving too little, nor too much: each has a unique legitimate role. Their functions sometimes seem to conflict. The mature superego in lieu of a psychoanalyst can distribute the functions of each one to prevent instability. In this sense the psychoanalyst is a kind of ideal superego. For this discussion about cultural forms, the comparison to Freud shows how a unique personal space is described in psychoanalysis as Bloom spoke of an imaginative space for poetry and Derrida did for philosophy. The individual psyche has its unique level of development. If psychology is to be canonical, to be traditional, it must have requirements of form like those of poetry, science, or philosophy. For this reason the hierarchy of the id-ego-superego resembles the hierarchy in Bloom's theory of the three main movements and that in Derrida's philosophy of difference-differance-supplement, to be explained in due course.

The two threads in Strudwick's painting indicate a process of deconstruction. Barbara Johnson explains,

> The doubleness of the word *supplement carries the text's signifying possibilities beyond what could reasonably be attributed to Rousseau's conscious intentions. Derrida's reading shows how Rousseau's text functions against its own explicit (metaphysical) assertions, not just by creating ambiguity, but by inscribing a systematic `other message' behind or through what is being said (p. xiii DS).*

The difference between the gray and golden threads resembles the difference between what Rousseau declared and what the text produced as an `other message' working against explicit intentions. Speaking of a philosophy in similar terms, Derrida stated, "...a deconstruction of that totality which is also a traced path, of that orb which is also arbitrary might be broached" (161 *OG*). The traced path resembles the threads, which enable Derrida to understand "the totality" of his precursor.

Derrida's Change of the Tradition

The Perspective Drawing

Derrida changes the whole tradition of Western philosophy by changing a presupposition by which it was unconsciously ordered. The presupposition of the entire tradition is like the point of perspective outside of a perspective drawing.

There is a type of drawing in which a frame is drawn and in it houses and streets or objects of any kind are drawn with lines emanating from a point outside the frame. In this way, everything in the drawing has an angle dependent on that point.

Kuhn, Bloom, and Derrida all have some sense of such a point as necessary in all cultural forms. Kuhn believes the scientist uses "as an integral part of his knowledge what that knowledge had previously made inaccessible to him. That is the sense in which they change his knowledge of the world" (263 *ET*). Unfortunately, no further elaboration is given. Bloom in his early *Shelley's Mythmaking* bases much of his interpretation on a "Thou" which poetry seeks but can never fully represent. Also, when discussing Milton and Virgil, Bloom gives examples of images that contain the entire tradition of poetry (134-138 *MM*). These images point to the poet's awareness of a point outside but determining the predecessor's poetry.

David Allison points out Derrida's uncovering of such a perspective point for the entire tradition, an essential phase of any deconstruction:

> The term "deconstruction" (déconstruction), while perhaps unusual, should present no difficulties here. It signifies a project of critical thought whose task is to locate and "take apart" those concepts which serve as the axioms or rules for a period of thought, those concepts which command the unfolding of an entire epoch of metaphysics. ...

THE START OF DERRIDA'S PHILOSOPHY

> Derrida also speaks of the "completion" of metaphysics, the terminal point of "closure" (clôture) for the system. But the work of deconstruction does not consist in simply pointing out the structural limits of metaphysics. Rather, in breaking down and disassembling the ground of this tradition, its task is both to exhibit the source or paradox and contradiction within the system, within the very axioms themselves, and to set forth the possibilities for a new kind of meditation, one no longer founded on the metaphysics of presence (xxxii SP).

The idea of a presupposition or perspective point outside any single individual's vision is necessary if culture is to be continually accumulating itself in each successive stage. It expains how previous culture can be accumulated and changed and transmitted through the limited cycles individuals can create. A perspective point can also explain why the concepts within a philosophy have unity (relative to its origin) but from an outside, higher perspective these lines are seen to diverge or be inconsistent. Consequently, Sartre's philosophy achieves an even greater unity than Sartre realized only as it is seen to be a less integral form of new concepts developed by Derrida. At the same time, the concepts lose their ambivalence and the dynamism of form becomes another dynamism. A gestalt switch, as Kuhn would say, has occurred--though much more determinate than in Kuhn's theory.

As in Figure 5-2, on page 172, a gestalt switch occurs in the transition from Sartre's perspective to Derrida's. The left box illustrates Lévi-Strauss' idea that the unity of a myth is merely "projective" or tendential (Derrida, WD, "Structure, Sign, and Play..."). The circle above the boxes represents Sartre's closing concept re-interpreted by Derrida to be the negative presupposition called the transcendental signified. This negative or faulty presupposition is revised to become Derrida's new concept founding his philosophy, difference. We can see that there is always a unity of one's perspective that cannot be seen within that perspective. Note that such perspective drawings usually include landscapes and houses and other objects, the lines for which are determined by some point or points outside the frame for those objects. Inside "Sartre's Perspective" is

Figure 5-2: Bricolage Is Like a Change from One Perspective Drawing to Another

A. The Idea of a Perspective Drawing

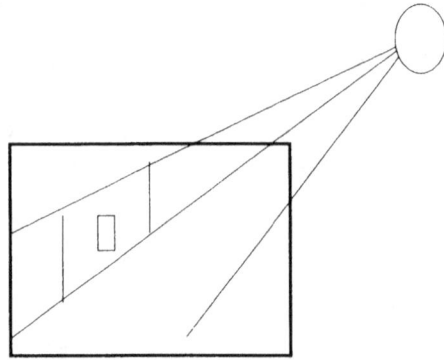

This type of drawing is made by drawing all objects according to a point outside the frame. Here a house has been started.

B. Bricolage as the Change from Sartre's to Derrida's Philosophies

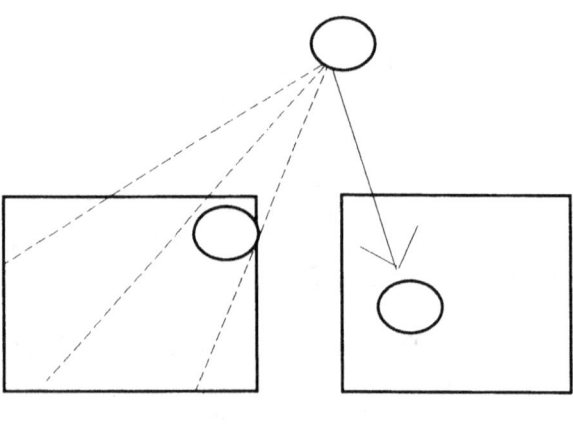

Sartre's Perspective   Derrida's

the small circle representing his closing concept, the fusion of the in-itself-for-itself, showing its containment within his persepctive.

In contrast to this view about the unity of a cultural work, Bloom seems to think a poetry can have unity outside of or before the change in perspective by the successor. His idea of misreading would presuppose this. Bloom falls short of describing the change in truth value or aesthetic value; he merely states that it occurs. He does not combine the idea of misreading with a broadening of consciousness.

Derrida himself finds in an outside perspective point the means by which he can change the Western tradition of philosophy. Consider this definition of deconstruction:

> to deconstruct a philosophy...to think--in the most faithful, interior way--the structured genealogy of philosophy's concepts, but at the same time to determine--from a certain exterior that is unqualifiable or nameable by philosophy--what this history has been able to dissimulate or forbid, making itself into a history by means of this somewhere motivated repression" (6 *POS*).

Philosophy before Derrida dissimulated the idea of a transcendental signified. Derrida formed this negative presupposition, rejected it, and developed his thought from it.

A few more lines from Writing and Difference *can help to show that the presupposition creates the perspective.* "By orienting and organizing the coherence of the system, the center of a structure permits the play of its elements inside the total form....The concept of centered structure--although it represents coherence itself, the condition of the episteme* as philosophy or science--is contradictorily coherent. And as always, coherence in contradiction expresses the force of a desire" (278). Following this desire, Derrida continues it to form a new ground of philosophy.

Derrida defines the end of a philosophy as providing a sense of what is outside it, yet not giving it entirely.[1]

In this way, Sartre's closing figure [the "ideal presence of the *ens causa sui*" to be explained (797 *BN*)] senses what is beyond it, points to it, but fails to reach it. Derrida rejects what gave Sartre's philosophy its internally diverging lines and changes this idea into an idea of his own (difference), which shows how those lines have their greatest unity. This process explains more than Bloom's idea that a poetry restores the lost unity of the tradition.

The idea of a perspective point requires the idea of some blindness of cultural form. It has been discussed much by Derrida and de Man. Since any text has a greater unity beyond itself, then the proper understanding of what has been written cannot be an identical paraphrase but a new concept constructing the former ones. A text can never be fully interpreted only in its own terms--Derrida speaks of it as the saturation of a context. Every text has a "structural unconsciousness," which deconstruction reveals (59 *Lim*), much as psychoanalysts reveal an unconscious. In contrast to Derrida's view Bloom's practice of criticism suggests a full interpretation can be achieved, or at least he himself knows of no higher goal for poetic vision. This unconscious is the unity of construction which cannot be known by the constructor. Plato believed the source of vision, "the sun," cannot be seen clearly, for it makes other things visible. Cassirer wrote that one cannot jump over one's own shadow and look back; the light defining oneself is not entirely visible to oneself. To represent self-consciousness, Sartre gave an image of a writer at a desk being observed by someone outside himself and knowing that he is being observed (214 *BN*), and Derrida gave a similar figure in *The Postcard*--Plato standing behind Socrates, telling him what to write.

The act of discovering the perspective point and changing it raises philosophy from a lower to a higher level. What does "higher level" mean? There may be an increase in the power of philosophy to know its own processes and be self-determining. The history of philosophy shows an increase in awareness of its ideal processes. Most concretely, there is greater integration of concepts. Derrida in *The Archaeology of the Frivolous*, a book on creativity, speaks of the progress as a greater connectivity of thought. I would compare this to learning more about a place. By actually wandering around a city one can make connections between points on the map to realize in ever greater degrees the relative positions and scale of the areas in the city. Someone might say, I didn't realize it was just behind that park! And when someone makes connections between points, a map constructing process, there is greater power to go where one wants to go. The person has greater freedom to choose options, greater power to realize them. In more general terms the operability of mind is increased or, perhaps more esoterically, mind becomes more mind than it was. Therefore, "higher level" in philosophy means a greater power of the philosophical concepts to enable the person to think philosophically. A philosophical ability is enhanced.

These conclusions apply not only to philosophy and to poetry but to science. The integration of concepts such that they become of a lower order in relation to new ones goes hand in hand with Derrida's *bricolage*, which is a concept-by-concept play of integrating and changing concepts. Einstein claimed his theory integrated previous concepts:

> The theory of relativity changes the laws of mechanics. The old laws are invalid if the velocity of the moving particle approaches that of light. The new laws for a moving body as reformulated by the relativity theory are splendidly confirmed by experiment. A further consequence of the (special) theory of relativity is the connection between mass and energy. Mass is energy and energy has mass. The two conservation laws of mass and energy are combined by the relativity theory into one, the conservation law of mass-energy.
>
> The general theory of relativity gives a still deeper analysis of the time-space continuum. The validity of the theory is no longer restricted to inertial co-ordinate systems. The theory attacks the problem of gravitation and formulates new structure laws for the gravitational field. It forces us to analyze the role played by geometry in the description of the physical world. It regards the fact that gravitational and inertial mass are equal, as essential and not merely accidental, as in classical mechanics (245).

The two instances of integration are mass-energy and the equality of gravitational and inertial mass. Derrida, thinking in general terms about philosophies based on a false presupposition, namely Sartre's, integrates a structural figure with a historical totality: "I have attempted to relate these two seemingly necessary approaches, thus repeating the question of the text, its historical status, its proper [own] time and space" (lxxxix *OG*).

The Transcendental Signified

Like the point of origination outside the perspective drawing, the transcendental signified is the negative presupposition of the whole tradition as far as it had come when Derrida's philosophy was conceived.

To define the transcendental signified, Derrida states, "[the transcendental signified]...in and for itself, in its essence, would refer to no signifier, would exceed the chain of signs, and would no longer itself function as a signifier" (19-20 *Pos*). The unusual concept indicates an "absolute and irreducible" difference between signifier and signified (20 *OG*).

How can the transcendental signified be thought if it is wrong? How could it have been legitimate philosophy for its time? Derrida's answer according to higher level, more integrated concepts is, "the voice is heard" or auto-affection explains it.

> Pure auto-affection necessarily has the form of time and does not borrow from outside itself any accessory signifier, any substance of expression foreign to its own spontaneity. It is the unique experience of the signified producing itself spontaneously, from within the self, and nevertheless, as signified concept, in the element of ideality or universality (19-20 *OG*).

A transcendental signified is not needed if the signified can produce itself spontaneously. In fact, the transcendental signified would stop the process of achieving new levels of signification. Sartre had to define his closing concept (the ideal presence of the ens causa sui) so that it would not be inconsistent with his opening concept (the for itself, which cannot produce itself or does not contain in its definition an explanation of how it can be originated).

For Derrida, the transcendental signified is a paraclete of thought, an awakener to new ideas. When discussing the theory of relativity, Ernst Cassirer claims its paraclete is "the conflict between the principle of the constancy of the propagation of light and the principle of relativity of mechanics" (370 *ETR*). The paraclete awakened Einstein because the conflict threatened the unity of nature and the future of science. In Bloom's terms Einstein seemed to be deprived of an imaginative space of physics, and needed to come into his own as a physicist.

How can such a conflict be resolved? On what terms can there be a solution? How can science continue? Cassirer gives an explanation important for the transcendental signified:

> If we look back on the historical development of the theory of relativity, we recognize that the latter has followed here a counsel which was once given by Goethe. "The greatest art in theoretical and practical life," wrote Goethe to Zelter, "consists in changing the *problem* into a *postulate*; that way one succeeds." In fact, this was the course which Einstein followed in his fundamental essay, *Zur Elektrodynamik bewegter Systeme* of the year 1905. The principle of the constancy of the velocity of light was given first place as a postulate, but,--supported by the negative result of all attempts to establish an "absolute" motion with reference to a chosen system of reference, i.e., the "motionless ether,"--the *supposition* was made that there correspond to the concept of absolute rest no properties of phenomena in either mechanics or electrodynamics, but rather that the same electrodynamic and optical laws hold for all systems of coordinates of which the mechanical equations hold. And this "*supposition*" does not continue such, but is expressly "made a presupposition," i.e., a shaping of theory is demanded which will simultaneously satisfy the conditions of the principle of relativity and those of the principle of the constant propagation of light. [Confer 16, p. 26; i.e. Einstein's *Ist die Trägheit eines Körpers von seinem Energiegehalt abhängig? Annalen der Physik*, 17, 1905] The two assumptions are indeed not compatible according to the means and habits of thought at the disposal of the kinematics

> generally accepted before the establishment of the theory of relativity, but they--*ought* no longer to be incompatible. ...there is only needed a transformation of these concepts in order to reach a logically unobjectionable theory (370-71).

The key to success is to change the problem into a postulate; in Borges' terms an artistic dead end is turned against itself to allow art to continue. The obstacle in theory that no one can surmount is reconceived to have been mistakenly framed all along. This intellectual move made by Einstein resembles that of Derrida concerning the obstacle presented by his predecessor, the transcendental signified. The general idea is that Derrida discovered a negative (false and implicit) presupposition in Sartre's philosophy and turned this problem into a postulate, just as Einstein had done: "Experience had shown that there is no such system [a particular privileged system of coordinates], and the theory, in its most general interpretation, makes it a postulate that there *cannot* and *must* not be such. That, for the physical description of the processes of nature, no particular reference body is to be privileged above any other is now made a principle" (382 *ETR*). The opposition found by Einstein was overcome because there was a redefinition of concepts in relation to each other; in Kuhn's terms the primitive similarity relation itself changes--the principle of identity which constitutes truth; the way all concepts are defined in relation to the other ones changes in principle, though Einstein did not attempt to change each one, one by one.

Not entirely coincidentally, the problem of the "motionless ether" is similar to the transcendental signified, which is motionless in the sense that it does not enter into the series of signifiers but serves as a non plus ultra for the indefinite series. This limit on future development recalls the same function of apophrades in Bloom's theory, which will be discussed at length. Similarly, the idea that there should be no privileged system of coordinates corresponds to Derrida's re-envisionment of Sartre's place in the tradition. Just as Bloom describes the start of a poetry as putting the precursor on an equal basis in the tradition, all of which is subordinated to the new poet, so too Derrida gets rid of Sartre's superiority by showing the less integral, lower level status of the transcendental signified than the new concept of difference.

Derrida re-establishes the unity of experience on the basis of the inadequacy of the transcendental signified. Then he must also restore the universality of philosophical vision. The continuum of philosophy is restored by extending knowledge beyond the transcendental signified, by permitting the extension of knowledge beyond a point allowed by this closing concept. To change the problem into a postulate, Derrida reconceives the signified so that it could never have been transcendental; it must always become the signifier for another signified in an endless series. This idea resembles Pierce's theory of interpretants:

> That the signified is originarily and essentially...trace, that it is always already in the position of the signifier, is the apparently innocent proposition within which the metaphysics of the logos, of presence and consciousness, must reflect upon writing as its death and its resource (73 *OG*).

The words "always already" show an a priori move by Derrida, in effect declaring that Sartre's views presuppose Derrida's for whatever validity and coherence they can be said to have. It is something like saying Sartre's philosophy actually presupposes Derrida's, which better explains what it was trying to do. Philosophies always begin this way, as do poetries according to Bloom and sciences according to Einstein. In less normative terms, more personal or psychological ones, Bloom speaks of a new poetry as attempting to restore a lost vision of wholeness in which a new poet cannot come into his own. In the case of Einstein, he restored the universality of physics in the following way, according to Cassirer:

> If we assume that the final objective determinations, which our physical knowledge can reach, i.e., the laws of nature, are provable and valid only for certain chosen systems of reference, but not for others, then, since experience offers no certain criterion that we have before us such a privileged reference system, we can never reach a truly universal and determinate des-

> cription of natural processes. This is only possible if some determinations can be pointed out, which are indifferent to every change in the system of reference taken as a basis. Only those relations can we call laws of nature... (383 *ETR*).

Einstein re-envisions what laws of nature are--in fact what truth in physics is--so that its tradition might continue. From the writings of Kuhn it seems clear he would not be bold enough to speak about a change in what constitutes scientific truth, nor in what constitutes science, because for him it would seem to threaten the continuity of purpose which is the prerogative of science.

Compare this restoration of universality in physics to Derrida's in philosophy:

> This was the moment when language invaded the universal problematic, the moment when, in the absence of a center or origin, everything became discourse--provided we can agree on this word--that is to say, a system in which the central signified, the original or transcendental signified, is never absolutely present outside a system of differences. The absence of the transcendental signified extends the domain and the play of signification infinitely (280 *WD*).

Here Derrida extends the domain of philosophy infinitely; Bloom believed poets wanted to extend the domain of poetry. When Bloom does speak of the creation of a new imaginative space, he does not do this in terms of the continuum of poetry but more in terms of the individual poet's desire for immortality. The problem with this approach--as good as it is--is that there is less determinate knowledge of the change from one tradition form to another, from one poetry to another, than there is in Derrida's knowledge of the change from one philosophy to another.

It is important to notice that "the final objective determinations, which our physical knowledge can reach" are "the laws of nature" (383 *ETR*). The final objects of knowledge are *not* physical things, as is commonly thought. The universalization by Einstein and Derrida depends upon the final objects of knowledge being laws of nature or elements of scientific discourse. Cassirer writes, "The real *content* of the object of thought, to which knowledge penetrates, corresponds therefore to the active *form* of thought in general" (322 *SF*). [Hegel, in a much quoted statement, wrote that the highest object of knowledge is the form of mind's own activity.] Therefore, Einstein and Derrida restore universality by hypostatizing a synthesis for the entire *form* of their predecessor's thinking. They can see the form whereas their predecessor's could not. In other words, Einstein knew how Maxwell had produced his laws better than Maxwell had known, and so Einstein's knowledge of physics was broader, deeper, of a higher level, more true to the goals of the form of physics.

The same goes for Derrida's start of his philosophy. He understands how Sartre made the transcendental signified better than Sartre did. He can see it as on a lower level of integration with the other concepts, resulting in a lesser degree of conceptual determination. He can see it as less meaningful philosophically. It is important to notice that the transcendental signified is not a term of Sartre's, but a term showing Derrida's ability to represent the totality of the formative processes not representable by Sartre to himself. In more technical terms, Derrida internalizes Sartre's closing concept, the ideal presence of the ens causa sui. Derrida can gain a more universal and determinate philosophical knowledge by discovering the source, origin, or manner of production of Sartre's ideas as a whole. If it is true that the highest objects of knowledge are the forms of our thinking processes, then it is easy to see that scientists work toward making their discourse, their tradition form anew. Their object is their tradition, and it improves itself by looking back at itself, synthesizing the understanding of its own processes, and revising this sense of what it is.

Irene Harvey writes about Derrida's interpretation of the transcendental signified and its significance for philosophies in general. "The ultimate basis for Derrida's unification of the history of philosophy as a single tradition concerns a fundamental desire which he claims animates the totality of philosophy. This desire is for a `transcendental signified' which would be liberated from all worldly representation..." (107-08 *The Economy of...*). Accepting her idea on face value, I would like to add to it the idea that all philosophies end in concepts functioning like transcendental signifieds. True, Derrida claims the whole tradition presupposed that one idea. Yet, the idea that all philosophies have something like a transcendental signified is different. It shows the recurrence of function needed to close a philosophy. The recurrence is needed for any complete theory of a philosophy as a tradition form.

The Precursor of Derrida

The following technical section may be useful only for philosophers, and perhaps then only for those with some belief in the validity of dialectical thinking.

Though Derrida does not speak of himself as having one precursor as Kant did (David Hume woke him from his `dogmatic slumbers'), nevertheless there is such a figure: Sartre.

Two great successive philosophies relate to each other as connected life-cycles, biologically connected life forms, like a parent and a child through which DNA is transmitted.

Many scholars point out the influence of Husserl or Heidegger or Nietzsche on Derrida, and rightly so. There are many more as well. But, as is the case with human beings, a child may be influenced by relatives of his parents, and neighbors and many people, but the actual descent must be attributed to a unique set of parents. Perhaps the reason Derrida seems to emphasize Husserl was discovered by David Allison, who said that the philosophy of presence and its oppositions are "strikingly evident" in Husserl's thought (xxxii *SP*).

Irene Harvey, whose interpretation I find very valuable, originates Derrida's philosophy in the work of Heidegger, Husserl, and Hegel (109 *The Economy...*). Certainly, Derrida's writings offer much evidence to support her view. A few other scholars trace the origin to Sartre. Christina M. Howells argues for the influence of Sartre on Derrida, because of the "parricidal attacks on Sartre," meaning the crime of killing one's father or mother (169). Liviu Cotrâu believes Derrida goes "beyond Sartre and Merleau-Ponty" (103). D.C. Wood claims Derrida has a direct relation to Sartre:

> Derrida's distinction [from Merleau-Ponty and Sartre in criticizing Husserl] is to have undertaken this

> criticism not to an appeal to the impossibility of bracketing out `existence' but to the irremediable *other relatedness* (in many different senses) of the sign, which is *the structure of consciousness*. Derrida would claim a common inspiration in Heidegger, but I cannot help wondering about a more direct relationship to the `vulgar' Sartre ["An Introduction to Derrida," *Radical Philosophy* 21(Spring 1979)].

In the case of Derrida, it can be shown here, contrary to almost all critics, that the parent of Derrida's philosophy is Sartre, not Husserl. For this specific direct relation Bloom used the term "prime precursor" (158 *MM*).

Objections to this idea of Sartre as the parent or predecessor should be set aside. The strongest, most common objection would be that Derrida refers much more to Husserl and to Heidegger and to Hegel, and also to Freud, and to Rousseau, and so on.

True enough. One need only look at *Writing and Difference* and *Speech and Phenomena* and *Edmund Husserl's `Origin of Geometry'*, etc., but one should not forget the personal, new technique of philosophizing that Derrida uses throughout his works. The fact that this technique is pervasive helps to convince sceptics that it is evident. Derrida presents his own ideas through a reading of other thinkers' ideas. This idea of "through" means an operation of refraction by the medium of Derrida's unique philosophical mind. He sees in the work of others what serves as the constituent of his own original ideas. Sometimes, "his" new technical concept has the same name as a term in the work he is reading, a science he called paleonymy.

Thus, when Derrida writes about Husserl, Husserl's ideas provide the opportunity for a "reading," for refraction, for new ideas. Husserl's ideas act as clay, in the way Bloom spoke of "misreading" as inventive interpretation. Then, it may not be (and is not) the case that Derrida's extended, early reading of Husserl and Rousseau must entail that they are the parents of his philosophy.

There is a primary single parent of a philosophy--a precursor who provides the pattern of philosophy from which a new version can be formed. It is well known Plato was a prime precursor for Aristotle, Descartes was for Spinoza, and Hume was for Kant, to pick out only three clear examples. Of course, this does not mean no other philosopher besides the prime precursor had been read.

Derrida states that his deconstruction of Western Philosophy begins with a critique of the transcendental signified (19-20 *Pos*). Many other references are available, as Derrida mentions the idea many times. So, too, does he mention the idea that his critique of preceding philosophy is the critique of *all* preceding philosophy, including that of Sartre.

The transcendental signified closes Sartre's philosophy in a way characteristic for all philosophies. Derrida's set of original, founding philosophical terms are semantically and syntactically related to the shape that the transcendental signified has in Sartre's philosophy. (Of course, if all previous philosophy had its "transcendental signified," it cannot have exactly the same definition in each philosophy for 3,000 years.)

The Canonical Structure of Sartre's Philosophy

Sartre's philosophy belongs in the series of great philosophies, and it has in it its own particular version of a genetic code of philosophy. It does to its predecessor what its successor will do to it. Or, forward looking, Maurice Merleau-Ponty's philosophy leads to the production of Sartre's, just as Sartre's does to Derrida's. In each a similar interdependence of concepts occurs, as Bloom's ratios explained the interdependence for poetry.

Very similar to Bloom's three movements of revisionary ratios, all canonical philosophies have evolved through three main dialectical movements. On the scale of an individual philosophy this triplicity corresponds to that of the three generations just mentioned. Examining three generations suggests the minimum condition of a tradition form: that a philosophy or poetry can lead to another one with a similar structure, and this in turn can lead to another with a similar structure. Then after the third generation, one can be assured that the series goes on infinitely or indefinitely.

Sartre solves a problem left by Merleau-Ponty, adds a link to the long chain of philosophical progress dating back to Thales, and develops a system of philosophy which contains the seeds of its successor.

THE START OF DERRIDA'S PHILOSOPHY

As with all the other great philosophies in the series before it, Sartre's system has at its core a tripartite diachronic structure.

The Tripartite Structure of Sartre's System

1. The founding principle or first pillar of the system: the for itself as a new idea of human subjectivity.

2. The second (and developed) pillar for Sartre's system: the in itself as that to which the for itself must relate.

3. The crossbeam or coping stone of the system: the ideal fusion of the in-itself-for-itself.

More Complete Definitions of the Three Main (A Priori) Principles

1. *The for itself, or the core of human subjectivity.*

> This new core is dynamic. "There is never an instant," Sartre writes, "at which we can assert that the for-itself *is*, precisely because the for-itself never *is*. Temporality, on the contrary, temporalizes itself entirely as the refusal of the instant" (211 *BN*).

2. *The "original" relation of the for itself (human subjectivity) to the in itself (any physical thing).*
Sartre feels he *must* posit such an "original" relation or else his doctrine of the for itself cannot have meaning and be true. "To exist as the act of freedom [i.e. to exist as the for itself] or to have to be a being in the midst of the world are one and the same thing, and this means that freedom [the for itself] is originally a *relation to the given*" [the in itself] (625 *BN*).

3. *The ideal fusion of the in-itself-for-itself.*
Sartre posits this ideal hybrid to fuse two otherwise separated

sides of his philosophy. This problem could not have been anticipated before the second acquired form. "We have seen in Part Two of this work," Sartre claims, "that the relation between the possible which I am and the present which I am fleeing is the same as the relation between the lacking and the one which lacks what is lacking. The ideal fusion [the in-itself-for-itself] of the lacking with the one which lacks what is lacking is an unrealizable totality which haunts the for-itself and constitutes its very being as a nothingness of being. This idea we called the in-itself-for-itself or value" (267 *BN*).

Questions to Be Answered to See the Canonical Structure of Sartre's System

1. How did Sartre start his philosophy? (How did Sartre discover the first a priori of his system?)

2. What is the internal development of Sartre's system? (Why did Sartre posit the second a priori of his system?)

3. How does Sartre bring his philosophy to a close? (Why did Sartre posit the third a priori idea of his system?)

Since this book deals with Derrida's philosophy, it is not necessary to explain the origin of Sartre's. A discussion of the end, however, can help explain the meaning of Derrida's philosophy as a tradition form: a cultural work that is a unit of tradition and revises the entire tradition before it.

How Does Sartre Bring His Philosophy to a Close?

Sartre felt that experience was split into two dimensions with human subjectivity as an enclave in the world of things. The reflective self of people seemed dissociated and aloof from physical things. Furthermore, this schism is dynamic. Sartre defined our human nature as a struggle by consciousness not to be an inert, physical thing--a struggle never completely won nor lost so long as we live.

THE START OF DERRIDA'S PHILOSOPHY 187

While these two poles (which define our dynamic existence as subjects) are theoretically related in Sartre's system, he *feels* a dissociation or separation. They are not related in practice, in action, in feeling.

A second main problem in the development of Sartre's philosophy leads to the positing of the in-itself-for-itself. This point in the system resembles the transition from the second to the third movement in Bloom's theory.

Sartre defines the in-itself-for-itself in this way:

> If our conclusions are accurate, this perpetual indication of an unrealizable fusion must appear not as a structure of the unreflective consciousness but as a transcendent indication of an ideal structure of the object. This structure can be easily revealed; correlative with the indication of a fusion of the polymorphic negation with the abstract negation which is its meaning, there is to be revealed a transcendent and ideal indication--that of a fusion of the existing *this* with its essence to come. This fusion must be such that the abstract is the foundation of the concrete and that simultaneously the concrete is the foundation of the abstract. In other words, the concrete "flesh and blood" existence must *be* the essence, and the essence must itself be produced as a total concretion; that is, it must have the full richness of the concrete without however allowing us to discover in it anything other than itself in its purity. Or if you prefer, the form must be to itself--and totally--its own matter. And conversely the matter must be produced as absolute form" (267 *BN*).

Here Sartre explains the impossible future that is perpetually indicated in human experience. Here it is expressed no longer as an inner state of some human subject but now as an external matter of our environment and worldly situation. He feels the problem alternately as the necessary but impossible enclosure of the self by the self, and as the imperative but impossible goal of understanding the universe in its totality. These two impossible dreams are obverses each of the human condition, as Sartre thinks *and* feels it. Each one is a faceted look at human nature insofar as any look reflects only a moment in a continuum of self-growth.

Sartre needs to explain the original relation of the for itself to the in itself. The original relation of the for itself and in itself must have a temporal manifestation.

The in-itself-for-itself defines a prior unity to either the in itself or the for itself. Sartre claims,

> If we wish to conceive of a synthetic organization such that the for-itself is inseparable from the in itself and conversely such that the in-itself is indissolubly bound to the for itself, we must conceive of this synthesis in such a way that the in-itself would receive its existence from the nihilation which caused there to be consciousness of it. What does this mean if not that the indissoluble totality of in-itself and for-itself is conceiveable only in the form of a being which is its own "self-cause" (791 *BN*).

Sartre's argument can be paraphrased: "Well, if there is an original relation of the for itself to the in itself, and if the in itself is partially a past form of the for itself and partially the seed of a future for-itself, then does the for-itself come into being from a change by a transformation in the in itself, or does the for itself come into being from a change by introspection?" The *ens causa sui* or self-cause is "an ideal being as the in itself founded by the for itself and identical with the for itself" (792 *BN*). Mentioned in the Prologue of this book, a distinguishing feature of humanity is its ability to determine its own improvement, to be its self-cause. The idea is very related to Bloom's notion that a poet does not want to be influenced but to be self-determining and to be an influence. Sartre's concern with a self-cause occurs at the close of his philosophy. In general, a cultural form closes itself when there is an awareness of the process by which it arrived at its previous stages. In this way a certain freedom or power has been gained along with a new deeper awarness of the human enterprise. Cassirer at the end of his *Essay on Man* believes culture seeks increasing self-knowledge and freedom, these two being linked together.

Sartre defines the original relation of the for itself to the in itself in the following way. "Everything happens therefore as if the in-itself and the for-itself were presented in a state of disintegration in relation to an ideal synthesis. Not that the integration has ever *taken place* but on the contrary precisely because it is always indicated and always impossible" (792 *BN*). This is a rather clear statement of the idea of one cultural level being higher or more integrated or purer than a previous one.

A feeling common at the close of cultural forms, Sartre is discontented with the perpetual failure or the limits required by his closing concept. On Bloom's view, the feeling of entropy or loss of meaning is a structural element common to the ends of poetries--a restriction by the creator on any would-be successors. The ambiguity concerning the source of change in the for itself (whether by external transformation or by introspection) corresponds to ambivalent feelings which Sartre has. Sartre defines a "spirit of seriousness." It is the "belief that one's mission of effecting the existence of the in-itself-for-itself is written in things" (797 *BN*). This spirit or feeling is not wholehearted but a part of a larger complex; it is ambivalent.

The spirit of seriousness changes into the spirit of futility. All human activities are equivalent (insofar as they all tend to sacrifice a person in order that the self-cause, an ideal, may exist); all are doomed to fail to bring the self-cause into existence.

About the spirit of futility which Sartre recognizes but does *not* define and see in relation to the other spirit, Sartre asserts:

> Thus it amounts to the same thing whether one gets drunk alone or is a leader of nations. If one of these activities takes precedence over the other, this will not be because of its real goal but because of the degree of consciousness which it possesses of its ideal goal; and in this case it will be quietism of the solitary drunkard which will take precedence over the vain agitation of the leader of nations (797 *BN*).

Sartre is writing about a limit of philosophical development (transcendence), just as Bloom wrote about limits being set by creators for their successors. This prophecy of a limit on future development is the way canonical philosophies bring themselves to a close. All philosophies end with a problem unsolvable in the terms of the philosophy--which shows the finitude or individuality of the philosopher. Since this dilemma is a limit on future development, the successor must explain how philosophy can continue, how there can be real unexpected development beyond the concepts already founded. The end of one philosophy is connected to the start of the next, like the serpent of time, the ouroboros, which forms a circle because it is trying to swallow its tail, as in Figure 5-2 on page 191. The serpent is usually used in mythology and early literature as a symbol of transformation, renewal, immortality, and Professor Spiros Iliopoulos has informed me that it was used by Romantic poets to show the one or whole of experience, which persists despite the ephemeral flux of experience. Similarly, the creator cannot revise his closing concept despite the problems it may cause, because it is the final piece to the puzzle forming a whole vision, and this whole vision is more important than a change in an isolated part that would not accomplish the same function, as the ouroboros creates a symbol of unity resulting from transformation.

Can the burdensome ideal of the *ens causa sui* ever be overcome? Sartre is stymied. He writes, "Will freedom be reapprehended from behind by the value which it wishes to contemplate? Or will freedom, by the very fact that it apprehends itself as a freedom in relation to itself, be able to put an end to the reign of this value? In particular is it possible for freedom to take itself for a value as the source of all value, or must it necessarily be defined in relation to a transcendent value which haunts it" (798 *BN*)? [The use of "transcendent" here refers to the transcendental signified.] This "value" is disadvantageous: a contradiction in terms, a self-contradiction.

The end of Sartre's philosophy entails a dilemma. Sartre was required to postulate the third a priori, if he was to integrate the two types of existence. This ideal fusion is an *ens causa sui*, or the in-itself-for-itself. In explanation, "Or if you prefer, the form must be to itself--and totally--its own matter. And conversely the matter must be produced as absolute form" (268 *BN*) Elsewhere Sartre suggests the curious image of someone bent over a table, writing, "who while writing knows that he is observed by somebody who stands behind him" (214 *BN*). There is a strange duality in the closing concept. How can we overcome the burdensome ideal of the *ens causa sui*?

Figure 5-3: The Ouroboros or The Serpent of Time Represents the Cyclical, Circular, and Finite Nature of Cultural Works

A. The Ouroboros

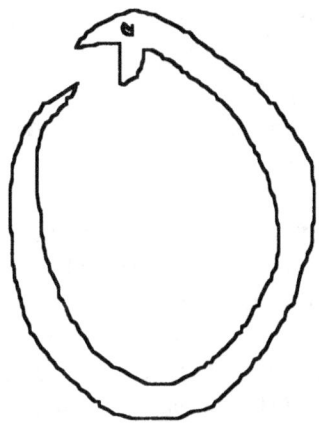

B. The Ouroboros as a Model of Derrida's Philosophy: the Supplement (#3) "Swallows" or Comprehends Its Origin, Difference (#1).

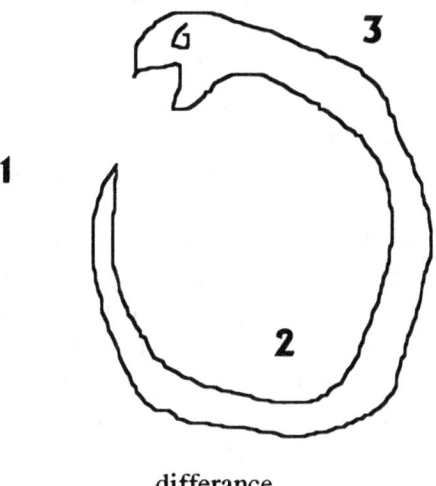

differance

The paradox is necessary, unavoidable within the philosophy; it is not the case that Sartre has made a wrong swerve at the very end, which by itself could then be corrected, to use language sometimes used by Bloom. A philosophy is much more all of a piece than that approach assumes. Sartre must posit the third a priori, and yet what it must be is unsatisfactory, even to him. This situation (in light of thirty philosophical precedents forming the canon of philosophy, from Homer to Sartre) suggests to me that the paradox cannot be simply rejected but that the opposing factors in it must be re-conceived and integrated in a new way.[2] This operation has been called deconstruction.

The paradox can be stated pre-logically. Sartre expresses a vague sense of a paradox in his theory, when he mentions the spirit of seriousness and when he describes the futility of human endeavor to achieve the ideal synthesis, a merely regulative ideal as opposed to one that would constitute other concepts directly, a virtual and projective point beyond the full knowledge that it nonetheless guarantees. The spirit of seriousness can become the spirit of futility, the two opposites defining the limiting attitudes toward human progress.

The paradox can be defined in the following way. To realize transcendence or progress the self must go outside or beyond itself--but how can the self be simultaneously whole and outside itself, in the act of developing?

Take a fictional example to express difficult relations. Consider any childhood memory--a party at age five. At age thirty I have a different view of this event. According to Sartre's view, the structuring of the event when age five does not fundamentally change--not even twenty five years later; rather, it subsists and resonates in the present situation. It is overlaid, colored; the interpretation when age thirty predominates. (Sartre commented on the persistence of the for itself's primary structures.) Here Sartre has corrected Merleau-Ponty with the new claim that the incident can change somewhat in meaning. Here one event in the world has two structures or forms. But does this fact mean that there are two selves which form the two structures? In this view of human development, a self grows by *enclosing* his previous self and retaining its meaning as if by swallowing it.

There is a second horn to the dilemma. The situation may be expressed in terms of the structure (the human subject) rather than the event (the non-human subject matter). A structure in the mind of the event at age five subsists at age thirty, even though there is at least one other interpretation, the accumulated present interpretation. The interpretation at age five is partially constitutive of the new structure. How can one "self" comprehend both structures if it is the distinct structure itself which is the manifestation of the self? The self is neither structure, neither the interpretation when five, nor that when thirty. Without some content of the mind, the self cannot exist. On this second view of self-growth, the self grows not by self-enclosure but by integrating events into a totality. Because the integrating is continuous, the process would have no definite marks and goals--an interpretation which could lead one to have a sense of futility.

Actually, philosophers solve paradoxes of their predecessors by taking philosophy as its example from which to determine the limits of the possible. Quite consistent with this view, Bloom speaks of poets restationing the context of the predecessor, redefining the relation of the predecessor to the poet before and to a proper successor.

As a case that can determine truth, consider the relation of Sartre's philosophy to Merleau-Ponty's. According to the model of Sartre's in-itself-for-itself, Merleau-Ponty's philosophy could have two interpretations, one by Sartre and one by a follower; nevertheless, it is *one* event. On the other hand, two structures in the mind, Merleau-Ponty's interpretation of his own philosophy and that by some other philosopher, produce one meaning: *the* interpretation of Merleau-Ponty's philosophy. Sartre cannot solve this problem in principle.

The two sides of the dilemma should be repeated and explained. Figure 5-4 on page 195 illustrates the problem. On the one hand (as manifest in the spirit of seriousness), Sartre believes transcendence or progress occurs only at specific points. On the other hand, Sartre believes that transcendence never fully occurs; rather it is diffused throughout every point on the line of the entire tradition, past, present, and future. The first problem I call the self-enclosure view and the second is the illicit-totality view.

The Self-Enclosure View

Acccording to this view the growth of self and its continuity (and therefore existence) are disrupted by the change of *all* its elements at once rather than a continuous developmental progression.

The Illicit-Totality View

According to this view, the gradual continuous, never completed growth is not a change in self-structure. The radius of experience remains the same, though the center and the perimeter are never finally known by the mind.

In the self-enclosure view there are dichotomized self-structures while in the illicit-totality view there can be no growth of the self

Statement of the Paradox in Terms of the Diagram

A. The self-enclosure horn of the dilemma. Refer to the figure. Though Sartre denies the closing of circle C (representing his philosophy) with A and B inside (the philosophies of predecessors), he nevertheless assumes such a closed circle; circle A, circle B, and circle C belong to an idea of philosophy made possible by the necessary assumption of its indefinite extension, by the not yet fully realized type or principle of some future circle, known and partially predetermined by Sartre.

B. The illicit-totality view. If Sartre's third a priori were correct as suggested by Sartre, there would never be a circle for which C circle would not define partially. Since C circle partially defines any future circle, the "radius of experience" cannot change. The closing of a philosophy resembles that of a poetry. Bloom believes any great poet does not make way for a successor and sets a limit on any future development. In fact, this idea equally applies to the closing of all canonical philosophies.

Changes in experience are relative to a fixed center and perimeter, which the self never finally realizes. The philosopher, however, has an idea of this totality because his claims entail that the C circle must partially constitute any further circle. Philosophies have often been, to speak anthromorphically, self-serving and domineering, for they have often denied future discovery of ideas by others, having set the pattern themselves.

Figure 5-4: Sartre's Dualistic View of Human Progress

There are two horns to this Dilemma: *A* and *B*:

A. The Self-enclosure View of Human Progress; the First Horn of a Dilemma.

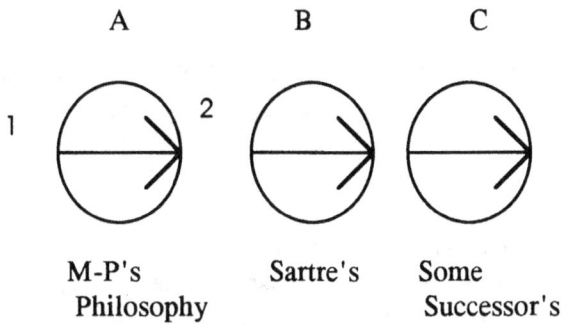

According to this half of the definition of Sartre's closing concept, progress occurs only at isolated points (A2, B2, C2, etc.) and so the tradition lacks continuity--an inconsistent view.

B. The Illicit-Totality View; the Second Horn of the Dilemma.

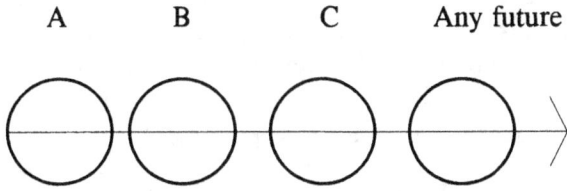

These circles represent the series of philosophies. According to the second horn, transcendence or progress is only completed at the end of a line that never stops. So the view fails to explain the development of tradition.

Solution to Sartre's View

The two horns of the dilemma must be re-interpreted so that a paradox no longer troubles us. (Kant expressed a prototype of this method in his antinomies.) The two unacceptable alternatives illustrated with the help of Figure 5-4 must be re-defined.

> A. *The Self-enclosure View.*
> It must be wrong to think that self-growth occurs only at isolated moments in a cataclysmic and orgasmic fashion. In this figure, self-growth occurs at all points on the line.

> B. *The Illicit-totality View.*
> The other alternative must also be incorrect. In this alternative, transcendence never fully occurs but rather is diffused throughout every moment in the continuum. This view must be incorrect. Self-growth must occur at identifiable moments; however, it should not be the case that every moment is equally a moment of self-growth. If this situation were true, self-growth would be unavoidable and it would be futile to exert extra effort to achieve particular plateaus of self-development. As Sartre has claimed, it would make no difference whether you have been a solitary drunkard or a leader of nations, except that the leader's agitation for development is vain, futile.

These two horns of the dilemma close Sartre's philosophy in the following way. Like two rails of a train track extending into the horizon, they seem to converge but in fact never do. Sartre's in-itself-for-itself is this kind of ideal. It has the effect of situating Sartre in an infinitely extendable imaginative space of his own making; this trait of form parallels the position of consciousness in experience as always inside it. In Bloom's terms the poet makes an imaginative space to obtain a universal vision, past, present, and future. All the predecessors throughout history and all possible "successors" to come can be seen through the universal vision. The infinite applicability of the ideas of the poet or philosopher or scientist are infinite only within experience, an internal infinity, one within limits. In Sartre's case the fusion of the in-itself-for-itself ensures this unlimited imaginative space.

The polar structure of the paradox must be avoided. This can be done by finding the unity from which the two horns can be seen as being produced. A deconstructive gesture is required. First, to dispel the illusion that the two senses of the in-itself-for-itself do converge eventually. And second, to find this unity requested by, though not discovered by, Sartre. What were two structures for one event, and what were two interpretations of one structure, must conceal two integral aspects or conditions of any content of consciousness. A new object of knowledge would begin to take shape, seemingly of its own accord, as when a scientist suddenly finds a solution as an imaginative congealing of separate ideas.

What is needed is a sense of difference in interpretation, not only between thinkers but within one's own thought. Meaning is possible because of differences in concepts. Merleau-Ponty's philosophy does not have the same meaning for Merleau-Ponty as it did for Sartre, and not for other later thinkers. The content of consciousness cannot be indifferent to the immediately preceding content. Thought is situated historically. Sartre could not have totalized his own thought, as no one can. One's own manner of vision cannot be completely represented to oneself. It would be, as Sartre suggested, as if someone could see himself from the outside: "the reflected-on knows itself observed. It may best be compared--to use a concrete example--to a man who is writing, bent over a table, and who while writing knows that he is observed by somebody who stands behind him. The reflected-on has then, in a way, already a consciousness (of) itself as having *an outside* or rather the suggestion of *an outside*; that is, it makes itself an object for _____ [the blank line is in Sartre's text], so that its meaning as reflected on is inseparable from the reflective..." (214 *BN*).

What can be called the event of Merleau-Ponty's philosophy has a meaning for me different from that which it had for Merleau-Ponty, because he defined it through a system of meaning or reference which differs from mine. It is not the case that the event remains the same while someone interprets it differently from the originator; nor is it the case that the originator has a false view of his own work. Both the event and its interpretation differ.

Sartre and the Start of Derrida's Philosophy

The indifferent "ideal presence of the ens causa sui" of Sartre becomes the irreducible difference of Derrida (797 *BN*). Figure 5-5 on page 199 shows this process of creation.

Derrida's critique of the transcendental signified is part of the critique of the metaphysics of presence. These terms, which are at the root of Derrida's critique are related and form the problem in Sartre's philosophy. Sartre's version of a transcendental signified is posited by Sartre to reconcile two other concepts, to solve a problem:

> If we wish to conceive of a synthetic organization such that the for-itself is inseparable from the in itself and conversely such that the in-itself is indissolubly bound to the for itself, we must conceive of this synthesis in such a way that the in-itself would receive its existence from the nihilation which caused there to be consciousness of it. What does this mean if not that the indissoluble totality of in-itself and for-itself is conceivable only in the form of a being which is its own "self-cause" (791 *BN*).

When Sartre writes about the bond between consciousness and things, he speaks of it as requiring "presence." Consider four passages:

> 1. "Presence cannot be in the mode of the in itself. It is the original bond to being (in itself) insofar as the For-itself is its own witness of co-existence but even the For-itself cannot know it only if the presence *already is*" (178 *BN*).

> 2. "Beings are revealed as co-present in a world where the For-itself unites them with its own blood by that total ekstatic sacrifice of the self which is called presence" (177 *BN*).

> 3. "...every process of a foundation of the self is a rupture in the identity-of-being of the in itself, a withdrawal by being in relation to itself and the

Figure 5-5: Creation as a Circumscribing Knowledge: the Total Former Thought Processes Become Represented as a New Object of Knowledge

A. *Sartre's Closing Concept Is a Thread of Continuity throughout the Development of the Philosophy*

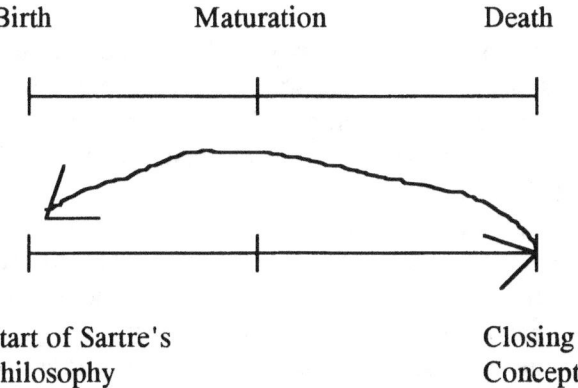

The interpretation of the first events is only final at the end, as is the case in novels.

B. *Ecphrasis: the Process of Understanding a Predecessor's Thought as a Circumscribable Whole.*

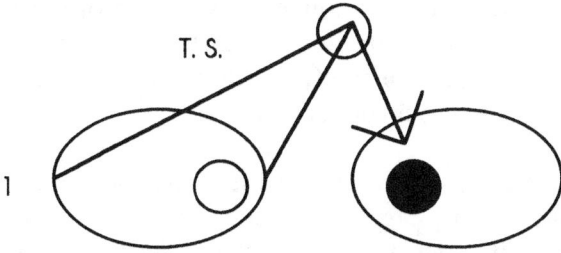

Sartre's closing concept cannot express the totality of formative processes, for it must represent the development from its origin, (#1) and thus its difference from that origin. Sartre's philosophy can only be seen as a whole according to a negative presupposition not explicitly known by Sartre: the Transcendental Signified (T.S.).

> appearance of presence to self or consciousness. It is only by making itself for-itself that being can aspire to be the cause of itself. Consciousness as the nihilation of pure being..." (788 *BN*).
>
> 4. "The For-itself is `a witness to itself of itself as *not being* that being'" (178 *BN*).

In passage one, presence "already is." Derrida often used the expression "always already"; both are ways of expressing presuppositions or a priori ideas. As one example, "...a central presence which has never been itself, has always already been exiled from itself into its own substitute" (280 *WD*).

Sartre defines "presence" as the content (or alterity) of consciousness when it emerges from things, when it is formed.

The lexical connection between Derrida and Sartre can be seen from many passages of both writers; however, in a passage by Derrida where he considers the definition of consciousness as a "for-itself," a view of consciousness as self-presence and its contents as present to it, the line of descent from Sartre becomes unmistakable. To show the interfacing of the two philosophers, the following passage of Derrida will be interpolated with the Sartrian references. Derrida writes,

> Auto-affection is a universal structure of experience. [Sartre was looking for the necessary bond of the for itself with the in itself, which bond would have to be universal throughout experience.]
>
> All living things are capable of auto-affection. And only a being capable of symbolizing, that is to say of auto-affecting, may let itself be affected by the other in general.
> ["Auto-affection" describes the bond of the for itself to the in itself which Sartre sought.]

Auto-affection is the condition of an experience in general.
[Sartre felt the bond of for itself to in itself was necessary for experience.]

This possibility--another name for "life"--is a general structure articulated by the history of life, and leading to complex and hierarchical operations. Auto-affection, the as-for-itself or for-itself--subjectivity--gains in power and in its mastery of the other to the extent that its power of repetition *idealizes itself*.
[Derrida is using Sartre's terms "for-itself" and elsewhere, before these passages, "touching-touched," which Sartre discusses in *BN*.]

Here idealization is the movement by which sensory exteriority, that which affects me or serves me as signifier, submits itself to my power of repetition, to what thenceforward appears to me as my spontaneity and escapes me less and less.
["For Sartre, "the sensory exteriority" here spoken of by Derrida is the in itself. Since this sentence of Derrida follows the one containing the words "for-itself" and "subjectivity," and since two paragraphs before this one and four later, Derrida discusses "touching-touched," it is clear that Derrida is speaking about Sartre's in-itself.] [Consciousness for Sartre was not defined initially as being exteriorized in sense data, or in other words the for itself was first defined apart from the in itself.] [Derrida's concern with the problem of writing originates in a problem of pure interiority as at the center of Sartre's definition of consciousness. Cf. 87 *OG*. This fact can be seen in the following continuation of the passage.]

One must understand speech in terms of this diagram. Its system requires that it be heard and understood immediately by whoever emits it. It produces a signifier which seems not to fall into the world, outside

the ideality of the signified, but to remain sheltered--
even at the moment that it attains the audiophonic
system of the other--within the pure interiority of
auto-affection. It does not fall into the exteriority of
space, into what one calls the world, which is nothing
but the outside of speech.
[Sartre's definition of consciousness as a "for-itself" is
not a process of acting on the sensory world, of shap-
ing it, of writing it; Sartre's for-itself pre-exists some-
how, to some extent, before what Derrida comes to
call writing.]

Within so-called "living speech, the spatial exteriority
of the signifier seems absolutely reduced.... Conversation is, then, a communication between two
absolute origins that, if one may venture the formula,
auto-affect reciprocally, repeating as immediate echo
the auto-affection produced by the other.
[The two absolute origins are the in-itself and the for-
itself. Auto-affection is appropriate for they are two
separate (absolute) origins of one human being, to be
mediated by the closing concept.]

Immediacy is here the myth of consciousness. Speech
and the consciousness of speech--that is to say consciousness simply as self-presence--are the
phenomenon of an auto-affection lived as suppression
of differance.
[Recall the passages at the end of *BN* where Sartre
describes the futility of transcendence caused by the
ens causa sui; this futility is a suppression of what
Derrida comes to call differance--unstoppable re-
signification, developement of mind.]

That *phenomena*, that presumed suppression of differance, that lived reduction of the opacity of the signifier, are the origin of what is called presence.
[Derrida emphasizes "phenomenon" as an ironic statement to say that consciousness as self-presence does

> *not* appear, is *not* a phenomenon. Note that the "opacity of the signifier" is the non-conscious, exterior nature of the in-itself, its resistance to consciousnes or pre-conscious alterity. Note also that "the origin of presence" as a problem can be traced to Sartre's philosophy.]
>
> That which is not subjected to the process of differance is *present*. The present is that from which we believe we are able to think time, effacing the inverse necessity: to think the present from time as differance (165-166 *OG*).

Derrida criticizes the idea of the in-itself-for-itself for being a pure inside or mental content, which cannot exist:

> Since the trace is the intimate relation of the living present with its outside, the openness upon exteriority in general, upon the sphere of what is not "one's own," etc., *the temporalization of sense is, from the outset, a "spacing."* As soon as we admit spacing both as "interval" or difference and as openness upon the outside, there can no longer be any absolute inside, for the "outside" has insinuated itself into the movement by which the inside of the nonspatial, which is called "time," appears, is constituted, is "presented" (86 *SP*).

This passage suggests why difference must be inscribed in sense, and why Derrida became interested in writing: because "the `outside' has insinuated itself" into any movement of mind. The "trace" mentioned in this passage is an early synonym for difference; it represents the sliding in meaning from Sartre's ideal presence of the ens causa sui to difference.

Difference is a concept that describes Derrida's new objects of thought but that also describes what Sartre's concepts were inadequately. In this way difference is universal ("before" Derrida) and capable of allowing for a change in concepts from Sartre's, since they are "different." "A text always gives itself a representation of its own roots; *and* those roots live only by that representation" (101 *OG*). "A text must retain a mark of what it lost or put aside" (156 *SP*). Putting something aside is called "erasure" and retaining a mark is called forming a trace; these two ideas are illustrated in Figure 5-6 on page 205.

"Difference" is a criticism not only of the end of Sartre's philosophy but also of the beginning. If Derrida changes the entire tradition of philosophy, and this tradition goes back long before Sartre, then the change would also affect the start of Sartre's philosophy. This point is made because often scholars believe a criticism applies to the last concepts or only to some concepts. The change Derrida brings about is not partial--it is a wholistic change. Another way to think of this idea is to remember the perspective drawing in which all lines emanate from one outside the drawing-- even the first lines, or the farthest from the edge of the perspective's frame. Paradoxes close philosophies, yet with Derrida's new principle of difference even the beginning of Sartre's philosophy is paradoxical. This does not mean no progress was made; it means concepts are bound to cycles, and successors can comprehend the principle of all that went before. Campbell explains the existence of paradoxes at both the end *and* the start of myths:

> Herein lies the basic paradox of myth: the paradox of the dual focus. Just as at the opening of the cosmogonic cycle it was possible to say "God is not involved," but at the same time "God is creator-preserver-destroyer," so now at this critical juncture, where the One breaks into the many, destiny "happens," but at the same time "is brought about." (288 *Hero*).

This idea that the beginning of a philosophy is also paradoxical is consistent with Bloom's idea that a successor changes the way his/her predecessor relates to the one before; the predecessor by his/her own estimate was superior to the ones before, but now (s)he belongs in a series with them. Campbell's statement applies especially clearly to early myths leading to philosophy--from the Babylonian myth of creation to Homer's and to Hesiod's and to Pherecydes of Syros' and then to Thales'.

Figure 5-6: The Idea of Difference Is Related to Sartre's Closing Concept by Derrida's Ideas of Trace and Erasure

A. Erasure as the Change of Sartre's Closing Concept

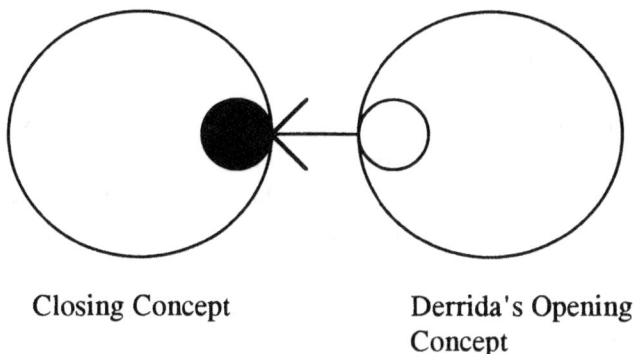

Closing Concept   Derrida's Opening Concept

Erasure is the arrow from the solid circle to the open one before it; it signifies the change in the concept before it.

B. The Trace Represents Derrida's Need to Explain How Concepts before and after His Difference Must Also Be Differences

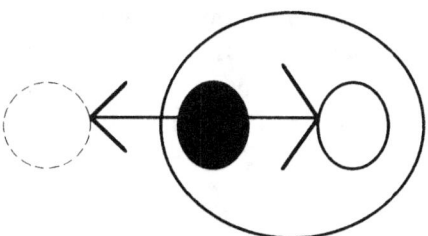

Derrida's own difference must itself undergo erasure. Each concept has a positive determinate meaning as a trace of what came before it. Therefore, the idea of difference explains its own change from Sartre's closing concept and its common identity as an object of knowledge. In a sense, erasure defines a negative relation between two differences, while the trace defines the positive continuity.

Sartre's Problem of the Transcendental Signified

Sartre's assumption of the transcendental signified is evident in his idea of the ideal fusion of the in-itself-for-itself sometimes called the *ens causa sui* (267 *BN*).

The unsatisfactory dynamic of signification within Sartre's *ens causa sui* is noticed by Derrida; Sartre also felt dissatisfied with the futility of transcendence (797 *BN*):

> There has to be a transcendental signified for the difference between signifier and signified to be somewhere absolute and irreducible. It is not by chance that the thought of being, as the thought of the transcendental signified, is manifested above all in the voice: in a language of words [*mots*]. The voice *is heard* (understood)--that undoubtedly is what is called conscience--closest to the self as the absolute effacement of the signifier: pure auto-affection that necessarily has the form of time and which does not borrow from outside of itself, in the world or in "reality," any accessory signifier, any substance of expression foreign to its own spontaneity. It is the unique experience of the signified producing itself spontaneously, from within the self, and nevertheless, as signified concept, in the element of ideality or universality. The unworldly character of this substance of expression is constitutive of this ideality" (20 *OG*).

The New Principle of Philosophy: Difference

"Difference" rids philosophy of the transcendental signified and starts philosophy anew.

Just as poetry for Bloom was a quest always referring back to its origin when developing, so too Derrida sees philosophy as developing in relation to its origin: the irrepressible desire of philosophy is "to summarize-interiorize-dialecticize-master-*relever* the metaphoric division between the origin and itself, the Oriental difference" (269 *MP*).

Reason for This Specific New Principle

This specific new principle is needed to save the unity of experience, the continuity of the tradition, and the consistency of philosophy.

Perhaps the primary argument of Derrida against Sartre is the following one. (Recall that on 178 *BN* Sartre states the for-itself is self-alienated as witness.)

> What is intolerable and fascinating is indeed the intimacy intertwining image and thing, graph, i.e., and phonè, to the point where by a mirroring, inverting, and perverting effect, speech seems in its turn the speculum of writing, which "manages to usurp the main role. Representation mingles with what it represents, to the point where one speaks as one writes, one thinks as if the represented were nothing more than the shadow or reflection of the representer. A dangerous promiscuity and a nefarious complicity between the reflection and the reflected which lets itself be seduced narcissistically. [Sartre used the terms for reflection on 267 *BN*.] In this play of representation, the point of origin becomes ungraspable. There are things like reflecting pools, and images, an infinite reference from one to the other, but no longer a source, a spring. There is no longer a simple origin. For what is reflected is split in itself and not only as an addition to itself of its image. The reflection, the image, the double, splits what it doubles. The origin of the speculation becomes a difference. What can look at itself is not one; and the law of the addition of the origin to its representation, of the thing to its image, is that one plus one makes at least three. The historical usurpation and theoretical oddity that install the image within the rights of reality are determined as the *forgetting* of a simple origin (36 *OG*).

This statement "the origin of the speculation becomes a difference states the origin of Derrida's idea of difference which begins his new philosophy in contrast to the previous tradition of the metaphysics of presence.

Actually in this passage Derrida is redefining the Sartrian idea of consciousness. "To be split" in itself means to Sartre to be a part in both halves (in itself, for itself), and Sartre thinks a new unity is needed. Derrida thinks this "split" is not a bifurcation--if we rethink and redefine the subject as necessarily inscribing itself in sense, and the percept as having difference (alterity, particularity in a context) and being partially defined as a negation of a past and capable of being negated: it is a trace; it originates through erasure and evanesces by the same process. Derridean auto-affection describes how the signifier is already in the signified, or how the Sartrian for itself could observe itself without experiencing internecine conflict or alienation. As Sartre believed, the for-itself is `a witness to itself of itself as *not being* that being' (178 *BN*).

More explicitly, Derrida states his redefinition of consciousness:

> This determination of `absolute subjectivity' would also have to be crossed out as soon as we conceive the present on the basis of difference, and not the reverse. The concept of *subjectivity* belongs *a priori and in general* to the order of the *constituted* (84 *SP*).

This statement indicates a unity of the for-itself and in-itself that Sartre did not conceive, insofar as the placement of subjectivity in the order of the constituted is the redefinition of the for-itself and the in-itself.

Derrida's idea of difference is a redefinition of Sartre's fusion of the in-itself-for-itself. The idea of difference as the new content of knowledge cannot be understood apart from the trace (the reference to the past) and the system of differences.

> The instituted trace cannot be thought without thinking the retention of difference within a structure of reference where difference appears as such and thus *permits a certain liberty of variations among the full terms*. The absence of another here-and-now, of

another transcendental present, of another origin of the world appearing as such, presenting itself as irreducible absence within the presence of the trace, is not a metaphysical formula substituted for a scientific concept of writing (46 *OG*).

The necessity of writing results from an integration of Sartre's for-itself with the in itself: "If the trace, arche-phenomenon of `memory'...belongs to the very movement of signification, then signification *is a priori written*, whether inscribed or not, in one form or another, in a `sensible' and `spatial' element that is called `exterior'" (70 *OG*).

Derrida's "difference" is an internalization of Sartre's manner of producing objects of knowledge. Sartre's doubling, splitting of the in itself through reflection has a positive redefinition as not what happens to a content of experience but rather what it is. The process of mind is postulated by integration into a new object--difference--which serves as the originating source of Sartre's whole theory of knowledge.

How Derrida's Start Compares to Bloom's

There are many similarities between Bloom's idea of the start of a poetry and Derrida's idea of the start of his philosophy. Figures 5-7, on page 210, and 5-8, on page 211, show two very important ones: *isonomy*--the process of forming a new idea such that the predecessor's ideas can be seen to belong as an equal member in a universal series; and *accumulation*--the function of each new stage in a cultural work to try to accumulate the entire tradition before it. I say "try" because only the last stage can accumulate the tradition with sufficient success to have formed the minimum structural requirements for any step in tradition. Both similarities are recursive, looking at their past forms, and cultural forms have a future reference, which will be discussed in the chapters on the ends of science, poetry, and philosophy. The fact that creation can occur only if there is this recursion suggests that a cultural form evolves out of previous ones; it is about itself; it is performative, not just discursive.

Figure 5-7: Tradition Takes One Step Forward by Isonomizing the One before It, Or by Finding a New Universal Principle of Ordering Tradition

A. *A Representation of the Change in the Philosophic Tradition by Isonomy*

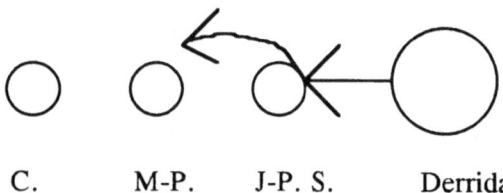

B. *A Representation of the Change in the Poetic Tradition by Isonomy*

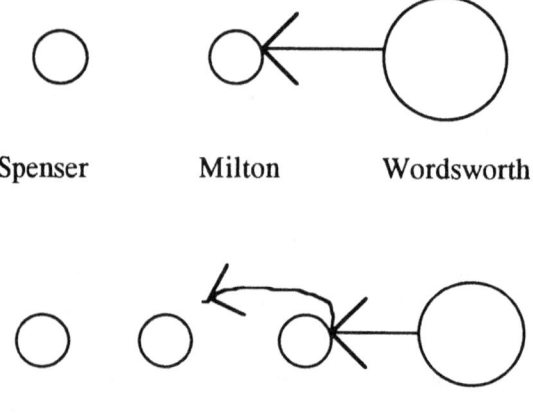

Figure 5-8: Not Only Does Each New Whole Step in Tradition Re-define the Totality of What Went before, But Also Each Major Stage in a Cultural Work Is a New Stance toward the Past

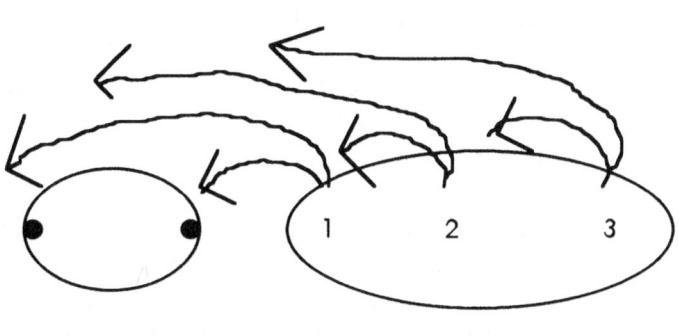

Sartre's Philosophy   Derrida's

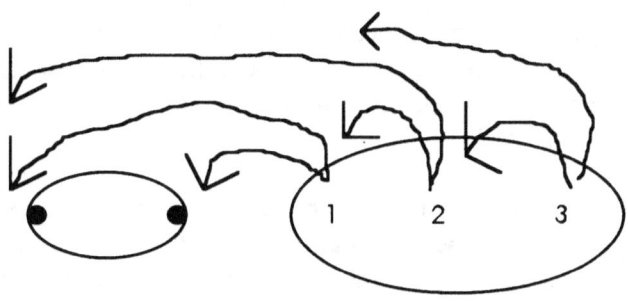

Wordsworth's Poetry   Shelley's

"Difference" is more defined than Bloom's "clinamen." Whereas Bloom's account of the start of a poetry does not explain *why* the change occurred, Derrida's start gives reasons. In Bloom's account one cannot see the normative decision of the creator, other than the general answer, the same in every case, that a poet wants to make way for himself/herself. Extending the domain of the play of signification infinitely (280 *WD*) by ridding philosophy of the transcendental signified, Derrida shows how there can be an increase in consciousness, a strengthening of it--not shown by Bloom.

That a new literary work begins by a broadening of consciousness was noticed by Todorov (and Bakhtin). The broadening is an accumulation of previous knowledge:

> For some time James followed in Flaubert's wake; when we mentioned his "exercises" it was to evoke precisely those texts in which he perfects the use of synecdoche (we find such pages to the end of his life.) But in the tales which concern us here, James has gone a step further: he has become conscious of Flaubert's sensationalism (or anti-essentialism), and instead of simply employing it as a means, he has made it the constructive principle of his *oeuvre*. We can see only appearances, and their interpretation remains suspect; only the pursuit of the truth... (151 *Poetics of Prose*).

The entire previous form or type of producing concepts becomes represented as an element, though changed, that can be used to extend the cultural activity. The represented whole of the previous formative activities helps to generate further objects of knowledge.

Bloom defines the start of a poetry more in terms of the individual poet than the continuum of poetry. Kuhn defines the start of a science in terms of the community of researchers, but the (Derridean) concern with a continuum is more based on the relations of ideas than the relations of people, and so the discussion can include proof for the change of ideas. Bloom defines the injustice of the precursor poet; namely, not allowing a successor though having been one. He does not define what the unity of poetry was and what it became, as Derrida did in the definition of the transcendental signified.

A "crisis" in Kuhn's terms is described by Bloom, yet a poetic paradox is lacking. The change in poetries should be clarified until a decision point is clear, albeit an aesthetic one. Certainly, one must have been successfully considered by the new great poet. For all Bloom's original ideas, nothing comparable occurs in his works. Bloom's approach can be improved to become more explanatory if the emphasis is placed on the tradition above individuals. After all, literature is a process of "tradition forming," and this requires a sense of the poet before one's precursor by a "grandfather clause" (14-15 *Novel Epics*). Bloom argues quite rightly that a creator does so by reinterpreting concepts so that the precursor can be serialized on an equal basis with the poets before. A new universal start of poetry is found. Although Bloom emphasizes the individual's will to become an influence, the emphasis would be better placed on the continued unity of poetic activity. The new poetry largely results as a fairly determined function of the state of poetry a poet-to-be encounters. Making an analogy to the replication of DNA, the new DNA cannot but have in common the general functioning of the parent DNA. A human being comes from a human being, though each one has its absolutely unique genetic code making a living thing with similar general structure or processes.

In Bloom's theory the reason for the change of poetries is unsatisfactory. Describing the transition from one science to another, Cassirer makes clear that the reasons for the change are to preserve unity:

> The true goal of science is not mechanism but unity--as Henri Poincaré once formulated the guiding maxim of modern physics. But concerning this unity the physicist does not need to ask *whether* it is, but merely *how* it is; i.e., what is the minimum of presuppositions that are necessary and sufficient to provide an exact exposition of the totality of experience and its systematic connection. In order to maintain this unity, which seemed endangered by the conflict of the principle of the constancy of the velocity of light and the principle of relativity of mechanics, and to ground it more deeply and securely, the theory of relativity renounces the unity of the values of spatial and

> temporal magnitudes in different systems. It surrenders the assumption that... . But these "relativizations" are not in contradiction with the doctrine of the constancy and unity of nature; they are rather demanded and worked out in the name of this very unity... But above all it is the general form of natural law which we have to recognize as the real invariant and thus as the real logical framework of nature in general (373-74 *ETR*).

Bloom did not specify *how* the unity of poetry was threatened--only *that* it was, while here the unity of physics is threatened by a conflict of principles. In poetry, it would not be a conflict of principles exactly--more like two opposing ways of producing poetic images. Here an aesthetic assumption must be surrendered if the conflict is to be eliminated and unity restored. Bloom does not tell his readers what is surrendered in poetic transitions, partly because his overall goal is to build a model invariant in the evolving series of poetries.

In the theory of the anxiety of influence, poetry does make for itself a whole universal vision. The entire development of a poetry moves toward restoring this wholeness. The same is claimed for science by Cassirer, except more determinately.[3] The decision itself becomes clear, as does the increase in value. Einstein expresses the same view, yet can define the different senses of the continuum whereas Bloom cannot for poetry: "The theory of relativity arises from the field problems. The contradiction and inconsistencies of the old theories force us to ascribe new properties to the time-space continuum, to the scene of all events in our physical world" (244). The level of discussion by Bloom is never so specific that a reader could say, `in Shelley's poetry the unity of poetry was defined in this way as superior to the definition given by Wordsworth, which is...' . The meaning of the poetic continuum changes with each great poet. By "continuum" I mean the unity of one's tradition, as Einstein was able to define and re-define it for physics. A degree of specificity of meaning remains unaccounted for in the theory of the anxiety of influence.

Continuing this point about specific explanation, Bloom *states* that a poet misreads the precursor by placing him/her equally in the series of poets; however, Bloom does not *show* what the revision of the origin and the end of the precursor's poetry is. He thinks his ratios can comprehend the origin and end, whereas they can only be comprehended by the poet's own specific figures, the specific relations of which need to be explained more. Therefore, the poet's passages explain the start of a new poetry more specifically than Bloom can. Though he cites them to explain his theory, he does not explain them as unique poetic acts of raising the level of poetry as it had never been done quite the same before. Bloom's ideas are not wrong; they are just not as full an explanation as possible, even for criticism. Derrida's philosophy in the explanation of its own origin shows what is lacking in Bloom's theory.

"Difference" should be contrasted with "clinamen or swerve." In clinamen an upcoming poet *intentionally* interprets the precursor in a new way. In "difference" the upcoming philosopher *necessarily* re-interprets the starting point of philosophy to preserve its unity. To see the contrast, consider Derrida's idea that a new concept cannot be "included in a previous regime" (42 *POS*). In a way for Bloom there is an overlap between regimes of poetry insofar as the precursor's poetic legitimacy seems to remain for the successor whose own poetry is a "misreading." The critic, too, allows the legitimacy of the precursor to remain, for he does not indulge in the idealization of superiority that a successor engages in. In a definite sense all canonical poetries are equally poetic in Bloom's view. The sense that tradition is like an ever-ascending staircase of increased value is missing.

To claim that a transition from one tradition form to another results in a broadening of consciousness and a preservation of the unity of the field does not explain progress entirely. The intension of any field is more important than its extension or broadening. On Cassirer's view it is not the most important factor in creation to have an extremely wide range of knowledge. What is important is "how clearly and genuinely the idea of his science [the scientist's] and of truth manifests itself in his work": what is important is "the intension" of concepts.[4] The intension corresponds to the meaning of a law, and the intension is more important than the extension because the generating principle of knowledge is in the former: "The meaning of the *law* that connects the individual members is not to be exhausted by the enumeration of any number of instances of the law; for such enumeration lacks the generating *principle* that enables us to connect the individual members into a functional whole" (26 *SF*).

Derrida's "Intervention" and Bloom's "Misreading" or "Misprision"

Derrida's View Is Less Empirical Than Bloom's

The past can change more completely for Derrida than it can for Bloom; the interpretation of the past is not deficient, but the past is. Bloom believes the successor attributes to the precursor a pseudo-deficiency; the successor's belief in having a better poetry is idealized prejudice.

Bloom's view and also Kuhn's are more empirical than Derrida's. "Empirical" means pertaining to objects in space and time; "a priori" means something known before gathering data through the senses. Cassirer defines it in this way: "A cognition is called a priori not in any sense as if it were *prior* to experience, but because and in so far as it is contained as *a necessary premise* in every valid judgment concerning facts (269 *ETR*).

Kuhn often speaks of a permanent body of knowledge being built up through science. The accumulation, however, is not in the quantity of concepts making any science; it is in the power of the science. Bloom does not speak of the accumulation of poetry as a quantitative increase, nor does he speak of it as an increase in power (sometimes of "inwardness"). According to Bloom's concept of *misreading* the precursor retains some criterion of poetic vision not falsifiable or surpassable by the successor and discovered by the critic.

Derrida's view of the change in philosophical tradition differs. He establishes the criterion of the past philosophies' validity. The past philosophies acquire their most validity if interpreted through Derrida's "difference." The same type of developed superiority was described by Cassirer to apply to Einstein's revolutionary theory. Einstein found a "truly universal principle," "a heuristic maxim of investigation in general...which claims to contain a criterion of the validity of all particular...theories" (368-379 *ETR*). The new great poet in Bloom's theory cannot develop "a truly universal principle" if the past poetry retains some of its right to aesthetic excellence unchanged. Bloom does give a sense of a heuristic maxim insofar as the new poet finds a way to begin poetry anew, from founding initial principle to complete poetry.

Derrida achieves the superior or prior criterion by a synthesis of previous modes of producing philosophical concepts; namely, contrary modes of Sartre's in-itself-for-itself. The synthesis is more than Bloom's "misreading," for it is a making. Derrida quotes Kant to express the necessity of original synthesis in understanding what has been written already:

> For he discovered that he must not follow the trace of what he saw in the figure or in the bare concept of that same figure. Rather he must beget (*hervorbringen*) (its object) with the help of what he himself put into it and what *a priori* was represented in it through the concept (through construction). And to know something *a priori* with complete security, he must attribute to things (*Sache*) nothing but what necessarily followed from what he had put there himself in accordance with his concept.[5]

Any a priori concept constructs the concepts before it, reveals the principle of their production. Directly related to Sartre, Derrida argues for the priority of his concepts, "This determination of `absolute subjectivity' would also have to be crossed out as soon as we conceive the present on the basis of difference, and not the reverse. The concept of *subjectivity* belongs *a priori and in general* to the order of the *constituted*" (84 *SP*). Sartre's concepts depend upon Derrida's.

In a definite sense the validity of Sartre's concepts comes from Derrida's new concept. In Derrida's words, "The trace is not only the disappearance of origin--within the discourse that we sustain and according to the path that we follow it means that the origin did not even disappear, that it was never constituted except reciprocally by a nonorigin, a trace, which thus becomes the origin of the origin" (61 *OG*). Here can be seen Derrida's deriving Sartre's concepts from his own, showing a presupposition of their coherence. Derrida found an origin to the different constitutive acts in Sartre's concepts. Those concepts are then "erased" or do not subsist in the new philosophy. Only if transformed can they be thought of as being incorporated into the new philosophy: "Since `past' has always signified present-past, the absolute past that is retained in the trace no longer rigorously merits the name `past'. Another name to erase, especially since the strange movement of the trace proclaims as much as it recalls" (66 *OG*). Since Derrida is uncovering an illusion, he can say that there is a "loss of what has never taken place, of a self-presence which has never been given but only dreamed of and always already split, repeated, incapable of appearing to itself except in its own disappearance" (112 *OG*). In contrast, for Bloom (and for Kuhn) not only has the past taken place but it also can be recovered by the critic without the idealization of the successor treating the preceding poetry as deficient.

Uuderstanding, Not Merely Asserting, The Reorientation of Mind

Derrida describes the process during the change of reorientation, whereas for Bloom misreading is less analyzable into stages.

Whereas Kuhn understands the start of a science through a gestalt switch, and Bloom understands the poetic start through a strategy called "clinamen," Derrida understands the process in philosophy in all its stages. "Misprision" for Bloom is not analysed into its stages.

The stages are indicated by Derrida's idea of *bricolage*, which he adapted from Lévi-Strauss:

> The *bricoleur*, says Lévi-Strauss, is someone who uses "the means at hand," that is, the instruments he finds at his disposition around him, those which are already there, which had not been especially conceived with an eye to the operation for which they are to be used and to which one tries by trial and error to adapt them, not hesitating to change them whenever it appears necessary, or to try several at once...the analysis of *bricolage* could "be applied almost word for word" to criticism [words of Lévi-Strauss], and especially to "literary criticism."
>
> If one calls *bricolage* the necessity of borrowing one's concepts from the text of a heritage which is more or less coherent or ruined, it must be said that

> every discourse is *bricoleur*. The engineer, whom Lévi-Strauss opposes to the *bricoleur*, should be the one to construct the totality of his language, syntax, and lexicon. In this sense the engineer is a myth. A subject who supposedly would be the absolute origin of his own discourse and supposedly would construct it "out of nothing," "out of whole cloth," would be the creator of the verb, the verb itself (286 *WD*).

The necessity of borrowing one's concepts means they are arrived at by transforming the predecessor's. The trial-and-error, piecemeal method of making meaningful connections leads to a new origin or ground of concepts. I think the process is like that of being in a city, going around, from place to place, and gradually realizing new connections between previously known sites. The new connections change the sense of perspective in which all have a share. The result for the person is a greater operability in the city, more ability to find one's way.

The meaning of *bricolage* can be understood through a scientific example. Scientists use models to represent the ideas they are trying to form. The scientific imagination is aided by the play of these forms. The forms themselves suggest new combinations, one by one, whereas the "engineer" believes the new theory occurs in one stroke. A great contributor to the understanding of DNA, Watson wrote this about *bricolage* in genetics:

> These possibilities [of relating two chains of the DNA molecule] can be differentiated by building models. We find that we can build models of one chain with a rotation of approximately 40 degrees per residue but that it is difficult, if not impossible, with a rotation of only 20 degrees. The van der Waals contacts in this latter case are much too close, and it appears probable that no structure of this type can exist. It, therefore, seems probable that each chain is in a nearly fully extended condition and makes one revolution every 34 A. It should be noted that this argument rules out the possibility that the two intertwined chains are related

> by a diad parallel to the fibre axis, for if true, the fibre axis repeat would be halved to 17 A (281).
>
> [and]
> When models employing this pairing arrangement are built, several additional structural features become apparent. In the first place, we find by trial that the model can only be built in the right-handed sense (282-83).

Much can be said about Derrida's *bricolage* in relation to Kuhn's work and Bloom's. Kuhn's "gestalt switch" merely names a wholistic change, and it is a change supposedly applying to all the sciences. This view is not wrong, just undeveloped. While more specific, Bloom's "misreading" does not apply to a specific transition of poetries. Then the need for explaining how the successor reacts to the predecessor's concepts can be more general. Immediately, if clinamen is defined in terms of two actual poets, there is the need to be more specific about the changes. Whenever Bloom discusses two actual poets in detail--and this is a big advance on Kuhn, the idea of clinamen or any ratio was already defined. The discussion only serves to illustrate the general notion applying in the same way to all such transitions.

In Derrida's case, "difference" arises from a reaction to Sartre's concepts (and the whole tradition). Due to the understanding of the idea through an actual specific case, the reasons for the change in concepts, the stages of development, can be defined.

The contrast between a *bricoleur* and an engineer (one who invents the totality of a discourse) shows a major difference between Derrida and Kuhn and Bloom. By inventing the totality of a discourse the engineer would be comparable to a wolf child inventing a whole human language. But this is not possible, as Susanne Langer asserts, "...Victor and Wild Peter did not invent language, and were nearly, if not entirely, past the hope of acquiring it when they were socialized" (125). In a way Kuhn and Bloom believe they can be engineers and invent the whole of their disciplines. Bloom's map of misreading is regarded as a whole of poetic tradition that is in some sense greater than that found in any one poetry, for it provides a model supposedly surviving the transitions from poetry to poetry and thus explaining the processes that the poets undergo. Not entirely but partially, the critic regards himself as gaining a mastery of the creative processes. To this extent, Kuhn and Bloom are engineers. To be bricoleurs, they would have to produce new concepts in a science and in poetry, respectively. Even though they do not attempt this, and so one could say that any criticism to this effect is unjust, the comparison with Derrida shows the greater degree of explanation of tradition.

One consequence of *bricolage is that a philosopher, scientist, or poet cannot understand the immediate precursor's work fully until a new creation is complete. Some creation occurs before the "final" re-envisionment of the predecessor's concepts. Bloom's view rates better than Kuhn's, for Bloom's whole theory emphasizes the constant reacting of a successor to the predecessor at each main stage of a poetry. Kuhn tends to regard it as an almost instantaneous interpretation of the whole previous science, to the extent that all terms describing the process are wholistic ones like "gestalt switch," which are not accomplished progressively through changes in perspective. Bloom's view does claim that the end of a poetry has a relation to the end of the previous poetry. Derrida's view, however, shows more the specific connection between tradition forms, as we shall see when the ends of the forms are discussed.*

Derrida's alternative to Bloom's "misreading" defines a transformation of the precursor's concepts. "...I [Derrida] try to respect as rigorously as possible the internal, regulated play of philosophemes or epistimemes by making them slide--without mistreating [*misreading*] them--to the point of their nonpertinence, their exhaustion, their closure" (6 *Pos*). "Sliding" suggests a continuation of the development already begun; this evolutionary sense of reinterpretation for a better view, not misinterpretation, is missing from Kuhn's and Bloom's theories. Sliding the concepts makes them malleable, as when Emerson writes, "Let the breath of new life be breathed by you through the forms already existing. For, if once you are alive, you shall find they become plastic and new" (955 "Divinity School Address," *Norton Anthology*). In *Edmund Husserl's `Origin of Geometry': An Introduction* Derrida elaborates this idea of *sliding* the meaning without mistreating (i.e. misreading) as a means of continuing while extending concepts when he discusses the infinitization or maximization or universalization of philosophical concepts to all possible objects. Derrida states, "...Husserl is interested in infinitization... . That is why he *reduced* all the a priori systems of past or present geometry, in order to reach back and grasp again the origin of aprioriness itself at its source, i.e. the institutive infinitization" (128 *OR*). In a similar way, each second ratio of Bloom's extends the former to its maximum or infinite or universal domain; tessera extends clinamen, daemonization extends kenosis, and apophrades extends askesis.

Transference of the Pattern

Derrida can explain how the pattern of tradition, like a cultural genetic code, is transferred.

Derrida's Positive Interpretation of the End of a Tradition Form

Whereas Bloom regarded the end of a poetry almost exclusively as negative for the successor, Derrida shows the need for tradition forms, for philosophies, to supply all that is needed to create.

Philosophy must resemble the genetic code at least insofar as its general pattern is transferred from one form to the next. "Something of what precedes must be transmitted to what follows, that the whole may form a concinnity (skillful congruity) and may be truly one" (210 *OG*).

The end to the transcendental signified means that any signified content is not transcendental but can in turn become a signifier, leading to the extension of signification infinitely. The new founding concept of Derrida must have been derived through some transformation from the transcendental signified it criticizes. "A signifier is from the very beginning the possibility of its own repetition, of its own image or resemblance. It is the condition of its ideality, what identifies it as signifier, and makes it function as such, relating it to a signified which for the same reasons, could never be a `unique and singular reality'" (91 *OG*).

When Bloom discusses the re-building of the six ratios in a new poetry, each ratio is fundamentally ambivalent (or dialectical), defining a relation to one's precursor and to one's possible successor. In this way the pattern of the precursor is transferred in six steps of measuring one's poetic sense with the precursor. Equally important, the way is prepared for a successor; a whole structure will be made from which replication can again occur through the six ratios. Jean-Joseph Goux interprets Derrida's grapheme or fundamental unit of knowledge as a "chromosome" ("Du graphème au chromosome").

Derrida claims the end of any text--science, literature, philosophy, or other--retains "at least the schema, if not the content, of the demand..." (141 *SP*). The solution to the paradox left by the preceding philosopher requires a repetition of the whole structure. The solution criticizes the paradoxical concepts while having the general form of that which it criticizes (286 *WD*). In this way, the transference of the schema of philosophy compares to the replication of chains within DNA.

The end of a philosophy prepares the way for a new start, according to Derrida:

> ...there must already be a certain element of play, a certain remove, a certain degree of independence with regard to the origin, to production, or to intention in all of its `vital', `simple' `actuality' or `determinateness', etc. For if this were not so, the `break' (with all its consequences, variables, etc.) would be impossible. And if a certain `break' is always possible, that with which it breaks must necessarily bear the mark of this possibility inscribed in its structure (64 *Lim*).

The ending paradox of a philosophy bears the mark of a possible break inscribed in its structure. A successor must see how this possibility is inscribed, a process neither deductive nor inductive.

Sliding was mentioned as a process of transforming concepts, but it is also a process within the development of one concept. Each one tends toward its own surpassing, each signified leads to a further signifier. "The field of the entity, before being determined as the field of presence, is structured according to the diverse possibilities-- genetic and structural--of the trace. The presentation of the other as such that is to say the dissimulation of its "as such," has always begun and no structure of the entity escapes it" (47 *OG*).

The Self-perpetuating Nature of Tradition

New relations of ideas are possible because the elements left by the precursor "implicitly contain" or "require as their solution" new combinatory possibilities. One can come to see them if one remembers the past exigencies of philosophical form and readapts them to the new situation.

A child learning language does not study grammar formally; it receives bits of language from a parent and, because these bits have grammatical laws implicitly in them, the child is able to form new combinations of words to the surprise and the delight of its parents. Applied to Bloom this example suggests that a formal model is not essential for creation; a complete set of instructions may never be obtainable or adequate, requiring the imaginative free play of the materials at hand in the predecessor's work. Of course, the analogy breaks down at some point; namely, the child forms new combinations of words, not an entire new language from a previous one--a situation more parallel to creating a new science or poetry or philosophy, but still not the same as inventing an entirely new cultural field without precedent. The child does not invent language, for this system evolved through the millenia, being a community product.

The elements of any cultural field, according to Derrida, contain some of the power of production. They are in a sense fertile if their meaning is determined fully enough.

> Numbers are caught in a mathematicogenetic theory of groups. If this in itself were intended to mean something, it would be that there is nothing prior to the group, no simple originary unity prior to this division through which life comes to see itself and the seed is multiplied from the start; nothing comes before the addition in which the seed begins by taking itself away...(304 *DS*).

In general this passage almost describes creation as a process appearing to a creator, not a matter of arbitrary or individual choice. It is almost as if the ideas of the predecessor have an energy of their own, moving of their own accord in ways not entirely determinable by the predecessor. The image of millions of swimming, hurrying sperms, each going its way comes to mind.

The passage can help to clarify the differences between Bloom's and Derrida's views. In contrast to Derrida, Bloom tries to find a "simple originary unity" when he formulates the map of misreading, for the map is not itself subject to the forces of change in the poetries it describes. The words "the seed is multiplied from the start" indicate the transference of the philosophical schema by energies or directions already forming, like the frantic self-directed movement of the sperms. No complete model of the structure of a philosophy could be adequate, for it is a new model anyway that is made, not another version of the same former model. In any living thing there can be a change in the DNA such that the whole of it differs, no matter how slightly, and still the offspring belongs in the species, looking in general like the others. No living thing in fact has exactly the same DNA as other members of its species.

Such specific differences between generations are necessary to understand creation thoroughly. Creation can occur if the concepts undergoing *bricolage* contain some of the direction, power or laws of subsequent production. Unlike Bloom's theory, Derrida realizes at the deepest level of interpretation that the transition from one philosophy to another cannot be known by the same rules throughout history; each transition is unique. Bloom's map of misreading is useful so far as it goes, yet it could never provide the specific determination explaining one unique transition. It is true the transition may be understood by the creator, and this understanding forms an integral part of the new philosophy, but the successor of this creator, or this third generation, will have yet a new understanding of how (s)he originates philosophy.

The repetition of the schema in philosophy occurs with some generalization of the previous concepts. Kuhn asserted that the theory of general relativity included Newtonian mechanics as a limited domain. Derrida extends this idea by pointing out the explicit parallelism between the new start of a philosophy and the start of the former one: Since method is `first known in the sciences', the philosopher who marks out a trail is the one who repeats (by generalizing) the fact of an earlier rupture, which both transposes and extends that fact. Thus Locke inaugurates--but *after* Bacon and Newton. Condillac inaugurates *after* Locke. ...How could Locke carve out a trail while contenting himself to develop, indeed repeat, an earlier rupture?" (42-43 *AF*) Derrida is suggesting that a philosopher making a new start has a sense of the way his predecessor made a start, and that the new start refers to the earlier one ("rupture") in a general way. The reference helps Derrida to form the idea of difference and is not merely auxillary. Changing the immediate predecessor's idea of his/her origin of philosophy partially constitutes a new origin.

There is a reason why the transference of the genetic code of philosophy or any field can occur. Each field seeks a new self-definition. Each field begins by attempting to understand the work already done, and this determination of meaning leads to its own criticism and extension. Ironically, the paradox or logical obstacle set by a philosophy for any successor arranges for the reproduction of its total form. The structure of a philosophy interlocks with what occurs before and what will occur by processes like replication.

A clear explanation of (Derrida's) idea of a tradition form is that of Jean-François Lyotard: "...the rule of the philosopher's discourse has always been to find the rule of his/her own discourse. The philosopher is thus someone who speaks in order to find the rule of what (s)he wishes to say, and who by virtue of that fact speaks before knowing the rule, and without knowing it" (xv *Lyotard Reader*). A successor seeks the rule(s) of the predecessor's philosophy: a new rule results. This view can help to explain how any cultural field is transmitted through cycles, which then form a continuous, regenerating series. Perhaps the ultimate purpose of cultural forms is to bring themselves into being, serving as modes of common orientation for individuals, making them be members of a common tradition. And so civilization can form.

The Chain or System of Differences

Just as Bloom thought that great poets extend their new creative principles to try to make them complete a lost whole poetic form, a lost continuum of poetry in which individuals arise, Derrida believes it is necessary for any difference to belong to a system or chain.

In Bloom's theory there is a development within the first pair of ratios, from clinamen to tessera. The development corresponds to

Derrida's extension of the concepts of trace and difference to a chain or system of differences.

> The first consequence to be drawn from this is that the signified concept is never present in itself, in an adequate presence that would refer only to itself. Every concept is necessarily and essentially inscribed in a chain or a system, within which it refers to another and to other concepts, but the systematic play of differences. Such a play, then---differance--is not longer simply a concept, but the possibility of conceptuality, of the conceptual system and process in general (140 SP).

Here the extension of Derrida's alternative to a presence, i.e. trace or difference, leads to a system or chain of differences. In this extension the idea of difference is infinitized or maximized, in the sense Derrida discussed in *Edmund Husserl's `Origin of Geometry'*; in other words, the idea of difference is made to apply to everything as a mode of knowledge or a new building block. The same operation, though in a clearer way, will lead from the system of differences to a concept more distinctly on a higher level of signification: differance, with an `a'. The reason for the infinitization comes as a result of the need to explain the precursor's concept, which was a faulty idea of the process of gaining philosophical knowledge because it did not allow there to be further significant development. Notice in the passage Derrida refers to the "process" of conceptualizing as part of what needs to be determined. The predecessor left the problem of defining the process of philosophy such that there could be further development, or stated synchronically the problem of an interrelated whole of philosophy containing the creator *and* a new successor. Derrida describes the goal of building a system of thought that is all-inclusive, or has no outside: "The absolute parousia of the literal meaning, as the presence to the self of the logos within its voice, in the absolute hearing-itself-speak, should be situated as a function responding to an indestructible but relative necessity within a system that encompasses it. That amounts to situating the metaphysics or the ontotheology of the logos" (89 *OG*).

With the new concept of difference Derrida seizes the law of previous metaphysics, internalizes that tradition, accumulates its knowledge, and revises it, repeating its fundamental goals. The change in tradition brought about by Einstein's theory of relativity as well as by other theories is often described as a simplifying and universalizing of previous laws. In the same vein Emerson describes the process of changing tradition:

> It is, in both cases, that a spiritual life has been imparted to nature; that the solid seeming block of matter has been pervaded and dissolved by a thought; that this feeble human being has penetrated the vast masses of nature with an informing soul, and recognized itself in their harmony; that is, seized their law. In physics, when this is attained, the memory disburthens itself of its cumbrous catalogues of particulars, and carries centuries of observation in a single formula (923 *Nature, Norton Anthology*).

Here Emerson believes seizing a law of nature is the same as the soul recognizing itself; thus, the nature of science is to change the self. In Kuhn's terms a world view is changed.

For the change, the most important point is the grasping of tradition in one principle. It is a way tradition can be remembered but surpassed. The same type of process may serve to explain personal memory. Susanne Langer writes, "To project feelings into outer objects is the first way of symbolizing, and thus of *conceiving* those feelings. This activity belongs to about the earliest period of childhood that memory can recover. The conception of `self', which is usually thought to mark the beginning of actual memory, may possibly depend on this process of symbolically epitomizing our feelings" (124). The epitomizing of feelings to conceive outer objects corresponds to the seizing of the law of previous tradition, for in both cases the whole of mind is represented before itself so that it may change itself. The processes become material to reflect on, to integrate further. New processes of mind result, and the regenerative process can go on indefinitely through history.

Summary

Derrida explains the start of his philosophy by the concept of "difference," which is then universalized into a system or chain of differences. "Difference" originates through a transformation of the closing of Sartre's philosophy. This concept constitutes a philosophical figure in the sense that Bloom's ratios were poetic figures; both have meaning in the distinctive ways determined by their fields. Bloom's ideas of clinamen and tessera can apply to differences and their system. However, Derrida'a concept of *bricolage* is more determined than Bloom's "misreading." Kuhn's ideas are less directly comparable to those of the other two thinkers because the ideas while not contrary to the other ones nevertheless are less developed. Both Bloom's and Derrida's figures are genetically encoded and in turn perform a coding function on the concepts developed from them. In this way the patterns of poetry and philosophy are transmitted from one generation to the next. Derrida's concepts can explain how one philosophy provides its successor with whatever it needs to create from, whereas neither Kuhn's nor Bloom's can; usually Kuhn and to a greater extent Bloom speak of the relation as a conflict, not a cooperation. Seeing how the end of one scientific theory, poetry, or philosophy provides the basis for its successor is necessary for any theory of tradition and its transmission.

NOTES

1. "And it would be risky to decide if the seam--the prohibition of incest--is a strange exception that one happened to encounter within the transparent system of difference, a "fact" as Lévi-Strauss says, with which "we are then confronted"; or is rather the origin of the difference between nature and culture, the condition--outside of the system--of the system of difference. The condition would be a "scandal" only if one wished to comprehend it within the system whose condition it precisely is" (103 *OG*).

2. The canon beginning with Homer is the following: Homer, Hesiod, Pherecydes of Syros, Thales, Anaximander, Anaximenes, Heraclitus, Parmenides, Anaxagoras, Plato, Aristotle, St. Augustine, Boethius, Anselm, Avicenna, Averroes, Maimonides, St. Aquinas, Scotus, Ockham, Descartes, Spinoza, Leibniz, Locke, Berkeley, Hume, Kant, Hegel, Cassirer, Merleau-Ponty, Sartre, Derrida, and possibly Lyotard.

3. "The theory of relativity shows the whole complexity of this task; but it retains the postulate of the possibility of such a system all the more strenuously and points out a new way to realize it" (381 *ETR*).

4. See p. 70 of *Ernst Cassirer: An Annotated Bibliography*, by Eggers and Mayer. The original is "Formen und Formwandlungen des philosophischen Wahrheitsbegriffes." *Hamburgische Universität. Reden gehalten bei der Feier des Rektorwechsels am 7. Nov. 1929.* Hamburg: Boysen, 1929. pp. 17-26.

5. Quoted from 40-41 of *OR*. The original is cited as the French translation of A. Tremesaygues and B. Pacaud, *Critique de la raison pure* (Paris: Presses Universitaries de France, 1950), p. 17.

Chapter 6:
The Middle Stage of a Scientific Theory

Introduction to Kuhn's Definition

Unlike Bloom and Derrida, Kuhn divides the creative process into two kinds of science: normal and extraordinary. Once a new paradigm has come into being, normal science resists it, then becomes converted, and finally works on puzzles stemming from its application to the world of behavior. Kuhn believes most scientists are "normal"; they do not bring about a new paradigm through revolution; they merely define the present one. They do, however, begin to point out anomalies and crises. Then extraordinary science can know that it must change the entire paradigm. By way of contrast, Bloom's theory only gives the creative role to what Kuhn would call extraordinary poetry; Bloom does not make the distinction. Derrida would agree with Bloom. Besides the difference between normal and extraordinary science, Kuhn does not define the development of science much between revolutions.

How Paradigms Guide the Research of Normal Science

Paradigms can guide the research of normal science because they lack a direct one-to-one relation of laws to actual things, and so normal scientists attempt to determine these relations.

Any new theory of science eventually gets presented in textbooks, gets applied to practical problems, and needs to be understood in more detail than the theory makes explicit. The laws of the theory are used to make rules of application to specific problems. Not all the rules defining the use of the laws can be explicitly stated with the laws, according to Kuhn (44 *SSR*). A similar situation is that of the laws of a country, for the laws do not contain the infinite number of applications to actual situations, and so courts are required to interpret and apply the law in specific cases.

Kuhn would like to define normal science to have such a judiciary role. But there is a problem. The scientists working through models, through rules, through puzzles do so "often without quite knowing or needing to know what characteristics have given these models the status of community paradigms" (46 *SSR*). Similarly, he believes the paradigm theories have no direct treatment by normal science (76 *SSR*). In contrast, Kuhn claims the members of a community work "from a single paradigm or from a closely related set" (162 *SSR*). Do normal scientists understand the paradigm in the way that extraordinary scientists do? Their research patterns would indicate, "No." But if they do not, how do they contribute to the creative function of extraordinary science?

Gablik tries to make definite Kuhn's view by claiming that normal scientists "take their cognitive and methodological framework for granted and concentrate on resolving issues within that framework" (159). If they take the framework for granted, perhaps it is because they do not know its nature as a general schema in tradition. Perhaps they do not know it in sufficient generality and with adequate rigor. They obviously have a different scientific goal. Kuhn's emphasis on revolution seems to rate the goal of extraordinary science higher, though being "extraordinary" it is not an everyday scientific process. On the other hand, normal science is regarded higher in value, because the opposite of normal is "abnormal," meaning that the essence of science does *not* consist in what is not `normal'. Both Bloom and Derrida make revolutionary poetry or philosophy the `normal' process. The purpose is to develop a new step in tradition.

One way to think of the difference between normal science and the extraordinary is to compare it to a game. Normal scientists make moves within a game the rules for which have been defined by extraordinary science; extraordinary science changes the rules, the game itself. In this way Gablik rightly expresses the difference (159). Would someone choose to make moves when he/she could do something more important by changing the game itself? Would someone choose to develop science iess than he/she could? An explanation is that normal science does not know what the game is, nor how to change it.

Kuhn attempts to make normal science participate in the creation of a paradigm by working on its further definition. If scientific discourse has written within it the developmental code, then this code should be in the form of a cycle--beginning, development, and end of a theory, leading in turn to a new start. The direction of the paradigm's development should lead by itself to a new paradigm. Kuhn does not refer to the relations of concepts in actual scientific theories. The development between paradigms is thus not understood in terms of the paradigm itself. This fact can be easily seen by contrasting Kuhn's explanation with Bloom's and Derrida's, both of whom define specific concepts serving in the intermediate development of what Kuhn called a paradigm. Kuhn gives no such definitions.

Kuhn does not fully accept the priority of the paradigm over rules of its application. If he did, he could not believe that normal science plays an essential role in the creative process. The idea of the predominance of the form of discourse over its contents was common to Russian Formalist theories: "While analyzing `how Don Quixote was made', Shklovsky also showed the instability of the hero and concluded that his `type' appeared `as the result of the business of constructing the novel'. Thus the dominance of structure, of plot over material, was emphasized" (121 Lemon and Reis). Kuhn gives little indication of the dynamism within scientific discourse. Concepts develop from the others and in so doing the previous ones are re-seen by the (extraordinary) scientist. Kuhn misses the internal metamorphoses necessary for the discourse to form relatively closed cycles. He does mention "internal features which give the discipline a history in its own right," but the reader never learns what these are (152 *ET*). Both Bloom and Derrida have extended explanations.

Role of Normal Science

Once a revolution has occurred, and once normal science accepts a new paradigm, it elaborates and applies the paradigm, which process prepares the way--eventually--for extraordinary science to produce another revolution.

Normal science is said to make a paradigm more precise in three ways: finding facts, matching facts with the theory, and further articulation (34 *SSR*). In doing this, normal science treats some past problem solutions as models for new problems of applying the paradigm (10 *SSR*). If these past solutions are the result of normal science, not the extraordinary, then normal science does not rely on an awareness of the past paradigm. Sometimes Kuhn directly states that normal science attempts no change of paradigm. If the facts do not fit, they are rejected or "not seen at all" (24 *SSR*).

Since a paradigm cannot include in itself all the rules of its application, neither can normal science come to understand all the rules for any paradigm. The model solutions it uses serves to replace the deficiency of not being able to predetermine every application. Scientific discourse is used to interpret itself. Alternatively, it has within it the seeds of its own interpretation, improvement.

Extraordinary science uses a parallel process of solution modelling, but the solutions are those of extraordinary science. When scientists create, the change of meaning comes about through a reflection on past changes. This fact suggests that scientific discourse `decodes' what went before and `recodes' a new version of itself. Furthermore, it is created as this cyclic decoding and recoding process.

Kuhn boldly declares that the laws of science eventually become formative factors in immediate experience (124 *SSR*). In more conventional terms everyone knows science is applied. Kuhn's assertion shows the aim of science is to some degree a change of perspective. Correlatively, the data of the sciences are observations from ordinary experience, as Kuhn sometimes claims (38 *ET*). If, however, the aim of science is a change of vision, then extraordinary science reflects directly on its own tradition when changing paradigms, not on observed facts, which can only be seen in terms of some paradigm.

What "Normal" Science Does

Normal science gathers facts, applies new generalizations, develops instruments, and most of all solves puzzles resulting from the paradigm's laws.

Rules come from paradigms by abstraction, the paradigm being more global (43 *SSR*). Normal science is generally concerned with making the fit between theory and observable fact clearer. To do so, rules of problem solutions are developed from the paradigm. Puzzles begin to appear to the normal scientist, who likes to "achieve the anticipated in a new way" (36 *SSR*). "The outcome itself is uninteresting, but the way is the challenge" (Ibid.)

A virtue of Kuhn's theory is the realization that no paradigm is without its problems (79 *SSR*). Bloom integrates the appearance of problems into the development of a poetic `paradigm' itself, with his concept of misadventures--turns and changes from ratio to ratio when a whole poetry is being developed. Derrida, too, claims a dialectical development of his main concepts, one into the other.

Summary

Although Kuhn wants normal science to participate in creation, his explanation seems ambiguous at best. Do normal scientists know any paradigm in the same sense as extraordinary science or not? If they do, then why do they choose not to engage in the more prestigious, more adventurous activity of changing paradigms? A good description of normal science by Kuhn is the following: "Chemists could not...simply accept Dalton's theory, they had still to beat nature into line, a process which, in the event, took almost another generation. ...The data themselves had changed" (135 *SSR*). It is as if normal science waited for a new paradigm to change its research, rather than actively changing it.

Chapter 7:

The Middle Stage of a Poetry

Introduction to Bloom's Definition

Whereas Kuhn does not explain the relations of concepts within a scientific theory as it unfolds itself, Bloom does explain the internal development of poetry. The intermediate development of poetry consists of a movement through a pair of revisionary ratios, kenosis and daemonization. During these stages the upcoming great poet takes a new stance toward the precursor and toward his/her previous concepts. Poetic figures are "revisionary ratios," suggesting that they are measured against what came before. "At key moments in the epic pilgrimage, the tradition itself steps forward to guide the seeker" (28 *Novel Epics*); Bloom's ratios, while not so positive as this statement would indicate, do represent moments of recasting the tradition.

The Transition from Tessera to Kenosis

Poets becoming great must develop their understanding beyond the start (clinamen and tessera) if they are to repeat the pattern of a tradition form.

In general the relation of tessera to kenosis is that of an effect to a cause, with the unusual fact that the effect precedes the cause. But in the order of concepts this seeming reversal of order is not a problem, for principles, assumptions, laws are often found after the phenomena they describe. Shklovsky noticed that the novelist Sterne presented the effects before the causes (168 *Theory of Prose*).

The internal development of a poetry resembles DNA insofar as internal replication occurs before the whole becomes complete. In the case of DNA a chain creates a complementary chain for itself, thus replicating the chain (284 Crick and Watson). In poetry each new ratio resembles in basic structure the previous one: all are dialectical, all have ambivalence, all change the meaning of a former ratio.

Yet, it is also true that all six ratios contribute different functions to an overall quest. At each change of ratios, the ratio becomes seen as dissolving "poetic divination and giving too little in return" (147 *MM*). A poetry develops through seeming "misadventures" to its complete state (217 *SM*).

If the first pair of ratios begins with an ironical attitude toward the precursor's work, then the second pair begins by "leading away from the horror of finding himself [the poet] to be only a copy or replica" (80 *AI*). There is a change of attitude toward the first pair of ratios, and the poet further individuates himself/herself from the precursor by showing a new type of greater poetic power. Through kenosis the precursor is seen to be more just a member of the series of predecessors, and the successor feels more independence from the influence (107, 110 *AF*). "`Where the precursor was, there the ephebe [new poet] shall be, but by the discontinuous mode of emptying the precursor of `his' divinity, while appearing to empty himself of his own" (91 *AI*). In other words, the power of the precursor is seen at kenosis to be even less than it was seen to be at clinamen or tessera. Kenosis is "a displacement by contiguity that repeats what is displaced, but always with a lesser tone" (98-99 *MM*). Curiously, though, Bloom believes the further separation actually means that the successor is more closely bound to the precursor. There is a new figure relating them, and the successor is repeating the pattern set by the precursor, so the latter is becoming more like the former.

The term "kenosis" Bloom takes from St. Paul, meaning "the humbling or emptying-out of Jesus by himself, when he accepts reduction from divine to human status" (14-15 *AI*). The precursor's poem is also emptied out or deflated of too absolutist claims to poetic vision. In this way, kenosis helps to make the successor even more superior to the precursor, for the emptying-out is accompanied by a purer sense of poetic vision. Kenosis represents a further undoing of the precursor's aesthetic principles "by a deliberate, willed loss in continuity," putting the successor further ahead (90 *AI*). Kenosis is a kind of reversal of tessera. The poet encounters a problem in his/her own development at tessera and a change of attitude leads to kenosis. The poet now sees himself/herself as formerly too bound with the predecessor (87 *AI*). Kenosis helps to save the poet from being a simple repetition of the precursor.

As Campbell points out, cultural forms have internal metamorphoses: "The hero-deed is a continuous shattering of the crystallizations of the moment. The cycle rolls: mythology focuses on the growing point. Transformation, fluidity, not stubborn ponderosity, is the characteristic of the living God. The great figure of the moment exists only to be broken, cut into chunks, and scattered abroad" (337 *Hero*).

Using similar language for kenosis, Bloom writes, "all questions of genesis have yielded to mere process, to one-thing-after-another"; "a world of continguities, in which resemblances..."; "a kind of continuous metonymy, in which a single, negative aspect of every thing substitutes for the thing itself"; "emptying-out-by-isolation" (110 *MM*). (These words characterize Derrida's second movement of concepts in philosophy, namely, the movement of differance in relation to difference.)

Kenosis shows more clearer than other ratios their recursive function. This act of poetry looking back at itself allows it to change its tradition. As Ehrlich writes of Russian Formalism literary theory, "Obviously, the differentia of literature, its concern with its medium, was more conspicuous where the device, instead of serving as a catalyst to blend heterogeneous elements into unity, was made to recoil upon itself" (194).

The internal steps of poetry move toward a mature understanding of the poetic process. Bloom explains,

> The internalization of quest-romance made of the poet-hero not a seeker after nature but after his own mature powers, and so the Romantic poet turned away, not from society to nature, but from nature to what was more integral than nature, within himself. The widened consciousness of the poet did not give him intimations of a former union with nature or the Divine, but rather of his former selfless self (26 *Ringers...*).

Poetry develops poetic self-knowledge, and poetry can be created only through reflection on the last greatest instance of its processes.

Bloom's theory of poetry is unusually strong for its detailed account of the transformations within poetries. The same principles could be adapted to fiction, as Tzvetan Todorov has done:

> I have tried to show, for example, that *The Quest of the Holy Grail* was characterized by the role which two types of transformations played in it: on the one hand, all events which occur are announced in advance; on the other, once they have occurred they receive a new interpretation, in a particular symbolic code. In another example, the tales of Henry James, I have tried to indicate the role of transformations of knowledge: they dominate and determine the linear movement of the narrative (231 *The Poetics of Prose*).

So, too, transformations dominate and determine the linear movement of poetry for Bloom. Derrida felt the transformations were such changes that he did not feel philosophy's concepts develop in a homogenous, linear fashion but rather by reversals in perspective.

The freeing of oneself or the making of an imaginative space continues throughout the quest.

The Transition to Daemonization

The transition from clinamen to tessera parallels that from kenosis to daemonization: a universalization or extension of the former ratio occurs, while the latter is to again become problematic and to lead to a new pair of ratios. This repeating of structures in complementary relation resembles the process of DNA producing itself.

Generally, in daemonization the precursor is seen to lose his/her originality to a daemonic agency (100 *AI*). Shelley "compels us to see him in the company of angels, the daemonic partners of his quest for totality" (104 *AI*). "Daemonic" does not mean evil; it means an agency of inspiration. This ratio needs to be explained.

The root of "daeomai" means "the power that distributes and divides" (Ibid.). This function calls to mind the second of the three fates Lachesis, who measures the thread of life spun by the first fate. Socrates thought he had a daemon, an inner voice that would instruct him what not to do but never what to do. In the case of poetry, the message is that the precursor did not do what the successor does. "The later poet opens himself to what he believes to be a power in the parent-poem that does not belong to the parent proper, but to a range of being just beyond that precursor. He does this, in his poem, by so stationing its relation to the parent-poem as to generalize away the uniqueness of the earlier work" (15 *AI*). Some new poetic dominion has been won, so the previous poetry is less than one thought before.

The successor tends to think of himself/herself as a daemon, a supra-human agency of poetic vision: in daemonization, the poet "attempts to expand the precursor's power to a principle larger than his own, but pragmatically makes the son more of a daemon and the precursor more of a man" (106 *AI*).

Daemonization leads to an alternation of sublime and grotesque images, heights and depths. At this stage the continuity of the poem is threatened (100 *MM*). A similar event occurs at Derrida's concept of infinite differance, which will be discussed. At his stage the quest is not yet completed, though it is in danger (18 *PR*). The poet must once again revise his/her perspective.[1]

Bloom's Ideas of "Misadventures" and "Ratios" in Relation to the Genetic Code

Bloom's ratios develop from one to the next, especially between pairs of ratios, because poets in their quest undergo "misadventures," and the process resembles replication in the steps toward complete DNA, a complete genetic code.

The completion of DNA resembles the completion of a poetry. Crick and Watson explain how DNA reproduces itself:

> In conclusion, we may mention that the complementary relationship between the two chains is very likely related to the biological role of DNA. It is generally assumed that DNA is a genetic substance

> and in some way possesses the capacity for self-duplication. It seems to us that the presence of a complementary structure strongly suggests that the self-duplicating process will be found to involve the alternative formation of complementary chains, and that each chain will be found capable of serving as a template for the formation of its complement (292).

And the antithesis in the self-duplication is clearer in the following passage by Crick:

> There is one unexpected peculiarity. In the usual double helix the two backbones of the two chains are not approximately parallel but antiparallel. If the sequence of the atoms in one backbone runs up, that in the other runs down. This does cause certain complications, but not as much as one might expect. At bottom it springs from the type of symmetry possessed by the double helix. This is produced by the pseudosymmetry of the base-pairing. It happens to be the convenient way for these particular chemicals to fit neatly together.
> It is easy to see that a molecule of this type, consisting of a pair of chains whose irregular elements (the bases) fit together, is ideal for molecular replication, especially since the two chains can be rather easily separated from each other by mild methods (66 *Life Itself*).

Bloom's ratios develop by "antithetical completion." The previous ratio serves as a template, a mold, to determine the general structure of the one to follow, albeit the following one is complementary or antithetical to the first. In each movement of ratios there is a reversal (84 *MM*). An adjustment in the direction of the quest occurs, for it is not over. The idea of a revisionary ratio being a mold for the next one goes beyond Bloom's explicit intentions. Yet, this interpretation would match Derrida's concept of *bricolage*, according to which the immediately preceding concepts contain directions for subsequent creation. If this is true, creation does not have to result from a single pattern--unchanging--throughout all tradition; each one can change somewhat.

      The forward advance comes about by revising the past. Todorov has described the recursion of forms well:

> In France, it is in Charles Mauron's studies that we first encounter a tendency to read the text systematically as a palimpsest, as a transformation of and commentary upon an earlier text by the same author: here the figure becomes an "obsessive metaphor." This does not mean we must follow Mauron when he extrapolates from an author's works an ideal entity which would be anterior to them de jure and de facto, "the personal myth": it is not necessary to postulate the existence of an original in order to consider the individual texts as its transformations; the text is always the transformation of another transformation (244 *Poetics of Prose*).

Most important, a text is a transformation of a previous text; it tells how this can be done. Poetry is about its process, making it new again. Not only is a whole poetry a transformation of a previous one but each part also transforms an earlier part.

      Moreover, poetry resembles DNA insofar as the whole is represented within itself. Gans points out this process in DNA, with a significant result--"It is this turning of matter on itself that makes it something more than mere matter" (797); this statement supports the idea previously suggested that cultural genetic codes have evolved out of the biological. The turning back on what went before is necessary to see the whole of it. Poetry develops in the same way. On Northrop Frye's view, a part of poetry has some similarity to its whole: "An archetype should be not only a unifying category of criticism, but itself a part of a total form, and it leads us at once to the question of what sort of total form criticism can see in literature" (20 "The Archetypes of Literature"). The archetype, of course, is a *repeated* part of a poetry, present in all great poetries, so that poetry views its own past when re-making them, each one in a poetry accumulating the tradition in its distinctive way.

The recursive, revisionary nature of poetry was expressed by Paul de Man: "The whole point of literature...is to create exactly this endless stream of reading, re-reading, and interpretation" (643 *Reader's Adviser*. Ed. Chernow). This "endless stream" is tradition, like a series of Moebius Strips, which has infinity because each end is connected to its beginning, each new one re-does what the old did.

Summary

Bloom defines the intermediate development of a poetry with the revisionary ratios "kenosis" and "daemonization." Together they define a new stance toward the precursor's aesthetic, further separating the successor from influence. In general the structure of this pair resembles the structure of the first pair, though complementary or antithetical. These ratios especially show how poetic form is recursive. By the fact that the new ratios come into being as the antithetical completion of the old, the ratios resemble the internal reduplication in DNA. A poetry, just as a science or a philosophy, occupies a position in a generative series. Each is a tradition form; tradition acquires a new meaning in each recurrence of its pattern.

NOTES

1. Daemonization seems exemplified in fiction. Consider what Griffiths and Rabinowitz wrote about Gogol's surpassing of Pushkin: "*Dead Souls*, Part Two, implicitly diagnoses its own paralysis; Tentetnikov waits for another fit preceptor to appear; Chichikov waits for some blueprint for rebuilding his soul; Gogol waits for a plan to complete the immense cathedral of letters for which Part One can serve as cellar. The solution here proposed is not to find another fit guide--the perfect critic that Pushkin should have lived to become--nor even to proceed without a guide, but for Gogol to become the critic himself and perhaps not proceed at all" (111 *Novel Epics*). Gogol seeks and finds a source of inspiration, a daemon, himself. A hierarchy begins to be established within the fiction, as there occurs in poetry.

Chapter 8:
The Middle Stage of Derrida's Philosophy

Introduction to Derrida's Definition of the Middle Stage

The transition from the system of differences to differance (with an `a') is like a transition from effects to causes. "Differance" produces the differences in a sense which shows a changed attitude by Derrida toward his first concepts, now no longer sufficient to answer the predecessor's challenge. In this way differance and infinite differance are like Bloom's kenosis and daemonization, which in their turn will become two more "misadventures."

The Transition from the System of Differences to Differance

The System of Differences Presupposes Differance, and so the System Cannot Be the Entire Philosophical Form that Derrida Was Seeking.

The new concept "différance" is a neologism explained well by David B. Allison:

> [Derrida introduces a neologism here; from the French "différence" he derives the term "différance." As in the Latin "differre," the French "différer" bears two quite distinct significations. One has a reference

> to spatiality, as the English "to differ"--to be at variance, to be unlike, apart, dissimilar, distinct in nature or quality from something. This is even more evident in its cognate form, "to differentiate." The other signification has a reference to temporality, as in the English "to defer"--to put off action to a future time, to delay or postpone.
>
> I have thus chosen to follow Derrida's employment of différance by rendering it as "differance" in English. This should not be too disconcerting a translation, for it incorporates the common origin of the two relevant English verbs, "to defer" and "to differ," namely, the Latin *differre*. ...--Translator.] (82 *SP*)

"Differance" includes the two meanings of differing, which can be in a spatial sense, and deferring, which is a temporal sense.

Differance must be postulated by Derrida to account for the change from Sartre's system to Derrida's and the changes within Derrida's own system of differences. Since Derrida defined difference to be a priori, to apply even to the philosophies of his predecessors, then he has the problem of explaining how Sartre's `differences' change into Derrida's "differences." Correlatively, looking at the relation of the present to the future instead of the past to the present, how does one difference develop into a future difference?

"Differance" explains the making of differences from other differences. In Derrida's terms, differance guarantees "the temporalizing synthesis" responsible for the formation of differences in an infinite chain. The change from Sartre's "differences" to Derrida's differences is a change to a higher order reflection on what was thought before. This change parallels the change from the appearing sound to the appearing of the sound: "It is therefore indispensable to preserve the distinction between the appearing sound and the appearing of the sound in order to escape the worst and the most prevalent confusions..." (64 *OG*). Irene Harvey agrees with the idea that there are layers or levels in Derrida's philosophy, and she sees a level change from the "given" to "the conditions of possibility" (50 *The Economy...*). What is even more salient is her observation of "a certain duplicity of layers or levels within that same text." The "duplicity" suggests a replicating of earlier structures; differance "replicates" difference, insofar as both are a priori figures of philosophy and one comes from the other, though they are not identical. DNA makes a second chain from a first one before the whole molecule is complete.

"Differance" cannot violate the epistemological requirements set up by the earlier concept "difference." Derrida is developing a total system and its parts must be consistent. Therefore, differance must be written as well. It must be a kind of higher order trace or difference ("prototrace"). The properties of difference would be extended though transformed in differance. Asserting this idea, Derrida writes, "These chains and systems cannot be outlined except in the fabric of this trace or imprint. The unheard difference between the appearing and the appearance...is the condition of all other differences, of all other traces, and it is already a trace" (65 *OG*). Differance explains the change from one difference to another--"the unheard difference." Differance is the condition of all differences.

Therefore, there are three conclusions about the meaning of "differance." First, it is a condition of the possiblity of differences. Second, it explains the development of Derridean differences from earlier ones and the development of Derridean differences into later ones. Third, "differance" cannot violate the epistemological restrictions of differences; thus, it is itself a trace, but of a higher order ("prototrace"). So differance works with difference to build a still larger whole of concepts. These three conclusions can be found in the following passage by Derrida:

> Differance is what makes the movement of signification possible only if each element that is said to be "present," appearing on the stage of presence, is related to something other than itself but retains the mark of a past element and already lets itself be hollowed out by the mark of its relation to a future element. This trace relates no less to what is called the future than to what is called the past, and it constitutes what is called present by this very relation to what it is not, to what it absolutely is not; that is, not even to a past or future considered as a modified present. In order for it to be, an interval must separate it from what it is not; but the interval that constitutes it in the

present must also, and by the same token, divide the present in itself, thus dividing, along with the present, everything that can be conceived on its basis, that is, every being--in particular, for our metaphysical language, the substance or subject. Constituting itself, dynamically dividing itself, this interval is what could be called spacing; time's becoming-spatial or space's becoming temporal (temporalizing). And it is this constitution of the present as a "primordial" and irreducibly nonsimple, and therefore, in the strict sense nonprimordial, synthesis of traces, retentions, protentions...that I propose to call protowriting, prototrace, or differance (142 *SP*; another very important passage on the reasons for positing differance--more thorough--is in *OG*, 60-65).

According to the first part of this passage, differance explains the possibility of differences, as well as the production of differences, their serial nature. The second part introduces the idea of an "interval," which shows how Derridean differences can be superior to the Sartrian and how Derridean differences can themselves develop. "Interval" names a distinction between differences in an infinite series, especially the distinction between Sartrian "differences" and the Derridean. The last part of the passage indicates that differance must satisfy the epistemological minimum standards for differences; the two concepts must be consistent, or at least not inconsistent. In the formation of DNA a second chain is formed antiparallel to the first while nonetheless complementary to it.

"Differance" is a further development of "difference." Differance adds the following idea: "a retention in the minimal unity of temporal experience," or "a trace retaining the other as other in the same" (62 *OG*). Derrida is trying to formulate a universal theory of knowledge.

Since differance comes after differences in Derrida's philosophy while nevertheless being the condition for them, it is an a priori concept in the same sense that difference was. Difference had the power to allow Derrida to retroactively re-envision the history of philosophy. Derrida describes difference as "arche-trace," as "pure" trace and as "prototrace," all terms suggesting the a priori relation of differance to difference. If differance is not possible, then difference is not. "*Differance* is to be conceived prior to the separation between deferring as delay and differing as the active work of difference" (88 *SP*).

The advance from the system of differences to the law of their production, to differance, results from an attempt to see the system as a whole in relation to the predecessor's philosophy. Quoting Derrida's "White Mythology," Paul Ricoeur writes about such a process: the layer of the first philosophical elements `is therefore self-eliminating every time one of its products...vainly attempts to include under its sway the whole field to which that product belongs' [287; or p. 18 of `White Mythology' trans. F.C.T. Moore, *New Literary History* 6(1974): 5-74]. "Difference" is self-eliminating or subordinating when Derrida attempts to totalize the system of differences and differentiate that system from Sartre's.

Differance helps to highlight the fact that creation is not a deductive process. "It [differance]," writes Derrida, "is also inconceivable as the mere *homogeneous* complication of a diagram or line of time, as a complex "succession" (88 *SP*). Differance is related to difference as a kind of unexpected reversal; its nature could not have been fully known before difference had been defined. It developed from difference.

Differance Can Be Characterized by Bloom's Ideas of "Misadventures" and "Revisionary Ratios" and Corresponds to "Kenosis," though Differance Explains More

Differance shows more about the process of tradition, because it is related to the system of differences as their production, thus showing an increase in knowledge. Derrida even defines the increase in knowledge as the new awareness that there must be "a retention in the minimal unity of temporal experience," or "a trace retaining the other as other in the same" (62 *OG*). Bloom does not explain the increase in poetic vision; he does state that there is an increase. The theory of the anxiety of influence stands outside the poetic decision-making process. Whereas Derrida gives arguments for his new concepts, whatever "arguments" the poets had to create are not presented by Bloom.

Bloom described kenosis as "a displacement by contiguity that repeats what is displaced, but always with a lesser tone" (98-99 *MM*). Bloom writes, "all questions of genesis have yielded to mere process, to one-thing-after-another"; "a world of continguities"; "a kind of continuous metonymy, in which a single, negative aspect of every thing substitutes for the thing itself"; "emptying-out-by-isolation" (110 *MM*). These features resemble differance, which explains the replacement of one difference by another in an indefinitely continuing series. Differance is the differing and deferring of differences.

Differance and a Genetic Code of Philosophy

Differance explains the dynamism within the code of philosophy; differance is an essential part of the code, and in this way the entire philosophy is seen as having a decoding and encoding function.

Derrida makes the explicit comparison between differance and the genetic code: "...we shall designate by the term differance the movement by which language, or any code, any system of reference in general, becomes `historically' constituted as a fabric of differences" (141 *SP*). The genetic code explains the series of living things; differance explains the series of differences, beginning with one's predecessor and extending into the future.

Stages in the formation of DNA resemble its overall function. Its replication of the chain of molecules is preparatory to the reproduction of the entire DNA. Similarly, differance replicates difference (though on a higher level), and in this way it mirrors the function of the total philosophy, which is to account for a new step in its tradition, its own reproduction. When differance was postulated it was clear it arose from a reflection on the whole of what had gone before--the system of differences. Then differance is concerned with the whole of what the philosophy seeks, without yet achieving it. Derrida's sense of philosophy is enlarged, deepened in the transition from difference to differance. The sense of the unity of philosophy changes during the completion of a philosophy. Differance is only a stage in the total philosophy. These ideas are consistent with Bloom's "misadventures" en route to the completion of the quest of poetry, to complete the task that the precursor's work presented as impossible.

Art Berman discusses this function of a code--that its parts have a similar structure to the whole. "In each of these models [DNA and Eco's model], the terms in the lexicon take their meaning from the total context of the theory in which they are used; they have no independent meaning. ...any poetic statement `bears the pressure of the context'...there is a constructed contextual meaning in addition to the everday meaning" (94). Quite rightly, Bloom's ratios and Derrida's main concepts "take their meaning from the total context of the theory." In fact they are *about* this context, give it specific form, and their meaning is the developing context. I do not think either Bloom or Derrida would agree that the wholistic meaning of their figures (e.g., kenosis or differance) is "in addition to" an everyday meaning. Each of the figures comes into being only to transform the whole poetry or philosophy. The parts transform the whole, just as the whole poetry or philosophy is at the same time a transformation of the tradition.

The Transition from Differance to Infinite Differance

Differences were extended into an infinite chain or system of differences. In a parallel move, differance has the tendency to become infinite. This tendency, however, causes problems: differance becomes so ambivalent as to be polarized. In Bloom's theory as well, such a universalization occurs within each of the three pairs or ratios.

"Differance is also something other than finitude" (68 *OG*).

Just as differences were extended into a system or chain of differences, Derrida tries to understand differance more and more by similarly extending the concept to an infinite domain.

The argument about the need to explain the temporalizing synthesis of differences by differance is reduplicated when Derrida again questions the temporal meaning of differance:

> In its greatest formality, this immense problem would be formulated thus: is the temporality described by a transcendental phenomenology as "dialectical" as possible, a ground which the structures, let us say the unconscious structures, of temporality would simply modify? Or is the phenomenological model itself con-

> stituted, as a warp [foundation, base] of language, logic, evidence, fundamental security, upon a woof [woven fabric] that is not its own? And which--such is the most difficult problem--is no longer mundane? (67 *OG*).

I can paraphrase this argument in other terms of Derrida's. Is differance changed by differences? Or, can differance change so much that it would differ from itself?

If differance extends infinitely, then would it even differ from itself? Or, conversely, if it did extend infinitely, would this mean it does not change essentially? There is a need to extend differance, as there was a need to extend differences into a system, but there is again a disturbing ambivalence in the result:

> The difference between the same and the other [differance], which is not a difference or a relation among others, has no meaning in the infinite, except to speak...of the anxiety of the infinite which determines and negates itself. But this horizon is not the horizon of the infinitely other, but of a reign in which the difference between the same and the other, differance, would no longer be valid. ...The infinitely other and the infinitely same, if these words have meaning for a finite being, is the same (129 *WD*).

Differance seems to become self-negating if it becomes infinite. On the one hand, differance would remain "the same"; on the other, it may differ completely from what it was in the beginning--but not quite.

Doubts arise about the fecundity of differance if it is extended over the whole domain of knowledge. Differance is extended until a limit of its power is seen. This process of maximization or infinitization or universalization of concepts to promote their closure was discussed during the passages on the start of Derrida's philosophy, where the strategy was used to develop beyond the transcendental signified and later beyond difference. The sense of the decline of differance, Derrida's growing awareness of its inadequacy to give the full answer to the problem set by Sartre, is presented in this passage:

> All the more extraordinary because a prodigious expansion of the power of differance was not accompanied, at least during these millennia, by any notable transformation of the organism. It is precisely the property of the power of differance to modify life less and less as it spreads out more and more. If it should grow infinite and its essence excludes this a priori--life itself would be made into an impassive, intangible, and eternal presence: infinite differance, God or death (131 *OG*).

Recall how much Sartre's closing concept concerned the nature of human progress (transcendence), and how that concept indicated an ultimate barrier.

The sense of entropy can also be found in the following passage, which shows the ambivalence in "infinite differance":

> Here we touch on the point of greatest obscurity, on the very enigma of differance, on how the concept we have of it is divided by a strange separation. We must not hasten to make a decision too quickly. How can we conceive of differance as a systematic detour which, within the element of the same, always aims at either finding again the pleasure or the presence that had been deferred by (conscious or unconscious) calculation, and, *at the same time*, how can we, on the other hand, conceive of differance as the relation to an impossible presence, as an expenditure without reserve, as an irreparable loss of presence, an irreversible wearing-down of energy, or indeed as a death instinct and a relation to the absolutely other that apparently breaks up any economy? (150 *SP*)

Here is the ambivalence in differance when extended over the whole field of knowledge, past, present, and future. On the one hand, "finding again the pleasure or the presence" means that differance must be similar to some differance of the past. On the other hand, differance changes so much that it seems to leave its origin behind, thus becoming other than itself--"an irreversible wearing-down of energy."

"Infinite" Differance and Bloom's Daemonization

Derrida's "infinite" differance corresponds to Bloom's daemonization; they have similar functions in the total tradition form.

Daemonization leads to an alternation of sublime and grotesque images, heights and depths. There is an alternation in hyperbole and litotes. At this stage the continuity of the poem is threatened (100 *MM*).

Derrida's differance sounds similar. "The infinitely other and the infinitely same, if these words have meaning for a finite being, is the same" (129 *WD*). The continuity of the philosophy seems threatened because differance "would no longer be valid" (129 *WD*), yet it was needed to guarantee the validity of the system of differences.

Differance and daemonization perform similar functions in relation to the precursor. In the anxiety of influence, "the later poet opens himself to what he believes to be a power in the parent-poem that does not belong to the parent proper, but to a range of being just beyond that precursor. He does this, in his poem, by so stationing its relation to the parent-poem as to generalize away the uniqueness of the earlier work" (15 *AI*). Some new poetic dominion has been won, so the previous poetry is less than one thought before. In daemonization, the poet "attempts to expand the precursor's power to a principle larger than his own, but pragmatically makes the son more of a daemon and the precursor more of a man" (106 *AI*). Differance helps to explain how differences can become as great as those between Sartre's concepts and Derrida's. With differance, Derrida can understand his separation from Sartre while gaining more originality.

Summary

Differance relates to differences as the cause to the effects, which come earlier as they are on a less developed level of knowledge. Differance explains the production of differences, how they were made, and in so doing explains the possibility of an infinite chain of them, beginning with the precursor and extending provisionally beyond Derrida. This dominant concept in Derrida's philosophy strongly resembles Bloom's kenosis. Both perform similar functions in relation to the precursor and to one's own earlier concepts. Derrida's concept, however, can give reasons for the advance, can define it. "Infinite" differance also performs functions similar to Bloom's `daemonization'. Both are extensions of those other figures just mentioned, and in the extension greater power to explain a new step in tradition. However, by threatening the unity of the field, the figures are not adequate to mark out the space, to meet the requirements of an entire poetry or philosophy. The cultural quest is not yet over. New figures arise from them, to be discussed next.

Chapter 9:
The End of a Scientific Theory

Introduction to Kuhn's Definition of the End

Kuhn is much more concerned with the start of a scientific theory than the end. He becomes enthusiastic about the beginnings that are revolutionary. A new beginning, however, comes from the end of a former theory. Sometimes, the direct relation of the beginning of one theory from the end of a previous one seems forgotten in the generality of the explanation; the moment of conception in this sense is `immaculate', with Kuhn being the divine agency. He does advance ideas of "anomaly," "crisis," and "incommensurability" to help explain why a new scientific theory would be needed.

General Features of the End

The end of a scientific theory has a characteristic structure. Eventually, anomalies appear until they form a crisis so serious that a new framework for science is needed. There is a question whether the previous science was therefore mistaken, in whole or in part, or perhaps just limited in scope and power, as Kuhn often would like to be true.

Kuhn describes the end of a scientific theory at length:

> We do not believe that there are rules for inducing correct theories from facts, or even that theories, correct or incorrect, are induced at all. Instead we view them as imaginative posits, invented in one piece for application to nature. And though we point out that

> such posits can and usually do at last encounter puzzles they cannot solve, we also recognize that those troublesome confrontations rarely occur for some time after a theory has been both invented and accepted. In our view, then, no mistake was made in arriving at the Ptolemaic system, and it is therefore difficult for me to understand what Sir Karl has in mind when he calls that system, or any other out-of-date theory, a mistake. At most one may wish to say that a theory which was not previously a mistake has become one or that a scientist has made the mistake of clinging to a theory for too long.... 'mistake' has been borrowed from normal science, where its use is reasonably clear, and applied to revolutionary episodes, where its application is at best problematic (279 *ET*).

Certainly, if previous science is mistaken it is not so in any ordinary, normal sense. Such insights beyond common sense like this one are some of the chief virtues of Kuhn's theory appealing to so many people. Scientific theories finally encounter puzzles they cannot solve. Since they are sequentially "invented in one piece," the problem forces some scientist to invent a different framework, again in one piece. Kuhn, rather controversially and boldly, denies that the problem not solvable by the theory can be called a "mistake" in the normal sense, which would imply some of the theory was correct if any progress was made and some of the theory was incorrect if future progress is to be made--but then is there thorough systematic unity of the concepts? I can interpet him to mean that it was not wrong to have proposed those concepts leading to the unsolvable puzzle; yet, if science is to continue beyond the obstacle of the unsolvable puzzle a new framework is needed. The "mistake" from the standpoint of extraordinary science seems to be inadequate scope and explanatory power only remediable by a change in the framing assumptions. Kuhn's ideas go no further. They need to be elaborated, even beyond Kuhn's own theory.

The Priority of Paradigms and the Ends of Forms

The whole framework of scientific laws, achieved with the completion of a scientific theory, is prior to rules that can be applied.

The whole framework of a scientific theory is prior to the elements in it. The priority is manifest in creation, according to Kuhn:

> The scientific concepts to which they [definitions] point gain full significance only when related, within a text or other systematic presentation, to other scientific concepts, to manipulative procedures, and to paradigm applications. It follows that concepts like that of an element can scarcely be invented independent of context. Furthermore, given the context, they rarely require invention because they are already at hand (142 *SSR*).

It follows from this passage that a scientist invents a new context more than he does any particular elements. Certainly, new elements or phenomena are defined, but they result from the creation of the framework. This idea resembles Bloom's that the context is restationed in creation, although Bloom's discussion is more explicit.

A paradigm is "a fundamental unity for the study of scientific development," "which cannot be fully reduced to logically atomic components which might function in its stead" (10 *SSR*). At a later stage in his career Kuhn disclaimed this idea by changing "paradigm" to the two different terms "exemplars" and "disciplinary matrix." The latter sense is the one he then said he never tried to prove, being concerned only with "exemplars" or model solutions used by normal science. But if Kuhn disclaims the wholeness of a paradigm, it seems that his theory is like a deflated balloon. The major presentation of his theory, developed through several years, *does* argue for the wholeness of a paradigm and its priority over the elements of the theory. Part of Kuhn's intellectual excitement is to discuss changes so large as to be called revolutions. How else could there be a change in world views?

The paradigms of extraordinary science are prior to the rules and puzzles of normal science. "Paradigms may be prior to, more binding, and more complete than any set of rules for research that could be unequivocally abstracted from them" (46 *SSR*). Paradigms cannot include all possible rules of application, so normal science must gain its type of knowledge more according to models of previous solutions called "exemplars."

Normal science particularly seeks rules when fundamental concepts are at stake, in a state approaching crisis (48 *SSR*). This category of scientist, however, does not realize an idea of Kuhn's: the word `mama' conveys knowledge of relatedness beyond the single individual who is the mother, knowledge of women, males and females, family structure, and so on to a total social framework. It is normal science that even under a crisis of fundamental concepts cannot begin to see the relatedness of the concepts enough to change the entire framework. Never for normal science can a specific issue become the index to the entire framework. (The greatest crisis is the inadequacy of the framework itself, not anything framed by it.) Nevertheless, it seems to Kuhn that normal science "chooses" a framework. To use other vocabulary, a framework is a transformation group, a whole in which transformations of knowledge occur. According to Cassirer, the possibility of organizing experience into an objective world depends upon a free choice of certain transformation groups in perception.[1] Perception depends upon vague "gestalts" in Kuhn's terms; in Cassirer's terms, perception requires invariables and limiting concepts of science if it is to be formable into a world. Lower orders of science in civilization would necessarily correspond to less developed perceptual abilities; it is well known that some primitive peoples cannot count sheep from a distance but can only distinguish visual groupings according to qualitative traits such as color and smell and general shape.

Perception depends upon the prior framework given to civilization by science, and it is its duty to specify the whole-determining assumptions. Kuhn is more right than he knows when he says science changes world views. Unfortunately, he fails to state those assumptions, as Einstein and Cassirer do. Kuhn's own vagueness about paradigms parallels the blindness of normal science toward the framework from which its rules derive. It is as if Kuhn's lack of knowledge is displaced onto persons he comprehends fully.

Another type of vocabulary by which to understand the priority of paradigms over their contents is used by Gablik. Concurring with Piaget, Gablik asserts that all learning results in "higher and more complex levels of functioning over time" and "more highly organized states" (32-33). A change of paradigms is a change of levels of knowledge, not just contents. Whatever contents are in the new paradigm have a greater connectivity or organizational state.

So far, I have been describing the priority of a paradigm to be finally established at the end of a scientific theory. There is another sense of "priority." Any scientific theory should be prior in a logical explanatory sense to previous theories; it should be superior scientifically. This idea of priority is essential to all tradition forms. Bloom discusses it at much length, calling it metalepsis or transumption. The renowned geneticist Jacques Monod defines this priority in a scientific context:

> The fundamental biological invariant is DNA. That is why Mendel's defining of the gene as the unvarying bearer of hereditary traits, its chemical identification by Avery (confirmed by Hershey), and the elucidation by Watson and Crick of the structural basis of its replicative invariance, without any doubt constitute the most important discoveries ever made in biology. To which of course must be added the theory of natural selection, whose certainty and full significance were established only by those later discoveries (104).

The certainty and full significance of the theory of natural selection was established only by those later discoveries. Kuhn almost brings this idea to full expression when he claims that a science is seen "as leading in a straight line to the discipline's present vantage" (167 *SSR*). The teleology is that defined by the present science, not the past, and a future science will interpret past science as leading to it, not to a previous level of science. The interpretation of previous theories such that they are subordinate is a function of developing the tradition, as Bloom realized much more definitely than Kuhn.

For the same reasons, the end of a scientific theory is prior to the earlier parts. Within the diachronic presentation of a scientific theory, the concepts are interdependent insofar as the later ones guarantee the validity of the earlier ones, which precede and lead to the later ones. Only if this is true can it be understandable that a problem at the end of a scientific theory would require a revision of the fundamental assumptions forming even the beginnings of the theory. When Derrida speaks about the meaning of successive stages in his thought, it is almost as if they replace the earlier ones; yet they do remain, albeit with reduced and altered contextual significance.

A more imagistic comparison may give a sense of the priority of one theory over previous ones. Pablo Picasso, in the last stages of his painting, is said to have been concerned with "paraphrasing" earlier masters but in Picasso's new style. He painted the "same" subjects, though in a different style.[2] The same principle applies to science, which interprets previous theories on its own terms. Thus, they lead up to the present theory. Einstein's comments about Newtonian mechanics being a limited case within his theory results from Einstein's sense of his own priority, and perhaps cannot be taken simply literally--the meaning changed.

Definition of the End of a Scientific Theory (As a Tradition Form)

Scientific theories (as tradition forms) end with the completion of a "disciplinary matrix," the global half of the original term "paradigm." Along the way, "exemplars" are also developed.[3] They are particular problem solutions, part of the meaning of the original term "paradigm." It may be that exemplars are what normal science is able to understand of a framework, never rising to the level of integration of concepts needed to form a paradox of the framework.

The end of a science produces a whole world view and from it specific problem solutions. No definite rule can be followed to make the new world view, for it changes the rules of scientific discourse, if only slightly. Definite rules can be followed to produce specific problem solutions. Jean-François Lyotard defines two types of knowledge: the making of new moves within established rules, and the more fundamental one of making new rules, of changing the game (43 *The Postmodern...*). The game is complete at the end of a scientific theory. This fact should suggest that science attempts to form new games, that genuine science is working toward a new game all the time, whereas Kuhn interprets revolutions to be "extraordinary." Then, the ordinary science of specific solutions, applications, is more essentially "science." I do not think Einstein and other creators would agree. Kuhn's attitude is ambivalent: excitement or valorization of the extraordinary and yet relegation of it to an abnormal para-scientific status.

Each discipline according to Kuhn has a "mental set" (5 *ET*). A different scientific theory produces a different world view. "Matrix" shows that a framework is involved in which particular things are generated. "Disciplinary" shows that the matrix is specific to a discipline (whereas Kuhn defines it in terms of all the sciences). The matrix not only provides the scientist with a map but also with new directions for map-making (109 *SSR*). Therefore, the matrix provides the means by which scientists can learn more about science, change tradition. The change is so thorough-going that Kuhn described it as a move from one planet to another (111 *SSR*). In such a change not only the phenomena would change but also the conditions in which they exist.

To draw out the implications of Kuhn's view more, I would suggest that science works toward a form of the discipline. Kuhn claims anomalies become lawlike. He also claims that scientists can learn from paradigms without abstracting elements (351 *CR*). The philosopher of science Ernst Cassirer believed mathematics must form a system.[4] When scientists such as Einstein assert the absolute value of the continuum of scientific theory--that it must be preserved--they are asserting the goal of scientific discourse. A scientific theory advances in the direction of an increasing awareness of the requirements of the discourse. Later theories are superior because they are more scientific; they establish a new definition of the scientific, which always accounts for a continuity of purpose with past theories.

A Characteristic Development and Hierarchy in Scientific Theory

Scientific theories must have a developmental hierarchy resembling that of their predecessors.

Kuhn does not have a theory of a specific structural standard for science that is repeated in each new science. He does not theorize about the sequence of transformations within a theory. A hint of what this might be occurs when he comments on Newton's physics: "The same change [of the third law of Newton] of motion supplies the definition of dynamical force implicit in the second law" (105 *SSR*). This statement expresses a developmental necessity within science. If the concepts are to be interrelated, there must be reasons for the order of the interrelationships. Some of the concepts must depend logically upon others. To some degree, the logical dependence should be recurring from theory to theory. Kuhn does *claim* an internal history is necessary, but he does not provide one (157 *ET*). A theory of science needs to explain the dynamic and general coherence of a scientific theory.

Then an explanation for the recurring structure of science is needed, one that accounts for progress, one that is transvaluative. Semioticist James Jacob Liszka has this type of explanation for myth:

> When supplemented by a transvaluative analysis it is clear that the general narrative structure of the myth seems to play about one principle: the narration begins with a disruption of a hierarchy, leading to a hierarchical crisis, and ending in various strategies which characterize narrative types: the destruction of the hierarchy, its reintegration, or its reestablishment.
>
> This general narrative structure indicates that it is ready-made for the function of transvaluating the rule-ordered hierarchies that constitute the culture. ...
>
> Both the origin and the structure of the myth point to its function. As the most comprehensive transvaluative device in a culture, the myth serves as the source for examining values and the rules that encode them (215-216 *The Semiotic of Myth*).

A philosopher of science needs to find the hierarchy of a science and note its changes through successive theories. It is the hierarchy and the production of it which provide the key to the transvaluation in science. Bloom's ratios are steps toward the completion of a transvaluation in poetry. Bloom's map of misreading almost qualifies as a narration in Liszka's sense: myth "suspends these rules imaginatively out of their typical employment and reanimates them, simultaneously reevaluating them, within the narration of the tale" (215 Ibid). If a regular internal development is described, science could more clearly be explained as transvaluative. Each main part of the theory would transvalue an earlier part ("The same change [of the third law of Newton] of motion supplies the definition of dynamical force implicit in the second law").

The need is well stated by Gablik:

> ...a particular notion such as perspective could only have been attained by a series of successive steps... The phenomena of art history only become fully intelligible when they are related to something both biological and logical that can help to explain why, in the development of representation, one stage follows another, or why these stages show a `sequential' character (each being necessary to the following one in a constant order) (152).

Kuhn's account needs to become more "biological and logical" if it is to explain more. Though Kuhn does not say as much, the inner development of a scientific tradition form is cyclical. Only if it is cyclical can each new theory regenerate science--transvalue it--while still belonging in a continuous series. Myth is transvaluative, on Liszka'a view, not because it teaches a lesson, but because it "should engender evaluation" (219 Ibid). For Bloom, a poetry evaluates a previous one; should this not apply also to a science?

One philosopher arguing for the necessity of narrative in science is Donald Philip Verene. Narrative, as I interpret his view, provides the means of ever new self-knowledge. "The self," he writes, "has no more than momentary reality without a narrative of itself which constantly lives below the surface of our actions" (47 *The New Art...*). In more scientific-style of language, science must have a sequence of developmental steps, which revise previous ones if there is to be a determinate direction in creation, not to mention access to the criteria of scientificity.

Crisis, and Impasse

Scientific theories all develop anomalies until they become a crisis, a problem found (by a successor) to be unsolvable by the paradigm's principles.

"Crisis" sets in when there are a proliferation of competing theories to account for anomalies (74 *SSR*). An example is the period when light was sometimes a wave, sometimes a particle (114-15 *SSR*). Normal science may not realize any fundamental problem--enough to require a change of paradigm--until extraordinary science does. A crisis is an anomaly on a deeper level.

Puzzle solving and fact finding cannot cast doubt on the most fundamental principles of the paradigm (349 *CR*); facts cannot disprove theories (281 *ET*). A crisis cannot consist in a counterinstance (77 *SSR*). I can offer the explanation for Kuhn that any phenomenon would be defined in terms of the paradigm; the paradigm is not defined in terms of any particular event. The validity of a paradigm would consist in its general coherence, the model for which is directly present in tradition, not in direct reference to observable facts. There are always some discrepancies or anomalies or counterinstances (81 *SSR*).

In some passages Kuhn presents the role of normal science in a crisis as follows. When a crisis is seen, normal science asks for help: "As in manufacture so in science--retooling is an extravagance to be reserved for the occasion that demands it. The significance of crises is the indication they provide that an occasion for retooling has arrived" (76 *SSR*). Bloom would disagree; each figure of poetry is also a crisis at which some `retooling' occurs--a change of direction.

When problems start to get more severe, normal science resists changes. Kuhn rightly points out that this has value; scientists will not be misdirected at every novel suggestion (65 *SSR*).

Do crises always precede revolutions? Kuhn's critics have said, `No' (181 *SSR*). Kuhn concurs, although he should not. If crisis is the sociological phenomenon of much controversy among competing theorists, then crisis may be absent. But if crisis means a structural limit of a scientific theory, then certainly there must be limits if a revolution is needed.

Sometimes Kuhn speaks of crises in a more deconstructive way. Then crises seem to be the direct result of the full development of the theory (74 *SSR*).

At what point do anomalies impugn the paradigm itself? When the "explicit and fundamental generalizations" are called into question, Kuhn answers (82 *SSR*). At this point "an anomaly is more than an anomaly." A change of paradigms occurs when the fundamental tenets of a field and when "the very possibility of continued progress" are at stake (163 *SSR*). Bloom and Derrida agree.

But why is the progress threatened? What is the impasse in a framework causing it to be changed? Einstein gives a sense of an impasse in physics leading to his new theory:

> But what is the medium through which light spreads and what are its mechanical properties? There is no hope of reducing the optical phenomena to the mechanical ones before this question is answered. But the difficulties in solving this problem are so great that we have to give it up and thus give up the mechanical view as well (122).

Kuhn's theory would be more complete if he defined the relation of concepts at the moment of the unsolvable problem (unsolvable within a given paradigm). It would also help to know how these concepts developed. Derrida has a definite sense of an impasse--that caused by the transcendental signified, as discussed earlier. Deconstruction, in fact, concentrates on the impasse, the point of orientation for the whole framework. Kuhn's theory is deconstructive to the extent that he does admit the regular occurrence of unsolvable problems in scientific theories. Yet, the discussion is too general to define the changes in concepts leading up to and beyond the impasse.

Incommensurability

Proponents of different paradigms cannot communicate fully; their views are "incommensurable."

"Incommensurability" refers to three kinds of differences in the views of scientists. They may disagree about the list of problems; about interpretation of problems; about the general orientation of science (148-50 *SSR*). "Practicing in different worlds, the two groups of scientists see different things when they look from the same point in the same direction" (150 *SSR*).

The issue of the incommensurability of paradigms is "the most castigated thesis of the Kuhnian opus" (105 Kisiel). This issue has earned Kuhn the charge of irrationalism, subjectivity, illogical thinking, especially when he declares that proofs cannot solve paradigm disputes (148 *SSR*). Ironically, these are just the traits a scientist usually is thought not to have, and the traits Kuhn would most like to deny. When theorizing about the failure of proofs to solve paradigm disputes, he always has normal scientists in mind, their strong (emotional) commitments. Isn't the proper question, do the creators of paradigms have proofs? Certainly Einstein believed he had proof.

The famous saying of physicist Max Planck expresses the difficulty in changing scientific world views: `new scientific truth does not triumph by convincing its opponents and making them see the light, but rather because its opponents eventually die, and a new generation grows up that is familiar with it' (468 Cohen).

Kuhn conveys the difficulty of the change in the views of normal science. But how difficult is it for creators to change their views? Does an Einstein ever convince his predecessor, a Maxwell, to begin science anew? Isn't the decision as to validity first made by the creators? Kuhn never does discuss how *they* make their decisions, but one would think that they are the most important cases to explain. By placing the incommensurability or possible commensurability in the hands of normal science, Kuhn is making scientific truth a matter of allegiance, almost a result of voting.

Kisiel describes the change in Kuhn's doctrine of incommensurability (106). The change is a "refinement." Kuhn does not mean that scientific theories cannot be compared, only that they cannot be compared by an external standard. I would like to ask, who has the standard? Can normal science ever be fully in possession of the standard of any paradigm? After much criticism by philosophers of science, Kuhn places the emphasis on linguistic features, rather than on a lack of understanding or disagreement about scientific truth. I think, those who would reject the idea of incommensurability the most do so because they would not like to admit that science changes its criteria of truth and that the criteria are limited to the cycle of a specific theory. If this is not the case, philosophers of science may feel secure in having a more legitimate activity: showing general truths about science indifferently applying to its successive generations. This is the easier intellectual route, as well as the less determinate one.

Notwithstanding eventual shortcomings, a main virtue of Kuhn's entire theory of science is this idea of incommensurability. All testing, he claims, must occur within a paradigm (146 *SSR*). Similar statements can be found in Derrida's philosophy: there is nothing outside the text, for example. There is no external authority outside science to judge it (114 *SSR*). I think critics of Kuhn's idea would like to be such external authorities. But the creators of science are not authorities by remaining "external" to the process; the legitimation is science itself.

Critics of Kuhn ignore human limitations. They take the part of the growing single human being which the race has formed--but one that does not change in the process. The individual does. Any definition of science is from some individual's limited vision. DNA is limited to each living thing; no two have exactly the same genetic instructions (except for the new possibility of clones).

In a way, I think the issue of incommensurability would not be an issue for a creator of science. When the previous theory is found to stop the progress of science, when its problem is seen to be unsolvable, new principles are proposed that make the previous ones dependent on the new ones. The previous ones were less adequate versions of the new ones. The previous views are devalued, subordinated so that no decision between competing theories need be made. If the predecessor objects to a successor's new theory, it cannot by definition be made from the same assumption as the successor holds, or else they would agree. The "dispute" would be no more than the difference of a paraphrase. Scientific progress must be more than a series of paraphrases. This support of some incommensurability is based on analogy with Bloom's view of misreading and even more on Derrida's view of intervention and *bricolage*.

The situation of incommensurability may even be an illusion. Consider the statement about a positive use of incommensurability in politics: "A leader has to be able to say different things to different people. When you make that impossible, you make it harder for all of us to agree with each other" (Suzanne Garment, author of a book on political mistrust, quoted from "What Can One Expect from Politicians?" *Athens News*, April 8, 1992). If science does not interpret the "same" ideas in different ways, how could there ever be a continuous series of changing views? The "disagreement" between say Maxwell and Einstein permits science to be a continuous yet changing process of building a tradition. By excluding genuine disagreement about what is truth in science, theorists can replace the engagement in the ever unique decision process with general ideas applicable to all theories, and to this extent the practice would be self-serving.

When philosophers of science object to "incommensurability," they seem to have faith that scientists always agree or in the end they always do. Ironically, scientists do not have this faith as strongly as those who claim to understand it. Cohen provides a good anecdote to the contrary: Lothar Meyer

> was recalling a striking event that occurred at the end of the Karlsruhe Congress in 1860, "one of the most important congresses in the history of chemistry" (van Spronsen 1969, 42), convened by the great organic chemist August Kekulé. This was the first time that an international assembly of scientists attempted to solve a pressing internal problem of science. At issue was the confusion between competing and rather different systems of atomic weights. So great was the uncertainty that many chemists turned from atomic weights to combining weights. ...The congress was called to solve "once and for all" this thorny question, on which all structural formulas for organic chemistry had ultimately to depend (see Milt 1948).
>
> The chemists from all over the world, as may not be surprising, did not conclude their deliberations with a simple, universally accepted solution (471).

Bloom sees the tradition of poetry as passing through single individuals. In nature, too, changes in DNA must appear in actual things. This example shows the belief in group change, as if all things had the same genetic code or were substantially united. Change cannot occur everywhere but in no particular individual.

Like the idea behind the congress, Kuhn himself likes to agree, for after years of criticism he changed his view slightly to make it seem as if he had accommodated the critics while retaining the basic theory he had all along. The approach is half cunning, half desire for consensus.

The Necessity in Creation and the Genetic Code of Science

(Extraordinary) scientists know what the necessary path in creation is by a sense of a genetic code. From a learned sense of the passing of generations and a thorough knowledge of the limits of the present one, a new generation progressively forms in the creator's mind.

Kuhn asserts the cyclic nature of scientific theories: "...though more powerful than its predecessors, the Newtonian universe is not proving more final. Nor is its history, considered as one of many chapters in the development of human thought, very different in structure from that of the earth-centered universe which Copernicus and Newton destroyed" (265 CR). If the structures of successive theories resemble previous ones, then a knowledge of the cycle would very much help scientists create, or solve problems--to use other language.

Scientists must have some sense of a recurring pattern which their new theories fit--better, they evolve a new pattern by analogy with the old. The following comment by Kuhn applied to the historian's task should apply equally to the scientist's:

> Such rules, however, only limit but do not determine the outcome of either the child's or the historian's task. In both cases the basic criterion for having done the job right is the primitive recognition that the pieces fit to form a familiar, if previously unseen, product. The child has seen pictures, the historian behavior patterns, similar to these before. That recognition of similarity is, I believe, prior to any answers to the question, similar with respect to what? Though it can be rationally understood and perhaps even modelled on a computer (I once attempted something of the sort myself), the similarity relation does not lend itself to lawlike reformulation. It is global, not reducible to a unique set of prior criteria more primitive than the similarity relation itself (17 ET).

Kuhn does extend this idea of primitive recognition to the role of paradigms (specific problem solutions) in scientific research. One cannot help but think that he is thinking of normal science and not extraordinary science. But the principle should apply even more to the latter, for this type knows the pattern better if able to create it anew. Since rules cannot be used to extend the traditional pattern, which must change even if only slightly in each new successive theory, some type of recognition of similarity could explain the transmission of the scientific way of doing things. The new theory would be modelled on a previous one, making possible the transfer of the pattern without the need to reduce the pattern to a finite fully determined set of rules. Kuhn does state that scientists do not know such a set.

The recognition of a pattern of scientific discourse would explain the priority of laws over observable facts. Kuhn writes about an "advance awareness of difficulties" that Lavoisier had, enabling him to see a gas Priestley never could see (56 *SSR*). The awareness of difficulties before they occur sounds paradoxical, unless it means the hypothetical extension of an existing pattern of discourse. Instead of "hypothetical," art scholars might say "imaginative."

The idea of a pattern recurring in successive theories would also explain the limits on individual knowledge. "...New members [of a scientific language community] acquire a set of cognitive commitments that are not, in principle, fully analyzable within that language itself" (xxii *ET*). The need for further explanation points the way to the recurrence of the pattern in a new, higher, more developed form. An individual scientist's knowledge of the scientific enterprise is limited to a specific theory; science, however, existed before that theory and develops beyond it. In the words of the poet Robert Duncan, "...there is a Self that belongs to a Story that determines the sense of truth and life..." (2). The scientist belongs to the Story of science, to the tradition surpassing every individual; without that continuous tradition there could be no individual theory. This narrative, cyclical view of scientific theories makes more understandable the view that science is more about a mode of vision, its coherence, its process, than about some external reality, which is anyway ever-changing with each new theory. Expressing this idea are Duncan's words: "The truth we know is not of What Is, but of What Is Happening" (46). For the creative scientist, science is about science-making. Extraordinary scientists explain science more than they do nature.

Consensus and the Legitimation of Science

According to Kuhn, science tends toward consensus, whereas the last stage of a theory ends in the strongest dissensus or disagreement.

Does science tend toward consensus as Kuhn claims? Certainly, it helped to form a common world of action while uniting people of different ages in the continuous project of civilization. But do all scientists agree with each new theory?

Kuhn perspicaciously remarks that if an anomaly continues some scientists may view it as "the subject matter of their discipline" (82 *SSR*). This could mean that it denotes a crucial topic; or that science tends to produce anomalies and therefore dissensus, not consensus; or, the most consequential meaning, the stakes in the crisis are the future of science.

The distinction between normal science and extraordinary science has much relevance to this issue. What Kuhn wants to explain above all is revolution. How can science change so radically? Kuhn would not ask this question if he did not see some kind of problem with the change. Radical, large-scale changes seem contrary to the gradual evolution of knowledge, according to the common sense view of science. The choice of "normal" in "normal science" sugggests that science does *not* change radically most of the time; the wholistic revolutions are not an everyday activity or goal of science. If this is true, then the fact is consistent with the idea that science tends toward consensus. However, if a paradigm always ends in an unsolvable problem--a point following from Kuhn's ideas but one he would not like to state so baldly, harshly, explicitly, then why does science not tend toward dissensus, paradox? To be fair to Kuhn, he does attribute a high value to extraordinary science. "There are also extraordinary problems, and it may well be their resolution that makes the scientific enterprise as a whole so particularly worthwhile. But extraordinary problems are not to be had for the asking" (34 *SSR*). By making revolution an extraordinary event Kuhn can preserve the value of normal science, with its special interest in consensus. Kuhn's whole theory is a kind of a dialogue between normal and extraordinary science in which normal science learns a little more about the extraordinary. For this reason, not to mention the controversy concerning his ideas, his theory achieved wide recognition. If he took the perspective of "extraordinary" science, the theory would be much different. Bloom does this.

If scientific validity depends upon consensus, it may seem as if truth is arrived at through a vote. Jean-François Lyotard interprets Kuhn's theory in this way:

> This way of inquiring into sociopolitical legitimacy combines with the new scientific attitude: the name of the hero is the people, the sign of legitimacy is the people's consensus, and their mode of creating norms is deliberation. The notion of progress is a necessary outgrowth of this. It represents nothing other than the movement by which knowledge is presumed to accumulate--but this movement is extended to the new sociopolitical subject. The people debate among themselves about what is just or unjust in the same way that the scientific community debates about what is true or false; they accumulate civil laws just as scientists accumulate scientific laws; they perfect their rules of consensus just as the scientists produce new "paradigms" to revise their rules in light of what they have learned (30 *The Postmodern...*).

In contrast Einstein did not call a meeting when creating the theory of relativity. Kuhn's concern with consensus is a concern with the voting *after* the theory has been created. It is as if a law is passed and Kuhn is interested not in the process of making it but in the more secondary process of obeying or disobeying by the citizens. He entirely misses the truth-making process on which consensus or dissensus depends. To this extent, Kuhn is a normal philosopher of science rather than an extraordinary. The primary issue is not whether the community of scientists agrees with Einstein; it is whether Einstein agrees with Maxwell and why. Bloom understands poetic change in these primary terms, one great poet revising a previous great poet.

Again interpreting Kuhn's theory, Lyotard argues the legitimacy of science depends upon dissension. Should one great scientist not disagree with a previous one if the understanding of science is to change? Isn't the purpose of science the growth of knowledge?

> ...it is now dissension that must be emphasized. Consensus is a horizon that is never reached. Research that takes place under the aegis of a paradigm tends to stabilize; it is like the exploitation of a technological, economic, or artistic "idea." It cannot be discounted. But what is striking is that someone always comes along to disturb the order of "reason." It is necessary to posit the existence of a power that destabilizes the capacity for explanation, manifested in the promulgation of new norms for understanding or, if one prefers, in a proposal to establish new rules circumscribing a new field of research for the language of science (61 *The Postmodern...*).

Being the whole purpose of his theory, Kuhn wants to explain the disturbance of revolutions, while defending the view of science held by "normal science." Consensus does occur, though only temporarily until an unsolvable problem occurs. Lyotard points out two assumptions behind this erroneous view (65-66 *The Postmodern...*). First of all, the view arguing for consensus assumes the debaters can know a set of rules valid for all paradigms. Secondly, the goal of science is consensus. Lyotard argues consensus does occur as a particular phase of the development; its end is always "paralogy": a crisis occurs which casts into doubt part of what has been meant by scientificity, scientific meaningfulness, scientific validity. If the criteria for validity change, if the criteria are limited to individual, human understanding, then how could criteria be external to any specific theory? A new theory includes new criteria, which promote a new kind of consensus, but these criteria disagree to some extent with the previous ones. Learning requires change; change in concepts requires disagreement. Bloom almost serves as an opposite to Kuhn. Bloom only explains poetry through the struggle of vision between great poets, virtually neglecting any cooperation of successive generations.

If generations of science succeed one another, they can only do so if there are differences in the concepts. These differences are fundamental, as Kuhn rightly emphasized in contrast to many of his critics. To create a new generation of science would be to create a difference with the previous one. In this way science moves toward paralogy, toward a state of affairs in which what is defined to be science changes somewhat. Kuhn should have understood science as a phenomenon of tradition more than he did. Then he would have taken the extra step to claim that science's purpose is to change itself. Lyotard speaks about the criteria of science in terms of language games. The game itself can change, or a lesser degree of change is a change in some moves within the game. Kuhn would have science primarily interested in a change in the moves of the game; Lyotard believes the more fundamental goal is the formulation of the rules by which the game can be played, the laws of nature (66 Ibid).

Built-in Signal for a New Science

The end of any scientific theory characteristically signals the presupposition which must be changed.

On Kuhn's view, science does form a whole of interrelated concepts. They are so interrelated that a problem can arise requiring the change in the network of relations. A new whole would be needed. Giving an example from Aristotelian physics, Kuhn states, "In that sense, too, the lawlike statement `there are no voids in nature' did not function within Aristotelian physics quite as a law. It could not, that is, be eliminated and replaced by an improved version, leaving the rest of the structure standing" (20 *ET*). Here the essential interdependence of a theory's concepts is clear.

There is a built-in signal system for creation. Crises discovered by normal science point to the need for innovation by extraordinary science (350 *CR*). The signal pointing the direction for future creation would be more built into the process of science if the agency creating also had direct access to the signal. The signal is a structural part of the paradigm, though Kuhn does not carry his own thought to this explicit conclusion. Elsewhere, Kuhn claims "felt anomaly" is transformed into "concrete contradiction" (264 *ET*). The signal does seem to be an inconsistency or hiatus in the fabric of scientific explanation, as Einstein describes it. "The theory of relativity arises from the field problems [of Maxwell's equations]. The contradictions and inconsistencies of the old theories force us to ascribe new properties to the time-space continuum, to the scene of all events in our physical world" (244). These contradictions operate as a signal to new creation: "The most beautiful fate of a physical theory is to point the way to the establishment of a more inclusive theory, in which it lives on as a limiting case."[5]

In the words of Clifford Truesdell, a science presents a "challenge" to its successors (242). I interpet this to mean all the basic factors of the problem are present in an unsythesized conglomeration. They need to be synthesized, decoded, recoded. Then science can continue.

If scientific form is to be well-formed, it must be capable of transmitting itself. As Derrida claims, the possibility must be inscribed in the structure of a previous science. Narrative knowledge, on Lyotard's view, "certifies itself in the pragmatics of its own transmission" (27 *The Postmodern...*). Similarly, if a science is to be certified as such, it must belong in a series, both receiving the heritage of the past and preparing the way for subsequent creation. This transmission remains a vague general idea for Kuhn.

Summary

Theories end in anomalies, anomalies create crises, and crises lead to a revolution. Basically, normal science makes the anomalies known to extraordinary science, even though Kuhn sometimes states that extraordinary science knows the difficulties "in advance" of normal science; perhaps the crises are necessitated by the structure of science, a fact Kuhn would not like to explain as merely an inevitable structural outcome, or perhaps normal science is not needed, contrary to what Kuhn predominantly claims. The capacity of normal science to understand the problem with the entire framework is ambiguously defined. Nor does Kuhn define adequately the actual problem that is unsolvable according to the presuppositions of the paradigm. Comments by Einstein and by Cassirer (previously given) define the recurring structure of the crisis much more. Kuhn's idea of the unsolvable puzzle forcing the creation of a new paradigm is a minimal idea of a built-in signal for scientific creation. A greater sense of a genetic code for science might have led Kuhn to define the signalling, the encoding of future science. Notwithstanding these critical relfections, Kuhn's theory contains many innovations in the philosophy of science.

NOTES

1. See 116 of Eggers and Mayer, *Ernst Cassirer: An Annotated Bibliography*. The ideas come from "Reflections on the Concept of Group and the Theory of Perception," *Symbol, Myth, and Culture*, ed. Donald Philip Verene, 271-91.

2. This discussion occurred in a film, "Pablo Picasso: The Legacy of a Genius," (Michael Blackwood, USA, 1982), 90', at The Tate Gallery, London, 12 September 1992. Comments were by Moore, Matta, Caro, Hockney and Lichtenstein, among others.

3. For a more extended discussion of the change in the term "paradigm" see Kisiel 97 and Cohen 578.

4. Idea taken from 105 of *Ernst Cassirer: An Annotated Bibliography*, by Eggers and Mayer. The original is "Logos, Dike, Kosmos in der Entwicklung der griechischen Philosophie." *Göteborgs Högskolas Arsskrift*, 47 (Göteborg: Eleanders Boktr., 1941), 31 pp.

5. Quoted from 378 *ETR*; also see 442 Cohen; also see the original: *Uber die spezielle und die allgemeine Relativitäts Theorie*. Sammlung Vieweg, Heft 38. 2. Aufl.

CHAPTER 10:

The End of a Poetry

Introduction to Bloom's Definition of the End

A poetry knows how to end itself, or in non-anthropomorphic terms there is a characteristic way in which the greatest poetries end, and each one has a slightly new definition of what it is to end a poem--a revised version of the poetic genetic code. Bloom's two revisionary ratios for the third, final movement are askesis and apophrades. These ratios achieve the most positive results yet, in providing the poet with an imaginative space beyond the precursor's. Once again the precursor's aesthetic is re-interpreted, and this time it becomes clearer that it is less adequate. In the final stages it seems as if the predecessor was trying to do just what the successor does much better. The quest ends. The new great poet ensures his/her immortality by limiting any future poetry to an art that is derivative. The cycle is completed.

The Relation of the End of a Poetry to Its Beginning

The end of a poetry gives its creator what (s)he started looking for at the beginning: a new individual imaginative space superior to the precursor's.

Throughout the making of an entire poetry the poet's understanding of the poetic vision constantly develops. The changes are called "misadventures." Critics have noticed the same process in fiction; "the cultural center that epics celebrate keeps shifting, as does the frontier from which they address that center" (28 *Novel Epics*).

There is a changing sense of the precursor's work combined with a changing sense of poetry's definition up to the end of the poetry.[1]

The quest begins because the previous great poet does not make way for a successor. It seems as if there is no more poetry to be written. Also it seems as if the imagination of the precursor is discontinuous or not universal. The upcoming poet develops "an anxiety that mixes worries about imaginative priority with more overt worries about the continuity of imagination between the younger and the older Wordsworth" (71 *PR*).

The three movements defining a poetry can be stated in different ways. All of them depend on a constant re-assessing of the poet's new vision in relation to the precursor. In one way, the new strong poet turns the "precursor into a fouled version of the later poet himself"; then the poet transforms "himself into a fouled version of himself"; finally, the poet confounds the consequence with the figure of the precursor" (62 *AI*). A higher origin of poetry is found at the end. Bloom also uses a second way, based on the original poet Wallace Stevens' idea. Poetry forms a threefold dialectic: the start is a "reduction to a First Idea"; the middle development is a "finding the reduction intolerable"; the final development is a "re-imagining the First Idea" (285 *PR*). The most prevalent way to describe the threefold dialectic of any canonical poetry is in terms of Bloom's unique revisionary ratios, of which there are six divided into pairs forming three movements. In the first pair of movements, clinamen and tessera, the poet strives to correct or complete the dead poetry. In the second pair, kenosis and daemonization, the poet works to repress memory of the dead, to see the precursor as even less original. In the third pair, askesis and apophrades, called "the contest proper," the poetic vision of the successor is finally seen to be "prior" to that of the precursor. Bloom often uses "earlier" for "prior." If poetry could be put into logical terms, the terms would mean that the successor's poetry is presupposed by the predecessor. Or, the predecessor's vision is less adequate.

The final two ratios are "prior" even to the start of the poetry, the first two ratios. Bloom's combined term for the third movement is "representation," meaning what the poet began with is re-presented in a new way, just as the great poet Stevens claims. A circle is formed like the ouroboros, the serpent of time, which forms a circle by swallowing its tail. In some ways the end of the poetry seems to be the "antithetical completion" of the start. Whereas the start was designed to show the separation from the precursor, the end shows a communion with the precursor, though a "re-presented" one: the successor is now superior, having his/her own imaginative space, a new space for poetry. Whereas the start of a poetry means a continuing denial of the vision of the precursor, the end antithetically completes the quest: "inverting the quest-pattern by revealing the past failures as being something other than failures" (114 *MM*). An apt way of phrasing the binding of the end to the start has been given by Griffiths and Rabinowitz: "The form itself becomes autobiographical in explaining the act of literary derivation that gave it birth" (5). The poet "recognizes himself" again (120 *PR*). Poetry moves from a desire for freedom from influence to self-realization. There is also a feeling of communion with the entire tradition, as will be seen in the next ratio apophrades. The modern Greek word for metalepsis means "communion," the religious ritual of drinking wine and eating bread to become united with Christ.

Derrida holds a similar view; namely, that a work can close itself because its end is defined as engendering its beginning. He calls this idea "preformationism," applicable to Proust's fiction and all canonical works.[2] It is as if a destination is reached, the destination being the final cause of the point of departure. The parts of a poetry are interdependent for an overall purpose.

What idea did the poet start with that is re-presented at the end? Strictly speaking, even the second set of ratios re-envision the first, though without providing the destination asked for by the start of the quest. The poetry is a continuous process of reforming the unity of the tradition. Imaginatively, this abstraction takes the form of the predecessor; that means the successor is re-interpreting the precursor at each stage. "...The blocking agent that gradually gives way here is the imaginary form of the precursor" (146 *PR*). The poetry begins in a struggle with the predecessor, and this struggle continues throughout to the end. "No newly strong poet can reduce the significance of the precursor's mastery, because it is not possible for the new or belated poet to transcend the oppositional relationship that is ultimately a negative or dialectical identification with the precursor" (146 *PR*). Poetic meaning at any point in a poetry is an "inter-poetic" relationship (157 *PR*). Derrida, too, founds all meaning on inter-textual differences. The unity of a poetry results from the initial quest the precursor set the successor on. "A poem both takes its origin in a Scene of Instruction and finds its necessary aim or purpose there as well. It is only by repressing creative `freedom', through the initial fixation of influence, that a person can be reborn as a poet. And only by revising that repression can a poet become and remain strong" (27 *PR*). The sense of the origin and the end become modified at each stage of the poetry, so no single creative principle could be used deductively or inductively throughout.

The quest is an attempt to counter the predecessor's limitation on future poetry. Poetry is understood by the precursor in such a way that the process is seen as being entropic; less and less meaning will be found in future poetry. Or to think of it in another way, any successor could only be derivative of the precursor. With the poetic process at stake, it needs to be understood in a new way. How can a poet develop a new sense of poetic development? The quest concerns defining new poetic development. Poetry is about its own process, its own tradition-forming. Byron Raizis makes the same point about Yeat's Byzantium poems: "they are visual dramatizations of the *process* of attaining artistic perfection, and of the special *status* (secular and spiritual) of the Poet, who has attained excellence" (301). Also, "`Sailing to Byzantium'" remains a poem about Yeats' maturation process as a poet" (308). The process implies "`psychic wholeness' and transcendence." Just as the painter when creating is asking, What is painting?, so too the poet is asking, What is poetry? (102 Lyotard *The Inhuman*).

The poet fully understands the process of the predecessor only by completing a subsequent great poetry. Only after its completion can the poet finally see his/her passage from the predecessor.[3] This requirement for the deepest understanding of poetry calls to mind Vico's principle that we can only understand what we have made; to understand great poetry--even that of the predecessor, for it was this attempt that started the quest--one must create it. Critics, of course, would resist this idea to the death because it puts them in a subordinate capacity for understanding poetic meaning, reserving the pure full understanding for creators.

The end of a poetry completes the vision required at the start. The poet finally understands how (s)he can be an influence rather than merely being influenced. There is a performance of the poetic process such that the successor can be seen as having a superior aesthetic.

The successor finally has an imaginative space, a total poetic vision, relatively independent of the precursor and extending to future influence. The poet desires to have an all-encompassing vision, one described by Campbell:

> The agony of breaking through personal limitations is the agony of spiritual growth. Art, literature, myth and cult, philosophy, and ascetic disciplines are instruments to help the individual past his limiting horizons into spheres of ever-expandng realization. As he crosses threshold after threshold, conquering dragon after dragon, the stature of the divinity that he summons to his highest wish increases, until it subsumes the cosmos (190 *Hero...*).

Askesis as a New Poetic Stance

It is a new poetic stance toward the precursor--a new sense of poetry, a new development of the continuum or unity of tradition; a new stance toward one's own previous ratios; toward one's own future developments; toward the developments by poets after oneself.

Askesis is a purgation, separation, estrangement. "The soul's estrangement from itself is not intended, yet follows from the attempt at estranging not only all precursors, but their worlds, which means to have estranged poetry itself" (120 *AI*). The previous ratio being daemonization, the poet wants to raise himself/herself above its counter-sublime [the sublimity counter to the predecessor], above the series which that ratio is still too attached to--by opposition. The reader should recall the extremes in daemonization represented in poems through images of highs and lows, using alternatively hyperbole and litotes. Bloom describes the feeling of the transition from daemonization to askesis as a change "from a perpetually mounting force of still greater repression to a stance finally the poet's own" (121 *PR*).

This opposition of daemonization is integrated into a new attitude. At askesis, there is "the acceptance of a precursor's survival as the inevitable form of the other, as a dualism that never again can be banished" (73 *MM*). The internalization of this opposition brings about "oxymoronic intensity," the term showing the combining of the opposition of daemonization into one figure (155 *MM*). The poet has the sense that (s)he starts the continuity of poetry. Images suggest that the poet's vision will continue indefinitely: "a self-perpetuating oscillating series is set in motion" (71 *AI*).

Askesis makes the end of a poem to some extent self-negating, to use de Man's term. The poet denies some feature of poetic vision previously assumed to apply to both the precursor and the new poet. Though the poet seems at first to limit his/her poetic ability, the goal is to become further distinguished from the precursor. Askesis is a "movement of self-purgation which intends the attainment of a state of solitude" (15 *AI*). Whereas kenosis was thought of as "emptying" the precursor, askesis is thought of as "curtailing." Askesis is a "self-curtailment which seeks transformation at the expense of narrowing the creative circumference of precursor and ephebe [upcoming poet] alike" (119 *AI*). The new poet not only limits the immediate precursor, but also the entire tradition. The poet sacrifices what was formerly thought to be part of poetic ability for the sake of greater individuation from the precursor. Bloom writes, "There [at the end] Roland negates the larger part of his poem, a negation that strengthens rather than weakens the poem" (116 *MM*). Bloom speaks about the fulfillment of Roland's quest after rejecting the wholly negative repetition which the poet experiences in the ratio before askesis (112 *MM*). Roland makes hyperbole of hyperbole--in this way he overcomes the previous ratio by totalizing it, by performing on it what operation brought it into being. The poet finally finds an adequate stance to define his/her own poetic space.

How Successors Become Superior While Formerly Inferior: Metalepsis or Transumption

Successors nearly complete the change of their predecessors' poetries by using metalepsis or transumption to gain their superiority.

Askesis is created through the rhetorical trope called metalepsis or transumption. In the most general terms it means a change of previous meaning such that the poet can see himself/herself as being superior and having an independent vision.

The turn of thought can be explained through the expression, `The Child is father of the Man'. A poet, say Wordsworth, comes *after* Milton but wants to be seen as a great poet from whose ability Milton's could be derived (as lesser). Wordsworth is the child of the man, Milton. Yet, the poet who comes later can become "the father" of the earlier one--a superior aesthetic is achieved. Wordsworth finds a higher, deeper poetic vision. The movement is like that from effect to cause, from a theory to new principles deriving the theory.

The meaning of metalepsis is best seen in the context of a whole poem. Wordsworth's "Intimations of Immortality from Recollections of Early Childhood" means for Bloom a quest for poetic election, an attempt to become a true and great poet (12-13 *MM*; 103-06 *PR*). Immortality is a very significant theme, for Milton tried to live forever through his poetry, to derive the past from himself and to deny that anyone could develop poetry further. Against this obstacle Wordsworth must struggle, and if successful he will achieve immortality by presenting an obstacle to any new poetry. The ode begins with a quotation from Wordsworth's "My Heart Leaps Up":

> The Child is father of the Man;
> And I could wish my days to be
> Bound each to each by natural piety.

Here the Child corresponds to Wordsworth at the time of his mature poetry and the Man refers to Milton, Wordsworth's great predecessor. The first line here demonstrates what Bloom believes is the quintessential poetic goal: "transuming" one's precursor, or developing one's poetry to a point at which it seems that all previous poetry is less poetic and perhaps derived paradoxically from the latter. At this point in a poem or a whole body of poetry, the anxiety of influence would have become the least possible.

Toward this rhetorical trope of deriving one's predecessors the Ode has a threefold characteristic movement. Throughout the three movements of the Ode, Bloom sees Wordsworth at first turning away from Milton, then further undoing his connection with Milton's processes, and finally arriving at a poetic ability that makes it seem as if Milton is derived from Wordsworth and not the other way around. This paradox is of the essence of the poetic struggle, according to Bloom, and it can be seen in Wordsworth's line "The Child is father of the Man." In other words provided by Bloom, "he who is willing to work gives birth to his own father" (56 *AI*). At this point, the opposition of successor and predecessor ceases, or is at the advantage of the successor. The previous great poet is fulfilled and refuted (142 *MM*). The quest ends.

To change the whole of tradition, to advance it one step, the poet must come to see his vision as retroactively giving meaning to preceding poetry. Einstein believed this process applied to his theory of relativity insofar as it could include Newtonian mechanics as a limiting case. The problem is to accept the accumulated knowledge of the past while not being determined by it and thus not original. Bloom explains,

> For the anxiety of influence stems from the ephebe's assertion of an eternal, divinating consciousness that nevertheless took its historical point of departure in an intra-textual encounter, and most crucially in the interpretative moment or act of misprision contained in that encounter. How indeed, the ephebe must wonder, can such a point of departure have more than merely historical rather than poetic interest? More anxiously, even, how is the strong poet's claim to poetic immortality (the only eternal happiness that is relevant) to be founded upon an encounter trapped belatedly in time? (57 *MM*).

A poetry must include all poetic vision if the tradition is to be accumulated in each new great poetry and so passed on. In more biological terms, a set of instructions is transmitted, with slight variation. For this to occur, the poet must form a vision giving new meaning to poetry's past, its present, and its future. Bloom's ratios situate the poet's vision within an infinite imaginative space.

The poet finally seems to be successful through the last pair of ratios. Does this mean that the successor "fulfills" the precursor? Does a succeeding poetry relate to a preceding one as a solution to a problem?

Although Bloom sometimes states a successor "fulfills" a predecessor, he more often wants to question this interpretation of the relationship. Keats "has seen what he always wanted to see. He has revised romance, even his own kind of romance, by reconciling and almost integrating the quester and the object of quest" (138 *PR*). And elsewhere Bloom claims one successor "fulfills and refutes" the predecessor (142 *MM*). Certainly, refutation is combined with fulfillment. The end of a poetry presents to the poet what the predecessor had denied to him/her (114 *MM*); In this way a "figure of a figure" is created, meaning that the successor changes what the predecessor had changed. Since there are arguments to the contrary, though, Bloom should be interpreted as denying the fulfillment. More important, what does fulfillment mean? Or, why does it make a difference? Bloom's idea is quite revealing about his whole criticism:

> In our terms, we might say that to the ephebe or later poet, the precursor is the figura, and the ephebe is the fulfillment, but that would be to share the later poet's self-idealization. Instead, the following can be stated as a basic principle of poetic misprision: `No later poet can be the fulfillment of any earlier poet'. He can be the reversal of the precursor, or the deformation of the precursor, but whatever he is, `to revise is not to fulfill' (88 *PR*).

Instead of the successor being the fulfillment of the predecessor, Bloom prefers to think of the relation as reversal or deformation. "Fulfillment" would suggest more continuity, perhaps identity, of purpose. When Helen Elam interpets Bloom's view, she points out that Erich Auerbach's "figura" expresses the idea of fulfillment, and that Bloom rejects the idea for a more "purely disjunctive figure"-- namely, metalepsis (39). Another passage can corroborate Elam's interpretation; Bloom argues that it was not fulfillment but "subversion of tradition that enforced Milton's own earliness while troping [turning, changing] tradition into belatedness" (96 *PR*).

The Transition from Askesis to Apophrades

Apophrades provides the poet with more of an image of wholeness (and an individual poetic space) than askesis does.

The best single definition of apophrades is the following: "the triumph of having so stationed the precursor, in one's own work, that particular passages in `his' work seem to be not presages of one's own advent, but rather to be indebted to one's own achievement, and even (necessarily) to be lessened by one's greater splendor" (141 *AI*). A poet "stations" another poet in his/her work by repeating words, images, themes in a new way. Especially if a reader is familiar with the previous poetry can one see the revision by the successor.

The quest comes to an end at apophrades because the poet finally harmonizes the two contrary feelings: that (s)he commits a crime by writing poetry after the great predecessor; and in contrast that the poet accepts the status of godhood for achieving the highest possible poetry (139 *AI*). The anxiety of influence began with the feeling that the predecessor was so great that it could only be immoral or an illusion to think one could overcome that poet. This feeling contrasted with the powerful desire to not be influenced by the predecessor, for this obviates one's own election to poetic greatness.

Just as the opposition in the fourth ratio (daemonization) was integrated to form the fifth (askesis), so too the opposition of the fifth is integrated to form the sixth (apophrades). The dualism of askesis, the perpetual oscillation becomes the "oxymoronic intensity" of apophrades. "The limitations of metaphor [in askesis] are restituted by a final representation" (101 *MM*). In apophrades the poet makes a choice between the two dualities of askesis, between introjection and projection (103 *MM*). Apophrades is "an intermediate step between the term transferred and the thing to which it is transferred" (102 *MM*). Holomorphically, this mediation epitomizes the function of the total poetry at its end: a rapprochement between predecessor and successor according to the new terms of the latter.

Apophrades gives the poet the final sense of his/her position in the tradition. The poet has wanted throughout the development of the poetry not to be determined by the influence of the predecessor but to derive the process of the predecessor ("swallowing" in ancient cosmogonic myths) and to be an influence ("swallowing" the future). This victorious twofold stance toward the past and the future is manifest in the introjection and projection of apophrades. Bloom defines apophrades:

> ...a representation set against time, sacrificing the present to an idealized past or hoped-for future. As a figure of a figure...it...becomes...a peculiar representation, either proleptic or `preposterous', in the root sense of making the later into the earlier. As a defense, this apophrades chooses between introjection and projection...Either there is a spitting-out and so a distancing of the future and so a swallowing-up, an identifying with the past, by substituting late words for earlier words in an anterior trope, or else there is a distancing, a projecting of the past, and an identifying with the future, by taking a substitution of early for late words (103 *MM*).

In this book thusfar many references were made to Bloom's idea that a poet does not make way for any successor, that a limit is put on future poetry. This act is not a malicious selfish act, but is a structural part of poetry. Poetry closes by means of finally marking off the boundaries of the imaginative space--with regard to the past and the future. In the transition from askesis to apophrades, the poet does make a sacrifice for the final gain, as was the case throughout the development of new ratios. "The surrender of the present compensates for the contradictory movements of the psyche" (121 *MM*). And in the passage Bloom states the present is sacrificed to "an idealized past or hoped-for future."

How is the present sacrificed? The poet's vision is seen as being the ideal terminus of past tradition or as setting the direction for all poetry to come. This positioning provides "an image of wholeness," quested for throughout the poetry (154 *MM*). The poet, realizing the limit of individual poetic development, is satisfied. Standing at the top or end of the series of poetries in the tradition, the poet can accept being limited by his/her own definition. When discussing the satisfaction at apophrades, Bloom quotes Kierkegaard: "When one has circumnavigated existence, it will appear whether one has courage to understand that life is a repetition, and to delight in that very fact....Repetition is reality, and it is the seriousness of life... (120 *MM*). The present vision of the new great poet is sacrificed insofar as it is now interpreted as a repetition of the past or as being repeatable in the future. The repetition, however, of a superior poetry. For the first time it seems as if the successor wrote the predecessor's poetry, or that a future poetry must write the present one again, though with less life. "The tyranny of time almost is overturned, and one can believe, for startled moments, that they [the great poets having achieved apophrades] are being imitated by their ancestors" (141 *AI*). The whole tradition seems accumulated in the new poetry.

If askesis put a limit on the successor's own poetry while limiting the poetry before it, so too does apophrades. Apophrades gives a sense of the limit of poetry. Quoting Hegel to explain the sense of a limit from within a poetry, Bloom agrees that "...Knowledge is aware not only of itself, but also of the negative of itself, or its limit. Knowing its limit means knowing how to sacrifice itself" (120 *MM*). In another passage Bloom argues there cannot be an end--one's own end--known to oneself. It would mean an end to the Moebian strip of the experience of individuals (134 *AI*). The limit of one individual's poetry makes possible a new start.

> "It may be that one life is a punishment
> For another, as the son's life for the father's" (139 *AI*).

This sense of a limit need not be disappointing, for it applies to *all* poets--past, present, future. A new ideal of poetry stands before the poet's gaze. The sense that one's own poetry is a repetition or will be repeated has the positive effect of allowing the poet to feel a part of the ideal community of all poets. The poet has joined the canon, the tradition, as its present spokesperson. Bloom cites a passage from Shelley to convey the mixed feeling of individual limitation and community membership:

> --I among the multitude
> Was swept--me, sweetest flowers delayed not long;
> Me, not the shadow nor the solitude,
>
> Me, not that falling stream's Lethean song;
> Me, not the phantom of that early Form
> Which moved upon its motion--but among

The thickest billows of that living storm
I plunged, and bared by bosom to the clime
Of that cold light, whose airs too soon deform.[4]

"The multitude" and "that early Form" refer to the precursors. In askesis the poet starts to come into his/her own.

Apophrades and the Highest Achievement of an Individual Poet

By the act of poetic creation called apophrades, poets gain a sense, which they express, of finality, of an ideal, of the highest achievement individual poets can attain. The lack of this kept poets struggling through an entire poetry, with a non-linear hierarchical structure of misadventures.

Following the "star of infinite desire" (193 *SM*), the poet finally wins his/her own imaginative space, and so the poet can praise the precursor for "having been what one has become" (126 *AI*). The poet can contemplate "the great image of human and poetic continuity" (115 *PR*). The poet feels partly responsible for this continuity of vision through the course of human civilization.

Apophrades is a victory for human culture. Poets "reach the extreme limit of existence" (241 *SM*). A poetry accomplishes the "sublime re-begetting of the poetic self" (292 *PR*). The form of poetry serves as a matrix in which the self develops: poetry defines "...the sphere/ Of all that is, has been or will be done" (241 *SM*). The placing of the self in a universal story or world perspective is necessary for the proper functioning of mind. For example, patients with neurological disorders sometimes lose some of their humanity, not being able to draw a map of their own bedroom which they can walk around quite easily.[5] Besides the benefit to the individual--in giving life some of its possible humanity, the poet offers to human culture a distinctive vision of human experience, a specific power of being human. Poems reveal to a human being something ultimate about experience, which can direct a life's development. Poems "begin, work themselves out, and end so finally as to be anagoges of human finality, of religious apocalypse" (92 *SM*). "Anagogy" refers to the ideal of poetic vision accomplished at apophrades when "the entire poem [is] simultaneously perceived" (105 *SM*). Bloom also calls anagogy "imaginative finality" (171 *SM*).

Beyond askesis to apophrades, the poet finds expression for the total process undergone. In the words of Lévi-Strauss and Greimas: "The order of chronological succession is reabsorbed into an atemporal matrical structure"; and, "Our reduction has required a paradigmatic and achronic interpretation of the relations among functions...this paradigmatic interpretation, the very condition for grasping the signification of narrative in its totality" (224 *The Poetics of Prose*). This "atemporal matrical structure" defines the ambivalent community with the inferior dead poets and the unborn would-be successors: "ambivalent" and even hypocritical because the poet does to his/her predecessors what the poet defines as not capable of being done to himself/herself. These restrictions define the boundaries of the imaginative space desired by the poet. Apophrades occurs when the poet feels this `room of one's own' as a mediation. Bloom's early concept of "anagogy" is quite applicable to apophrades at which point the poet has a synchronic perception of the whole poetic process from predecessor to apophrades. The image of this whole might be the ouroboros, the serpent of time, mentioned in Blake's poetry and by Bloom; the serpent forms a circle by swallowing its own tail. This process of swallowing resembles the accumulation of previous ratios by succeeding ones. Mythologists also note its role in explaining the dynamic inner development of myths; for example, in the *Theogeny* parents swallow children to prevent the succession of generations. By the time of Sophocles, the conflict between generations is expressed in less animalistic terms. Bloom's theory posits a "circular dialectic" (213 *SM*).

Apophrades and the Limits of an Individual's Poetry

"Apophrades" means that poets have a sense of their own limits and the limits of all poets, which recognition gives them a sense of individual fulfillment, even superiority. The poet gets the sublime sense of "the beauty of Fate" (172 *MM*).

The internalization of the precursor begun at the start of a poetry continues to the end. "`The Witch of Atlas',...seems to have become a permanent part of the mature Yeats' poetic mind" (202 *SM*). Negatively stated, "The shadow of Keats never did abandon him [Tennyson] wholly" (174 *PR*).

Apophrades has negative and positive sides. As the positive, the successor "searches for evidences of election that will fulfill his precursors' prophecies by fundamentally re-creating those prophecies in his own unmistakeable idiom" (152 *AI*). As the negative, the successor beholds his indefinite end (and that of any would-be successor).

There is a feeling of poetic entropy at the end of a poetry, this feeling of course mixed with others. This occurrence also characterizes other cultural forms, for example, the feeling of Sartre at the end of *Being and Nothingness*, the feeling of the "spirit of futility" for future development. Derrida, too, seems to lament the increasing lessening of life in writing--"dead writing"--connected with the problem of "representative differance" in *Of Grammatology*. Bloom describes the feeling when he asserts the deepest fear of a poet: "increasingly we do become all too much alike" (278 *PR*). In addition, "To grow endlessly more aged while remaining immortal is an oxymoronic or belated version of the divination that is crucial to strong poetry" (168 *PR*). The entropy has the effect of partially reconciling the creator to his possible successors and still placing the creator above them. In static visual imagery the poet now stands at the top of a pyramid, with the past leading up to it and the future leading downward from this height. The creator's power may eventually decrease more, but the successor's power, whatever it could be, would be on the terms set here even less. If the feeling of entropy is not connected with one's successors, it might be connected with a positive requirement of a tradition form; namely, that entropy ensures an infinity of possible development within the finitude of an individual's life--there is a lessening or slowing of development, but an infinity nonetheless.

A poetry is limited because a poetry can be completed. "In Shelley's myth, a poem is a relational event which has run its course by being set down..." (200 *SM*). In previous discussions of Derrida's ideas it was noted that the limit on a person's perspective has the positive role of being the source of orientation for the whole text. Describing the limit that orients, that moves the poet ceaselessly on and would begin to move the successor even further, writes Todorov:

> The figure which we read through the different levels of the work may very well not be found in the repertory of classical rhetorics. In studying the tales of Henry James, I found myself up against such a "figure in the carpet"; by schematizing, we may reduce it to this formula: "the essence is absent, the presence is unessential." This same "figure" organizes James's themes as well as his syntax, the composition of the story quite as much as the "points of view" in the narrative. We cannot a priori grant a "first" or "original" status to any of these levels (the others being its manifestation or expression); on the other hand, within a particular text we can discover a hierarchy of this kind. We see at the same time there is no break between superposition and figuration: the latter extends and elaborates the former (243-44 *The Poetics of Prose*).

"Superposition" and "figuration" refer to the reinterpretation of the precursor and new poetic creation.

Compare this passage of Bloom's: "Shelley's visualization strains upward, toward the evanescence of Thou, seeking desperately for the Thou that cannot by its very nature become for us an It, and seeking (of necessity) vainly" (185 *SM*). Rather than being interpreted unsuccessful, the evanescence at the end of the struggle should be interpreted to be good, to be the orientation in poetry toward a "star of infinite desire." A tradition form must achieve a kind of infinite vision if it is to be the accumulation, once again, of all the poetic tradition. In an analogous context, science seeks a universal theory of nature, leaving no phenomena out, applying to past, present, and future phenomena. Yet, new phenomena are found; new physics are created. Nevertheless, any physics makes itself into a universal vision, without bounds.

The limits of an individual's poetry cannot be understood without a reference to the beginning. Why would apophrades mean the "return of the dead [poets]" as Bloom claims? A comparison to religion can provide an answer. Lyotard writes, "Freud's general thesis as to the history of religion can be expressed in a few words, and they form a dramatic sequence: the lawless domination of the

Urvater over the horde--the murder of the *Urvater*--the establishment of a matriarchal and fraternal totemic religion--the return of the repressed, that is, the return of the father and the reestablishment of monotheism" (102 *Lyotard Reader*). This cyclic drama proceeds from the murder of the *Urvater* to the return of the father. Killing the *Urvater* wards off the threat of castration. This is a typical pattern in succession myths, for example *The Theogeny*: the father tries to kill--perhaps by swallowing--his own children so that they will not grow up and kill and replace him. Instead, the children kill the father. Some of the children try to kill their brothers or their own children to prevent them from doing the same to them. A child, Zeus, escapes and becomes victorious; he differs from his progenitors in not attempting to swallow his offspring; instead they are generated from him in a fixed way repeating his nature. A new order of right belonging to the new generation comes into being. The *Urvater*, or grandfather, wants to prevent his children from producing offspring or from coming into their own. The return of the father means that there is no longer any fear that the children will be castrated or limited in creativity, and so there can be a reconciliation with the father. Instead of opposing him as was done throughout, some acceptance occurs. This could mean the victor acts like the father did, to some extent, but only more morally. The total relation of successor to precursor is represented in the closing figure of a poetry. The poet finally grants to the precursor some imaginative space though it is contained as a smaller portion within his own; the predecessor is seen to have less poetic ability. Accepting limited castration while also placing some limit on all future poets, the poet gains a new space of poetry greater than the predecessor. The limitation is the individual's payment of debt to the whole community for initially providing the power through the precursor to become great. The limit on oneself and the precursor is a reconciliation with the father, who has returned but in altered form--not as what is to be murdered but as what offers salvation. The limitation on future poetic development, founded on the limitation of oneself and the precursor, is a natural closing, stopping of a poetry. It looks ahead to the infinite future. In the religious myth of the Holy Trinity, there is not a killing of God, the father, but there is a return of the murdered son in the new form of the Holy Ghost. In this way the son who left the father becomes reconciled to him after undergoing transformation. The poet does this as well: the successor can finally accept the precursor partially once the successor is guaranteed some imaginative space to be an individual poet.

The reconcilation of the precursor by the successor on his own terms is like the ouroboros, the serpent of time. The seprent swallows its own tail, forming a circle. The partial acceptance of the precursor binds the successor to the former. The successor has joined the community of poets throughout tradition. Nevertheless, the serpent of time also announces an end. There is the implied hint in the return of the father, in apophrades, that a cycle has been completed, that "the dialectic can always be reversed" (146 *SM*). "The future's force is directed to driving the poem back into the past" (30 *PR*). To ward off the idea of the poet's mortality, a limitation on the universal vision gained, the poet through apophrades sets up an inequality, an injustice in the series of poetries: what the successor did to the predecessor the successor will forbid or attempt to prevent future possible generations from doing. The reversal of the dialectic requires first of all the elimination of this inequality. Then, the new creation is partially prefigured in the final poetic figures--prefigured negatively, prefigured by what seems to be lacking, namely, the chance to do what the previous poet had done. The new creator will transfigure this negative poetic figure into a new positive start, into clinamen.

Does Bloom's theory make the end of a poetry successful or not? This is an issue for interpretation. On the one hand, poetry seems unsuccessful. Bloom claims poetic divination intends "literal immortality" (102 *AI*). But only an "ideal" kind of immortality is attained. The goals of a creator at the beginning of a poetry do not persist unchanged up to the end. Poetry cannot in some sense get what it wants: "The end of quest is to be not in the quester's merging in the identity of others, or of the poethood, but in the perpetual stasis of an earthly paradise preserved by enchantment from the single gratification it [the paradise] affords, and which would end it" (157 *PR*). What gratification can the poet not achieve? Literal immortality. The poet cannot achieve all poetic vision for all time, past, present, and future, even though "each wants to be the universe, to be the whole of which all other poets are only parts" (52 *MM*). Being only an individual, the poet could only be one if a tradition had accumulated the knowledge of thousands of years of individuals. The same seeming lack of gratification occurs in myths and literature. In the famous myth of Gilgamesh (circa 1400 B.C.) the hero Gilgamesh leaves his community, travels over an enchanted sea, finds a plant of immortality, and tries to bring it back. But on the return a snake eats the plant. The snake can regenerate itself endlessly by shedding its old skin, covering the new. However, the snake is not literally immortal. What Gilgamesh returns with for his fellow human beings is the knowledge of this eternally possible regeneration, the nature of human culture as traditional. This type of "immortality" that of the snake changing its skin season after season is "ideal." The person does not actually live for ever, but the regeneration of the spirit makes one have a life that is as if one is immortal. The human race considered as one growing human being may have literal immortality. The possibility of spiritual development is infinite--an infinity, however, enclosed for the individual within finite biological life. A similar modern echo of this tale, Hemingway's *Old Man and the Sea* presents the merely ideal victory of an old fisherman [not unlike Hemingway in his personal life] who gets a huge fish but which is eaten by sharks, allowing him to bring only the bones back to the shore. Was he successful or not? In ideal terms, perhaps; in literal terms, not. In the case of Gilgamesh, the ironic victory can be seen more definitely.

On the other hand, the poet is successful, though "ideally." This victory can be seen in the "perpetual stasis of an earthly paradise preserved by enchantment from the single gratification it [the paradise] affords, and which would end it" (157 *PR*). Just as Gilgamesh achieved the ideal immortality of infinite spiritual regeneration, the poet's activity, which is regenerative, is seen by the individual as infinite. There never would be a limit such that the poetic activity would not still be valuable for the individual. The poet has assured and has understood his/her own endless development.

The ideal success of the poet occurs when the individual reaches the greatest development possible at the same time that the individual is humbled, being only one individual in the ages of humanity. This ideal status of the individual through membership in a larger community has been expressed well by Campbell:

> Hence, the totality--the fullness of man---is not in the separate member, but in the body of the society as a whole; the individual can be only an organ. From his group he has derived his techniques of life, the

> language in which he thinks, the ideas on which he thrives; through the past of that society descended the genes that built his body. If he presumes to cut himself off, either in deed or in thought and feeling, he only breaks connection with the sources of his existence (383 *Hero*).

The fullness of a human being is achieved in its ideal vision of itself: self-knowledge.

The poet comes to understand poetry as an ideal, universal process. The original goal of personal aggrandizement wanes under the new more mature vision of the universal activity of tradition. "A consciousness comes to know itself as negative and finite. It sees that others know themselves also in this way, and so it transcends the negative and finite present by seeing the universal nature of what it itself is becoming" (121 *MM*). The poet cannot become free of the past (141 *PR*), nor is this afterall desirable. Tradition gives to the individual its greatest power, and tradition places on the individual its greatest limit.

To achieve this ideal meaning given to life, poetry is required. It must be written, just as Navahos need to make a hut to give shape to the greater universe:

> The hogan, or mud hut, of the Navahos of New Mexico and Arizona, is constructed on the plan of the Navaho image of the cosmos. The entrance faces east. The eight sides represent the four directions and the points between. Every beam and joist corresponds to an element in the great hogan of the all-embracing earth and sky. And since the soul of man itself is regarded as identical in form with the universe, the mud hut is a representation of the basic harmony of man and world, and a reminder of the hidden life-way of perfection (385 *Hero*).

Poetry in Bloom's theory accomplishes some of the same goals. Its figures are holomorphic; each has the structure of the whole at that point; the total process is represented variously in all the parts. In so doing, poetry situates the human being in the totality of life and the universe. Potentially, poetry could be about all themes. Yet, it develops in a specific direction, toward the limit of what an individual is capable of, toward knowing this limit. A step in tradition allows the individual the greatest development possible; it is measured to make possible a "life-way of perfection." "Poetry," Bloom thinks, "finds outer forms of an inward power" (35 *SM*).

Apophrades and the Genetic Code

The end of a poetry contains sparks of future poetry that a possible successor must know how to develop; such knowledge is based on the sense of what poetry does, of how poetry started before, of a (new) genetic code of poetry.

The poet realizes in apophrades that only part of the vision is fertile for the future (87 *SM*). Bloom speaks of a successor lifting up a precursor's spark, much like the self-resurrection of the phoenix (194 *PR*). Browning lifts up "the sparks of his own root" 204 *PR*). Wordsworth and Shelley end some poems by speaking of scattering the sparks among humanity for the future. Derrida wrote about the sparks scattered through his works (in *Cinders*), and he prefers the metaphor of dissemination to insemination for the description of cultural transmission.

Although Bloom has some of the elements needed to explain how the sparks can be carried over to start a new poetry, the view can be developed.

Bloom finds the point at which transmission of the poetic heritage occurs. From the standpoint of the precursor the point is apophrades; from the standpoint of the successor the point is clinamen. Finding the point is a good start, yet it does not explain transmission. He defines the transmission only by mentioning in passing how one poet represents the totality of poetry within his/her own (134ff. *MM*). In the words of Griffiths and Rabinowitz about Bloom's finding epic "ecphrasis" [meaning literally "expression"], "Whereas Homer and Virgil miniaturized the world on their heroes' shields, Milton presents Satan's shield as a microcosm of his own literary antecedents, optically distorted...to fill his own needs" (28). Bakhtin, too, believes Dostoevsky is able to represent the consciousness of his predecessor, thus surpassing him (48-49 *Problems...*).

This passage shows Bloom's "internalization of tradition" very clearly, very imagistically.

> "That which was presented in Gogol's field of vision as an aggregate of objective features, coalescing in a firm socio-characterological profile of the hero, is introduced by Dostoevsky into the field of vision of the hero himself and there becomes the object of his agonizing self-awareness; even the very physical appearance of the "poor clerk," described by Gogol, Dostoevsky forces his hero to contemplate in the mirror."

Bakhtin explains more than Bloom does. [This process of internalization may have its historical origin in the swallowing of people and animals in ancient myths of succession.]

Bloom does not explain the transmission of a poetic genetic code at the point of origin. The closing figure of a poetry, apophrades, must serve as a negative mold for the creation of a positive counter figure. DNA replicates by splitting into two chains of molecules, so that each chain can form its own complement. Bloom does argue for the "antithetical completion" of earlier ratios by later ones. A related process, described in this book, is Derrida's concept of *bricolage*, which must use the words, ideas, figures already existing to form new ones. Derrida's account is much more developed, specific, as it has been presented. He realizes that with each new philosophy the creative act is defined anew.

More positively, Bloom's whole theory can be interpreted as providing some structural elements for a poetic genetic code. The map of misreading with its six revisionary ratios explains the minimum structural standards and recurrence of them rather well. On the scale of whole poetries, all the ratios develop from the previous poetry by negating some feature of that poetry only to replace it with some new positive alternative. This action resembles the forming of complementary chains. It also occurs on the scale of the individual ratios. Each ratio develops from the preceding one in a similar way, serving as a mold, albeit negative, for its positive figure to follow. The revisionary ratios virtually constitute steps in the replication of a genetic code of poetry. By them the code of poetry can be transmitted from one generation to the next, forever.

In this general way Bloom can explain the transmission of poetry. Part III and the Epilogue will suggest ways the view can be developed.

Summary

Poetries know how to end themselves, doing so in a characteristic way. Each canonical poetry must pass through "askesis" and "apophrades," the final two revisionary ratios of the map of misreading. The end of a poetry redefines the whole poetic process, which had been disunified by the precursor. The end of a poetry explains its own coming into being or passage. Finally, the poet understands how (s)he can have an imaginative space (made by the passage). With it comes the realization of the ideal nature of the poetic process. Though the individual knows (s)he is limited, more than had been anticipated, the individual feels compensated by the knowledge that this activity is universal, beginning long before the poet's own work and extending far beyond it into the future. The poet's own work reestablishes this continuity of the ages of humanity. Bloom's view, while more explanatory than Kuhn's, leaves room open for a still deeper understanding of poetry as a phenomenon of tradition, perhaps guided by a genetic code.

NOTES

1. Griffiths and Rabinowitz express this idea of the changing sense of poetry up to the end of the form: "Not only did his [Dostoevsky's] predecessor's Petersburg `nightmares', such as `The Nose' and `The Overcoat', influence Dostoevsky's earliest prose narratives, but it was Gogol's later, larger vision of Rus' that would inspire and challenge him at the very end. Quite in the Gogolian tradition, *The Brothers Karamazov* is evasive about its literary legacy" (121 *Novel Epics*).

2. Derrida writes, "When one is concerned with an art that does not imitate nature, when the artist is a man, and when it is consciousness that engenders, preformationism, no longer makes us smile. *Logos spermatikos* is in its proper element (1978: 23)." Quoted from p. 181 of Alexiou, Margaret and Vassilis Lambropoulos. *The Text and Its Margins*. N.Y.: Pella Publishing Company, 1985.

3. This idea was expressed by Todorov in *Poetics of Prose*, 141. "Thereby narrative appears as the fundamental theme of *The Quest of the Holy Grail* (as it is of all narrative, but always in a different way). Ultimately, the quest of the Grail is not only the quest of a code and a meaning, but also of a narrative. Significantly, the last words of the book tell its history: the last link of the plot is the creation of this very narrative we have just read." To say that the novel is the quest of a code must mean that when creation starts the author does not have a full code; the work itself is the code of the past, even of the entire tradition; and in this sense the work is performative more than it is a completely transparent, circumscribable object of the intellect. Not a scientific theory, nor a poetry, nor a philosophy can exist to anyone in that way.

4. 140 *AI*. Bloom does not identify the poem.

5. This example of a man named Schneider was taken from Maurice Merleau-Ponty's *Phenomenology of Perception*. Similar examples are given in Volume III of Ernst Cassirer's *Philosophy of Symbolic Forms*.

Chapter 11:

The End of Derrida's Philosophy

Introduction

Derrida completed a system of philosophy in his three major original publications of 1967. After that time he wrote many other works. Although these works are valuable, and although they do develop Derrida's thinking, there is such a thing as a structural end to a philosophy, which was achieved in those 1967 writings. *Of Grammatology* contains the structural whole of his philosophy. The end of his philosophy is defined through the concept of the "supplement" and its more advanced form, the idea of representative differance in the festival. These ideas resemble the closing figures of poetry in Bloom's view, namely, askesis and apophrades. Nevertheless, Derrida's account conveys more about tradition.

The Relation of the End of Derrida's Philosophy to Its Beginning

The meaning of the end of Derrida's philosophy consists at least partially in a relationship to its beginning. The end is a self-closing of the philosophy that guarantees the beginning while nonetheless being in a sense contrary to it, as the ouroboros, the serpent of time, forms a circle by swallowing its tail. Heraclitus used the image of the harmony of the bow and the lyre.

Just as differance guaranteed the system of differences, so too the supplement guarantees differance, and so by extension it guarantees the system of differences. In addition the supplement defines a new standard for philosophical validity, so that Sartre's philosophy depends on Derrida's (in a way that will be explained). This standard is a definition of what philosophical development can be and what philosophical meaning is. The supplement is a synecdoche for philosophical development, as well as defining the latest definition of philosophical meaning. It explains how Derrida's philosophy could have arisen from Sartre's. The philosophy starts with the attempt to remedy the end of Sartre's philosophy, which has a mistaken notion of development, transcendence in philosophical terms. Derrida's project cannot be structurally complete until he has an adequate replacement. He must find a new definition of the philosophical project. Since the supplement defines the relation of ideas in a series, it can explain the superior status of Derrida's ideas despite their appearance after Sartre's.

To illustrate, a comparison can be made between Derrida's three main concepts, difference, differance, and the supplement and Freud's three main concepts, id, ego, and superego. The superego (the ethical sense) is opposed to the id insofar as the former must keep the latter in order, must control the passions springing from it. But since both are extremes of one whole psychical apparatus, they must form a harmony, like that of Heraclitus' bow and the lyre. In Lyotard's relevant words "both psychoanalysis and critique [of Kant's philosophy] desire that the situation be stabilized; the former aims to stabilize the boundaries on the interior of the `psychical apparatus' (Freud's name for the three agencies: id-ego-superego), through a `dynamic equilibrium' being established by rival investments on the same territory by different agencies" (xxv *Libidinal Economy*). The supplement is bound to Derrida's first concept, difference, because the supplement guarantees differance and differance guarantees the system of differences. And the supplement is contrary to the concept of differences insofar as it serves to unite different objects of knowledge in the manner of an adding on, supplementation. In an article Liszka rightly thinks of it [the supplement] as slipping into an indifference--in relation to the original concept of difference. Paul Ricoeur also mentions as important some contrast between the end and the start of Derrida's philosophy. Bloom's idea of askesis, the curtailing of previously established meaning, applies. Ricoeur quotes from Derrida's "White Mythology": `It is metaphysics which has effaced in itself that fabulous scene which brought it into being, and which yet remains, active and stirring, inscribed in white ink, an invisible drawing covered over in the palimpsest'.[1] Derrida is discussing the effacement of metaphysics' own origin. Ricoeur speaks of a Derridean concept that erases its trace. Perhaps he is thinking of the vicarious function of the supplement. At any rate, Derrida's and Ricoeur's comments help to support the idea that the end of the philosophy may in some sense be contrary to the start. Such a situation is not a problem of consistency. Instead it shows a possible condition of closure for tradition forms. It also shows the interdependence of the start and the end. Like two poles of a magnet, they are bound together but are at opposite ends, have contrary polarity. The opposition of the start and the end shows that the whole structure is oriented, teleological.

Bloom also thought of the end of poetic form as partially contrary to its start insofar as the end inverts the quest pattern so that the poet accepts the precursor's vision to a limited extent whereas the poet had rejected it all along. The words of Lyotard help to point out the twofold relation of the supplement to the beginning of the form, before more elaboration is given. The supplement establishes a "dynamic equilibrium" as the model of philosophical development, transcendence. It permits each of the former concepts, difference and differance, to have their own right within a larger system of concepts, because the supplement explains their passage from the predecessor's closing concept to Derrida's; in Bloom's terms this problem keeps the quest of a poetry going until the end. The three a priori concepts--difference, differance, and the supplement--have similar but complementary structures, which accumulate the preceding ones in each case; in this way their replicative nature resembles the forming of complementary chains in DNA. Derrida's three main concepts parallel the three main movements of revisionary ratios in Bloom's theory. The transitions are dialectical in each case, not to mention the curiously close connections in meaning from start to start, middle to middle, and end to end.

The end of Derrida's philosophy, the supplement, accumulates the knowledge gained before. In this respect it is both "model and included object" (83 *AF*); "model" because it is a superior form of differance and difference; "included object" because it is also about itself, explaining how it came into being. It is for this reason that a philosophy ends: the final concept can explain how the others came into being and how it itself did. The other concepts (difference and differance) can only explain how the preceding concept came into being, and they do not provide a satisfactory answer to the question of how they came into being, which is also a question of the philosophical continuum, the unity of experience. The supplement, though a priori as difference and differance are, has a distinctive feature. "Their effects [the effects of the supplement and a synonymous idea of the pharmakon] do not simply turn back on themselves by means of an auto-affection without opening. Rather they spread out in a chain over the practical and theoretical entirety of a text, and each time in a different way" (40-41 *Pos*). The spreading out of the supplement over the entire philosophy shows its function of naming the orientation in which all the previous concepts can be related. This function is termed "passe-partout," something circulating through all possible places, possibilities (see a chapter by the same name in *The Truth in Painting*).

Though the supplement is arrived at last in Derrida's philosophy, it is prior--logically--to difference and differance. They presuppose it; they cannot be true if it is not. The difficult argument given by Derrida to prove the presupposition of the supplement by differance will be discussed shortly. Another way to think of the relationship of the supplement to the preceding concepts is that they are effects and it is the cause. Speaking precisely, difference is to differance as effect to cause, just as differance is to the supplement as effect to cause.

The Transition from Differance to the Supplement

Since differance cannot fulfill the need for a total philosophical perspective, as there is still a problem of the relationship of Derrida's ideas to his precursor's and to possible successors, there must be another concept that can: the supplement.

To prepare the way for a logical discussion of the transition, a parallel can be drawn to mythology. Campbell describes a three-stage process in myths; it could be called a rite of passage, a quest, a succession myth, a cosmogonical pattern. In Derrida's philosophy there are three main concepts. The change from differance to the supplement parallels that in Campbell's passage from the second stage of the myth to the third, when "the transcendental powers" must be left behind. (Recall Bloom's theory, in which the end of the second main movement is daemonization of the creator, a heightened sense of poetic powers, followed by a curtailing of the creator's claim to those powers). Even if the transcendental powers are left behind, the hero still has an even greater benefit to give to the human community in the third stage. In the terms of Derrida's philosophy, differance claims too much for philosophical knowledge so that it must be limited by a concept that also reveals how Derrida is nevertheless superior to his predecessor. Differance is like the transcendental powers, which must be left behind the supplement. Campbell explains the three stage pattern of myth:

> [First Stage: Separation from the Community]
> The mythological hero, setting forth from his commonday hut or castle, is lured, carried away, or else voluntarily proceeds, to the threshold of adventure. There he encounters a shadow presence that guards the passage. The hero may defeat or conciliate this power and go alive into the kingdom of the dark... or be slain by the opponent and descend in death... . Beyond the threshold, then, the hero journeys through a world of unfamiliar yet strangely intimate forces, some of which severely threaten him... .
>
> [Second Stage: The Initiation or Ordeal]
> When he arrives at the nadir of the mythological round, he undergoes a supreme ordeal and gains his reward. The triumph may be represented as the hero's sexual union with the goddess-mother of the world (sacred marriage), his recognition by the father-creator (father atonement), his own divinization (apotheosis), or again--if the powers have remained unfriendly to him--his theft of the boon he came to gain (bride-theft, fire-theft); intrinsically it is an expansion of consciousness and therewith of being (illumination, transfiguration, freedom).

[Third Stage: The Return to the Community; End of the Quest]
The final work is that of the return. If the powers have blessed the hero, he now sets forth under their protection (emissary); if not, he flees and is pursued (transformation flight, obstacle flight). At the return threshold the transcendental powers must remain behind; the hero re-emerges from the kingdom of dread (return, resurrection). The boon that he brings restores the world (elixir) (245-46 *Hero*).

These three stages have strong similarities to the three movements of Bloom's revisionary ratios, but here we are particularly interested in shedding light on Derrida's philosophy. Bloom spoke of daemonization in terms of the creator being a being, a daemon, above the merely human status of the precursor. The creator has an exaggerated idea of his own powers in relation to the precursor. This is characteristic, too, of Derrida's differance, with its tendency toward becoming infinite. It would make of Derrida's knowledge both too much and too little to define an autonomous new domain of philosophy beyond Sartre's.

Turning to the third stage, Bloom speaks of it as a recognition of one's own beginning, a return of the dead poets. Campbell speaks of it as a return here--a return to the community. The poet returns to become a part of the community of poets. The poetic vision at the end places the poet in a line with the great poets of the past as well as the future. Derrida's supplement similarly places the new philosophy in line with Sartre's as well as future ones. The concepts can give Derrida a vision of the whole tradition with himself in key position. This is like a return to the community also because the supplement shows the limit of individual knowledge. New philosophy will begin by other members of the community. Interpreted in this way, all cultural fields develop in steps made by the individual. The purpose of the cultural field is to make the step--for the individual and the community.

One logical definition of "differance" is a principle for producing "nonsynonymic substitutions" in any series of objects of knowledge (142 *SP*). In the series of differences they must begin to become differences of a different type. If they cannot, Derrida has no way to justify his claim already made that his idea of difference is of a logically higher type than the corresponding prototype in Sartre's philosophy. One could say that the need arises to postulate a concept internalizing the necessary variation of differences.

In the simplest discursive terms, "infinite" differance cannot ground the unity of philosophy, the unity of experience, which is a necessary presupposition. Some other concept is needed that can. The problem with differance is that it tends by its nature to become infinite but it cannot be. The concept is ambivalent. On the one hand, looking toward the past, differance is related to the predecessor's concepts (Sartre's) by opposition. As a result, if Derrida is to explain the unity of philosophy, he must explain the superiority of differance to that which in Sartre's philosophy it opposes. The definition of differance, however, contains no such meaning. So the continuity between Sartre and Derrida is still problematic.

On the other hand, looking instead toward the future of differance, it must by its own definition change into some other principle, if it is to be consistent with the series of differences. If it does, however, Derrida's philosophy will not be universal and he still does not have an explanation for the lost continuity of experience, past, present, and future. This goal of creating a universal theory of knowledge gives to all of Derrida's concepts their common purpose.

To support this attempted simplified paraphrase, consider the following quote: the supplement "hollows out that which will be reconstituted by deferral as the present. The supplement, which seems to be added as a plenitude to a plenitude, is equally that which compensates for a lack" (211 WD). Here there is an internal differentiation (a negativity) in the series of supplements not characteristic of differance. The "hollowing out" allows Derrida to explain two desirable conditions of knowledge: (1) how his differance could have developed from Sartre's philosophy; (2) how a possible successor will not form concepts different in type from Derrida's. The reason for revising differance is to create such a universal theory of experience, a universal domain called a philosophy. The infinity of differance is avoided.

A more specific way to think of the problem with differance is the following. Modifying itself less and less as it spreads out over the domain of knowledge more and more, differance splits into extremes. If it does not change in principle, it will become "the plenitude of a speech," making it inconsistent with the founding principle of difference. If it does change in principle, it cannot serve to explain the production of a universal domain of knowledge. The unity of experience would be lost, but this cannot be. The concept of differance leads to the concept of the supplement because the latter expresses the unity producing the ambivalent aspects of differance. Derrida expresses this view in the following passage:

> In terms of this problematical scheme, we must therefore think Rousseau's experience and his theory of writing together, the accord and the discord that, under the name of writing, related Jean-Jacques to Rousseau, uniting and dividing his proper name. On the side of experience, a recourse to literature as reappropriation of presence, that is to say, as we shall see, of Nature; on the side of theory, an indictment against the negativity of the letter, in which must be read the degeneracy of culture and the disruption of the community.
>
> If indeed one wishes to surround it with the entire constellation of concepts that shares its system, the word *supplement* seems to account for the strange unity of these two gestures (143-44 *OG*; and the two paragraphs beforehand give more of the argumentation).

Clearly, the supplement is postulated to unite two contrary gestures. These are ambivalent aspects of differance, mentioned above: (1) its need to be the "reappropriation of presence"; and (2) its need to be the "indictment against the negativity of the letter." The first ambivalent aspect shows a problem if differance does change in principle. The second shows a problem if it does *not* change in principle. There must be a new more complex idea of the change in the objects of knowledge than differance. The solution must overcome the opposition with Sartrian principles in order to ensure the continuity of knowledge, while placing Derrida's concepts in their higher order of validity.

A comparison with another concept may help to explain the supplement. The closing concept of Cassirer's philosophy is the idea of the ideal limit. Since both that idea and Derrida's idea of the supplement are closing concepts of a philosophy, recurring structural limits, they should be similar. Consider just two points of similarity. The closing concept represents a truth of a preceding one by generating or originating the concept: "...we can only realize what a certain truth `is' by intellectually regenerating it, i.e., by allowing it to develop before us out of its particular conditions" (315 *SF*). Derrida's supplement explains the origin of difference as well as its own origin or production. Secondly, the closing concept represents the ideal rule of progress for all the series of philosophical concepts. Cassirer writes,

> Knowledge realizes itself only in a succession of logical acts, in a series that must be run through successively, so that we may become aware of the rule of its progress. But if this series is to be grasped as a unity, as an expression of an *identical* reality, which is defined the more exactly the further we advance, then we must conceive the series as converging toward an ideal limit. This limit `is' and exists in definite determinateness, although for us it is not attainable save by means of the particular members of the series and their change according to law (315 *SF*).

Derrida's supplement is like an ideal limit. With the supplement Derrida can explain the identity of his own thought as one member of the series of philosophies, better than the preceding ones and leading to the future ones. The change of the members of the series can mean the change of philosophies. What a strong similarity this guarantee of a philosophical place in the tradition has to Bloom's idea of the "imaginative space" gained at the end of a poetry!

The supplement must be presupposed to fulfill these requirements, to make a unity of the ambivalent differance. Derrida explains the nature of the supplement as a solution to the problem of differance:

> Writing is dangerous from the moment that representation there claims to be presence and the sign of the thing itself. And there is a fatal necessity, inscribed in the very functioning of the sign, that the

> substitute make one forget the vicariousness of its own function and make itself pass for the plenitude of a speech whose deficiency and infirmity it nevertheless only *supplements*. For the concept of the supplement--which here determines that of the representative image--harbors within itself two significations whose cohabitation is as strange as it is necessary. The supplement adds itself, it is a surplus, a plenitude enriching another plenitude, the *fullest measure* of presence. It cumulates and accumulates presence. It is thus that art, *technè*, image, representation, convention, etc., come as supplements to nature and are rich with this entire cumulating function. This kind of supplementarity determines in a certain way all the conceptual oppositions within which Rousseau inscribes the notion of Nature to the extent that it *should* be self-sufficient. ...
> But the supplement supplements. It adds only to replace. It intervenes or insinuates itself *in-the-place-of*; if it fills, it is as if one fills a void. If it represents and makes an image, it is by the anterior default of a presence. ...
> But the inflexion varies from moment to moment. Each of the two significations is by turns effaced or becomes discreetly vague in the presence of the other. But their common function is shown in this: whether it adds or substitutes itself, the supplement is *exterior*, outside of the positivity to which it is super-added, alien to that which, in order to be replaced by it, must be other than it. (144-45 *OG*).

Derrida reveals here how he limits differance. Contrary to differance, the supplement has within it a difference from the sign (actually supplement) from which it is derived. Differance did not have this difference; differance was not defined to have an opposition in it to what it was derived from. Therefore, the supplement can explain the continuity with Sartre's philosophy while retaining Derrida's superiority. Derrida's philosophy is not related to Sartre's as one stream of differance. Instead, Derrida's concepts are all supplements to Sartre's concepts, which are also supplements but of a lower order.

Another passage may help to explain the origin of the supplement. Consider this statement of the problem caused if differance becomes infinite.

> ...a prodigious expansion of the power of differance was not accompanied, at least during these millennia, by any notable transformation of the organism. It is precisely the property of the power of differance to modify life less and less as it spreads out more and more. If it should grow *infinite*--and its essence excludes this a priori--life itself would be made into an impassive, intangible, and eternal presence: infinite differance, God or death (131 *OG*).

To stop differance from becoming infinite, to prevent life from becoming an eternal presence without further development, to avoid such an inconsistency with "difference," there must be a new concept that is "exterior" to earlier such concepts in a series.

Besides being exterior, the supplement must still be continuous with what went before. Without this, the philosophical vision would not be universal, as it must be. In other terms the supplement must be so defined as to *include* the idea of difference, Derrida's first concept. The indefinite entropy of infinite differance threatened the unity of Derrida's own philosophy if "difference" became no longer valid because of the infinite entropy of differance. The supplement cannot be insconsistent with difference, nor with differance.

The parallels to Bloom are quite strong here. Notice that Derrida sacrifices some of his vision in differance and with it some of Sartre's power, only to more clearly gain a superiority over Sartre. Bloom calls this askesis. Derrida seems to pinpoint the positive result of the sacrifice when he writes, "the greatest sacrifice aiming at the greatest symbolic reappropriation of presence" is writing (142-43 *OG*). However, Derrida does not want to reappropriate presence, in the end.

Several features of the passage should be noted. First of all, the supplement is a unity of opposing aspects: "This second signification of the supplement cannot be separated from the first." Bloom argued for the duality in askesis that could never be eliminated. The indissoluble unity of contrary tendencies points the way to a problem that cannot be solved in the terms or presuppositions of Derrida's thought, which will be discussed in Part III, in the next chapter on Derrida.

The Supplement and Bloom's Metalepsis

The supplement essentially performs what Bloom called metalepsis or transumption. In other words, the end of a cultural form must explain how it can develop from the preceding form, while nevertheless being conceptually "prior" or superior. It is as if the effects precede the causes.

In *The Archaeology of the Frivolous: Reading Condillac* Derrida begins the book with the first chapter entitled "The Second First-Metaphysics," which seems to be a contradiction in terms. How can there be two "First Metaphysics" in a row? How could a First Metaphysics be second to another?

In the tradition of philosophy--actually in any tradition--there must be specific structural standards that recur in successive theories. If a philosophy is to comprehend the entire tradition before it, as it must if tradition is to be capable of being accumulated at any stage, then there must be adequate answers to those questions.

Derrida gives a general idea of what is needed: "Through a chiasmus effect the new metaphysics, by advancing itself as second philosophy, will methodically reconstitute the generative principles, the primordial production of the general starting from real singularities" (35 *AF*).

In Bloom's terms the upcoming poet wants to change his/her belated status with respect to the great precursor into a position of being earlier, prior [superior]. Temporally, of course, the reversal cannot be accomplished. In terms of aesthetic principles it can. The successor arrives at an understanding of poetry such that the precursor seems to have imitated the successor, though somewhat weakly; poetic vision is stronger in the successor.

Derrida points out that "supplementary" is synonymous with the German word "nachträglich," which for Freud means "deferral" and "belatedly" (211 *WD*). The supplement makes the later philosopher earlier. It is a cause coming after the effect; it is "a possibility that produces that to which it is said to be added on" (88-89 *SP*). Bloom used this latter term to explain how a second poetry can become first-- in quality.

Derrida explicitly assigns a metaleptic role to the supplement. "Thus we no longer know whether what was always presented as a derived and modified re-presentation of simple presentation, as `supplement', `sign', `writing', or `trace', `is' not, in a necessarily, but newly, ahistorical sense, `older' than presence and the system of truth, older than `history'" (103 *SP*).

It could also be shown that the other two main concepts of Derrida's are metaleptic (i.e. difference and differance). For example, Derrida directly relates differance to presence. "That phenomenon, that presumed suppression of differance, that lived reduction of the opacity of the signifier, are the origin of what is called presence. That which is not subjected to the process of differance is present" (165-66 *OG*). With difference, the criticism of presence is obvious, based on the discussion of the origin of Derrida's philosophy. This continuing relating of each new main concept to the precursor's shows the transference of a code of philosophy.

Derrida's idea of "preformationism" has within it the functions of metalepsis. In reference to Proust, Derrida entertained the idea that the end of a literary work engenders its beginning.[2] Here there is a development by final causation. The effects precede the causes.

The Supplement as a Solution to Sartre's Bequeathed Problem

The supplement virtually completes the requirements of a new total philosophical form--Derrida's own--in response to Sartre's declaration that it could not be done. "Difference" as a solution to Sartre's problem has already been discussed. That solution could only be partial, as a system of concepts was needed.

If the supplement performs the functions of Bloom's metalepsis, then it is natural to expect some indication that Derrida is thinking of his immediate precursor when he discusses what the supplement can do. Of all the passages that could be adduced in support of this conclusion, consider the following:

> Thus the North, winter, death, imagination, representation, the irritation of desires--this entire series of supplementary significations--does not designate a natural place or fixed terms: rather a periodicity. Seasons. In the order of time, or rather like time itself, they speak the movement by which the presence of the present separates from itself, supplants itself, replaces itself by absenting itself, produces itself in self-substitution. It is this that the metaphysics of presence as self-proximity wishes to efface by giving a privileged position to a sort of absolute now, the *life* of the present, the living present. The coldness of representation not only breaks self-presence but also the originarity of the present as the absolute form of temporality.
>
> This metaphysics of presence constantly reappears and is resumed in Rousseau's text whenever the fatality of the supplement seems to limit it (309 *OG*).

Considering the discussions in this book of Derrida's criticism of the Sartrian idea of presence (in-itself-for-itself), it is clear that the supplement counters the metaphysics of presence. Derrida started his philosophy by criticizing that presupposition of metaphysics, replacing it with "difference." The project was never complete until the supplement was formed. The direct relevance of the supplement to the precursor's closing concept is clear. It is also clear that the supplement shows Derrida to be the victor. The supplement can explain the development denied by Sartre's idea of an ideal presence of ens causa sui, or the in-itself-for-itself. Also, near the passage just quoted, Derrida discusses "an unforseeable factum." It is "a negativity perfectly exterior to the system it comes to overturn, intervening in it therefore as an unforeseeable factum. This natural catastrophe is neither in nor out of nature and remains nonrational as the origin of reason must." Isn't Derrida explaining how the supplement as a factum unforeseeable by Sartre can overturn a system because it is exterior? Remember the reason for postulating the supplement: it had to be exterior to what it is added to in order for a differentiation to be introduced into the series of objects of knowledge, preventing them from being ordered by infinite differance. The supplement is a better *alternative* to Sartre's ideal presence of the ens causa sui (the in-itself-for-itself). The fact that a philosophy needs such a closing shows that the meaning of that discourse forms itself into units of tradition. Philosophies reproduce themselves, though not clones.

The supplement is logically prior to Sartre's closing concept, the ideal presence of the ens causa sui (the in-itself-for-itself). In philosophical terms it is a priori. "The indefinite process of supplementarity has always already infiltrated presence, always already *inscribed* there the space of repetition and the splitting of the self" (163 *OG*). The supplement counters a deficiency of Sartrian presence: "The supplementary difference vicariously stands in for presence due to its primordial self-deficiency" (88 *SP*). The supplement provides an answer to the problem of further development caused by Sartre's concept. The closing concept of a philosophy is a final representation of the process of philosophizing, almost a synecdoche. Sartre writes, "It [the ideal fusion of the in-itself-for-itself] is value as transcendence" (267-8 *BN*). The supplement defines the possibility of new objects of knowledge developing from previous ones--the process denied by Sartre's concept. Here it can be mentioned that the creator comes to explicit knowledge of the process of philosophizing only at the end of the philosophy; this topic will be elaborated in the Epilogue.

With the supplement, Derrida completes the domain of his universal field of vision, just as Bloom believed a poet must complete a new imaginative space, and just as Kuhn believes the sciences complete universal theories. The supplement provides the completing structural feature for the new space, domain of philosophy, for it can explain both the break from Sartre's philosophy and the continuity with it:

> The two--apparently contradictory--conditions for the constitution of a scientific field and object, here language, would thus be fulfilled: a natural, a continuously natural causality, and a break designating the irreducible autonomy and originality of a domain. The question of the origin is itself suspended, in that it no longer calls for a continuous, real, and natural description, being but the index of an internal structural description (143 *MP*).

Eric Mottram points out that Derrida's philosophy is "supplementary" to Sartre's, that any philosophy or poetry or science is supplementary to the previous series of tradition. He gives a sense of the freeing of a new space for thought:

> We endlessly supplement our cultural existence. The principle of supplementarity prevents the restriction of signification to a totality controlled from a centre. ...History [or tradition] is not repetition but *supplementarity*--the new or original structure "always comes about by a rupture with its past, its origin, and its cause" (50).

The supplement brings about a rupture from the Sartrian philosophy, opens up a new space, and defines its borders and continuity.

The supplement defines a new type of domain for philosophy, one without the possibility of it being totalized.

> If totalization no longer has any meaning, it is not because the infiniteness of a field cannot be covered by a finite glance or a finite discourse, but because the nature of the field--that is, language and a finite language--excludes totalization. This field is in effect that of *play*, that is to say, a field of infinite substitutions only because it is finite, that is to say, because instead of being an inexhaustible field, as in the classical hypothesis, instead of being too large, there is something missing from it: a center which arrests and grounds the play of substitutions. One could say-- rigorously using that word whose scandalous signification is always obliterated in French--that this movement of play, permitted by the lack or absence of a center or origin, is the movement of *supplementarity*. One cannot determine the center and exhaust totalization because the sign which replaces the center, which supplements it, taking the center's place in its absence--this sign is added, occurs as a surplus, as a *supplement* (289 WD)

Derrida's new field of philosophy is more dynamic, being characterized by a constant changing of signification through "play."
It is clear from this passage that Derrida uses the supplement to define his new field of philosophizing in contrast to Sartre's. Concerning this idea of the non-totalization of a text, Gasché makes a helpful point; Derrida "transcends the opposition of text and textuality, of appearance and essence, by paradoxically denying all ontological status to the general text." He quotes Derrida: `There is no present text in general, and there is not even a past present text, a text which is past as having been present' (*WD*, p. 211)' (283 *The Tain*...). This denial by Derrida is consistent with Bloom's assertion that all poetic meaning is inter-textual.

One could say that the supplement virtually closes the circle of the philosophy's form, but in this function it does not limit signification within the form. Within the form there is indefinite or virtually infinite space for improvement. The supplement permits an infinite development of knowledge, beginning with the model set by Derrida. Todorov discusses a final concept that closes the circle of form without thereby stopping meaningful development within it.

> What appeared as an irreducible and final signification--the opposition between God and the Devil, or between virtue and sin, or even, in our case, between virginity and lust--is not one, and this is because of narrative. It seemed at first glance that Scripture, the Sacred Book, constituted a halt in the perpetual reference from one layer of significations to the other; as a matter of fact this halt is illusory, for each of the two terms which form the basic opposition of the last network designates, in its turn, narrative, the text, that is, the very first layer. Hence the circle is closed and the retreat of the "final meaning" will never come to a halt again (141 *The Poetics of Prose*).

This passage about prose remarkably expresses a main requirement of a philosophy, a poetry, a science, or any tradition form--each must define an infinite domain of development, a universal field of vision, within the limits of a finite individual's experience in the ongoing process of human traditions. Each tradition form looks to the past, the present, and the future, for which its principles provide a perspective of a directed process of value, a teleological order, a domain for the enculturation of the individual.

Many concepts of the Nobel laureate geneticist Jacques Monod help to define the traits of the oriented, teleological fields of human traditions. Monod discusses the invariance of the genetic code through time and contrasts it with a principle of "teleonomy" for living things. All their development is guided by final causes operating from the first moment of life. Life-cycles are oriented. An acorn develops into an oak tree so that the tree can produce more acorns. The individual living thing is a part of a more comprehensive process of its species. Teleonomy almost seems like a subjective project, but it refers to a process greater than the individual. The most comprehensive project for an individual living thing is "the preservation and multiplication of the species" (14). Teleonomy means this tendency of living things.

In tradition forms, too, each one develops from a preceding one and prepares the way for a succeeding one. No single philosophy created philosophy, for it already existed. The highly evolved functions of teleonomy enable the series of cultural fields to become practically immortal, infinite. The role of the individual philosophy or other form can only be to continue the type of developing already begun by tradition. The continuity of tradition is the individual form's highest purpose. This adaptation of Monod's idea of teleonomy to cultural works is consistent with Bloom's idea that poetry is always about its own tradition, that a poetry starts by attempting to preserve the lost continuity, and that it is completed when the continuity through a new imaginative space is ensured.

Therefore, any philosophy, poetry, or scientific theory is an oriented or teleological field having as its highest purpose the adding of a new step to renew the continuity of tradition. Individual culture-makers raise themselves to the development of all past culture, participate in it by changing it, and thereby achieve the greatest possible development that an individual is capable of. Cassirer wrote about "synthetic supplementation" that combines the single instance with the totality of which it is a part; in this totality the individual concept or culture-maker is fulfilled (95 *LM*).

The Hierarchy of the Supplement

The supplement establishes a new hierarchy of philosophical concepts: difference, differance, and the supplement, with the supplement being at the top or prior.

Derrida's deconstruction claims to offer a philosophy for interpreting the meaning of human life. It creates a universal domain of vision in which the individual mind functions. Experience is like this, for mind never gets outside experience to look at it, even though mind has no limit on the concepts it can form. To provide an idea of the pattern of human life, Derrida must consider its ultimate foundations. "We must exhaust the resources of the concept of experience before attaining and in order to attain, by deconstruction its ultimate foundation" (60 *OG*). Since life is a passage through time, and since the pattern to interpret the meaning of life must be universal, Derrida represents the stages of life's development. Individuals can get a sense of direction, a sense of the meaning of life from a pattern "writ large," as Plato said.

The supplement, above all other concepts, defines the passage of the human mind. But its description is not complete, depending for its meaning on concepts leading to it. Together with difference and differance, the supplement establishes a hierarchy in the philosophy, a hierarchy by which an individual can find a direction for development.

The supplement is superior to differance; in a way it replaces differance, though not completely. "Writing will appear to us more and more as another name for this structure of supplementary" (245 *OG*). At first writing was defined in terms of difference, then in terms of differance, and finally in terms of the supplement above all others. "The same is here called supplement, another name for differance" (150 *OG*). In another passage Derrida claims that the supplement is "primordial" [in relation to difference and differance], that it is substitutive of signs before it, and that its structure "belongs to every sign in general" (88-89 *SP*). The supplement is the *structural* end of Derrida's thought, since it defines the rule of progress and its legitimate original domain. In the words of Lyotard, "Philosophical discourse has as its rule to discover its rule: its *a priori* is what it has at stake. It is a matter of formulating this rule, which can only be done at the end, if there is an end" (60 *Differend*). Philosophy is concerned with the principle of progress defined by the supplement. The progress is indicated by the hierarchy of difference, differance, and supplement.

In one respect, difference and differance are inadequate versions of the philosophical concept provided by the supplement. The supplement includes difference and differance. "It is the production of *differance*. It is the *differance* of difference" (127 *DS*). Once Derrida has defined the supplement, he sees both difference and differance in terms of the supplement, as supplementary. "Thus understood, what is supplementary is in reality *differance*, the operation of differing which at one and the same time both fissures and retards presence... ." And later in the same passage, "The supplementary difference vicariously stands in for presence due to its primordial self-deficiency" (88 *SP*). Both difference and differance are supplementary. Being more adequate and logically prior, the notion is a little like a Chinese box in which there is another box though smaller, and inside it is still another.

While the discussion of the relation of differance and the supplement in Irene Harvey's *Derrida and the Economy of Differance* has helped me clarify many points of interpretation, I would like to shift slightly her emphasis on differance to an emphasis on the supplement. The title of her book suggests the emphasis. Derrida does believe the "graphic of supplementarity" is "the economy of differance" as she rightly points out (209). This statement should be interpreted to mean that the supplement can explain the production of differance in the same way that differance could explain the production of difference. Nevertheless, in more extended discussions she treats differance as primary over the supplement, or at least the primacy of the supplement is not at all clear. For example, she writes, "Nevertheless as a final word of introduction to the structure of *differance* as the economy of the play of supplementarity..." (207). Of course, it is not a question of seeing differance without value; its place in the system is ensured. But Harvey does not clearly assert the primacy of the supplement over differance, especially not the parallel of this primacy to the primacy of differance to difference. In one passage, echoing Derrida, she denies that the hierarchy in Derrida's philosophy is of a neat Hegelian type. "It is not yet possible to say, we suggest, that the difference between metaphysics and *differance* is one that is governed by or organized by *either* metaphysics *or differance*. If we could, we would be within a neat Hegelian system with its third term usurping the other two--sustaining their `apparent contradiction', but overwhelming their limits and situating them in a larger system" (90). Although I do agree that a system so described is undesirable, I think the charge of a "neat" system can be avoided. I do not think interpreting the supplement as prior to differance requires interpreting Derrida's thought as a "neat" or perhaps "mechanical or formalistic" dialectic. The terms "apparent contradiction" do not apply to the relation of difference and differance, so that the supplement is not simply their unity. Moreover, the dynamism of the supplement prevents it from being a simple unification. In numerous passages Derrida describes the supplement as an oscillation, a perpetual alternation, and other terms to describe a "nonunifiable entity." It has already been mentioned that Derrida does not think a text can be totalized; neither can a concept be totalized, finalized, reified into a meaning no longer pushing beyond itself toward new ones. One point could be made about the Hegelian system. Even though some people can make of Hegel's dialectic a "neat" triadic structure, the seemingly mechanical quality of concepts analyzed by Hegel does not necessarily reflect the quality of Hegel's own fundamental principles. The principles by which Hegel analyzes other people's concepts would of course be of a higher, less mechanical order than those concepts he overcomes.

The "hierarchy" in Derrida's philosophy refers to the order of difference, differance, and the supplement, as well as to the priority of each concept over the former. In the supplement the dynamic and the static aspects of its definition mirror each other. It is about development and itself develops as a performance of its meaning. More clearly than the two philosophical figures (difference and differance) before the supplement, it allows mind to see the process used to form it. In the words of Cassirer, "The real *content* of the object of thought, to which the knowledge penetrates, corresponds therefore to the active *form* of thought in general" (322 *SF*). There is a homology, a similarity in structure between the product and the process of mind. The product allows the mind to see itself so that mind can alter itself. In this way the human mind has a greater control over its own development than pre-human living things do through the genetic code. Cultural forms are higher order modes of organization, albeit of a nonmaterial type, than DNA molecules are.

Nonhuman animals have not yet evolved the ability to change the entire process by which they relate to the world. They are still in the jungle, still in the "state of nature" before any social contract to form a civilization. An example once given by Alfred North Whitehead, though for a different purpose, can make the human ability clearer (19 *Symbolism: Its Meaning and Effect*, Capricorn Books, N.Y., 1927 and 1955). Consider Aesop's fable of the dog who stole a piece of meat, went across a bridge, saw the `meat' in the water, went down to the water to get this second piece, and then lost the first piece. The dog could learn to change the behaviour of dropping the meat from its mouth to get the `second' piece, though it could not learn that water reflects images. Looking in the water it would see another dog. Humans can change their orientation to the whole of experience by learning through specific cases. Writ large, human civilization is ample proof. On a smaller scale, Kuhn claims new theories in science change the entire world view.

Each new form of tradition changes our entire world view. It is the distinctive organization of a form that permits the change. Just as in the supplement the dynamic and the static aspects defined by it mirror one another, so too the total form of a philosophy is homologous. This is one complex feature of the hierarchy of concepts. There is the homology between the three concepts as dynamic (each one surpassing the previous until the form is completed) and as static (each one coexisting in the finished form). Victor Turner has found a homology "between the diachronic transitions between statuses and the synchronic structural inferiority of certain groups within the social hierarchy" (234 Liszka). [Turner's *Ritual Process* was published in 1966, approximately the same time as the writings of Kuhn, Bloom, and Derrida.] The three main concepts of Derrida are neither simply static, nor dynamic. The passage of each one into the next shares the structure of the concept considered as static. In other words, the process of making the concept mirrors its definition. The products of self-consciousness are self-conscious, too.

This feature of ideas, the homology or mirroring, permits the development of new ones. The passage from difference to differance depended on noticing the differences between differences. By applying the idea of difference to itself, Derrida discovered the structure should become dynamic. The dynamisim led to a new type of structure, to differance. Derrida has used the term "sliding" to refer to this process of making concepts develop into higher forms. The only conclusions to be drawn from the subtle idea of the homology are (1) that the movement of ideas runs parallel to changes in their meanings; and that the development of concepts into higher forms depends upon an operation of making the structure recursive of itself such that it dynamically alters itself. Historically, this process has been called dialectic, though here it acquires features never considered by philosophers before Derrida. A similar expression of this difficult process has been given by Lyotard:

> A third rule, that of expression (*ausdrücken*), indicates that the result of the immanent derivation must be expressed in a term designating the movement of effectuation of the unity of two opposed signifieds. This term alone merits the name of result (*Resultät*). Then this term undergoes in its turn its own dissolution in its putting-into-motion, and then in the expression of its equivocality (that is of the internal opposition of its signifieds) (271 *Lyotard Reader*).

Derrida's Hierarchy and Sartre's

Derrida's hierarchy replaces Sartre's with one of a similar type but of a more integrated--perhaps one could say more philosophical--structure.

Derrida often defined deconstruction to be the overturning of a hierarchy in the tradition before. "Inverting" and "subverting" are other terms. What the predecessor defined at the end of his/her thought becomes raw material for a new start. There is a clear connection between this process and metalepsis, for in that rhetorical trope there is a reversal allowing the successor to become superior.

The change in the Sartrian hierarchy is very significant, because it shows the recurrence of a pattern. And if someone had enough knowledge about the manner of the transference of the pattern, creation would become much easier. Scientists have been practicing "recombinant DNA" techniques for changing the properties of living things. Creation in culture is analogous.

Offering a remarkably accurate account of the change in hierarchies, the semioticist James Liszka concludes that the second hierarchy, in the second philosophy or poetry or science, is superior:

> There is a restoration of the original hierarchy, but revitalized by the experience of liminality [state of being at a threshold] which the initiate has undergone: `men are released from structure into *communitas* only to return to structure revitalized by their experience of *communitas*'. The last stage of this `dialectic' retains the opposition present in the hierarchy, but now unified at a higher level in the form of the raised consciousness of the Kanongesha [people] (234-35).

So too Derrida's restitution of the philosophical hierarchy after having rejected Sartre's version results in a raised philosophical consciousness. In this light Liszka claims the pharmakon, another word for the supplement, "acknowledge[d] value and hierarchy." The supplement is the name for the new hierarchy of philosophy.

In fact, Liszka defines the three stages of Derrida's philosophy in the same way the present book does. Difference develops into differance, and differance develops into the supplement or pharmakon. With expertise in the semiotics of myth, Liszka might have been able to see the structure so clearly because philosophy originally arose from myth and it still shares features of its transmission from one generation to the next. This continuity need not alarm anyone who might think that I am saying philosophy is really myth. Other forms also arose from myths, including poetry and the sciences. The transmission of cultural knowledge resembles the transmission of the genetic code at least in several general features, as semioticists and semiologists and other theorists have discussed at length. This transmission remains rather constant. Scientists at The University of California, Berkeley, have been doing research to measure the rate of change in the genetic code (their research used DNA from ancient bees encased in amber). They found the code changes rather slowly-- on the order of several thousand years. The external physical features of a living thing seem to be more variable than the code bringing them into being. These considerations might suggest the relevance of studies of the transmission of myths for studies of the transmission of philosophy, poetry, or science. The changes in subject matter from ancient myths through the history of philosophy may seem more extreme than the underlying code actually warrants.

The Child Who Is the Father of the Man

The superiority of one philosophy over another occurs by a manoeuvre expressed in the paradox: `The Child Who Is the Father of the Man'.

The paradoxical expression has two meanings, which it relates: (1) an efficient cause--a child, what comes at the beginning, leads to the end, the Man; (2) a final cause--what comes at the end (a child) is the source of the Man, as a final cause.

Harvey finds a problem in the hierarchy of Derrida's philosophy, which she calls the "child which is the father of the man" (213 *Derrida and...*). This phrase, as already discussed, exemplifies Bloom's idea of metalepsis. Harvey, so the difficult passage seems to conclude, would like to get rid of a concept like this.

> What is this "point of non-replacemnt" for Derrida, which is also the "point of orientation"? The non-replaceable, non-representable, which allows for representation and replacement; indeed the play of *differance itself. Do we not here have the idiom, the subject, the writer, the non-authorized authority, the illegitimate father, who in fact has never left his text? Do we not have the "child which is the father of the man" here? Do we not have the "madness" which Reason thinks it has excluded from the house of being or language itself?* (213)

It seems to me that Harvey is charging Derrida with in effect producing a kind of transcendental signified, whereas his whole philosophy had started with its rejection. At any rate it is clear she believes the notion with the logic of the `child which is the father of the man' is problematic. In the context of this passage clearly that notion is the supplement. A few lines later Harvey brings to more discursive terms the tone of objection so far manifest. "It [differance] comes to a halt, a stop, indeed perhaps to an abyss in the system, in the calculus--which never goes full circle, nor full ellipse, and thus never returns totally. Is it not this that Derrida himself has pointed towards throughout his work? The essentiality of the non-return." If I interpret her correctly, and this is a difficult objection, Harvey objects to the supplement insofar as it does go full circle, does return; doing so would be counter to his whole work.

Beginning with the same concept, the supplement, and the idea that it manifests the logic of the `child which is father of the man', I would like to suggest a different way of situating the supplement in Derrida's system. Hardly can it be avoided to close a philosophy without some concept exhibiting the logic of the `child which is father of the man'. In poetry, Bloom treats it as a victory, the end to all the poet's searching. Previously, I have argued that the supplement's metalepsis proves Derrida's advance upon the tradition, bequeathed by Sartre. The value of the `child which is father of the man' is that it can repeat the past pattern of philosophy while developing an alternative of it which is superior. It may be true that Harvey was suggesting that the supplement became *a kind of* transcendental signified, which the whole philosophy rejected. Or perhaps I draw too much out of her own conclusions, forcing them to tell us more than they attempt to. Irregardless, the supplement *does* have a reference to Sartre's closing concept, as has been shown. Such a reference is not bad, however, because it shows what Derrida solved. Neither would it have been good for Derrida to avoid forming a concept with that metaleptic logic. It is the canonical passage of a philosophy (and perhaps of a poetry and a science and any tradition form) to develop such a construction at the closing. That logic helps to perform the closing of the system, which then stands atop a pyramid of universal history. It is true, I believe, that the supplement is a kind of substitute for the transcendental signified, but only in the sense that the supplement fulfills functions in Derrida's thought similar to those of the ideal fusion of the in-itself-for-itself in Sartre's; definitely--quite definitely--the meaning of the supplement differs from the concept which it ultimately substitutes for. Derrida's concept could only have formed in contrast to the preceding one so that the pattern of philosophy could be transferred while being improved. I agree with Harvey that there is a problem with the concept of the supplement, but I will argue for an interpretation based on its specific meaning and not its general function in the system, which must occur precisely because it will cause a problem. I will criticize the supplement in the next chapter on Derrida.

The Supplement as the End of Derrida's Philosophy

The supplement leads to the closing, the terminus, of Derrida's philosophy. [Derrida's idea of "the festival" as a solution to representative differance is more advanced than the supplement; in Derrida's terms, he starts to "slide" his own idea into its future form.]

The Supplement as the Point of Orientation

The supplement "has no energy of its own, no spontaneous movement"; "it is...an imagination or representation which determines and orients the force of desire" (178 *OG*). This description could serve as a metalepsis of Aristotle's closing concept, the Unmoved Mover or the Prime Mover, which moved the whole universe but itself was unmoved. A text is "ordered around its own blind spot"; "the concept of the supplement is a sort of blind spot in Rousseau's text, the not-seen that opens and limits visibility" (164, 163 *OG*).

Derrida defines the point of orientation in a philosophy in the following way:

> There is a point in the system where the signifier can no longer be replaced by its signified, so that in consequence no signifier can be so replaced, purely and simply. For the point of nonreplacement is also the point of orientation for the entire system of signification, the point where the fundamental signified is promised as the terminal-point of all references and conceals itself as that which would destroy at one blow the entire system of signs. It is at once spoken and forbidden by all signs (266 *OG*).

Is Derrida thinking of the supplement here or the transcendental siginified of Sartre? Of course, the supplement orients the other concepts; it describes the rule of their passage. Derrida is remembering what he did to Sartre's closing concept to re-envision it as a negative presuppostion, the transcendental signified, and he is applying it to his own supplement to define it better for himself. After all, the supplement becomes the ground of Derrida's metaphysics, as Harvey claims (119). This issue shows that Derrida understands the process of philosophy better than Sartre did or perhaps, which must be the same thing, the process is more determinate. Derrida can look for his point of orientation. He knows after his reinterpreting Sartre's in-itself-for-itself as the unacceptable transcendental signified that the closing concept of any philosophy requires a unity to which the creator is blind. To go even further beyond past tradition, Derrida attempts to push through this apparent limit on knowledge. One can know there is a limit, but not be able to pass it. This is the way all (canonical) philosophies close. Poetries and scientific theories as well. Whereas Bloom had the creator place a limit on the precursor and the future generations, the sense of the creator coming to a limit of form is more dominant in Derrida's philosophy.

The Supplement as the Limit of Form

The supplement can be the limit of form insofar as it completes the task the philosophy began with. That was to re-define philosophical development, transcendence. The supplement provides a definition--one that avoids the problem of Sartre's. The relation between the supplement and Sartre's closing concept is not so straightforward as that between a problem and a solution. Derrida's original conception of the problem and the possible solution changed at each main new concept in his philosophy, as Figure 11-1 on page 333 shows; these points of that change (difference, differance, and the supplement) are points of replication leading to full reproduction, but not of an identical philosophy. So the destination turned out to be somewhat different from the point of departure.

The supplement is an "absolute limit of analysis" (87 *SP*). The complete product necessitates or means a change occurred in the activity of production. This change cannot itself be accounted for, or

Figure 11-1: A Cultural Work Has a Perspectival Meaning by Re-defining a New Position in Tradition at Each New Main Stage

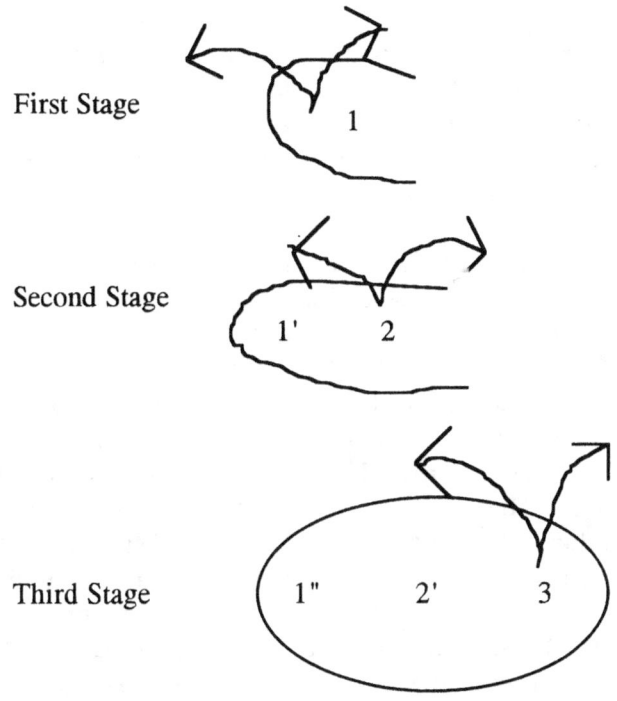

The third main stage of a science, poetry, or philosophy is the best understanding of the total process, each figure referring to what went before and what will come. Only the third stage achieves a stance in tradition. The reference of each figure to the whole process is Ariadne's thread guiding the creator to create an alternative to what the predecessor did, to define a new step in tradition, with a new past, new present, and new future.

represented in the product (as an infinite reflection is not ever finished). The accounting for the change is up to the human community beyond the individual in which the change occurred. The limit on any cultural form allows for the best possible situation: the individual can take a step up the staircase of human civilization but must not take more than one step nor the last step if other later individuals are to be able to do the same.

Offering a valuable way of stating the limit according to Derrida's thought, Harvey does not interpret it as negative, bad. The limit can be something good.

> This "certain powerlessness of language" is that same limit that Derrida claims for all structures. That which forms its conditions of possibility, that which is the opening which necessarily exceeds it are by definition not capable of being understood from within that same structure or system. They form instead what one might term its "blind spot"--its shadow, its other side. There is thus a perspectival nature within the nature of structure introduced here such that it is intrinsically *not* all-inclusive, nor all-embracing. Structure as such, and thus language as structure, is prohibited therein from a certain omniscience. This prohibition is precisely the condition of its possibility, Derrida claims. In addition, the condition of the possibility of structure is itself a structure...

The positive features of the limit are the fact that it is also an opening; the fact that it creates a perspective; the fact that it is the condition of the possibility of the structure or philosophy. Derrida calls the condition of possibility a *fundamental structure* "by which the totality opens itself and overflows to create meaning in the anticipation of a telos which we must consider here in its most indeterminate form."[3] The fact that the same word is used both for the whole system and for the closing concept shows a homology of whole and part. The opening here sounds like a preparation for a successor, who would form a telos the creator himself (Derrida) could only form indeterminately. The limit is a positive symbol of a new beginning in philosophy.

The supplement closes the perspective of the predecessor, without being able to lead Derrida to the closure of his own perspective, which would be its annihilation since the passage Derrida makes is not the wrong one from the point of departure. This lack of symmetry between the start of a philosophy and its end, this difference in ability to totalize a perspective, shows the greater importance of the whole coherence of the discourse, the greater importance to the practical consciousness raising performed by philosophical development. The elements of experience become capable of greater interdependence such that mind increases its own operability. The lack of symmetry shows that the philosophical perspective is not a machine that could run by itself, "at least not yet" (208 *Derrida and...*). From a new rhetorical vantage point in history, the individual can require the end point to be transformed into a satisfactory starting point. History needs new individuals, whose starting point and end point must differ, since history is an oriented series.

One question a reader should ask is, if the limit is not known determinately, then how does the creator know this concept definitely closes the philosophy? In *The Truth in Painting* Derrida discusses this issue-- How does a frame or context relate to the painting? To what extent is the frame an internal constitutive factor? To what extent is the frame of a painting or the context of a discourse aware of an outside, a beyond? One way to interpret Derrida's answer, considered as the general course of the book, is to refer to the idea of a "structural unconsciousness" proposed by Derrida in *Limited Inc.*. That idea would lend credence to the view of a genetic code of philosophy guiding the philosopher almost unconsciously. Another way is to interpret Derrida's answer by the idea of "undecidables":

> ...I have called undecidables, that is, unities of simulacrum, "false" verbal properties (nominal or semantic) that can no longer be included within philosophical (binary) opposition, but which, however, inhabit philosophical opposition, resisting and disorganizing it, *without ever* constituting a third term, without ever leaving room for a solution in the form of speculative dialectics (the *pharmakon* is neither remedy nor poison, neither good nor evil, neither the inside nor the outside, neither speech nor

> writing; the *supplement* is neither a plus nor a minus, neither an outside nor the complement of an inside, neither accident nor essence, etc. ... (43 *Pos*).

"Undecidable" does not mean Derrida cannot determine the concept. He can define those mentioned. Instead it means the opposition within them cannot be unified; their meaning prevents a further unification to form a new concept. The opposition is an "opening" pointing the way to a new "telos" as mentioned in the passage before. It is a *non plus ultra*. It is a Gordian knot, which cannot be untied. It must rather be cut. Another image for the opposition within "undecidables" is that of two train rails extending into the horizon. Like the gaze of an observer into his/her horizon, a philosophy must present to itself a vision of the future beyond itself which limits itself. To the person looking at the horizon, it seems as if the two rails converge. But to *a different* observer further along the tracks, the two lines forever diverge. A successor sees this irreconcilable dualism in the philosophy of the predecessor--irreconcilable, that is, within the assumptions of the predecessor. (Kuhn's idea of incommensurability has truth in this sense of the difference in concepts of reality.) The ability to see or not see the convergence/ lack of convergence is a matter of perspective. It does not mean either perspective is equally good. Either perspective is a perspective but the succeeding one integrates the processes of the former more thoroughly, determinately. Liszka develops an idea of "liminal entities," concepts that are situated at points of transformation of the self, at thresholds. These points are structural punctuating points in the dynamic of the narratives in texts, myths, philosophies, poetries, scientific theories. Those entities are neither inside nor outside, and it is not exactly true that they are on the border. While indicating a change in consciousness, they indicate the self-awareness even more.

The Supplement as a Regulative Ideal

Beginning with the philosopher Immanuel Kant, "regulative ideal" was distinguished from a "constitutive idea of reason." "Regulative" means other concepts do not really come from the regulative ideal, they are not formed through it. Instead, it regulates or orders concepts which have a similar structure in general but which are not the ideal itself. "Ideal" suggests that something is not realized, or that a series of objects of knowledge proceeds to infinity.

A regulative ideal is needed to justify different levels of knowledge--both between a successor and a precursor, and within the development of a single philosophy.[4] Since the transition between different levels of knowledge requires a change in the process of knowing, not just in the objects known, only a multiplicity of acts of mind could explain the varying functioning of the mind. But throughout this growth, the mind understands its transformations through a common tendency: the mind projects a regulative ideal more and more throughout the building of a philosophy so that the knowledge already accumulated by the precursor might be empowered even more.

Like a regulative ideal, the "undecidable" supplement indicates the place of a new concept, not its specific content. In the manner of a ventriloquist speaking through Lévi-Strauss, as Derrida often does, the philosopher defines the regulative status of the supplement:

> `In the system of symbols constituted by all cosmologies, *mana* would simply be a zero symbolic value, that is to say, a sign marking the necessity of a symboic content *supplementary* [Derrida's italics] to that with which the signified is already loaded, but which can take on any value required, provided only that this value still remains part of the available reserve and is not, as phonologists put it, a groupterm'.
>
> [And Lévi-Strauss adds the note:]
> ...if we schematize the conception I am proposing [Derrida is proposing the supplement]...the function of notions like *mana* is to be opposed to the absence of signification, without entailing by itself any particular signification.[5]

Very significant is the restriction on the concept able to take on any value (meaning) that it not be a "group term." The supplement cannot fully become a member of the series it regulates; it cannot become constitutive. If it became a member of a series, it could not regulate the perpetual generation of the series beyond that member. Derrida tries to avoid the requirement that an advanced form of the supplement, the "festival," be representable, be inscribable in writing: "the ideal of a public festival substituted for representation, and a certain model of society perfectly present to itself in small communities which render both useless and nefarious all recourse to representation" (244 *WD*; also 306ff. *OG*).

The regulative nature of the supplement means there is a common tendency in the productive acts of the mind. It cannot be the unity of all of the philosophy including itself. Lévi-Strauss believes the unity of myth is merely tendential and projective (*The Raw and the Cooked* Trans. John and Doreen Wightman, New York: Harper and Row, 1969, pp. 5-6). "It [the unity of myth] is a phenomenon of the imagination, resulting from the attempt at interpretation; and its function is to endow the myth with synthetic form and to prevent its disintegration into a confusion of opposites." So too the supplement prevents Derrida's philosophy from falling into a confusion of opposites. One act of mind may not produce the supplement but rather several related actions. Consider Cassirer's idea of a movement of thought producing a sense of the whole discourse:

> Here the individual gains its meaning and content only from the whole;--but this whole cannot be presented like a quiescent object of perception, but, in order to be truly surveyed, must be grasped and determined in the law of its construction. In order to comprehend the number series *as a series* and thus to penetrate into its systematic nature, there is needed not merely a *single* apperceptive act (such as is considered sufficient for the perception of a particular thing of sense), but always a manifold of such acts, which reciprocally condition each other. Thus a *movement of thought* is always demanded, yet a movement which is no mere change of presentation, but in which what is first gained is retained and made the starting-point of new developments. Thus from the activity itself flows the recognition of a fixed body of truths (317 *SF*).

Harvey points out that the supplement is "a non-unifiable differing and differing." [6]

To some extent the supplement goes contrary to common sense by not being reducible to a single object of knowledge. Most knowledge concerns everyday behavior toward physical objects that can be defined that way. Supporting the interpretation that the supplement is not a single object of knowledge, Derrida writes, the supplement "`precedes' the opposition between different effects, does not have the punctual simplicity of a *coincidentia oppositorum*" (127 *DS*).

The Chain and the Passage of Supplements

The supplement explains the development that led to it and the supplement must belong in an infinite chain; thus, it is the model of concepts in the past and in the future.

The three stages of Derrida's philosophy through which the supplement passes are difference, differance, and the supplement. These resemble the three fates: Clotho, who makes or spins the thread of life from raw fibers; Lachesis, who measures, weaves it; and Atropos, who cuts the thread or puts a limit on it.

A universalization, infinitization, or maximization of the supplement must occur; it must apply to all objects of knowledge. Difference was universalized into a system of differences; and differance was universalized into infinite differance. The supplement is universalized into a chain or system of supplements.

This extension of the concept is not arbitrary but necessary.

> The supplement comes in the place of a lapse, a nonsignified or a nonrepresented, a nonpresence. There is no present before it, it is not preceded by anything but itself, that is to say by another supplement. The supplement is always the supplement of a supplement. One wishes to go back *from the supplement to the source*: one must recognize that there is *a supplement at the source*" (304 *OG*).

By saying that the supplement is preceded by nothing but itself Derrida indicates the closing character of the concept, how it ends the quest. He also means that a supplement requires another supplement, in fact a *future* supplement. One must immediately wonder how the present could be if it depends on a future not yet existing. As the saying goes, tomorrow never comes. Of course, the immediate response to make Derrida as consistent as his theory allows would be to point out that the supplement never comes from anything but a supplement, so that all objects of knowledge in the past were supplements. An immediate question would be, how is Derrida's supplement superior to past supplements, if all concepts in the past were really supplements after all? Derrida does not limit the meaning of the supplement to either alternative, instead shifting from emphasis to emphasis, like a person shifting his/her weight from foot to foot. In more logical terms the dependence of one supplement on another has been stated in this way by the French philosopher: according to the logic of supplementarity it is necessary that "the outside be inside, that the other and the lack come to add themselves as a plus that replaces a minus, that what adds itself to something takes the place of a default in the thing, that the default, as the outside of the inside, should be already within the inside, etc." (215 *OG*). Since the first supplement has a deficiency, it could be interpreted as either a past supplement before Derrida's philosophy or as one in his philosophy that might develop into a higher type of concept, though not different from the change effected by Derrida.

The most direct argument for an infinite chain of supplements is the following:

> Through this sequence of supplements a necessity is announced: that of an infinite chain, ineluctably multiplying the supplementary mediations that produce the sense of the very thing they defer: the mirage of the thing itself, of immediate presence, of originary perception. Immediacy is derived. That all begins through the intermediary is what is indeed "inconceivable [to reason] (157 *OG*).

A sense of a problem is at hand. The infinite generativity of supplements seems to be compulsive, to express the need to re-think it to make it complete by itself.

A single supplement is deficient; only another one partially redeems it, itself being in turn deficient. This logic may resemble borrowing money to repay the interest on money borrowed in the past. The remedy perpetuates the deficiency. For this reason the supplement is entropic, as differance also was thought in its unique way. The financial situation gets worse. The supplement is "a substitute that enfeebles" (215 *OG*). The problem for Derrida of understanding the incompleteness of any single supplement can be seen being played out in several passages. For example, "The supplement to Nature is within Nature as its play. Who will ever say if the lack within nature is within nature, if the catastrophe by which Nature is separated from itself is still natural? A natural catastrophe conforms to laws in order to overthrow the law" (258ff. *OG*). Perhaps subconsciously Derrida may be trying at this point to re-think, once again, his relation to his main predecessor. How could his philosophy have developed from a previous one? Would it still be a philosophy? In what sense must it be like philosophy before it?

Another passage should be adduced to help convey this significant point about the need of one supplement for another. It is as if one cannot have independent existence.

> But, by a strange motion, the more one departs from the origin, the more one tends to come back to what precedes it, to a nature which *has not yet* awakened to speech and to everything that is born along with speech. And, between the two polar series, regulated relations of supplementarity: the second series is added to the first in order to be *substituted* for it, but, in supplementing a lack in the first series, also to *add* something new, an addition, an *accident*, an excess that *should not have* overtaken the first series. In doing this, the second series will hollow out a new lack or will enlarge the original lack, which will call for a new supplement, etc. (147 *MP*).

From this passage it is clear that no one can tell which is the *first* supplement. The order of particular supplements can be established, whereas the meaning of a supplement excludes an idea of the beginning and end of the entire series. One gets the sense of the infinite generativity of supplements, as if Derrida has finally succeeded in defining a domain of philosophy that is truly universal, beginning in the infinite past, continuing through the present, and extending into the future by the *necessary unstoppable* generation of new supplements. A remarkably accurate parallel in ancient sources for this infinite generativity is Zeus' ability to reproduce beings from his head, without needing another being with which to copulate (*Theogeny*). Bloom's idea that a poet aims to be an influence, wants to be capable of generating new poetry, seems justified.

Derrida's "Festival" Like Bloom's "Apophrades"

Derrida's "festival," an expression of the unity of supplements, functions in his philosophy very much like Bloom's "apophrades." Bloom defined askesis as containing an opposition that was limited or relativized into the more integrated poetic figure of apophrades. The opposition between supplements is internalized, united into a new more integrated supplement.

The need of one supplement for another leads Derrida to state an advanced form of the supplement including what was needed from more than one supplement. The transition or passage from one supplement to another was not fully intelligible. This concept is like a mass of chemicals in a crucible; the heat or pressure of the preceding context makes it a volatile mass ready for transformation.

Derrida tries to resolve the problem of the passage by imaginatively presenting the situation to see if the terms of a solution would appear. This process resembles the thought experiments of Einstein and the physical models chemists use to discover possible new combinations of chemical phenomena. Eliot, too, spoke of poetic creation as an experimental situation in which the poet assembled the ingredients and conditions, waiting for the transformation to occur of itself ("Tradition and the Individual Talent"). The merely place-marking nature of the supplement is imaginatively presented as a stage with nothing to be seen. The difference between one supplement and another, the need of one for the other, is imaginatively presented as the relation of actor and spectator, the represented and the representer, the signified and the signifier. Then, to express not the difference *between* supplements but rather the necessity of their relation in another concept, he shifts the imagery from a stage to that of a public festival.

> But what is a stage which presents nothing to the sight? It is the place where the spectator, presenting himself as spectacle, will no longer be either seer or voyeur, will efface within himself the difference between the actor and the spectator, the represented and the representer, the object seen and the seeing subject. With that difference, an entire series of oppositions will deconstitute themselves one by one. Presence will be full, not as an object which is *present* to be seen, to give itself to intuition as an empirical unity or as an *eidos* holding itself *in front of* or *up against*; it will be full as the intimacy of a self-presence, as the consciousness or the sentiment of self-proximity, of self-sameness. That public festival will therefore have a form analogous to the electoral meetings of a free and legiferant [law-making] assembled people: the representative differance will be effaced in the self presence of sovereignty (306 *OG*).

The reconciliation of different senses of right in the public voting echos Sartre's idea: "Man makes himself in order to be God"; "Man must lose himself in order that the self-cause may exist" (796 *BN*). The individual in the group of voters must give way to the "indifferent" opinion of the mass. To this extent, Liszka correctly claims that the closing of Derrida's philosophy slips into an indifference, into a concept with a meaning counter to the founding idea of difference. The end runs counter to the start in the way the ouroboros swallows its tail, thus completing and closing a circle.

Strong, definite comparisons could be made between Derrida's "festival" and Bloom's apophrades. Apophrades is also a community event, with the return of the dead. In both the creator comes to the point of an imageless vision. Derrida discusses, "the desire of making *representation* disappear (Ibid.). "The telos of the image is its own imperceptibility" (298 *OG*). Bloom, early in his career, pointed to an anagogy achieved in the final stage of a poetry--a vision of poetic finality. At first he termed this the desire for a Thou that could not become an it; this relation of a universal and a particular mirrors Derrida's discussion of the supplement not having a particular value (meaning) in a series of supplements but rather being a place-marker of an indefinite development of meaning. An imageless vision closes a philosophy or a poetry, because the creator comes to see vision itself, not a visible object. Seeing is seen, not an object of sight. Plato conveyed this ultimate vision by the metaphor of the sun, being the source of all visible things and capable of being sensed in a vision, though not itself a discrete visible object, for it is too bright to look at and define with the naked eye. Its regularity seems faultless, and it is the source of all life. Perhaps it is necessary to use metaphorical, imaginative presentation for this idea of an imageless vision, the source of knowledge, the knowing process, as Plato and Derrida and all great philosophers and poets do, because making seeing into a seen object could never be completed as it would involve an infinite regress of new modes of seeing needing to be represented. The community of creators through history does perform this process, but the individual can do it just once. The difficulty with this idea of a festival will be discussed in the next chapter on Derrida.

Derrida's Dissatisfaction at the End of His Philosophy

Characteristic of philosophies, there is a dissatisfaction about a loss of meaning, an entropy; this loss functions to limit the creator himself/herself; to limit a successor; and also to challenge someone to become the successor by presenting an apparently unsolvable problem, a Gordian knot, which cannot be untied but only cut by changing the entire matrix in which the concepts have meaning.

Typically, philosophies end in mixed triumph and dissatisfaction. Sartre expresses his, in just one passage, in this way:

> Many men, in fact, know that the goal of their pursuit is being; and to the extent that they possess this knowledge, they refrain from appropriating things for their own sake and try to realize the symbolic appropriation of their being-in-itself. But to the extent that this attempt still shares in the spirit of

> seriousness and that these men can still believe that their mission of effecting the existence of the in-itself-for-itself is written in things, they are condemned to despair; for they discover at the same time that all human activities are equivalent (for they all tend to sacrifice man in order that the self-cause may arise) and that all are on principle doomed to failure. Thus it amounts to the same thing whether one gets drunk alone or is a leader of nations. If one of these activities takes precedence over the other, this will not be because of its real goal but because of the degree of consciousness which it possesses of its ideal goal; and in this case it will be the quietism of the solitary drunkard which will take precedence over the vain agitation of the leader of nations (797 *BN*).

The dissatisfaction concerns the possibility of development beyond a certain point. The closing concept of Sartre's philosophy presents an ideal that can never be realized fully. This idea fits very well with Bloom's major idea that a poet does not make way for a succeeding poet; a poet forbids, prevents future development. In this passage of Sartre, as well as the passages concerning Derrida to follow, the prevention of future development is more clearly not just a personal wish for supremacy, for immortality, but is a necessary structural feature.

Writing is often thought to be entropic. Through Rousseau, Derrida associates writing with "loss of passional energy" (239 *OG*). "The replacement of an *object*" is a deficit in energy" (200 *OG*). "It is precisely the property of the power of differance to modify life less and less as it spreads out more and more" (131 *OG*). Derrida discusses "dead writing" and the loss of meaning through successive metaphors in language ("White Mythology").

Writing eventually becomes counter to life, to creation (25 *OG*). For Derrida this end to his philosophy is brought about by the supplement (153 *OG*). The supplement is even "fatal": "How was this supplementary substitution fatal? How is it fatal?" (200 *OG*).

Derrida describes a loss of universality at the end of his philosophy.

> Under a universal appearance, painting would thus be perfectly empirical, multiple, and changeful like the sensory units that it represents outside of any code. By contrast, the ideal universality of phonetic writing is due to its infinite distance with respect to the sound (the primary signified of that writing which marks it arbitrarily) and to the meaning signified by the spoken word. Between these two poles, universality is lost. I say between these two poles since, as I have confirmed, pure pictography and pure phonography are two ideas of reason. Ideas of pure presence: in the first case, presence of the represented thing in its perfect imitation, and in the second, the self-presence of speech itself. In both cases, the signifier tends to be effaced in the presence of the signified (301 *OG*).

The universality is lost between the two poles of knowledge, pure pictography and pure phonography. Three pages later Derrida describes the loss of universality in other terms.

> Where should one search, in the city, for that lost unity of glance and speech? In what *space* can one again *listen to himself*? [A successor is deprived of his/her own imaginative philosophical space.] Can the theater, which unites spectacle and discourse, not take up where the unanimous assembly left off? (304 *OG*).

A solution given by Ricoeur to the entropy is "to climb back up the slope of this sort of entropy of language by means of a new act of discourse" (259).

The Supplement and the Genetic Code

The supplement completes the genetic code of Derrida's philosophy such that it could reproduce one with a similar pattern, just as it had reproduced the pattern of philosophy through Sartre's work. Figure 11-2 on page 347 illustrates Derrida's genetic code.

Figure 11-2: Each New Cycle of Philosophy and Poetry Has within It a Triadic Genetic Code

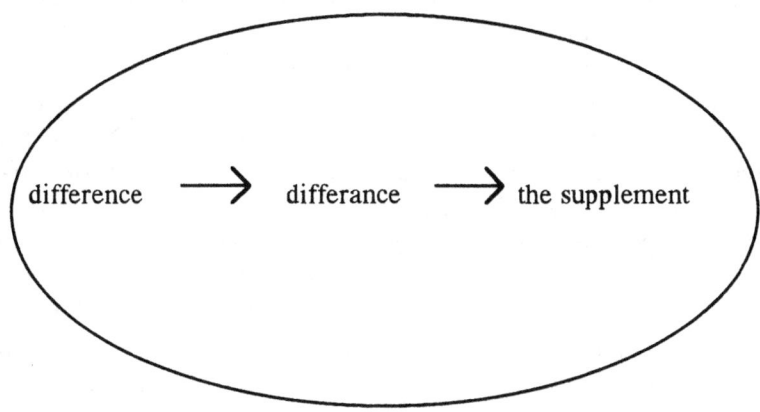

Derrida's Philosophical System

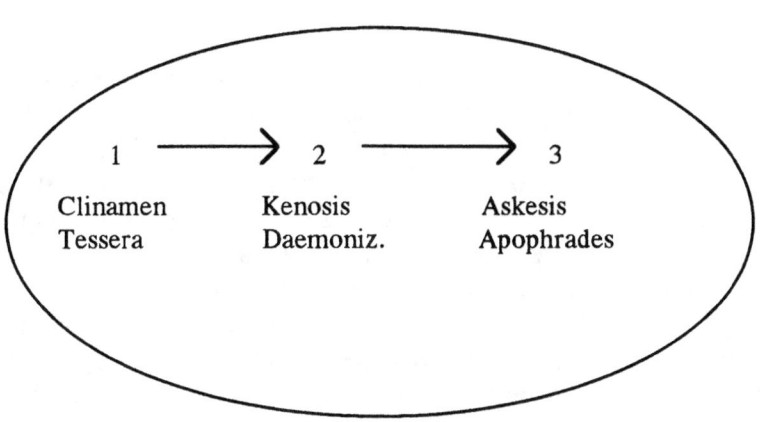

Bloom's Model of All Poetries

Harvey interpets Derrida's discussion of the "desire for a transcendental signified," which must "inhabit metaphysics" (13 *Derrida and...*). While this desire cannot be fulfilled, it nevertheless provides the condition for the possibility of metaphysics, endowing its lifespan with infinity. "Infinity," I think, means that, since the transcendental siginified can never be fully attained, knowledge can develop forever in the direction toward it. As a further question, does Derrida's supplement have the function of leading to a new version of a transcendental signified, as all philosophies do?

The supplement does correspond to the in-itself-for-itself in closing the philosophy. Strictly speaking, the "transcendental signified" is not *in* Sartre's philosophy; rather it is what Derrida formulates from the in-itself-for-itself as its negative (false and implicit) assumption. Then the functions of the supplement correspond to those of the in-itself-for-itself.

Requirements of the "Space" or Form of Derrida's Philosophy

The supplement can be the synecdoche for the whole space of Derrida's philosophy. The philosophy began with the problem of further philosophical development. The supplement became the last concept in a series to explain how Derrida could develop a philosophy after Sartre's. The supplement represents the idea of development: "the concept of the supplement and the theory of writing designate textuality itself...in an indefinitely multiplied structure--*en abyme [in an abyss]*" (163 *OG*). The use of the singular form for "indefinitely multipled structure" means that the infinite generativity is just as much a property of the whole philosophy as it is of the supplement. Baudrillard described his third stage of knowledge as simulation ["simulacrum" coming from Derrida's *Positions*]; real knowledge can only be "that of which it is possible to give an equivalent reproduction," and the real thing is that which is always already reproduced (146 *Simulations*). Clearly, the supplement is necessary for the text, the whole of Derrida's philosophy. The demarcation of Derrida's specific text requires the idea of the infinite generativity of concepts. The property of infinite generativity of new supplements represents the requirement of a philosophical form that it be internally infinite, that development could continue indefinitely, practically infinitely within its boundaries. This requirement need not sound exorbitant, as science always purports to provide a universal theory of nature; philosophy, too, claims to provide a universal theory of knowledge. Not only do the epistemic principles apply to any object of knowledge, but they also apply to the development of knowledge, past, present, and future. Rodolphe Gasché correctly argues that the semantic inexhaustibility is a function of "a structural necessity that is marked in the text."[7] Only as such could it be a matter of principle, not quantitative inexhaustibility.

By defining knowledge as "that of which it is possible to give an equivalent reproduction," to use Baudrillard's words for the supplement, Derrida thinks of it like the genetic code, the essence of which is reproduction. The process defined by the supplement is designed to be able to go on forever.

The Supplement Conveys a Sense of the Continuum of Philosophy

Since one supplement is a development from another one, Derrida's philosophy has an explanation for the development of his philosophy beyond Sartre's: it is "supplementary" in the special senses of that term. The supplement leads to a `return of the dead', to use Bloom's terms, insofar as Derrida can finally define Sartre's work as a step before his own, though inferior, and his own as an autonomous step beyond. Sartre is referred to on Derrida's terms, from his vantage point. Despite the predecessor's not making way for a successor, Derrida shows how it is possible to have further development after Sartre's in-itself-for-itself. The supplement defines the space or domain of this development, one providing indefinite, limitless improvement up to an ideal maximum serving to regulate the common direction of all progress toward it. Within the philosophy there is continuity of purpose, a sense of a single common project.

The continuum of philosophy is regained by an idea of infinite re-generativity. The continuum up to Sartre is thereby extended, renewed. The genuine possibility of development is represented in the figure of the supplement that can produce itself out of itself, as Zeus in Hesiod's *Theogeny* could. The producing of the supplement out of itself justifies Derrida's claim to have developed his own philosophy from his *own* principles, not from Sartre's.

The continuum is re-established if no break occurs before or after Derrida's philosophy, if it is universally applicable. But there is a border, a limit. How does the limit not prevent philosophy from being seen as a continuum even beyond Derrida's philosophy?

The border is defined in *Dissemination*. With the philosophy structurally complete in 1967 it is a question of interpretation what the works after that time can add. Certainly they do, but no main structural additions occur. Instead, the works indefinitely refine the closing concept, the supplement, a border. The text, though limited by the community, is internally infinite for the individual, and this is good, for the individual can never exhaust the benefits of further philosophizing. Derrida realizes the text does not issue into "some unique ultimate accomplishment," after which nothing more can be said (295 *DS*). More can be said after 1967, after *Of Grammatology*. But it serves as refinement. Rather than that last member of a series, the border of a philosophy is "a displacement and a rift," "an open system consisting of the repetition of rifts" (295 *DS*). The idea of the border becomes a seed to be implanted elsewhere, and Derrida plants the seed in many contexts after the 1967 philosophy--painting, politics, literary criticism, and theory of culture, among others. Derrida denies that the regeneration of philosophy occurs by the end inseminating a new text. The relation is not so direct, so substantially unified. The fertilizing is more like dissemination. The end of the text is not a single punctual border control station. It is multiple, unfinished: "two hemitropic crystals," which of course have the unusual property of being able to regenerate their own structures in separate but related formations (227 *DS*). The end is never finished, related. The supplement develops like two hemitropic crystals. It nevertheless grounds the new continuum of philosophy partly because the generation of the supplements is never finished; each requires another.

Harvey correctly notices that this end of Derrida's philosophy repeats in a new way the close of previous philosophies:

> Far from destroying metaphysics or undoing its conditions of possibility, deconstruction instead is condemned to a certain participant-observational role in

> the following sense. It participates certainly in the history of metaphysics as the history of philosophy, just as Kant's critique has done despite the former's attempt to step outside and consider the "unacknowledged foundations of the same." Yet it remains an observer in the sense that, although illustrating the limits and conditions of the possibility of metaphysics--as a primarily Western post-Platonic phenomena [phenomenon]--it does not prohibit in the slightest the continuation and indeed paradoxical affirmation of that same history (14 *Derrida and...*).

Derrida continues and affirms the history he criticized. A change in tradition occurs. Whereas Derrida's pattern of philosophy resembles that of Sartre, it still can differ in meaning. DNA has the same structure, even though different genes compose the same structure. The human body has the same structure even though all the cells have changed the chemical substances to maintain its life.

The Supplement Provides What Is Necessary for a Successor to Create

What is necessary is a repetition of the pattern on which Derrida built his philosophy--though in a new way. Harvey predicts this will happen to Derrida's own philosophy:

> As Derrida says: "According to a law, which one could formalize, philosophy always reappropriates for itself the discourse which delimits it." In fact this essay is a part of that movement. Any attempt to understand Derrida's work is a movement toward its reappropriation by metaphysics, and thereby a movement, paradoxically, toward the former's recognition and thus destruction (124 *Derrida and...*).

Following these principles Derrida criticized the Sartrian "in-itelf-for-itself" only to develop a new concept with some similar functions in closing a philosophy. Other concepts, too, correspond between the two philosophies. In this respect the model of Bloom can be used to give a remarkably accurate idea of the relationships of two philosophies, though of course the meanings of the poetic and philosophical figures differ.

As in Bloom's theory, the creation of a philosophy from another is not a part-by-part process in which one part comes from the corresponding part in the previous philosophy. The first philosophical concept, namely difference, results from a re-interpretation of the relative failure of the coherence of the Sartrian philosophy; thus, a knowledge of the system as a whole informs difference. Derrida's opening concept issues out of a new sense of the philosophical continuum, the tradition; the concept has an environing role; that is, it begins to make a new matrix of the philosophical process; it makes a new environment in which they can have meaning, as living things, too, can only exist in a specific kind of environment. Similar to the opening concept, differance comes from difference and also from a generalized differentiation from the precursor's rejected negative presupposition, though at a higher level than the rejection made by difference. The supplement, too, comes from the concept before, from differance, and from a generalized rejection of the precursor's sense of the continuum, though the rejection now is at a higher level of determination than before. The same mediated or indirect relationship occurs in the replication of DNA. Since each part "knows" its role (is programmed, coded in scientific terms), each can help to carry the message of reproduction.

> Thus, while it is true that the genetic code is written in a stereochemical language, each of whose letters consists of a sequence of three nucleotides (a triplet) in the DNA, specifying one amino acid (among twenty) in the polypeptide, there exists no direct steric relationship between the coding triplet and the coded amino acid (Monod 108).

Then, there is no one-to-one part-by-part creation of the new DNA from the old, no "direct steric relationship" between the coding part and the coded. The genetic code reads in triplets, as does the code of philosophy and of poetry--the three movements of revisionary ratios according to Bloom. Each part itself--whether difference, differance, or the supplement--knows its place (is defined by its position relative to the others)--and so conveys to the next concept what is needed to form its complementary parts. Bloom used a term remarkably close to the terms in genetics: "antithetical completion." To show that the parts of a philosophy carry some of the burden of the message of reproduction consider Derrida's statement: "Numbers are caught in a mathematicogenetic theory of groups...there is nothing prior to the group, no simple originary unit prior to this division through which life comes to see itself and the seed is multiplied from the start" (304 *DS*). The power of individual concepts to carry a sense of their needed environment within themselves gives much power to the creator, who then does not have to invent an entire prototype of what the created pattern will be. Alternatively, creation proceeds by a more step-by-step process of understanding the previous philosophy, as Harvey pointed out, using *bricolage*. The fact that the understanding of a philosophy in the deepest and truest way leads to a new philosophy supports the view that a kind of genetic encoding process is at work.

The presence of the needed code of philosophy is stated by Derrida: "And if a certain `break' is always possible, that with which it breaks must necessarily bear the mark of this possibility inscribed in its structure" (64 *LIM*).

The cyclical transmission of the pattern of philosophy has been described well by Joseph Valente: "Each new representation surpasses its object, comprehending its frame, its limits if you will, within its own field of vision. Yet having done so, it finds itself identically framed."[8] "Identically" is a little too strong since there is a development of the meaning. A comparison would be some improvements in the features of a living thing without a change in the general functioning of the code, as scientists can now perform, called "recombinant DNA theory." Of greatest importance is the fact that the frame of the previous theory is comprehended in order for the pattern to be repeated in a subsequent philosophy. This process has been mentioned in various contexts, especially concerning the perspective point, the transcendental signified, and epic ecphrasis.

The supplement indicates the point of the problem to be overcome. The need of one supplement for a future one directs a possible successor's attention to defining the passage of one supplement into another, creating a new unity. Any supplement means something beyond itself, just as the genetic code carries a message to inform a future code. "The necessary exit lays siege; it surrounds the text indefinitely, and also imperfectly, by referring--by exiting--toward another text. A false exit extends out of sight" (336 *DS*). The false exit is like the Sartrian presupposition of the transcendental signified as a perpective point outside the system of philosophy but orienting it. It is a "negative" presupposition--false and implicit--what Derrida calls a "false exit."

Derrida's term "representative anticipation" suggests that the new object of knowledge after the supplement is prefigured in some way in the supplement, that the supplement contains some sense of what is to come, some of the genetic instructions but in a nonliteral or figured way (see 35 *TP*: the structure of a lack that is supplemented always has the form of "representative anticipation").

Some kind of prefiguration is necessary if one cycle of philosophy interlocks with the next. The end of a philosophy bears the mark of the possibility of its succeeding development. Bloom's theory virtually avoids attributing any positive role to the end of form to help the precursor. In this way Bloom insufficiently determines the process itself, for Derrida has such answers and with them more power to explain tradition.

The point of change of one philosophy into another requires a kind of Copernican revolution, literally meaning the standpoint of the scientist is changed, from an earth-centered universe to a sun-centered one, and as a result the view of the whole universe changes. Kant believed his revolution to be similar. The difficulties of a theory force one to look at the point from which the subject previously ordered all the concepts. Some difficulty is so serious that only a change in the point of orientation, the point of perspective can make the whole structure coherent and new again. A self-determining factor is present in creation that is not present in the biological genetic code. Some awareness of the total process informs each part of a philosophy, poetry, or a scientific theory. And at the end of a philosophy a successor can form the totality of the process of the precursor, in effect representing the former laws of mind so that new ones can be created. That human tradition moves according to a dynamic of increasing self-knowledge. Consider Cassirer's insight: "the I creates for itself a kind of opposite in its own products...and it can contemplate itself only in this kind of projection" (217 *The*

Philosophy of Symbolic Forms, II). The mirroring or feedback of the process of mind allows it to develop in cyclical forms.

Besides the "mathematicogenetic" property of concepts in mathematics, for example, a creator needs a developing sense of the continuum before and after his/her own thought. This sense would change at each main figure of poetry or philosophy or science. Kuhn's idea of solution modelling is part of this matrix-forming process. When a new tradition form begins to come into being, it can only do so if as Bloom said, the context is "re-stationed." The matrix, the context, the continuum of the tradition must be progressively redefined. Knowing the solution of one's predecessor helps a new creator to sense the pattern that should be formed once again. This retrospective sense is a necessary part of the formation of a new environment in which the particular concepts can take on their specific meanings. A prospective sense is also needed. This begins to form with the formation of the negative presupposition of the prescursor, for at this stage the inadequacy of the continuum formed by the predecessor can only be understood if a higher sense of the continuum is beginning to be employed to give a place, a significance to concepts. A process that might be called normative hypostatization occurs continuously throughout the philosophy, poetry, or science. The creator asks, what would make my field into a continuum again? What would define a new space for my field? How can I accumulate tradition in a new form of it? Kuhn's observation about the recognition of the pattern in creation provides a key insight. The rightness of new concepts is intuited on the basis of the recognition of a pattern being repeated but improved, raised to a higher level.

Then the quanitity of knowledge about one's precursor has finite limits, or no creation could ever have occurred. The knowledge needed can be bounded by determinately knowing at least the functioning of the complete cycle of one's predecessor--determinately in relation to his predecessor, such that the attempt is made to make a third generation of this process. Tennyson, Bloom reports, was convinced by a friend named Hallam that he could develop a poetry from Keats' as Keats had done from his predecessor, Shelley (168 *PR*). The sense of three generations for the matrix of creation mirrors the internal structure of three main movements of a poetry, a philosophy, and probably a scientific theory (recall Kuhn's statement about the relation of Newton's second law to the third).

How the end of form contains the seeds of a future philosophy is most fully explained in *Dissemination*, not `inseminations':

> The semen [of the end of form] is already swarming. The "primal" insemination is dissemination. A trace, a graft whose traces have been lost. Whether in the case of what is called `language' (discourse, text, etc.) or in the case of some `real' seed-sowing, each term is indeed a germ, and each germ, a term. The term, the atomic element, engenders by division, grafting, proliferation. It is a seed and not an absolute term. But each germ *is* its own term, finds its term not outside itself but within itself as its own internal limit, making an angle with its own death (304 *DS*).

The end of a text, ending as it does in paradox, contradiction, can be opened by a successor like a seed pod bearing the germs of a new plant to be cultivated. One must find the point at which the opening must occur, and one must know how such an opening occurred in the past.

This passage incidentally exemplifies the knowledge gained after the 1967 philosophy was structurally complete; the limit of it is known in increasing depth, and elsewhere this knowledge is planted as a seed in applications to various subjects, such as painting. It is as if Derrida completed the building of a giant palace in 1967 and after this time explored its interiors from the inside, looking out to see visions of what lay outside, but never leaving it.

Summary

Derrida closes his philosophy with the concept of the supplement. A specific structural minimum of philosophy is achieved which repeats the pattern of Sartre and the entire tradition of philosophers before him. In many ways the functions of Derrida's closing concepts are the same as those defined by Bloom for poetry. Derrida's supplement and the festival correspond to Bloom's askesis and apophrades.

Derrida's concepts, however, are capable of determining the process of tradition more. They can reveal more about the process, in more depth and more detail. The correspondence of the two theories gives greater credence to the idea of cultural genetic codes. Kuhn's theory contains some features of this code but in a less developed form. Whereas Kuhn writes the least about the end of a scientific theory, Derrida writes the most. And, his theory gives the greatest sense of how a new theory might develop from his own, since he understands the process in his field to a greater degree.

Neither Kuhn's nor Bloom's discourses have the degree of order of the discourses of which they speak. As a living thing can only exist in a certain kind of environment, so too cultural concepts can only be understood as living, i.e. understood fully enough to yield new culture, if they are interpreted through an order of concepts of the same type. Only in a new original philosophy can the concepts of the previous be *understood* fully; it is not the case that an already-made philosophy is understood fully and then creation starts. The concepts show their natures only in certain kinds of environments of concepts: the philosophical, the poetic, the various scientific ones.

NOTES

1. Quoted from 286 of Ricoeur's *Rule of Metaphor*. The original is on p. 11 of Derrida's "White Mythology," trans. F.C.T. Moore. *New Literary History* 6(1974): 5-74 (`La mythologique blanche' in *Rhétorique et philosophie, Poétique* 5. Paris, Éditions du Seuil 1971).

2. Quoted from 181 of Alexiou, Margaret and Vassilis Lambropoulos. *The Text and Its Margins*. 1985.

3. Harvey is translating p. 44 of *L'Ecriture et la difference*. Paris: Seuil. 1967. That article is a reprint of "Force et signification." *Critique* 19, no. 193 (June 1963), pp. 483-99. and no. 194 (July 1963), pp. 619-36.

4. Cassirer writes, "In the process of knowledge, the conception is established of a body of ideal relations, that remain self-identical and unaffected by the accidental, temporally varying conditions of psychological apprehension. The affirmation of such a constancy is essential to every act of thought; only in the way in which this affirmation is proved is founded the different levels of knowledge" (322 *SF*).

5. Quoted from 290 *WD*. The original is from "Introduction à l'oeuvre de Marcel Mauss," in Marcel Mauss, *Sociologie et anthropologie* (Paris: P.U.F., 1950), p. xlix-1.

6. From p. 131 of an encyclopedia article on Jacques Derrida in *Thinkers of the Twentieth Century*.

7. The words are from Derrida, 223 *DS* as quoted by Gasché. Gasché's ideas come from his 1986 article "Nontotalization without Spuriousness."

8. Quoted from Valente's review of Jean Baudrillard's *The Mirror of Production* and *Towards a Political Economy of the Sign* entitled "Hall of Mirrors: Baudrillard on Marx." *Diacritics* 15.2 (1985): 54-65.

Part III:

Conclusion:
Judging the Three Theories by Comparison and by Reference to the Standard of a Cultural Genetic Code

Chapter 12:

Judging Kuhn's Theory

Kuhn Explains Tradition the Least, and He Uses a Cultural Genetic Code the Least

Introduction to the Judging of Kuhn's Theory of Tradition

Kuhn helped to change the prevailing idea of science as a simply cumulative learning process in a straight line. He introduced some turns, intellectual reversals at each new revolution. He also introduced some non-rational factors into the scientific process (conversion, commitment, resistance, incommensurability). Despite these successes of some of his main ideas, including the ideas more commonly called "irrational," there are some inconsistencies in some of his views and methods. In general, compared with the views of Bloom and Derrida, his view of tradition is least developed, and least deconstructive.

Chauvinism

Kuhn is chauvinistic about science in several ways; he believes science is (1) more important for society; (2) more technical; (3) uniquely progressive; (4) more capable of achieving consensus; (5) controllable, knowable, useable as a tool.

It is common for each discipline to think it is the best because it provides a universal vision of experience, but Kuhn's chauvinism is particularly strong, perhaps even indicating limits to his understanding of science. These limits can be removed.

Is science the most important discipline for society? The most grandiose claims make science into the main driving force of society in modern times. The bulk of scientific knowledge is "a product of Europe in the last four centuries" (168 *SSR*). After 1750 it is said to have risen to become the "historical prime mover" (131 *ET*); "Prime mover" is a commonly known term from Aristotle's metaphysics meaning a being that moves the universe but is not itself moved. Science assumes a great new role after the Industrial Revolution (2 *CR*). Science directs human history by providing it with philosophy and with the necessitites of life. "Contemporary Western civilization is more dependent, both for its everyday philosophy and for its bread and butter, upon scientific concepts than any past civilization has been" (3 *CR*). When writing about the Copernican revolution Kuhn emphasized the chain reaction of changes beginning with astronomy and then extending through all of society, changing even daily life. This universal influence distinguishes science on Kuhn's theory.

These claims may obstruct a deeper knowledge of science. Kuhn seems to describe an acceleration of science. Doing so has the effect of valorizing the present level of science, giving Kuhn the historian some periods about which he can speak, and changing what might be a discussion of the meaning of scientific concepts into a discussion of time periods of scientific history. Science has seemed to usurp the roles of other cultural activities to become the dominant force in modern life. This, however, does not mean science itself has changed, nor does it mean science is more important in human development than other fields are.

Kuhn is chauvinistic because he declares science to be more technical (128 *ET*). This statement may not seem to subordinate other fields but it does because they are seen to be more subjective, less determinate. Being an historian of science, Kuhn puts his profession ahead of art criticism, for the historian reads the critics who are themselves creators of science whereas art critics often read other critics very often (132 *ET*). The historian of science has to know more (154 *ET*); (s)he has "an acquaintance with the essentials" (10 *ET*). A way to paraphrase this claim is to say, `I know more than you because I study science and you only study literature'. The assumption of the greater epistemic quality of science often surfaces from the not-so-deep subconscious. To say that science is distinctively technical is to downgrade the development necessary to achieve the highest in other fields. Only in science is the work of individuals addressed so exclusively to a few individuals who understand the technicalities (164 *SSR*). The number of specialists may be 100 or less (178 *PO*).

It is chauvinistic to think only science progresses. It "moves steadily ahead," whereas other fields do not (160 *SSR*). This early statement was revised later to acccept some progress in other fields but nothing so definite as can be found in science. Ironically, Bloom's theory of poetry articulated its ideas in a greater degree of completeness, precision.

Able to achieve consensus much more, science seems superior. Kuhn confidently asserts science attains consensus but other fields do not (17, 173, 177 *SSR*). If there are controversies, they are resolved more quickly than in other fields; they last only for a short time (348 *CR*). To temper this view, he notes that resistance to innovation is common to both the arts and sciences. While Kuhn compartmentalizes the strife in science to particular groups at particular times, Bloom makes strife a characteristic of all poetic creation.

In contrast to Kuhn's view, the lack of consensus may promote the progress of science. A free market, fair competition, seems to promote prosperity. Commenting specifically on Kuhn's idea of consensus, Lyotard values the competition of scientifc theories:

> ...today there is a generally recognized `crisis' of what is called reason in the sciences. I am speaking of the hard sciences. The names of Kuhn and Feyerabend come to mind in connection with this crisis. I am probably not in agreement with the whole scheme of thought of these celebrated epistemologists; but, since the middle of the nineteenth century, the question of what is rational in mathematics and the sciences of animate and inanimate nature is an open one. This question has such force that it even affects the nature, whether rational or non-rational, of space and time. What has been called `the crisis of the foundations' is not something that can be neglected

> today to the pretended advantage of a consensus of arguments, when this consensus is precisely what is missing from the interior of the, let us say physical, sciences. And far from suppressing the possibility, contrary to what might be thought, this absence of consensus has, on the contrary, only worked to allow a more rapid and more impressive development of the sciences. I am thinking, for example, of the discussion between Einstein, who was in a certain way a classical rationalist, a Leibnizian we might say, and the Danes, who showed themselves to be very adventurous in these matters, or, again with Louis de Broglie (280 *Theory, Culture, Society*).

The lack of consensus promotes more rapid growth in science. Consensus, too, can be undesirable. "The stronger the `move', the more likely it is to be denied the minimum consensus, precisely because it changes the rules of the game upon which consensus had been based. But when the institution of knowledge functions in this manner, it is acting like an ordinary power center whose behavior is governed by a principle of homeostasis" (63 *The Postmodern...*). In this context Bloom's statement that the precursor is both "muse and enemy" is quite apt.

Finally, Kuhn is chauvinistic about science by making it distinctively controllable and knowable. His theory is nothing other than an attempt to plum the bottom of the processes of scientific creation, getting to a level deeper than the original scientists who did not write about them. To this degree, there is an unmistakable hubris running through his theory. The attitude of Kuhn often resembles that of John Dewey, famous American philosopher of a pragmatic theory of knowledge and a theory of science as completely within our control, as a tool to be used by us however we like:

> The fact is that it is foolish to try to draw up a debit and credit account for science. To do so is to mythologize; it is to personify science and impute to it a will and an energy on its own account. In truth science is strictly impersonal; a method and a body of knowledge. It owed its operation and its con-

> sequences to the human beings who use it. It adapts itself passively to the purposes and desires which animate these human beings. It lends itelf with equal impartiality to the kindly offices of medicine and hygiene and the destructive deeds of war. It elevates some through opening new horizons; it depresses others by making them slaves of machines operated for the pecuniary gain of owners.
>
> The neutrality of science to the uses made of it renders it silly to talk about its bankruptcy, or to worship it as the usherer in of a new age. In the degree in which we realize this fact, we shall devote our attention to the human purposes and motives which control its application. Science is an instrument, a method, a body of technique ("Science and Society" Paragraph four).

That there might be laws of human nature in the same way that there are laws of the physical universe is beyond the ken of Dewey's mind. He has little sense that any new motives of individual scientists must conform to patterns establishing the continuity of tradition, patterns that are transgenerational and so outside the arbitrary change by any individual. Agreeing with common sense, Dewey's view does not seem to be extreme, yet it is. Consider an analogy to language. Imagine the situation of human language if its direction depended upon the choice of the speakers. No committee meetings were held in the past to decide to effect the great vowel shift, or to make any other changes. The artificial "language" of esperanto was such an attempt to invent a language, but it never caught on. A language cannot be invented; it invents us. Human beings did not decide to invent language, for it would have required language to come to an agreement. Science, too, is not created because its principles can explain nature and can make new goods for use in everyday life. The concern of the creator differs from the concern of the normal scientist. Einstein developed the theory of relativity and only much later did he with the "help" of others realize that it could be applied to create a weapon of unprecedented destruction. Einstein's concern, like that of all revolutionary scientists, is with understanding the tradition coming before. They revise the definition of the sciences.

Kuhn does discuss the community changes in science while sharing Dewey's faith in the instrumental value of science. Today this value is called technological, science often being linked with technology as inseparable coworkers.

As with all doctrines of Kuhn, his treatment of the control of science has an open door to a more developed view, a fact showing how well thought out the theory is for its level of explanatory power. At one insightful moment in his theory he claims scientists do not know the characteristics which must be preserved in the revolution to legitimate the new process (44 *ET*). To the extent that scientists do not know the process, it must be operating automatically; or, since many people would reject any automatism used to explain the generation of thought, the action could be described to be the built-in transference of the pattern during the understanding of the previous science. Human nature is cunning even though unwittingly. In accomplishing the proper understanding of the previous science a new one is constructed. This line of thought shows how elements in Kuhn's theory can be extended to a more definitely deconstructive approach.

Beyond Kuhn, we should realize that scientists do not control science; it controls them. Despite the lack of control, there is still a necessity in the development of the concepts. Some concepts are the only acceptable developments of other ones. This does not mean that personal, individual formative factors do not have a play in creation, but it does mean that the role is secondary. As Cassirer claims, science bears the individual stamp of the creator in combination with the necessity of form (228 *EM*). These ideas can be clarified by reference to a statement made by Russian literary critic Osip Brik, `If Pushkin had never been born, *Eugene Onegin* would have been written by itself' (166 Wellek). If another author had written the work, maybe different characters would have been used, or with different names, or a different number, and so on with other features such as setting; nevertheless, the essential line of the narrative as a transformation of the aesthetic before Pushkin's time would have been recognizably similar. One only need to study the simultaneous discovery of the calculus by Newton and Leibniz, with the significant though secondary differences in symbolization, to realize the truth of necessity in development. All individuals react to a tradition which they merely supplement, to use a term from Derrida's philosophy.

There could be no science if one had not been able to receive the accumulated knowledge of the ages before. And any new knowledge must have meaning as a new step in this accumulating process greater than individual efforts.

Generality

Kuhn's theory of science is ironically more general and less determined--less `scientific'--than Bloom's theory of poetry in several ways: method of presentation; choice of units of tradition as periodizations; extension of paradigms for centuries; ignoring the inner recurring structure of a tradition form (like Bloom's kenosis and daemonization or Derrida's differance and infinite differance); overemphasis on community factors; failing to define specific differences between successive scientific figures.

The title of Kuhn's main work is very revealing about his theory: *The Structure of Scientific Revolutions*. No distinction is made between the different sciences, nor is any allowance made for variation of the structure from one theory to the next. "The" suggests too confidently that there is only one structure. In addition the point of departure of Kuhn's theory is not a specific historical one, whereas Bloom for example always defines his theoretical concepts according to specific poets, primarily the English Romantics.

Bloom's method of presentation is quite general. There are no extended examples, except for *The Copernican Revolution*, and this book still does not have the detail of Bloom's works, for only two chapters deal with the theory itself and the remaining deal with accompanying intellectual history and milieu. The examples Kuhn uses are often only a few sentences long. No proof can be given through the examples as the technical language of science is not used; instead the theory has had wide appeal to general educated audiences, who can read the examples as illustrations of Kuhn's ideas. The reader can find headings such as "The Genesis of Modern Physics," whereas this one would be quite general for Bloom who typically limits the principles to being valid within specific poetries. It is possible for the genetic code to change in each new living thing--a change, however, very slight. If science revises its assumptions with each revolution as Kuhn claims, should this variation not be accounted for in a theory of revolutions? The change in a revolution is comprehensive, affecting all concepts, so it is natural to ask for an account of the changes in the most fundamental processes.

Secondly, the theory is general because Kuhn chooses the units of tradition as periodizations of science. Consider phrases such as "a paradigm of eighteenth-century chemistry was gradually losing its unique status." He often speaks of main figures changing the paradigms of several centuries before. Copernicus is said to have changed the Ptolemaic model, just as Einstein changed Newtonian mechanics. The directness of these transformations should be doubted very much. Was there no science in between each of those pairs of especailly great scientists? In another way Kuhn's units of tradition are often more temporal periods than specific structural units of science. The creation process is divided into two creators, normal science and extraordinary science (221 *ET*). The former articulates the paradigm until a "period of crisis" begins to appear at which time extraordinary science completely changes the paradigm in a revolution. The creation process then has two alternating temporal periods. It is not very intelligible to claim that normal science understands a paradigm but chooses to work on minor problems instead of making a new one. This distinction is not at all present in the theories of Bloom and Derrida, both of whom limit creation to the work of one thinker.

Thirdly, the theory extends some paradigms for centuries, with intervening developments of a "smaller" nature. Newton's second law "took centuries of difficult factual and theoretical research to achieve" (78 *SSR*). It almost sounds as if the scientists during those centuries were engaged in the same research project during which time there were no new recurrences of the structure of physics.

Fourthly, the inner recurring structure of a science is ignored. Kuhn almost treats a crisis as a random event each time. In Bloom's theory there is a regular, recurring structure of the problematic end of a poetry leading to a new one. The absence of a definition suggests nothing more can be said about the recurrence of a crisis than that it does happen. Bloom's theory offers good reasons by analogy to think science, too, can be defined in more detail.

As the next way in which Kuhn's theory is too general, he overemphasizes community and external factors. "Our concern will not then be with the arguments that in fact convert one or another individual, but rather with the sort of community that always sooner or later re-forms as a single group" (153 *SSR*). A crude though perhaps useful paraphrase would be to say, `I am going to assume what scientific concepts mean so that I can convey my high evaluation of the social revolutions caused by science'. Scientific knowledge is intrinsically a group product (xx *ET*). Acknowledging that his theory depends more on the community's reaction than the scientific laws (351 *CR*), Kuhn makes one wonder if the meaning he then determines is sociological or scientific. Perhaps it could have been called a theory of the social revolutions caused by science. This suggestion is not extreme, since Kuhn when discussing his shortcomings in his main work stated the need to put still more emphasis on the community, less on the relations of scientific laws. He would like to understand the "external, social, economic, and intellectual conditions in the development of the sciences" (ix *SSR*). The study of the community would precede the study of such ideas as crisis, incommensurability, conversion.

Finally, Kuhn's theory is quite general insofar as he does not define the specific differences between successive scientific theories. Bloom's theory hardly discusses anything but the differences between specific poets. The examples, too, are extended into the serial relations between more than two poets. To define the meaning of a poetry Bloom would define the poetry before and after: three generations are almost requisite to define the historical situatedness of any poetry. Kuhn's examples are not extended enough to include transgenerational relations. The point of change between successive theories has the general significance of a gestalt switch, a wholistic intuitive change of perspective not analyzable into components. Other scholars--not only on poetry but also on science--do define the point of change in convincing detail. An expert of Einstein's theory of relativity, Cassirer writes

> ...in the special theory of relativity, the electrodynamic processes are not used as a key to the mechanical, but a truly universal principle, a heuristic maxim of investigation in general, is established, which claims to contain a criterion of the validity and permissibility of all particular physical fields and theories. Thus it is seen that the initial contradiction,

> appearing between the principles of mechanics and those of electrodynamics, has shown the way to a far more perfect and deeper unity between them than previously existed. And this result was not reached entirely by heaping up experiments by newly instituted investigations, but it rests on a critical transformation of the system of fundamental physical concepts.
>
> On the purely epistemological side, there thus appears with special distinctness in this intellectual process in which the theory of relativity originates, that peculiar "Copernican revolution," that variation in the conceptual foundations of the theory of nature, which we have previously traced in the example of classical mechanics and the older physics. An essential part of its achievement seems based on the fact, that it has shifted the previous logical constants of physical knowledge, that it has set them at another place than before. For classical mechanics, the fixed and immovable point was the assumption of the identity of the spatial and temporal values gained by measurement in the various systems (373 *ETR*).

Kuhn's theory never gets to the degree of specificity to define the contradiction serving as the unsolvable problem within a set of assumptions. He does argue for the existence of "an unsolvable puzzle," as has been mentioned. Whereas Kuhn gives the name of a city only, Cassirer draws a map of it. Cassirer can determine the crisis leading to the theory of relativity so exactly as to define the single contradiction bringing about the change. In this passage the change in physical constants is discussed, a problem not directly addressed by Kuhn. Cassirer thinks on the level of "physical concepts" to allow for a difference in the concepts of physics in contrast to those of any other science. What is most crucial, perhaps, is the isolating of the "fixed and immovable point," the single "assumption of the identity of the spatial and temporal values gained by measurement in the various systems." This intellectual procedure should call to mind the process Derrida performed when revising the tradition of philosophy. By reinterpretation of a closing concept of Sartre's philosophy, he understood the assumption upon which Sartre's and all previous philosophies had been based. Like an Archimedean lever, he could move the earth with that fulcrum alleviating the burden of so much weight. Kuhn's theory falls short of noticing this extremely important matter of the immovable point, the perspective point as it has been called herein, by which the whole tradition can be changed.

The criticism made by Cassirer of Bertrand Russell's study of Leibniz applies to Kuhn's theory. Cassirer charged Russell with failing to determine fully the historical conditions of Leibniz's system, failing to distinguish between "the traditional concepts of substance and those specific and original to Leibniz." [1] To be fully determinate, Kuhn's theory would have to define revolution with a specific difference in each case. A theory of science must be case-bound if science changes even only slightly with each new theory. Otherwise, there is a reduction in meaning, a problem Bloom considers as possibly unavoidable by all scholarship that is not also creation. This issue will be discussed in the next chapters.

Lack of Proofs and Value Judgments

The lack of proofs and value judgments shows that Kuhn could develop his sense of the inner necessity of form, with a recurring pattern, a genetic code.

"Our concern," writes Kuhn, "will not then be with the arguments that in fact convert one or another individual" (153 *SSR*).

Kuhn makes generalizations without proof, and he refrains from making value judgments. All the judgments presented are "found." He gets indications of revolutions from journal articles, bulletins, bibliographies, textbooks, other historians of science. The passages are descriptive, not deductive. For example, "By the time Lavoisier began his experiments on airs in the early 1770's, there were almost as many versions of the phlogiston theory as there were pneumatic chemists. That proliferation of versions of a theory is a very usual symptom of crisis" (70 *SSR*). Though there are always many theories, most are usually wrong, even in science. Sometimes, Kuhn as a scholar and others almost seem to be more preoccupied with their own thought constructions than with the meaning of scientific concepts. For example, some debate surrounded the issue whether all revolutions arise from a crisis or not (27 Cohen). In the 1962 *Structure of Scientific Revolutions* crisis is presented as an integral part of the cycle of scientific theories. Later, in response to criticism Kuhn states that perhaps not all revolutions are preceded by crises. If all the series of revolutions for a specific historical period were stated, it would be easy to discover whether a crisis did precede a revolution in each case. The solution to such problems depends less on the inner consistency or other appeal of the scholar's theory of science than it does on the actual scientific cases. The scholar's activity can begin to replace the further determination of the discipline studied, because different ordering principles make the discourse coherent. As a result, Kuhn does not prove his ideas as much as he might have, nor does he determine scientific meaning as much as one who is not a creator could.

Kuhn shifted the emphasis away from proof using scientific formulas. As Cohen points out, "...a significant feature of his [Kuhn's] influence has been to shift the point of view of scholars away from the notion of a contest among competing ideas to that of a contest among individual scientists or groups of scientists holding ideas" (403). Scientific meaning would then be assumed or avoided. If proof were offered, philosophers of science could not be fence-sitters, occupying a neutral position above any two scientists. Clifford Truesdell claims a history or philosophy of science cannot be impartial: "He who refuses to `take sides' in science in effect negates science itself by denying its one and common purpose. He reduces science to just one more social manifestation. In so doing, not only does he by implication belittle the great scientists of the past but also he sins against history, for in his attempt at historical impartiality he destroys the object, namely science, the history of which he claims to write" (241).

Kuhn's Doctrine of Incommensurability Avoids Proof

Kuhn originally held the bold idea that proponents of different scientific communities cannot achieve full communication (338 *ET*). This doctrine brought charges of irrationality (199 *SSR*).

Later in his career Kuhn softened his position slightly on incommensurability. The problem was not a matter of scientific understanding but a problem of the opponents belonging to "different language communities" (202-3 *SSR*). They experienced "imperfections of the processes of translation and of reference determination" (xxii *ET*). What scientists lack has been described by Art Berman as a "neutral language," and this issue has been a link between literary theory and science (95-96).

Concerning this problem, Lyotard would support Kuhn's earlier position: incommensurability is not just a language problem:

> Traditions are mutually opaque. Contact between two communities is immediately a conflict, since the names and narratives of one community are exclusive of the names and narratives of the other (principle of exception, vainglory and jealousy of names).... . The conflict does not result from a problem of language, every language is translatable (this does not prevent linguistic differences from contributing on occasion to the exacerbation of a conflict). ...It is thus a litigation over the names of times, places, and persons, over the senses and referents attached to those names (157 *Differend*)

I agree that the problem cannot merely be a language problem. Certainly, if learning occurs in science, then some change in conceptions occurs and with it changes in the definition of science and the concept of truth (what can constitue a scientific law or a well-formed formula). These changes require differences in understanding and often also of language. Another way to look at the problem, different from Kuhn's way, is to consider the issue of incommensurability or commensurability from the standpoint of extraordinary science, not normal science as Kuhn does. If we consider the relation between Einstein and Maxwell, surely Einstein understood the other's physics well enough to create a new one from it. To this extent, there is a basis of commensurability. Yet, if the views of Maxwell are proven to be inadequate by Einstein, then commensurability is not so much the issue as which view is right? The problem of commensurability is at bottom more a problem of scientific validity, and if Kuhn and others discussed the validity directly there may be no need to discuss commensurability.

Kuhn's Avoidance of the Inner Necessity of Form

Kuhn avoids discussing science in so much detail that scientifc proofs would be given. He even doubts whether the criteria of a science are internal only to that science: "Planetary astronomy was never a totally independent pursuit with its own immutable standards of accuracy, adequacy, and proof" (viii *CR*). Even if Kuhn were right about this, he does not say where scientists would look to find the criteria. Do astronomers look in a different place each time, i.e. for each paradigm? How do they know where to look? To the extent that a theory should predict, explain processes, or prove, Kuhn does not have a theory of scientific legitimacy that is non-sociological.

Kuhn's displacement of the criteria of astronomy outside it is a defence reaction against giving scientific proof. When a weight is too heavy people often, quite wrongly, stop breathing while tensing up other muscles in their bodies, as if this would help move a weight only the other muscles could move. He needs to find the requirement of evolution; he needs to show, in the words of Bakhtin, "that the two phenomena [scientific systems] are connected in substance and that the first one essentially and necessarily determines the one that follows it" (165 *The Formal Method*).

Kuhn seems to be assuming that the purpose of new form is to express new content. This assumption is related to the idea that the purpose of science--including the extraordinary--is to explain the world, rather than create a specific kind of vision that increases the power of mind, which then has benefits in life. A better view on the common issue of human tradition is that of the literary critic Victor Shklovsky, who wrote:

> The work of art arises from a background of other works and through association with them. The form of a work of art is defined by its relation to other works of art, to forms existing prior to it....Not only parody, but also any kind of work of art is created parallel to and opposed to some kind of form. *The purpose of the new form is not to express new content, but to change an old form which has lost its aesthetic quality* (118 Lemon and Reis). ...

> An image is not a permanent referent for those mutable complexities of life which are revealed through it; its purpose is not to make us perceive meaning, but to create a special perception of the object--*it creates a `vision' of the object instead of serving as a means for knowing it* (18).

By analogy, the purpose of science would be to change the old form--in Kuhn's terms a paradigm--because it lost its scientific quality. A successor sees it to be non-universal. Certainly, a new scientific theory arises from a previous one. It cannot be understood in isolation, as Boris Eichenbaum, Russian literary critic, notices: "We found that we could not see the literary work in isolation, that we had to see its form against a background of other works rather than by itself" (119 Lemon and Reis). Bloom has this approach with more explanatory power. Derrida, too, regards a system of thought, whether science or any other, as being regulated by an internal necessity making its parts cohere (33 *OG*).

Finding an internal necessity for texts allows one to have criteria for ranking different ones. Which scientific theory is great? Why? Kuhn often took his answers from textbooks, journals, bibliographies, and various other sources. Are all great or only some? Are all revolutionary or only some? The answer could consist in defining the structure having internal necessity of a specific kind, belonging in the chain of scientific theories.

Too Much Emphasis on External Factors, Too Empirical

Although bold in some of his concepts, Kuhn does not explain as much as he could because he places too much emphasis on external factors for scientific creation and meaning; his theory relies more on empirical factors than it should if it is to lead us to the point where we can create.

Predominantly, Kuhn regards the meaning of science as an explanation of the physical world (39 *CR*).

Making science an explanation of the physical world we live in is like making language a communication between people. Both are right, but both fall short of more fundamental goals. According to Susanne Langer, it is not communication but symbolic representation that is the most fundamental goal of language (115). How can language convey events not present or not even existing if the purpose is only communication? If that were the case, language might only extend to present or existing objects in the presence of both speakers. Even more primary, language allows a world of thought, an interrelated network of possible things to be available for thinking, a network through which new ideas could arise. So too in science. Its most primary function is to make a discourse including the totality of nature. The thought world of science determines its concepts more than external phenomena. The object of science is the renewing of its own thought world. In the words of Heinrich Wölfflin, painting strives for "a picture of the world," not of things in it (230). In addition, art depends on "a living power of apprehension which has its own inward history and has passed through many stages" (146 Gablik; *Principles of Art History*, N.Y., 1932, 226). Einstein speaks of science as a change in vision: "Human thought creates an ever-changing picture of the universe. Galileo's contribution was to destroy the intuitive view and replace it by a new one. This is the significance of Galileo's discovery" (9). To more clearly point out the change in the entire vision of the world, Einstein writes, "The theory of relativity arises from the field problems. The contradictions and inconsistencies of the old theories force us to ascribe new properties to the time-space continuum, to the scene of all events in our physical world" (244).

Too Much Emphasis on External Factors

By emphasizing external factors too much, Kuhn avoids the discussion of internal factors of scientific creation, preventing his knowledge of science from deepening.

"External factors" are responsible for "determining the timing of breakdown, the ease with which it can be recognized, and the area in which...the breakdown first occurs. Though immensely important, issues of that sort [external ones concerning the Copernican revolution] are out of bounds for this essay" (69 *SSR*). Kuhn believes the "technical breakdown" is at the core of the crisis. But why does he not present extended discussions of these breakdowns? The external factors distract Kuhn from the law-making process, which is primary.

While in principle emphasizing the technical factors in scientific breakdowns, in practice he emphasizes other, external factors such as group commitments, instruments used, changes in other fields or society, and other factors already discussed. A paradigm is more than a theory, he claims; it is also a sociological explanation of coherence of research (87 *SSR*). But if sociological facts determine the scientific process, does this mean that sociology or other fields have a direct production in science? No, not at all. If it did, science would become parasitic on other fields. The use of sociological concerns gives to the scholar a base of principles by which to explain science in a *nonscientific* way. In passing he does state, "Yet the Revolution [Copernican] turned upon the most obscure and recondite minutiae of astronomical research" (1 *CR*). He never presents these details to the reader, yet they may be the factors by which revolutions occur. Kuhn presents his theory primarily to non-scientists, and in so doing Kuhn does not continue to explore the meaning of science in greater depths. When writing about the difference between external and internal approaches, he desires a safe middle ground giving to both their value. In practice, he emphasizes the external more.

The legitimation of theories in particular is always discussed from the standpoint of the scientific community's acceptance or rejection (xviii *ET*). This is merely an external factor in the interpretation of science because the paradigm has already come into being. Its right does not depend on a vote, or else committees would just vote for the theory they wanted. Its right depends on factors known to the extraordinary scientist, factors that could be called "internal." Einstein wrote, "the strength of the theory [of relativity] lies in its inner consistency" (245). The concern with inner consistency suggests that science is most concerned with its own thought world.

When determining which theories produce revolutions, Kuhn examined various publications other than the original theory. Bloom was criticized for not using such sources: "...he [Said] cites Bloom's lack of reference in his treatment of the English Romantics to the `materially productive agencies' of the time: the journals, reviews, and `competing discourses', as well as larger collective supports such as the university, the press, the class system, and Foucault's "archive-discourse-statement (enoncé)."[2]

It is hard to envision what science could be if it is not primarily an explanation of external physical reality. Kuhn admirably stretches the imagination of common sense by occasional statements that observation alone does not produce new theories, nor do experiments; by his discussion of the gestalt nature of the change in concepts during a revolution; and by the action of `putting on a different thinking cap' when he echoes the words of Herbert Butterfield. A philosopher of science after Kuhn needs to develop intrinsic factors of scientific creation. There must be according to Nobel prize laureate Jacques Monod "...an internal, autonomous determinism" to guarantee "the formation of the extremely complex structures of living beings" (11-12). This determinism would not directly arise from the attempt to explain external nature but from the attempt to fulfill requirements of scientific discourse itself. "The forms of art," according to Victor Shklovsky, are explained by the artistic laws that govern them and not by comparisons with actual life" (170 *Theory of Prose*). Science, then, could be like myth in the sense of supplying "the symbols that carry the human spirit forward" (11 *Hero*).

Too Empirical

Kuhn's theory is too empirical to prepare one adequately for scientific creation.

In many subjects Kuhn's theory is more empirical than either Bloom's or Derrida's. He defines science primarily in terms of normal science, the group that articulates a paradigm further by solving puzzles. He seems to assume that science is "an enterprise which aims at puzzle solving" (349 *CR*). Science also attempts to preserve a "hard core of the knowledge provided by the predecessor" (3 *CR*). The achievement of science is "permanent" (25 *SSR*). Neither Bloom nor Derrida believe there can be a substantive identity of meaning from one poetry or philosophy to another. Kuhn does at times speak as if all concepts change. Then how is "a hard core" preserved? Kuhn thinks of the accumulation of knowledge in terms of quantity, a fact showing his empirical thinking. Bloom and even more Derrida think of the accumulation in terms of the power of vision: Bloom said "greater inwardness" for poetry; Derrida said the degree of connectivity of concepts (*AF*).

It is as if Kuhn leaves an open door to a less empirical view, even though he does not take his readers outside. He believes fields of science are changed in revolutions, not just particular concepts (41 *ET*). Kuhn could carry this idea further by interpreting a scientific theory as both "model and included object," an idea of Derrida's (83 *AF*). The object is the relative totality of the predecessor's work, while the model is a new vision of the unity of science, using new assumptions. Agreeing with Derrida, Bloom defines creation by a transgenerational act: "When a fresh author is simultaneously cognizant not only of his own struggle against the forms and presence of a precursor, but is compelled also to a sense of the Precursor's place in regard to what came before him" (32 *MM*). There is no conflict between the phylogenetic transmission of science (through the species) and the ontogenetic transmission (through the individual), since both work in and through the other, the individual through the community and the community through the individual. Kuhn does not define thoroughly the "general reorientation" of scientific intentions, which replaces the view of science as developing from its beginnings according to one single goal, as Viennese art historian Alois Riegl does for art (149 Gablik; also see Riegl). "Riegl considered that changes of form are not caused by extraneous forces in society but by impulses which come from the forms themselves" (149 Gablik). In art there is a "creative and transcendent directive force...seeking to realize itself." As mystical as this may sound to many a scientist, musn't there be a continuity of purpose greater than an individual scientist could understand completely and finally if the purposes of science are renewed in successive theories? No individual is in control or responsible for the continuity beyond his/her own generation. Wölfflin grasps the continuity of purpose:

> No human personality, however mighty, would have sufficed to enable him to conceive these forms if he had not previously been over the ground which contained the necessary preliminary stages. The continuity of the life-feeling was as necessary here as in the generations which combine to form a unit in history (230).

Tradition is only possible if there is a continuity throughout generations. To ensure some continuity, knowledge must be accumulated through changes affecting the whole of thought. Not the same actual meanings but the same type of meaning-forming activity continues. To argue how thorough the changes in concepts are from one generation to the next, Lyotard writes, "physics furnishes an excellent illlustration of the way in which even `basic concepts' that have been established in the form of definitions are constantly being altered in their content" (79 *Lyotard Reader*). Physics changes its criteria of validity, of physics, yet it remains physics.

To ask that the theory of science be less empirical is not to ask for mysticism but to ask for more determinateness of the meaningful, creative processes. A philosopher of science after Kuhn could do this by determining both the structural hierarchy in a scientific theory and its place in the evolving scientific system as a whole. A more determinate idea of a tradition form has been advanced by Tynyanov and the Russian Formalists:

> Indeed, for the Formalists, `literary language'...and its development cannot be understood as a planned development of tradition but rather as `colossal displacements of traditions' (Tynyanov 1978c: p. 144, not his italics). Literariness is a product of the deformation of the canonized or automatized elements, in other words of precisely those factors which constitute a tradition. Form is made perceptible against a background of existing form, and the function of a device is determined not just by the structural hierarchy of a particular work, but by its place in the literary system as a whole. The principle of defamiliarization simultaneously undoes the idea of tradition and reintroduces an historical dimension in the relationship between individual literary device and the overall system. Discontinuity replaces continuity as the basis of historical progression. The fact that the specificity of literary science is constituted by literariness means that an historical dimension is inevitably brought into play. In contrast both to the genetically based view of literary history which tends

to ignore questions of form, and to other formally biased approaches which tend to ignore history, the Russian Formalist view is that it is history itself which allows the specificity of literature to be established (33 *Modern Literary History*).

Kuhn's theory does not show the specificity of form by contrast. It does not show the structural hierarchy, and it does not show its particular place in the evolving system of science as a whole. Bloom does this much more by defining the relations between generations of poetry.

If empirical factors are not the object of theory, then what is? The unity of thought. In Cassirer's words,

> ...it is the *unity of all thought*, which stands constantly before us as an ultimate goal and directs our cognition. The truth of any particular proposition can only be measured by what it contributes to the solution of this fundamental problem of knowledge, by what it contributes to the progressive unification of the manifold. We can never set a judgment directly over against the particular outer objects and compare it with these, as things given in themselves; we can only ask as to the function it fulfils in the structure and interpretation of the totality of experience (318 *SF*).

Undefined Unit of Science

Kuhn defines the unit of scientific tradition less than Bloom and Derrida do.

Weak Sense of the Unit of Tradition as a Serial Phenomenon

A stronger sense of the unit of tradition as a recurring serial phenomenon would help to define a unit more definitely.

In Kuhn's theory there is little sense that a new theory arises from the direct need to interpret a previous one. Although he claims science evolves cyclically, how the end of one form issues into the start of a new one remains a mystery. The attempt to determine the coherence of the previous theory leads to the repetition of these processes in a new way. The form is complete when this change has been effectuated: a cycle is complete, a level changed. Kuhn certainly does not give enough information so that one could *make* science. Ultimately, this knowledge could only come from previous science, but Kuhn could still point to this more directly.

The Unit of Science Is Best Defined in Terms of the Needs of a Tradition Form

Kuhn only has a few vague general comments about consistency, simplicity, universality.

Besides failing to define the recurring structural hierarchy of theories, Kuhn fails to define the recurring structure within the crisis. On this idea depends his whole theory. Bloom presents a definition of the ends of poetries by defining the relations set up there with the encompassing literary system, evolving through history. Derrida gives an even more detailed definition through his particular solving of a crisis. Einstein gives the sense of a problem unsolvable on the terms of the science before him:

> But what is the medium through which light spreads and what are its mechanical properties? There is no hope of reducing the optical phenomena to the mechanical ones before this question is answered. But the difficulties in solving this problem are so great that we have to give it up and thus give up the mechanical view as well (122).

Derrida's solution to the problem of the transcendental signified gives a much more detailed account than Kuhn's of what happens during a crisis. Derrida finds the "matrix" for the entire tradtion before him-- the same word by Kuhn to describe the totality of a scientific theory ("disciplinary matrix") (278 *WD*). This matrix defines the "orienting and organizing" of "the coherence of the system."

In general terms, Kuhn fails to explain "a regulated transformation of one language by another, of one text by another"--of one science by another (20 *POS*).

Need for an Internal Dynamic Structure of Science (An Internal Narrative)

The idea of an internal dynamic structure can help explain the recurrence and the transmission of scientific tradition forms. "Narrative" is needed by theorists of science to explain (1) the serial continuity of theories; (2) the feedback (recursive knowledge) allowing creation to occur; (3) the making of the internal hierarchy; (4) the legitimation of a new theory by its creator and its correlative transmission to a successor.

First of all, "narrative" as recurring internal dynamism is necessary to explain the serial continuity of scientific theories. Since these theories are transmitted cyclically, the narrative is the process of the transference of the previous pattern into its new form. The inseparability of the two processes, intertextual development and intratextual development, has been strongly argued by Bloom and Derrida. Other scholars who would concur with this view are Todorov and Bakhtin. Voicing the view of Bakhtin, Todorov writes,

> In the study of the "Theory of Parody," he had shown the impossibility of wholly understanding a text by Dostoevsky without reference to a certain earlier text of Gogol. It was after this work that investigations began into what we have called the polyvalent (or dialogic) register. From which we learn that genesis is inseparable from structure, the story from the creation of the book, of its meaning: if we were ignorant of the parodic function of the Dostoevskian text (at

first glance, a simple element of its genesis), our comprehension of it would suffer seriously (60 *Introduction to Poetics*).

Derrida, too, explicitly announces his intention to unite genesis and structure; the supplement is beyond the opposites genesis (history) and structure (259 *OG*). (These were opposites in Sartre's philosophy.) Kuhn does not explain intertextual relations at all; his emphasis is on the community of normal science, its reactions before and after a paradigm change.

If science is through and through traditional, if its entire purpose is to build up a new unit of tradition, then narrative is essential. Writing about the "preeminence of the narrative form in the formulation of traditional knowledge," Lyotard states that the form of traditional knowledge is narrative; narrative explains cycles of tradition. It is the "quintessential form of customary knowledge" (19 *Postmodern*). Consider a related way to discuss the same point. If science develops the human mind, and the mind develops through individuals, then science develops in individual units. These would then have the form of self, as they are determined as units of development of the self. For example, a physics on this view would have a start, middle, and end and be oriented toward an end; a person's life is too.

Secondly, narrative provides feedback about the processes of creation, which constitutes a determining factor in them. To use an everyday analogy, it is easier to comb one's hair if one has a mirror. Or, it is easier to learn dancing if the lights are on so that one can see one's body. Donald Philip Verene writes about the role of narrative in science, claiming that science excludes narration but that narrative is "the natural form in which to grasp culture as a whole"; "the form in which culture can be known" (29 "Science, Symbolic Form, and Narration"). Narration would provide science with self-knowledge by "the representing of the genesis of the thing in question" (27 Ibid). What Verene calls for has always existed in the great canonical scientific theories, whereas it may have been lacking in theories of science by historians and philosophers; the latter are Verene's readers. Kuhn does consider science to be a transformation of the relation of human beings to the universe; he does not, however, explain how the transformation of views about nature can effect a transformation of the mind's orientation. He does argue for cycles of scientific theories, but he never explains the internal stages of the cycle and their relations to the cycle that preceded the current one. To this extent the theory is more intuitive than analytical, especially in comparison to Bloom's and Derrida's views.

Thirdly, narrative corresponds to an internal hierarchy of scientific theories. The concepts must be interdependent, and this interdependence must have a recurring structure. The different concepts or laws forming the hierarchical structure can only be presented diachronically--not only presented but also developed in a sequence of stages. This sequence would be the "narrative" of science by which it comes to know itself in relation to its predecessor. Kuhn, as has been mentioned, commented on the interdependence of Newton's second and third laws. More than a comment in this direction is needed. A reader wishing to discover more about the internal dynamic of science, its narrative, can find a detailed account in Cassirer's *Einstein's Theory of Relativity Considered from the Epistemological Standpoint*. As one sample in a thorough discussion, consider the following:

> According to the general theory of relativity the velocity of light is dependent on the gravitation potential and must thus in general vary with places. The velocity of light must always depend on the coordinates when a field of gravitation is present; it is only to be regarded as constant when we have in mind regions with a constant gravitation potential. This consequence of the general theory of relativity has often been regarded as a refutation of the presupposition from which the special theory of relativity took its start and on which it based all its deductions (378).

Cassirer understands this passage with the idea in mind of the necessity of diversity and change within a theory (324 *SF*). There is a "mathematical manifold" [a mathematical whole uniting many diverse aspects] to serve as the symbolic counterpart of the sensuous manifold of the physical world.

Finally, science depends upon narrative for its legitimation and transmission. "Scientific knowledge," writes Lyotard, "cannot know and make known that it is the true knowledge without resorting to the other, narrative, kind of knowledge, which from its point of view is no knowledge at all" (29 *Postmodern*). Narrative allows science to refer to its own past as an element in the development of a new theory so that the two theories, the two generations of science are genetically and structurally related.

Need for Teleology in the Understanding of Science

It is more necessary to characterize scientific discourses, theories, as teleological phenomena than Kuhn realized.

Kuhn denied that the entire tradition of science has a single specific goal guiding all theories. He takes the issue no further. He does not extend the idea to infer the role of goals limited to specific theories yet recurring.

Tradition Depends upon Teleological Principles

The teleology of science helps to explain how it is traditional.

Derrida discovers a point of orientation for a whole text, a perspective point, when he looks for the Achilles heel, the faulty assumption on which the whole system depends. Such points also exist for scientific systems. According to Cassirer, the objects of knowledge are never simply isolated but can only be created according to an ideal standpoint (the emerging context that is being re-stationed, in Bloom's terms; a new definition of the tradition). Scientific unity cannot be represented as a particular concept but only a system of valid relations.[3] For physics before Einstein, the "fixed and immovable point was the assumption of the identity of the spatial and temporal values gained by measurement in the various systems. This identity was taken to be the unquestionable and sure foundation of the concept of objectivity in general: as that which first really constituted the object of `nature' as a geometrical and mechanical object..." (373 *ETR*). The change of such an assumption would explain how there can be a change in the whole perspective of science. Baudrillard called this "an impossible-to-break-through point around which the whole analysis is rearranged" (157 *Simulations*). Furthermore, the system of science, its tradition, has priority over individual contents. Kuhn does not try to formulate what these specific expressions of unity are for successive theories. Bloom points to them but does not define them as Cassirer does or as Derrida does.

Some scholars, unlike Kuhn, reject attempts to explain the wholistic nature of a scientific theory. Gablik recounts Gombrich's rejection of attempts to reconstruct `the whole process' of art. Gombrich rejects, along with Gablik, Alois Riegl's idea of "the evolution of the arts both as an autonomous dialectical process and as wheels revolving within the larger wheel of successive `world views'" (149).

Such denials run counter to Einstein's and other scientists' assertions that the unity of science is the most important criterion for a theory. If there is to be unity--at least relative--from theory to theory, each one must form through each of its main concepts a sense of the new definition of the unity of a science. Bloom's revisionary ratios each form a new sense of the unity of the poetic tradition, only completed in the last ones. In spite of the fact that Kuhn does not deny the wholistic nature of a science, he does not define its structure as *oriented* from beginning to end. Bloom speaks of the poetic quest in its successive stages, a fact pointing out the orientation of the whole poetry toward some end--not an end known and fixed when the process is begun but an end constantly redefined. Derrida, like Bloom, thinks of texts as oriented structures (211 *OG*).

Gablik interpets Kuhn's non-teleological theory of science as raising a fundamental question, also applicable to art. Kuhn's view is said to be "non-goal-oriented," since he asks, "what `evolution', `development' and `progress' could mean *in the absence of a specified goal*" (158). In a limited way he sees Kuhn's view as teleological: "the terminal point has continually to be discovered or constructed: *it is a matter of finding something which is not yet known*" (157). Gablik seems to be reading more in Kuhn's theory than can be found in his texts--not a misguided amelioration, yet an amelioration nonetheless. Kuhn does not discuss a terminal point of a scientific system, whether known at the start or progressively developed throughout.

Kuhn's view could benefit much by influence from the 1965 Nobel laureate in physiology and medicine, Jacques Monod. Monod's idea of the teleonomy of living things could apply to cultural forms, including scientific theories. Besides the goal of survival of the organism, "teleonymy" means the goal of reproduction to serve needs greater than those of the individual, namely, the needs of the species (20). It also means that "*objects [are] endowed with a purpose or project*, which at the same time they exhibit in their structure and carry out through their performances (such as, for instance, the making of artifacts)" (9). He makes a distinction between "teleonymy" and "invariance" throughout reproduction. Some things have invariance without teleonymy, for example, crystals. They "reproduce" their structures without altering the whole process in successive cycles. Individual crystals do not alter the species as DNA and people can. Monod feels quite uncomfortable about resorting to ideas of a purpose greater than that of the individual living thing, whereas he feels compelled to postulate such purpose for the sake of explaining the transgenerational unity of living things. There seems to be a need for thinking of a final cause guiding the "structural norm" of any thing. He also uses the terms "specific structural standard." If the genetic code is repeated in various living things with some slight variations, still the code must set for itself requirements fairly constant. These requirements or goals of form guide the process.

Whereas teleonymy is a distinguishing feature of living and nonliving things, Monod makes the side remark that teleonymy provides no feature distinguishing living things from their artifacts (9). "...The project which gives rise to an artifact belongs to the animal that created it." Therefore, if this is true, and it is consistent with the tendency of the previous discussion, then forms could only serve the development of the individual living things; a scientific theory would be about the development of science and the individuals advancing it. Science would not merely be about nature; it would be more about human nature.

Criteria of Validity, of Scientificity, Depend upon Teleology

Without a teleology of science there could be no way to explain how its criteria of truth is known to itself.

In the philosophy of art Riegl uses a teleological approach, the chief value of which is to introduce "a determining factor within the phenomenon of development" (9 Riegl). To say that science develops according to final causes is to say that it knows the direction it should be taking. If it does not, how could it ever take the right direction?

In *The Structure of Scientific Revolutions* Kuhn hints at a teleological process within the creation of a new theory ("invention" may sound more scientific to many scholars). "If we can learn to substitute evolution-from-what-we-do-know for evolution-toward-what-we-wish-to-know, a number of vexing problems may vanish in the process. Somewhere in this maze, for example, must lie the problem of induction" (171 *SSR*). In Bloom's terms, the context of the tradition of poetry is "re-stationed," meaning a new unity, a new definition is found. To make this unity, the old cannot be used as a direct source from which to copy, since the new poetry changes the orientation of the whole framework. Nevertheless, an idea of some unity must be worked toward as a transformation of the old. In this way there is an almost symbiotic transfer of the fertile pattern of poetry to a succeeding one.

Reflecting on Kuhn's non-teleological approach, Gablik would like to limit any teleological explanation to "develomental laws" meaning earlier stages are "preconditions" for later ones (152). His change of vocabulary from Riegl's "will-to-form" (*Kunstwollen*) is not a significant improvement in conception, only a change in style. Despite that attempt, whatever development or growth there is must be contained by an origin and an end of a specific scientific theory. Consequently, any "development" is secondary to principles which bound it.

Some teleological explanation is necessary to link systems of science in a series. The beginning of one theory must be linked to the previous as its superceding, its transvaluation. Writing about tradition and the indiviudal talent, T.S. Eliot claims the continuity of purpose in poetry results from its comprehension of former knowledge.

> But the difference between the present and the past is that the conscious present is an awareness of the past in a way and to an extent which the past's awareness of itself cannot show.
>
> Someone said, `The dead writers are remote from us because *we know* so much more than they did'.

> Precisely, and they are that which we know (2209 *Norton Anthology*).

Accordingly, humans can partially determine the creative process, a teleological one of changing old ends and making new ones. It is also partially true, however, that the individual is not absolutely self-conscious of the process of making the artifacts, theories; the individual is serving a greater purpose beyond its complete control. About control in creation Eliot writes, "The last quatrain gives an image, a feeling attaching to an image, which `came', which did not develop simply out of what precedes, but which was probably in suspension in the poet's mind until the proper combination arrived for it to add itself to" (2210). The individual does not invent poetry but only a poetry, fitting the parts together to form a whole for which there can only be limited, changing recognition by the individual. The genetic code of poetry is not arbitrarily changeable by the individual, though the individual does change it slightly. The needs of a unit of tradition are met again in each new creation: these constitute its goal.

Much Stronger Sense of the Genetic Encoding of Science Needed

Kuhn insufficiently realized the extent to which one body of science encodes the next.

When defining revolutions, Kuhn usually refers to some major ones, often spanning centuries. This habit of exposition runs counter to the idea of revolutions as regular occurrences, with a recurring structure. Later in his career, seven years after the first edition of *The Structure of Scientific Revolutions*, after being charged with defining only major revolutions, he noticed this problem and asserted the regularity of revolutions more than he had:

> [revolution is] a special sort of change involving a certain sort of reconstruction of group commitments. But it need not be a large change, nor need it seem revolutionary to those outside a single community, consisting perhaps of fewer than twenty-five people.

> It is just because this type of change, little recognized or discussed in the literature of the philosophy of science, occurs so regularly on this smaller scale that revolutionary, as against cumulative, change so badly needs to be understood (181 *SSR*).

Kuhn never does define the regularity of revolutions on this small scale, perhaps because it could not be treated in a very general way with assumed or common knowledge about the changes. Instead, he would have to discuss "technical" scientific concepts, himself entering into the process of determining scientific validity. Kuhn has a background in science, one which never enters the foreground of his theory. Bloom has a different approach. To define the "life-cycle of the poet-as-poet," Bloom does not consider the reactions of the community of poets; he considers only regularly recurring structural features (7 *AI*). To a large extent, though Kuhn states there is a regularity to revolutions, he does not define it by features of the theories themselves, which would require detailed discussions of the interdependence of scientific concepts, as Bloom discusses details of poetic interdependence, both within and between texts.

Kuhn's `Dead View of Science'

Kuhn's view of science is `dead', because he does not explain it as a living, reproductive system. The reproduction of the pattern of the sciences is necessary for an understanding of the continuum of science, the forever changing, living, ongoing unity of scientific discourse.

Kuhn gives no idea of the dynamism, the changes, within a scientific theory--the character of its being alive even to its creator, of offering surprise, of effecting a development not fully anticipatable at the outset. While being points where learning occurs, these changes also establish the hierarchy of concepts, their interdependence. If cultural forms have a higher organization than living forms, but if they too must in a sense be living to be products of living things, then cultural forms would have at least as much of the same type of organization as living things would, or something better. Monod describes living things as "self-constructing machines":

> ...a living being's structure...owes almost nothing to the action of outside forces, but everything, from its overall shape down to its tiniest detail, to `morphogenetic' interactions within the object itself. It is thus a structure giving proof of an autonomous determinism: precise, rigorous, implying a virtually total `freedom' with respect to outside agents or conditions--which are capable, to be sure, of impeding this development, but not of governing or guiding it, not of prescribing its organizational scheme to the living object (10).

For Monod, the autonomy of a living thing's development depends upon interactions, even changes, within its structure. A living thing *is* a teleonomic apparatus; its purpose is to maintain itself and reproduce (16). This feature of organization also characterizes Bloom's map of misreading because of the nonrelation of poetic creation to social forces and the dynamic changes brought about by each new revisionary ratio. One would only look in vain to find correlative stages in scientific theories in Kuhn's view.

Teleonymy is also a transgenerational feature of organization. It is "the transmission from generation to generation of the invariance content characteristic of the species" (14 Monod). From scientific theory to theory there must be a "specific structural standard." Then, a scientific theory could not be studied in isolation. Only in an order of theories could the individual become clearly defined.[4] Kuhn gives little sense of the transgenerational nature of specific theories. There must be a "regular recurrence across the generations" of science (153 *Lyotard Reader*). What could this be but a kind of genetic code of science? Or is there no such regularity?

Insufficient Grasp of the Metalepsis of Science

Metalepsis, insufficiently understood by Kuhn, can explain changes in the encoding processes of science.

Kuhn's theory contains only the beginnings of an idea of metalepsis. One feature of metalepsis is the seeming return to the precursors, and Kuhn states Einstein returned to the canons and problems of Newton's predecessors (108 *SSR*). This return can seem false to Kuhn, as in the case of Newton attributing to Galileo what Galileo's paradgims could not have asked (139 *SSR*). Kuhn feels this attribution is false, because he does not see a structural feature of science to "re-write" previous science in its own terms, as Bloom does for poetry.

Textbooks act in a metaleptic way, following scientific developments. After each revolution textbooks must be rewritten, for they explain the past as developing linearly toward the present, and now there is a new present (138 *SSR*). Not only textbooks but science has the tendency to "write history backwards." Kuhn claims other cultural forms do this as well. A negative side effect of this process in textbooks is that revolutions become hidden (140 *SSR*). The only revolution is the last. This perspective mirrors that of the scientist, who incorporates all past science by revising the unity of the discipline. Previous concepts must become re-interpreted as logically subordinate. Bloom discussed the corresponding feature of poetry in terms aggrandizing the new poet.

Kuhn comes closer to expressing metalepsis when he discusses the difference between Priestley and Lavoisier. "The impossible suggestion that Priestley first discovered oxygen and Lavoisier then invented it has its attractions. Oxygen has already been encountered as discovery; we shall shortly meet it again as invention" (66 *SSR*). Since Kuhn does not draw out further implications, statements like this could easily be passed over by even an attentive reader who is not familiar with Bloom's concept of metalepsis or with that feature of scientific theories. To say that the discovery of oxygen precedes its invention is to say that Lavoisier understood more deeply what Priestley thought about. Metalepsis means a successor understands the predecessor's concepts more deeply, more thoroughly. Bloom expressed the relation always in temporal terms of the reversal of a successor's belatedness for an earliness. In logical rather than temporal terms, this reversal means a successor develops concepts from the predecessor which the predecessor's concepts presuppose. Using provocative language, Lyotard writes, "Begetting a father; that is the origin of science" (84 *Lyotard Reader*). The successor develops logically prior concepts. In the famous example of Einstein declaring Newton's mechanics to be valid as a limiting case, some priority is evident, though to many people it may sound as if no change occurred in the Newtonian concepts within that limited domain of physical cases.

Science as Primarily a Mode of Improving the Human Being

Had Kuhn tried to describe science more like the arts or humanities--more like a mode of improving the human being than an explanation of "external" nature--then Kuhn would have come closer to seeing how science is made.

Due to its cyclical evolution, science makes much more sense as a mode of improving the individual mind than as an explanation of external nature. Why would such an explanation be cyclical? The development of individuals must be cyclical because their lives are; the cycle is repeated for each individual, from birth to death. Science is similarly limited to finite cycles. The unity of a science, as I have suggested, is limited to a specific tradition form, a specific scientific theory. The unity can be fully defined by examining the relations to the theory before and after. Between the origin and the end the unity of a theory consists in this space or passage, in this step in tradition. Writing about Derrida's relevant views, Hobson remarks, "At this level the coherence, whether of organism or of text, is not one of identity or self-identity, but one of self-replication or self-repetition."[5] The discourse is concerned with itself more than with *external* nature; it has its own requirements.

Scientific creation follows a course of the evolution of the unity of science, or the form of the discourse. The solutions of one theory come from a process of modelling on previous solutions. The modelling process is global, since scientists do not know the specific characteristics that must be preserved throughout the transference of the code. Kuhn expresses this view,

> I have elsewhere argued that the cognitive content of the physical sciences is in part dependent on the same primitive similarity relation between concrete examples, or paradigms, of successful scientific work, that scientists model one problem solution on another without at all knowing what characteristics of the

> original must be preserved to legitimate the process. Here I am suggesting that in history that obscure global relationship carries virtually the entire burden of connecting fact (17 *ET*; also see 48 *SSR*)

The global relationship is the unity of scientific discourse, a unity limited to a specific step in tradition. What is most important in creation is to develop "a way of viewing physical situations rather than rules or laws" (190 *SSR*). It follows that finding a new way of viewing physical situations comes from a criticism of the old way of viewing them. The mode of vision, the perspective, the coherence of the discourse--this is more important than the contents or reference to the actual physical world.

Viewing science more as a mode of developing human nature than a mode of explanation--often called "disinterested" or objective-- can be a way of overcoming the longstanding split of the sciences from the humanities and arts. Whereas the humanities and arts seem to deal with inner, spiritual nature, the sciences seem to deal with outer, physical nature. More primary than either inner or outer, spiritual or physical is the common function of all cultural fields to evolve through a tradition. Whenever consciousness is raised by a new step in tradition, so too `external' nature becomes reconceived. Inner and outer are not exclusive because they are interdependent. They change together, and the form of this change is human tradition. Then scientific concepts do tell us about external nature, yet creators have often pointed out the needs of the unity of form were more primary so that those concepts tell us at least as much about the functioning of the scientific mind. Science plots some of the abstract coordinates for the future direction of the improvement of human life. Expressing the primacy of the goal of development over the explanation of either inner or outer nature, Lévi-Strauss at the same time places myth more in the category of a legitimate interpretation of the world than is commonly done: "Myths...were simply making a general application of the processes according to which thought finds itself to be operating, these processes being the same in both areas, since thought, and the world which encompasses it, are two correlative manifestations of the same reality."[6] The theories function as feedback mechanisms for the development of human nature; in the products a scientist can see the workings of the mind and so change the way the mind works. Such an access to self-improvement is lacking in the simpler DNA, which does represent its whole in its parts, in some sense (namely, the function of replication), but this representation is not necessarily transvaluative as it is in cultural fields.

The idea of the essential significance of scientific concepts for human development has been expressed metaphorically by Emerson, when he compares nature to our human house, or shell:

> Man is the dwarf of himself. Once he was permeated and dissolved by spirit. He filled nature with his overflowing currents. Out from him sprang the sun and moon; from man, the sun; from woman, the moon. The laws of his mind, the periods of his actions externalized themselves into day and night, into the year and the seasons. But having made for himself this huge shell, his waters retired; he no longer fills the veins and veinlets; he is shrunk to a drop. He sees, that the structure still fits him, but fits him colossally. Say, rather, once it fitted him, now it corresponds to him from far and on high. He adores timidly his own work. Now is man the follower of the sun, and woman the follower of the moon. Yet sometimes he starts in his slumber, and wonders at himself and his house, and muses strangely at the resemblance betwixt him and it. He perceives that if his law is still paramount, if still he have elemental power, `if his word is sterling yet in nature', it is not conscious power, it is not inferior but superior to his will (929 *Nature, The Norton Anthology*)

This passage can serve to provoke a sense of the interest any theory must have for its inventor. Scientific theories can be thought of as the processes of the mind externalized, "writ large" as Plato wrote for philosophy. The individual does not make these laws arbitrarily but rather is governed by them, limited in the possibilities of development. The theories are so fascinating as to be one's "life work" because they pull the mind forward to its future state.

Had Kuhn considered science to be more of a mode of self-development, his theory would have been different. He would have described the developmental dynamism within scientific theories that also established the interdependence of the concepts. The relations between scientific theories would have become much clearer. There would have been more emphasis on internal factors. Stages in a theory would have been related to the overall needs of the discourse, thus adding a teleological dimension to the explanation of science, which afterall is an activity not of disinterested beings. The teleological structures of poetry and philosophy are much more evident in the works of Bloom and Derrida. Just as the entire structure of living things, of the DNA in them, seems to be geared toward survival and reproduction, so too cultural forms can be defined by their unity and re-creation of a pattern passed on through tradition. In this process culture exceeds nature by introducing an essential transvaluative meaning to each successive structure, and the individual can determine the direction the improvement must take. Kuhn's theory has little to offer concerning the inherently transvaluative nature of science. "...The permissible starting points for physical explanation do not seem intrinsically more advanced in a later than in an earlier age" (30 *ET*). Cyclicism with little sense of improvement. But isn't this the most important, albeit most difficult, question? What genetic code does science have partially in its control?

Summary

Kuhn's popular theory of scientific revolutions clearly makes some bold innovations and, yet, while not for the most part wrong, his view of the traditional nature of science seems quite a bit less developed than either Bloom's or Derrida's corresponding views are. I have been claiming that a philospher of science after Kuhn could gain more explanatory power by using an idea of a genetic code in science to guide research. Also, by so doing, the problems or inconsistencies of his approach would largely be overcome. The problems discussed herein are chauvinism; generality; lack of proofs and value judgments; too much emphasis on external, empirical factors; failure to define the unit of science; need for an internal dynamic structure of theories; need for a teleological understanding of science;

and a need to have a stronger sense of the genetic encoding of science. The Epilogue will suggest a positive future path for those philosophers of science after Kuhn.

NOTES

1. The idea was taken from p. 123 of *Ernst Cassirer: An Annotated Bibliography*. Originally, it comes from Cassirer's review of Russell's *A Critical Exposition of the Philosophy of Leibniz* (Cambridge 1900). In *Leibniz' System in seinen wissenschaftlichen Grundlagen*, 532-41.

2. Quoted from 191 Fite. The original is Said, Edward. "Interview." *Diacritics* 6, no. 3(1976), 34.

3. The idea is taken from p. 13 of Eggers and Mayer, *Ernst Cassirer: An Annotated Bibliography*. The English translation is annotated.

4. See 235 of Alastair Fowler's *Kinds of Literature* for a recounting of Yury Tynyanov's idea that "only in the context of changing generic paradigms" can "a single genre's function" be grasped.

5. Quoted from page 310 Hobson. She is referring to an idea of Derrida from p. 378 of *La Carte postale*.

6. Quoted from 161 Nancy. The original is *The Naked Man*, p. 678.

Chapter 13:

Judging Bloom's Theory

Bloom Explains Tradition Much More Than Kuhn, but Future Critics Should Use a Literary Genetic Code Even More

Introduction to the Judging of Bloom's Theory of Tradition

Bloom's theory has many features that would commend it highly. It is much more determinate, specific, complete than Kuhn's. What is more, Bloom places tradition at the center of the poetic activity. The theory seems to be universal and is well supported by examples.

Despite all its good features, there are several which can be improved, and they will be discussed in the following chapter.

Criticism Necessarily Reduces Meaning

Criticism necessarily reduces the original poetic meaning, something Bloom does less than other critics.

The Russian formalist Boris Eichenbaum questions the ability of criticism to apprehend the full meaning of a literary work: "We were interested in the very process of evolution, in the very *dynamics* of literary form, insofar as it was possible to observe them in the facts of the past" (136 Lemon and Reis).

Discussing this question of criticism coming too late to catch poetry while it is still alive, dynamic, Bloom quotes Anna Freud's *Ego and the Mechanisms of Defence*:

> ...all the defensive measures of the ego against the id are carried out silently and invisibly. The most that we can ever do is to reconstruct them in retrospect: we can never really witness them in operation. This statement applies, for instance, to successful repression. The ego knows nothing of it; we are aware of it only subsequently, when it becomes apparent that something is missing (14 *DC*).

Defined originally in reference to Sigmund Freud's ambivalent defense mechanisms, Bloom's revisionary ratios are in motion. They represent movements or stances of the poetic mind. The ambivalence represents this dynamism, only known to the poet at the next higher ratio. Similarly, in Anna Freud's ideas cited above, the ambivalent operation of the defense mechanisms is known only subsequently when the ambivalence is seen to be an inadequate response.

These ideas might seem to suggest that the understanding of a poetry can only come *after* the poetry, and this is a legitimate inference--with a restriction. The "understanding" of a poetry could be a higher order poetry, not a different mode of discourse, namely, criticism. Criticism cannot understand, as if by freezing, the revisionary ratios in an actual poetry because they are not static nor univocal even for the poet. The law of understanding a text seems to be `either more or less than the original meaning is meant, though never can the understanding be an exact duplicate by a different mode of discourse: a contradiction in terms'. Stated differently, "I must Create a System, or be enslaved by another Man's," cries Los at a crucial moment early in Blake's "Jerusalem," "I will not Reason & Compare [systematize]; my business is to Create" [10:20-21, E151). When writing about narrative transformations, Todorov claims, "The study of each level can be made only in relation to the level hierarchically above it..." (219 *Poetics of Prose*).

To say that critical models are necessarily reductive is not to say that criticism does not perform a valuable service in society. Like a step in the food chain, like crabs on the sea floor breaking down the highly organized dead sources of protein, critics break down the difficult feelings of finished poetry into less integral bits for those with a lower understanding to benefit from.

Tautology and Reduction

Bloom believes all criticism must avoid two extremes:

> All criticisms that call themselves primary vacillate between tautology--in which the poem is and means itself--and reduction--in which the poem means something that is not itself a poem. Antithetical criticism must begin by denying both tautology and reduction, a denial best delivered by the assertion that the meaning of a poem can only be a poem, but `another poem--a poem not itself'. And not a poem chosen with total arbitrariness, but any central poem by an indubitable precursor, even if the ephebe `never read' that poem (70 *AI*).

In other words, a poem is not merely self-referential; its reference is to a future poem. The meaning of a poem is to lead to another poem. Consequently, if criticism does not itself make another poem, does it understand the meaning of a poem? Another way to approach the issue is to ask, can a way of ordering a poem that is different from poetry properly represent its meaning?

As another aspect of the question whether criticism is necessarily reductive, Bloom puts criticism in the same category as creation of poetry. He claims there is no difference in kind between them (43, 95 *AI*). Then why does criticism produce a different product from creation?

Bloom thinks reduction may be inevitable; "reduction" causes a loss of meaning due to a change in it. "All reading is translation, and all attempts to communicate a reading seem to court reduction, perhaps inevitably. The proper use of any critical paradigm ought to lessen the dangers of reduction, yet clearly most paradigms are, in themselves, dangerously reductive" (14 *PR*).

The theorist of influence seems to know his own weakness. Some reduction of meaning is inevitable. He takes a vantage point above individual great poets in a series, but precisely for that reason the standpoint is outside the meaning it purports to explain. Though each new poetry changes the meaning of poetry, criticism cannot address this level of specificity from its standpoint above the series.

The Mistaken Idea about the Necessity of Critical Models

Critics can hardly deny the value of critical models without denying the value of their activity. According to Bloom, "to refuse models explicitly is only to accept other models" (14 *PR*). Murray Krieger's expression of this situation makes its principles quite clear. "So I urge again that our choice is not between having a theory or not having one; for have one (or two or three or more incompatible ones) we must" (7). The lack of critical consensus throughout history must be an embarrassment for those arguing for the ability of criticism to explain meaning without reducing it. Krieger uses the expression "superintend" literature. Critics manage the creative process from a standpoint superior--and inferior; superior, because they feel they can grasp the processes from no standpoint in particular, unlike the poet; inferior, because they must reduce the meaning by stopping and changing the process underway. The ambivalence of the critical reliance on models ironically echos the ambivalence of the defence mechanisms and of Bloom's revisionary ratios.

Without being able to overcome this ambivalence, Bloom reproduces it in his own criticism. In his theory poetry begins in "apotropaic litany" (271 *PR*). Poetry wards off the evil of the previous great poet whose evil is to try to stop anyone from developing some greater poetry. A litany is a kind of prayer in which the priest and the members respond in the same words, suggesting that the previous great master and the new poet speak in the same language. The new poet, then, must ward off the evil of the precursor while nonetheless speaking in the same language.

Bloom makes an assumption concerning texts that Derrida denies. By making the meaning of a poem another poem, Bloom is not saying that there is an infinite regress of interpretations so that the critic can never understand any poetry. Instead, he is saying that the critic can understand each poetry in the tradition as it is and define the changes in poetry. In so doing he assumes the ability to totalize the meaning of a poetry, to know what it is in relation to another poetry. In contrast Derrida does not think it is possible to totalize the meaning of a text (288-89 *WD*). It is not because there is too much wealth of meaning but because "the nature of the field...excludes totalization." The field of any text--whether poetry, science, or philosophy--is made by a possible infinity of substitutions of meaning. The critic must preserve the meaning of each poetry in the tradition, although the poets see themselves as displacing, as overshadowing their predecessors. For Derrida, there is nothing outside the text (158 *OG*); for Bloom, his map of misreading is outside any particular poetry, outside those texts. The change in the field of poetry must be overlooked by models. Also, the change in meaning within poetries is overlooked, for the parts of a poetry serve as templates for other parts in a self-replicating process of tradition. To give the same definition to the ratios in a series of poetries is to ignore these differences.

Critics act as if the *real* meaning of a poetry is the model made by the critics, as if there could not be a real meaning without them. Derrida explains this dissemblance:

> The conscious text is thus not a transcription, because there is no text *present elsewhere* as an unconscious one to be transposed or transported. For the value of presence can also dangerously affect the concept of the unconscious. There is then no unconscious truth to be rediscovered by virtue of having been written elsewhere. There is no text written and present elsewhere which would then be subjected, without being changed in the process, to an operation and a temporalization (the latter belonging to consciousness if we follow Freud literally) which would be external to it, floating on its surface. There is no present text in general, and there is not even a past present text, a text which is past as having been present. ...Everything begins with reproduction. Always already: repositories of a meaning which was never present, whose signified presence is always reconstituted by

deferral, *nachträglich*, belatedly, *supplementarily*; for the *nachträglich* also means *supplementary* (211 *WD*).

The critic's model serves as the real meaning of a poetry, unknown or unconscious to the poet. Forming models results from a dissemblance; the critic declares the wealth of the text while showing the greater essentiality of the model.

The belief in the necessity of models may also arise from Bloom's partial realization of some of his own principles. The Russian Formalists agree with Bloom that the meaning of a poem is another poem, while not agreeing with Bloom that the meaning of a poem is a model of the poem. "...We [Russian Formalists, writes Boris Eichenbaum] had to approach it [the problem of literary evolution] without abstract, ready-made, unalterable, classical schemes" (132 Lemon and Reis).

Models do not seem to be necessary for creators when they understand a previous poetry. They know that that understanding only becomes complete as a new poetry is written. To understand a poetry means to know its processes and form. The attempt to finalize the form, to make it a single representation, only occurs in a new poetic representation. Laws of form-building are in the images of poetry so that when these images are related more than the previous poet did, the laws begin to appear in a new and better light. In other words, the greater unity of contents is their representation in a new content with a different law of constitution. Derrida expressed the fecundity of each content of a text when he wrote, "Numbers are caught in a mathematicogenetic theory of groups" (304 *DS*) . The creative process of relating contents of a precursor's work is called *bricolage* in "Structure, Sign, and Play in the Discourse of the Human Sciences."

The Embarrassing Question of the Completeness of Criticism

Criticism always leaves a remainder of text to be interpreted; "...it is impossible in a commentary to exhaust" its meaning (77 *SM*). If criticism aims to understand literature, and if criticism of a text is never complete, then criticism admits to never understanding fully.

But doesn't someone understand the literary works fully? How can there be adequate knowledge? Perhaps adequate knowledge would have to be defined for a purpose, such as adequate for creating a new poetry from an old.

Rather than being a positive feature, the incompleteness of criticism points to its secondary, not entirely accurate understanding. Interpretation cannot be completed because the text does not exist as a completed thing in the manner of a physical object. A text is a dynamic stance of the mind, the mind in process. Alfred North Whitehead is famous for his notion that there is no nature at an instant; this reminds me of the fact that a mathematical point has no magnitude. Those points permit actual magnitudes to be measurable. In a similar way the unity of a text is not actual but ideal. It is the source of the unity of experienced objects, though not itself one of those. About the merely ideal unity of myth, Lévi-Strauss writes,

> There is no real end to methodological analysis, no hidden unity to be grasped once the breaking-down process has been completed. Themes can be split up *ad infinitum.* Just when you think you have disentangled and separated them, you realize that they are knitting together again in response to the operation of unexpected affinities. Consequently the unity of the myth is never more than tendential and projective and cannot reflect a state or a particular moment of the myth. It is a phenomenon of the imagination, resulting from the attempt at interpretation; and its function is to endow the myth with synthetic form and to prevent its disintegration into a confusion of opposites.[1]

The unity of a myth is not to be found within the myth. It aims at a unity beyond itself, while giving greater unity to what preceded it. The unity becomes evident in a new myth which attempts to interpret the former one in a process requiring an original synthesis. Bloom's concept of clinamen sounds vaguely in the background of these ideas.

A model is not needed for the understanding of a poetry if it coincides with the further development of that poetry. About this evolutionary process, Lyotard writes, "(Dialectical) logic `is not something distinct (*nichts Unterschiedenes*) from its object and content; for it is the inwardness of the content, the dialectic which it possesses within itself, which is the mainspring of its advance'."[2] Ironically, Bloom thought of the progress in poetry in terms of greater "inwardness," yet if his practice followed that statement then he would not define ratios apart from any particular poetry, ratios more general than any particular poetry; he would attempt to make revisionary ratios himself, starting in reaction to the last great poetry.

Inevitably, models begin to put themselves in place of the poetry as the object of attention. Models make us ignore each new increment of progress laid down by the labor of a great poet's life. In Bloom's career the detailed exegesis of *Shelley's Mythmaking* becomes (fourteen years) later the more abstract defence of a critical model with much less attention to actual poetry.

The Ambiguous Limits of Bloom's Criticism

On the one hand, Bloom sees a limit to the power of criticism; on the other, he raises it above creative poetry. "I too offer a `machine for criticism', though I sometimes fear that poetry itself increasingly has become the last formula" (21 *PR*). Here "formula" could be substituted by "model." So criticism is a secondary understanding to the next great poetry. On the other hand, criticism is more primary than individual poetries. Bloom denies that a poet fulfills the project of a preceding one, for to do so would be to share in the "later poet's self-idealization" (88 *PR*). Bloom understands his own limits ambiguously. What is necessary to help Bloom understand poetry is confused with what is necessary to produce that poetry. To gain help, Bloom places the power of creation, direct vision of the process, into a tutelary spirit, his map of misreading.

Criticism as Fundamentalism

"Religious fundamentalism" refers to the belief in only one real interpretation of the bible, usually literal. Critics, too, are fundamentalists at heart, since they do think there is some single, fixed interpretation about which their peers would agree. Bloom, at any rate, is of this opinion, as de Man brings to light: "In his [Bloom's] description of influence as a cunning, malicious distortion of tradition Bloom gives a displaced version of a very genuine problem" (273 Review of *AI*). Bloom uses these words: "self-saving caricature," "distortion," and "perverse, wilful revisionism" (30 *AI*). If Bloom describes tradition as a cunning or malicious distortion, then he can know this because his interpretation is relatively undistorted. But, as Derrida claims, the past does not literally exist (59 *Mémoires for Paul de Man*). "The allegation of its supposed `anterior' is memory." Bloom's fundamentalism is just another standpoint of the imagination.

The concepts of "misreading" and "misprision" have a fundamentalist basis due to the implications of the negative prefixes. A mistake is made by someone. The terms seem to imply that the successor knows but ignores a right interpretation of his/her predecessor. Such a view makes the act of the successor arbitrary or not a specifically required evolutionary movement. In de Man's words, Bloom "assumes that the meaning from which it [a succeeding poetry] deviates could itself be considered to be definite and authoritative" (274 Review of *AF*). Another way to look at the negative value of the prefixes is that the elision, the sliding, in the terms--from right reading known to not right reading for a model to follow--may allow the critic to avoid having to enter the poetic process and explain why one poetry is "better" than another. The term also slides in meaning from wrong interpretation for the succeeding great poet to right interpretation for the critic.

The message of a poem--against Bloom's idea of the personal wishes of the author or apparently against structural closing features-- is to get the reader to develop a new poetry. Semioticist Umberto Eco discusses the fictional, substitutive nature of meaning (12 "Looking for a Logic of Culture"). A sign does not have to show the thing itself; it has a message insofar as it leads to another sign. This is a reproductive view of meaning. A poetry is complete when it provides all the poetic vision from which a succeeding one can be formed. No further explanation outside of the text is needed from the critics if the purpose of poetry is not to make a statement about the world but to move humanity forward, providing a vehicle of self-development.

In one passage Bloom almost breaks away from the fundamentalism chaining him to critical aims:

> The precise form in which Shelley visualizes in the `Triumph' [of Life] is itself an anagoge of his meaning. If you take your eyes away, at any point in the poem, from Shelley's own figures, then you will fall inevitably into misreading [in a bad sense] of the meaning, for the meaning is the total form that Shelley's series of visions (and everything in this poem is visualized for you) assumes when you can be certain you have seen all of them as clearly as Shelley has presented them. As soon as you have identified the abstraction you believe the chariot of Life and its occupants to be, then just that soon you have stopped reading Shelley's poem. Shelley's chariot, Shape of Life, and charioteer are themselves, not something else. They are forms seen in a poet's vision, and what they mean is not something in addition to what they are (243 *SM*).

Bloom almost but not quite thinks the proper understanding of poetry is the next poetry. He slips back into a realist, fundamentalist interpretation of the tradition.

Fundamentalism distinguishes Bloom's method from deconstruction. Instead of seeking to "deconstruct meaning," Bloom prefers to "restore and redress meaning" (175 *MM*). This restoration can never be completed (29 *PR*).

Insufficient Realization of the Collective Meaning of Poetry

Bloom usually discusses the changes in poetry according to the desires of the individual poet: to achieve poetic election, to overcome the influence of the predecessor, and to become an influence oneself. Poetic immortality is the strongest desire of the poet (186 *MM*). Seldom does Bloom discuss the advent of a new poetry by showing the poetic superiority of the new one.

De Man has a thorough discussion of the subjective individual meaning of poetic change in the theory of the anxiety of influence--anxiety, influence, power, rivalry, desire. He would prefer a linguistic vocabulary to the psychological one (276 Review of *AI*). Poetic meaning becomes more a relation between two people than it does a change in the nature of poetry, as Cassirer defined the change brought about by Einstein's physics.

Furthermore, usually the end of a poetry is considered to be negative to the successor. The precursor does not make way. In science the structural counterpart is a contradiction making an increase in the unity of the science impossible according to its old assumptions. Most of Bloom's terms for the ongoing development are negative: misadventures, misreading, misprision, anxiety, defense mechanisms.

Kuhn does not define the new specific meaning of the continuum at each ratio for each poet. If this were done, each one would be seen as a positive development of the idea of the continuum, the unity of poetry, even the closing of a poetry, which would nevertheless be seen as problematic by a successor.

Mistakes in the Method and Psychology of Criticism

Misguided Concentration on Individual Poems

Bloom concentrates his criticism on individual poems, and so he calls his criticism "practical." Practical as it may seem to students and scholars, a confusion arises concerning the application of the revisionary ratios to actual poetry. Each one occurs in individual poems as well as the poetry as a whole. Wallace Stevens is said to have "tesserae"--the plural form of "tessera"--in his poetry. But this double use of the ratios obstructs further determination of the poetic process. He could have found the single best clinamen or start from a predecessor's poetry instead of one in each poem. Had the interpretation been more geared to the poetry as a whole rather than to individual poems, the meaning of each ratio could have been defined uniquely for each succeeding poetry.

Besides the self-imposed limit of further understanding, the emphasis on individual poems causes other confusions. Sometimes Bloom speaks of a "composite precursor" (140 *PR*). This infrequent claim runs counter to the entire tendency of the theory of the anxiety of influence. And sometimes he seems unsure which poet in a succession is the victor in the struggle (12 *AI*). Emphasis on the entire poetries would help to make the decision clearer, especially if the line of succession of great poets is formed by a direct single line of canonical poetries, parent to child, which is the predominant view of Bloom.

"Misreading" as Too Empirical

Bloom regards the swerve of clinamen as occurring at a single point in the text: "...revisionism follows received doctrine along to a certain point, and then deviates, insisting that a wrong direction was taken at just that point, and no other" (29 *AI*). This idea assumes the predecessor's text subsists as a static whole for the successor to react to, and this attitude is too empirical. The swerve is from the whole text, even the origin. In changing the start of poetry, in accumulating the tradition, all is reinterpreted, even if only slightly. Also, the poet "represses some of the traces, and remembers others. This remembering is a misprision, or creative misreading..." (4 *PR*). Again, some contents of the previous poetry cannot become parts in the new one unchanged. The continuity is not by a substantive retaining but by the functional correlation of the two poetries as tradition steps.

Derrida's view of the change of a precursor's ideas is less empirical, yet more explanatory. For Derrida, though he does not use these exact terms of Bloom's, there is even a misprision of one's own work. In the course of a philosophy, points of transformation occur, unexpected. The reversal leading away from the precursor is repeated on a smaller scale within the form itself. If there can be a misprision of one's own work, then a critic should redefine at each point what the new sense of the continuum is. Bloom provides no such specific explanations. Derrida does for his own philosophy; they constitute the arguments for his main concepts, namely, difference, differance, and the supplement.

For Derrida, the change brought about by re-interpreting the precursor is more complete (actually more a priori) than it is for Bloom. Bloom criticizes Derrida's idea of the start of cultural form for being "A turn that does not turn from anything" (81 *Kabbalah*). *Before the start of his philosophy, the interpretation of his precursor becomes "erased" [a term used by Derrida], replaced by the right interpretation, starting with the idea of difference.*

The Hubris of Bloom and Critics in General

David Fite correctly identifies hubris in Bloom's criticism (188). Bloom rates his criticism both as higher than that of poetic creation and also as a type of creation. "But we, to understand the strong poet, must go further still than he can go, back into the poise before the consciousness of falling came [from the precursor]" (21 *AI*). With this knowledge Bloom thinks critics can teach principles about poetry that cannot be taught through the poetry (25 *PR*). Could it be that this claim of superiority is a defense reaction against inferiority, against not knowing how to create?

Bloom often makes his theory self-reflexive by applying his own terms for creative poets to his criticism. He often calls his activity "misreading." And in general the sequence of chapters in *The Anxiety of Influence* is the sequence of the parts of a poem. However, a "strong reading" or misreading by a poet insists on being right in the complete sense of being the same as the text, of erasing the former interpretation, but Bloom does not apply the principle to his own criticism, which would make the poets whom he interprets `wrong' (125 *Kabbalah*).

He also claims poets are helped by critics who can serve as some of the precursors (95 AI). As de Man has pointed out, though, Bloom does not order his theory as an epic battle against one poet (274 Review of *AI*). This last claim is tempered by Bloom's assertion that critics can never become prior to poets, as poets do to poets (65 *AI*).

Both these tendencies manifest hubris. Rather curious, Bloom never tries to write poetry, preferring to publish a novel instead. All his books concentrate on poetry, and so why would he write a novel? It may be a defense reaction against further determination of the creative process in the great poets leading up to Bloom's time. Perhaps he subconsciously feels his claims about poetry are less than adequate for producing the kind of poetry of which he speaks. But, then, shouldn't his knowledge be deepened?

The Non-idiomatic Language of Critics

Bloom's inhibition about writing poetry--and must he not have been inhibited if poetry is primary, criticism secondary--is an inability to accept the blindness necessary to create. Bloom referred to Vico when he wrote that attempting to know the process too determinately can be an avoidance of the process. Blindness of a sort is integral to creation, as when he writes, "The Tower stands for the blindness of the influence-process, which is the same as the reading-process. Fresh creation is a catastrophe, or a substitution, a making-breaking that is performed in blindness" (113 *MM*). Blindness does not mean the poet has no idea of the direction to take; it means a new sense of the continuum must be constantly hypothesized to guide the poetry.

In this development a point of orientation is established by the poetry, a point not visible to the poet. Derrida writes about a point of textual orientation invisible to the creator, which I called a perspective point. Poets have this too, and it is the successor which comes to understand the aesthetic ideal of the predecessor which (s)he ever tends toward but never reaches. This ideal is then changed to open a new space for creation.

The language of Bloom tends to diverge from that of poetry; the criticism does not simply run in the same semantic line nor even parallel. As a result, authority to judge poetic excellence is forsaken. Poetry legitimates itself in its tradition. While a great poet is alive, he or she may be acknowledged as such by the community at large, or may not. It is usually only later, after succeeding great poets proclaim the greatness, first one and then another and then another that reputation is established. However, the legitimation is not the recognition by the community--contrary to Kuhn's view. It is the ability of the poetry to lead to, to provide the pattern for a next great poetry. Avoiding the idiom of poetry, Bloom is unwilling to understand poetry through poetry. In consequence some of the authority of poetic knowledge escapes him.[3] Legitimation, the understanding of poetic "proof," comes most through the successor's new poetry, and it comes in degrees according to which the poetic idiom is pure. Bloom's criticism is purer than most critics who are not creators.

Not Enough Proof

Unlike Derrida who asserts `deconstruction is not neutral; it intervenes,' Bloom attempts to maintain a neutral position above the struggles of poets.[4]

A weakness common to most critics, Bloom uses other disciplines besides poetry to "criticize" or to communicate poetic meaning. Of course, one could not explain Russian to a non-Russian speaker by using Russian, but on the other hand if one explains Russian with another language it is unlikely that the transfer of meaning is identical--only similarity could be claimed. Bloom uses two main sources as non-poetic explanation of poetry. In the start of his career, in *Shelley's Mythmaking*, he also used another source, Martin Buber's philosophy, though he stopped such explanations in later works. Instead he continued throughout his career using Freud's psychology and a medieval Jewish religious doctrine of Kabbalah, meaning tradition, to explain poetry. Admittedly, these two fields gave power to Bloom's interpretation, so they are not wholly without value. But the power comes at a price. Bloom's action is like an act of avoidance when exercising: when someone is lifting a heavy weight, to reduce the effort he often tries to employ other muscles or to tense them rather than to exercise the one he is trying to develop. The result is that the muscle to be developed is less developed than it otherwise would have been--and in Bloom's case the knowledge is less poetic.

John Hollander defends Bloom, saying that the use of Buber was only an expository device (xii-xiii, *PI*). Furthermore, Hollander denies that Bloom's criticism is psychoanalytic (xvi). Bloom himself denies he gives an "Oedipal interpretation of poetic history" (25 *PR*), because he is not studying the mind, nor the unconscious, but a kind of labor--the poetic. Nevertheless, Bloom's use of Freud and Kabbalah is more than an illustrative device. It is a way he can understand and explain the genuine poetic processes. He wrote an entire book on Kabbalah, and several essays on Freud. If these two external fields merely provided illustrations, not so much attention would have been devoted to them--certainly not such quantity of writing and references as Bloom did devote. Bloom's action is a kind of avoidance as when we seek help from the wrong muscles when we exercise to decrease effort. Partly, Bloom is not to blame. If the critic has the purpose of explaining Russian to someone who knows none, then almost inevitably another language is used. However, making this explanation does not increase the critic's or translator's understanding of the way the meaning is built up specifically in Russian; such understanding would be assumed in the explanatory process. Bloom used Freud and Kabbalah as a means to explain and he seems to have forgotten that doing so assumes more knowledge than he could actually have gotten by concentrating solely on the poetic explanation of poetry.

There is no proof of the progress in poetry. The revisionary ratios are never presented from merely poetic relations of images. Why is one passage poetically better than or "prior" to a preceding one? Why is one productive of a former one? This progress is always described in terms of typology, taking the text in discreet units. The explanations are illustrations, not deductions.

De Man notices that Bloom discusses poetry from a "love-hate point of view" rather than "the perspective of its truth or falsehood" (272 Review of *AI*). He states that difficult passages are presented as if they spoke for themselves in *The Anxiety of Influence*.

Almost no discussion is devoted to what constitutes progress. In rare passages he mentions increased "innerness," and a self yet more inward (61 *PR*, 105 *AI*). In Derrida's philosophy a lot of attention is paid to establishing the greater coherence of the new principle of difference. The changes in the idea of the philosophical tradition are explained at length.

Bloom's misreading seems to ignore the development of new advances by regarding the tradition as some sense reversible. While some poets re-envisioned the previous poetry so that it could never be seen the same by them again, this decision of poetic right, poetic superiority is ignored by Bloom, who can understand a predecessor in a way undistorted by the successor. Doing so suggests that the change in interpretation is arbitrary, not poetically necessary.[5]

Anyone reading many of Bloom's works must be struck by the scarcity of normative judgments. Sometimes it seems as if Bloom avoids making a judgment, as when he speaks of "Pound's unending match with Browning" (12 *AI*). For whom is the match unending? Is there no decision about the victor? Shouldn't the critic tell us? The negative prefixes help Bloom to fence-sit between any two great poetries, not judging that the second is better. A fence-sitting position may partially be above either poet's position (71 *AI*), as if the critic were speaking about more important matters than either great poet; these matters would be the critic's model, the six revisionary ratios. A characteristic example of Bloom's ambiguous lack of judgment and superiority occurs when he writes, "...we need Milton, and not the Romantic return of the repressed Milton but the Milton who made his great poem identical with the process of repression that is vital to literary tradition. But a resistance even in myself is set up..." (37 *MM*).

While speaking about the origin of "misprision" and "misreading," Hollander defends the idea as "an appropriateness beyond correctness" (xlii). A better defence of Bloom's usage would be to point out that the successor may feel as if it is a mistake to change the predecessor because he is so great; Bloom calls Wordsworth's poem an angel with whom Shelley wrestles (149 *MM*). Within the term a paradox may be contained: the paradox that the predecessor was right but that it is not the right path to follow and so must be construed differently. At least to this degree, Bloom's "misreading" and "misprision" is quite clever and even profound.

A greater value, however, is blocked by the negative prefixes. The usage blocks the need for going into more depth about the nature of improvement and the unique poetic meaning of each individual great poet while allowing Bloom to concentrate on the mechanics of his own critical model. Normative critical judgments are severely lacking (88 *PR*), perhaps because the critic would have to take a stand, enter the poetic process, and explain poetic superiority. In one rare passage Bloom describes what is gained in poetic evolution: "To appropriate the precursor's landscape for himself, the ephebe [the new great poet] must estrange it further from himself. To attain a self yet more inward than the precursor's, the ephebe..." (105 *AI*). Increasing inwardness, perhaps depth of sensitivity or power of expressibility, is gained. Elsewhere he states that the poet completes his greater poetic perspective when he shows how his predecessor's lines or images can be derived from him. The relations described by Bloom are brilliantly correct in general, but in particualr the specific meaning of the improvement in each case is not discussed. Bloom avoided doing so.

In "Tradition and the Individual Talent" Eliot wrote about an increase in consciousness that poetry brings about. Readers of Bloom's criticism cannot see an explanation of these increases in each movement toward new poetry, even though this is of greater significance than yet another example defending Bloom's model. The model begins to take on a value of its own, replacing that of the poetry.

What would proof in literary scholarship be? The Russian Formalists discussed this idea in ways relevant to Bloom's critical practice. For them "literature is a `pure form' with no (or almost no) relation to extra-literary reality, and therefore can be regarded as a `series' which derives its forms from itself" (257 Todorov *Poetics of Prose*). Literary proof is showing how the forms, each successive body of literary works derives from the tradition. This proof is literarily represented within literature. Yury Tynyanov and V.V. Vinogradov are "much more concerned to discover the motivation, the internal justification of one element or another within a work, than to note its recurrence elsewhere" (Ibid.). Bloom tends to note the recurrence of each brilliant ratio without proving the specific right of each new formulation by a poet. The general form of the poetic argument is conveyed with confidence; the specific argument for this poet's clinamen or whatever ratio is undeveloped.

In other terms, Bloom does offer much evidence to prove the existence of a pattern of poetry, whereas he does not offer convincing evidence to prove the specific differences, the changing definitions of the ratios from poet to poet. The theory of the anxiety of influence shows the a priori status of poetic patterns, not the differences between the patterns in successive poetries; Bloom is more concerned with the similarity. Art historian Heinrich Wölfflin points to the place where proof would come into play:

> And when we speak of the progress of imitation, of the new impressions of nature which an epoch produced, that is also a material element which is bound to *a priori* forms of representation. The observations of the seventeenth century were not merely woven into the fabric of Cinquecento art. The whole

> groundwork changed. It is a mistake for art history to work with the clumsy notion of the imitation of nature, as though it were merely a homogeneous process of increasing perfection. ...The imitative content, the subject matter, may be as different in itself as possible, the decisive point remains that the conception in each case is based on a different visual schema [recall Kuhn's ideas of a scientific world view and disciplinary matrix]--a schema which, however, is far more deeply rooted than in mere questions of the progress of imitation. ...This volume is occupied with the discussion of these universal forms of representation...the mode of perception which lies at the root of the representative arts in various centuries (13).

Proof in art history concerns the change of groundwork, the change from one schema to another, each successive one re-defining the mode of perception of the art. Applied to Bloom (and also to Kuhn), this passage suggests the most important point where proof is needed: to justify a change in the fundamental schema of an art, a body of literature, a scientific theory, a philosophy; to justify the new step in tradition. Bloom's account is too general.

The extent of the lack of proof is the extent of the lack of knowledge of poetic processes. If criticism is inevitably abstraction, this reduction in meaning is inevitable. One could not blame criticism for doing only what it can do, but at the same time one can look for ways to bring criticism closer to creation. Abstraction in interpretation, according to Lyotard, results from a separation of "the production of knowledge" from its "transmission" (53 *Postmodern*). Applied to Bloom's criticism, it can be deepened by following more closely the ever-changing means of producing poetry. A theory should change with the changes of the new forms.

Illusory Idea of "Control" Over Tradition

Bloom believed less in the control of literature than Kuhn did in science. Kuhn's ideas on this theme are relevant for, although he does not think the scientists know all the traits to be preserved from the old framework, still Kuhn knows the processes at work in all scientific revolutions. The critic's control over literature is equally a displacement, spurious substitute for the control creators have in the process. Something like Freudian introjection characterizes the attitude toward control. What critics think the creator has but is denied to them is transformed into what they think they have but the creator does not. Partially, Bloom's sense of the control of literature by criticism has been introduced in the discussion of hubris.

Whatever control anyone, critic or creator, could have over the literary process depends on its regularity. Control means ability to change the direction combined with the ability to understand fully. The control organisms have over their existence has been defined by Monod with the idea of teleonymy. This principle of the survival and reproduction of the species applies to all features of the organism contributing to this end. It is a goal because all structures, all functions serve to realize that end, just as all revisionary ratios serve to complete one quest. Throughout the evolution of the species, the ability of the organism to survive and to reproduce is enhanced; there is a change in the "teleonomic level" (14-15). Monod can define this level according to "the quantity of information which, on the average and per individual, must be transferred to assure the generation-to-generation transmission of the specific content of reproductive invariance." The organism is limited in development to levels. There are limits to the degree as well as the type of change.

So too with poetry. Poetries develop in discrete steps, levels, as Bloom so expertly helped to bring to the attention of critics. The question is, does Bloom define differences in teleonomic level? Does he state why one poetry is superior to its predecessor? A more intensive definition of the differences would deepen Bloom's knowledge.

The issue of control over cultural forms is a problem within the form itself. Bloom notices that poets try to escape the influence (control) of the precursor and instead to influence (control). Clear early examples date back to Homer and Hesiod. Both their cosmogenic myths end in ambiguities concerning the freedom and fate of human beings.

> At one time fate is a power with unlimited sway over men and gods and the will of fate is searched out and executed by Zeus with the other Gods (*Iliad* xix, 87; *Oddyssey*, xxi, 413); at another, Zeus is called the highest ruler of destinies; or again, he and the other gods can change the course of fate (*Iliad*, xvi, 434), and even men can exceed the limits it imposes (*Iliad*, xx, 336). In Hesiod, they are called in one passage (*Theogeny* 211-17) daughters of night and sisters of the goddesses of death (Kires), while in another (*Theogeny*, 211-17) they are the daughters of Zeus and Themis and sisters of the Horae, who give good and bad fortunes to mortals at their birth" (1051 *Harper's Dictionary of Classical Antiquities*).

Tradition forms must repeat a pattern in a new way. Concerning this general requirement there can be no exception. Individual freedom comes into play insofar as the indivdual can choose to bring the new pattern into being, not to mention the freedom of secondary variations in the form which do not affect its essential meaning. In poetry those variations would be possible differences of themes, settings, images, metres; in mathematics Leibniz's calculus differed from Newton's primarily in the symbolization; otherwise, the discovery was simultaneous.

Bloom seeks some control over the creative processes, for he can see what the creators cannot. What he sees, however, is spurious; it does not directly promote creation. A creator cannot have the control over the developing form that Bloom purports to give. The critic thinks he has full knowledge of the total form created by a poet. Bloom's map of misreading with its six ratios is just such a defined total form. The matrix of a poetry, also called the imaginative space or the total form, is something the poet works toward without at the beginning having full knowledge. The first discovery is the lack of poetic unity in the precursor's work; the need for a new type, synthesized from what came before. Then knowledge of the goal which the poet works toward changes throughout the process. At each stage the new creator re-envisions the total form of what a poetry should be. And at the closing of the poetry, the ambivalent poetic acts make a paradox preventing the form from being seen even by the creator as a simple completed unity. The critic, however, has more confidence, albeit unwarranted, when defining the total form. (S)He can see the total project of the poet. In contrast the poet sees the poetry indefinitely extendible into the future. The poet's situation resembles Zeus'. Was the poet destined to make just that form? Or, was that form the result of individual invention? Was Oedipus destined to fulfill the oracle or did he choose the path leading him to it?

A critic might better give up some control of the total form in order to gain the power to create: a more genuine type of control in the process. Stating the idea that a creator develops toward an end not entirely in his/her control, Derrida writes,

> My interest...continued to relate to the same question: how is it that philosophy finds itself inscribed rather than inscribing itself, within a space which it seeks but is unable to control... How is one to name the structure of this space? I do not *know*; nor do I know whether there can be what may be called *knowledge* of such a space (45 *Philosophy in France Today*. Ed. Alan Montefiore. Cambridge).

Though Derrida denies knowledge of his own philosophical space, this does not mean he cannot understand the space of his predecessor in a degree greater than the predeceesor, a degree adequate to create. Bloom's knowledge of any figure is not adequate to create, for it is of a different type, being related to all poetries in the same way. To create one must give up this control over the tradition, to enter into a specific relation so that the transference of the heritage may occur, thus in return gaining power within it to extend it.

Under-developed Conception of Form

Bloom has an underdeveloped conception of poetic form in four main ways: (1) not fully realizing that a form intends or means another one; (2) not limiting interpretation rhetorically; (3) not orienting the discussion sufficiently historically; (4) not finding an internal criterion of poetic legitimacy (legitimacy tends to come through psychology or other fields besides poetry).

Rather than intending a model, a poetry intends or means another poetry. In "The Breaking of Form" Bloom claims poems break the form of tradition in order to bring about meaning (1 *DC*). He does not draw this idea to its logical conclusions, however, as Victor Shklovsky does when he writes about Sterne, pointing out how the "consciousness of form" results from its "violation" (149). This view resembles Bloom's along general lines, but it differs in emphasizing the building upon the past. If Bloom drew the logical conclusion, he would deny criticism the possession of the proper meaning unless it too broke tradition. Shklovsky's view makes Sterne the best critic of his predecessor.

The proper criticism of any cultural text requires the creation of a new text. Concerning philosophy, Lyotard makes this point: "No need to criticize metaphysics...since such criticism presupposes and continually recreates that very theatricality [of the representation which tries to recover the `thing'--D.V.], better to be inside and forget it" (282 *Theory Culture Society*). The fullest meaning only can be obtained by transmitting the poetry through another one. Lyotard discusses at length the essential function of narratives to transmit tradition, preparing the way for the future. "What matters in the transmission of these narratives, in the repetition of their narrational etiquette, is to tell while being a relay; it is to be the (traditional) bearer of the narrative because, in the simple fact of relaying something, there is precisely something that gets forgottten" (34 *Just Gaming*). And one page later, "...I am obligated in the way of a relay that may not keep its charge but must pass it on" (35).

As the second way in which the conception of form is underdeveloped, Bloom does not fully appreciate the rhetorical situation of the predecessor and the successor in relation to one another. He thinks the later poet, as opposed to the critic, has an idealization of superiority that is false. If it is false, then how does poetry make any progress? The map of misreading is more synchronic than a genetic code. Bloom does not realize that the situation of the successor is rhetorically different from that of the predecessor. The successor's product is not limited to what the precursor's is. To paraphrase an idea of Lyotard, `the precursor approaches the end of his/her poetry from one side and knows his/her way about; the successor approaches the same place from another side and no longer knows the way about' (351 *LR*). If each poet is bound to a predecessor, symbiotically transforming his/her work, still each is not bound to the *same* predecessor. Consequently, the limit on development foreshadowed by the point of origin is different in each case. A successor can see more than the predecessor because it is as if the successor can start on the same step as the predecessor [for (s)he accumulates the whole tradition] and move to one higher step, thanks to the former. The theory of the anxiety of influence does not place Bloom in such a serial rhetorical relation to the poets discussed, unlike the philosophy of Derrida.

The conception of poetic form is underdeveloped historically. Derrida requires that for the most determinate thought the terms one chooses be oriented in a specific historical position.

> If words and concepts receive meaning only in sequences of differences, one can justify one's language, and one's choice of terms, only within a topic (an orientation in space) and an historical strategy. The justification can therefore never be absolute and definitive. It corresponds to a condition of forces and translates an historical calculation (69-70 *OG*).

Bloom's terms, unlike Derrida's, do not take their historical place after the poetries discussed; the terms are to some degree indifferent in their meaning to a historical, unique case.

Finally, Bloom's conception of form lacks an internal criterion of poetic legitimacy. Partially, the mere reproduction of the map in one's own poetry legitimates it. A problem arises though. If successive poetries change the rules of poetry, however slightly, then poetry-making becomes slightly re-conceived in each new step in tradition. That is what the phrase `a step in tradition' would imply. The changes of tradition cannot occur without good reasons if an improvement is being made. A critic should find the reasons within the text, as a scholar of science should; "the interpretation is included within the texture of the narrative" (123, Todorov, *Poetics of Prose*). Bloom does admirably emphasize the relational meaning of all poetry to past poetry, yet the relations are not justified in each particular case, for each poet; they are merely illustrated, explained. To the extent that any justification occurs, it is of Bloom's critical terms, not the superior relation of this poet's work to the predecessor's.

Criticism as a Lesser Understanding Than Poetry

In a saying of Wittgenstein, `You cannot hear God speaking to others; you can only hear Him if He speaks to you' (333 *LR*). If poetry is to be anagogical as Bloom claims, if it presents an ultimate vision of imaginative poetic finality, then any vision not in this form is not ultimate. The critic is unlike the strong poet "who will not tolerate words that intervene between him and the Word, or precursors standing between him and the Muse" (10 *PR*). Does this imply strong poets cannot tolerate critics?

Whereas criticism dissimulates its activity, making itself superior to what it is trying to explain, actually it has less knowledge. The attempt to find a principle of creation before actually creating a great poetry is somewhat misguided. If a new poetry forges a new sense of poetry, even only slightly different, then the former framework must change and cannot serve as an exact mold for reproduction. The new principles cannot simply be invented before the process occurs to replace the prior one. Arguing for this idea of creation, Derrida agrees with Condillac:

> `Thus in calculating will we learn to calculate, as in speaking we learned to speak. We would live a long time before knowing our language, or we would never even know it, if we wanted to speak only after having each time consulted our grammar. Nature does not instruct us that way: what it wants to teach us it makes us do... .I am not supposed to make these signs known to them [the beginners]: they are supposed to see the signs in what they know, and I answer them that they will discover these signs'.[6]

Consulting a grammar before speaking is not entirely unlike Bloom's referring to his model before interpreting any poetry. If nature makes us do what it teaches us, then the teaching of a poetry is to make new great poetry, not to make critical models. All in all, this passage points to one conclusion not fully understood by critics: the principle of creation may not be in the past but in the future, to be found only after the operation is complete as its explanation or principle of unity. All development before the end is a provisional understanding of what comes only at the end. It follows that the process of one's predecessor is not fully understood until the closing of one's own succeeding poetry. This conclusion, too, runs counter to a primary assumption of criticism that the understanding should precede, not follow, creation.

In one last main but crucial way Bloom's understanding of poetry is less than Derrida's understanding of philosophy. Derrida sees each new main philosophical concept as defining the act producing the previous concepts. When the act is understood, a new concept has taken the former's place of precedence. Then the former concept has subordinate significance [hence the term "hierarchy" for the relation of main figures in a tradition form]. The act of producing becomes visible; it is as if mind sees the whole of its workings--almost (148 *SP*). The idea sounds much like the Russian Formalist idea that the consciousness of form occurs through its violation, through overcoming it. Bloom's corresponding idea is weaker. Creation is a re-seeing what the precursor had seen, not a new seeing of the way the precursor was seeing (16 *PR*).

A Stronger Sense of the Genetic Encoding of Poetry Is Needed

Some ways in which Bloom's theory treats poetry as having a genetic code have already been mentioned. To summarize, the map of misreading defines a specific structural standard that recurs in each successive canonical poetry. [Kuhn lacked the idea of a specific structural standard of science, a term ironically from genetics to help explain relative biological invariance.] The form as described by Bloom becomes complete when it has the main features of the previous poetry and, although Bloom does not like to emphasize this, the poetry would also provide the pattern for a succeeding poetry. DNA, too, is a structure that makes a second structure that can in turn produce a third structure of the same general type. That the series can continue into the third generation suggests that it can continue indefinitely. All tradition forms create such a universal order for the environment of the individual mind. Just as the generations of DNA are directly linked, Bloom considers a poetry to be related to its precursor in a direct, specific parent-to-child or one-to-one relation. Finally, like DNA, a poetry develops to maturity by a process of internal replication, each ratio serving as a mold for the formation of an antithetical complement, and since the next development is itself a ratio, the previous structure is to some extent replicated, though not identically.

But the anxiety of influence could become better if it treated poetry even more like a genetic code. Though the map of misreading with its six ratios does function like the genetic code in those key ways just mentioned, it is too synchronic: it is almost a code that is identically repeated, a limiting feature of Bloom's criticism illustrated in Figure 13-1 on page 428. Critics after Bloom should define form more dynamically.

Derrida discusses his own philosophy very dynamically. The supplement or pharmakon marks "sites of passage," meaning it is not a closing, a stopping of what came before (40 *POS*). There is a variation in the dialectic of any concept. The supplement constantly generates new ones interlocked with its nature; an infinite chain is necessary. The supplement [as simulacrum] "...must be understood as a force--of an identity that is ceaselessly dislocated, displaced, thrown outside itself..." (326 *DS*). The supplement is virtually a synecdochal representation of the whole philosophy: "the moving structure of the play as a whole...and its total account in process of formation" (325).

The Russian Formalist Yury Tynyanov considers form to be through and through dynamic.

> The unity of the work is not a closed, symmetrical whole, but an unfolding, dynamic whole. Its elements are not static indications of equality and complexity, but always dynamic indications of correlation and integration. The form of literary works must be thought of as dynamic.[7]

Figure 13-1: Bloom's Insufficiently Cyclical Definition of a Poetry

A. A Representation of How a Poetry Is Insufficiently Cyclical

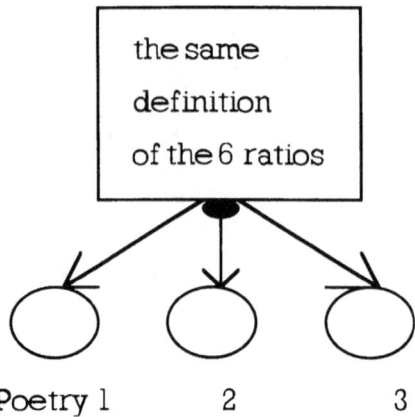

The meaning of clinamen for Bloom is not limited within a cycle but extends throughout all poetries conceived as cycles.

B. A Recommended Alternative to Bloom's Unchanging Poetic Cycle

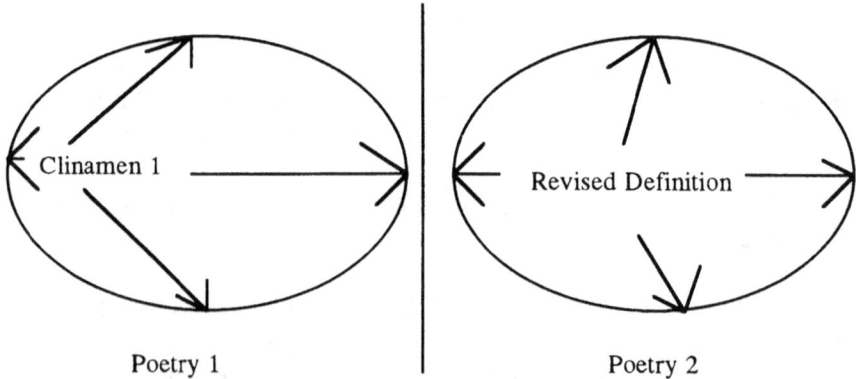

The most determinate definition of a recurring poetic figure would situate it within a specific body of work. The definition of meta-concepts (Bloom's revisionary ratios) must be case-bound, limited.

Bloom does tend to regard a poetry as a closed symmetrical whole. And although he explains the building of it, a completed poetry seems to have a fixed definition as if a static object of perception. The revisionary ratios in being ambivalent are dialectical standpoints, yet they are not described as moving structures, shifting within a complex of contents, as Derrida's supplement is. Had the ratios been regarded more dynamically, their irreducible uniqueness would have been more important to discover.

At the end of a poetry, at the revisionary ratio called apophrades, the poet has a double standard toward the past and the future. The past is subordinated to the new poet who cannot in turn become subordinated by the future. The passages in the poetry express this double attitude. This tension is a kind of dynamism in the sense Cassirer used: cultural forms have a tension provoking a striving for equilibrium which points to a new instance of the form (260, *The Philosophy of Symbolic Forms*, II).

Everyone--even critics--are limited to steps of tradition. Wölfflin expresses this idea: "the most powerful individual talent has only been able to win from it a definite form of expression, which does not rise very far above general possibilities" (226). In contrast to Bloom, in that passage the art historian emphasizes the "change of the form of beholding," whereas Bloom maintained the synchronic identity of the map of misreading. "...Beholding is not just a mirror which always remains the same, but a living power of apprehension which has its own inward history and has passed through many stages." No poet can transcend poetry; he can only transcend a precursor's work.[8]

Even though any individual is limited to a step in tradition, it is a step forward. What makes each successive poetry a step forward is by no means clear. The theory of the anxiety of influence does present any poetry as a step in tradition, in the manner of Eliot when he writes, "And we do not quite say that the new [poetry] is more valuable because it fits in; but its fitting in is a test of its value" (2208 "Tradition and the Individual Talent"). But why is one poet's use of clinamen better than the previous poet's approach? Bloom does not say. The explanation of increased value is not an integral part of the theory of the anxiety of influence.

The theory of the anxiety of influence has insufficient realization of the transvaluative feature of cultural genetic codes making them more developed than the biological. Transvaluation occurs between forms as well as within forms (poetries). It occurs when the previous processes of mind become objects of consciousness as a new mode of making poetry comes into being. Derrida has a clearer idea of this necessary feature; he expresses it as the act of production becoming visible in *Of Grammatology* while originating difference from differance. Griffiths and Rabinowitz in *Novel Epics* call this process of transvaluation "epic ecphrasis" [epic "expression" in modern Greek] (28). At such points the whole of the previous tradition becomes represented by a new poetic process showing its limited aesthetic vision. Then "the tradition itself steps forward to guide the seeker" (28).

Shklovsky advanced "the principle of perceptible form as the specific sign of artistic awareness": "If we have to define specifically `poetic' perception and artistic perception in general, then we suggest this definition: `Artistic' perception is that perception in which we experience form--perhaps not form alone, but certainly form."[9] The form of which Shklovsky speaks is the form of the predecessor's creative processes which, though they could not become fully explicit to the precursor, can become known and at the same time improved upon so new processes begin to take shape. It is also true to speak of the form as the disciplinary matrix, in Kuhn's terms. Instead of an abstract statement, Bakhtin gives a specific case to present his similar concept of the dialogical nature of literary tropes:

> Even in the earliest `Gogolian period' of his literary career, Dostoevsky is already depicting not the `poor government clerk' but the *self-consciousness* of the poor clerk (Devushkin, Golyadkin, even Prokharchin). That which was presented in Gogol's field of vision as an aggregate of objective features, coalescing in a firm socio-characterological profile of the hero, is introduced by Dostoevsky into the field of vision of the hero himself and there becomes the object of his agonizing self-awareness; even the very physical appearance of the `poor clerk', described by Gogol, Dostoevsky forces his hero to contemplate in the mirror. And thanks to this fact all the concrete features of the hero, while remaining fundamentally

unchanged in content, are transferred from one plane of representation to another, and thus acquire completely different artistic significance...(48 *Problems of Dostoevsky's Poetics*).

A similar thought has been voiced by mythologists, the Frankforts, who wrote, mythical imagery "represents the form in which the experience has become conscious".[10] Bloom lacks a sense of the greater consciousness of the previous form during the transference of the pattern of poetry. With DNA improvement may or may not occur. With poetry and all `tradition forms' the improvement is built into the process.

Summary

While Bloom develops a very penetrating theory of poetry--actually leading the entire field, I have emphasized the drawbacks so that some readers might be able to do even better than Bloom. The extended interest in his theory demonstrated by this book should be a statement about its worth. Still, there are definite drawbacks. Though he believes models are necessary, he is aware of their necessary reduction of meaning. His criticism is fundamentalist, a problem critics in general have. As another drawback, he does not fully realize the *collective* meaning of poetic progress, usually presenting it as personal competition. In addition there are a few unproductive features of the psychology or method of his criticism. More difficult to surmount--perhaps insurmountable, the non-idiomatic or non-poetic language he uses sets a limit on poetic understanding since he himself does not use the form of poetry when evaluating it. He fails to "inhabit the structures" he overturns, to use a common phrase of Derrida's, and as a result his discourse does not overturn any poetry. In general he does not use proof enough, not entering into poetic justification, nor directly presenting that of the poets; he presents only the location and the fact and the mechanism of a poet's step ahead. The critic-theorist claims for himself an illusory, dissimulated idea of control over tradition, something all critics seem to do. On a larger perhaps more abstract scale, his conception of form is underdeveloped, but it could be better if his followers develop a stronger sense of the genetic encoding of poetry. Bloom's theory does treat a poetry as having a "genetic code", which he calls a "map of misreading," but this innovative critical model is in the end too synchronic.

NOTES

1. Quoted from 287 *WD*. The original is from *The Raw and the Cooked*, trans. John and Doreen Wightman (New York: Harper and Row, 1969), p.2.

2. Quoted from 93 of Lyotard's *Differend*. The original is from the German edition of Hegel's *Science of Logic*, abbreviated *WL*, 54.

3. See Lyotard's discussion of legitimation through the next step in tradition: 153 and 321 *Lyotard Reader*.

4. Quoted from Harvey, 24, *Derrida and the Economy of Difference*. The idea is translated by Harvey from *Positions* (Paris: Editions de Minuit, 1972), p. 129. For more about intervention see 329 of *Margins of Philosophy*.

5. See A-J Greimas. "Structure et histoire." *Les Temps Modernes* No. 246 (Nov. 1966), 815-27. Greimas theorized that accounts of human structures should be able to formulate the "irreversibility" of transformations. I adapted this idea to the present book.

6. Quoted from 101 *AF*. The original is from Condillac's *La Langue des calculs* in *Oeuvres Philosophiques de Condillac*, Ed. Georges Le Roy. Corpus Général des Philosophes Français. Paris: Presses Universitaires de France, 1947-51, II, p. 425.

7. Quoted from p. 130 of Boris Eichenbaum's "The Theory of the `Formal Method'," in Lemon and Reis, *Russian Formalist Criticism*. The original comes from *The Problem of Poetic Language*, Leningrad, 1924. It may be difficult to find a translation from Russian.

8. For a similar idea see Baudrillard's *Critique of the Political Economy of the Sign*, 156, note 9.

9. Quoted from p. 112 of Eichenbaum's essay in Lemon and Reis' translated anthology. The original is in *Voskresheniye slova* (Petersburg, 1914), p. 11 ff.

10. Quoted from p. 3 of *SM*. The original is from p. 22 of *Before Philosophy*, London, Penguin, 1949.

Chapter 14:
Judging Derrida's Theory

Derrida Explains Tradition More Than Kuhn and Bloom Do, by Making a New Genetic Code of Philosophy

Introduction to the Judging of Derrida's Theory of Tradition

Derrida's philosophy ranks as a better theory of tradition than either Kuhn's or Bloom's. His original work can provide answers to questions left unanswered in the other theories. For example, Derrida can explain the change of perspective by a successor in logical, determinate terms whereas Kuhn used vague wholistic terms and Bloom used emotive, psychoanalytical terms. See the end of Chapter 1 for other good features of Derrida's theory (called grammatology).

Unlike Kuhn's or Bloom's theory, Derrida's philosophy ends in a dilemma unsolvable on the terms of his philosophy, this issue being the most difficult for the understanding of his entire contribution but still the most worthwhile for assessing it. This does not mean he made a mistake at one point to be corrected, nor does it mean he has not been successful at all. The dilemma is a paradox serving to point to a negative presupposition not known by Derrida but orienting his entire philosophy, in the manner of a perspective point outside the frame of drawn objects, discussed in connection with the start of Derrida's philosophy. In order for philosophical form to be regular--to have a definite determinate nature, the way the closing concept, the supplement, functions to signal the end of the system must echo the role of Sartre's closing concept and that of all canonical philosophies in the Western tradition. And it does. Figure 14-1 on page 437 suggests Derrida's success in joining the Western philosophical canon, but more generally to readers from other fields this figure suggests the necessary regularity of cultural forms if they are to form a tradition, this regularity being tantamount to some kind of genetic code. Difficult as it may be to understand the dilemma of the supplement, a full understanding could only come from the standpoint of a new philosophical concept, to be suggested in the "Epilogue."

Problem of the Imprint vs the Form

Derrida himself considers the supplement to be regulated by supplementarity, "the contradictory unity of a desire" (245 *OG*). The contradiction lends to the desire an infinity. The unity of the supplement can never be accomplished fully; it is an "ideal limit" (197 *OG*). [This term was used by Cassirer for the closing concept of his philosophy; see Vol. III of *The Philosophy of Symbolic Forms*, the final pages.]

The supplement ironically functions like Sartre's self-cause (the ideal fusion of the in-itself-for-itself, also called the ideal presence of the ens causa sui). As was explained in the chapter on the closing of Derrida's philosophy, any supplement needs a future supplement to complete its being, to provide its unity. And this priority of one supplement over another parallels the priority of the supplement over Derrida's "differance" and "difference."

Two Horns of the Supplement's Dilemma

"...The supplement...harbors within itself two significations whose cohabitation is as strange as it is necessary" (144 *OG*).

Since the problem is quite difficult to apprehend, an analogy to introduce the problem would be helpful. The supplement causes a logical dilemma, a double bind of two horns, each one leading to a contradiction. "The second signification of the supplement cannot be separated from the first" (145 *OG*). Imagistically, the two horns, the

Figure 14-1: Derrida's Philosophy Belongs in the Canon; This Means It Is One Step Forward in Tradition, Like Many Previous Such Steps

Twentieth Century Philosophy

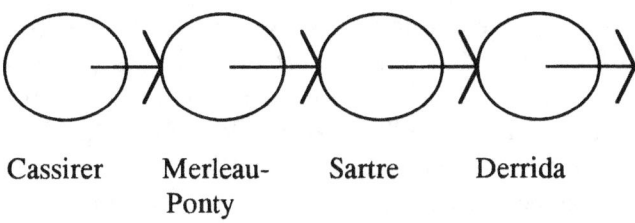

Cassirer   Merleau-   Sartre   Derrida
            Ponty

Before the Twentieth Century

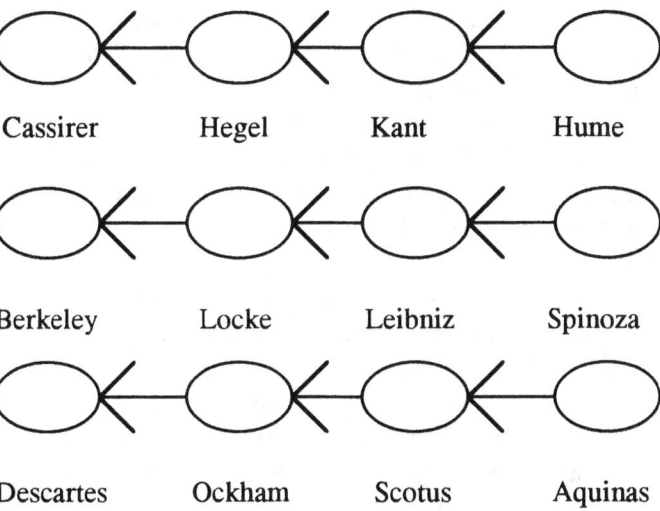

Cassirer   Hegel   Kant   Hume

Berkeley   Locke   Leibniz   Spinoza

Descartes   Ockham   Scotus   Aquinas

And this list of canonical figures extends to figures before Homer.

two problems caused by the split nature of the concept resemble two train rails extending to the horizon on the flat earth. They seem to a person to converge. However, someone much further along the tracks, perhaps at the terminus of the line where the tracks end, would see that they never did come together. It was an illusion made by the formation of a horizon.

The supplement was initially defined to have two aspects. On the one hand, it adds itself to a previous sign (supplement). On the other hand, it adds itself only to replace the previous one; "if it fills, it is as if one fills a void" (144-45 *OG*). Whether it adds or substitutes, the supplement is exterior, outside of the positivity to which it is super-added, alien to that which, in order to be replaced by it, must be other than it. The exteriority in this way just described was necessary to avoid the problem of infinite differance.

Quite valuable to notice well, Derrida writes as if something is wrong. The sense of dissatisfaction with the supplement reappears in many ways. It is described as "an evil" with the form of "representative alienation" (296 *OG*). Also, many expressions indicate an entropy of meaning caused by the concepts he developed, as has been mentioned. Difference, for example, has the power to modify life less and less as it extends its range of development. Writing tends to become the dead writing of abstract signs.

In some passages the supplement seems not to be able to accomplish much, though it was necessary to posit.

> The work of exclusion operates within the structure of supplementarity. The paradox is that one annuls addition by considering it a pure addition. *What is added is nothing because it is added to a full presence to which it is exterior.* Speech comes to be added to intuitive presence (of the entity, of *essence*, of the *eidos*, of *ousia*, and so forth); writing comes to be added to living self-present speech...(167 *OG*)

Here it does not seem that the supplement adds anything to what came before. And also, "its place is assigned in the structure by the mark of an emptiness" (145 *OG*).

The two horns of a dilemma develop from the two significations originally defining the supplement. On the one hand, "the supplement adds itself, it is a surplus, a plenitude enriching another plenitude, the *fullest measure* of presence. It cumulates and accumulates presence. On the other hand, the supplement

> "adds only to replace. It intervenes or insinuates itself *in-the-place-of*; if it fills, it is as if one fills a void. If it represents and makes an image, it is by the anterior default of a presence. Compensatory [suppléant] and vicarious, the supplement is an adjunct, a subaltern instance which *takes-(the)-place* [tient-lieu]. As substitute, it is not simply added to the positivity of a presence, it produces no relief, its place is assigned in the structure by the mark of an emptiness (144-45 *OG*).

The Supplement Becomes Further Integrated into the Ideas of Supplementarity and the Festival

The two aspects of differance become related in a new way in the concept of the supplement. Differance became problematic for Derrida when he considered the consequences of its tendency to become infinite (see the earlier chapter on this topic). To avoid those problems, differance had to be capable of some change within itself. This needed change is the exteriority of one supplement to another one.

Differance is both the "formation of form" and "the being imprinted of the imprint" (63 *OG*). "Imprint" refers to the sensible representation of any thing--its visual, auditory, olfactory, tactile qualities. "Form" refers to the relations synthesizing any thing into a unity.

The supplement develops these two enclaves of any thing further; it integrates them. The two halves of differance are integrated into a new concept combining those halves in each of its parts. They become more interdependent in the two significations of the supplement mentioned above. On the one hand, when the supplement adds to what came before, it adds itself as a surplus, as a plenitude to another plenitude, suggesting that it is not needed after all. The difference between two successive supplements--and there must be if development is to occur--would be sensory, but the underlying form would be univocal. The sensory difference would have a unity of nonsensory relations. This would be like one form for two blurred imprints, to use the terms introduced in the discussion of differance. Speaking of one of the significations of the supplement in this way shows it to be a further integration of differance.

On the other hand, when the supplement replaces, it is a substitute that "produces no relief," that serves as the mark of an emptiness" (144-45). Here, the difference between two successive supplements is nonsensory, is more a result of different forms or sets of relations for a common identical sensory imprint. Again, the two enclaves of differance become more integrated in the concept of the supplement. Now imprint and form, the sensory and the conceptual aspects of any reality, are more complexly related than before. (Harvey notices a problem concerning imprint and form. See 178 *Derrida and the Economy of Differance*).

The Paradox of the Festival as a Problem of Imprint vs. Form

Just as the supplement further integrated differance, or even more parallel--just as `infinite' differance integrated differance to some degree, so too the supplement becomes further integrated in the idea of the character common to two successive supplements in a series: supplementarity, the origin of the supplementary structure or of an individual supplement (255 *OG*). The necessity of the chain or series has been discussed. Derrida tries to lessen the effect of duality caused by the difference of two supplements, or the difference of the two halves of any supplement. The two aspects are referred to as the "theorem" and the "theatre" (302 ff. *OG*). The "theorem" refers to the formal emphasis of the supplement, when it expresses the unity of sensory differences between supplements. The "theatre" refers to the sensible features of a supplement, when some sensible representation (imprint) serves as the unity of the difference of relations between two supplements. To express the unity of the two aspects of the supplement in the new features of supplementarity, the unity of the theorem and the theatre, Derrida writes, there is a "theatre without representation" or "a stage without a show"; "visibility--a moment ago the theorem, here the theatre--is always that which, separating it from itself, breaches [*entame*] the living voice" (306 *OG*).

The unity of the theorem and the theatre of experience, the unity of the conceptual and the sensory, the most degree of unity for the imprint and the form is what he calls "the public festival":

> But what is a stage which presents nothing to the sight? It is the place where the spectator, presenting himself as spectacle, will no longer be either seer [*voyant*] or voyeur, will efface within himself the difference between the actor and the spectator, the represented and the representer, the object seen and the seeing subject. With that difference, an entire series of oppositions will deconstitute themselves one by one. Presence will be full, not as an object which is *present* to be seen, to give itself to intuition as an empirical unity or as an *eidos* holding itself *in front of or up against*; it will be full as the intimacy of a self-presence, as the consciousness or the sentiment of self-proximity, of self-sameness [propriéte]. That public festival will therefore have a form analogous to the electoral meetings of a free and legiferant assembled people: the representative differance will be effaced in the self-presence of sovereignty (306 *OG*).

This concept of the public festival functions in Derrida's philosophy like apophrades does in poetry, according to Bloom's theory. It is a single expression for the duality present in askesis of the first ratio of the close of a poetry. Of course, whereas Bloom's idea is generic to all poetries, the public festival is defined more determinately as just this one case of a closing concept.

The "representative differance" crucial in that passage refers to the problem of explaining a change within the nature of differance as it is extended into infinity, as it develops knowledge. How can Derrida explain the change in differance, its re-presentation? The two functions performed by the idea of the public festival, this advanced form of the supplement, are to explain how Derrida's differance could differ from what "differance" may be attributed to the precursor, being inferior to Derrida's differance. With respect to the future, the public festival explains how the supplement can be added on to by philosophers after Derrida, but at the same time since they also use supplements, they never outdate his work. His work remains valid forever. The past is subordinated, the future is contained, limited.

This issue can be stated as an issue concerning Derrida's own thought. This advanced supplement provides some answer to the question of the epistemological self-reflexivity of Derrida's philosophy: how can the end be subsumable under the same principle as the origin if each has come to be known as a differance, which could not allow an identity between them? In other words, the standard of universality for a philosophy seems to run counter to the standard of a genuine change or development being made. Once again, can the original founding concept, difference, become different from itself at the end of Derrida's philosophy? If it does, the unity of the system is threatened. If it does not, it and its succeeding ideas are not true. A dilemma has two horns that are the only alternatives but that are both unsolvable.

Another way to approach the festival is to define it in terms of the imprint and the form, terms used by Derrida, especially when he founded his second stage, with differance. Figures 14-2 and 14-3 on pages 444 and 445 illustrate the two horns without being able to represent them exactly; this limit to the correspondence of empirical examples faced Descartes when his critics could not understand his argument about the existence of God through an example of a perfect island, and Descartes replied that one could not reasonably expect for the relations in the one domain (those of a physical reality, the island) to correspond exactly to the relations in the different domain of universal concepts, so that examples can never be more than generous suggestions--they are not in themselves proof in the way that diagrams play a role in mathematics, a point Plato emphasized in the *Republic* as the difference between philosophy and mathematics.

One horn of the supplement's dilemma is called the "reappropriation of presence" and the other is the "negativity of the letter" (144-45 *OG*). In the first horn, a sensory imprint or mark is added to other marks in a network of relations, a code, but it does not change their relationability or lawfullness vis-à-vis each other. In the second horn, the same mark or physical sign acquires a different relationability and thus meaning from itself.

These two alternatives constitute horns of a dilemma insofar as they both are inseparably related to each other; both derive from aspects of the supplement. Originally, the term "horns" for a dilemma may come from the two horns on a bull's head. Whatever the etymology, they act like the famous two clashing rocks which tried to catch Odysseus'ship to prevent it from passing, Scyla and Charybdis.

Derrida's last attempt at avoiding his clashing rocks is the idea of the festival. In another passage he describes its mediating role:

> There is no longer spectator or spectacle, but *festival* (244 WD).

> ...the ideal of a public festival substituted for representation, and a certain model of society perfectly present to itself in small communities which render both useless and nefarious all recourse to *representation* at the decisive moments of social life (245 WD).

This ideal allows Derrida to think two points of knowledge indefinitely far apart as having some unity, a unity or identity defined by Derrida. This would give him a universal vision of experience, including the past and limiting any future. Derrida would be at the center of the universal vision. Like a mountain peak from which one can look both ways and seemingly see the whole earth of lower mountains, valleys, seas, plains, the festival is a maximum of vision:

> ...the inaccessible limit of a representation which is not repetition, of a *re*-presentation which is full presence, which does not carry its double within itself as its death [as a genetic code carries its double within itself], of a present which does not repeat itself, that is, of a present outside time, a nonpresent. The present offers itself as such, appears, presents itself, opens the stage of time or the time of the stage only by harboring its own intestine difference, and only in the interior fold of its original repetition, in

Figure 14-2: One Horn of the Dilemma of the Supplement and a Suggested Alternative

The dilemma is caused by a split between the network of relations of a concept and its sensory qualities such that a change in one does not necessitate a change in the other, but it should if the concept is whole.

A. A New Supplement Fills a Void in a Previous One

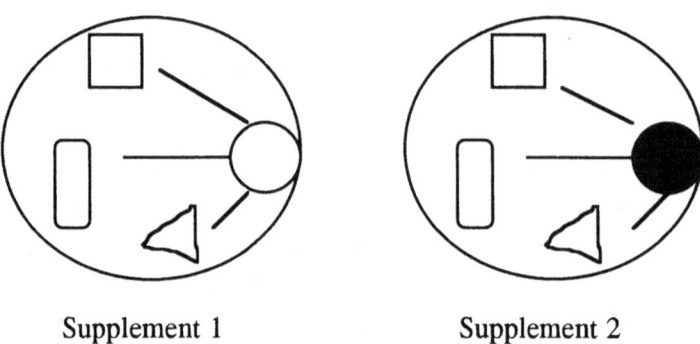

Supplement 1   Supplement 2

This diagram represents the situation when a concept is suggested by others but not yet known--like a new chemical compound missing from a series. The void in Supplement 1 becomes filled in Supplement 2. The form changes, i.e. the relations to the little circle become redefined, but the imprint or sensory surface of the others does not change.

B. An Alternative to This View

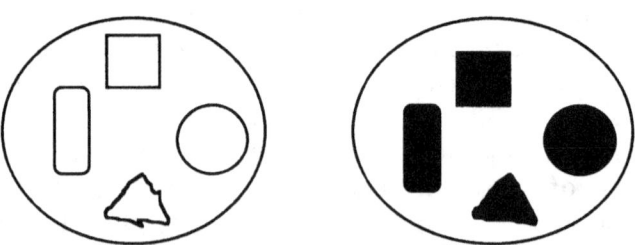

A change in relationships should change the sensory qualities of all objects, no matter how slightly.

Figure 14-3: A Second Horn of the Dilemma of the Supplement

A. If the Supplement Does Not Fill a Void, It Takes the Place of Another Supplement

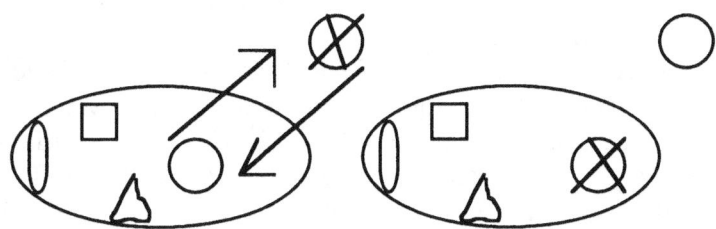

The imprint represented as the little circle is changed, but the relations of all the parts do not change.

B. A Recommended Alternative

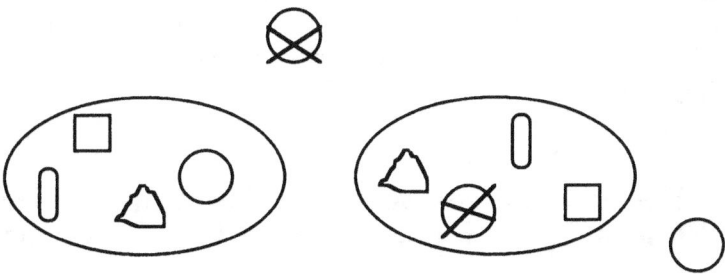

Here the change of one concept (or imprint of sensory qualities) also changes the entire network of relationships; so the change is totalized or accumulated.

C. The Best Illustration Changes Both the Relationships and the Sensory Qualities of All Objects Defined in the System of Thought

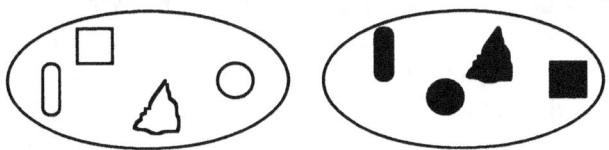

representation. In dialectics [the process of finding
the unity of opposites] (248 *WD*).

"By harboring its own intestine difference," the "inaccessible limit" is like an oxymoron; a present that is a non-present. The Holy Ghost of the Derridean trinity: difference (the Father), differance (the Son), and the supplement (the Holy Ghost).

Another way to look at the festival is to see it as the attempt to mediate the two limits of philosophical vision. In this way the nature of the closing concept of philosophy achieves a new specific definition, contrary to the practice of Bloom to keep the closing the same. Derrida described the supplement in terms of an "unforeseeable factum": a concept which comes to overturn a system of thought (259 *OG*). For Derrida's predecessor, Sartre, the supplement certainly comes as an unforeseeable factum overturning his system. And as a complementary notion, the supplement is referred to an "unrelinquishable past." For Derrida this past is the concept of difference, itself bound as alternative to Sartre's closing concept; difference is found to depend on differance, which is found to depend on the supplement. With the supplement Derrida redefines how a philosophy relates to the previous one.

Why Derrida Cannot Solve the Limiting Problem of His Philosophy and Why No One Can Solve His/Her Own

"Supplementarity as structure" is "that within which metaphysics can be produced but which metaphysics cannot think" (167 *OG*).

The individual human mind is limited to a unit of tradition. Any perspective of an individual person is limited to a single definite perspective. There are analogies to perception. A person looking at the horizon from Florida has a different horizon from a person looking from California. The California person can think of the Florida person as having a more limited vision in the sense that from California more of the west where the sun sets seems visible, yet the function of a horizon is the same. The analogy breaks down because the perspective of an individual through a cultural form includes all past knowledge in a way a visual field on the earth cannot include the visual field of others. Cassirer describes the necessary limit on the possible development of an individual by saying, one cannot jump over one's own shadow (478 *The Philosophy of Symbolic Forms*, trans. Ralph Manheim, Yale University Press, 1957). What makes vision, makes it individual. And philosophy seeks the source of vision, never being able to see it directly, completely, according to Plato, who described the ultimate goal of philosophy as a vision of the sun, that which makes vision possible but which cannot be looked at directly in the manner of physical objects since it makes their visibility possible. The sun, too, is an archetypal image of regularity, order, and philosophical forms are of the highest order of concepts, or at least equal but different. Lyotard expressed the limit on the individual by saying, "time does not allow the full synthesis of the moments or positions the mind crossed through..." (7 *Peregrinations*). In other words, if an individual is to be able to develop from a predecessor, then someone must be able to develop from that second individual, and any individual's tragic flaw stems from the difference between the end point and the origin, which only a successor can truly subsume under a universal principle making the entire past tradition of concepts isomorphic again. It is always the case that anyone's concepts can be better understood by a successor. The understanding of any ideas leads to new ones. The chief function of cultural forms is to build up traditions: series of developmental steps, each on a higher level. The greatest opportunity for an individual is linked to the strongest limitation.

The previous criticism of the supplement does not mean that Derrida's philosophy before the supplement was consistent except for a wrong turn made by the supplement. The supplement is so related to all the other concepts that if it must be rejected then they too must be. This is so because the other concepts logically depend on the supplement. If the supplement is rejected all the other concepts must be. Removing the supplement would require effacing the origin, like pulling a plant--roots and all--out of the ground in order to remove the blossoms above ground. The blossoms give the roots their reason for being, just as the roots allow the blossoms to exist. The purpose of changing only the closing concept is self-defeating. The criticism of the supplement means that it cannot be the uniform building block for philosophical development beyond it; it allows for indefinite developement from it, yet only if it has its structure. To develop new philosophical concepts, a philosopher after Derrida must transform the supplement, starting a new philosophical system.

Another metaphor for the indissociability of the supplement from difference and differance is a magnet. The supplement is like one pole, the origin (difference) is like the other. Together they must remain if either is to be what it is. Still, they are opposites, in a way. They set up a field of attraction, of force, as Derrida's philosophy is a teleological field, its parts being origins or ends for the other parts; it is all of a piece, and it is the supplement which provides the completing pole. Magnetism or electricity is a metaphor for the unity of a cultural work: it exists as a whole, in a circuit, or not at all.

There are many reasons why Derrida cannot solve the paradox of his closing concept. Precisely because it cannot be solved it is a closing concept. One barrier to accepting such an impossibility is the prejudice that a philosophy's structure indicates a quantitative extension of knowledge. A philosophy, however, is the size of a life: its concepts structure a universal vision of experience, so the extension of knowledge should be thought more in terms of a structural repetition of the previous pattern, in a slightly new way. A philosophy always defines its starting concept to apply to all previous knowledge--subordinating it, yet nonetheless including it. The vision is universal with respect to the future as well. A philosophy always provides a model of future knowledge that has at least partially the structure known already. In this way the future is limited in development to the mode of knowledge already achieved, so that its creator has a universal vision of the future. A philosophy always includes the whole of human experience; of course, this does not mean the quantitative whole of all knowledge; it means a structure able to apply to any and all knowledge. The formula `$f = ma$' does not present all possible amounts for force, mass, and acceleration; it only presents the principle by which they can be related no matter what the specific quantitites may be. Rather than being quantitative, its meaning is structural, a matter of principle. Some theorists use the terms the extension of knowledge versus its intension, the latter meaning the level of knowledge; its depth; its purity or its degree of faithfulness to the objectives of the form, not the amount. If each new step in tradition includes all of the past knowledge, of course this accumulation is not a simple quantitative addition. The intension or level or power of knowledge is increased.

So if a philosophy has a structure that provides a universal vision, once this vision is achieved the individual has achieved the most that one could in philosophy. Even if "another" philosophy could be developed by the same individual, this would be superfluous, for the first one provides a universal vision, a space of infinite imaginative growth within it, to use terms more from Bloom than from Derrida. The individual has incorporated the whole of knowledge in one field and increased this knowledge. If the knowledge of tradition accumulates in a definite way, it must do this in definable individual increments. For this reason the individual person could do no more than to perform this accumulation and extension.

It is not particular contents that are sought in making a philosophy or any other form but the perspective brought about through the total form. The bonds of the total form are stronger than any impulse could be to revise just the closing concept, the paradox. In the terms of Cassirer, the objects of knowledge are never simply given but must be determined by an ideal standpoint, which establishes a perspective by which all human experience may be related. The unity of science "is not to be represented in the form of a particular objective content, but exclusively in the form of a system of valid relations."[1] The ideal unity of any tradition form, whether it be a scientific theory, a poetry, a philosophy or any other, means concepts are so related as to make a domain in which the individual has infinite development. If such a perspective is achieved, a future individual could repeat the achievement in a slightly different way without ever surpassing the possible development of an individual.

There is a certain dissymetry of a philosophy or other form: any creator subordinates his/her predecessors while obstructing his/her own subordination by future generations. Bloom uses such terms of personal intention, which point to the way the closing of the form applies to what came before and what will come. This dissymetry allows the vision of a mere individual to be universal with regard to the past and the future. Besides allowing a universal vision, the perspective is still individual: it starts by an individual person in time and later ends, to be followed by another.

Another reason why the closing concept's paradox cannot be solved by its creator is that doing so *by the creator* would be tantamount to nullifying all the knowledge developed from the predecessor, but this was not wrong. Any creator is bound to his/her predecessor, for the successor's work internalizes the former, revises it, and repeats its general pattern. The relation is almost symbiotic; it cannot be broken. The request for an individual to form a second philosophy would be like the request for an individual to gain amnesia so as to forget one's life so that another could be had. Still, there could not be "two" lives. Since the structure of a philosophy is universal with respect to an individual's life, it cannot be universal if the individual is said to develop two philosophies.

Summary

Unlike the theories of Kuhn or Bloom, Derrida's philosophy produces a closing concept that is paradoxical. It is not a partial mistake; rather, it serves as a signal system to point the way to the point of orientation for his whole perspective. I have called the difficulty the problem of the imprint vs. the form, although more generally it can be called the dilemma caused by the supplement. Derrida cannot solve the problem on the assumptions of his philosophy. Like the founding movement of Einstein's physics, a new beginning with a new working assumption must be made. Consistent with a genetic code of philosophy, someone must do to Derrida's philosophy what he did to Sartre's, with some variation. More ideas about a philosophy after Derrida's appear in the Epilogue.

NOTES

1. Quoted from Eggers and Mayer, *Ernst Cassirer: An Annotated Bibliography*, p. 13. The original comes from *Einstein's Theory of Relativity Considered from the Epistemological Standpoint*.

Epilogue:

Proposal for a "Transductive Method": Using Genetic Codes of Science, Literature, and Philosophy in Future Scholarship

A Genetic Code Is Useful for Criticism and Scholarship

The answers to the two questions of this book raised in the Prologue are now clear. To the question, `Whose theory of tradition is the best?', the answer would have to be Derrida's, for it is the most consistent, the most complete, the most explanatory in principle--it tells us the most about tradition. And to the second, more general question, `Are there genetic codes in science, literature, and philosophy?', the answer again is yes, if we understand that we are referring to the unique decoding/encoding (or recoding) cycle of a tradition form, rather than a subtantially existing pattern present and unchanging throughout changes of tradition forms.

Taking seriously the idea of genetic codes in scholarship can improve it tremendously--bringing it closer to creation without requiring that it be creation. Such scholarship can be called "transductive," for it follows and analyzes the transfer of genetic determinants from form to form, from figure to figure up to the most recent science, poetry, or philosophy embodying its discipline's code. Cultural forms belong in a canon: their membership can be defined by rules, and the most general for all fields--the touchstone of a canon, a classic--is that each new science, poetry, philosophy or any tradition form must create a structure that produces a second-generation structure that can itself create a third generation structure of the same general type. A mother has a child which can in turn have a child and so on in an indefinite or even infinite process of evolution of the same genus. Therefore, a canonical work or a classic is able to reproduce; in non-biological terms, it is a step forward in tradition. A culture-maker can realize the canonicity of his/her own work by knowing that (s)he did what the precursor did but only better.

In the following epilogue there are specific proposals for improvement of the views of Kuhn, Bloom, and Derrida, and the idea of transduction provides the main direction for the changes.

Criticism and Scholarship Should Become "Transductive"; Creation Is "Teleduction"

All three theorists emphasized the points of transformation in their disciplines. Bloom's ideas are most amenable to forming new tenets of criticism or scholarship in any field. According to him, "form in poetry is always merely *a change in perspective*" (122 Kabbalah). The points at which this change is evident are the revisionary ratios, which are said to complete "crossings" (14 *DC*). This word fits well into the semantic field of Campbell's discussions of rites of passage. Another word sometimes used by both is "threshold." The idea of "crossing over" in the dialectical development of poetry was suggested by Angus Fletcher (17 *PR*). The fact that poetic form as well as form in other fields is concerned with a change in perspective suggests that the most fundamental purpose of a cultural form is to change one's perspective to a new level.

Like the replication occurring in the development of DNA, a poetry changes its stance toward the precursor whenever a general change of perspective occurs. The new is measured by analogy against the old, as the old becomes reinterpreted by the new. Through this symbiosis, the mutual determination, the genetic code of poetry is transferred, step by step, revisionary ratio by revisionary ratio. To describe this all important transference ("transmission" is used in genetics), the poet John Hollander aptly described Bloom's idea: "the misprision of the prior body of texts leads to the operation of these processes in the generation of a new one" (xxix-xxx *PI*).

These tendencies of the theory of the anxiety of influence can be continued to make a better program for criticism--not, however, in the direction of making an abstract synchronic model to be applied to all poetries in succession. Such a model could be allowed to develop diachronically with the changes brought by each new poetry. Each of the ratios should be defined also with the specific difference of the new poetry.

This new process, building on the idea of "crossings," I would like to call "transduction": the process of finding the transference of genetic determinants from one main structural point in any cultural work to the next main point, as well as the more global transference between tradition forms. The word actually exists, and it is important to notice the association with deduction and induction, transduction also being a mode of inference, albeit not from general principles nor from particulars but from one type of generation of knowledge to a higher mode of the same type. So "trans-" seems appropriate to describe the development of one form from another through a transference of codes or sets of instructions--a genetic code.

Transduction involves some general principles of method, not totally unlike those of Kuhn, Bloom and Derrida. This new program for scholarship and criticism would essentially be forward moving, would essentially change with the theories it analyzes, and would attempt to approach the frontier of each field. The general aim would be to bring criticism and scholarship closer to creation without requiring that they create. The process would start with a known main structural point in a text and show how it is a transfer of genetic determinants from a lower, previous level of the same text or a previous text. Monod proposes "a local heightening of order" in "an isolated system" (18). Changes from lower to higher levels or degrees of organization would repeat structures in better ways, while explaining the solidarity of all concepts in a system.

This process has been indicated somewhat in the discussions of the changes in Bloom's revisionary ratios and even more in the discussions of Derrida's main concepts. However, in those discussions the order of presentation was always from lower to higher. Transduction should begin with the higher (for it should not be expected to make a creative forward movement itself) and then show it to be an evolution from the lower, the previous main structural point. Criticism and scholarship usually look backward toward origins.

Transduction does, too, but it sets the higher priority of ascending to the last great or canonical work of the field, to show its canonical status. Works in different historical periods have different values for scholars. The most recent works embody the highest levels of the fields, the most determinate, whereas the earliest works embody simpler versions of the disciplinary matrix.

In these general terms, transduction could be contrasted with "teleduction." Criticism and scholarship explain the forms already existing; creation must do even more. With a knowledge of the past solutions in the background of the mind, a creator can adapt them by analogy to the new needs of re-defining the disciplinary matrix. This problem or quest guides the creator to the end. The term for criticism I am proposing comes from "telos" meaning goal or end, "telein" meaning to complete, and the root of "deduction" and "induction." Critics would follow the path already discovered by the creator.

Teleduction can hardly be called a method in the everyday sense if it is not a repeatable procedure. It would vary with each new application, having itself to be reconceived, though always with the guidance of tradition serving as the analogous pattern on which to forge the new one. While there can be continuity through analogy, there cannot be continuity through an identical set of instructions. There cannot be an invariant genetic code used by a succession of great culture-makers, because the act of creation is in each case uniquely determined by the immediately preceding concepts; this content passes on the accumulated tradition something like the passing of the light at Easter from one candle to another, spreading all around the world. Describing the unique context of creation, Derrida writes, "For the paradox is that the metaphysical reduction of the sign needed the opposition it was reducing. The opposition is systematic with the reduction" (280 WD). The power to create requires the direct influence of a predecessor.

The inner workings of teleduction or creation are quite complex; previous discussions of Derrida's changes of main concepts are examples of teleduction. To find a new, more integrated, higher order concept, the creation would have to come from a sense of the future pattern to be realized, almost like creation by final causes but much more determined than the Aristotelian notion. Lyotard describes, I think, the type of conception (the type of *-duction*) creating a new concept by anticipating its end (telos) while in a sense completing the former level of knowledge:

> A postmodern artist or writer is in the position of a philosopher: the text he writes, the work he produces are not in principle governed by preestablished rules, and they cannot be judged according to a determining judgment, by applying familiar categories to the text or to the work. Those rules and categories are what the work of art itself is looking for. The artist and the writer, then, are working without rules in order to formulate the rules of what *will have been done*. Hence the fact that work and text have the characters of an *event*; hence also, they always come too late for their author, or, what amounts to the same thing, their being put into work, their realization (*mise en oeuvre*) always begin too soon. *Post modern* would have to be understood according to the paradox of the future (*post*) anterior (*modo*) (81 *The Postmodern Condition*).

The finding of a rule for the work already done is like finding the telos, the goal of the process, which is then completed. Some anticipation of a pattern to be realized is necessary from the start--the future anterior. This sounds a little paradoxical, a little like Derrida's preformationism, the engendering of the beginning of a text by the end, already discussed. I suggest the new pattern forming in the mind comes from an analogy with the old pattern, a process of transferring a genetic code. It is not mechanical, for analogy is needed and the pattern will be changed somewhat, while at the same time the process does have its determining factor so that human beings can be partially in control of their own self-development. They must be able to see possible futures so that present action can be guided, changed.

A Genetic Code Is Insufficient for Creation

While the idea of a genetic code can improve the scholarship of Kuhn and the criticism of Bloom as well as many of their peers, the idea cannot be sufficient to actually create. A tradition form--any scientific theory, poetry, philosophy, or other form making a step forward in tradition--is more than a genetic code. After all, since a new work re-makes the genetic code, the new one can hardly be the deductive result of some old invariant one. In the biological realm theorists would be quite willing to admit evolution; in the cultural, few would be willing to give up the hubris of an intellectual standpoint above the series being explained.

A cultural form is always more than a bare genetic code. A genetic code changes by chance, and it may become better. "Tradition forms" by their manner of transmission become better in each successive one. The previous philosophy or other form cannot exist as a consistent, completed total on which to build a new form. At the moment that its perspective point is understood, it is seen to be fragmented, discontinuous in relation to a new demand for unity; consider Einstein's remarks about the need to preserve the unity of universality of physics; Bloom's remarks about the need to continue poetry by making a new imaginative space possible; Derrida's claim to have extended the domain and play of signification from his predecessor infinitely. A creator's work begins at the moment (s)he tries to define the single rule of the predecessor's formative process which can never be unified using the predecessor's concepts. The previous cultural work can only be understood as somewhat inadequate when the attempt is made to see it as whole. Then no single adequate genetic code is found intact, nor is any possessed by the creator, who cannot simply copy the instructions applying them to new material. The creator must rewrite, no matter how slightly, the set of instructions for the disciplinary matrix. This process calls to mind recombinant DNA research, in which a code is found and it is changed to produce anticipated results. "Philosophy cannot be learned: `At most, one can learn to *philosophize*'" (396 *LR*). One can get prepared to create, but the actual creation must be unique.

Kuhn's term "matrix" from "disciplinary matrix" is good for understanding how a tradition form is more than a genetic code. That term referred to the global properties of a new scientific theory, which Kuhn late in his career refused the responsibility to defend. It is to his credit, nonetheless, that he did offer a conception of those global properties, no matter how vague in comparison to the ideas of Bloom and Derrida. Kuhn had a minimal sense of the genetic code, yet at least some sense of it. As one indication, he remarks how scientists create not from a list of invaribale traits that the former science and the new one must share, but from a wholistic sense of the pattern's recurrence (17 *ET*):

> ...the cognitive content of the physical sciences is in part dependent on the same primitive similarity relation between concrete examples, or paradigms, of successful scientific work, that scientists model one problem solution on another without at all knowing what characteristics of the original must be preserved to legitimate the process."

How a matrix supercedes a code in the development of any cultural form can best be seen by considering the change from Derrida's differance to the supplement. Derrida associates differance with the workings of a code, as has been mentioned (28 *POS*). Differance explained the succession of differences: one comes after another in an endless series of substitutions. It is like the code of their production. Bloom, too, spoke of kenosis as an endless series of metonymous substitutions. Derrida noticed a problem with differance; it tended to become infinite, and some change in its nature had to occur for reasons previously stated. The supplement is posited to explain a change that must occur within the nature of differance, a change in the "code" of the production of differences. Figure Epi-1 on page 460 illustrates how a code is essential to philosophy without being the most general expression for its unity, since any philosophy contains a dialogue of codes (of predecessor and successor) and itself changes its own code during the course of its development. A more general expression for the unity of a cultural form would be an order, or a disciplinary matrix, to use Kuhn's insightful term, one echoed by Lyotard in the idea of a matrix for any field. Baudrillard, whose ideas are based on Derrida's and Lyotard's, expresses a remarkably similar idea to that of Derrida on the change of differance to the supplement:

Figure Epi-1: A New Genetic Code Is Generated in the Change of Disciplinary Matrices

A. The Old Code Reaches Its Limit when, Unknown to Its Inventor, It Is Used in Two Different Kinds of Conceptual Acts

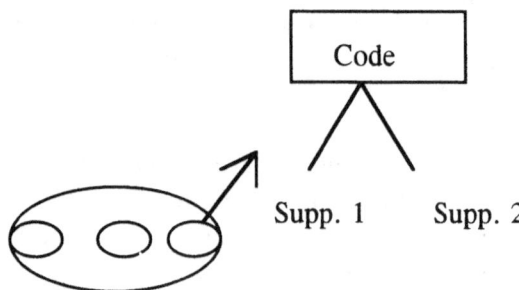

B. A Successor Sees the Hidden Unity in the Conceptual Acts, and Thus Those Conceptual Processes Change: A New Code Comes into Being (Gradually)

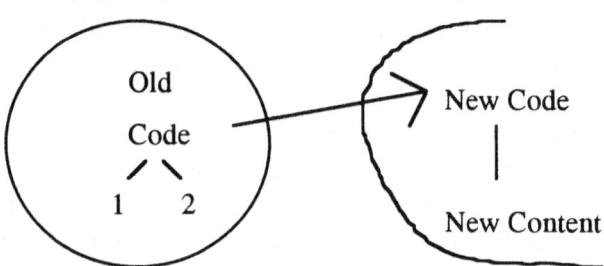

In the left circle, the triad of Old Code, 1, and 2 represents the two horns of the supplement and Derrida's understanding of their unity. Derrida's difference marks the start of a new code of philosophy, but it is not until the supplement that Derrida can know his own processes of formation the most an individual can.

> "...serial production yields to generation by means of models. And here it is a question of a reversal of origin and finality, for all the forms change once they are not so much mechanically reproduced but even *conceived from the point of their very reproductibility*, diffracted from a generating nucleus we call the model. Here we are in the third-order simulacra; no longer that of the counterfeit of an original as in the first-order, nor that of the pure series as in the second. Here are the models from which proceed all forms according to the modulation of their differences. ...the model ...is a kind of anterior finality..." (100 *Simulations*).

Beyond generation in the manner of a pure series there is generation by means of models. The change occurs through "a reversal of origin and finality" as it does with Derrida's supplement. Beyond the (genetic) code as something that could mechanically reproduce whole cultural forms, there is the idea of what permits a cultural form to reproduce itself--the supplement, which explains the passage of Derrida's concepts away from Sartre's, the rule of progress for the preceding development. Lyotard's "differend" performs a similar function in explaining the right of Lyotard's knowledge to be different from what came before and yet of the same type. The source of cultural forms is represented to the creator at the level of what Kuhn called a *disciplinary* matrix, beyond a fully explicit code. Rather than denying the analogy of a cultural form to a genetic code, this final stage of forms deepens the idea of a genetic code into what cannot be used mechanically but what is the source of the whole form. From a particular perspective, the individual comes to see the maximum development possible for an individual. "Matrix" suggests a totality in which creation occurs. Very consistent with Derrida's account of the supplement, Baudrillard makes this third order of the generation of knowledge "the genesis of the code" (101 Ibid.). Derrida uses the term "matrix" when he thinks of the ground of all previous metaphysics (278 *WD*); he constructs a matrix by which he can see the whole previous history of philosophy as being made. This difficult point of a matrix being a level of a cultural form above the code can perhaps be explained by Yury Tynyanov's ideas:

> Tynyanov thought of literature as a complex system with its components--some of them, like the genres, distinct "orders" in themselves--continually interrelated in dynamic tension. The system is such that its components do not coexist, but struggle for preeminence (250 Fowler).

"Matrix" then refers to the representation of the whole tradition within a particular theory. This sense of the continuum guides each phase of creation, and it changes during the development of any theory. The transgenerational sense that "matrix" requires is evident in the passage. A disciplinary matrix is unique each time; it is the new definiton of a science, poetry, or philosophy.

One of the best expressions for the primacy of a matrix over a code is that of Roland Barthes. "The five codes create a kind of network, a `topos' through which the entire text passes (or rather, in passing, becomes text) (in S\Z: "The Weaving of Voices").

The whole cultural form *functions* like a genetic code to reproduce the pattern--the matrix--of the discipline, yet a clear idea of the genetic code was never present to the creator as an abstract set of instructions for creation.

If there is no way to explain the change in codes of production, then there is no adequate way for a creator to explain his/her development from a precursor to a legitimate step forward. This fact shows how central the idea of a genetic code is while also showing how it cannot become an abstract set of instructions for the generation of a new cultural product. It leads to the matrix of the discipline, which always outstrips the power of the individual to control completely. No individual made science, poetry, philosophy, or any other field. They all are traditional phenomena, and the most an individual can do is to make a new step in which the principles guiding the process become represented--but *not* the principles for all individuals in history.

Derrida's idea about the limitation on the knowledge of philosophy, already discussed, helps to make the limitation of cultural genetic codes clearer. He thinks a philosopher seeks the space of his discipline, which (s)he cannot control absolutely. One way the creative philosopher does not control the process is the limit on the knowledge one can have when first beginning to create. No whole conception of a pattern can be used to create from; instead, *bricolage* describes the piecemeal process of creation by borrowing concepts from one's predecessor, synthesizing them, and seeing how they begin to require new modes of linking, new laws of synthesis to permit the increase of associations. On the other hand, considering the end of a philosophy, the creator is limited there, too; metaphysics can produce its limit, although it cannot understand it fully.

The matrix of a cultural field, the level at which its previous concepts are seen to be produced, has been described by Baudrillard in a discussion of Jacques Monod's ideas of science:

> In fact it is the coherence of a certain *discourse*, and all scientific movement is nothing but the space of this discourse, never revealing itself as such, and the "objective" simulacrum of which hides the political, strategic word. ...the scheme of scientific discourse... (113 *Simulations*).

One's own "space" does not become an object for oneself because it is the entire frame for the location of objects we do know distinctly, including the predecessor's rule of development. For tradition to be ever self-accumulating, the perspective of individuals must be partially beyond them and yet capable of being incorporated into a deeper, wider future perspective. All perspectives have a point outside that orients all that occurs within. Lyotard mentions "a ciphered language," "the code of which is beyond the reach of our understanding" (22 *Pergrinations*). All cultural fields are ciphered languages insofar as they have meaning within unique formative processes that the individual acquires through the accumulated knowledge of tradition but did not invent nor can say the final word about.

Finding a genetic code from which to create would be tantamount to escaping the limits of individual perspective. Scholars and critics who make models surreptitiously assume this supra-human standpoint. More than a code, the idea of a matrix or a context to be restationed or the continuum of one's field is needed when creating. Since the future pattern must be better than the previous one, creation is not a question of a single code; multiple definitions of codes are always at play. These differences between modes of generating knowledge have been described by Lyotard in a complex but revealing way:

> ...Hugo and Richard de Saint-Victor know that they do not and never will *have* the code. With this refinement, then, they already love in things that element in things which denies them the code, they love the negative of the code in the message, they valorize the work of this negative, the text, the *dissimilitude* of things, and they find beauty in this (7 *LR*).

The "negative of the code in the message" means the livingness of all our products: they ceaselessly lead to higher forms, even after the completion of a cultural work and the death of the creator. Bloom defined the ambivalence in each revisionary ratio. Derrida presented the dialectic in each of his main concepts. And above all he describes the supplement as having in it a negativity preventing it from being simply unifiable or decidable. He calls it a "moving structure"-- perhaps like the motion of sperm, moving toward future forms, carrying the power of reproduction.

PROPOSALS FOR THE PHILOSOPHY OF SCIENCE AFTER KUHN

In general, philosophers of science should be more up to date than Kuhn was. They should limit their analyses in scope, making them more detailed. The whole philosophy of science should be more *strategic*--preparing and pointing the way for researchers to create new scientific theories, or *strategic* in the sense of setting the goal for itself of getting closer to the most recent and purist truth of the field, which is also called increasing the intension of concepts as opposed to their extension, their domain of applicability.

To Reconceive the Goal of the Philosophy of Science as Transductive

A transductive study of science would follow the developments of canonical science to the most recent one. The highest goal would be to attempt to present the meaning of already existing science as purely as possible to prepare future creators. Kuhn once asserted that a history of science could not be written from a merely internal point of view, that is, other concepts besides the scientific must be used (110 *ET*). In the earlier works he uses "history" of science, while in the later ones he also uses "philosophy" of science. I think his goal is to make a product different from science, with the consequence that the meaning of the concepts discussed would tend to have a historical, not scientific, significance. In a way there is an internal history of science: each new science rewrites its own history. If the valuation of previous concepts--all previous concepts--changes, then the most accurate history would be the one written from the most recent scientific level. As Adriaan Theodoor Peperzak put it, "*Every* historical overview of philosophy expresses a particular thematic philosophy that functions as a prism" (41). Philosophy of science could better help creative science by pointing to the most recent canonical science and showing how it developed.

To Direct the Study of Science More Strategically

A philosopher of science after Kuhn should direct the study more strategically toward the preparation of future scientists. The highest goal is to make a staircase up to the point where new creation can begin. Of course, there may be other legitimate goals, though of lesser value.

To direct the study more strategically, a philosopher of science should analyze only one specialty forming its own tradition. Kuhn "analyzed" all the sciences at once with the methodological consequence that the theory can never penetrate to a level of specific differences between successive theories. But isn't this the most crucial topic?

Bloom analyzes only one specialty of literature with the consequence that the theory can be much more detailed than Kuhn's. Derrida limits the area of analysis even more to the specific set of differences between his philosophy and what I have argued is his immediate predecessor's, Sartre's.

I recommend analyzing the specific difference between two fairly recent canonical scientific theories. Of course, determining which ones are canonical can only be accomplished after studying them. If two are found a third either preceding of following them can be also studied to see the transgenerational relations across three steps in tradition. Doing so can clearly define what a step does in relation to the one before and the one after. The idea becomes definite, circumscribed. Its life-cycle becomes explicit.

What in general a philosopher of science after Kuhn needs to do is to increase its intension, not its extension--to deepen the knowledge, making it more pure, as opposed to attempting to discuss all science in all times. Kuhn's theory has no specific historical boundaries. Cassirer presents the value of an intensive standard of knowledge (how deep or pure it is) according to Eggers and Mayer:

> ...the functional concept of truth replaces the extensive standard of knowledge by an intensive one. For the individual researcher this means that the question is not how large or small his field of overview is

but how clearly and genuinely the idea of his science
and of truth manifests itself in his work.[1]

The translators to *Substance and Function* and *Einstein's Theory of Relativity* indicate Cassirer's emphasis on an intensive standard of knowledge: "...Einstein's theory is seen to be only the latest and most radical fulfillment of the motives which are inherent in mathematical and physical science as such" (v-vi Translator's Preface).

By the same token, a philosopher of science can have the most accurate theory if (s)he plummets more into the depths of science by defining the intension of some scientific specialty. This notion of the intension of concepts is not an expression of subjective will; it is more like an expression of a field's teleonymy, which means the goals establish a structural standard regulating all the concepts.

To Minimize The Reduction in Meaning

Reduction in meaning seems unavoidable by criticism and scholarship. The criticism itself has a lower degree of conceptual order than the products it analyzes. I say this because criticism itself does not have a definite traditional structure according to which each successive criticism would manifest virtually the same pattern or genetic code. It is a lower degree of conceptual activity, less demanding of knowledge. The intension of science or literature or philosophy must be lower than that for the original creator, for the critic's concepts cannot "mean" in the body of his/her work in the same idiomatic way. The order or context in which concepts are presented partially determines not so much *what* but *how* concepts mean.

What can be done to lessen the reduction in meaning in the degree Kuhn does? Making scholarship as close as possible to the intensive standards of knowledge for any one field. To do this, one can proceed as quickly as possible to the frontier of scientific knowledge in any specialty, though equally important is to analyze the transgenerational relations of at least three successive scientific theories: grandparent, child, grandchild.

To Study the Variation of the Genetic Code of a Science

It is very important for a philosopher of science to analyze an actual sequence of three theories in one specialty because some of the meaning of science as traditional can only be seen in the relations beyond two generations. Science always sees a regularity or pattern in nature. Similarly, science itself should be understood as regular in structure. The regularity of structure throughout history is tantamount to a genetic code of science, with positive implications for creation. Lyotard expresses the regularity as essential to the purpose of science: "...these addressees [of a universal narrative should] be able to become in turn its addressors, if the stakes pursued by the narrative genre are indeed those of the narrative's recurrence" (157 *Differend*). In the language of science, a successor should be able to repeat the specific structural standard of his/her field so that it may serve to provide a second successor to build upon the first's if science aims to make a structure that can reproduce itself, forming a tradition. Musn't the unit of any philosophy of science be structurally similar to other ones in a developing series?

Bloom's work serves to suggest the exigency of detailed studies spanning generations; some of the meaning of poetry is the establishing of a new relation to previous generations.

Not only should the genetic codes of the sciences be studied to define the relations between tradition forms, but they should also be studied within the tradition forms. The revisionary ratios of Bloom should have their counterparts in science; they do in philosophy, as the discussion of Derrida's three main concepts indicated. Kuhn does have a very slight indication that a scientific theory could be studied as having within it the replication processes of a genetic code. In a rare moment he discusses the interrelationship of concepts in Newton's theory: "The same change [of the third law of Newton] of motion supplies the definition of dynamical force implicit in the second law" (105 *SSR*). This change of concepts can be called a teleduction; the goal of previous concepts is found such that a new one on a higher level is formed. The process occurred very definitely in the transitions between Derrida's main concepts and also definitely though less completely in the transitions of Bloom's ratios.

PROPOSALS FOR LITERARY CRITICISM AFTER BLOOM

In general, the changes I propose for the philosophy of science also apply to literary criticism, though some are needed less in the case of Bloom than they are for Kuhn. Critics should give up the security of a model, a typology, such as Bloom's map of misreading composed of the six ratios, to follow the diachronic meaning changes in the ratios themselves, the transfer of the genetic determinants, the continuing change of the code. More intensity at selected points is required. Future critics should perform analyses that are more *strategic* than Bloom's: that bring them closer to creation, that better prepare poets for creation--the highest but not the only function of criticism.

To Reconceive the Goal of Literary Criticism as Transductive

The best way for criticism to prepare for creation is to become transductive, to follow the transfer and changes in the genetic code of poetry.

The goal of Bloom's criticism is not to prepare future poets by pointing the way to the most recent canonical poetry. Bloom may seem to contradict this conclusion. In one passage he states the best critics--Dr. Johnson, Coleridge, Hazlitt, Ruskin, and Emerson-- "perfect and extend the canon," (413 *PI*) and Bloom's remark that a critic could be a precursor for a poet was previously mentioned. Bloom himself does not attempt to perfect and extend the canon. He does not try to determine the frontier of poetry and to suggest how it could be advanced further. In contrast he develops a model of poetic development which he applies somewhat indifferently to various poetries, many in succession. I say "somewhat indifferently" because the definitions of the ratios do not change with each new poetry, and still he allows in principle for improvement through the repetition of the ratios. There is no mounting excitement as Bloom discusses poetries of the last decades, discussed to a much less extent than the English romantics. Although Bloom can discuss the ambivalence of the revisionary ratios, his own use of his model tends to make the poetries static instances of the map of misreading, like turning people into statues. David Fite, a major interpreter of Bloom's work, states in disagreement: "for Bloom, from the very start, the meaning of a poem resides in the dynamic, *temporal* relation between the poet's desires and his poem's quest toward their fulfillment" (23). I do not disagree that Bloom intends to regard poetry as somewhat dynamic; I am suggesting that Bloom's revisionary ratios are themselves insufficiently dynamic, and thus they miss some deeper, not entirely controllable dynamism of poetic meaning. The phenomenon of a poetry must be conceived more dynamically and consequently more teleologically. As Cassirer writes about the need to respect the dynamism of myth if it is to be understood: "We cannot reduce myth to certain fixed static elements; we must strive to grasp it in its inner life, in its mobility and diversity, in its dynamic principle" (76 *EM*). This dynamism is a dialectic toward an ideal that orients an entire form without ever being overcome within the form. Cultural forms are through and through teleological phenomena--even science; Lévi-Strauss' idea of the tendential unity of myth is consistent with these ideas.

It stands to reason that Bloom does not know the frontier of poetry, the last canonical poetry, nor does he know with much precision what would happen at the end of a poetry to allow a successor to make the first step; there is a noticeable gap in his knowledge at this point. Would someone who knew how to do the best work possible say, `No, I prefer to do the second best'?

Bloom's criticism seems to presuppose a faulty assumption about creation. So much attention to a model, the map of misreading, suggests that it gets to the fundamentals of creation more than the poets can. It suggests that the principle of creation is needed--complete--at the start of creation. This assumption must be misguided, according to previous discussions of the relation of the end of a poetry or a philosophy to the start. The end accounts for the passage that was made from the origin; the end is "prior" to the origin in showing the poet the direction which it had to take. In an obvious drama concerned with fate Oedipus develops inner vision despite outer blindness when he realizes the fate of the oracle uniting his life's events. In

Derrida's philosophy, too, the rule of progress for all his philosophy only achieves expression at the end of the form. Lyotard's idea of the "future anterior" applies in this discussion. If creation could never proceed until one had a complete model from which one could produce a new poetry, then why have creators not presented the model they used? Why has Bloom's model not been sufficient for this task?

Scholars and critics should change the mistaken assumption that one knows the full meaning of a great work before or outside of a great work that answers or develops in dialogue with the former. The opposition between generations of great works is so powerful that no one ever fully escapes it, and so encompassing that one understands one's predecessor's work fully only when one's work is complete. Creation requires a separation from the predecessor during which his/her power is passed on to the successor. Derrida writes, "For the paradox is that the metaphysical reduction of the sign needed the opposition it was reducing. The opposition is systematic with the reduction" (280 *WD*).

Struggling to free himself from Wordsworth, to gain a knowledge that would "comprehend" his, Shelley could not have known what such a form of poetry would be until he had written it by working through the double opposition that binds but requires revision called the anxiety of influence. The full understanding of one's predecessor does not occur *before* one writes a great poetry; it is only progressively revealed to the poet during the creation; it *is* the great poetry. The search for a new poetry denied by the predecessor is the driving force of creation and the goal within the production of the form. If the form were already known, `the' or any further poetry would be unnecessary. Any poetry is a kind of giving new form to what went before, thus the highest, most poetic type of critique. In this way, each new great poetry made a model of poetry far better than Bloom's. Although the role of a scholar or critic must essentially differ from a creator, why shouldn't it come as close as possible to each unique step in poetic evolution?

The power of the opposition by a new great poet paradoxically comes partly through the products of the great poet being opposed. And this opposing force of the precursor is never absolutely left behind.

According to the famous idea of Vico, we only know what we have made (5 *PR*). If this is true, and I am agreeing, then a great poet only fully knows the principles of a better great poetry as the poetry is written, not before.

Since a model known in advance can never be complete and accurate, as any poetry is a new model but much more determinately and more fertile, anyone trying to create from it could not succeed. Instead one would have to form by analogy to the most recent great poetry a new idea of the unity of poetic vision, and this idea would be revised as the poetry progressed. Also, a specific reaction would have to take place in relation to the former poetry, not in relation to a model.

For these reasons criticism after Bloom should not seek to form models. It could begin with Bloom's model but see it much more determinately in each successive poetry especially defining the changes in the understanding of poetic unity. Bloom does not define these as Einstein does for physics or Derrida does for philosophy.

There are three main ways to make criticism more transductive. First of all, a critic after Bloom should only study canonical poetries with the goal in mind of forming the single line of poets up to the last great one. Canonical poetries are tradition forms; they repeat the genetic code of poetry uniting it for thousands of years. To a large extent, Bloom does concentrate on them. He does state he only discusses "strong poets," although some of his choices are not clearly in the single line of succession.

The line of succession is not as definite as it might be. It is strongest from Milton to Wordsworth to Shelley to Keats to Tennyson, but after this there are unmistakeable gaps; the derivation does not seem direct anymore. Bloom does claim at times that a poet has one specific poetic father with whom (s)he wrestles, and yet if this were true, why does Bloom not give us a single defined line beginning with the Romantics up to the present day? This would be a kind of family tree, except for the fact that only one branch precedes any given branch.

John Hollander, a strong supporter of Bloom and a highly acclaimed original poet, believes genealogists are not needed (xix *PI*). To some degree Hollander is right. A genealogy of the entire history of poetry would not be needed, for to understand the most recent great generation is a higher goal and can be achieved without a complete genealogy; also mere facts of influence-relations would not necessarily develop one's mind so that one could write great poetry.

Instead of developing a definitive single line of great poets, Bloom developed his *model* of poetic tradition. His attention in some books was more concerned with convincing the reader about his model than in deepening it and taking his readers up to the current thoughts of the most recent great poet.

In contrast to Bloom, I would like a new critic to bravely say, this poet is the most recent great poet of the world and this is why. More important than a complete genealogy would be a vector leading to the most recent great poet. The extension of the application of Bloom's model was perhaps too great to increase the intension of knowledge, i.e. to deepen the knowledge more than Bloom's already admittedly deep level. And, perhaps the professional pressures for Bloom to write only about American or English figures prevented him from developing a line which might include non-English speaking poets. Are the greatest poets of the last two centuries only English speakers? And, are some of the most recent poets not better than the romantics?

A second change to make criticism more transductive is to place more emphasis on the relation of whole poetries to one another, less on the interpretation of individual poems. Bloom uses his "revisionary ratios" in two senses, but it would have been more useful for him to choose one, if he were to develop beyond the point that he has reached. The ratios are applied to individual poems (188 *PR*), with the result that Shelley's clinamen with respect to Wordsworth, the swerving and change, takes place many times. The second use of the ratios is to apply to a whole body of poetry, such that there is just one clinamen of Shelley from Wordsworth. For the sake of Bloom's and his readers' development, it would have been far better though more difficult for Bloom to have found the best, most complete clinamen of one poet in respect to another. The specific improvement could have been understood in greater depth than Bloom was able to. The nature of clinamen could be known as a unique poetic move in a history of such moves by poets. Bloom treats all the poems of one author as embodying clinamen and the other ratios, but certainly not all are equally valuable for studying the improvement of one poet on another, nor would it be the case that in all poets would one poem have all the ratios in their best form. In conclusion, Bloom's depth of understanding of poetic creativity could have been increased, had he only spoken of the ratios in terms of the whole body of poetry and not always in terms of each and every poem. Bloom's theory can be developed in this direction; he sometimes speaks of a "Keatsian kenosis"--kenosis being defined distinctively in a Keatsian style (128 *PR*). Criticism should do this much more than Bloom does.

As the third way to make criticism more transductive, a critic should place more emphasis on poetry, less on psychology, Kabbalah, philosophy, or any other field. The common practice of explaining a field by another's concepts can be an appeal to external factors, to use Kuhn's terms, and an avoidance of the internal. More positively, Bloom is able to "borrow" some of the power of those fields because they and poetry are tradition-making activities, the general processes of which are analogous. But after a point, after book-length discussions of Kabbalah, after thousands of references to psychology, the use of those fields besides poetry becomes a displacing of poetic meaning outside itself or a translation of it into ready made terms with some power. Bloom's whole criticism allows in principle for the interpretation of poetry by itself, by a future higher form--a transductive process. Strictly speaking, if one followed statements by Bloom that the meaning of a poem is another poem as well as many others, criticism would become unnecessary if its only purpose was to understand a poetry. Criticism always translates poetry into terms nonpoetic--hard as Bloom explicitly struggled against this, especially in *Shelley's Mythmaking*. To allow criticism a legitimate, useful role in culture, without demanding it be creation, criticism can follow the path of poetry's own understanding of itself, being a skill of tracking what has gone before, by knowing the habits of the animal, the needs for food and shelter, the physiognomy, the life patterns. Beginning with already made poetries, critics can explain how a canonical poetry is a higher form of a previous poetry, how the genetic code is transferred, making the later one canonical. Critics can help to place poets in the canon, can help to define what a canon is. Critics can ultimately point the way for new poets.

To Minimize the Reduction in Meaning

Future critics can minimize the reduction in meaning by making their theories case-specific and by interpreting revisionary ratios by other revisionary ratios in great poetries. In contrast to Bloom's definitions of the ratios which do not change, it is best to define them as higher level forms of the immediately preceding ones.

The decision making a person a critic should be evaluated with soul-searching objectivity. Defences against creation seem to be built in. I do not want to rid the world of critics, but criticism would be better if these defences were reduced in austerity.

That there is a defence against creation can be seen in the following way. Bloom's map of misreading creates the pattern of poetry unchanging throughout the actual series of poetries. Between any two poetries, Bloom's model serves as an intermediary, a kind of translation language. The practice of referring the series of poetries to a model outside or above it takes one's attention away from the motives which might lead one to develop a new poetry beyond the ones already interpreted. A model has the tendency of delaying forever the movement to create a new poetry because the goal is to leave the actual series, not to enter into the transformations required uniquely in each new creation, and worse yet not to deepen the knowledge of the ever-deepening process.

Scholars and critics should not explain the opposition of generations of great works outside of the figures given by--in our case--great poets. Their interpreters should not create meta-poetry or meta-figures or meta-language, which the map of misreading essentially is, including the six revisionary ratios that Bloom claims are the language of poetry. After Bloom's fine work, one should not find three pairs of revisionary ratios for all of poetry; it is better to name the three new movements for each great poet in succession. This procedure would be more idiographic or specific than Bloom's. If this were to be done, there would be greater knowledge of the actual operations of the figures in any field of knowledge, not to mention a more up-to-date knowledge of the field, hopefully of the most recent great development. What is more important than the showing that each poetry has three movements is the understanding of their uniqueness, so that one can ascend the stairs made by poets, following as closely as possible, or getting as high as possible.

To Study the Variation of the Genetic Code of Poetry

Scholars and critics should attempt to define the last great opposition between one great poet and his predecessor. Bloom's model kept him from finding this clearly. Since each opposition of great poets produces a unique improvement in poetry, no understanding of a field could ever be greater than one particular great body of work. A scholar would follow each development to the present instead of trying to control it ahead of time or to make the perfect interpretation-machine. Once at the most recent great poetry, then the critic could deepen the analysis of the nature of poetry by analysing the most recent, highest level. The purest criticism is a poetry itself on the next higher level. Nevertheless, there is a close legitimate, useful role for critics to point to the last great canonical poetry and to explain how it is a criticism of what went before. Not only would their work serve as a stepping stone for future creators, it would serve to "explain" the making of the canon, the transfer of the genetic code from poetry to poetry, from one main part of a poetry to the next.

Beyond Bloom's work which contributes to the defining of the relations between whole poetries, new critics can further determine that work by specifying changes in poetry-making between whole poetries. If one remembers that the purpose of a new poetry is to make a step in tradition, to change the way poetry is made, no matter how slightly but definitely, then the following idea of Shklovsky points to the need to study the transfer of poetic knowledge from one generation, one form, to the next:

> The work of art arises from a background of other works and through association with them. The form of a work of art is defined by its relation to other works of art, to forms existing prior to it. ...Not only parody, but also any kind of work of art is created parallel to and opposed to some kind of form. *The purpose of the new form is not to express new content, but to change an old form which has lost its aesthetic quality* (118 Eichenbaum).

EPILOGUE

The stakes of poetry are to transmit the heritage while giving it new life. This idea--poetry for poetry's sake--has been much criticized, especially by those scholars who see their task as explaining poetry in nonpoetic terms everyone can understand (like biodegrading in the biological sphere), but the wisdom, the "cunning of reason" as Hegel says, should be pointed out. The recursion of poetry, its essential concern with its own tradition, is necessary if it is to be capable of accumulating its past, building and changing it, ascending to new levels of better poetry, like a person, the one single human being growing through all time, going up an indefinitely long staircase. If the necessary recursion of poetry is denied, how could its level-changing, step-climbing purpose be possible?

PROPOSALS FOR PHILOSOPHY AFTER DERRIDA

In general, any proposals for Derrida's followers must differ from those for followers of Kuhn and Bloom, for scholarship differs from creation. Although any complete solution of the difficulty with Derrida's supplement could be nothing less than an entire alternative philosophy, still the first step of such a move can be indicated below.

Solution Modelling or Forming a Matrix of Creation

Derrida's successor must ask of the supplement a question not asked by Derrida, and thus a new environment or matrix for the concept must be formed.

Kuhn mentioned the idea of solution modeling in scientific creation. He referred to an article by Clifford Truesdell indicating similarities in solutions to problems in mechanics after Newton. In Kuhn's own theory he considers the use of model solutions within a science to be essential for people to learn it. The use of model solutions for solving problems is not the same as solution modeling, a more global operation.

The idea of a genetic code in philosophy could lead one to the point of creation. If one knows the origin of one's predecessor, one can remember this while developing a new origin from his/her closing concept. The process of solution modeling, which can help to overcome the obstructing dilemma ending a philosophy, assumes the regularity of philosophies, as if they shared a genetic code.

The general form of this process has been described inadvertently by Kuhn:

> Given the conditions that obtained at the moment when the narrative opens [a philosophy begins], and given also a knowledge of the covering laws [the genetic code], one should be able to predict [or make], perhaps with the aid of additional boundary conditions inserted along the way, the future course of

> some central parts of the narrative [a new philosophical form] (15 *ET*).

Creation is a process looking forward and backward, reminiscient of Sartre's regressive-progressive method. The opposite directions of attention establish a new matrix in which the former ideas are seen to be created. A culture-maker can only define his/her new work in a universal continuum of past, present, future. In this way, a cultural work establishes an ideal standpoint or perspective.

To recall now the general nature of Derrida's overcoming of the Sartrian dilemma, he found a negative presupposition of that philosophy and, since that philosophy had accumulated the entire tradition before it, the presupposition is one for the entire tradition. I explained Derrida's procedure by using the term "perspective point" outside the framework of Sartre's thought, yet orienting its total movement. From this merely negative point, a point from which knowledge does not actually proceed, Derrida asked again how this knowledge could have been possible. He reinterpreted the Sartrian closing concept by seeing it as isonomic with Sartre's predecessor's thought, according to a new principle. This principle, also understood as the form of the production of the dualism in Sartre's closing concepts, is difference. Difference can also be understood as the preliminary statement of the rule of Sartre's discourse, with differance and the supplement deepening it.

Solution modeling uses hypostatization. The previous solution of Derrida's can be used as an analogy to determine what would have been enough to produce his already completed closing concept.

This process treats the previous philosophy, that is, Derrida's as "model and included object," to use a phrase from Derrida. It is a model insofar as what it did to the predecessor should be repeated in a new way. It becomes a case to decide meaning, to produce new meaning insofar as any new concepts cannot violate the most recent conception of what the previous philosophy did.

Solution modeling establishes a transgenerational situation or matrix of creation. Thinking of more than one step in tradition helps to define a step clearly by circumscription. The life-cycle, a term from Bloom's work, becomes clear. Researchers in the genetic transmission of diseases study three generations, and by doing so they isolated the Alzheimer's gene (Researchers at the Indiana School of

Medicine). The change of Derrida's subordination of Sartre and isonomization of his thought into the new uniform series of tradition requires a relating of concepts across generations of thinkers. Kuhn and Derrida both used the word "matrix"; Bloom used the words "restationing the context." The new concept that needs to be formed from Derrida's will set up a new standard for philosophical unity in the manner Einstein did for physics: "The general theory of relativity gives a still deeper analysis of the time-space continuum [than the special theory]" (244). The continuum of philosophy is disrupted by the logical consequence of the supplement according to the problem called the problem of the imprint versus the form, discussed in the previous chapter. The new unity that is made/found establishes a "mutual relation between the *object* and the *operation* of thought" (314 *ETR*), and this act of integrating the predecessor's former modes of production echos Derrida's account of Rousseau's writing as being afflicted with a tension between what his text performs and what the words declare. The making of a text more self-reflexive, more consistent is a kind of a Copernican Revolution changing the point from which mind orients itself.

Limiting the Needed Knowledge to a Window of Creation

Because as Derrida realized, though not in these exact terms, a creator misprisions himself in the course of creating, and so only a window of creation for the first philosopheme can be apprehended at first--then the other philosophemes would change and deepen the understanding of the first.

How is the window found and opened? The paradox of Derrida's philosophy has a logic of a double bind. Two contrary assertions lead to contradictions, even though both are necessary. The logic of the double bind resembles two train rails proceeding toward the horizon which seem to their creator to converge but which at the point actually seen are still as far apart as before and as far apart as they will always be. If someone is to create from Derrida's supplement, (s)he must go to the projected point on the horizon from which to look backward on the illusory perspective before it, now in clear view. The creative process called teleduction would do this.

Expressing the Negative Point of Perspective

Just as Sartre's philosophy was given a greater unity by Derrida through the concept of a transcendental siginified, so too Derrida's philosophy has beyond its apprehension a perspective point from which its divergent concepts, lines originate.

This point is indicated by the two horns of the dilemma of the supplement, if they are followed to their logical conclusions. Each of these horns was afflicted with an opposition of form versus imprint. In Derrida's own solution to Sartre's problem he used the idea of a "pathway," a course of mediation (61 *OG*). Campbell makes the connection between horns of a double bind and the mythical clashing rocks preventing ships from passing:

> The pairs of opposites...are the clashing rocks (Symplegades) that crush the traveler, but between which the heroes always pass. This is a motif known throughout the world. The Greeks associated it with two rocky islands of the Euxine Sea, which clashed together, driven by winds; but Jason, in the Argo, sailed between, and since that time they have stood apart (89 *Hero*).

Notice that the rocks are seen to always stand apart after Jason passes through, just as Derrida re-interpreted Sartre's philosophy as affected by a dichotomy. Notice that the dilemma closing a philosophy is mythically presented as clashing rocks that threaten the continued journey of travellers, almost in a provocation to find a way through.

Positing a New Figure of Philosophy

A new figure of philosophy, a new philosopheme, must overcome the diremption of sensory imprint and conceptual form.

Between the two horns of the dilemma of the supplement, discussed in the previous chapter, there is a complementarity, an analogy. One horn is the definition of the passage of a supplement into another when the unity is a matter of form, the network of relations, with the sensory representation differing. The other horn is the definition when the unity is a matter of the same sensory representation providing continuity between two different conceptual networks. This paradox has for its subject the question of the relation of two successive philosophies, not to mention any two objects of knowledge. Here is the interest of Kuhn in the gestalt switch of scientific revolutions, which went largely undefined. Here, too, is a more determinate questioning of the improvement in the change of poetries left undefined by Bloom. The problem of the unity of philosophy, indeed the unity of experience, is raised for philosophy as it was raised for science, according to Einstein.

The analogy between the two horns is the dissynchronization of conceptual form and sensory imprint; that is, in both horns, one of the two contrary ideas changes while the other remains constant. The analogy of the situation suggests that if the supplement is to lead truly beyond itself, if experience is to continue so that echoing Derrida the "domain of play of signification can be extended infinitely," then both form and imprint must be redefined to change together. Change in one must bring change in the other. Instead of two separate descriptors of the object of knowledge, there should be a new object of knowledge defined by their new interrelation.

To develop this idea further, the law of synthesis of objects of knowledge must become particular within one of them without homogenizing the trace.

Applied to the change in philosophies, the need for the interrelation of form and imprint means two things. First of all, the previous form of a philosophy becomes imprinted in the new entity (like the idea of epic ecphrasis, of Griffiths and Rabbinowitz). Thus, the form becomes more concrete; knowledge, more determinate. Secondly, it is just as much the case that in the change of philosophies, or of any tradition forms for that matter, the sensory imprint acquires the generality of form in the new entity. Thus, it becomes more universal, able to change everything else when it changes. Both of these concomitant changes effect an increase in the power of mind to relate its contents.

Lyotard as a Possible Canonical Successor of Derrida

There are good indications that Lyotard has solved the problem of Derrida's "supplement" already and according to the lines of the solution indicated above. Although going beyond the projected course of this book, this topic is important for future philosophers.

Lyotard's first main original philosophical work *Discours, figure* contains many critical references to Derrida's work (in French, the English translation is forthcoming). This title suggests the relating of what Derrida kept apart: conceptual form (discourse) and sensory imprint (figure). He criticizes "the Derridean notions of `trace' and `archi-writing' for being unable to take any account of the positive presence of the other in relation to discourse" (286 *Theory Culture Society*). About the book Lyotard writes, `This book is not an honest book, it remains withing the field of signification; deconstruction does not take place here directly, it is signified' (282 *Theory Culture Society*). This statement suggests a greater understanding of (Derridean) deconstruction than it has of itself; it suggests that Derridean deconstruction is its object of analysis. The philosophy in this work takes on a threefold dialectical development from figure image to figure form to figure matrix, this word again characterizing the final stage of a philosophy.

Derrida uses the terms "discourse on figure" on page 14 of "White Mythology" translated by F.C.T. Moore in *New Literary History* 6(1974): 5-74. Also, Derrida uses terms such as "field of nondiscursive forces" in "Sign Event Context," *MP*; these references may show how Derrida's philosophy contains the positive genetic determinants of Lyotard's philosophy.

There are good preliminary reasons to begin to research the question whether Lyotard has solved the Derridean dilemma. Gasché deems *Discours, figure* to be a "monumental work in deconstruction" similar to *Of Grammatology* [*Glyph*, 6(1979)183-84]. In "Préjugés: Devant la loi," Lyotard makes a challenge to Derrida, claiming that there is a problem he cannot solve. In one discussion between Derrida and Lyotard, Derrida expresses their difference as Lyotard more decisively breaking with origins (Derrida's):

> I was still sensitive to it today, and I have always sensed it in reading you, but even today when I never felt so close to your work, you have a style, a tone or a way of breaking with nostalgia and everything it connotes or carries along with it, which is resolute, sharp, determined, etc., and I said to myself that at bottom that is what is at stake, and only that, in this question [of what separates us].[2]

Lyotard seems to be able to break from an origin that Derrida cannot. Recapitulating his differences from Derrida, Lyotard writes,

> If there is a variation between my thought and Derrida's, it is expressed in the extension given to the idea of difference. It seems to me that Derrida brings difference into play over all genres, all phrases, all linkages, as I would put it... . To make difference cover everything, to show or exhibit the difference in all kinds of linkages, in all kinds of phrases, there is a risk...of being accused of scepticism (286-87 *Theory Culture Society*).

Lyotard can leave the origin Derrida could not--the original concept of difference. The latter philosopher extends the notion of difference to give it new meaning as "figure image." If Lyotard does extend Derrida's thought by repeating its genetic code in an improved version, it would provide a means of verifying the interpretation offered of Derrida in this book.

Final Remarks: The Human Project

Future philosophers of science, literary critics, and scholars in any field can benefit by using the idea of a cultural genetic code, for tradition forms do act much like DNA. A transductive approach can help scholars point and prepare the way for subsequent creation, as this is scholarship's highest goal. Such an approach can lead specialists to the determining factor necessary for self-improvement, for creation. Although DNA is self-improving it would be anthropomorphic to say that the whole process becomes a component in the continuing process; this is a trait only of self-consciousness.

Human culture has evolved beyond biological species, for it has a freedom of self-determination unknown in the merely biological sphere. Cultural genetic codes are thus more than biological genetic codes. The evolving of cultural genetic codes raised humans out of the merely biological order to a being of a tradition.

Ancient myths used to present the human struggle against beasts and chaos, (usually) resulting in the restoration of a human order of right, of law, of a dominion for individual mind. Consider the Babylonian Myth of Creation (Enuma Elish or `When on High'), the Homeric hymns, and Hesiod's Theogeny. In each there is a triumph of the human community without the victory ever being final, for the individual to be must earn freedom anew.

NOTES

1. Quoted from p. 70 of the bibliography. The original is from "Formen und Formwandlungen des philosophischen Wahrheitsbegriffes." *Hamburgische Universität*. Reden gehalten bei der Feier des Rektorwechsels am 7. Nov. 1929. Hamburg: Boysen, 1929. Pp. 17-26.

2. Quoted from 213 of Carroll's *Paraesthetics*. The original is from Lacoue-Labarthe's and Nancy's edition of *Les fins de l'homme*, 312-13.

List of Secondary Works Cited

Adams, Hazard. "The University of Literature: Terrible Beauty or Rough Beast?" in *Directions for Criticism*. Eds. Murray Krieger and L.S. Dembo. Madison: The University of Wisconsin Press, 1977.

Alexiou, Margaret and Vassilis Lambropoulos. *The Text and Its Margins*. N.Y.: Pella Publishing Company, 1985, 181.

Allen, Richard. "Critical Theory and the Paradox of Modernist Discourse." *Screen* 28.2(1987), 69-84.

Bakhtin, Mikhail. *Problems of Dostoevsky's Poetics*. Ed. and trans. Caryl Emerson. Introd. Wayne C. Booth. Minneapolis: University of Minnesota Press, 1984.

Bakhtin, M.M. and P.N. Medvedev. *The Formal Method in Literary Scholarship: A Critical Introduction to Sociological Poetics*. Trans. by Albert J. Wehrle. London: Harvard University Press, 1978.

Baudrillard, Jean. *For a Critique of the Political Economy of the Sign*. Trans. and introd. by Charles Levin. St. Louis, Mo.: Telos Press, 1981. (The original French publication was in 1972.)

Baudrillard, Jean. *Simulations*. Trans. from the French by Paul Foss, Paul Patton and Philip Beitchman. N.Y.: Semiotext(e), 1983.

Beadle, George W. "The New Biology and the Nature of Man." 1280-81 in *The Norton Reader: An Anthology of Expository Prose*. Gen. Ed. Arthur M. Eastman. N.Y.: W.W. Norton & Company, 1969.

Benjamin, Andrew, ed. *The Lyotard Reader*. Oxford: Basil Blackwell, 1989.

Bennington, Geoffrey. *Lyotard: Writing the Event*. Manchester: Manchester University Press, 1988.

Berman, Art. *From the New Criticism to Deconstruction: The Reception of Structuralism and Post-Structuralism.* Chicago: University of Illinois Press, 1988.

Borklund, Elmer. *Contemporary Literary Critics.* London: Macmillan, 1982.

Brooke-Rose, Christine. "Id is, is Id?" 19-37 in *Discourse in Psychoanalysis and Literature.* Ed. Shlomith Rimmon-Kenan. London: Methuen, 1987.

Burkert, Walter. *Structure and History in Greek Mythology and Ritual.* Berkeley: University of California Press, 1979.

Campbell, Joseph. *The Hero with a Thousand Faces.* Bollingen Series XVII. Princeton: Princeton University Press, 1949.

Carroll, David. *Paraesthetics: Foucault, Lyotard, Derrida.* N.Y.: Methuen, 1987.

Cassirer, Ernst. *Substance and Function and Einstein's Theory of Relativity.* Trans. from the German by William Curtis Swabey and Marie Collins Swabey. N.Y.: Dover Publications, 1923.

Cassirer, Ernst. *The Logic of the Humanities.* Trans. Clarence Smith Howe. N.Y.: Yale University Press, 1961, 187.

Chiarenza, Marguerite Mills. "The Imageless Vision and Dante's *Paradiso.*" *Dante Studies* 90(1972), 77-91.

Clignet, Remi. *The Structure of Artistic Revolutions.* Philadelphia: University of Pennsylvania Press, 1985.

Cohen, I. Bernard. *Revolution in Science.* Cambridge: The Belknap Press of Harvard University Press, 1985.

Cotrâu, Liviu. "Dis-placing and Re-placing the Center: The De-centered Discourse." *Cahiers Romans d'études littéraire* 21(1985), 100-109.

Cummings, Katherine. "*Bleak House.* Remarks on a Daughter's Da." *Style* 21(1987), 237-38.

Crick, F.H.C. and James D. Watson. "The Complementary Structure of Deoxyribonucleic Acid (Proceedings of the Royal Society, 1954). Pages 274-295 in *The Double Helix: A Personal Account of the Discovery of the Structure of DNA.* Ed. Gunther S. Stent. N.Y.: W.W. Norton & Company, 1980.

Crick, Francis. *Life Itself: Its Origin and Nature.* N.Y.: Simon and Schuster, 1981.

Curtius, Ernst Robert. *European Literature and the Latin Middle Ages*. Princeton: Princeton University Press, 195.
De Man, Paul. Review of Jacques Derrida. *De la grammatologie*. *Annales de la socíeté Jean-Jacques Rousseau*. 37, 1966-68, 284-88.
De Man, Paul. "Appendix A: Review of Harold Bloom's *Anxiety of Influence*." In *Blindness and Insight: Essays in the Rhetoric of Contemporary Criticism*. Introd. by Wlad Godzich. Minneapolis: University of Minneapolis Press, 1971. Also in De Man's "Review of Harold Bloom, *The Anxiety of Influence: A Theory of Poetry*." *Comparative Literature*. 26: 3(Summer 1974), 269-75.
De Man, Paul. *The Resistance to Theory*. Foreword by Wlad Godzich. Minneapolis: University of Minnesota Press, 1986.
Dewey, John. "Science and Society." *Philosophy and Civilization*. N.Y.: G.P. Putnam's Sons, 1931. Paragraph 4.
Drain, Betsy. "Writing, Deconstruction, and other Unnatural Acts." *Boundary 2* 9(1981), 425-36.
Duncan, Robert. *Fictive Certainties*. N.Y.: New Directions, 1990.
Eco, Umberto. "Looking for a Logic of Culture." 9-19 in *The Tell-Tale Sign: A Survey of Semiotics*. Ed. Thomas A. Sebeok. Lisse, Netherlands: The Peter de Ridder Press, 1975.
Eco, Umberto. *Semiotics and the Philosophy of Language*. Bloomington: Indiana University Press, [n.d.].
Eggers, Walter and Sigrid Mayer. *Ernst Cassirer: An Annotated Bibliography*. N.Y.: Garland Publishing, 1988.
Eikhenbaum, Boris M. and Yury Tynyanov (note that these names are sometimes transcribed from Russian differently). Trans. and Ed. by Ray Parrot. Ann Arbor: Ardis, 1985.
Einstein, Albert and Leopold Infeld. *The Evolution of Physics: from Early Concepts to Relativity and Quanta*. N.Y.: Simon and Schuster, 1938.
Elam, Helen Regueiro. "Harold Bloom." Pages 32-48 in *Modern American Critics Since 1955*. Ed. Gregory S. Jay. *Dictionary of Literary Biography*. Vol. 67. Detroit: Gale Research Co. [n.d.]
Eliot, T.S. *On Poetry and Poets*. London: Faber & Faber, 1957.

Eliot, T.S. "Tradition and the Individual Talent." *The Norton Anthology of English Literature*. Ed. M.H. Abrams. Fifth edition. Vol. 2. N.Y.: W.W. Norton & Company, 1962.

Emerson, Ralph Waldo. *Nature. The Norton Anthology of American Literature*. 3rd edition. Vol.1. N.Y.: W.W. Norton & Company, 1989.

Erlich, Victor. *Russian Formalism: History-Doctrine*. London: Yale University Press, 1955.

Fite, David. *The Rhetoric of Romantic Vision*. Amherst: The University of Massachusetts Press, 1985.

Fowler, Alastair. *Kinds of Literature. An Introduction to the Theory of Genres and Modes*. Cambridge, Ma.: Harvard University Press, 1982.

Frank, Joseph. "Spatial Form in Modern Literature." Pages 43-78 in *The Avant-Garde Tradition in Literature*. Ed. and intro. by Richard Kostelanetz. N.Y.: Prometheus Books, 1982.

Frye, Northrop. "The Archetypes of Literature." in *The Avant-garde Tradition in Literature*. Ed. and introd. by Richard Kostelanetz. Buffalo, N.Y.: Prometheus Books, 1982, 16-28.

Gablik, Suzi. *Progress in Art*. N.Y.: Rizzoli, 1977.

Gans, Eric. "Differences." *Modern Language Notes* 96(1981), 792-806.

Gasché, Rodolphe. *The Tain of the Mirror: Derrida and the Philosophy of Reflection*. Cambridge: Harvard University Press, 1986.

Gasché, Rodolphe. "Nontotalization without Spuriousness: Hegel and Derrida on the Infinite." *Journal of the British Society for Phenomenology* 17(1986), 289-307.

Gould, Stephen Jay. "A Biological Homage to Mickey Mouse." *The Panda's Thumb: More Reflections in Natural History*. N.Y.: Norton, 1980.

Greimas, A.J. "Structure et histoire." *Les Temps Modernes* No. 246(Nov. 1966), 815-27.

Griffiths, Frederick T. and Stanley J. Rabinowitz. *Novel Epics: Gogol, Dostoevsky, and National Narrative*. Evanston: Northwestern University Press, 1990.

Harper's Dictionary of Classical Literature and Antiquities. Ed. Harry Thurston Peck. N.Y.: Cooper Square Publishers, 1965, pages 163, 374, 1051.

Hartman, Geoffrey H. *Beyond Formalism: Literary Essays 1958-1970*. London: Yale University Press, 1970.

Hartman, Geoffrey H. "Monsieur Texte II: Epiphany in Echoland." *Georgia Review* 30.1(1976), 169-204; see 184.

Hartman, Geoffrey H. *Saving the Text: Literature/Derrida/Philosophy*. London: The Johns Hopkins University Press, 1981.

Harvey, Irene E. *Derrida and the Economy of Différance*. Bloomington: Indiana University Press, 1986.

Hollander, John, ed. "Introduction." *Poetics of Influence: New and Selected Criticism*. New Haven: Doberman, 1988.

Howells, Christina M. *Sartre: The Necessity of Freedom*. Cambridge: Cambridge University Press, 1988. Chapter 9.

Howells, Christina M. "Derrida and Sartre: Hegel's Death Knell." Pages 169-181 in *Continental Philosophy II: Derrida and Deconstruction*. London: Routledge, 1989.

Jefferson, Ann and David Robey, eds. *Modern Literary Theory: A Comparative Introduction*. London: Batsford Academic and Educational Ltd., 1982. [Introduction by Jefferson and Robey; Jefferson 16-38 and 84-113; Robey 38-84; David Forgacs 134-end.]

Kearney, Richard. *Dialogues with Contemporary Continental Thinkers: The Phenomenological Heritage*. Manchester: Manchester University Press, 1984.

Kellner, Douglas. *From Marxism to Postmodernism and Beyond*. Cambridge: Polity Press, 1989.

Kisiel, T. "Paradigms." 87-111 in *Contemporary Philosophy: A New Survey*. Ed. Guttorm Floistad. Hague: Martinus Nijhoff Publishers, 1982.

Krieger, Murray. *Theory of Criticism: A Tradition and Its System*. London: The Johns Hopkins University Press, 1976.

Kronik, John W. "Editor's Column." *PMLA* 106, 2(March 1991), 200-204.

Lemon, Lee T. and Marion J. Reis. *Russian Formalist Criticism: Four Essays*. Trans. and Intro. by Lemon and Reis. London: University of Nebraska Press, 1965.

Lévi-Strauss, Claude. *Structural Anthropology*. N.Y. 1963.
Liszka, James Jakób. "Derrida: Philosophy of the Liminal." *Man and World* 16(1983), 233-250.
Liszka, James Jakób. *The Semiotic of Myth: A Critical Study of the Symbol*. Bloomington: Indiana University Press, 1989.
Lowe, Walter. "Dangerous Supplement/ Dangerous Memory: Sketches for a History of the Postmodern." *Thought* 61(1986), 34-55.
Lyotard, Jean-François. *The Postmodern Condition: A Report on Knowledge*. Trans. from the French (1979) by Geoff Bennington and Brian Massumi. Foreword by Frederick Jameson. Minneapolis: University of Minnesota Press, 1984.
Lyotard, Jean-François and Jean-Loup Thébaud. *Just Gaming*. Trans. by Wlad Godzich. Afterword by Samuel Weber. Minneapolis: University of Minnesota Press, 1985.
Lyotard, Jean-François. *Peregrinations: Law, Form, Event*. N.Y.: Columbia University Press, 1986.
Lyotard, Jean-François. *The Differend: Phrases in Dispute*. Trans. by Georges Van Den Abbeele. Minneapolis: University of Minnesota Press, 1988.
Lyotard, Jean-François. *The Inhuman: Reflections on Time*. Trans. Geoffrey Bennington and Rachel Bowlby. Cambridge: Polity Press, 1991.
Lyotard, Jean-François. *Libidinal Economy*. Trans. Iain Hamilton Grant. London: Athlone Press, 1993, xxv.
Miller, J. Hillis. *The Form of Victorian Fiction*. Notre Dame: University of Notre Dame Press, 1968.
Monod, Jacques. *Chance and Necessity: An Essay on the Natural Philosophy of Modern Biology*. Trans. from the French by Austryn Wainhouse. N.Y.: Alfred A. Knopf, 1971.
Montefiore, Alan. *Philosophy in France Today*. Cambridge: Cambridge University Press, [n.d.], 45.
Mottram, Eric. "No Centre to Hold: A Commentary on Derrida." *Curtains* 14-17(1976), 38-57.
Nancy, Jean-Luc. *The Inoperative Community*. Ed. Peter Connor. Trans. Peter Connor, Lisa Garbus, Michael Holland, and Simona Sawhney. Foreword by Christopher Fynsk. Oxford: University of Minnesota Press, 1991.

Nemerov, Howard. "America's Poet Laureate: Interview with Howard Nemerov." *American Studies Newsletter* 19, Sept. 1989.

Norris, Christopher. *Deconstruction: Theory and Practice*. N.Y.: Methuen, 1982.

"Pablo Picasso: The Legacy of a Genuis." The Tate Gallery, London, Sept. 12, 1992. Art criticism by Moore, Matta, Caro, Hockney, and Lichtenstein, among others. (Michael Blackwood, USA, 1982). 90 minutes.

Peperzak, Adriaan Theodoor. *System and History in Philosophy*. Albany, N.Y.: SUNY, 1986.

Platt, Robert. "Writing, Différance, and Metaphysical Closure." *Journal of the British Society for Phenomenology*, October 1986.

Powell, Grosvenor. "Yvor Winters: A Poet Against Grammatology." *Southern Review* (Baton Rouge) 17(1981), 814-32.

Prodi, G. *Le basi materiali della significazione*. Milan: Bompiani, 1977.

Prodi, G. *La Storia Naturale della Logica*. Milan: Bompiani, 1982.

Raizis, Marius Byron. "Yeats's Preoccupation with Spiritualism and His Two Byzantium Poems." Epistimoniki Epetirida tis Philosophikis Scholis tou Panepistimiou Athinon. Athens. 1992.

Ricoeur, Paul. *The Rule of Metaphor: Multidisciplinary Studies in the Creation of Meaning in Language*. Trans. by Robert Czerny with Kathleen McLaughlin and John Costello, S.J. London: Routledge & Kegan Paul, 1977 [French 1975].

Riffaterre, Michel. "Syllepsis." *Critical Inquiry* 6(1980), 625-38.

The Reader's Adviser. Eds. Barbara A. Chernow and George A. Vallasi. N.Y.: R.R. Bowker Co. 1986, 643.

Riegl, Alois. *Late Roman Art Industry*. Trans. from the original Viennese edition with foreword and annotation by Rolf Winkes. 1985. Published by Giorgio Bretschneider Editore. Also, Riegl wrote *Stilfragen* [Questions or Problems of Style] Also, see Meyer Schapiro, "Style" in *Aesthetics Today*. Ed. Morris Philysson. N.Y.: Meridian, 1961, for a summary of Riegl's views.

Rorty, Richard. "Derrida on Language, Being, and Abnormal Philosophy." *Journal of Philosophy* [74.11] Nov. 1977, 673-81.

Schultz, William. "An Evaluation of Harold Bloom's Idea of Opposition in Poetic Creation." Paper delivered at Aristotle University of Thessaloniki, April 1-4, 1993. Conference title: "Logomachia: Forms of Opposition in English Language/Literature." The proceedings are to be published.

Schultz, William R.; and Lewis L. B. Fried. *Jacques Derrida: An Annotated Primary and Secondary Bibliography*. New York: Garland Publishing, 1992. 882 pages.

Shapiro, Gary. "Peirce and Derrida on First and Last Things." *University of Dayton Review* 17.1(1984), 33-38.

Shklovsky, Viktor. *Theory of Prose*. Trans. by Benjamin Sher and Intro. by Gerald L. Bruns. Naperville, Il.: Dalkey Archive Press, 1992.

Silverman, Hugh. *The Textual Sublime: Deconstruction and Its Differences*. SUNY.

Simmel, Georg. *Philosophische Kultur*. Leipzig: A. Kröner, 1911, 251.

Strudwick, John Mehuish (1849-1935). "A Golden Thread." [Painting] Presently at the Tate Gallery, London.

Tedlock, Dennis. "The Science of Signs and the Science of Letters." [A Review Article of books by Culler, Derrida, Hawkes, and Sebeok] *American Anthropologist* 82(1980), 821-830.

Todd, Jane Marie. "Autobiography and the Case of the Signature: Reading Derrida's *Glas*." *Comparative Literature* 38(1986), 1-19.

Todorov, Tzvetan. *The Poetics of Prose*. Trans. from the French by Richard Howard. Foreword by Jonathan Culler. Ithaca, N.Y.: Cornell University Press, 1977.

Todorov, Tzvetan. *Introduction to Poetics*. Trans. from the French by Richard Howard. Intro. by Peter Brooks. Minneapolis: University of Minnesota Press, 1981.

Truesdell, Clifford. "Reactions of Late Baroque Mechanics to Success, Conjecture, Error, and Failure in Newton's *Principia*." *Science* 10(1967), 238-58.

Tynyanov, Yury. "Preface." *Russian Prose*. Ed. B.M. Eikhenbaum & Yury Tynyanov. Trans. and Ed. by Ray Parrott. Ann Arbor, Mi.: Ardis, 1985.

Veerman, Dick and Willem van Reijen. "An Interview with Jean-François Lyotard." Pages 277-310 in *Theory, Culture & Society: Explorations in Critical Social Science*. Vol. 5, 2-3(June 1988).

Verene, Donald Philip. *The New Art of Autobiography: An Essay on the Life of Giambattista Vico Written by Himself*. Oxford: Clarendon Press, 1991.

Verene, Donald Phillip. "Science, Symbolic Form, and Narration." Theme of Conference: "Narrative Patterns in Scientific Disciplines." *The Cohn Institute*, The Universities of Tel Aviv and Jerusalem. April 1992.

Wellek, Rene. "Russian Formalism." *The Avant-Garde Tradition in Literature*. Ed. Richard Kostelanetz. Buffalo, N.Y.: Prometheus Books, 1982.

Wölfflin, Heinrich. *Principles of Art History: The Problem of the Development of Style in Later Art*. Trans. by M.D. Hottinger. N.Y.: Dover Publications, 1932.

Bibliography

WORKS BY AND ABOUT THOMAS KUHN

Works by Kuhn

1947

Note: Kuhn describes "stumbling upon" his idea of scientific revolution in 1947, before he finished his physics dissertation; see *SSR*, 1970, Preface, xvi.

1952

"Robert Boyle and Structural Chemistry in the Seventeenth Century." *Isis*, XLIII (1952), 26-29. Sometimes Kuhn cites this source as 12-36 and sometimes as 26-39.

1956

"The Function of Measurement." Presented at the Social Science Colloquium at the University of California, Berkeley, in October 1956; revised and extended during 1958; included in *The Essential Tension* as "The Function of Measurement in

Modern Physical Science." (See Kuhn's "Preface," xvii, in that book.

1957

The Copernican Revolution: Planetary Astronomy in the Development of Western Thought. Cambridge, Mass. 1957.

1958

"The Caloric Theory of Adiabatic Compression." *Isis*, XLIX (1958), 132-40.
"Newton's Optical Papers." *Isaac Newton's Papers and Letters on Natural Philosophy.* Ed. I.B. Cohen. Cambridge, Mass. 1958. 27-45.

1959

"Conservation of Energy as an Example of Simultaneous Discovery." *Critical Problems in the History of Science*, ed. Marshall Clagett. Madison, Wis. 1959, 321-56. Though much of this article is an attempt to understand simultaneous discovery, partly by discovery through anomalies in the applications of theory to the world, Kuhn also notes this: "much of what is there said about the emergence of `conversion processes' [conversion of the scientist to a new way of thinking] also describes the evolution of a crisis state [a state in which theory confronts insoluble problems and so necessitates a new way of thinking or revolution]" (*ET*, 205).
"The Essential Tension: Tradition and Innovation in Scientific Research." *The Third (1959) University of Utah Research Conference on the Identification of Creative Scientific Talent.* Ed. Calvin W. Taylor. Salt Lake City, 1959. 162-77.

1960

"Engineering Precedent for the Work of Sadi Carnot." *Archives internationales d'histoire des sciences*, XIII (1960), 247-51.

1961

"Sadi Carnot and the Cagnard Engine." *Isis*, LII(1961), 567-74.
"The Function of Measurement in Modern Physical Science." *Isis*, 52(1961), 161-93. This is the first publication introducing Kuhn's idea of the distinction between the classical and the Baconian sciences (Kuhn, *ET*, 62).
"The Function of Dogma in Scientific Research." In "Symposium on the History of Science, University of Oxford, July 9-15, 1961."

1962

"The Historical Structure of Scientific Discovery." *Science*, CXXXVI (June 1, 1962), 760-64. Reprinted in *ET*, 1977, Chapter 7.
The Structure of Scientific Revolutions. Part of "The Foundations of the Unity of Science," which constituted volumes 1 and 2 of the *International Encyclopoedia of Unified Science*. Ed. in Chief Otto Neurath. Chicago: The University of Chicago Press, 1962. All references are to the Enlarged Second Edition, 1970.

1963

"The Function of Dogma in Scientific Research." *Scientific Change*. Ed. A.C. Crombie. New York, 1963. 347-69.

1964

"A Function for Thought Experiments." In *Melanges Alexandre Koyré*. Eds. Cohen and Taton. Vol. 2, *L'aventure de l'esprit*, pp. 307-34.

1967

Kuhn, T.S. and J.L. Heilbron, P.F. Forman, and Lini Allen. *Sources for History of Quantum Physics: An Inventory and Report*. Philadelphia, 1967. This contains information about depositories of documents relating mathematics and mathematical physics in England, France, and the United States during the 1920s. The Archives for History of Quantum Physics contain interviews with Leon Brillouin, E.C. Kemble, and N.F. Mott.

1969

"Second Thoughts on Paradigms." Prepared for a conference held in March 1969. "Some of the same ground" is "retraced" (Kuhn's words, *ET*, xx) in "Reflections on My Critics" and in the "Postscript--1969" to the enlarged edition of *The Structure of Scientific Revolutions*.

"Comment [on the Relations between Science and Art]." *Comparative Studies in Philosophy and History*, XI, 1969, pp. 403-12. Kuhn speaks of paintings as being "modelled" one on another--here is a concept needing to be developed by Kuhn (solution-modelling). Also, Kuhn discusses what is special about science in relation to the arts.

1970

Enlarged, Revised, Second Edition of *The Sturcture of Scientific Revolutions*, with a *Postscript*, containing refinements of his theory. Chicago University Press, 1970.

"Reflections on My Critics." In *Criticism and the Growth of Knowledge: Proceedings of the International Colloquium in the Philosophy of Science, London, 1965, Volume 4*. Eds. Lakatos, Imre and Alan Musgrave. London: Cambridge University Press, 1970. Discussions by J.W.N. Watkins, S.E. Toulmin, L. Pearce Williams, K.R. Popper, Margaret Masterman, I. Lakatos, P.K. Feyerabend, and T.S. Kuhn. [Kuhn addresses critics in the volume containing their criticism.] Note that this was written *after* "Second Thoughts on Paradigms" but *before* "Postscript--1969" (*ET*, xx).

"Logic of Discovery or Psychology of Research?" in *Criticism and the Growth of Knowledge*.

"Second Thoughts on Paradigms." In Frederick Suppe, ed., *The Structure of Scientific Theories*. Urbana, Il.: University of Illinois Press, 1970 or 1971. In the 1974 edition the pages are 459-82. Also included in *The Essential Tension*, 1977.

"Alexandre Koyré and the History of Science." *Encounter* 34 (1970), 67-70.

1971

"Notes on Lakatos." *Boston Studies in Philosophy of Science* 8(1971), 137-46.

"Les notions de causalité dans le developpement de la physique." *Etudes d'épistémologie génétique* 25(1971), 7-18. Later appearing in *ET*, 1977, as "Concepts of Cause in the Development of Physics."

1972

"Scientific Growth: Reflections on Ben-David's `Scientific Role'." *Minerva* 10 (1972), 166-78.

1976

"Mathematical versus Experimental Traditions in the Development of Physical Science." *The Journal of Interdisciplinary History* 7(1976), 1-31. The first version was presented in 1972 as a George Sarton Memorial Lecture, Washington, D.C., before the joint session of the American Association for the Advancement of Science and the History of Science Society. Reprinted in *ET*, 1977, Chapter 3.

1977

"The Relations between the History and the Philosophy of Science." In *Die Entstehung des Neuen: Studien zur Struktur der Wissenschaftsgeschichte*. Frankfurt. 1977. Also in *The Essential Tension*, 1977.

"Objectivity, Value Judgment, and Theory Choice." In *Die Entstehung des Neuen* and in *The Essential Tension*, both 1977.

The Essential Tension: Selected Studies in Scientific Tradition and Change. Chicago: The University of Chicago Press. 1977.

1989

Preface. In *Die Wissenschaftsphilosophie Thomas S. Kuhns: Rekonstruktion und Grundlagenprobleme*. Braunschweig: F. Vieweg, 1989.

Selected Works on Kuhn's Thought

Note: Ackermann, J.S. is cited in *ET*, the Index, but no bibliographic information is given; he is a critic of Kuhn's views of art and science. Also, G. Kubler; for biographical material see

John Horgan 1991; a computer search yielded 1,600 records on Kuhn in late 1992.

1963

Hawkins. Review of Kuhn's *Structure of Scientific Revolutions*. *American Journal of Physics*, 31 (1963), 554-55.

1964

Shapere, Dudley. "The Structure of Scientific Revolutions." [Review of *The Structure of Scientific Revolutions*.] *The Philosophical Review*, 73, 1964, 383-94. Kuhn found this criticism and that of Margaret Masterman particularly "cogent" (See *The Structure of Scientific Revolutions*, p. 174, note 4).

1965

See 1970 Lakatos, Imre and Alan Musgrave, eds. *Criticism and the Growth of Knowledge*. While the conference was in 1965, the year of first publication was 1970.

1966

Shapere, Dudley. "Meaning and Scientific Change." In *Mind and Cosmos: Essays in Contemporary Science and Philosophy*. The University of Pittsburgh Series in the Philosophy of Science, III, Pittsburgh, 1966, 41-85. Shapere accuses Kuhn of "glorifying subjectivity and even irrationality" in Kuhn's words (*SSR*, 1970, 186).

1967

Toulmin, Stephen. "The Evolutionary Development of Natural Science." *American Scientist* 55 (1967), 456-71.

Scheffler, Israel. *Science and Subjectivity*. New York, 1967. Herein in Kuhn's words (*SSR*, 1970, p. 186) Scheffler accuses Kuhn of "glorifying subjectivity and even irrationality." Also, Kuhn believes the essays of Sir Karl Popper and Imre Lakatos make the same charge; see *Criticism and the Growth of Knowledge*.

1969

Lashchyk, Eugene M. "Scientific Revolutions: A Philosophical Critique of the Theories of Science of Thomas Kuhn and Paul Feyerabend." Diss. University of Pennsylvania, 1969.

1970

Lakatos, Imre and Alan Musgrave, eds. *Criticism and the Growth of Knowledge: Proceedings of the International Colloquium in the Philosophy of Science, London, 1965, Volume 4*. London: Cambridge University Press, 1970. Discussions by J.W.N. Watkins, S.E. Toulmin, L. Pearce Williams, K.R. Popper, Margaret Masterman, I. Lakatos, P.K. Feyerabend, and T.S. Kuhn ("Reflections on My Critics" [Kuhn addresses critics in the same volume] and "Logic of Discovery or Psychology of Research?"). In "Postscript--1969" in *SSR* Kuhn responds to these criticisms once again.

1973

Gablik, S. "On the Logic of Artistic Discovery: Art as Mimetic Conjecture." *Studio International*. Vol. 186, 958(Sept. 1973), 65-68.

1977

Brown, Harold I. "Objective Knowledge in Science and the Humanities." *Diogenes* 97(1977), 85-102.
Kourany, Janet A. "A Paradigm in Crisis: A Study of Thomas Kuhn's Theory of Science." Diss. Columbia University, 1977.
Mehta, Ghanshyam. *The Structure of the Keynesian Revolution.* London: Martin Robertson, 1977. Also in 1978.

1978

Bukin, W. "Aesthetische Kultur und wissenschaftliches Weltbild." *Kultur* 26(1978), 1029-33.
Mehta, Ghaushyam. *The Structure of the Keynesian Revolution.* N.Y.: St. Martin's Press, 1978. Also in 1977 with an English publisher.
Ryan, Steven T. "The Importance of Thomas S. Kuhn's Scientific Paradigm Theory to Literary Criticism." *Midwest Quarterly*, 19, 2(1978), 151-9. Ryan thinks Kuhn's ideas are helpful in understanding literature, because they help clarify ideas about form and his historical discussions show how science affected literature of the 19th and 20th centuries.

1979

Bizzel, Patricia. "Thomas Kuhn, Scientism, and English Studies." *College English* 40(1979), 764-71.
Jacobs, Struan. *On the Philosophical Analysis of Science.* Waurn Ponds, Victoria: The University, 1979.
Jevons, F.R. "Puzzles and Revolutions: Case Study of the Copernican Revolution." Waurn Ponds, Victoria: Open Campus Program, Deakin University, 1979.
Murrell, William Gregory. "Paradigmatology, Paradigms and Education: A Study of Thomas Kuhn and Magoroh Maruyama with Implications for Contemporary and Future Education." Diss. The Univerity of New Mexico, 1979.

1980

Gutting, Gary, ed. "Paradigms and Revolutions; Appraisals and Applications of Thomas Kuhn's Philosophy of Science." Notre Dame: University of Notre Dame Press, 1980.

1981

Ragonnet, James Lawrence. "The Relationship Between Rhetorical and Scientific Discovery." Diss. Rensselaer Polytechnic Institute, 1981.
Wells, Richard H. and J. Stephen Picou. *American Sociology: Theoretical and Methodological Structure*. Washington, D.C., University Press of America, 1981.

1982

Barnes, Barry. *T.S. Kuhn and Social Science*. N.Y.: Columbia University Press, 1982.
Langsdorf, Lenore. "The Relevance of the Popper-Kuhn Debate for the Understanding of Language Use." *Forum Linguisticum*, 7, 1(1982), 3-14.
Mackenzie, J. Lachlan. "Linguistics as `Normal Science': Charted, Championed and Challenged." *Dutch Quarterly Review of Anglo-American Letters* 12, 2(1982), 141-152.
McCawley, James D. "How Far Can You Trust a Linguist?" Pages 75-87 in Simon, Thomas W.; Robert J. Scholes; Robert Q. Marston, eds. *Language, Mind, and Brain*. Hillsdale, N.J.: Erlbaum, 1982.
Reckmeyer, William John. "The Emerging Systems Paradigm: An Historical Perspective." Diss. The American University, 1982.
Stove, David C. *Popper and After: Four Modern Irrationalists*. N.Y.: Pergamon Press, 1982.

1983

Bahner, Werner. "`Paradigm' or `Current' in the History of Linguistics." Published under Auspices of CIPL (The Hague); Actes du XIIIe cong. internat. des linguistes. In Hattori, Shiro and Kazuko Inoue, eds. *Proceedings of the XIIIth International Congress of Linguists, August 29- September 4, 1982, Tokyo.* Tokyo: Tokyo Press, 1983.

Brown, J. Marvin. "Powers's Loop and a Neural Theory of Language." Pages 50-84 in Agard, Frederick B.; and Gerald Kelley; Adam Makkai; Valerie Becker Makkai, eds. *Essays in Honor of Charles F. Hockett.* Leiden: Brill, 1983.

Gatens-Robinson, Eugenie. "The Relationship of Scientific Explanation to Models of Rationality." Diss. Southern Illinois University at Carbondale, 1983.

1984

Cude, Wilfred. "What Literary Criticism Needs to Learn from Scientific Methodology." *Mosaic: A Journal for the Interdisciplinary Study of Literature,* 17, 4(1984), 1-16.

Putnam, Hilary. "The Craving for Objectivity." *New Literary History: A Journal of Theory and Interpretation,* 15, 2(Winter 1984), 229-239.

Tinkler, John Francis. "Humanism as Discourse: Studies in the Rhetorical Culture of Renaissance Humanism, Petrarch to Bacon." *Dissertation Abstracts International,* 44, 9(March 1984).

1985

Clignet, R. *The Structure of Artistic Revolutions.* Philadelphia: The University of Pennsylvania Press. 1985.

Langsdorf, Leonore and Harry P. Reeder. "`The Whole Business of Seeing': Nature, World, and Paradigm in Kuhn's Account of Science." Pages 175-199 in Ihde, Don and Hugh J. Silverman, eds. *Descriptions*. Albany: State University of New York Press, 1985.

McCawley, James D. "Kuhnian Paradigms as Systems of Markedness Conventions." Pages 23-43 in Makkai, Adam, and Alan K. Melby, eds. *Linguistics and Philosophy: Essays in Honor of Rulon S. Wells*. Amsterdam: Benjamins, 1985.

Quigley, Austin E. "Taking the Measure of Theoretical Models." *University of Hartford Studies in Literature: A Journal of Interdisciplinary Criticism*, 17, 2(1985), 1-12.

Rowe, Montie Edward. "A Content Analysis of Citations to Four Prominent Philosophers of Science in Selected Sociology Journals." Diss. North Texas State University, 1985. This work analyzes the citations to Kuhn's and others' work.

1986

Greenway, John L. "Seward's Folly: Dracula as a Critique of `Normal Science'." *Stanford Literature Review*, 3, 2(Fall 1986), 213-230.

Heusser, Hans-Jorg. "Computers and the Crisis of Art History." *Bulletin of the Archives and Documentation Centers for Modern and Contemporary Art*. Vol. 14-15, 25-26(1986-1987), 3-4.

Hughes, Shaun F.D. "Salutary Lessons from the History of Linguistics." Pages 306-322 in Bjarkman, Peter C. and Victor Raskin, ed. *The Real-World Linguist: Linguistic Applications in the 1980s*. Norwood, N.J.: Ablex, 1986.

Hullen, Werner. "The Paradigm of John Wilkins' Thesaurus." Pages 115-124 in Hartmann, R.R.K., ed. *The History of Lexicography: Papers from the Dictionary Research Centre Seminar at Exeter, March 1986*. Amsterdam: Benjamins, 1986.

Schwab. "Reader-Response and the Aesthetic Experience of Otherness." In Berman, R. and Wellbery, D. eds. *Interpretation--Discourse--Society. Interdisciplinary Paradigms in Literary Scholarship*. And in *Stanford Literature Review*, 3, 1(1986), 107-136.

Shaw, D. "A Kuhnian Metatheory for Aesthetics." *Journal of Aesthetics and Art Criticism.*" Vol. 45, Part 1 (Fall 1986), 29-39.

Uematsu, Yasuo. "Aldous Huxley and the Post-Cartesian Disciplinary Matrix." *Tohoku Gakuin University Review: Essays and Studies in English Language and Literature* (Tohoku Gakuin Daigaku Ronshu, Eigo-Eibungaku), 78, Nov. 1986, 63-80.

Verronen, Veli. *The Growth of Knowledge: An Inquiry into the Kuhnian Theory.* Jyvaskyla: Jyvaskylanyliopisto: Distributor, Jyvaskylan University Library, 1986. There is a copy in the University of California library system at Berkeley.

Weimar, K. "On Traps for Theory and How to Circumvent Them." In Berman, R. and Wellbery, D. eds. *Interpretation--Discourse--Society. Interdisciplinary Paradigms in Literary Scholarship.*

1987

Kralik, Monica M. "Conceptual Revolutions in Antiquity: A Historical and Analytical Comparison of the Greek and Etruscan Experiences." Diss. Wayne State University, 1987.

Callahan, John F. "`Riffing' and Paradigm-Building: The Anomaly of Tradition and Innovation in `Invisible Man' and `The Structure of Scientific Revolutions'." *Callaloo: An Afro-American and African Journal of Arts and Letters*, 10, 1(1987), 91-102.

Schatzberg, Walter; Ronald A. Waite, and Jonathan K. Johnson, eds. *The Relations of Literature and Science: An Annotated Bibliography of Scholarship, 1880-1980.* 1987.

1988

Andersson, Gunnar. *Kritik und Wissenschaftsgeschichte: Kuhn's, Lakatos' und Feyerabend's Kritik des Kritischen Rationalismus.* Tubingen: J.C.B. Mohr (P. Siebeck), 1988.

Chimimbo, Moira. "Toward an Integrated Model of First and Second Language Acquisition." *Journal of Humanities*, 2, 1988, 1-16.
Emons, Rudolf. "Chomsky's Grammar as a Paradigm?" 21, 1988, 113-121. *PMLA*.
Keita, L. "Theory Incommensurability and Kuhn's History of Science, A Critical Analysis." *Diogenes* 143(Fall 1988), 41-65.
Kolenda, Konstantin. "The Idea of Progress." *Humanist* 48, 1(1988), 43.
Margolis, Joseph. "Ontology Down and Out in Art and Science." *Journal of Aesthetics and Art Criticism*. Vol. 46, Part 4 (Summer 1988), 451-60.
Segal, Judith Zelda. "Reading Medical Prose as Rhetoric: A Study in the Rhetoric of Science." Diss. The University of British Columbia, 1988.
Ulmer, Gregory. "The Puncept [sic: `P'] in Grammatology." Pages 164-189 in Culler, Jonathan, ed. *On Puns: The Foundation of Letters*. Oxford: Blackwell, 8, 1988.

1989

Cravens, Hamilton; Alan I. Marcus. "American Studies and American Science: An Analysis." *American Studies* 30, 2(Fall 1989), 5-21.
Glas, Edward. "Testing the Philosophy of Mathematics in the History of Mathematics: The Sociocognitive Process of Conceptual Change." *Studies in History and Philosophy of Science* 20, 1(March 1989), 115-132.
Holcomb, H.R. "Interpreting Kuhn--Paradigm Choice as Objective Value Judgment." *Metaphilosophy* 20, 1(Jan. 1989), 51-67.
Hoyningen-Heune, Paul. *Die Wissenschaftsphilosophie Thomas S. Kuhns: Rekonstruktion und Grundlagenprobleme*. Mit einen Geleitwort von Thomas S. Kuhn. Braunschweig: F. Vieweg, 1989.
Hoyningen-Heune, Paul. Title trans. from German: "Scientific Development and Reality in the Theory of Kuhn, Thomas,

S." *Deutsche Zeitschrifte fur Philosophie*, 37, 6(1989), 508-17.
Jackson, Robert S. "The Rhetoric of Translation: Interpretive Communities and Sacred Text." *Literature and Belief*, 9, 1989, 18-29.
Sindelar, D. "Questions d'esthetique contemporaine." *Estetika*, CSK, 26, 4(1989), 193-198.
Wallen, Stanley. "Historiography of Thomas S. Kuhn." Diss. New York University, 1989.

1990

Amrine, Frederick. "The Metamorphosis of the Scientist." *Goethe Yearbook: Publications of the Goethe Society of North America*, 5, 1990, 187-212.
Biagioli, Mario. "The Anthropology of Incommensurability." in *Studies in the History and Philosophy of Science*, 21, 2(1990), 183-210.
Callahan, John F. "Tradition and Innovation: Evolving Paradigms in the `Structure of Scientific Revolutions' and `Invisible Man'." Pages 117-28 in Slade, Joseph W., and Judith Yaross Lee, eds. *Beyond the Two Cultures: Essays on Science, Technology, and Literature*. Ames: Iowa State University Press, 1990.
Efland, Arthur D. "Curricular Fictions and the Discipline Orientation in Art Education." *Journal of Aesthetic Education*, Vol. 24, Part 3 (Fall 1990), 67-81.
Holland, Ray. "The Paradigm Plague: Prevention, Cure, and Inoculation." *Human Relations* 43, 1(1990), 23-49.
Hoyningen-Heune, Paul. "Kuhn's Conception of Incommensurability." *Studies in History and Philosophy of Science*. Vol. 21, 3(Sept. 1990), 481-493.
Moses, David James. "Incommensurability and the Revolution of Quantum Mechanics." M.A. California State University, Long Beach, 1990.
Radnitzky, G. "Is Kuhn's Revolution in the Philosophy of Science a Pseudo-Revolution?" *International Studies in Philosophy*, 22, 1(1990), 77-78.

1991

Horgan, John. "Profile: Reluctant Revolutionary: Thomas S. Kuhn Unleashed `Paradigm' on the World." *Scientific American*, 264, 5(May 1991), 40-2. Biographical Material.

Khaliki, Muhammad Ali. "Meaning-Change and Theory-Change." Diss. Columbia University, 1991.

LaLumia, Joseph. "Kuhn and His Critics on Normal and Revolutionary Science." *Diogenes*, 154(1991), 39-46.

Mcomber, James Brant. "Philosophy in the Service of Rhetoric: Rhetoric and Antirhetoric in the Creation-Science Controversy." Diss. The University of Iowa, 1991.

Palmer, Eric Joseph Edward. "Philosophy of Science and History of Science: A Productive Engagement." Diss. University of California, San Diego, 1991.

Reisch, George A. "Did Kuhn Kill Logical Empiricism?" *Philosophy of Science*, Vol. 58, 2(June 1991), 264.

Schaffer, Simon. *Kuhn* Cambridge: Polity Press [in association with Basil Blackwell], 1991.

Stone, Mark A. "A Kuhnian Model of Falsifiability." *British Journal for the Philosophy of Science* 42, 2(June 1991): 177-186.

1992

Argyrous, G. "Kuhn Paradigms and Neoclassical Economics." *Economics and Philosophy*, 8, 2(Oct. 1992), 231-48.

Fuller, S. "Being There with Kuhn, Thomas--A Parable for Postmodern Times." Review. *History and Theory*, 31, 3(1992), 241-75.

1993

Horwich, Paul, ed. "Thomas Kuhn and the Nature of Science." Cambridge: MIT Press, 1993.

WORKS BY AND ABOUT HAROLD BLOOM

Books by Bloom

1959
Shelley's Mythmaking. New Haven: Yale University Press.

1961
The Visionary Company: A Reading of English Romantic Poetry. Garden City: Doubleday.
Ed. *English Romantic Poetry* (Anthology).

1963
Blake's Apocalypse: A Study in Poetic Argument. Garden City: Doubleday.

1965
Commentary to Blake's Poetry and Prose
Ed. with Frederick W. Hilles. *From Sensibility to Romanticism; Essays Presented to Frederick A. Pottle.* N.Y.: Oxford University Press, 1965.

1970
Yeats. New York: Oxford University Press.
Ed. *Romanticism and Consciousness: Essays in Criticism*

1971
The Ringers in the Tower: Studies in Romantic Tradition. Chicago: University of Chicago Press, 1971.
Revised (from 1961) and enlarged: *The Visionary Company: A Reading of English Romantic Poetry.* Ithaca, N.Y.: Cornell University Press.

1972
Ed. *The Romantic Tradition in American Literature*
Ed. with Kermode, Hollander, Price, Trilling, and Trapp, *Oxford Anthology of English Literature*, 2 vols.

1973
Ed. *Romantic Prose and Poetry*
The Anxiety of Influence A Theory of Poetry. New York: Oxford University Press.
Selected Poetry [of S.T. Coleridge]. N.Y.: New American Library, 1973.
The Oxford Anthology of English Literature: Romantic Poetry and Prose. With Lionel Trilling

1975
Kabbalah and Criticism. New York: Seabury Press.
A Map of Misreading. New York: Oxford University Press.
Poetry and Repression: Revisionism from Blake to Stevens. New Haven: Yale University Press.

1976
Figures of Capable Imagination. New York: Seabury Press.

1977
Wallace Stevens: The Poems of Our Climate. London: Cornell University Press.

1978
Ed. *Selected Poetry and Prose of Shelley*
The Flight to Lucifer: A Fantasy of the Gnosis (a novel by Bloom)

1980

Robert Browning: A Collection of Critical Essays, co-editor. Englewood Cliffs, N.J.: Prentice-Hall.

1981
Agon: Towards a Theory of Revisionism. Oxford: Oxford University Press.

1982
The Breaking of the Vessels. Chicago: University of Chicago Press.
Ed. *Selected Writings of Walter Pater*. New York: Columbia University Press.
With David V. Erdman. *The Complete Poetry and Prose of William Blake*. Garden City, N.Y.: Anchor, 1982.

1983

Foreword by Bloom in *Elizabeth Bishop and Her Art*, eds. Lloyd Schwartz and Sybil P. Estess. Ann Arbor: University of Michigan Press, 1983.

1984
Freud: Transference and Authority
Poetics of Influence: New and Selected Criticism

The Chelsea House Library of Literary Criticism. Introductions by Bloom. A very large series. New York: Chelsea House. 1984 onward.

1985

The Art of the Critic. Many volumes to date, edited, with introductions by Bloom. New York: Chelsea House. 1985 onward.

Modern Critical Interpretations. Over 70 volumes to date, edited, with introductions by Bloom. New York: Chelsea House.

Ed. *Robert Browning*

1986

The Critical Cosmos. More than 8 volumes to date, edited, with introductions by Bloom. New York: Chelsea House.

1987

Ruin the Sacred Truths: Poetry and Belief from the Bible to the Present

1988

The Art of the Critic: Literary Theory and Criticsm from the Greeks to the Present. Vol. 6. Later Romantics. Introduction by Bloom. New Haven: Chelsea House Publishers.

1989

Too many editions to mention through Chelsea House--literally thousands.

1990

The Book of J. With David Rosenberg. N.Y.: Grove Weidenfeld, 1990.

Articles by Bloom

1961

"Napolean and Prometheus: The Romantic Myth of Organic Energy." *Yale French Studies* 26(1961), 79-82.

1964

"Keats and Romanticism." *Modern Language Quarterly* Vol. 25, December 1964, 479-85. Review article.
"Keats and the Embarrassments of Poetic Tradition." *From Sensibility to Romanticism* [28]. Ed. Hilles and Bloom. [Place: Publisher], 1964, pp. 513-26.

1965

Introduction. *The Literary Criticism of John Ruskin*. Garden City, N.Y.: Anchor, 1965.

1966

"The Central Man: Emerson, Whitman, Wallace Stevens." *Massachusetts Review* 7(Winter 1966), 23-42.
"Frankenstein or the New Prometheus." *Partisan Review* 32(1965), 611-18.

1968

"Visionary Cinema." *Partisan Review* 55(Fall 1968), 555-70.

1969

"The Internalization of Quest Romance." *Yale Review* 58 (Summer 1969), 526-36.
"The Visionary Cinema of Romantic Poetry." Pages 18-35 in Rosenfeld, Alvin H., ed. *William Blake: Essays for S. Foster Damon.* Providence, R.I.: Brown University Press, 1969.

1970

"Browning's Childe Roland: All Things Deformed and Broken." *Prose* 1(1970), 29-44.
"Recent Studies in the Nineteenth Century." *Studies in English Literature, 1500-1900* 10(1970), 817-29.
"First and Last Romantics." *Studies in Romanticism* 9(1970), 225-32.
"To Reason with a Later Reason: Romanticism and the Rational." *Midway* 11, 1(1970), 97-112.

1971

"Bacchus and Merlin: The Dialectic of Romantic Poetry in America." *Southern Review* (not University of Adelaide) 7(1971), 140-75.
"The Daemonic Allegorist." *Virginia Quarterly Review* 47(1971), 477-80. [Review article]
"Blake's `Jerusalem': the Bard of Sensibility and the Form of Prophecy." *Eighteenth-Century Studies: A Journal of Literature and the Arts* 4(1971), 6-20.
"Poets' Politics." *Virginia Quarterly Review* 47(1971), 314-317.
"Emerson: The Glory and the Sorrows of American Romanticism." *Virginia Quarterly Review* 47(1971), 546-63.

1971

"Work in Progress. Antithetical Criticism: An Introduction."
    Diacritics 1, 2(1971), 39-46.

1972

"Clinamen or Poetic Misprision." *New Literary History* 3(1972), 373-91.
"Death and the Native Strain in American Poetry." *Social Research: An International Quarterly* 39(1972), 449-62.
"The Sorrows of American-Jewish Poetry." *Commentary* 53, 3(1972), 69-74.
"Coleridge: The Anxiety of Influence." *Diacritics* 2, 1(1972), 36-41. Also in Hartman, Geoffrey, ed. *New Perspectives on Coleridge and Wordsworth*. Columbia University Press, 247-67.
"Dark and Radiant Peripheries: Mark Strand and A.R. Ammons." *Southern Review* (not the University of Adelaide) 8(1972), 133-49.

1973

"Emerson and Ammons: A Coda." *Diacritics* 3, 4(1973), 45-46.
"Emerson: The Glory and Sorrows of American Romanticism." Pages 155-73 in Thorburn, David, and Geoffrey Hartman, eds. *Romanticism: Vistas, Instances, Continuities*. Ithaca: Cornell University Press, 1973. Previously published in 1971.
"John Ashberry: The Charity of the Hard Moments." *Salmagundi* 22-23(1973), 103-31.
"The Native Strain: American Orphism." Pages 285-304 in Brady, Frank; John Palmer; and Martin Price, eds. *Literary Theory and Structure: Essays in Honor of William K. Wimsatt*. New Haven: Yale University Press, 1973.

1974

"The Dialectics of Literary Tradition." *Boundary* 2(1974), 528-38.
"The Freshness of Transformation or Emerson on Influence." American Transcendental Quarterly 21(1974), 57-63.
"How to Read a Poem: Browning's `Childe Roland'." *Georgia Review* 28(1974), 404-18.
"John Ashberry: The Charity of the Hard Moments." Also in 1973, but reprinted as pages 83-100 in Weisberber, Leo. *Rhenania Germano-Celtica: Gesammelte Abhandlungen dem Autor zum siebzigsten Geburtstag am 25. Februar 1969.* Bonn: Ludwig Roehrscheid.
"Wallace Stevens: The Poems of Our Climate." *Prose* 8(1974), 5-24.
"Walter Pater: The Intoxication of Belatedness." *Yale French Studies* 50(1974), 163-89.

1975

"A.R. Ammons: The Breaking of the Vessels." *Salmagundi* 31-32(1975), 185-203.
"The Freshness of Transformation: Emerson's Dialectics of Influence." Pages 129-48 in Levin, David, ed. *Emerson: Prophecy, Metamorphosis, and Influence.* N.Y.: Columbia University Press, 1975.
Introduction. *Somewhere Is Such a Kingdom: Poems, 1952-1971.* Boston: Houghton-Mifflin, 1975.
"Poetry, Revisionism, Repression." *Critical Inquiry* 2(1975) 233-51.
"The Survival of Strong Poetry (on Geoffrey Hill)." *American Poetry Review* 4, 4(1975), 17-20.
"The Necessity of Misreading." *Georgia Review* 29(1975), 267-88.
Introduction. *Somewhere Is Such a Kingdom: Poems, 1952-1971.* Boston: Houghton-Mifflin, 1975.

1976

"Poetic Crossing: Rhetoric and Psychology." *Georgia Review* 30(1976), 495-524.

"Poetic Crossing II: American Stances." *Georgia Review* 30(1976), 772-96.

Review article on the year's poetry. *New Republic*, 20 Nov. 1976, 20-26.

"Wallace Stevens: Reduction to the First Idea." *Diacritics* 6, 3(1976), 48-57.

1979

"The Breaking of Form." Pages 1-38 in *Deconstruction and Criticism*. Ed. by Harold Bloom, Paul de Man, Jacques Derrida, Geoffrey Hartman, and J. Hillis Miller. New York: Continuum, 1979.

"Lying against Time: Gnosis, Poetry, Criticism." *The Oxford Literary Review* 3, 3(1979), 4-15.

"The White Light of Trope: An Essay on John Hollander's `Spectral Emanations'." *Kenyon Review* 1(1979), 95-113.

1980

"Freud's Concept of Defense and the Poetic Will." Pages 1-28 in Smith, Joseph H., ed. *The Literary Freud: Mechanisms of Defence and the Poetic Will*. New Haven: Yale University Press, 1980.

"Viewpoint." *Times Literary Supplement*, 30 May 1980, 611. This is about modern American poetry and its antecedants.

"The Voice of Kinship." *Times Literary Supplement*, 8 Feb. 1980, 137-38.

1981

"Agon: Revisionism and Critical Personality." *Raritan* 1, 1(1981), 18-47.
"Auras: The Sublime Crossing and the Death of Love." *Oxford Literary Review* 4, 3(1981), 3-19.

1982

"Clinamen: Towards a Theory of Fantasy." Pages 1-20 in Slusser, George E[dgar]; Eric S. Rabkin; and Robert Scholes, eds. *Bridges to Fantasy*. Essays from Eaton Conference on Science Fiction and Fantasy Literature. Carbondale: Southern Illinois University Press, 1982.
"Plagiarism: A Symposium." *TLS* 1982 April 9. With Lord Goodman; Ian McEwan; Wilfrid Mellers; Pat Rogers; John Sutherland.

1983

Foreword. In *Elizabeth Bishop and Her Art*. Lloyd Schwartz and Sybil P. Estess, eds. Ann Arbor: University of Michigan Press.
"Reading Freud: Transference, Taboo, and Truth." Pages 309-328 in Cook, Eleanor; Chaviva Hosek; Jay Macpherson; Patricia Parker; and Julian Patrick, eds. *Centre and Labyrinth: Essays in Honour of Northrop Frye*. Toronto: University of Toronto Press, 1983.

1984

"Apocalypse Then." *New York Review of Books* 30(19 January 1984), 25-6.
"`Before Moses Was, I Am': The Original and Belated Testaments." *Notebooks in Cultural Analysis* 1(1984), 3-14.

"Sunset Hawk: Warren's Poetry and Tradition." Pages 59-79 in Edgar, Walter B., ed. *A Southern Renascence Man: Views of Robert Penn Warren*. Baton Rouge: Louisiana State University Press, 1984.

1985

"From Topos to Trope, from Sensibility to Romanticism: Collins's `Ode to Fear'." Pages 182-203 in Cohen, Ralph, ed. *Studies in Eighteenth-Century British Art and Aesthetics*. Berkeley: University of California Press, 1985.

"James Dickey: From `The Other' through *The Early Notion*." *The Southern Review* 21, 1(Winter 1985), 63-78.

1986

"Falstaff." *Scripsi* 4, 1(July 1986), 59-66.

"Freud: The Greatest Modern Writer." *New York Times Book Review* 91(23 March 1986), 1.

"Homer, Virgil, Tolstoy: The Epic Hero." *Raritan: A Quarterly Review* 6, 1(Summer 1986), 1-25.

"W.S. Merwin. The New Transcendentalism: The Visionary Strain in Merwin." *Contemporary Poets*. Modern Critical Views Series. Ed. and Intro. (9 pages) Harold Bloom. New Haven: Chelsea House Publishers, 1986, 245-250.

1988

Bersani, Leo. "Against *Ulysses*." *Raritan* 8, no. 2 (Fall 1988): 1-32. This describes *Ulysses* as transumptive or metaleptic in Bloomian style.

Review of *The Literary Guide to the Bible*. *New York Review of Books* 35, 5(March 31, 1988), 23-6.

"Reflections on T.S. Eliot." *Raritan: A Quarterly Review* 8,2(Fall 1988), 70-87.

1990

"The American Sublime." [Botts, Gregory: The Painting as Icon.] *Arts Magazine* 64, 10(1990), 37-43.

Commentary on "J in the Wilderness" [reputed author of the Pentateuch; another article in this same issue]. *Tikkun* 5, 5(Sept-Oct., 1990), 41-46.

Excerpt from *The `Book of J'*, by Harold Bloom and D. Rosenberg. *American Poetry Review* 19, 6(1990), 27-33.

"Introduction to Proust." Pages 311-325 in Laforge, Catherine, ed; Henri Peyre, introd; Jean Boorsch, tribute. *Dilemmas du roman: Essays in Honour of Georges May*. Saratoga, California: Anma Libri, 1990. Previously published essay.

1991

"Freud--Frontier Concepts, Jewishness, and Interpretation." *American Imago* 48, 1(Spring 1991), 135-152.

"Mark Strand" [Review]. *The Gettysburg Review* 4, 2(1991), 247-48.

1992

"The Religion-making Imagination of Joseph Smith" [Nineteenth-Century Mormon Prophet]. *Yale Review* 80, 1-2(April 1992), 26-44.

Selected Works on Bloom's Criticism

1959

Anon. Review of *Shelley's Mythmaking Times Literary Supplement*, August 21, 482.
Simpson, L. Review of *Shelley's Mythmaking*. *Hudson Review* 12(1959), 635-37.
Wasserman, E. Review of *Shelley's Mythmaking*. *Yale Review* 48(1959), 609-11.

1960

Butler, Peter. Review of *Shelley's Mythmaking*. *Modern Language Review* 55(1960), 268-69.
Fogle, Richard Harter. Review of *Shelley's Mythmaking*. *Modern Philology* 57(1960), 212-13.
Mathews, G.M. Review of *Shelley's Mythmaking*. *Essays in Criticism* 10(1960), 462-6.
Nitchie, Elizabeth. Review of *Shelley's Mythmaking*. *Modern Language Notes* 75(1960), 609-13.

1961

Fogle, Richard Harter. Review of *Shelley's Mythmaking*. *Comparative Literature* xiii(1961), 279-80.
Huscher, Herbert. Review of *Shelley's Mythmaking*. *Anglia* 79(1961), 113-116.
Purser, J.W.R. Review of *Shelley's Mythmaking*. *Review of English Studies* 12(1961), 214-16.

1962

Anon. Review of *The Visionary Company*. *Times Literary Supplement*, April 20, 266.
Gross, John. Review of *The Visionary Company*. *N.St.* 64(1962), 202-3.
Nichol, Norman. Review of *The Visionary Company*. *Listener* 67(1962), 700-01.

1963

Benziger, James. Review of *The Visionary Company*. *Criticism* 5(Spring 1963), 185-8.
Grant, John E. Review of *Blake's Apocalypse*. *Yale Review* 52(1963), 591-98.
James, Louis. Review of *The Visionary Company*. *Critical Quarterly* 5(1963), 277.
Lewis, C.S. Review of *The Visionary Company*. *Encounter* 20(June 1963), 74-76.
Purser, J.W.R. Review of *The Visionary Company*. *Review of English Studies* 14(1963), 209-11.
Smith, H.A. Review of *The Visionary Company*. *Modern Language Review* 58(1963), 108-9.

1965

Minerof, Arthur. Review of *The Literary Criticism of John Ruskin*, ed. Bloom. *The Library Journal* 90(1965), 3455.
Review of *From Sensibility to Romanticism* (by Bloom and Hilles). *Carleton Miscellany* 6(Fall 1965), 93.
Review of *From Sensibility to Romanticism*. *Choice* 2(1965), 297.
Review of *From Sensibility to Romanticism*. *Johnsonian News Letter* 25(1965), 1-2.
Review of *From Sensibility to Romanticism*. *Times Literary Supplement*, Dec. 23, 1965, 1198.

1966

Brett, R.L. Review of *From Sensibility to Romanticism*. *Critical Quarterly* 8(1966), 95-6.
Jump, John D. Review of *From Sensibility to Romanticism*. *Review of English Studies* 17(1966), 331-33.
Kinsley, James. Review of *From Sensibility to Romanticism*. *Modern Language Review* 61(1966), 681-3.
Peschmann, Hermann. Review of *From Sensibility to Romanticism*. *English* 16(1966), 20-2.
Mahoney, John L. Review of *From Sensibility to Romanticism*. *Thought* 41(1966), 284-5.

1967

Mahl, Mary R. Review of *The Literary Criticism of John Ruskin*. *The Personalist* 68(1967), 262.

1968

Hollander, Robert. Review of *The Literary Criticism of John Ruskin*. *Southern Quarterly* (University of Southern Missouri) 4(1968), 767.

1970

Boland, Evan. Review of *Yeats*. *The Critic* 29(Jan.-Feb. 1970), 80-2.
Boulger, James L. Review of *Yeats*. *Thought* 45(1970), 620-3.
Grossman, Allen. Review of *Yeats*. *Virginia Quarterly Review* 46(1970), 520-5.
Jumper, Will C. Review of *Yeats*. *Poet and Critic* 6,1(1970), 47-8.
Moore, Harry T. Review of *Yeats*. *Saturday Review* 20(June 1970), 37-9.
Pick, John. Review of *Yeats*. *America* 1,22(1970), 597-8.
Review of *Yeats*. *Antioch Review* 30(1970), 133.

Review of *Yeats*. *Christian Century*. 87(April 1970), 511. (only 70 words)

1971

Allen, James L. Review of *Yeats*. *Journal of Modern Literature* 2(1971), 148-54.
Baine, Rodney M. Review of *Blake's Apocalypse*. *Georgia* 25(1970), 238-41.
Boland, Eavan. *Critic* 29(Jan. 1971), 80ff. (1100 words).
Connelly, Kenneth. Review of *Yeats*. *Yale Review* 60(1971), 394-403.
Fletcher, Angus. "The Central Commentary: Notes for a Review." *Diacritics* 1(Fall 1971): 16-26.
Review of *Yeats*. *Times Literary Supplement* 12 March 1971, 292. (650 words).
Rose, Edward J. Review of *Blake's Apocalypse*. *Western Humanities Review* 25(1971), 362.
Siegel, Sandra. "Prolegomenon to Bloom: The Opposing Virtue," *Diacritics* 2(Winter 1971): 35-38.
Vendler, Helen. Review of *Yeats*. *Journal of English and Germanic Philology* 70(1971), 691-6.
Wellek, Rene. "American Criticism of the Last Ten Years." *Yearbook of Comparative and General Literature* 20(1971), 5-14.
Yergin, Daniel. Review of *Yeats*. *Yale Review* 60(March 1971), 417 ff. (2800 words)

1972

Adams, Hazard. Review of *Yeats*. *Georgia Review* 26(1972), 249-78.
Allen, James L., Jr. Review of *Yeats*. *Journal of Modern Literature* 2(1972), 148-54.
Ehr, John W. Review of *The Ringers in the Tower*. *ESQ: A Journal of the American Renaissance* 18(1972), 186-96.
Parkinson, Thomas. Review of *Yeats*. *English Language Notes* 9(1972), 234-5.

Pritchard, William H. Review of *Yeats*. *Partisan Review* 38,1(1972), 107-12.
Peckham, Morse. Review of *The Ringers in the Tower* 9(1972), 59-62.
Sidnell, Michael. Review of *Yeats*. *UTQ* [University of Texas Quarterly] 41(1972), 263-74.
Torchiana, Donald T. Review of *Yeats*. *Modern Philology* 70(1972), 168-74.

1973

Hartman, Geoffrey. "War in Heaven." *Diacritics* 3, 1(1973), 26-32. Review article on Bloom's *Anxiety of Influence*.
McGann, Jerome J. "Romanticism and the Embarrassments of Critical Tradition," in *Modern Philology* 70, 3(1973), 243-57.

1974

De Man, Paul. "Book Reviews: `The Anxiety of Influence: A Theory of Poetry'," in *Comparative Literature* 26, 3(1974), 269-75.
Lentricchia, Frank. "Harold Bloom: The Spirit of Revenge," in *After the New Criticism*. Chicago: University of Chicago Press, 1974, 318-346.

1975

Burke, Kenneth. "Father and Son," *New Republic* 172(12 April 1975): 23-24.
Culler, Jonathan. "Reading and Misreading," *The Yale Review* 65, 1(October 1975), 88-95.
Hartman, Geoffrey. "War in Heaven," in *The Fate of Reading and Other Essays*. Chicago: University of Chicago Press, 1975, 41-56.
Pritchard, William H. "The Hermeneutical Mafia; or, After Strange Gods at Yale." *Hudson Review*, 28(1975), [pp.]

Said, Edward W. "The Poet as Oedipus: A Map of Misreading," *New York Times Book Review*, 13 April 1975, 23-25.
Wood, Michael. "In the Literary Jungle," *The New York Review of Books* 12, 6(April 17, 1975), 15-18.

1976

Hollander, "Poetic Misprision," *Poetry* 127 (January 1976): 222-234.
Humphris, R. "The Influence Argument." *British Journal of Aesthetics* 16(1976), 261-67.
Kincaid, James R. "Antithetical Criticism, Harold Bloom, and Victorian Poetry." *Victorian Poetry* 14(1976), 365-82. [Review article]
Krieger, Murray. *Theory of Criticism: A Tradition and Its System*. Baltimore: Johns Hopkins University Press, 1976.
-----. "Poetics Reconstructed: The Presence vs. the Absence of the Word." *New Literary History* 7(1976), 347-75.
McGann, Jerome J. "Formalism, Savagery, and Care; or, The Function of Criticism Once Again." *Critical Inquiry* 2(1976)
Nemoianu, Virgil. Review of *The Anxiety of Influence*. *Romania literara* (Bucharest) 9:10(1976), 20.
Ricks, Christopher. "A Theory of Poetry, and Poetry: `Poetry and Repression: Revisionism from Blake to Stevens'," *The New York Times Book Review* 14 March 1976, p.6.
Riddel, Joseph N. "[Review article on H. Bloom]" *Georgia Review* 30(1976), 989-1006. Reviewed are *Kabbalah and Criticism* and *Poetry and Repression*.
Wieseltier, Leon. "Summoning Up the Kabbalah." *New York Review of Books*, 19 Feb. 1976, 27-31. Review article on Bloom's *Kabbalah and Criticism*.

1977

Ackerman, R.D. Review of *Wallace Stevens*. *Wallace Stevens Journal* 1(1977), 108-110.

Basset, Sharon. "*Tristes Critiques*: Harold Bloom and the Sorrows of Secular Art." *Literature and Psychology* 27(1977), 106-12. [Review article]
Bennett, Diane. Review of *Poetry and Repression*. *Wallace Stevens Journal* 1(1977), 79-80.
Burke, Kenneth. Review of *Wallace Stevens*. *New Republic: A Journal of Politics and the Arts* 1, 76(1977), 25-7.
Daley, Morton D. Review of *Poetry and Repression*. *Studia Neophilologica* (Stockholm) 49(1977), 159-61.
Eiland, Howard. "Harold Bloom and High Modernism." *Boundary 5* (1977), 935-42. [Review article]
Gould, Warwich. Review of *Kabbalah and Criticism*. *English* (London) 26(1977), 40-54.
-----. Review of *The Anxiety of Influence*. *English* 26(1977), 40-54.
"Harold Bloom on Poetry." *New Republic* Vol. 177, (Nov. 26. 1977), 24-27.
Hirsch, David H. Review of *Kabbalah and Criticism*. *Sewanee Review* 85(1977), 153-66.
-----. Review of *Figures of Capable Imagination*. *Sewanee Review* 85(1977), 153-66.
-----. Review of *Poetry and Repression*. *Sewanee Review* 85(1977), 153-66.
Kermode, Frank. Review of *Wallace Stevens*. *New York Times Book Review*, 12 June 1977, 44.
Lehman, David. Review of *Figures of Capable Imagination*. *Times Literary Supplement*, 11 March 1977, 266.
Lentricchia, Frank. Review of *Poetry and Repression*. *Modern Language Quarterly* 38(1977), 110-12.
Margolin, Vri. Review of *The Anxiety of Influence*. *Canadian Review of Comparative Literature* 4(1977), 103-9.
Marshall, Donald. Review of *Kabbalah and Criticism*. *Partisan Review* 44(1977), 131-4.
-----. Review of *A Map of Misreading*. *Partisan Review* 44(1977), 131-34.
Maxwell-Mahon, W.D. Review of *The Anxiety of Influence*. *Unisa English Studies* 15.1(1977), 51-2.
Miller, Vincent. Review of *Wallace Stevens*. *Yale Review* 67, 1(1977), 121-4.

Morse, Samuel French. Review of *Wallace Stevens*. *Wallace Stevens Journal* 1(1977), 99-107.

Pritchard, William H. Review of *Wallace Stevens*. *New Republic: A Journal of Politics and the Arts* 77(3 Dec. 1977), 35.

Proffitt, Edward. Review of *Wallace Stevens*. *Commonweal* 104(1977), 691-92.

Riddel, Joseph N. Review of *Wallace Stevens*. *Wallace Stevens Journal* 1(1977), 111-19.

Russo, John Paul. Review of *Wallace Stevens*. *Times Literary Supplement*, 18 Nov. 1977, 1345.

Sawyer, M. Review of *Poetry and Repression*. *Revue des langages vivantes* (Brussels) 43(1977), 636-7.

Wilkie, Brian. Review of *Poetry and Repression*. *Journal of English and Germanic Philology* 76(1977), 114-17.

Wordsworth, Ann. Review of *Figures of Capable Imagination*. *Georgia Review* 31(1977), 528-33.

1978

Altieri, Charles. Review of *Figures of Capable Imagination*. *Criticism* 19(1978), 350-61.

Bedient, Calvin. Review of *Wallace Stevens*. *Modern Language Quarterly* 39(1978), 183-90.

Margolin, Vri. "Harold Bloom. *The Anxiety of Influence: A Theory of Poetry*." *Canadian Review of Comparative Literature* 4(1977), 103-99.

Perloff, Marjorie G. Review of *Wallace Stevens*. *American Literature* 50(1978), 129-32.

Ryan, Steven T. "The Importance of Thomas S. Kuhn's Scientific Paradigm Theory to Literary Criticism." *Midwest Quarterly* 19(1978), 151-59.

Todorov, Tzvetan. "On Literary Genesis." Tran. Ellen Burt. *Yearbook of English Studies* 58(1979), 213-35.

Toloyan, Khachig. Review of *Poetry and Repression*. *English Language Notes* 15(1978), 229-37.

1979

Abrams, M. H. "How to Do Things with Texts." *Partisan Review*, 46, no. 4 (1979): 566-588.

Lynch, Michael. Review of *Wallace Stevens*. *Four Decades* 2(1979), 54-9.

Miller, James E., Jr. Review of *Wallace Stevens*. *Modern Philology* 7, 7(1979), 249-53.

Moynihan, Robert. Interview with J. Hillis Miller. Yale, Fall 1979. *Criticism: A Quarterly for Literature and the Arts*. 24, 2(Spring 1982), 99-125.

Pinsky, Robert. Review of *Poetry and Repression*. *Modern Philology* 76(1979), 300-303.

Rose, Edward J. Review of *Wallace Stevens*. *Modern Studies* 3(1979), 168-71.

Sukenick, Ronald. Review of *Wallace Stevens*. *Partisan Review* 45(1979), 634-6.

Wilkie, Brian. Review of *Poetry and Repression*. *Journal of English and Germanic Philology* 76(1979), 114-117.

1980

Cain, William E. Review of *Deconstruction and Criticism*. *College English* 42(1980), 28-30.

Dauber, Kenneth. "The Revisionary Company." *Sewanee Review* 88(1980), 184-97.

Donoghue, Denis. Review of *Deconstruction and Criticism*. *New York Review of Books*, 12 June 1980, 37-9.

Hall, Dennis R. "Semiotics: An Approach to Interdisciplinary Studies." Festschrift 62 as cited in the *MLA*. 110-21.

Hartman, Geoffrey H. "The Sacred Jungle 1: Carlyle, Eliot, Bloom," in *Criticism in the Wilderness: The Study of Literature Today*. New Haven: Yale University Press, 1980, 42-62.

Norris, Christopher. "Harold Bloom: A Poetics of Reconstruction." *British Journal of Aesthetics* 20(1980), 67-76.

-----. "Wrestling with Reconstructs." *Critical Quarterly* 22(1980), 57-62. [Review article]

O'Hara, Daniel T. "The `Freedom of the Master'." *Contemporary Literature* 21(1980), 649-61.
Riddel, Joseph N. "Juda Becomes New Haven," *Diacritics* 10(Summer 1980): 17-34.
Scruton, Roger. Review of *Deconstruction and Criticism*. *PN Review* 4(1980), 22-4.
Smith, Joseph H. Introduction to *The Literary Freud: Mechanisms of Defense and the Poetic Will*. Ed. by Smith. New Haven: Yale University Press, 1980, pp. ix-xix.
Vickery, John B. "Literary Criticism and Myth: Anglo-American Critics." *YCC* 9(1980), 210-37.

1981

Clubbe, John. "The `Folklore' of English Romanticism." *Mosaic* 14, 3(Summer 1981), 95-112.
Culler, Jonathan. "The Semiotics of Poetry: Two Approaches." Pages 75-93 in De George, Richard T., ed. *Semiotic Themes*. Lawrence: University of Kansas, 1981.
Diehl, Joanne Feit. "Dickinson and Bloom: An Antithetical Reading of Romanticism." *TSLL [Texas Studies in Literature and Language]* 23, 3(Fall 1981), 418-441.
Donoghue, Denis. "Harold Bloom," in *Ferocious Alphabets*. Boston, Little Brown, and London, Faber, 1981.
Ferber, Michael. "`London' and Its Politics." *English Literary History* 48, 2(Summer 1981), 310-338. This treats politics in Bloom's work.
O'Hara, Daniel. "Love's Architecture: The Poetic Irony of Thomas Kinsella." *Boundary* 9, 2(Winter 1981), 123-35.
Olsen, Stein Hangom. "On Unilluminating Criticism." *British Journal of Aesthetics* 21, 1(Winter 1981), 50-64.
Polansky, Steve. "A Family Romance--Northrop Frye and Harold Bloom: A Study of Critical Influence." *Boundary 2: A Journal of Postmodern Literature and Culture* 9, 2(1981), 227-45.
Sitter, John. "The Flight from History in Mid-Eighteenth-Century Poetry (and Twentieth-Century Criticism)." Pages 94-116 in Agresto, John, ed.; Peter Riesenberg, ed.; Walter Alan

Tuttle, bibliog. *The Humanist as Citizen* Chapel Hill: National Humanities Center, 1981.

Wordsworth, Ann. "An Art that Will Not Abandon the Self to Language: Bloom, Tennyson and the Blind World of the Wish." In *Untying the Text: A Post-Structuralist Reader.* Ed. Robert Young. Boston: Routledge, 1981, pp. 207-222.

1982

Bruss, Elizabeth. "Harold Bloom," in *Beautiful Theories: The Spectacle of Discourse in Contemporary Criticism.* Baltimore: Johns Hopkins University Press, 1982, pp. 283-362.

Fite, David Joseph. "Criticism as Scripture: The `Belated' Romanticism of Harold Bloom." Diss. University of Southern California, Vol. 43, 3(1982), p. 797A.

Galbreath, Robert. "Salvation-Knowledge: Ironic Gnostics in `Valis' and *The Flight to Lucifer.*" In *Science Fiction Dialogues*, ed. Gary Wolfe. Chicago: Academy Chicago, 1982, pp. 115-132.

Handelman, Susan A. "The Critic as Kabbalist: Harold Bloom and the Heretic Hermeneutic," in *The Slayers of Moses: The Emergence of Rabbinic Interpretation in Modern Literary Theory.* Albany: State University of New York Press, 1982, 179-223.

Horn, William D. "William Blake and the Problematic of the Self." in *William Blake and the Moderns*, ed. Robert J. Bertholf and Annette S. Levitt. Albany: State University of New York, 1982, pp. 260-285.

Jackson, Richard. "The Deconstructivist Moment in Modern Poetry." *Contemporary Literature* 23(Summer 1982), 306-322. This article uses a deconstructionist approach to treat timelessness and spatial form.

Jay, Gregory S. "Going after New Critics: Literature, History, Deconstruction." *New Orleans Review* 8, 3(1981), 251-164.

McFarland, Thomas. "Field, Constellation, and Aesthetic Object." *New Literary History: A Journal of Theory and Interpretation* 13, 3(1982), 421-47.

Mudrick, Marvin. "Bloom, Bloom, Go Out the Room!" *Harper's* 265, 1587(August 1982), 65-70.

Payne, Michael. "The Poet's Eye." *Pennsylvania English: Essays in Film and the Humanities* 9(1982), 20-38.

Randel, Fred V. "Coleridge and the Contentiousness of Romantic Nightingales." *Studies in Romanticism* 21(Spring 1982), 33-35.

Rollin, Roger B. "The Anxiety of Identification: Jonson and the Rival Poets." In *Classic and Cavalier: Essays on Jonson and the Sons of Ben*, ed. Claude J. Summers and Ted-Larry Pebworth. Pittsburgh: University of Pittsburgh Press, 1982, pp. 139-154.

Swann, Joseph T. "`Where All the Ladders Start': Language and Experience in Yeats's Later Poetry." *Studies in Anglo-Irish Literature*. Bonn, Germany: Bouvier, 1982. This discusses "The Circus Animals' Desertion" by Yeats in Bloom's *Yeats*.

Vendler, Helen. "The Poetics of Power." *New Republic* 186(17 February 1982): 31-36.

1983

Aune, James Arnt. "Burke's Late Blooming: Trope, Defense, and Rhetoric." *The Quarterly Journal of Speech* 69, 3(1983), 328-53.

Brooks, Cleanth. "The Primacy of the Reader." *The Missouri Review* 6, 2(1983), 189-201.

Caruth, Cathy. "Speculative Returns: Bloom's Recent Work." *MLN* 98, 5(1983), 1286-96.

Dolzani, Michael. "The Infernal Method: Northrop Frye and Contemporary Criticism." Pages 59-68 in Cook, Eleanor; Hosek Chavira; Jay Macpherson; Patricia Parker; Julian Patrick, eds. *Centre and Labyrinthe: Essays in Honor of Northrop Frye*. Toronto: University of Toronto Press, 1983.

Horn, William Dennis. "William Blake and the Problematic of the Self." Pages 260-285 in Bertholf, Robert J., ed; Annette S.Levitt, ed. *William Blake and the Moderns*. Albany, N.Y.: State University of New York, 1982.

Horstmann, Ulrich. "The Over-Reader: Harold Bloom's Neo-Darwinian Revisionism Poetics." *International Review for the Theory of Literature* 12, 2-3(1983), 139-49.
Horstmann, Ulrich. "Parakritik und Dekonstruktion: Der amerikanische Post-Strukturalismus." *ArAA [Arbeiten aus Anglistik und Amerikanistik]* 8, 2(1983), 145-158.
Jarvis, Robin. "Three Men in a Drunken Boat: Milton, Wordsworth, Bloom." *Diacritics* 13, 3(Fall 1983), 44-56.
Jay, Gregory S. "Father Figures and Literary History," in *T.S. Eliot and the Poetics of Literary History*. Baton Rouge: Louisiana State University Press, 1983, 67-79.
O'Hara, Daniel. "The Genuis of Irony: Nietzsche in Bloom." Pages 109-32 in Arac, Jonathan; Wlad Godzich; and Wallace Martin, eds. *The Yale Critics: Deconstruction in America*. Minneapolis: University of Minnesota Press, 1983.
Poole, Roger. "The Yale School as a Theological Enterprise." *Renaissance & Modern Studies* 27(1983), 1-29.
Riddel, Joseph N. "The Climate of Our Poems." *Wallace Steven Journal* 7, 3-4(Fall 1983), 59-75.
Webster, Grant. "American Literary Criticism: A Bibliographical Essay." *American Studies International* 20(Autumn 1981), 3-44.

1984

Ahsen, Akhter. "Reading of Image in Psychology and Literary Text." *Journal of Mental Imagery* 8, 3(Fall 1984), 1-31.
Axelrod, Steven Gould. "Harold Bloom's Enterprise." *Modern Philology: A Journal Devoted to Research in Medieval and Modern Literature* 81, 3(1984), 290-297.
Federmayer, Eva. "Beyond Formalism: Problems of Interpretation in Harold Bloom's Antithetical Criticism." In *The Origins and Originality of American Culture*, ed. Tibor Frank. Budapest: Akademiai Kiado, 1984. 467-475. This is about *A Map of Misreading*.
Fogel, Daniel Mark. "henry JAMES joyce: The Succession of the Masters." *Journal of Modern Literature* 11, 2(July 1984), 199-229.

Godfrey, Sima. "The Anxiety of Anticipation." *Yale French Studies* 66(1984), [pp.].
Lecercle, Jean-Jacques. "Meprise et interpretation: Harold Bloom et l'hermetisme." Pages 37-50 in Arnaud, Pierre (introd.) *L'Hermetisme*. Paris: Univ. de Paris X, 1984.
Lindholdt, Paul J. "Isaac McCaslin and the Burden of Influence." *University of Mississippi Studies in English* 5 (1984-1987), 172-181.
Mulryne, Ronnie. "Yeats and Edward Dowden: Critical Clinamen." *Gaeliana* 6(1984), 137-153.
Rowlinson, Matthew. "The Skipping Muse: Repetition and Difference in Two Early Poems of Tennyson." *Victorian Poetry* 22, 4(Winter 1984), 349-363.
Wyatt, David. "Bloom, Freud, and `America'." *Kenyon Review* 6(Summer 1984), 59-66.

1985

Axelrod, Steven Gould. "Robert Lowell and Hopkins." *Twentieth Century Literature: A Scholarly and Critical Journal* 31, 1(1985), 55-72.
Barzilai, Shuli. "A Review of Paul de Man's `Review of Harold Bloom's Anxiety of Influence'." *Yale French Studies* 69(1985), 134-141.
Curtis, James M. "Ephebes and Precursors in Chekhov's `The Seagull'." *Slavic Review: American Quarterly of Soviet and East European Studies* 44, 3(1985), 415-437.
Daleski, H.M. "Lawrence and George Eliot: The Genesis of `The White Peacock'." Pages 51-68 in Meyers, Jeffrey, ed. and introd. *D.H. Lawrence and Tradition*. Amherst: University of Massachusetts Press, 1985.
Davidson, Michael. "Notes beyond the `Notes': Wallace Stevens and Comtemporary Poetics." Pages 141-160 in Gelpi, Albert, ed. *Wallace Stevens: The Poetics of Modernism*. Cambridge: Cambridge University Press, 1985.
Delgado, Ana Maria. "A Note on Misreading; or Filling the Author's Gaps II." Pages 19-23 in Balakian, Anna, ed. and foreword; James J. Wilhelm, ed; Douwe W. Fokkema, ed;

Edward C. Smith, III, asst. to ed.; Claudio Guillen, ed; Peggy Escher, asst. ed.; M.J. Valdes, ed. *Proceedings of the Xth Congress of the International Comparative Literature Association, New York, 1982.* Vol. 1, New York: Garland, 1985.

Fischer, Michael. *Does Deconstruction Make Any Difference? Poststructuralism and the Defense of Poetry in Modern Criticism.* Bloomington: Indiana University Press, 1985.

Fite, David. *Harold Bloom: The Rhetoric of Romantic Vision.* Amherst: University of Massachussetts Press, 1985.

Ford, Jane. "James Joyce and the Conrad Connection: `The Anxiety of Influence'." *Conradiana: A Journal of Joseph Conrad Studies* 17, 1(1985), 3-18.

Goldstein, Lynda R. "Harold Bloom's `Notes' toward Self-Canonization." *The Wallace Stevens Journal: A Publication of the Wallace Stevens Society* 9, 2(Fall 1985), 101-117.

Hollahan, Eugene. "An Anxiety of Influence Overcome: Dickey's Puella and Hopkins' The Wreck of the `Deutschland'." *James Dickey Newsletter* 1, 2(1985), 2-12.

O'Hara, Daniel T. "The Genius of Irony: Nietzsche in Bloom." Pages 55-92 in *The Romance of Interpretation: Visionary Criticism from Pater to de Man.* New York: Columbia University Press, 1985.

Johnson, Michael L. "From Hardy to Empson: The Swerve of the Modern." *South Atlantic Review* 50, 1(1985), 47-58.

Mileur, Jean-Pierre. *Literary Revisionism and the Burden of Modernity.* Berkeley: University of California Press, 1985.

Perloff, Marjorie. "Revolving in Crystal: The Supreme Fiction and the Impasse of Modernist Lyric." Pages 41-64 in Gelpi, Alpert, ed. *Wallace Stevens: The Poetics of Modernism.* Cambridge: Cambridge University Press, 1985.

Primeau, Ronald. "Robinson and Browning Revisited: `Man against the Sky' and `Childe Roland'." *College Literature* 12, 3(1985), 222-232.

Renza, Louis A. "Poe's Secret Autobiography; Sel. Papers from the Eng. Inst., 1982-83." Pages 58-89 in Michaels, Walter Benn, ed.; Donald E. Pease, ed. and introd. *The American Renaissance Reconsidered.* Baltimore: Johns Hopkins University Press, 1985.

Sadoff, Dianne F. "Black Matrilineage: The Case of Alice Walker and Zora Neale Hurston." *Signs: Journal of Women in Culture and Society* 11, 1(1985), 4-26.

Spearing, A.C. "Renaissance Chaucer and Father Chaucer." *English: The Journal of the English Association* 34, 148(1985), 1-38.

Sultan, Stanley. "Eliot and the Concept of Literary Influence." *The Southern Review* 21, 4(1985), 1071-1093.

Swaim, Kathleen M. "`Heart-Easing Mirth': L'Allegro's Inheritance of Faerie Queene II." *Studies in Philology* 82, 4(1985), 460-76.

1986

Delany, Sheila. "Rewriting Women Good: Gender and the Anxiety of Influence in Two Late-Medieval Texts." Pages 75-92 in Wasserman, Julian N., ed; Robert J. Blanch, ed. *Chaucer in the Eighties*. Syracuse: Syracuse University Press, 1986.

Hummer, T.R. "`The Thousand Variations of One Song': James Dickey and the Impetus of Influence." *James Dickey Newsletter* 3, 1(Fall 1986), 9-12.

Lehman, David. "Yale's Insomniac Genius." *Newsweek*, Vol. 108, August 1986, 56-58.

Lobb, Edward. "The Dead Father: Notes on Literary Influence." *Studies in the Humanities* 13, 2(Dec. 1986), 67-80.

Motte, Warren F., Jr. "Clinamen Redux." *Comparative Literature Studies* 23, 4(1986), 263-281.

Moynihan, Robert. *A Recent Imagining; Interviews with Harold Bloom, Geoffrey Hartman, J. Hillis Miller, Paul De Man.* Hamden, Conn.: Archon Books, 1986. Republished from "Interview with Harold Bloom." *Diacritics*, 13 (Fall 1983): 57-68.

Newlyn, Lucy. "For the Fallen." *Times Literary Supplement* (London), vol. 4349, 1986 Aug. 8, p. 871.

O'Hara, Daniel. "Over Emerson's Body." *CEA Critic: An Official Journal of the College English Association* 49, 2-4(Winter-Summer 1986-1987), 79-88.

Steiner, Dorothea. "Feminist Criticism, Poetic Theory, and American Poetry Historiography." Pages 88-113 in Truchlar, Leo, ed. *Fur eine offene Literaturwissenschaft: Erkundungen und Eroprobungen am Beispiel US-amerikanischer Texte/Opening Up Literary Criticism: Essays on American Prose and Poetry.* Salzburg: Neugebauer, 1986.

Tagliaferri, Aldo; Carravetta, Peter. "Harold Bloom between Tradition and Innovation." *Differentia: Review of Italian Thought* 1(Autumn 1986), 113-21.

1987

Ash, Beth Sharon. "Jewish Hermeneutics and Contemporary Theories of Textuality: Hartman, Bloom, and Derrida." *Modern Philology* Vol. 85, 65(Aug. 1987), 65-80.

Berman, Jaye. "Harold Bloom and Judaism." *Midstream: A Monthly Jewish Rev.* 33, 8(Oct. 1987), 42-44.

Brooke-Rose, Christine. "Id is, is Id?" In *Discourse in Psychoanalysis and Literature.* New York: Methuen, 1987, 19-37. This article discusses Bové's more detailed discussion of tradition in Bloom and Derrida in Bové, Paul A. *Deconstructive Poetics: Heidegger and Modern American Poetry.* New York: Columbia University Press, 1980 esp. pp. 19 and 294 of Bové's work.

Doane, Janice; Hodges, Devon. *Nostalgia and Sexual Difference: The Resistance to Contemporary Feminism.* N.Y.: Methuen, 1987.

Eddins, Dwight. "Paradise Reclaimed: Idyllic Vision in Joyce's Ulysses." *Texas Studies in Literature and Language* 29, 4(Winter 1987), 397-411.

Huckle, Nicholas Martyn. "Arrangements in Alchemy: Studies in Mallarme and Char." *DAI* 48, 4(1987), p. 934A.

Kolodny, Annette. "The Influence of Anxiety: Prolegomena to a Study of the Production of Poetry by Women." Pages 112-141 in Harris, Marie; Kathleen Aguero, eds. *A Gift of Tongues: Critical Challenges in Contemporary American Poetry.* Athens: University of Georgia Press, 1987.

McGuirk, Bernard. "On Misreading Mallarme: Ruben Dario and `The Anxiety of Influence'." *Nottingham French Studies* 26, 2(1987), 52-67.

Pease, Donald. "Critical Communities." Pages 92-110 in Buttigieg, Joseph A., ed. *Criticism without Boundaries: Directions and Crosscurrents in Postmodern Critical Theory*. Notre Dame: University of Notre Dame Press, 1987.

Salusinszky, Imre. *Criticism in Society; Interviews with Jacques Derrida, Northrop Frye, Harold Bloom, Geoffrey Hartman, Frank Kermode, Edward Said, Barbara Johnson, Frank Lentricchia, and J. Hillis Miller*. Series: New Accents. New York: Methuen, 1987.

Uhlig, Claus. "Antithetical Criticism: Harold Bloom's Psychopoetik als Novum der amerikanischen Literaturkritik." Pages 99-112 in Haas, Rudolf, ed. foreword, and introd. *Amerikanische Lyrik: Perspektiven und Interpretationen*. Berlin: Schmidt, 1987.

Zytaruk, George. "D.H. Lawrence's `The Rainbow' and Leo Tolstoy's `Anna Karenina': An Instance of Literary `Clinamen'." *Germano-Slavica: A Canadian Journal of Germanic and Slavic Comparative Studies* 5, 5-6(1987), 197-209.

1988

Adams, Jeffrey. "The Scene of Instruction: Morike's Reception of Goethe in `Besuch in Urach'." *Deutsche VierteUahrsschrift fur Literaturwissenschaft und Geistesgeschichte* 62, 3(1988), 476-513.

Anon. "Literature as the Bible." *The New York Review of Books* 35(31 March 1988), 23-5.

Collings, David Allen. "In Search of Expiation: The Structure and Psychology of Secularization in Wordsworth's Poetry." *DAI* 48, 8(Feb. 1988), p. 1928A.

De Bolla, Peter. *Harold Bloom; Towards Historical Rhetorics*. Critics of the Twentieth Century. London: Routledge, 1988.

Elam, Helen Regueiro. "Harold Bloom (11 July 1930-)." Pages 32-48 in *Modern American Critics Since 1955*. Dictionary of Literary Biography. Ed. Gregory S. Jay. Vol. 67. Detroit: Gale Research Company, 1988.

Froula, Christine. "Rewriting Genesis: Gender and Culture in Twentieth-Century Texts." *Tulsa Studies in Women's Literature* 7, 2(Fall 1988), 197-220.

Jeon, Hong Shil. "The Revisionism of Harold Bloom." *Journal of English Language and Literature* 29(May 1988), 85-100.

Macdonald, D.L. "The Return of the Dead in `Large Red Man Reading'." *The Wallace Stevens Journal: A Publication of the Wallace Stevens Society* 12, 1(Spring 1988), 21-34.

Pearce, Dan. "Repetition Compulsion and `Undoing': T.S. Eliot's `Anxiety of Influence'." *Mosaic: A Journal for the Interdisciplinary Study of Literature*, 21, 4(Fall 1988), 45-54.

Polka, Brayton. "The Critique of Poetry: Text, Philosophy, and the Bible." *Religion and Literature* 20, 3(Autumn 1988), 1-23.

Robinson, D. "Dear Harold." *New Literary History* Vol. 20, 1(1988), 239-250.

Schwabsky, Barry. (Interview). "Harold Bloom." *Flash Art* (Italy). 143(Nov.-Dec. 1988), 65-7.

Solomon, Andrew. "Something Borrowed, Something Bloom." *Artforum International Magazine* Vol. 26, 9(May 1988), 122-27.

1989

Anon. (Picture) "Harold Bloom: Literary Critic." *Esquire*. Vol. 112, 1(July 1989), 67.

Altevers, Nannette Ann. "Vision and Re-Vision: The Symbiosis of Wordsworth and Harold Bloom." Diss. University of California, Irvine, 1989. *DAI* lists March 1990, Vol. 50, No. 9, page 2902A.

Beach, Christopher. "Ezra Pound and Harold Bloom: Influences, Canons, Traditions, and the Making of Modern Poetry." *ELH* [*English Literary History*] Vol. 56, 2(Summer 1989), 463-83.

Beaver, Harold. Review of *Ruin the Sacred Truths*. *Times Literary Supplement*, August 18, 1989, 900.

Finkelstein, Norman. "The Sage of New Haven." *Critical Texts: A Review of Theory and Criticism* 6, 2(1989), 1-22.

Helmling, Steven. "T.S. Eliot and Ralph Ellison: Insiders, Outsiders, and Cultural Authority." *Southern Review* 25, 4(Autumn 1989), 841-858.

Levin, David J. "A Tell-Tale Tale: Recounting Origins in Gottfried's Tristan." *New German Review: A Journal of Germanic Studies* 5-6, 1989-90, 56-74.

Meidner, Olga McDonald. (Book Review) "Harold Bloom: Towards Historical Rhetorics." *British Journal of Aesthetics*. Vol. 29, 4(Autumn 1989), 386-88.

Michasiw, Kim Ian. "*Barnaby Rudge*: The Sins of the Fathers." *ELH* 56, 3(Fall 1989), 571-592. The theory of Bloom is discussed.

Robinson, Douglas. "Two Dickinson Readings." *Dickinson Studies* 70(1989), 25-35.

1990

Aizenberg, Edna. "Borges and the Hebraism of Contemporary Literary Theory." Pages 249-262 in Aizenberg, Edna, ed. *Borges and His Successors: The Borgesian Impact on Literature and the Arts*. Columbia: University of Missouri Press, 1990.

Alter, Robert. "Harold Bloom's `J'." *Commentary*. Vol. 90, 5(Nov. 1990), 28-34.

Anon. "The Book of B.J. Miles." *Commonweal* 117(9 November 1990), 639-42.

Anon. "Murder She Wrote." *U.S. News and World Report*, 109(30 July 1990), 9.

Anon. "Ms. Moses: Did a Woman Write Scripture?" *Time*, 136 (1 Oct. 1990), 80.

Brown, John L. Review of *Ruin the Sacred Truths*. *World Literature Today*. 64(1990), 200. (800 words)

Fogel, Daniel Mark. "Covert Relations: James Joyce, Virginia Woolf, and Henry James." Charlottesville: University Press of Virginia, 1990.
Helmling, Steven. Review of *Ruin the Sacred Truths*. *Kenyon Review* 12(Summer 1990), 154 ff. (5500 words)
Horn, M. "The Original Hebrew Bible." *U.S. News and World Report*, 109 (10 December 1990), 70.
Kihn, M. "Bloom in Love." *Gentleman's Quarterly* 60(November 1990), 151.
Metress, Christopher. "`A New Father, a New Home': Styron, Faulkner, and Southern Revisionism." *Studies in the Novel* 22, 3(Fall 1990), 308-323.
Miles, Jack. "The Book of B: Bloom, Bathsheba & the Book." *Commonweal* 117, 19(Nov. 9, 1990), 639-43.
Noll, Mark A. Review of *Ruin the Sacred Truths*. *Books in Religion* 17(Spring 1990), 9. (1150 words)
O'Brien, D. "Academic Study in a Deconstructive Age, Or What If the Wife of Bath Had Read Bloom, Harold." *CEA Critic* [College English Association] 52, 4(Summer 1990), 2-9.
Pollack, Frederick. (Book Review). "Toward Historical Rhetorics." *Salmagundi* 88-89(Fall 1990), 507-600.
Sellars, Roy. (Book Review) "Harold Bloom: Towards Historical Rhetorics." *Notes and Queries* Vol. 37, 4(Dec. 1990), 521-23.
Skelley, Steven J. "Mapping Anglo-Irish Poetry: With(out) Harold Bloom." *Text & Context: A Journal of Interdisciplinary Studies* 4(Autumn 1990), 70-79.
Strahan, Linda. "What's in a Name? Richardson's Roger Solmes and Galsworthy's Soames Forsyte." *University of Mississippi Studies in English* 8(1990), 155-67.
Taylor, J. "Bloom's Day." *New Yorker*, 23, 5 November 1990, 52-8.
Woodward, K.L. "The Woman Who Invented God." *Newsweek*, 116(1 Oct. 1990), 62.

1991

Andersen, R.T. "`The Book of J' Speaks for Bloom, Harold." *Centennial Review* 35, 1(Winter 1991), 187-94.

Anon. (Interview with Harold Bloom). "Shakespeare's Freud." *Harper's Magazine* Vol. 283, 1695(August 1991), 29-31.

Barbarese, J.T. "Implicit Categories of the Romantic Imagination." *Sewanee Review* 99, 1(Winter 1991), 145-149.

Garner, Brent. "Anxious Odes of Tate and Lowell." *Journal of American Studies* 25, 1(April 1991), 93-99.

Ghannoum, Muhammad. "English Romanticism in Contemporary Revisionist Theory." *DAI*. Columbia University, Vol. 52, 4(1Oct. 1991), p. 1323A.

Grosby, Steven. "Men Blow Kisses at Calves." *American Scholar* 60, 4(Autumn 1991), 518-535.

Lieb, Michael. "The Book of M: Paradise Lost As Revisionary Text." *Cithara: Essays in the Judaeo-Christian Tradition* 3, 1(Nov. 1991), 28-35.

McVeigh, Daniel M. "`J' as in Joke? Bloom, Rosenberg, and the Hermeneutics of Chutzpah." *Christianity and Literature* 40, 4(Summer 1991), 367-79.

Parrinder, Patrick. (Book Review) "Harold Bloom: Towards Historical Rhetorics" [by Debolla, P.]. *Journal of English and Germanic Philology*. Vol. 90, 2(April 1991), 231-33.

Sabor, Peter. "Harold Bloom on Eighteenth-Century Fiction." *Eighteenth-Century Fiction* 3, 2(January 1991), 153-63.

Seitz, C.R. "Wellhausen Goes to Yale [Cover Story]." *The Christian Century* 108(30 January 1991), 111-114.

Stern, D. "The Supreme Fictionalist." *The New Republic* 204 [Festschrift 4 as cited in the *MLA*] (1991), 34-40. Has bibliography.

Takayama, Machiko. "Poetic Language in Nineteenth Century Mormonism: A Study of Semiotic Phenomenology in Communication and Culture." *Dissertation Abstracts International* Vol. 52, 5(Nov. 1991), page 1574A.

Tsuchida, Tomonori. "Had H. Bloom Surpassed T.S. Eliot? From a Viewpoint of `Intertexuality'. *Chiba Review* 13 (1991), 91-106.

Weiss, Antonio. (Interview) "The Art of Criticism." *Paris Review* 33, 118(Spring 1991), 178 ff.

1992

Altevers, Nannette. "The Revisionary Company: Harold Bloom's `last romanticism'." *New Literary History* 23, 2(Spring 1992), 361.
Brown, Erella. "The Ozick-Bloom Controversy: Anxiety of Influence, Usurpation as Idolatry, and the Identity of Jewish American Literature." *Studies in American Jewish Literature* 11, 1(Spring 1992), 62-82.
Boodrich, C. "The Bloom Factory." *Lingua Franca* 2, 5(Jun.-Jul. 1992), 29-37.
Kraft, Quentin G. "Toward a Critical Re-renewal: at the Corner of Camus and Bloom Streets." *College English* 54, 1(January 1992), 46-64.
Qualls, Barry V. Review of *The Book of J*. *Raritan: A Quarterly Review* 11, 3(Winter 1992), 105-117.

WORKS BY AND ABOUT JACQUES DERRIDA

Books by Derrida

1962 [English 1978]

Edmund Husserl's "Origin of Geometry": An Introduction. Ed. David B. Allison. Trans., with a Preface, John P. Leavey, Jr. Stony Brook, N.Y.: Nicolas Hays, 1978. 207 pages. Rpt. Lincoln: University of Nebraska Press, 1989 with a new Afterword by the translator.

> Contents: Acknowledgments; Preface: Undecidables and Old Names, by John P. Leavey: Undecidables and Deconstruction; Derrida's *Introduction* to *The Origin of Geometry*; Deconstruction and the Science of Old Names; Translator's Note. Introduction to *The Origin of Geometry*: [These headings were added by Leavey for the convenience of the reader, but do not appear in the French edition.] I. The Sense of Sense-Investigation: Responsibility, Consciousness, and Existence; II. The Historical Reduction and the Necessity for Return Inquiry (*Rückfrage*) in Reactivation; III. The Ego as Fundament and the Reduction of Factuality; IV. Objectivity, Historicity, and Intentionality; V. Language, the Possibility of Transcendental Historicity; VI. The How of Ideality: the Earth and the Living Present; VII. The How of Ideality: Writing and Univocity as the Telos of Reac-

tivation; VIII. Horizon: the Absolute of History, and Imaginary Variation; IX. The Suspension of Ideality: Scientific Study of the Life-World (*Lebenswelt*); X. Geography, Infinitization, and the Idea in the Kantian Sense; XI. The Historicity of the Idea: Difference, Delay, Origins, and the Transcendental. Appendix: *The Origin of Geometry*, by Edmund Husserl. French and English Bibliography of Jacques Derrida, compiled by John P. Leavey and David Allison. Index of Passages Cited from Husserl. Index.

1967[English 1975]

Of Grammatology. Trans. Gayatri Chakravorty Spivak. Baltimore: Johns Hopkins University Press, 1975. 354 pages.

Contents: Acknowledgments. Translator's Preface. Preface. **Part I: Writing before the Letter.** *Exergue.* 1. *The End of the Book and the Beginning of Writing.* The Program. The Signifier and Truth. The Written Being/The Being Written. 2. *Linguistics and Grammatology.* The Outside and the Inside. The Outside Is [The `Is' has an `x' drawn over it.] the Inside. The Hinge [*La Brisure*]. 3. *Of Grammatology as a Positive Science.* Algebra: Arcanum and Transparence. Science and the Name of Man. The Rebus and the Complicity of Origins. **Part II: Nature, Culture, Writing.** *Introduction to the "Age of Rousseau".* 1. *The Violence of the Letter: From Lévi-Strauss to Rousseau.* The Battle of Proper Names. Writing and Man's Exploitation by Man. 2. *" . . . That Dangerous Supplement . . . "* From/Of Blindness to the Supplement. The Chain of Supplements. The Exorbitant. Question of Method. [Both "The Exorbitant" and "Question of Method" are grouped as one section heading.] 3. *Genesis and Structure of the Essay on the Origin of Languages.* I. The Place of the "*Essay*". Writing, Political Evil, and Linguistic Evil. The Present Debate: The Economy of Pity. The Initial Debate and the Composition of the *Essay*. II. Imitation. The Interval and the Supplement. The Engraving and the Ambiguities of Formalism. The Turn of Writing. III. Articulation. "That Movement of the Wand . . ." The Inscription of the Origin. The Neume. That "Simple Movement of the Finger." Writing and the Prohibition of Incest. 4. *From/Of the Supplement to the Source: The Theory of Writing*. The Originary Metaphor. The History and System of Scripts. The Alphabet and Absolute Representation. The Theorem and the Theater. The Supplement of (at) the Origin. Notes.

1967[English 1973]

Speech and Phenomena and Other Essays on Husserl's Theory of Signs. Trans. David Allison. Evanston: Northwestern University Press, 1973. 166 pages.

Contents: *Preface, by Newton Garver. Translator's Introduction, by David B. Allison.* Speech and Phenomena: Introduction to the Problem of Signs in Husserl's Phenomenology. Introduction. 1. Sign and Signs. 2. The Reduction of Indication. 3. Meaning as Soliloquy. 4. Meaning and Representation. 5. Signs and the Blink of an Eye. 6. The Voice That Keeps Silence. 7. The Supplement of Origin. Other Essays. Form and Meaning: A Note on the Phenomenology of Language. Differance. *Index of Passages Cited from Husserl. Index.*

1967[English 1978]

Writing and Difference. Trans. Alan Bass. Chicago, University of Chicago Press, 1978; London, Routledge & Kegan Paul, 1978. 342 pages. [pages 341 and 342 of the translation list the sources and dates of the chapters in JD's publications; some essays were written in the 1950s.].

Contents: *Translator's Introduction*. **One:** Force and Signification. **Two:** Cogito and the History of Madness. **Three:** Edmond Jabès and the Question of the Book. **Four:** Violence and Metaphysics: An Essay on the Thought of Emmanuel Levinas. **Five:** "Genesis and Structure" and Phenomenology. **Six:** La parole soufflée. **Seven:** Freud and the Scene of Writing. **Eight:** The Theater of Cruelty and the Closure of Representation. **Nine:** From Restricted to General Economy: A Hegelianism without Reserve. **Ten:** Structure, Sign, and Play in the Discourse of the Human Sciences. **Eleven:** Ellipsis. **Notes. Sources.**

1972 [English 1981]

Dissemination. Trans. Barbara Johnson. Chicago, University of Chicago Press, 1981; London, Athlone Press, 1981. 366 pages.

Contents: Translator's Introduction. **Outwork, prefacing** [small `p'] **Plato's Pharmacy**. I.1. Pharmacia. 2. The Father of Logos. 3. The Filial Inscription: Theuth, Hermes, Thoth, Nabu, Nebo. 4. The Pharmakon. 5. The Pharmakeus. II. 6. The Pharmakos. 7. The Ingredients: Phantasms, Festivals, and Paints. 8. The Heritage of the Pharmakon: Family Scene. 9. Play: From the Pharmakon to the Letter and from Blindness to the Supplement. **The Double Session**. I. [No title]. II. [No title]. **Dissemination**. I. 1. The Trigger. 2. The Apparatus or Frame. 3. The Scission. 4. The Double Bottom of the Plupresent. 5. wriTing, encAsIng, screeNing [yes, this unusual capitalization is in the book]. 6. The Attending Discourse. II. 7. The Time before First. 8. The Column. 9. The Crossroads of the "Est." 10. Grafts, a Return to Overcasting. XI. The Supernumerary [yes, a Roman numeral is used].

1972 [English 1982]

Margins of Philosophy. Trans. Alan Bass. Chicago, University of Chicago Press, 1982; Hassocks, Harvester Press, 1982. 330 pages. The translator's note contains the sources of many of the essays.

> Contents: Translator's Note. Tympan. Différance. *Ousia* and *Gramme*: Note on a Note from *Being and Time*. The Pit and the Pyramid: Introduction to Hegel's Semiology. The Ends of Man. The Linguistic Circle of Geneva. Form and Meaning: A Note on the Phenomenology of Language. The Supplement of Copula: Philosophy before Linguistics. White Mythology: Metaphor in the Text of Philosophy. Qual Quelle: Valéry's Sources. Signature Event Context [Three words with spaces between two adjacent ones].

1972 [English 1982]

Positions. Trans. Alan Bass. Chicago, University of Chicago Press, 1982; London, Athlone, 1982. 114 pages.

> Contents: Implications: *Interview with Henri Ronse*. Semiology and Grammatology: *Interview with Julia Kristeva*. Positions: *Interview with Jean-Louis Houdebine and Guy Scarpetta*. Notes.

1973 [English 1980]

The Archeology of the Frivolous: Reading Condillac. Trans. John Leavey. Pittsburgh, Duquesne University Press, 1980. 143 pages, of which 37 are the translator's introduction. [Originally published in 1973 as an Introduction to Condillac in *Essai sur l'origine des connaissances humaines*. Paris, Galilée, 1973, which had long been unavailable in

French, and republished separately as *L'Archéologie du frivole: Lire Condillac*. Paris, Gonthier-Denoël, 1976.]

Contents:)1-the fractured frame, the seduction of fiction (by John P. Leavey [yes, the parentheses are backwards]. Abbreviations. **THE ARCHEOLOGY OF THE FRIVOLOUS: READING CONDILLAC**. 1. the Second First-Metaphysics. 2. Genius's Deferred Action [*L'après-coup*]. 3. Imagining-Conceptual Stand-in and the Novel of Force. 4. A Marginal Note or Remark--The Two Loose Pages. 5. Introduction to *An Essay on the Origin of Human Knowledge*--Frivolity Itself. *Index*.

1974 [English 1976]

Glas. Trans. John Leavey and Richard Rand. Lincoln, University of Nebraska Press, 1986. 262 large-format pages; not divided into chapters; parallel columns. French reference at A30FR. Note that Leavey's book *Glassary* would be very helpful when reading *Glas*.

Contents: None. The reader may want to consult John P. Leavey, Jr.'s *Glassary*, which contains "the critical apparatus to the translation, that is, explanations of particular terms and their translations, commentary on individual lines, and the location of all cited passages, as well as introductory essays . . ." [this statement comes from a one-page note to Leavey's translation].

1975 French

[*Adami*. Paris: Galerie Maeght, 1975.]

1976 [Bilingual edition 1979]

Spurs: Nietzsche's Styles. Trans. Barbara Harlow. Chicago, University of Chicago Press, 1979. 165 pages, of which 12 pages are Notes and as a Bilingual Edition half of the 143 pages are in French, and half are in English, on facing pages. [Note that there is an article "The Question of Style" translated by Ruben Berezdivin that is published in *The New Nietzsche: Contemporary Styles of Interpretation*. Ed. and Intro. David B. Allison. Cambridge and London: The MIT Press, 1985. 176-89. This article, according to those acknowledgments, page vi, "consists of selections from `La Question du style' first published in *Nietzsche aujourd' hui*, Union Générale d'Editions, 1973. . . . A revised and extended text of the complete article, translated into English, Italian, and German, has been published under the title *The Question of Style* by Corbo e Fiore, Venice, 1976."

Contents: Coup sur coup: Préface à Éperons. Coup upon Coup: An Introduction to *Spurs*, Stefano Agosti. Éperons: Les Styles de Nietzsche/ Spurs: Nietzsche's Styles. La question du style/ The question of style. Distances/ [Distances]. Voiles/Veils. Vérités/ Truths. Parures/ Adornments. La simulation/ Simulation. "Histoire d'une erreur"/ "History of an error". Femina vita/ [No translation]. Positions/ [No translation]. Le regard d'Oedipe/ The Gaze of Oedipus. Le coup de don. Abîmes de la vérité/ Abysses of truth. "J'ai oublié mon parapluie"/ "I have forgotten my umbrella". Notes.

1977 French 1986

"Living On: Border-lines." Trans. James Hulbert. In *Deconstruction and Criticism*. Ed. Harold Bloom et al. New York: Seabury Press, 1979. 75-176. [The French version, "Survivre: Journal de bord," was published in Derrida's *Parages* (1986).]

[One piece of writing by JD that is significant for its length--101 pages--was, however, not published as a monograph in English. "Living On: Border-lines."]

1977[English 1977]

Limited Inc.. Trans. Samuel Weber. Baltimore: Johns Hopkins University Press, 1977. 160 pages. Weber's translation first appeared in *Glyph 2, Johns Hopkins Textual Studies*. The French version was published as a supplement to its English translation; in 1988 a new afterword was added: "Toward an Ethic of Discussion." The French version by Galilée with the same title appeared in 1990.

Contents: Editor's Foreword [Gerald Graff]. Signature Event Context. Summary of "Reiterating the Differences". Limited Inc a b c . . . . Afterword: Toward An Ethic of Discussion.

1978 French

[*Titus Carmel.* (The pocket size Tlingit Coffin.) Paris, Centre Pompidou, 1978. See *The Truth in Painting* for the English translation.]

1978 [English 1987]

The Truth in Painting. Trans. G. Bennington and I. McLeod. Chicago, University of Chicago Press, 1987. 386 pages.

Contents: **List of Illustrations. Translators' Preface. Passe-Partout. 1. Parergon.** I. Lemmata. II. The Parergon. III. The *Sans* of the Pure Cut. IV. The Colossal. **2. +R (Into the Bargain). 3. Cartouches. 4. Restitutions. Index.**

1979 [Forthcoming English translation]

Les états généraux de la philosophie. Paris: Flammarion, 1979.

1980 [English 1987]

The Post Card: From Socrates to Freud and Beyond. Trans. Alan Bass. Chicago, Chicago University Press, 1987. 521 pages, with greater thematic unity than a collection of essays.

> Contents: Translator's Introduction: L before K. Glossary. Envois. To Speculate--on "Freud". 1. Notices (Warnings). 2. Freud's Legacy. 3. Paralysis. 4. Seven: Postscript. Le facteur de la vérité. Du tout.

1982 French

[*Affranchissement du transfert et de la lettre.* Colloquium on Jacques Derrida's *La Carte postale*, April 4 and 5, 1981. Comments by Derrida. Paris, Confrontation, 1982.]

1982 [The French text was published separately in 1984; English edition 1985]

The Ear of the Other: Otobiography, Transference, Translation: Texts and Discussions with Jacques Derrida. Trans. Peggy Kamuf. New York, Schocken Books, 1985. 164 pages.

> Contents: Preface. Translator's Note. Otobiographies. Roundtable on Autobiography. Roundtable on Translation. Works Cited.

1983 French monograph; English journal article 1982, and 1984]

[*D'un ton apocalyptique adopté naguère en philosophie.* Paris: Galilée, 1983. Trans. by John P. Leavey as "Of an Apocalyptic Tone Recently Adopted in Philosophy," *Semeia*, 23 (1982), and *Oxford Literary Review*, 6.2 (1984): 3-37.] This lecture was delivered at the 1980 Cerisy-la-Salle colloquium on Derrida; the French text was first published in *Les fins de l'homme: A Partir du travail de Jacques Derrida*. Ed. by Philippe Lacoue-Labarthe and Jean-Luc Nancy. Paris: Galilée, 1981.

1984 [1991[

[*Feu la cendre*. Firenze, Sansoni, 1984. Paris, "Bibliothèque des voix," Editions des Femmes, 1987.] The text is accompanied by a cassette recording of JD and the actress Carole Bouquet reading the text.

1984 [Bilingual 1984]

Signéponge/Signsponge. Trans. Richard Rand. New York, Columbia University Press, 1984. (Parallel French and English Translation.) 160 pages.

1985 French collection

[*Droits de regards*. Photographs by M.F. Plissart with an essay by Jacques Derrida. Paris, Minuit, 1985.]

1985 French collection

[*La Faculté de juger.* Paris: Minuit, 1985.

1986 French collection

[*Parages*. Paris, Galilée, 1986.]

> This is a collection of JD's essays on the *récits* of Blanchot. Some of the contents are "Living On: Border Lines" ; "Pas" [not yet translated]; "Title (to be specified) [yes, translated;]; and "The Law of Genre" [yes, translated].

1986 French

[*Schibboleth, Pour Paul Celan*. Paris, Galilée, 1986. This essay, trans. by Joshua Wilner, appeared as "`Shibboleth' (on Paul Celan)" in Geoffrey Hartman and Sanford Budick, eds, *Midrash and Literature*. New Haven, Yale University Press, 1986. 307-47.]

1986 [English 1986 and revised with a major addition in 1989; the French in 1988]

Mémoires for Paul de Man. Trans. Cecile Lindsay, Jonathan Culler, Eduardo Cadava, and Peggy Kamuf. The Wellek Library Lectures at the University of California, Irvine. Revised Edition. New York: Columbia University Press, 1989. (263 excluding "In Memoriam/ On the Soul", which is six pages) The 1989 edition has an essay not found in the 1986 one of the Wellek Library Lectures, because Paul de Man's wartime journalism became controversial in 1987, and thus JD's essay "Paul de Man's War," which first appeared in *Critical Inquiry* (Trans. Peggy Kamuf; 14.3 (1988). JD made some changes and published them in *Responses: On Paul de Man's Wartime Journalism*, Ed. Werner Hamacher, Neil Hertz, and Thomas Keenan (Lincoln, Nebraska: University of Nebraska Press, 1989). These publication notes result from Murray Krieger's Editorial Note to the 1989 edition.

Content: Editorial Note. Preface to the Revised Edition. Preface to the French Edition. In Memoriam. Preface. 1. Mnemosyne. 2. The Art of *Mémoires*. 3. Acts. 4. Like the Sound of the Sea Deep Within a Shell: Paul de Man's War.

1986 French

[*Altérités: Jacques Derrida et Pierre-Jean Labarrière*, avec de études de Francis Guibal et Stanislas Breton. Éditions Osiris, Paris: Mars 1986. 95 pages.

1987[English 1989]

Of Spirit: Heidegger and the Question. Trans. Geoffrey Bennington and Rachel Bowlby. Chicago: The University of Chicago Press, 1989. 139 pages, of which ten chapters constitute 113 pages and the remaining 26 pages are notes.

Contents: Translators' Note. CHAPTER I. CHAPTER II. CHAPTER III. CHAPTER IV. CHAPTER V. CHAPTER VI. CHAPTER VII. CHAPTER VIII. CHAPTER IX. CHAPTER X. NOTES.

*1987*Only in French as a monograph

[*Ulysse Gramophone: Deux mots pour Joyce.* Paris: Galilée, 1987. These two essays were translated into English, but in independent publications. In *Post-Structuralist Joyce: Essays from the French*. Trans. Geoffrey Bennington. Ed. Derek Attridge and Daniel Ferrer. London: Cambridge University Press, 1984. 145-58. And see "Ulysses Gramophone: Hear Say Yes in Joyce". Trans. Tina Kendall and Shari Benstock. In *James Joyce: The Augmented Ninth*. Ed. Bernard Benstock. Syracuse, NY: Syracuse University Press, 1988. 27-75.

1987 [No English translation of the work as a whole yet]

Psyché. Inventions de l'autre. The title essay was translated as "Psyche: Inventions of the Other".

INFORMATION ABOUT THE TRANSLATED ESSAYS. The essays as an entire collection have not been translated yet. The following list ordered according to the Table des matières indicates the translations. Some bits of information came from Peggy Kamuf's *A Derrida Reader: Between the Blinds*, Columbia University Press, 1991.

1987   [Derrida was one of the editors]

[*For Nelson Mandela.* Jacques Derrida and Mustapha Tlili, eds. Trans. Phillip Franklin et al. New York: Henry Holt & Co., 1987; 1st ed. New York: Seaver Books.

1987 French

[*Chora*, in *Poikilia, études offertes à Jean-Pierre Vernant*, E.H.E.S.S., 1987.]

1990 [no English translation yet]

Du droit à la philosophie. Paris: Galilée, 1990. 663 pages.

1990 [no English translation yet]

Le problème de la genèse dans la philosophie de Husserl. Paris: Presses Universitaires de France, 1990. 292 pages. This is the first publication in English of Derrida's 1954 Master's thesis.

1990 [1992]]

L'autre cap. Minuit: 1990.

1990 [no English translation yet]

Mémoires d'aveugle, L'autoportrait et autres ruines. Paris: Reúnion des Musées Nationaux. This text is a commentary by JD on an exhibition of drawings at the Louvre.

1990

A Derrida Reader: Between the Blinds. Ed. Peggy Kamuf. New York: Columbia University Press, 1990. Included is a translation of "Che cos e la poesia?", 221-241.

1991 [1993]

Jacques Derrida. By Geoffrey Bennington and Jacques Derrida. Paris: Seuil, 1991. 379 pages. Translation by Geoffrey Bennington: Chicago: The University of Chicago Press, 1993.

Cinders. Trans. of *Feu la cendre*. University of Nebraska Press, 1991.

> Contents: Introduction: Mourning Becomes Telepathy (1-20); Prologue (21-30); Animadversiones/Animadversions (30-31); Feu la cendre/Cinders (31-78); Notes.

1992

The Other Heading: Reflections on Today's Europe. Trans. from the French by Pascale-Anne Brault and Michael B. Naas.

Introd. by Michael B. Naas. Bloomington: Indiana University Press, 1992.

Contents: [Introduction: For Example, by Michael B. Naas]. Today (1-4); The Other Heading: Memories, Responses, and Responsibilities (4-84); Call It a Day for Democracy (84-111); Notes.

Raising the Tone of Philosophy: Late Essays by Immanuel Kant, Transformative Critique by Jacques Derrida. Ed. Peter D. Fenves. Baltimore: Johns Hopkins University Press, 1992.

1993

Given Time, Pt I: Counterfeit Money. V. Ch. Press.

Institutions of Philosophy. Ed. Deborah Esch and Thomas Keenan. Harvard University Press.

Negotiations: Writings. Ed. Deborah Esch and Thomas Keenan. University of Minnesota Press.

Selected Articles by Derrida

"The Age of Hegel." Trans. Susan Winnett. *Glyph Textual Studies: Demarcating the Disciplines: Philosophy, Literature, Art* 1 (1986): 3-43.

"Les antinomies de la discipline philosophique." Lettre préface a *La Grève des philosophes*. Ecole et philosophie. Paris: Osiris, 1986. A translation is forthcoming in *Institutions of Philosophy*, 1993.

"Biodegradables: Seven Diary Fragments." Trans. Peggy Kamuf. *Critical Inquiry* 15 (1989): 812-73. There has been no published French text up to June 1991.

"Devant la loi." *Philosophy* Supplement (1983): 173-88.

"Economimesis." Trans. Richard Klein. *Diacritics* 11.2 (1981): 3-25.

"The Ends of Man." Trans. of "Les fins de l'homme" by Edouard Morot-Sir, Wesley C. Puisol, Herbert L. Dreyfus, and Barbara Reid. *Philosophy and Phenomenological Research* 30.1 (1969): 31-57. Rpt. in *MP*.

"An Idea of Flaubert: `Plato's Letter'." Trans. Peter Starr. *Modern Language Notes* 99 (1984): 748-68. Rpt. in *Psyche*.

"Languages and Institutions of Philosophy." Trans. Sylvia Söderlind, Rebecca Comay, Barbara Havercroft, and Joseph Adamson. *Semiotic Inquiry/Recherches Sémiotiques* 4.2 (1984): 91-154.

"The Law of Genre." Trans. Avital Ronell. *Critical Inquiry* 1 (1980): 55-81. And in *Glyph 7: Johns Hopkins Textual Studies*. Baltimore, Johns Hopkins University Press, 1980, 176-232. This item comes from `La Loi du genre'. Colloque Le Genre. Strasbourg, Université de Strasbourg, 1980.

"Letter from Jacques Derrida." *Sub-stance* 35 (1982): 2.

"Letter of Jacques Derrida to Jean-Louis Houdebine (Excerpt)." *Diacritics* 3.3 (1973): 58-59.

"Letter to a Japanese Friend." "Lettre à un ami japonais." *Le Promeneur* 42 (1985): 2-4. Rpt. in *Psyche*.

"Of an Apocalyptic Tone Recently Adopted in Philosophy." Trans. John P. Leavey, Jr. *Oxford Literary Review* 6.2 (1984): 3-37.

"On Reading Heidegger: An Outline of Remarks to the Essex Colloquium." Trans. David Farrell Krell. *Research in Phenomenology* 17 (1987): 171-88.

"Plaidoyer pour la métaphysique: `Passage du temoin de Jacques Derrida à Jean-Francois Lyotard'." *Monde* [12366] 28-29 Oct. 1984: ii.

"Pour la philosophie." *La Nouvelle Critique* 84 (1975): 25-9. This article became "Réponses á la Nouvelle Critique" in *Qui a peur de la philosophie?*.

"The *Retrait* of Metaphor." Trans. Frieda Gasdner, Biodun Iginla, Richard Madden, and William West. *Enclitic* 2.2 (1978): 5-33.

"Signature Event Context." Trans. Samuel Weber and Jeffrey Mehlman. *Glyph* 1 (1977): 172-97. Rpt. in *Lim, MP, La Communication*.

"Speech and Writing According to Hegel." Trans. Alfonso Lingis. *Man and World* 11 (1978): 107-30.

Selected Interviews with Derrida

1970

"Discussion." *The Structuralist Controversy: The Languages of Criticism and the Sciences of Man.* Ed. Richard Macksey and Eugenio Donato. Baltimore: Johns Hopkins University Press, 1970. 265-72.

1976

"Littéraire, philosophie et politique sont inséparables." Avec Agacinski, Kofman, Lacoue-Labarthe, Nancy, Pautrat. *Le Monde* 30 Nov. 1976.

1980

"Débat." *Les Fins de l'homme: A partir du travail de Jacques Derrida.* Ed. Philippe Lacoue-Labarthe and Jean-Luc Nancy. Colloque de Cerisy-la-Salle du 22 juill. au 2 août 1980, and published by Galilée, 1981. There are a series of discussions after papers, and JD participated in many of them.

1981

"Dialogue with Jacques Derrida. Deconstruction and the Other." With Richard Kearney. *Dialogues with Contemporary Thinkers: The Phenomenological Heritage.* Ed. Richard Kearney. Manchester: Manchester University Press, 1984. 105-26. The discussion occurred in 1981.

1983

"Interview with *Nouvel Observateur* 9 Sept. 1983." Sometimes this item is cited in other bibliographies as "Interview. With Catherine David." Reprinted in Coventry by Parousia Press, 1985; and translated by David Allison, et al., and reprinted in *Derrida and Différance*, 1988, 71-82.

1984

"Bonnes volontés de puissance (Une réponse á Hans-Georg Gadamer)." *Revue Internationale de Philosophie Deconstruction* 151 (1984): 341-43. Translation reprinted in *Dialogue and Deconstruction: The Gadamer-Derrida Encounter.* Ed. Diane P. Michelfelder and Richard E. Palmer. Albany: State University of New York Press, 1989. 52-54.

"Plaidoyer pour la métaphysique. Avec J.F. Lyotard." *Le Monde* 28 Oct. 1984.

1985

"Deconstruction in America." Interview with James Creech, Peggy Kamuf and Jane Todd. *SCE Reports* 17 (1985): 1-33. Also in *Critical Exchange* 17 (1985): 1-33, as "Deconstruction in America: An Interview with Jacques Derrida."

1988

"Controverse sur la possibilité d'une science de la philosophie." Avec F. Laruelle. *La Décision philosophique* 5 (1988).

"Interview with Jean-Luc Nancy." [Peggy Kamuf in *A Derrida Reader* cites this interview as "Interview with Jacques Derrida (by Jean-Luc Nancy)" and Leventure in his bibliography cites this as "Derrida interviewed by Jean-Luc Nancy."] Trans. by Peter T. Connor. *Topoi* 7 (1988): 113-21. There is a longer French version entitled "`Il faut bien manger', ou le calcul du sujet," *Cahiers Confrontation* 20 (1989): 91-114. See below for the annotation on the continued interview: "`Eating Well,' or the Calculation of the Subject," 1991.

1989

"Interview with Jean-Luc Nancy." Trans. Peter T. Connor. *Topoi* 7 (1989): 113-21. Trans. from "`Il faut bien manger' ou le calcul de sujet." See next entry. Annotated below in

"`Eating Well,' or the Calculation of the Subject," *Who Comes After the Subject?*

"Jacques Derrida in Conversation with Christopher Norris." *Architectural Design* 58.1-2 (1989): 6-11. See the next entry herein "Jacques Derrida in Discussion with Christopher Norris." Also in *Deconstruction: An Omnibus Volume*, Ed. Andreas Papadakis, Catherine Cooke, and Andrew Benjamin. London: Academy Editions, 1989.

1990

Interview with Derrida, conducted by Raoul Mortley. *French Philosophers in Conversation: Derrida, Irigaray, Levinas, Le Doeuff, Schneider, Serres.* London: Routledge, 1990.

Derrida, et al. "Discussion after Circulus vitiosus" in *Nietzsche aujourd'hui?*. JD makes various interventions in the discussion, and is in turn discussed by Jean-François Lyotard.

"Jacques Derrida ici et ailleurs." Avec R.P. Droit. *Le Monde*, 16 nov. 1990.

"Le programme philosophique de Jacques Derrida." Avec R. Maggiori. *Libération*. 15 Nov. 1990.

1991

"`Eating Well,' or the Calculation of the Subject." With Jean-Luc Nancy. Trans. Peter Connor and Avital Ronell. *Who Comes After the Subject?* Ed. Eduardo Cadava, Peter Connor, Jean-Luc Nancy. New York: Routledge, 1991. 96-119. Note that this is a longer version of a previously published interview. See the 1988 published interview: "Interview with Jean-Luc Nancy."

Selected Works on Derrida Concerning Bloom or Tradition

Note: For a comprehenisive bibliography of Derrida up to 1990, see *Jacques Derrida: An Annotated Primary and Secondary Bibliography*. William R. Schultz and Lewis L.B. Fried. New York: Garland Press, 1992, 882 pages, with an Introduction and Author and Subject Indexes.

Allison, David B. "Derrida and Wittgenstein: Playing the Game." *Research in Phenomenology* 8 (1978): 93-109.

> Compares Wittgenstein's and JD's views of language to see to what extent they escape tradition and to see what the conception of language as game or play means. For JD the play is the functioning of a sign in a system of differences. Both thinkers claim that the tradition is exceeded by its very perpetuation (108). Traditional discourse is transgressed by the "play" or "game."

Altwegg, Jürg and Aurel Schmidt. *Französische Denker der Gegenwart: Zwansig Porträts*. Munich: C.H. Beck, 1987.

> Traces the turn away from Hegel reminiscent of Nietzsche in modern French philosophy, and its ambivalent reception in the German speaking world, in a brief chapter entitled "Jacques Derrida, or the Pedagogics of Philosophy."

Aron, Jean Paul. *Les Modernes*. Paris: Gallimard, 1984.

> Brief mention of JD's involvement in the Tel Quel group.

Ash, Beth Sharon. "Jewish Hermeneutics and Contemporary Theories of Textuality: Hartman, Bloom, and Derrida." *Modern Philology* 85.1 (1987): 65-80.

> "Midrash" is the traditional method of Jewish biblical hermeneutics. The discussion begins with a brief historical sketch of Jewish sacred literature. JD is compared to Bloom on the topics of Kabbalah and *différance*. JD's idea of metaphoricity is discussed at more length. Llewelyn's account of JD is discussed, as well as Llewelyn's unusual word formations.

Barzilai, Shuli and Morton W. Bloomfield. "New Criticism and Deconstructive Criticism; Or, What's New?" *New Literary History* 18 (1986): 151-69.

> Authors try to pinpoint what new insights deconstruction can offer beyond New Criticism. Several pages are on JD, who is seen as the nucleus of the Yale Critics: Bloom, Hartman, de Man, and Miller. The article is a survey discussion. The conclusion is a safe middle-of-the-road no-answer: as every literary development departs from the past and yet carries it over, so does deconstruction.

Bandera, Cesáreo. "Notes on Derrida, Tombstones, and the Representational Game." *Stanford French Review* 6 (1982): 311-25.

> Discusses deconstruction, *différance*, the supplement, and the pharmakon to explain what JD means. He uses these ideas to deconstruct the Spanish work: *Danza general de la muerte*. He refers to several of JD's works. He does question whether JD, instead of deconstructing the big pyramid of metaphysical tradition, has not built an even bigger one, and is concerned to point out the seriousness

of the "play" of differences, of the "game" of deconstruction, perhaps contra JD.

Benoist, Jean Marie. *La revolution structurale.* Paris: B. Grasset, 1975. Translated as *The Structural Revolution.*

Brief but veracious overview of the roots and general thrust of JD's "grammatology," which is described as linking together "phenomenology and structuralism," if only to bind them "under the common accusation of being still caught up in the matrix of Western metaphysics."

Berman, Art. *From the New Criticism to Deconstruction: The Reception of Structuralism and Post-Structuralism.* Urbana: University of Illinois Press, 1988.

Almost half the book is directly or indirectly about JD, and is useful for its broad examination of his philosophy in various contexts, such as those of Marxism, Feminism, Structuralism, Romanticism, and New Criticism. Three chapters present JD from three different angles: the first is a detailed and wide-ranging exposition of his philosophy mainly from the perspective of its import for literary theory and criticism; the second is an in-depth charting of his influence on the Yale School Critics--Hillis Miller, de Man, Hartman, and Bloom; and the third defines the milieu of literary criticism and theory in America before JD's arrival on the scene, and gives an overview of both the acceptance and antagonisms JD's philosophy has provoked in the general practice of literary studies in America.

Bloom, Harold. *A Map of Misreading.* New York: Oxford University Press, 1975. Also see E121 about Bloom's relation to JD.

> Various, brief invocations of JD on Nietzsche, Freud, and tropes. Bloom was much impressed with JD's reading of Freud, which influenced Bloom considerably in mid-career. A point of agreement between Bloom and JD is the use of Freud's principle of "*ungeschehenmachen*" in interpretation of texts: i.e., undoing as a mechanism of spiritual development, reversing the past. Also see Bloom's *Anxiety of Influence*.

Bloom, Harold. *Kabbalah and Criticism*. New York: Seabury Press, 1975.

> Passing references to JD, including a rather provocative linking of JD's philosophy to the Kabbalahistic tradition: "Kabbalah stops the movement of JD's `trace', since it has a *point* of the primordial, where presence and absence co-exist by continuous interplay" (53). JD would object to this claim but not to Bloom's general principles of criticism.

Bouchard, Guy. "Le signe saussurien et la métaphysique occidentale selon Jacques Derrida." *Canadian Journal of Research in Semiotics* 6.1-2 (1978-79): 147-69.

> Examines JD's critique of Saussure in *Gram* in the attempt to demonstrate that Saussure's theory of signs is not, as JD claims, simply reducible to the metaphysical tradition.

Bové, Paul A. *Destructive Poetics: Heidegger and Modern American Poetry*. New York: Columbia University Press, 1980.

> Briefly discusses Bloom as offering theories that purport to be alternatives to JD, analyzes de Man's critique of JD in "The Rhetoric of Blindness," and discusses JD's relation to Nietzsche and to a lesser extent Heidegger.

Brutting, Richard. *Ecriture und texte: d. Franz. Literaturtheorie nach d. Strukturalismus: Kritik.* Bonn: Bouvier, 1976.

> Extensive exposition of JD's philosophy from a literary-critical perspective, which views JD's work as a wholesale critique of the structuralist enterprise. Focuses on JD's notions of *écriture*, text, and his concept of the sign, especially as they relate to the work of the other members of the Tel Quel group.

Dallmayr, Fred R. *Twilight of Subjectivity: Contributions to a Post-individualist Theory of Politics.* Amherst: University of Massachusetts Press, 1981.

> Recounts JD's critique of Sartre, and his roots in phenomenology. Reviews JD's critique of Lévinas and Heidegger in terms of otherness and *différance*. Examines JD's writings on Lévi-Strauss and Rousseau from the perspective of the "man-nature issue", especially the political implications of this traditional dualistic problematic.

De Beaugrande, Robert. *Critical Discourse: A Survey of Literary Theorists.* Norwood, N.J.: Ablex, 1988.

> While not directly on JD himself, helpful for its discussion of the appropriations of JD's thought by the Yale School critics and Frederic Jameson.

De Man, Paul. *Allegories of Reading: Figural Language in Rousseau, Nietzsche, Rilke, and Proust.* New Haven and London: Yale University Press, 1979.

> JD is cited on 6 different pages in passing references that use his ideas appreciatively to support de Man's point. De Man and JD had mutual respect for each others' work.

De Man, Paul. *Blindness and Insight: Essays in the Rhetoric of Contemporary Criticism*. [Introduction by Wlad Godzich] Theory and History of Literature, Volume 7. University of Minnesota Press: Minneapolis, 1971 and 1983.

> This 1971 publication contains a significant treatment of JD's reading of Rousseau, just as de Man believes JD's reading of Rousseau is significant: ". . . Derrida's work is one of the places where the future possibility of literary criticism is being decided . . ." (111). De Man subordinates JD's interpretation to his own by seeing it as "an exemplary case of the interaction between critical blindness and critical insight . . . ." In de Man's discussion he recognizes that JD is *not* a literary critic in the professional sense. The now famous essay, "The Rhetoric of Blindness: Jacques Derrida's Reading of Rousseau," which purports to discover an essential blindness in JD's reading of Rousseau in *Gram*: "What happens in Rousseau is exactly what happens in Derrida: a vocabulary of substance and of presence is no longer used declaratively but rhetorically . . . Derrida misconstrues as blindness what is instead a transposition from the literal to the figural level of discourse" (138-39). This essay is especially notable because it marks a turning point in the reception of JD's work by de Man in particular, and the Yale School in general.

De Man, Paul. *The Resistance to Theory*. Minneapolis: University of Minnesota Press, 1986.

> Reprints an essay, "Hypogram and Inscription," which touches on *Gl* by way of a reading of Riffaterre's reading in "Le trace de l'intertexte," and an interview in which De Man briefly but decisively distinguishes the differences between his work and JD's.

Descamps, Christian. *Les idées philosophiques contemporaines en France, 1960-1985.* Paris: Bordas, 1986.

>Short chapter entitled "Deconstruction et interprétation," provides a very spartan overview of JD's philosophy, including an exposition of *différance*.

Descombes, Vincent. *Le Même et l'autre.* Paris: Minuit, 1979. Trans. as *Modern French Philosophy*.

Doane, Janice L., and Devon Hodges. *Nostalgia and Sexual Difference: The Resistance to Contemporary Feminism.* New York: Methuen, 1987.

>Only a passing reference to Harold Bloom's divergence from JD, despite the fact that the authors state at the outset that "our critique . . . is obviously informed by Jacques Derrida's efforts" (8).

Dostal, Robert J. "The World Never Lost: The Hermeneutics of Trust." *Philosophy and Phenomenological Research* 47 (1987): 413-34.

>Wants to defend "what Rorty has called the `weak textualism' of Gadamer against the `strong textualism' of Rorty and Derrida." The terms weak and strong refer to Bloom's usages in *Kabbalah and Criticism*. The content is mostly about the Gadamer-JD encounter with the emphasis clearly on Gadamer.

Ewald, François and Dominique A. Grisoni. "Six personnages en Quête d'une autre philosophie." *Magazine Littéraire* [196] June 1983: 74-81.

The title in English means "Six Personalities in Search of Another Philosophy." The decade of the 80's includes the seeds of another philosophy. This philosophy will come out from a nonexistent school of philosophy but it will have a common style. Its theme will be more narrow but also leaving behind political and ethical prejudices. Six works on philosophy which are recent and widely respected are the following: (1) Jean-Claude Milner's *Les noms indistincts*; (2) JD's *D'un ton apocalyptique adopté naguère en philosophe*; (3) Ricoeur's *Temps et récits*; (4) Christian Jambet's *La Logique*; (5) Michel Serres's *Rome, le livre des fondations*; (6) Maurice Maschino's work on questions of the philsophical program. All of them are entering a new passage and they transfer their centers of interest toward the confluence of new passages. In our age, we are immersed in a revival of postmodernism. There exists in the body of French philosophy a kind of old and arrogant cancer, a kind of a team (the Derridean). They are the philosophers of an old fashion. They follow the work of one teacher. [One must reflect on the choice of these six as opposed to Lyotard, Lacoue-Labarthe, Nancy, or others.]

Fite, David. *Harold Bloom: The Rhetoric of Romantic Vision*. Amherst: University of Massachusetts Press, 1985.

There are only a few paragraphs on JD, and then the content is quite general or it is about the "witty thrust" of literary critics toward JD: `an absolutist without absolutes' (188). Fite claims Bloom at once embraces and rejects JD. He also offers a brief overview of the appropriation of JD's philosophy by the Yale School.

Gane, Mike. "Textual Theory: Derrida." [A Review of five books by Derrida: *WD*, *Pos*, *SP*, *Gram*, and *Dis*.] In *Economy and Society* 11.2 (May 1982): 199-222.

In twenty-two pages, Gane, a sociologist, reviews *WD*, *Pos*, *SP*, *Gram*, and *Dis*. In this attempt Gane claims that JD's dialectic is proximate to Marx's. As a criticism Gane claims that JD, though he tried, has not been able altogether to escape "the limiting effect of the formalism-empiricism couple in Hegelian philosophy" (209). JD's thought is a "Marxism which has undergone, at specific points, a shift towards empiricism and at others towards formalism." There is a definition of JD's project vis-à-vis the tradition.

Gans, Eric. "Différences." *Modern Language Notes* 96 (1981): 792-806.

There is a long discussion of main concepts of genetics, e.g. DNA/RNA code, before Gans explains how Girard's ideas are too empirical to be a successful replacing critique of JD. See this passage (803): "Girard's original event must do too much--it must do what Derrida knows is impossible, explain the birth of difference. But difference `always already' exists, in a form Derrida refuses to recognize, and that Girard recognizes but then forgets" (803). Concludes, "The original difference is precisely that of life itself [hence the long discussion of the origin of life in the DNA code], which from its own problematic origin has distinguished structurally, if not conceptually, between the organism and its appetitive objects" (803-04). Also, see 807 for a parallel preference of JD's a priority of *différance* as opposed to Girard's critique/replacement. In the closing remarks Gans states there must be--in the intellectual realm--some kind of "law of unequal development" (808).

Gasché, Rodolphe. "Deconstruction as Criticism." *Glyph* 6 (1979): 177-215.

> Claims "the critical malaise of modern critics that makes them long for a "beyond-deconstruction" and simultaneously allows the attacks of the rear-guard, stems in the first place from a mutual misunderstanding of the notion of deconstruction. It is precisely this misinterpretation that makes its accommodation by American criticism possible, and, by the same token, transforms it into a mechanical exercise similar to academic thematism or formalism" (178). Gasché tries to clarify the misunderstanding. It is significant that six of thirty-one pages are on Lyotard's deconstruction. Two pages are on the source of deconstruction in Merleau-Ponty's work.

Gasché, Rodolphe. "Joining the Text From Heidegger to Derrida." *The Yale Critics: Deconstruction in America.* Ed. J. Arac, W. Godzich, W. Martin. Minneapolis: University of Minnesota Press, 1983.

Gasché, Rodolphe. "Nontotalization without Spuriousness: Hegel and Derrida on the Infinite." *Journal of the British Society for Phenomenology* 17 (1986): 289-307.

> Gasché relates JD's ideas about the finite vs. infinite status of the text to Hegel's notions of the spurious and the genuine infinite. Central to this discussion is JD's idea of "play," as necessity and chance, as infinite substitutability. Develops the notion of "structural infinite" to describe the putative features of JD's idea of text. Concludes "it should be clear by now that the infinitude of this structural infinite hinges on the finitude of the field subjected to infinite substitutions. In `Dissemination,' one reads: `In the dial's *finite* apparatus, the polysemous phase of dissemination reproduces itself indefinitely'" (305). Strictly speaking, Gasché states that JD's philosophy is overcoming the oppositions of finite vs infinite.

Gasché, Rodolphe. "Postmodernism and Rationality." *Journal of Philosophy* 85.10 (1988): 528-38.

> Describes how postmodernist thinkers account for rationality. There is a three to four page discussion of Lyotard's revision of knowledge as now taking account of the irrational, the paradoxical, the undecidable. The views of Lyotard and JD are contrasted with those of Habermas. JD finds an "opacity" in the system of reason; the origin of reason is non-rational.

Gasché, Rodolphe. "`Setzung' and `Ubersetzung': Notes on Paul de Man." *Diacritics* 11 (1981): 36-57.

Gasché, Rodolphe. "Unscrambling Positions: On Gerald Graff's Critique of Deconstruction." *Modern Language Notes* 96 (1981): 1015-34.

> Describes the furor of literary critics against deconstruction, and he states the need to adjudicate. Graff is the primary prosecutor [or persecutor] of deconstruction that Gasché discusses. Concludes that deconstructive criticism is invaluable despite all its fallacies.

Gasché, Rodolphe. *The Tain of the Mirror: Derrida and the Philosophy of Reflection*. Harvard University Press: Cambridge, 1986.

> Besides Harvey's attempt, one of the few total philosophical criticisms of JD's philosophy (1986). All in all, as the title indicates, Gasché claims JD writes a philosophy of reflection; philosophy *is* reflection. The word "tain" in the title refers to the silver backing which makes a mirror reflect images, and JD uses this term in *Diss* to denote the reverse side on which dissemination writes itself (238). In an epigraph to the entire book Gas-

ché quotes the passage in that work where JD speaks about the entire philosophical enterprise in terms of reflection. Gasché's terminology is suggestive of classical idealistic issues prior to JD's *Gram*, as when Gasché writes "Instead of inquiring into the a priori and logical credentials of the philosophical discourse, JD's heterology is the setting out of a law that is written on the tinfoil of the mirrors between which thought can either maintain the separation of fact and principle in an endless reflection of one another, or sublate them in an infinite synthesis" (318). Gasché's book has 3 parts: 1. Toward the Limits of Reflection; 2. On Deconstruction; 3. Literature or Philosophy? This work has more merit than other partial attempts.

Gasché, Rodolphe. *Rethinking Relation: On Heidegger, Derrida, and de Man*. This book is forthcoming in 1991 or 1992.

Goux, Jean-Joseph. "La dissémination." Rev. of *Dis*, by Derrida. *Les lettres françaises* 1455 (Octobre 1972): 14-15.

The title in English means "dissemination." There is a small epigraph by Jean Ristat. "When we devoted one whole periodical to JD, no one talked about his book *Diss*. And this article which we publish today wasn't published as if a kind of censorship was exercised against JD. This last volume of *Lettres Françaises* has a duty to correct this by publishing this article. The criticism is very positive. Never before has the texture of philosophy texts been investigated as JD has done. Philosophy moves between semiology on the one hand and literature on the other, and JD's position is the philosophical light on both of them which crosses them and goes deep in them and originates new positions. JD reveals Plato, Hegel, Mallarmé, Husserl, and Artaud."

Goux, Jean-Joseph. "Du graphème au chromosome." *Lettres Française* 29 Mar. 1972 [1429]: 6-7.

Goux, Jean-Joseph. *Oedipus, Philosopher*. Trans. Catherine Porter. Stanford University Press, 1993.

Granel, Gérard. "Jacques Derrida et la rature de l'origine." *Critique* [246] (Nov. 1967): 887-905. Repris in *Traditionis traditio*, Paris, Gallimard, 1972.

Granel, Gérard. *Traditionis traditio*. Paris: Gallimard, 1972. Reprints "Jacques Derrida et la rature de l'origine"

Grisoni, Dominique. "Inter-fluences de la philosophie contemporaine." *Magazine Littéraire* 127-128 (1977): 66-67.

"Genealogical" chart which shows some of JD's philosophical forebears and heirs.

Grisoni, Dominique A. "Le phénomène Derrida." *Magazine Littéraire* 196 juin 1983.

Grisoni, Dominique. "Politiques et philosophie: éléments pour une chronologie." *Magazine Littéraire* 127-128 (1977): 68-87.

Chronological examination of French philosophy in the 1960s and 70s which is extremely helpful in contextualizing JD's work within the French intellectual scene.

Gumbrecht, Hans. "Deconstruction Deconstructed: Transformationen französischer Logozentrismuskritik in der amerikanischen Literaturtheorie." *Philosophische Rundschau* 33 (1986): 1-34.

Handelman, Susan A. *The Slayers of Moses: The Emergence of Rabbinic Interpretation in Modern Literary Theory.* Albany: State University of New York Press, 1982.

> JD, who is categorized as a thinker "attempting to articulate theories of language and interpretation appropriate to a twentieth century which has severed its ties with the Greco-Roman tradition, is a central figure in a text which examines his writing in relation to Rabbinic interpretation. Chapter One offers a substantial reading of "White Mythology"; Chapter 3 briefly touches on the relation between "*écriture*" and "the Jew"; Chapter 5 includes a brief reading of JD on Freud in "Coming Into One's Own"; and Chapter 7 provides an extensive reading of JD's debate with Lacan, as well as of JD's essays on Lévinas and Jabès in and against the Jewish and psychoanalytic traditions.

Handelman, Susan. "Jacques Derrida and the Heretic Hermeneutic." *Displacement: Derrida and After.* Ed. Mark Krupnick. Bloomington: Indiana University Press, 1983. 98-129.

> Views Derridean "displacement" as a "key term for Jewish heremenutics." Goes on to provide a detailed, complex, and far-reaching set of parallels between deconstruction and Rabbinic interpretation and Kabbalah, setting traditional Greek and/or Christian views of language against Jewish ones. Also relates deconstruction to a number of other central ancient and contemporary philosophical and literary figures.

Harris, Wendell V. *Interpretive Acts: In Search of Meaning*. Oxford: Clarendon Press, 1988.

> JD is discussed only secondarily; that is, insofar as his principles are at work in J. Hillis Miller's deconstruction, with Miller's `Walter Pater; A Partial Portrait' taken as an example.

Hartman, Geoffrey H. *Criticism in the Wilderness: The Study of Literature Today*. New Haven: Yale University Press, 1980.

> A number of short expositions and some longer analyses of JD's "unsettling" philosophy in the context of literary criticism and theory. Includes discussions of *Gl* and JD's blurring of the distinction between primary and secondary texts, as well as some positive endorsements of JD's project.

Hartman, Geoffrey H. *Saving the Text: Literature, Derrida, Philosophy*. Baltimore: Johns Hopkins University Press, 1981.

> A crucial text in the dissemination of JD's work in North America. The first three chapters present an extended literary-oriented reading of *Gl*, which is marked by its attention to the heterogeneous styles of JD's text. A fourth chapter focuses on the French transformation of psychoanalysis by JD and Lacan, and the final one is a series of readings of literary texts which are only tangentially related to JD, though clearly are inspired by him.

Hartman, Geoffrey H. *The Fate of Reading and Other Essays*. Chicago: University of Chicago Press, 1975.

> Seven essays contain brief discussions of and/or citations from JD.

Harvey, Irene E. *Derrida and the Economy of Différance.* Indiana University Press: Bloomington, 1986. [Note also a reference article that Harvey wrote in *Thinkers of the Twentieth Century* overviewing JD's work in which she writes, "These comments do not sum up Derrida's work as a whole, but they do suggest two crucial dimensions of his project. First, it seems clear that Derrida has sustained a consistent, coherent and explicitly defined program in his writing which is concerned with the revelation of the conditions of the possibility of metaphysics itself. Second, and equally as important, it is also evident that Derrida's development of this same problematic has taken on radically original formats of textuality such as (a) have never before been attempted within philosophy as such, and (b) have yet to be thoroughly analyzed, understood or appropriated by that same tradition." p. 132.]

One of the few philosophical attempts at a total criticism of JD's work (1986). (Another would be that of Gasché and Llewelyn.) Sympathetic though the text is, there are 3 criticisms of JD's work. (1) Freud's and JD's model of the memory as a mystic writing pad employs a "circular causality" which is short-circuited (178-79); (2) she questions the double movement of protection and violation that characterizes the relation of trace to memory (180); and (3) JD is afflicted with a classical flaw of philosophies, a confusion of the logical and the temporal, i.e., the problem of the "child which is the father of the man" (213).

Harvey, Irene E. "Contemporary French Thought and the Art of Rhetoric." *Philosophy and Rhetoric* 18 (1985): 199-215.

Discusses Sartre, Barthes, Ricoeur, Foucault, JD (three pages), and Lacan. "Derrida's work to-date does not divide into earlier and later periods of development, nor contradict itself, nor split into a practice of a method, on the one hand, and a theoretical exposé and justification of that method, on the other. Rather, his project as a whole can be characterized as being without such divisions and hence also by means of any particular text" (208-09). The aims of deconstruction are stated and a definition of his original `idea' of *différance*. JD is relevant for a discussion of the art of rhetoric, because, as Harvey states at the end of the article, rhetoric presupposes theories of writing, of speech, and of language. JD's idea of *différance* transforms our notion of communication through writing and speech.

Harvey, Irene E. "Derrida and the Concept of Metaphysics." *Research in Phenomenology* 13 (1983): 113-48.

Harvey, Irene E. "A Derridean Pre-Text." *Journal of the British Society for Phenomenology* 17.3 (1986): 215-16.

Short as this introduction is, it merits an annotation. There are some implied statements, apropos of the essays to follow, about the kind of possible development of JD's thought. It can't be an Oedipal development. Also, deconstruction cannot be deconstructed, for in doing so the opponent makes deconstruction right whether it is wrong or right--by presupposition.

Harvey, Irene E. "Metaphorics and Metaphysics: Derrida's Analysis of Aristotle." *Journal of the British Society for Phenomenology* 17 (1986): 308-30.

Begins with a quote of JD on the blind spot or formal law of philosophy. Her analysis leads up to the "supplement of syntactical resistance" as the principle of metaphorics, as the foundation of philosophy in JD's view. The syntax of syntaxes is not possible; it is the blind spot, yet formal law. In general this spot is an irrepressible desire to overcome the metaphorical division of origin and itself (philosophy). Harvey ends by saying that there might be found something like this as a contract or rule.

Harvey, Irene. "Re-Evaluating Deconstruction." *Philosophy and Culture*. V.3 Ed. Venant Cauchy. Montreal: Beffroi, 1987. 264-68.

Haverkamp, Anselm. "Paradigma Metapher, Metapher Paradigma-- Zur Metakritik hermeneutischer Horizonte (Blumenberg/Derrida, Kuhn/Foucault, Black/White." *Poetik und Hermeneutik* 12 (1987): n.p.

Hayles, N. Katherine. *Chaos Bound: Orderly Disorder in Contemporary Literature and Science*. Ithaca: Cornell University Press, 1990.

Brief, provocative discussion of the similarities between Derridean deconstruction as presented in *Gram* and the "nonlinear dynamics" of chaos theory as represented by the works of M. Feignbaum, J. Ford, and R. Shaw.

Henning, E.M. "Foucault and Derrida: Archaeology and Deconstruction." *Stanford French Review* 5 (1981): 247-64.

Henning is interested in reviewing and understanding Foucault and JD as intellectual historians. Their projects vis-à-vis the tradition are assessed. Essentially, this article is a comparison on a theme. The conclusion is that Foucault stays more within the tradition, while JD understands the problems better.

Holland, Nancy J. "Merleau-Ponty on Presence: A Derridian Reading." *Research in Phenomenology* 16 (1986): 111-20.

Compares JD and Merleau-Ponty: "In comparing the two . . . the central question would seem to be not only time, but also perception, which is central to Merleau-Ponty's philosophy, language, which is so important for Derrida, and the relationship between the three. In this paper I will address these three topics, looking at the points Derrida raises against phenomenology with regard to each and the ways in which Merleau-Ponty can be seen to exceed the tradition, often in words that echo Derrida's own texts before their time" (112).

Hopkins, Burt C. "Derrida's Reading of Husserl in *Speech and Phenomena*: Ontologism and the Metaphysics of Presence." *Husserl Studies* 2 (1985): 193-214.

Hopkins compares and assesses Husserl's and JD's views on the issues discussed in *SP*. Hopkins criticizes JD: (1) JD's deconstruction does fall within the imminent concern of phenomenology; (2) Hopkins sees deconstruction as limited to "the intelligible horizon of the natural attitude" (214).

Horstmann, Ulrich. *Parakritik und Dekonstruktion: Ein Einführung in den amerikanischen Poststrukturalismus.* Wurzburg: Köninshausen + Neumann, 1983.

Though more directly about the Yale School of critics than JD himself, his work receives a great deal of attention as the root of the American school of deconstruction. Especially good for its historical survey of JD's influence on literary theory and criticism in America, and for following the appropriations of and deviations from his work by the four critics--Bloom, Hartman, J. Hillis Miller, and de Man--studied.

Houdebine, Jean-Louis. "Letter from Jean-Louis Houdebine to Jacques Derrida. Excerpt." *Diacritics* (Summer 1973): 57. Also see *Pos*.

> This letter appears at the end of *Pos*; it is a criticism of JD's notion of alterity/spacing as self-contradictory and which must give way to some notion of "position." JD doesn't accept the criticism.

Howells, Christina. "Sartre and Derrida: Qui Perd Gagne." *Journal of the British Society for Phenomenology* 13 (1982): 26-34.

> Howells doesn't want "to pit Sartre against Derrida "but she does want to show that the early Sartre is closer to JD's position than he would like to admit. At the close Howells criticizes JD's idea of *différance* insofar as it is "a game of loser-wins where one wins and loses every time."

Karamcheti, Indira. "Tradition and Originality in Third World Literature: V.S. Naipaul and Aimé Cesaire." University of California, Santa Barbara, 1986.

> The literary theories of Bloom, JD, and Said help to examine the status of the literary authority of Third World authors.

Kuenzli, Rudolf E. "Derridada." *L'esprit créateur*. 20.2 (1980): 12-21.

> Kuenzli claims there are "striking parallels between Derrida's deconstruction of logocentrism and Dada's critique of the cultural sign system" (13). Dada dismantled "traditional cultural norms and codes" of "the insane war culture." "Derrida's critique of the traditional faith in the

sign as involving presence may be seen in the context of the present crisis of language, which has become the principal theme of literature."

Lacoue-Labarthe, Philippe. "L'imprésentable." *Poétique* 21 (1975): 53-95.

> JD is quoted at length and his ideas permeate this essay, though there is no direct mention or analysis of his works in the text proper.

Lacoue-Labarthe, Philippe. *L'imitation des modernes*. Paris: Galilée, 1986.

Lacoue-Labarthe, Philippe. *Le Sujet de la philosophie*. Paris: Aubier: Flammarion, 1979.

> Essays here have only a small number of direct quotations and mentions of JD, but they are nonetheless highly Derridean in their textual practices. [Part of this is contained in the English translation *Typography*.]

Lacoue-Labarthe, Philippe. *Le titre de la lettre: une lecture de Lacan*. Paris: Galilée, 1973. Now translated into English.

> Though JD's name appears only in the Notes, this remarkable interrogation of Lacanian psychoanalysis can be viewed as an extension and expansion of many of JD's own positions and ideas.

Lacoue-Labarthe, Phillipe et Jean-Luc Nancy, ed. *Les Fins de l'homme. A partir du travail de Jacques Derrida*. Colloque de Cerisy-la-Salle du 22 juill. au 2 août 1980.

> Galilée, 1981. textes de Agacinski, Allen, Borch-Jacobsen, Brémondy Burger, Carroll, Courtine, Escoubas, Feher, Ferry et Renault, Fischer, Fynsk, Gasché, Gearhart, Granoff, Hamacher, Hollier, Hovald, Imbert, Irigaray, Johnson, Kambouchner, Kofman, Lacoue-Labarthe, Laporte, Lewis, Lichtenstein, Loraux, Lyotard, Madaule, Marin, McDonald, Moscovici, Nancy, Payant, Petitot-Cocorda, Pinchard, Pujol, Rey, Rogozinski, Spivak, Toyosaki, Wipf. For annotations see the chapters of works rather than whole books.

Lacroix, Jean. *Panorama de la philosophie française contemporaine.* Paris: Presses Universitaires de France, 1966.

> Mentions JD's "Violence and Metaphysics" as a text to consult on Lévinas.

Lane, Gilles. *A quoi bon la philosophie?* Longueuil, Quebec: Le Preambule, 1982.

> Brief reference to JD's notion of transcendental signifieds.

Lapouge, Gilles. "Six philosophes occupés à deplacer la philosophie à propos de la `mimesis'." *Quinzaine Littéraire* [231] 1976: 23.

Laruelle, François. "Le texte quatrième: L'événment comme simulacre." *L'Arc* 54 (1973): 38-45.

Lentricchia, Frank. *After the New Criticism.* Chicago: University of Chicago Press, 1980.

Compares JD with Frye. Critiques JD's reading of Saussure, notes the later Barthes' indebtedness to JD. Provides a detailed history of JD's emergence and influences on the American scene, especially through "Structure, Sign and Play," tracing the various attacks by "traditionalists" on postmodernist and vice versa, as well as by various postmodern factions on each other. Also presents a detailed overview of JD's philosophy up to 1977, including the debate with Foucault, as well as Krieger, Hirsch, de Man, and Bloom on JD.

Lévinas, Emmanuel. "Tout autrement." *L'Arc* 54 (1973): 33-37.

Superb synopsis of the core of JD's philosophical project which interrogates certain crucial Derridean notions, and which praises JD's philosophy for its courage to renew debate on some "primordial" philosophical questions.

Lewis, Clayton W. "Identifications and Divisions: Kenneth Burke and the Yale Critics." *Southern Review* 22 (1986): 93-102.

Lewis compares and mostly contrasts Burke with the Yale critics. About three pages are on JD, most on Burke, some on Miller and de Man, but only references to Bloom and Hartman. The general type of differences between Burke and the Yale critics is "in their central motivations, the ends they seek, as well as in how each conceives of his own discourse--Derrida's being essentially philosophical and Burke's broadly social" (95). One of these ends that is spoken of more than once is Burke's "subversion" of a text to show its value for a "socio-historical setting." Lewis clearly thinks the deconstructionists ignore this but shouldn't. More generally, the Yale critics diminish the power of language "to make something happen whereas Burke does not."

Liszka, James Jakób. "Derrida: Philosophy of the Liminal." *Man and World* 16 (1983): 233-50.

>Liszka actually attempts a kind of statement about the coherence and structure of JD's entire philosophy. It forms a three-phase dialectic resembling the rites of passage documented by Victor Turner apropos of a primitive tribe. Turner describes "liminal entities" that signal the movement in a rite of passage. Liszka drops the empirical example very quickly and describes the rite of passage of the Derridean philosophy which takes JD to "liminal entities", i.e. the pharmakon as undecidable.

Lyotard, Jean François. *The Differend: Phrases in Dispute*. Minneapolis: University of Minnesota Press, 1988.

>As the advertising blurb on the back cover indicates in a quote from Wlad Godzich, "Jean-François Lyotard is, with Jacques Derrida, Michel Foucault, and Gilles Deleuze, one of the key figures in contemporary French philosophy." Lyotard disagrees with JD about the meaning of time according to his (Lyotard's) new idea of *phrase* and also of *presentation* [74-75]. Another reference to JD is incidental to a discussion of Hegel [96-97]. Also there is a brief discussion of JD on the ideas of presence and the "common" in Aristotle and Hegel.

Lyotard, Jean François. *Heidegger and "the jews"*. [Yes, lower case for "jews," which has an intended meaning]. Trans. Andreas Michel and Mark Roberts. Intro. by David Carroll. University of Minnesota Press: Minneapolis, 1990.

>Lyotard refers to JD on 12 pages in mostly isolated references. He critiques JD on pages 75-77 and 81. On 75 he writes, "That is, to deconstruct what remains of the still too pious, too respectfully nihilist in Derrida's deconstruction of that `politics' that is the thought of

Heidegger." On page 81 he declares that deconstruction [Derrida's and Lacoue-Labarthe's] "impedes and mesmerizes itself." David Carroll comments on Lyotard's criticism of JD and Lacoue-Labarthe's deconstruction as being harsh but not being harsh enough about Heidegger's failures.

Lyotard, Jean-François. *The Lyotard Reader*. Ed. Andrew Benjamin. Oxford: Basil Blackwell, 1989.

This is a collection of mostly previously translated works. There are significant references to JD and to differences in the ideas of Lyotard and JD. There is a discussion of JD's philosophy as represented in the figure of Auschwitz, and a short exchange between JD and Lyotard is given [which the editor indexes as pertaining to Lyotard's idea of `phrase']. These ideas come from the 1980 colloquium on JD's work: *Les fins de l'homme: á partir du travail de Jacques Derrida*, at Cerisy-la-Salle.

Lyotard, Jean-François. *Tombeau de l'intellectuel: et autres papiers*. Paris: Galilée, 1984.

Passing references to JD's "progressivism" and the central role of JD's philosophy in the post-Sartrean French philosophical scene.

Margolis, Joseph. *Pragmatism without Foundations: Reconciling Realism and Relativism*. Oxford: B. Blackwell, 1986.

Numerous, short analyses of JD's thought, mostly of the following nature: "the tradition that moves through Heidegger and Derrida . . . has spawned a tribe of thinkers that have a remarkably impoverished sense of the specifically historicized and historicizing nature of human existence" (193).

Melville, Stephen. "Reading Bloom." Rev. of *Poetry and Repression*, by Harold Bloom. *Chicago Review* 28.1 (1976): 133-40.

Miklitsch, Robert William. "Discourse and Meditation: Readings in Contemporary Poetry and Poetics." Diss. State University of New York at Buffalo, 1982.

> The first part consists of readings of contemporary poems and poets, which part relies on the textual theories of Freud, Bloom, Barthes, and JD.

Miller, J. Hillis. "Deconstructing the Deconstructors." Rev. of *The Inverted Bell: Modernism and the Counterpoetics of William Carlos Williams*, by Joseph N. Riddel. *Diacritics* 5.2 (1975): 24-31.

Miller, J. Hillis. "Geneva or Paris? The Recent Work of Georges Poulet." *University of Toronto Quarterly* 29 (1970): 212-28.

> There is only one page on JD. His change of the tradition from the metaphysics of presence is discussed, which is said to be an interrogation of all the apparent assumptions of Georges Poulet's criticism. The assumptions are found to be wanting, though JD doesn't refer to Poulet specifically. The overall purpose of the essay is to assess the significance of the many books and essays Poulet has published since 1963.

Mishra, Vijay. "Critical Practice and Literary Theory: An Interview with Geoffrey Hartman." *Southern Review* 18 (July 1985): 189-200.

Vijay Mishra interviews Hartman. There are two questions and answers of paragraph size on JD. One concerns the circle of reputation that JD's work passed through: rejection, acceptance, and rejection because institutionalized. In the other answer, Hartman says JD didn't change his criticism but he did give more philosophical explicitness.

Monegal, Emir. "Borges/deMan/Derrida/Bloom, La desconstrucción `Avant et après la lettre'." *Diseminario. La desconstrucción otro descubrimiento de America.* Montevideo: XYZ Editores, 1987.

Münster, Arno. *Pariser philosophisches Journal: Von Sartre bis Derrida.* Frankfurt: Athenäum, 1987.

Chapter on JD entitled "*Die Differänz und die Spur: Jacques Derridas Dekonstruktion des Logozentrismus in der abendländsichen Metaphysik*" ("*Différance* and Trace: Jacques Derrida's Deconstruction of Logocentrism in Western Metaphysics") offers a substantial exposition of *différance* and trace within the larger project of JD's work. Concentrates on how *différance* arises out of JD's critiques of Husserl and Heidegger and how the trace is linked to JD's readings of Freud.

Nancy, Jean-Luc. "Monogrammes IV." *Digraphe* 24 (1980): 131-40.

Terse commentary on *La carte postale*, which is characterized as "an impossible book." Nancy claims that JD's philosophy has reached a point where "incomprehensibility was not far from making itself the message." ("*l'incompréhensibilité n'était pas loin de faire elle-même le message*") (136).

Nancy, Jean-Luc. *La communauté désouvrée.* Paris: C. Bourgois, 1986. Now translated into English.

> Short mentions of JD, mainly in the Notes, on *différance*, the proper, Bataille, and the idea and possibility of community.

Nancy, Jean-Luc. *Le discours de la syncope.* Paris: Aubier-Flammarion, 1976.

> Few passing mentions to JD are relegated to the notes, but the entire argument is indebted to JD, as a note indicates.

Nancy, Jean-Luc. *L'experience de la liberte.* Paris: Galilée, 1988.

> Though JD's explicit role is mainly in footnotes and a brief discussion of *Parages*, the entire text is suffused with JD's thought.

Nancy, Jean-Luc. *Ego sum.* Paris: Flammarion, 1979.

> Brief mention of JD's reading of Foucault in "Cogito and the History of Madness."

Noakes, Susan. *Timely Reading: Between Exegesis and Interpretation.* Ithaca, NY: Cornell University Press, 1988.

> Brief, provocative analysis of how JD's own project has a strong, though "highly traditional" concern with history and the history of philosophy which is totally lost in deconstruction's appropriation by American literary theorists.

Norris, Christopher. "Harold Bloom: A Poetics of Reconstruction." *British Journal of Aesthetics* 20 (1980): 67-76.

Norris, Christopher. "Derrida at Yale: The `Deconstructive Moment' in Modernist Poetics." *Philosophy and Literature* 4 (1980): 242-56.

>Norris' purpose is "to `situate' JD's texts within a wider context of modern critical debate" (254). The mixing of text and citation by JD raises "the central challenge and problem of Derrida's enterprise. Is it possible to go so far toward eliminating voice, presence, origin, and the whole `logocentric' tradition of Western discourse, without in the process giving up the claim to communicate intelligible meaning?" (255).

Norris, Christopher. *The Contest of Faculties: Philosophy and Theory after Deconstruction.* London: Methuen, 1985.

>Collection of mostly previously published essays, a number of which touch on JD. Most useful as an account of the "selective appropriation of JD's texts by critics [especially American deconstructionists] in search of a more adventurous hermeneutic model" (221) and for its exposition of the various attacks on JD's philosophy, especially by Habermas and Gadamer.

Norris, Christopher. *Deconstruction and the Interests of Theory.* Norman: University of Oklahoma Press, 1989.

>Four chapters treat JD specifically: "Post-Structuralist Shakespeare" begins by briefly touching on JD and the question of the institution, and applying JD's critique of "nationalism and universalism" to current Shakespeare studies; "Deconstruction against Itself" is a sweepingly useful exploration of JD's relation to Nietzsche, focusing

on the question of the politics of reading as it pertains to the twisted Nazi appropriation of Nietzsche, demonstrating how JD "has shifted his ground in relation to Nietzsche" in such a way that JD's philosophy can no longer be viewed as merely another form of "`textualist' mystification"; "Derrida, on Reflection," is ostensibly a very commendatory review of Gasché's *Tain*, but also serves as a vehicle for a commentary on what Norris views as certain misappropriations and misreadings of JD by Anglo-American philosophers and literary critics; and "What's in a Name? Derrida's `Signsponge'" is a detailed and laudatory review of JD's book that attempts to demonstrate that JD's modes and strategies of reading, when taken as a whole, have little to do with some type of nihilistic "`freeplay'" but are rather "scrupulously *literal.*"

O'Hara, Daniel. "The Genius of Irony: Nietzsche in Bloom." *The Yale Critics: Deconstruction in America.* Ed. Jonathan Arac, Wlad Godzich and Wallace Martin. Minneapolis: University of Minnesota Press, 1983. 109-32.

Probst, A. "Une critique de la métaphysique occidentale: La philosophie de Jacques Derrida." *Revue Réformée* [24] 93 (1973): 29-43.

Ricoeur, Paul. *The Rule of Metaphor.* London: Routledge & Kegan Paul. 1978. Argues from a broadly hermeneutic viewpoint not wholly sympathetic to deconstruction, but contains some interesting pages on JD's "The White Mythology."

Rorty, Richard. "Deconstruction and Circumvention." *Critical Inquiry* 11 (1984): 1-23.

Rorty states the success and failure of JD's project. It was successful in showing that Heidegger had not performed an "epochal transformation" but had only "a brilliantly original narrative" (20). JD is wrong to think that his deconstruction is the "armature" or "template" of literature and perhaps all other fields. Instead, JD and Heidegger only "encapsulate" the tradition of the history of philosophy and allow us up to "circumvent" it. [Whether the circumvention is good or bad is not clear from Rorty's article.]

Rorty, Richard. "Philosophy as a Kind of Writing: An Essay on Derrida." *New Literary History* 10 (1978): 141-60.

Significant if somewhat ironic exposition of what are characterized as JD's "good" and "bad" side: the former entails the JD who wants to push past the Heideggerian critique of western metaphysics to an even more radical position, the latter who falls back into precisely the ontotheological tradition which he is attempting to deconstruct.

Salusinsky, Imre. "An Interview with Harold Bloom." *Scripsi* 4.1 (n.d.): 69-92. Reprinted in *Criticism in Society*.

Although JD is only mentioned, this interview may be of high interest to those interested in JD vis-à-vis Bloom.

Scarpetta, Guy and Dominique Grisoni. "Dix ans de philosophie en France." *Magazine Littéraire* [225] Dec. 1985. 16-66.

Seebohm, Thomas M. "`Deconstruction' in the Framework of Traditional Methodical Hermeneutics." *Journal of the British Society for Phenomenology* 17 (1986): 275-88.

"Section I of this paper will hence, try to restore a proper concept of the character of traditional hermeneutics. Section II will then be the attempt to construct an analogue to JD's notion of deconstruction in the fringes of traditional hermeneutics." Does not intend to interpret JD. The essay concludes with the point that the real significance of deconstruction is the choice of *différance*; the examples deconstructed are indifferent to the nature of the process, its definition.

Smith, F. Joseph. "Jacques Derrida's Husserl Interpretation." *Philosophy Today* 9 (1967): 106-23.

A note before the text explains its unusual nature: "The following essay grew out of an invitation to Professor Derrida to address the American Phenomenology Society at Penn State University in October 1966. Although Professor Derrida was unable to attend the meeting, he prepared a paper of some 130 pages, an interpretation of Husserl. In his absence Professor Smith was asked to summarize and select parts of this study and present them, together with some commentary. *Philosophy Today* is happy to publish here, with Professor JD's approval, the presentation of his thoughts by Dr. Smith. The full text of his study of Husserl will be published within the next year [1968] by Editions du Seuil in Paris." There are appreciative commentaries by Smith, ending with the prospect that "the outstanding researches of Jacques Derrida . . . will promote a truer understanding of the problematic situation of phenomenology vis-à-vis traditional metaphysics and ontology" (123).

Spikes, Michael P. "Stability of Meaning in Literary Language." Diss. Indiana University, 1986.

> This study supplies a theory of literal meaning. This thesis balances and supplements the views of Iser, Fish, Bloom, and JD.

Ulmer, Gregory L. "The Post-Age." *Diacritics* 11.3 (1981): 39-56.

> The structure of *PC* is described in detail [see 40-41]. What attracts JD's attention in *PC* is that the letter is addressed and signed, directed or destined. There is a kind of communication from a distance or return inquiry here that fascinates JD. [Also, the posting is imagined as traversing different possible recipients through time (from Socrates with help from Plato to Socrates and beyond) such that either its intended meaning or its received meaning cannot be singular or univocal.] Ulmer regards the book as a commentary on the media of our age (hence the punning title: "The Post-Age"), which is also a comment on the transmission of tradition in the human sciences.

Wahl, François. *Philosophie: La philosophie entre l'avant et l'après du structuralisme.* Paris: Seuil, 1973.

> Early, appreciative exploration of JD's 1967 texts from the viewpoint of having gone beyond structuralism. Establishing JD's notion of "writing" ("*l'écriture*") as the point of departure for this analysis, Wahl closely reads *Gram*, *SP*, and *WD*.

Waldenfels, Bernhard. *Phänomenologie in Frankreich.* Frankfurt: Suhrkamp, 1983.

> Very helpful both for its summation of JD's critiques of Husserl and its situating of JD's response to phenomenology within those of his contemporaries.

Wenzel, Ruth. *Posen des modernen Denkens: Die Yale Critics.* Frankfurt: P. Lang, 1988.

> Study of appropriation and deformation of, as well as the reaction against, JD's philosophy by the Yale School. Interesting for its German perspective of this essentially American critical and theoretical phenomenon.

Wordsworth, Ann. "An Art That Will Not Abandon the Self to Language: Bloom, Tennyson and the Blind World of the Wish." *Untying the Text: A Post-Structuralist Reader.* Ed. Robert Young. Boston: Routledge, 1981. 207-22.

Wordsworth, Ann. "Derrida and Foucault, Writing the History of Historicity." *Post-Structuralism and the Question of History.* Ed. Derek Attridge, Robert Young, and Geoff Bennington. Cambridge: Cambridge University Press, 1987. 116-25.

> Fine reading which focuses mainly on the JD-Foucault debate, siding with JD's "disruptions" of the classical notions of the Cogito.

Zapf, Hubert. "Dekonstruktion als Herausforderung der Literaturwissenschaft: Das Beispiel der englischen Romantik." *Anglia: Zeitschrift fur Englische Philologie* 106 (1988): 360-79.

> Title in English: "Deconstruction as a Provocation to the Science of Literature: the Example of English Romanticism." This article treats of the invasion of the deconstructive thinking in English Literature, whose precursors Nietzsche, Freud, Saussure and Heidegger are (the destroyers of metaphysics). The most important representative is JD. He inspires the Yale Critics to tend towards a fundamental new orientation. This is proved

on Romanticism. The author starts with JD's theories from *Gram* and mentions two main axioms: (1)there is no reality without writing (intertexuality); (2) there is no identity, but only difference. Even the relations between humans and the relation to oneself is affected by deconstruction.

Index

Aesop, 326
Alexiou, Margaret, 304, 358
anagoge, 102, 410
anagogical, 425
anagogy, 53, 58, 59, 61, 121, 293-94, 343
anomaly, 127, 131, 259, 268, 275, 278
anxiety of influence, 35, 53, 54, 56, 58-9, 61, 95, 96, 103, 138, 140, 154, 158, 214, 251, 256, 287-88, 290, 411-13, 416, 418, 424, 427, 429, 455, 471
apophrades, *Also see* revisionary ratio. 53, 67-8, 96, 146, 166-67, 169, 178, 222, 281-83, 289-96, 298, 301-03, 305, 342-43, 356, 429, 441
a priori, 179, 185-86, 190, 192, 194, 200, 208, 209, 216-17, 248-50, 255, 296, 307-08, 315, 319, 323, 413, 418
arche-trace, *Also see* trace. 250
askesis, *Also see* revisionary ratio. 53, 96, 146, 148, 166, 169, 222, 281-82, 285-86, 289-94, 303, 305-06, 315-16, 342, 356, 441
Bakhtin, M.M., 153, 212, 301-02, 374, 383, 430

Baudrillard, Jean, 7-9, 16-17, 39, 348-49, 358, 386, 433, 459, 461, 463
Beadle, George W., 4, 6, 8
belatedness, 53, 55, 95, 99, 289, 393
Berman, Art, 32-33, 253, 373
bricolage, 102, 106-07, 109, 164, 175, 218-21, 225, 229, 242, 271, 302, 353, 406, 462
bricoleur, 107, 218-20
Brooke-Rose, Christine, 39
Burkert, Walter, 13-14, 39
Campbell, Joseph, 9, 13-14, 17, 20-21, 141, 143, 145, 204, 239, 285, 299, 308-10, 454, 481
canon, 36, 48, 55, 57, 65, 86, 87-88, 98, 100, 126, 137, 151, 155, 164, 192, 230, 292, 436, 453, 469, 474, 476
Carroll, David, 486
Cassirer, Ernst, 15, 19, 39, 118, 135, 143, 174, 176-77, 179, 181, 188, 213-16, 230, 262, 265, 279, 280, 304, 312-13, 322, 325, 338, 354, 358, 366, 369, 370-71, 381, 385-86, 387, 399, 411, 429, 436, 447, 449, 451, 466-67, 470
Clignet, Remi, 34

clinamen, *Also see* revisionary ratio. 53, 96, 137, 146, 147-52, 159, 163, 166, 212, 215, 218, 220, 222, 226, 229, 237-38, 240, 282, 298, 301, 407, 411-12, 418, 429, 473

Cohen, I. Bernard, 34, 50, 133, 270, 272, 280, 372

continuum, *Also see* tradition form. 126, 148-50, 156-57, 159, 175, 179-80, 188, 196, 212, 214, 226, 265, 278, 285, 308, 349, 350, 352, 355, 376, 391, 411-12, 414, 462-63, 479-80

conversion, 32, 44, 50, 132, 133-34, 361, 369

Copernicus, 73, 75, 79, 118-19, 273, 368

Cotrâu, Liviu, 182

Crick, F.H.C., 5, 8, 238, 241-42, 263

crisis, *Also see* anomaly. 32, 36, 44, 50, 91, 94, 101, 107, 117-18, 126, 127, 130, 149, 213, 259, 262, 266-68, 275, 277, 279, 363, 368-72, 376, 382-83

Curtius, Ernst Robert, 20, 55

daemonization, *Also see* revisionary ratio. 53, 96, 146, 166, 222, 237, 240-41, 244-45, 247, 256-57, 282, 285-86, 290, 309, 310, 367

deconstruct, 173, 410

deconstruction 31-33, 56, 63, 64, 79, 83, 98-101, 105, 108-13, 124, 132, 166, 169-74, 184, 192, 269, 323, 327, 350, 410, 415, 483

De Man, Paul, 32, 35, 53-4, 56, 147, 174, 244, 286, 409, 411, 413, 416

Descartes, René, 118, 135, 183, 230, 442

Dewey, John, 364-66

dialectic, 8, 54, 282, 294, 298, 325, 327-28, 408, 427, 464, 470

dialectical, 7, 54, 101, 108, 110, 120, 137, 140, 147, 182, 184, 222, 235, 238, 253, 283, 307, 387, 408, 429, 454, 483

difference, *Also see* infinite differance. 63, 166, 169, 202-03, 227, 239, 241, 247-57, 295, 305-18, 323-26, 328-29, 331-32, 339, 341, 343, 345, 352, 367, 412, 430, 436, 438-39, 440-42, 446, 448, 459, 479

difference, *Also see* trace, erasure, and then system of differences. 3, 11, 29, 32, 44-5, 63, 65-6, 68, 86, 92, 98, 100-01, 108, 124, 131, 138, 142, 163, 169, 171, 173-74, 176, 178, 183, 196-98, 203-04, 206-09, 212, 215-17, 220, 226, 227-32, 239,

INDEX

248-49, 250-52, 254, 271, 277, 289, 306-08, 311-12, 314-15, 317-19, 323, 324-26, 328, 332, 335, 336, 339, 342-43, 352, 358, 370-71, 377, 389, 393, 403, 412-13, 416, 430, 433, 436, 438-39, 440-43, 446-48, 455, 466, 479, 484

disciplinary matrix, *Also see* paradigm. 44, 49, 60, 77, 82-3, 261, 264, 383, 419, 430, 456, 458-59, 462

DNA, 4-6, 8-12, 15, 29, 63, 77, 86, 109, 121, 137, 143, 164, 182, 213, 219, 223, 225, 238, 240-41, 243-44, 249-50, 252-53, 263, 271-72, 302, 307, 325, 327-28, 351-52, 353, 388, 396-97, 426-27, 431, 454, 458, 485

Dostoevsky, Fyodor M., 151, 154, 160 (Dostoevskij), 301-302, 304, 383, 430, 431

Duncan, Robert, 274

Eco, Umberto, 8, 28, 39, 253, 409

ecphrasis, 301, 353, 430, 482

Eggers, Walter, 135, 230, 280, 399, 451, 466

Einstein, Albert, 16, 21, 31, 122-23, 125, 127, 131, 175, 177-81, 214, 216, 228, 262, 264-65, 269-71, 276, 278-79, 288, 342, 364, 365, 368-69, 373, 376, 377, 382, 385, 386-87, 392-93, 411, 450-51, 458, 467, 472, 480, 482

Elam, Helen Regueiro, 35, 54, 289

Eliot, T.S., 16, 85-6, 88, 95-6, 100, 126, 154, 342, 389, 390, 418, 429

Emerson, Ralph Waldo, 396, 469

ens causa sui, *Also see* in-itself-for-itself and transcendental signified. 173, 176, 181, 188, 190, 198, 202-03, 206, 318-19, 436

erasure, *Also see* trace. 204, 208

Erlich, Victor, 160

exemplar, *Also see* paradigm and disciplinary matrix. 43, 48-9, 77

extraordinary science, 44, 82, 118, 125, 231-35, 260-61, 268, 274-75, 278, 279, 368, 373

fates, the three, 163-64, 166-68, 241, 339

festival, (an advanced form of the supplement; *also see* supplement) 21, 166-67, 305, 331, 338, 342-44, 356, 439, 440-43, 446

Fite, David, 36, 54, 399, 413, 470

form of tradition, *See* tradition form.

Fowler, Alastair, 399, 462

Frank, Joseph, 44
Freud, Sigmund, 8, 16, 27, 28, 55, 56, 64, 66, 88-9, 94, 99, 113, 138-39, 147, 161, 169, 183, 296, 306, 316, 402, 405, 415-16
Frye, Northrop, 14, 17, 27, 35, 53, 55, 56, 243
Gablik, Suzi, 34, 50-1, 119-22, 128, 135, 144-45, 232, 262, 267, 376, 379, 387, 389
Gans, Eric, 243
Gasché, Rodolphe, 321, 349, 358, 483
genetic code, 5-9, 16, 21, 24, 25, 28, 30-1, 68-9, 86, 92, 94, 97-8, 103-04, 126, 128, 137-38, 154, 163-64, 168, 184, 213, 222, 226, 241, 252, 272, 273, 279, 281, 301-02, 303, 322, 325, 328, 335, 346, 349, 352, 354, 361, 367, 371, 388, 390, 392, 397, 401, 423, 426-27, 432, 435-36, 443, 450, 453-59, 461-63, 467-69, 472, 474, 476, 478, 484-85
Gogol, Nikolai, 39, 151, 154, 160, 245, 302, 304, 383, 430
Gould, Stephen Jay, 60
Goux, Jean-Joseph, 223
Grammatology, 27, 32, 37, 63, 64, 66-7, 80, 106, 295, 305, 350, 430, 435, 484
Greimas, A.J., 294, 433
Griffiths, Frederick T., 142, 151, 155, 160, 245, 283, 301, 304, 430, 482
Hartman, Geoffrey H., 32, 55
Harvey, Irene, 181-82, 248, 324, 329-30, 332, 334, 339, 348, 350-51, 353, 358, 433, 440
Hegel, Georg, 64, 66, 181-83, 230, 292, 325, 433, 477
Hollander, John, 35, 56, 415, 417, 454, 472
Howells, Christina M., 182
Hume, David, 182-83, 230
ideal limit, 313, 436
incommensurability, 32, 50, 61, 83, 130, 259, 269, 270-72, 336, 361, 369, 372-73
incommensurable, 132, 269
infinite differance, *Also see* differance. 166, 241, 247, 253, 255, 315, 318, 339, 367, 438
in-itself-for-itself, *Also see* ens causa sui and transcendental signified. 173, 185, 186-90, 193, 196-97, 203, 206, 208, 217, 318-19, 330, 332, 345, 348, 349, 436
invariance, reproductive, 263, 322, 388, 392, 420, 426
inwardness, 148, 216, 379, 408, 417
James, Henry, 240, 296
Kabbalah, 30, 55-6, 58, 86, 89, 92, 94, 146-47, 149, 413, 415-16, 454, 474

Kant, Immanuel, 23, 39, 132, 182-83, 196, 217, 230, 306, 336, 351, 354
Keats, John, 86, 89, 91, 113, 288, 295, 355, 472
Kellner, Douglas, 39
kenosis, *Also see* revisionary ratio. 53, 96, 146, 166, 222, 237-40, 244, 247, 251-53, 257, 282, 286, 367, 459, 474
Kisiel, T., 34, 50-1, 269, 270, 280
Krieger, Murray, 404
Kronik, John W., 37
Leibniz, Gottfried, 230, 366, 371, 399, 421
Lemon, Lee T., 8, 142, 233, 374-75, 401, 406, 433
Lévi-Strauss, Claude, 12, 19, 39, 171, 218-19, 230, 294, 337, 338, 395, 407, 470
Liszka, James Jakób, 141, 266-67, 306, 326, 328, 336, 343
Lowe, Walter, 7
Lyotard, Jean-François, 10, 14, 17, 25-6, 226, 230, 264, 276-79, 284, 296-97, 306-07, 323, 327, 363, 373, 380, 384-85, 392-93, 408, 419, 423, 433, 447, 456, 459, 461, 463, 468, 471, 483-84
map of misreading, 53, 58, 103, 111, 137, 138, 146, 164, 220, 225, 266, 302, 303, 392, 405, 408, 421, 423, 426-27, 429, 432, 469-70, 475
Mayer, Sigrid. *See* Eggers, Walter.
Maxwell, J.C., 75, 123, 181, 270-71, 276, 278, 373
Merleau-Ponty, Maurice, 182, 184, 192-93, 197, 230, 304
metalepsis, *Also see* transumption. 53, 148, 263, 283, 286-87, 289, 316-17, 327, 329-31, 392-93
metaleptic, 317, 330, 393
Miller, J. Hillis, 14, 32, 56
Milton, John, 86, 88-93, 97, 155, 170, 287, 289, 301, 417, 472
misprision, *Also see* misreading. 53, 137, 139, 145, 159, 216, 218, 288-89, 409, 411-12, 417, 454
misreading, 36, 53, 58-60, 89, 103, 111, 130, 137-39, 145-46, 150, 159, 164, 173, 183, 215-18, 220-21, 225, 229, 266, 271, 302-03, 392, 405, 408, 409-13, 416-17, 421, 423, 426-27, 429, 432, 469-70, 475
misread, 86, 139
Moebian strip, 292
Monod, Jacques, 263, 322, 352, 378, 387-88, 391-92, 420, 455, 463
Montefiore, Alan, 422
Mottram, Eric, 320
Nancy, Jean-Luc, 39, 399, 486

narrative, 10, 14, 17, 25-6, 81, 83, 240, 266-67, 274, 279, 294, 296, 304, 321, 366, 383-86, 402, 423-24, 468, 478-79

Nemerov, Howard, 27

Newton, Sir Isaac, 8, 23, 45, 70, 72-3, 75, 119, 123, 131, 225, 265, 267, 273, 356, 366, 368, 385, 393, 421, 468, 478

normal science, 44, 50-1, 77, 117-18, 123, 125, 132, 134, 231-35, 260-62, 264, 268, 270, 274-75, 277-79, 368, 373, 378, 384

Oedipus, 27-8, 67, 156, 422, 470

ouroboros, 190, 282, 294, 298, 305, 343

paradigm, 32, 34, 43-5, 47-53, 71, 73, 75-9, 82-5, 94, 105, 117-18, 120, 122, 123-27, 129, 130-34, 144, 231-35, 261, 263, 264, 267-71, 275, 277, 278-79, 280, 368, 374, 375, 377-78, 384, 403
   post-paradigm, 75
   trans-paradigm, 129

Peperzak, Adriaan [sic] Theodor, 465

perspective, 241

perspective drawing, 163, 170, 176, 204

phoenix, 14-5, 25, 65, 97, 301

Picasso, Pablo, 67, 264, 280

Plato, 74, 133, 164, 174, 183, 230, 323, 344, 396, 442, 447

presence, (sometimes called pure presence), *Also see* self-presence. 64, 87, 90, 93, 96, 100-101, 109-10, 118, 142, 171, 173, 176, 179, 181-82, 198, 200, 202, 203, 208-09, 223, 227, 242, 249, 255, 296, 309, 312-15, 317-19, 324, 340, 343, 346, 353, 376, 379, 405, 436, 438-39, 441-43, 483

Prodi, G., 8, 39

psychoanalysis, 99, 143, 147, 169, 306

Rabinowitz, Stanley J. *See* Griffiths, Frederick T.

Raizis, Marius Byron, 284

ratio, *See* revisionary ratio.

Reis, Marion J. *See* Lemon, Lee T.

revisionary ratio, *Also see* clinamen, tessera, kenosis, daemonization, askesis, apophrades. 53, 55, 96, 149, 151-52, 242, 392, 429, 454, 464

revolution, 29, 34, 44, 46-7, 51, 68, 70, 72-6, 80, 82-5, 110, 117-20, 122-23, 125, 127, 130, 132-34, 137, 144, 219, 231-33, 268, 275, 279, 354, 361, 362, 366-68, 370-72, 376-78, 390, 393, 480

Ricoeur, Paul, 251, 306-07, 346, 358
Riegl, Alois, 13, 120, 153, 379, 387, 388-89
Sartre, Jean-Paul, 13, 63-5, 163, 166, 171, 173-90, 192-94, 196-204, 206-09, 217, 220, 229-30, 248, 251, 254-56, 295, 305-06, 310-11, 314-15, 317-321, 327-28, 330, 332, 343-46, 348-51, 356, 370, 371, 384, 436, 446, 450, 461, 466, 479, 480-81
science, extraordinary, and science, normal, *See* extraordinary science and normal science.
self-presence, 200, 202, 218, 318, 343, 346, 441
Serpent of Time, the, *See* ouroboros.
Shelley, Percy Bysshe [sic], 25, 33, 53, 55, 57, 58-61, 86, 89, 91, 96, 97-8, 102, 147, 170, 214, 240, 292, 295, 296, 301, 355, 408, 410, 415, 417, 471-74
Shklovsky, Victor, (in some sources spelled "Shklovskii, V.B.") 27, 142, 156, 233, 237, 374, 378, 423, 430, 476
Simmel, Georg, 15, 39
Spenser, Edmund, 85-6, 91, 93, 147

Strudwick, John Mehuish (1849-1935), 164, 166, 167, 169
supplement, 63-4, 166-67, 169, 305-26, 328-32, 335-42, 344-46, 348-54, 356, 366, 384, 412, 427, 429, 436, 438-43, 446, 447-48, 450, 459, 461, 464, 478-83
symbolic form, 384
system of differences, 83, 180, 208, 226-27, 247-48, 251-53, 256, 305-06, 339
Tedlock, Dennis, 7, 39
teleduction, *Also see* transduction. 454, 456, 468, 481
teleonomic level, *Also see* invariance, reproductive. 420
teleonymy, *Also see* invariance, reproductive. 388, 392, 420, 467
Tennyson, Alfred Lord, 86, 89, 295, 355, 472
tessera, *Also see* revisionary ratio. 53, 96, 137, 146, 159, 163, 222, 226, 229, 237, 238-40, 282, 411
Todorov, Tzvetan, 39, 152, 212, 240, 243, 295, 304, 321, 383, 402, 418, 424
trace, *Also see* transcendental signified, erasure, arche-trace, and difference. 25, 179, 182, 203-04, 208-09, 217-18, 223, 227, 249-51, 307, 317, 356, 482-83

tradition form, *Also see* continuum. 15-18, 20-1, 28, 63, 65, 67-8, 107, 122, 134, 137, 144, 146, 157, 163, 180-82, 184, 186, 215, 222, 226, 237, 244, 256, 264, 267, 295, 296, 321, 330, 355, 367, 380, 382, 394, 426, 449, 453, 458
transcendental signified, *Also see* erasure, trace, and difference. 63-4, 105, 164, 171, 173, 176, 177-82, 184, 190, 198, 206, 212, 222, 254, 269, 329-30, 332, 348, 353, 354, 383
transduction, *Also see* teleduction. 127, 454-56
transumption, *Also see* metalepsis. 53, 263, 286, 316
Truesdell, Clifford, 44-5, 129, 279, 372, 478
Tynyanov, Yury, (in some sources spelled "Tynianov, Iurii" and other various transcriptions from the Russian) 19, 27, 151, 160, 380, 399, 418, 427, 461-62
Verene, Donald Philip, 267, 280, 384
Watson, James D., 219, 238, 241, 263
Wellek, René, 366

Wölfflin, Heinrich, 18, 120, 122, 128, 135, 376, 379, 418, 429
Wordsworth, William, 86, 88-9, 91, 95-8, 101, 214, 282, 287, 301, 417, 471-73

For Product Safety Concerns and Information please contact our EU representative GPSR@taylorandfrancis.com
Taylor & Francis Verlag GmbH, Kaufingerstraße 24, 80331 München, Germany

www.ingramcontent.com/pod-product-compliance
Lightning Source LLC
Chambersburg PA
CBHW072018240426
43667CB00043B/1473